IMPACT EVALUATION IN INTERNATIONAL DEVELOPMENT

IMPACT EVALUATION IN INTERNATIONAL DEVELOPMENT

THEORY, METHODS, AND PRACTICE

Paul Glewwe and Petra Todd

WORLD BANK GROUP

1 2 3 4 25 24 23 22

ISBN (paper): 978-1-4648-1497-6
ISBN (electronic): 978-1-4648-1498-3
DOI: 10.1596/978-1-4648-1497-6

Cover and interior design: Yaneisy K. Martinez, World Bank.

Library of Congress Control Number: 2020901028.

Contents

Boxes

Figures

Tables

Preface

Governments in all countries spend trillions of dollars each year on a wide variety of programs that are intended to raise the welfare of their citizens. Nongovernmental organizations, both national and international, spend additional hundreds of billions of dollars per year on their own programs, which have similar goals. These programs and projects cover a wide variety of sectors and areas of interest, such as agriculture, credit, education, employment, energy, environmental protection, fertility, food and nutrition, health, housing, microenterprises, poverty reduction, public safety, transportation and communication, urban development, and water and sanitation. It is virtually certain that not all of these programs are as effective as their designers and implementers intended. Indeed, some of them could be completely ineffective, or even harmful. Thus, both governments and nongovernmental organizations should conduct evaluations of their programs and projects to measure their impacts so that they can understand what is working and what is not working. Evaluating rigorously, based on the methods presented in this book, has the potential to avoid wasteful spending on ineffective or weakly effective programs and projects. Redirecting those funds to more effective programming has the potential to greatly increase the welfare of the citizens of developing countries.

This book is written to provide detailed, rigorous guidance on how to conduct impact evaluations of government and nongovernment programs and projects. It covers all the leading quantitative impact evaluation methods, explaining the assumptions required for them to provide unbiased estimates and the data required to implement them. It also provides many examples of how these methods have been applied in developing economies. The book's contents are based on lectures given by the authors, and their collaborators, as part of a two-week intensive course conducted in China, Peru, South Africa, and Uganda between 2012 and 2017. The courses in China, South Africa, and Uganda were administered and supported by the Centers for Learning on Evaluation and Results (CLEAR) Initiative, a multidonor partnership program for evaluation capacity development with its secretariat at the World Bank and centers located in universities in different parts of the world; in 2020, the program and centers became part of the Global Evaluation Initiative.

The presentation of the material in this book is at a high technical level. It assumes that the reader is very comfortable with algebra and has an intermediate knowledge of statistical theory. It is essentially a graduate-level textbook for use in economics, public policy, or related academic programs, although it may also be useful for a course designed for advanced undergraduate students.

This book is divided into five parts. Part I, which consists of five chapters, provides an introduction to impact evaluation, including its purpose; an overview of how to conduct such evaluations; and an explanation of the "evaluation problem." It also discusses issues of internal and external validity and provides a nontechnical overview of the rest of the book. Part II provides a thorough, detailed, and rigorous exposition of the use of randomized control trials to conduct impact evaluations, including the use of regression methods, practical advice, and issues of sample size, sample design, and power calculations. This part also includes guidelines for conducting evaluations in an ethically responsible manner. Part III presents detailed expositions of several other impact evaluation methods, which are often used when randomized control trials are not possible or not recommended for other reasons. It covers difference-in-differences, matching methods, regression discontinuity, instrumental variables, quantile treatment effects, and control function methods. Part IV consists of three chapters that explain how to implement impact evaluations, including the design of questionnaires and other data collection instruments, the organization of data collection and data management, and overall survey management. Finally, Part V covers three special topics: dissemination of results and working with policy makers, use of qualitative methods, and cost-benefit analysis and cost-effectiveness analysis.

For readers who are university professors or trainers, an intensive 2-week course can cover almost all the material in this book. If following the approach taken by the authors, a typical course would consist of lectures on two chapters in the morning, with applications using real data sets—using Stata, R, SPSS, SAS, or other software applications for analysis—in the afternoon. Another way to cover the material would be in about 10 weeks, with 3 hours of lectures, and 1.5–2 hours of applications, per week. The material could also be covered in 14–15 weeks, with a total of about 3 hours of total class time (lectures and applications) per week. Of course, the amount of time required would be reduced if certain advanced topics (such as quantile regressions and control functions) are not covered. Data sets used in the courses offered by the authors are not provided in this book, but readers may contact the authors to obtain these data sets.

Finally, we owe a great debt to many individuals and organizations that helped with the courses that we taught and to the individuals who provided advice on writing this book. Nidhi Khattri, who headed the CLEAR Initiative's secretariat at the World Bank, first proposed that we teach this course in 2011. Ximena Fernandez-Ordoñez assisted in the first courses in China and South Africa. The courses in China, which brought together participants from around the world, were hosted by the CLEAR Center for East Asia at the Asia-Pacific Finance and Development Institute in Shanghai, under the direction of Li Kouqing and Zhao Min, with coordination by Scott Liu, Amy Chen, and Ningqin Wu. The courses in Africa were organized by the CLEAR Center for Anglophone Africa at the University of the Witwatersrand in South Africa, overseen at the time by Stephen Porter. The course in Peru was organized by the Universidad del Pacifíco. The programs offered through the CLEAR Initiative benefited from the support of 3ie in the form of scholarships to participants, under the direction of Howard White and later Emmanuel Jimenez, with scholarship administration from Jennifer Ludwig. The courses also benefited from trainers who joined the courses at different times, including Qihui Chen, Sarah Humpage Liuzzi, Howard White, Emmanuel Skoufias, Volker Schoer, Gareth Roberts, Janna Johnson, Thulile Zondi, Thandeka Thokozile Mhlantla, Johanna Fajardo-Gonzalez, and Bixuan Sun. At the book production stage, we benefited from an initial set of primary reviews from David Evans, Jeff Tanner, and Erwin Bulte, and later comments or assistance from Jos Vaessen, Estelle Raimondo, Ariya Hagh, Jessica Meckler, and Sylvia Otieno, the last of whom also served as project coordinator. The editorial and book production process was led by Michael Harrup and Susan Graham, with overall publishing work overseen by Jewel McFadden and design and print coordination contributions from Yaneisy K. Martinez. Lastly, Joan DeJaeghere and Sarah Humpage Liuzzi wrote chapters 22 and 10, respectively, and Qihui Chen and Maurya West Meiers went over every chapter, multiple times, in great detail, and thus we include all four as contributors to this book.

Paul Glewwe and Petra Todd

About the Authors and Contributors

Authors

Paul Glewwe is a Distinguished McKnight University Professor in the Department of Applied Economics at the University of Minnesota. His research interests are development economics, economics of education, and poverty and inequality.

Prof. Glewwe's research focuses on education, inequality, income mobility, and poverty in developing countries. He has conducted research on Brazil, China, Côte d'Ivoire, Ghana, Honduras, India, Jamaica, Kenya, Morocco, Nepal, Peru, the Philippines, Rwanda, Sri Lanka, Thailand, and Vietnam. He has also conducted research on education in the United States.

Before joining the University of Minnesota, he worked as a senior economist in the World Bank's Policy Research Group.

He received a BA in economics from the University of Chicago and a PhD in economics from Stanford University.

Petra Todd is an economist and professor in the University of Pennsylvania's Department of Economics. Her research interests are social program evaluation, labor economics, economics of education, and microeconometrics. She has published papers on program evaluation methodology, modeling the production function for cognitive achievement, testing for discrimination in motor vehicle searches, sources of racial wage disparities, school vouchers, pension system design, and methods for evaluating and optimally designing conditional cash transfer (CCT) programs. She has several papers that apply structural-modeling approaches to data derived from randomized control trial data. Her recent work analyzes the impact of the Prospera CCT program in Mexico on academic achievement and studies effects of grade retention in Portugal.

Petra has consulted with the Inter-American Development Bank, the World Bank, the Millenium Challenge Corporation, the U.S. Department of Labor, and the Mexican and Chilean governments.

She received her BA in economics and English from the University of Virginia, an MA in economics from the University of Chicago, and a PhD in economics from the University of Chicago.

Contributors

Qihui Chen is a Professor in the College of Economics and Management at China Agricultural University in Beijing, China.

Joan G. DeJaeghere is a Professor in the Department of Organizational Leadership, Policy and Development at the University of Minnesota in Minneapolis, Minnesota.

Sarah Humpage Liuzzi is a Senior Researcher in the International Unit at Mathematica in Minneapolis, Minnesota.

Maurya West Meiers is a Senior Evaluation Officer in the Independent Evaluation Group at the World Bank in Washington, DC.

Abbreviations

ATE	average treatment effect
ATT	average treatment effect on the treated
CAPI	computer-assisted personal interviewing
CAQDAS	computer-assisted qualitative data analysis software
DID	difference-in-differences
FDR	false discovery rate
FWER	family-wise error rate
GPA	grade point average
ID	identification
IRB	institutional review board
ITT	intention-to-treat effect
IV	instrumental variable
kg/ha	kilogram per hectare
LATE	local average treatment effect
MDE	minimum detectable effect size
OLS	ordinary least squares
PAP	pre-analysis plan
PDV	present discounted value
PSM	propensity score matching
QTE	quantile treatment effect
RCT	randomized controlled trial
RD	regression discontinuity
RDD	regression discontinuity design
SMART	specific, measurable, achievable, relevant, and time-bound
SUTVA	stable unit treatment value assumption

PART I

The Basics of Impact Evaluation

CHAPTER 1

The Purpose of Impact Evaluation

Introduction

Impact evaluations are studies that attempt to measure the causal impact of a project, program, or policy on an *outcome of interest* to governments and other interested parties. The purpose of this book is to provide a comprehensive set of skills that will enable the reader to conduct impact evaluations. The underlying assumption of this book is that impact evaluations are worth doing, even though they can be quite expensive and in some circumstances may not work. This raises the question of why they are worth doing, or more succinctly, why conduct evaluations?

There are several answers to this question, which are explained in greater depth in subsequent chapters, but for now the following answers should be fairly compelling. Foremost, projects, programs, and policies should be evaluated to see whether they work. They can be expensive, and if they are ineffective, either they should be modified to be more effective, or they should be ended so that the resources required to implement them can be used for other purposes. In extreme cases, impact evaluations can demonstrate that projects, programs, and policies can be harmful, and thus should be modified or stopped to put an end to their harmful consequences. One example of a harmful impact is a policy in Peru requiring employers to provide permanent employees (those with 6 or 12 months of job experience) with additional benefits; to avoid providing these benefits, employers would lay off employees before they reached the threshold for permanent benefits. Impact evaluations provide valuable guidance on whether to adjust, expand, or end specific projects, programs, and policies.

Evaluating projects, programs, and policies has other benefits. First, evaluations increase the transparency and accountability of the government to its citizens, and thereby increase social cohesion. Second, from the point of view of the government, evaluations demonstrate the government's commitment to using resources more effectively, which should increase political support for the government. This support can be useful when the government needs to implement reforms that may be unpopular or even painful to some of its citizens; citizens may be willing to accept such reforms if they have more confidence in their government.

Finally, in the past two decades, the international development community, governments, nongovernmental organizations, philanthropies, and others have given increased attention to results (see box 1.1 for examples). A strong push came at the turn of the century, when international development agencies were increasingly pressured by the wealthy nations that fund them to show that their programs are effective, and these agencies in turn increasingly required that the programs they support in developing countries be evaluated to determine whether they are effective. Examples of this emphasis on results include the following:[1]

- The Millennium Development Goals (2000)
- The Monterrey Consensus (2002) on "Better measuring, monitoring and managing for development results"
- The Paris Declaration on Aid Effectiveness (2005)
- The Accra Agenda for Action (2008)
- The Busan High-Level Forum (2011)
- The Sustainable Development Goals (2015)

At the same time, signals from academia and think tanks also pointed to the need for better evaluation. In 2006, an influential paper published by the Center for Global Development (2006) pointed out an evaluation gap in development; despite enormous investments in development policies, programs, and projects, the evidence base on what works was diagnosed as quite weak at that time. Although the "results agenda" push may have initially been driven by international and bilateral development agencies, with reinforcing insights from academia and think tanks, today there is considerable "local" buy-in and drive for results, with many government agencies leading and innovating their own results agendas.

BOX 1.1 Key organizations and agency departments that focus on impact evaluation in international development

Individual researchers and organizations have conducted impact evaluations for decades (such as in the health sector), but interest in impact evaluations among individuals and organizations in the international development community began to accelerate rapidly starting in the 1990s in response to donors' demands for evidence that the programs they were funding were in fact improving people's lives in developing countries. A key result of this increased interest was the founding of several organizations or agency departments devoted to impact evaluations. Examples of some of the most prominent of these include the following:

- The Abdul Latif Jameel Poverty Action Lab, which was founded in 2003, at the Massachusetts Institute of Technology (www.povertyactionlab.org)
- The International Initiative for Impact Evaluation (3ie), which began operations in 2008 (www.3ieimpact.org)
- Innovations for Poverty Action, which was founded in 2002 (www.poverty-action.org)
- Departments or teams within multilateral or bilateral agencies, such as three teams in the World Bank, including the Development Impact Evaluation team (https://www.worldbank.org/en/research/dime), the Africa Gender Innovation Lab (https://www.worldbank.org/en/programs/africa-gender-innovation-lab), and the Strategic Impact Evaluation Fund (https://www.worldbank.org/en/programs/sief-trust-fund)

These groups, along with many others and in cooperation with individual researchers, are funding and implementing hundreds of evaluations in countries every year. They are disseminating the results in a variety of different ways, and their work should be required reading for any person or organization involved in international development.

The rest of this chapter begins by describing the difference between monitoring and evaluation. The next section then presents a definition of impact evaluation, which is followed by a section that provides a brief overview of different types of impact evaluation. The subsequent section highlights key issues regarding impact evaluation, and the final section concludes.

The difference between monitoring and evaluation

The terms "monitoring" and "evaluation" are sometimes used together. For example, a program-implementing agency may produce a "monitoring and evaluation" report. Yet monitoring and evaluation refer to two different activities that have different objectives. Monitoring is a continuous or regular collection and analysis of information about the implementation of a project, program, or policy to review its progress. It compares actual progress with what was planned so that adjustments can be made in implementation in real time. It is usually an internal activity that is the responsibility of those who manage the implementation, although in some cases an external party performs monitoring services. Monitoring thus represents a good management practice. See Gugerty and Karlan (2018) for a very useful book on monitoring and related topics.

In contrast, evaluation is a periodic assessment of the relevance, efficiency, effectiveness, impact, and sustainability of a project, program, or policy. This task requires both a methodology for the evaluation and explicit criteria for judging whether the goals and objectives have been achieved (see Vaessen, Lemire, and Befani [2020] for an introductory overview of a range of methods applied in the broader field of evaluation).

A final point is that impact evaluations are just one type of evaluation. There are many other types of evaluations. For example, a process evaluation focuses on whether a project, program, or policy is implemented effectively. An outcome evaluation would look at the outcomes, or results, of a program. A good reference for other types of evaluations can be found in Imas and Rist (2009).

A definition of impact evaluation

Governments and nongovernmental organizations often implement projects, programs, or policies that are intended to change individuals' economic or social outcomes. An important—and difficult to answer—question is,

▶ How effective are programs in changing economic or social outcomes?

Governments and others would like to know the answer to this question so that they can compare the relative effectiveness of different programs and compare the benefits of these programs[2] to their costs.

A general definition

The above question can be modified to obtain the definition of impact evaluation that will be used in this book:

Definition: *An* **impact evaluation** *is a study that attempts to measure the causal impact of a project, program, or policy on an outcome of interest to governments and other interested parties.*

Several initial comments are helpful regarding this definition. First, some researchers, such as economists, often use the term "program evaluation" instead of impact evaluation. But others, especially professional evaluators, use the term "program evaluation" in a broader sense that includes not only impact evaluations but also process evaluations and other types of evaluations. For the former, this book can be viewed as a volume on how to conduct what they call program evaluations, although we prefer the more precise term "impact evaluations." Second, some use the term impact evaluation to mean randomized controlled trials (RCTs). However, there is no reason for such a narrow definition, and in this book "impact evaluation" has a wider interpretation, including many other types of methods and designs that are presented in detail in this book.

Third, conducting an impact evaluation is not an easy task (but hopefully not an impossible one) because it is not easy to measure the causal impacts of a project, program, or policy. Fourth, it is usually possible to measure outcomes of interest for people who participate in the project or program, or more generally are affected by the policy. The hard part is to measure what their outcomes would have been had they not participated, which is often referred to as the *counterfactual outcome*, or simply the *counterfactual*.

An example may make the idea of the counterfactual more intuitive. A policy question in the area of education may be, *Does providing students with eyeglasses increase their academic performance?* Students who wear eyeglasses may be observed to outperform students who do not wear eyeglasses on academic exams. But students who wear eyeglasses might study harder than those who do not, which may partly explain why they need eyeglasses in the first place. They may perform better simply because they spend more time studying. To determine whether a program (for example, providing eyeglasses) has a causal impact on an outcome of interest (student performance), impact evaluation methods are used to rule out the possibility that factors other than the program of interest (for example, students' study habits) explain the observed outcome. In this example, the counterfactual is what the performance of the students who wear eyeglasses would have been on academic exams if they had never had eyeglasses.

Much of this book uses certain notation to clarify the concept of the counterfactual in a more concise way. The causal impact of a program, with the latter denoted by P, on an outcome of interest, denoted by Y, for the unit of analysis (for example, an individual, a household, or a village) is the difference between the outcome with the program, denoted by $(Y \mid P = 1)$, and the outcome without the program, denoted by $(Y \mid P = 0)$, for that same unit. (The vertical bar denotes "conditional on.") This causal impact for a given person, denoted by Δ, can be defined as follows:

$$\Delta \equiv (Y \mid P = 1) - (Y \mid P = 0),$$

where the ≡ symbol indicates that this is a definition. The fundamental problem of impact evaluation is that both $(Y \mid P = 1)$ and $(Y \mid P = 0)$ can never be observed at the same time for the same person (or household or village). In particular, $(Y \mid P = 1)$ can be observed for program participants, but $(Y \mid P = 0)$ cannot be observed for participants; $(Y \mid P = 0)$ can be observed only for nonparticipants, who may be quite different from the participants and thus may not be a valid counterfactual for the participants.

The term $(Y \mid P = 0)$ represents the *counterfactual*, which is *what would have happened if a participant had not participated in the program*. Because $(Y \mid P = 0)$ cannot be directly observed for program participants, it must be estimated. $(Y \mid P = 0)$ is usually estimated from a comparison group that is similar to the treatment group. Later chapters in this book introduce different impact evaluation methods that, if certain assumptions hold, can be used to identify valid comparison groups that can be used to accurately estimate the counterfactual.

Brief overview of types of impact evaluations

Most of this book is devoted to explaining in great detail how to implement different types of impact evaluations. Therefore, it is useful to briefly describe the main methods so that the reader can have an idea of what this book is about.

The first method, which has a long history in both medical and social science research, is RCTs. RCTs are implemented by randomly dividing the population into two (or in some cases more than two) groups. The program is implemented for one group (the "treatment" group) but not for the other group (the "control" group, or "comparison" group), and outcomes of interest are compared for the two groups. The key feature of RCTs is that assignment to the two groups is completely random, which implies that any differences in the outcomes of interest between the two groups must be due to the program.

Although RCTs are sometimes considered the best methodology for impact evaluations, in many cases randomly assigning individuals, households, or communities to the program of interest is not possible. Thus many other methodologies have been developed that do not depend on random assignment to the program. One common method is difference-in-differences estimation, which compares changes in the outcome of interest over time, separately for individuals or groups who have participated in the program and for others who have not participated in the program.

Five other methods, which are used less often, are (1) matching methods, which match program participants to nonparticipants with similar characteristics; (2) regression discontinuity methods, which compare individuals (or households or communities) who just barely satisfy the eligibility criteria for a program with similar individuals who do not quite meet those criteria; (3) instrumental variables methods, which are based on characteristics that "predict" program participation but otherwise do not have any effect on the outcomes of interest; (4) control function methods, which modify regression methods by adding one or more generated control variables to a regression equation to minimize or eliminate bias; and (5) quantile regressions, which under certain conditions can be used to estimate the distribution of program impacts.

These methods are explained in great detail in chapters 6–17 of this book; chapters 6–10 focus on RCTs, and chapters 11–17 cover the other methods.

Other issues regarding impact evaluation

In addition to the various types of impact evaluation methods, other important aspects of impact evaluation merit discussion and thus are topics in other chapters in this book. One of the most important is comparing the impact of a project, program, or policy with its cost. Ultimately, a project, program, or policy is worth implementing only if its benefits exceed its costs. *Cost-benefit analysis* considers how to assign values to both the costs and the benefits of a program (or project or policy), so that they can be compared. In theory, any program for which the benefits exceed the costs is worth implementing, but if funds are scarce then priority should generally be given to programs for which the ratio of the benefits to the costs is the highest. A related concept is *cost-effectiveness analysis*, which compares the costs of different projects, programs, or policies that produce the same outcome and can be used to select the program that has the lowest cost for obtaining that outcome. The key advantage of cost-effectiveness analysis, relative to cost-benefit analysis, is that assigning a monetary benefit to the impact of the program is not necessary, but the key disadvantage is that it does not provide information on whether the costs are greater than the benefits. These issues are discussed in detail in chapter 23.

A related set of issues is the cost of evaluations. Over and above the costs of the project, program, or policy, implementation of an evaluation has additional associated costs. The most obvious are the monetary and resource costs, given that data must be collected and the time of researchers usually has an explicit cost. A second cost occurs when data are collected from program participants and comparable nonparticipants; obtaining information from these individuals may require a significant amount of their time, which they could have used for other activities that would have directly benefited them. A third cost is more political. Impact evaluations often show that programs are not very effective in producing the outcomes that they were designed to produce. This lack of effectiveness could embarrass the government, at least in the short run, and may result in loss of political support for conducting evaluations. On the other hand, in the long run a system of impact evaluations should improve outcomes that the population cares about, increasing political support for impact evaluations. In practice, one might wish to approach investments in impact evaluation from a portfolio perspective. Perhaps not all programs of a similar nature need to be subject to full-fledged impact evaluations. Instead, a limited number of programs across a region or country that are representative of a larger set of similar programs may be strategically selected for rigorous impact evaluation.

Yet another aspect of impact evaluations is that many projects, programs, and policies are implemented on a relatively small scale, and though they may work well on a small scale, whether they will work well when scaled up is not clear. *Efficacy evaluation* examines whether the project, program, or policy works on a small scale, under much supervision, and under very specific circumstances. Such evaluations are often carried out as pilot studies before the programs are implemented on a larger scale. In contrast, *effectiveness evaluation* examines whether the project, program, or policy works under normal circumstances, using regular implementation channels. This distinction is important because the conclusions drawn from an efficacy evaluation may not be valid for a different population, location, or implementation channel. See Chen (1990) for a discussion of the distinction between efficacy and effectiveness evaluations. This concept relates to the distinction between internal validity and external validity, which are covered in more depth in chapter 4.

Impact evaluations can also raise complex ethical issues because they involve conducting research on human subjects. Researchers should minimize the risks that participants face from participating in a study and, when necessary, inform them that they are participants in a study. If the research involves an RCT, the control group, which is equally deserving of the treatment, by definition will not receive the treatment at the same time as the treatment group (and may never receive the treatment), which may raise additional ethical issues. Finally, when collecting data, researchers must take care to protect participants' anonymity. Ethical issues are covered in detail in chapter 10.

Conclusion

The goal of impact evaluations is to measure the causal impact of a project, program, or policy on an outcome of interest to governments and other interested parties. This book provides a comprehensive exposition of how to conduct impact evaluations. In doing so it expands on the material in a very useful book by Gertler et al. (2016). More specifically, it provides more comprehensive coverage of impact evaluation methods, offers more technical detail on those methods, and thoroughly covers many practical topics related to implementation of those methods.

This chapter provides an introduction to this book, and more generally an introduction to impact evaluations. The rest of this book is divided into five parts. Part I, which consists of the first five chapters, provides an overview of impact evaluations. Part II presents, in chapters 6–10, a comprehensive discussion of the use of RCTs to conduct impact evaluations. Part III, consisting of chapters 11–17, presents the main nonexperimental methods that are used to implement impact evaluations when RCTs are not feasible or are not recommended for other reasons. Part IV then considers more practical issues when conducting impact evaluations, including designing questionnaires, data collection methods and survey management, and disseminating results to policy makers; these topics are covered in chapters 18–21. Finally, part V (chapters 22–23) addresses other topics in impact evaluation.

A final point about this book is that, although it does present several examples of impact evaluations that have been conducted in recent years, it does not provide a general summary of the findings of impact evaluations conducted in developing countries. A good source for detailed reviews on a wide variety of topics can be found in the systematic reviews that have been conducted by the International Initiative for Impact Evaluation (3ie), the Campbell Collaboration, and the Cochrane Collaboration.[3]

Notes

1. Information on the Millennium Development Goals can be found at http://www.un.org/millenniumgoals/. For the Monterrey Consensus, see https://www.un.org/en/development/desa/population/migration/generalassembly/docs/globalcompact/A_CONF.198_11.pdf. The Paris Declaration on Aid Effectiveness can be found at www.oecd.org/dac/effectiveness/34428351.pdf. Information on the Accra Agenda for Action is available at www.oecd.org/dac/effectiveness/45827311.pdf. For the Busan High-Level Forum, see http://www.oecd.org/dac/effectiveness/fourthhighlevelforumonaideffectiveness.htm. Finally, for information on the Sustainable Development Goals, see http://www.un.org/sustainabledevelopment/sustainable-development-goals/.
2. When conducting evaluations, we may examine small to medium-sized *projects*, a larger *program* or set of programs, or a *policy*. *Intervention*, a more generic term, is often used by evaluators in place of these three terms. Because the term "intervention" may not be as commonly understood by some readers, the term "program" is used frequently throughout the book, but is used in a general sense.
3. The relevant websites are 3ie, "Evidence Synthesis," https://www.3ieimpact.org/our-expertise/synthesis; Campbell Collaboration, https://campbellcollaboration.org/; and Cochrane, https://www.cochrane.org/evidence.

References

Center for Global Development. 2006. "When Will We Ever Learn? Improving Lives through Impact Evaluation." Report of the Evaluation Gap Working Group. Center for Global Development, Washington, DC.

Chen, Huey T. 1990. *Theory-Driven Evaluations.* Newbury Park, CA: Sage.

Gertler, Paul, Sebastian Martinez, Patrick Premand, Laura Rawlings, and Christel Vermeersch. 2016. *Impact Evaluation in Practice.* 2nd ed. Washington, DC: World Bank.

Gugerty, Mary Kay, and Dean Karlan. 2018. *The Goldilocks Challenge: Right-Fit Evidence for the Social Sector.* Oxford, U.K.: Oxford University Press.

Imas, Linda, and Ray Rist. 2009. *The Road to Results: Designing and Conducting Effective Development Evaluations.* Washington, DC: World Bank.

Vaessen, Jos, Sebastian Lemire, and Barbara Befani. 2020. *Evaluation of International Development Interventions: An Overview of Approaches and Methods.* Washington, DC: World Bank.

CHAPTER 2

How to Conduct an Impact Evaluation: Getting Started

Introduction

Almost all impact evaluations seek to answer the following question:

- What is the *causal* impact of the program (or project or policy) on the outcome variables of interest?

This question, however, raises other questions, such as *What are the outcome variables of interest?* It also assumes that the program (or project or policy) is clearly defined.

This chapter provides an overview of the first five steps to take to implement an impact evaluation:

1. Clarify what the *program* and the *outcome variables of interest* are.
2. Formulate a *theory of change* to define and refine the evaluation questions.
3. Depict the theory of change in a *results chain* (often called a *logic model*).
4. Formulate *specific hypotheses* for the impact evaluation.
5. Select *performance indicators* for monitoring and evaluation.

Note that the order of the steps is not rigid; at times it may be useful to go back to an earlier step because of unforeseen problems that arise at a later step. Once these five steps are complete, the next major decision is to choose the method or methods to be used to estimate the impact of the program on the outcomes of interest; this is discussed in detail in subsequent chapters.

The next five sections of this chapter describe each of these five steps; a final section concludes.

Step 1. Defining the program and the outcomes of interest

To avoid confusion regarding the results of the impact evaluation, the group or organization that is assigned to implement it must be completely clear about the following:

- What project, program, or policy is being evaluated?
- What are the outcome variables of interest?

Ideally, both questions should be answered in consultation with all groups that have an interest in the program (and thus have an interest in the program's evaluation). If not, the evaluation results may not be accepted, or may not be considered useful, by some of those groups.

Three groups will certainly have an interest in the program, and thus in its evaluation: policy makers, program managers, and program beneficiaries. All three of these groups should be included in the planning of the program, and thus in the planning of its evaluation. Note, however, that in some cases it is difficult to include program beneficiaries in the planning for the program and the planning for the evaluation.

What project, program, or policy is being evaluated?

The first question to address is, What is being evaluated? The answer to this question may appear to be obvious if the program (or project or policy) already exists, but even for existing programs, this question requires some discussion, for two reasons.

First, in some cases the program may have changed since the decision was made to evaluate it, either for administrative reasons or for the purpose of the evaluation. An example is Colombia's Gratuidad school fee reduction program; in 2004–05, the program changed the method used to determine eligibility. This change in the Gratuidad program was made for administrative reasons that were unrelated to any evaluation of that program.

Second, the program may take different forms in different parts of the country. In this situation, if the evaluation is performed in only one part of the country, the results apply only to the version of the program in that part of the country.

What are the outcomes of interest?

Any well-designed program should be clear about the social or economic outcome variables it is trying to change. Although the outcome variables that the program is expected to change may seem obvious, in many cases complications can arise for the evaluators. First, a program could be designed to change a large number of outcome variables. In this situation, it may be expensive to measure all of the outcomes. For example, a health program could affect many different types of health conditions, and some health conditions cannot be easily measured.

A second general problem, which is particularly likely for new programs, is that the set of outcomes that the program is intended to improve could change. Many programs change over time, especially in the first few years, and if the program changes, the relevant outcomes may also change.

A third complication in determining the outcomes of interest of a particular program is that outcome variables that the program was *not* designed to change may be affected. Some of these unintended outcomes may be desirable, while others may not. A simple example of the latter is that a program that promotes agricultural or industrial production could also lead to environmental damage. A more specific example comes from China. In the early 1980s, China manufactured and imported ultrasound B-machines on a large scale. Their purpose was to monitor pregnancy, check placement of intrauterine devices, and perform other diagnostic tasks. Yet Chinese couples' strong preference for sons and China's newly enacted one-child policy led people to use ultrasound to determine sex prenatally, which led to sex-selective abortions (Chen, Li, and Ming 2013; Chu 2001).

A final potential problem is that some outcomes are immediate (for example, an increase in hand washing) but the real or ultimate intended outcomes occur later (for example, reduced rate of diarrhea). For instance, Mexico's PROGRESA conditional cash transfer program focused on health and education outcomes, but other outcomes followed, such as changes in labor supply. Indeed, several studies have focused on outcomes that were not the original intent of that program, as summarized in table 2.1.[1]

Step 2. Forming a theory of change to refine the evaluation questions

The causes of program success or failure can be divided into two general types: those related to program design or theory, and those related to program implementation. This chapter is more concerned with the issue of program theory.

TABLE 2.1 PROGRESA outcomes evaluated

FOCAL OUTCOMES		OTHER OUTCOMES	
School enrollment and attendance	Schultz (2004)	Food consumption	Hoddinott and Skoufias (2004)
Test scores	Behrman, Sengupta, and Todd (2000)	Food and nonfood consumption	Hoddinott, Skoufias, and Washburn (2000)
Preschool child height	Behrman and Hoddinott (2001)	Work, leisure, and time allocation	Parker and Skoufias (2000)
Child height and child illness	Gertler (2004)	Adult labor supply and leisure, poverty	Skoufias and Di Maro (2008)
Schooling; child labor	Skoufias and Parker (2001)	Private interhousehold transfers	Teruel and Davis (2000)
		Women's status and intrahousehold transfers	Adato et al. (2000)
		Community social relationships	Adato (2000)
		Poverty, inequality, and spillovers	Handa et al. (2001)

Source: Original table for this publication.

After Step 1 is completed, the team doing the impact evaluation should have a good understanding of what the program is, what its expected outcomes are, and how the outcomes will be achieved—in essence, the program theory. Then the evaluation question (or set of evaluation questions) becomes

> What is the causal impact of the program (or project or policy), which can be denoted by the variable P, on the outcome variables X, Y, and Z?

As mentioned previously, the program can change, and the outcome variables of interest may also change. In reality, forming the evaluation questions should be thought of as an iterative process.

One way to begin understanding the program theory is to form a *theory of change*, which is simply an explanation of why, and how, the program (or project or policy) should have an effect on the outcome variables of interest. A theory of change describes—usually in a narrative form or supplemental document—the causal pathways of how the program intends to reach its goals.

While this chapter provides only a summary of program theory and theories of change, these topics are explored more fully in books devoted to this area of research, such as Funnell and Rogers (2011). Funnell and Rogers (2011, 31) define *program theory* as "an explicit theory or model of how an intervention contributes to a set of outcomes through a series of intermediate results. The theory needs to include an explanation of how the program's activities contribute to the results, not simply a list of activities followed by the results, with no explanation of how those are linked, apart from the mysterious arrow. We find it helpful to think of a program theory as having two components: a theory of change and a theory of action." Funnell and Rogers (2011, 31) describe theory of change as defining "the central mechanism by which change comes about for individuals, groups, and communities." They describe theories of action (about which we do not go into detail in this book) as explaining "how programs or other interventions are constructed to activate their theory of change" (Funnell and Rogers 2011, 31). In other words, the two components are (1) the change theory (what it is that leads to what), and (2) the action theory (what actions will accomplish the articulated change). Finally, Funnell and Rogers describe another tool used in program theory, the *logic model*, which usually displays the program theory in a diagram. This chapter shows such a diagram (see figure 2.1) but uses another term, *results chain*, which is often used instead of the term logic model.

One final background note on this discussion of program theory is that agencies and professionals working in evaluations and program planning might use different terminology, such as *causal chain, intervention theory, program logic, logical framework,* or *log-frame,* among many others. For instance, some agencies often use the terms "theory of change" and "results chain" interchangeably, even though they are differentiated here. There are many similarities—and some differences—in terms and tools, so one should check with the users of these terms to understand how they define them.

The step of formulating a theory of change is especially important if the program is new and has not been implemented elsewhere. Ideally, the program designers should have, at least implicitly, a theory of change, even if they have not written it down. If not, the evaluators will have to meet with the program designers to work one out. Over the past 20 years, it has become very common for programs sponsored by governments, international agencies, nongovernmental organizations, and others to require a theory of change at the program design or approval stages. A large literature on theories of change has been produced in the evaluation academic community, and many agencies have produced their own guides on how to develop theories of change. These guides have many common elements, but they may also have some differences in terminology, how to construct theories of change, and how they are visualized.

A theory of change does not have to be complicated. In its simplest form it describes the sequence of activities and outputs that the program (or project or policy) is expected to put into motion that will lead to the desired outcomes. This theory is particularly important for programs designed to change participants' behavior in order to set in motion a sequence of (desired) outcomes (e.g., from direct behavioral outcomes to intermediate outcomes such as crop yields, sales volumes, or incidence of diseases).

Several other recommendations are useful for developing a theory of change for the program under consideration. The first is that, ideally, it should be developed when the program is being designed, because working out the theory of change is beneficial for thinking through how the program should work to generate the desired outcomes. In other words, developing a theory of change will improve the design of the program. For programs covering a long period, or that adjust to a changing environment, it is very common and even recommended that theories of change be revised from time to time.

A second recommendation is to read reports on similar programs to get an idea of what has happened with those programs. Doing so is likely to uncover some missing pieces in the results chain that otherwise may have been overlooked. As mentioned previously, a results chain is usually presented as a diagram that shows how a program is intended to work; it is described in detail in the discussion of Step 3. Reading reports on similar programs, consulting experts in the program area under study, gathering the perspectives of the program's stakeholders, and other activities may also provide an idea of the magnitude (or importance) of the various links in the results chain.

A third general recommendation is to think about the conditions and assumptions necessary for the program to work as planned. Ideally, the team should be able to identify these conditions and assumptions and integrate them into the theory of change. A particularly important implication is that the evaluation team should collect data on these conditions and assumptions to see whether they are met. If the program does not work as planned, it may be because the required conditions and assumptions were not met; collecting such data should point to the likely weak link in the causal chain that led the program to be ineffective. Beyond identifying assumptions, during this stage it is also common to identify risks that could lead to failure or an inability to reach the intended goals.

A final note regarding a theory of change is that it can help the evaluation team identify additional expected indicators and measurement strategies in the results chain. That is, by fully specifying the way that the program should work, the theory of change is likely to bring to light additional data that should be collected to understand how the program managed to be a success, or why it failed to succeed.

A simple example of a theory of change is the evaluation of a program to use cameras to raise teacher attendance and student learning in India by Duflo, Hanna, and Ryan (2012).

The ultimate outcome of interest was student attendance and learning. The implicit theory of change posited that these student outcomes were low because teachers were often absent from school, with a teacher absence rate of about 40 percent. One reason why teachers were absent was the lack of incentives for them to be present in the schools where they taught.

The program was designed to provide such an incentive. Teachers were given cameras that automatically stamped the date and time for each picture that was taken on the film used in the camera. These teachers were instructed to have two pictures taken of them with their students (one at the beginning of the school day and one at the end of the school day) for every day that they were at the school. Each month the teachers mailed the film to the central office, which checked their attendance. For each (additional) day per month that the teachers' attendance exceeded 20 days per month, the teachers were provided a monetary reward. The causal chain underlying this intervention was that providing an incentive for teachers to be present in the schools would increase their attendance, and that this increase in teachers' attendance would increase the attendance and test scores of the students. In fact, the evaluation showed exactly that: the teacher attendance rate increased from about 60 percent to about 80 percent, and students' attendance and test scores increased substantially.

Step 3. Depicting a theory of change in a results chain (logic model)

Perhaps the best way to illustrate a theory of change is to build a "results chain" or "logic model" diagram. These diagrams usually have five standard components, as well as a box for assumptions and risks. Figure 2.1 provides the typical successive layout of a full program theory (theory of change plus theory of action) in the form of a results chain diagram, noting that the action and change processes are usually described more fully in a supporting program description document.

FIGURE 2.1 A results chain diagram: Basic layout and components

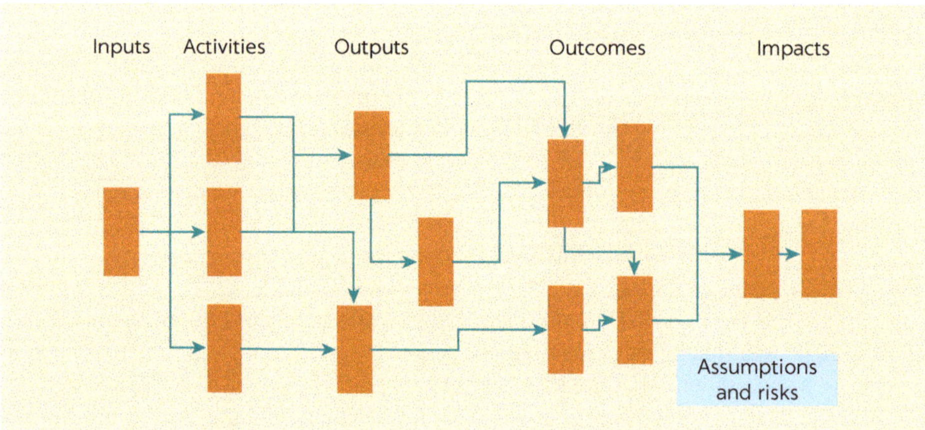

Source: Original figure for this publication.

Some organizations use somewhat different terms for the components, or they might subdivide components in different ways (for example, instead of identifying a single set of outcomes, they may break outcomes into short-, medium-, and long-term outcomes). This chapter depicts results chains using a successionist causation approach (*a* leads to *b* leads to *c*, etc.), but results chains could be presented in many different ways. Further, Bamberger and Mabry (2020, 155) note, "in the real world these simple linear models must be adapted to reflect the challenges of *emergence* (the changing internal and external context within which a program operates) and *complexity* (outcomes and impacts are affected by non-linear interactions among multiple factors)." While this chapter only introduces these concepts, authors such as Funnell and Rogers (2011) and Bamberger and Mabry (2020), among others, provide a deeper discussion and provide numerous nonlinear illustrations.

The first of the five components of the results chain or logic model diagram is the *inputs* (or *resources*) provided to implement various activities. These inputs usually include the funds, staff, facilities, equipment, and technical expertise that are needed to implement the program, project, or policy.

The second component is the *activities* that use the inputs to produce or deliver the services or products provided by the program. These activities are what the program does with the inputs. Examples of activities include building roads, vaccinating children, training teachers, and developing a variety of plans and partnerships.

Outputs are the third component, and they are the direct results of the activities. They are the supply-side services or products generated by a program's activities. Specific examples of outputs are 10 roads constructed, 5,000 children vaccinated, or 1,500 teachers trained.

The fourth component is *outcomes*. The program's outputs should cause something to change in the desired direction. The near- and medium-term effects of a program are its outcomes. They reflect the uptake, adoption, or use of the program's outputs by the program's intended beneficiaries. They are what are changed by the program. Examples of outcomes are reduced costs for farmers to transport their crops to major markets, reductions in childhood illnesses, and children who learn more because their teachers have been trained. In general, outcomes should be measurable; otherwise, evaluating the impact of the program is almost impossible.

The fifth component of the results chain is the longer-term effects of the program, which are referred to as *impacts*, and are sometimes called higher-level outcomes. They are the ultimate goals of the program. Examples include lower child mortality and higher economic growth. Achieving impacts is usually beyond the control of the project implementers, who are responsible only for the outputs and perhaps the outcomes; they should not be held accountable for a program's failure to achieve the program impacts if they successfully provided the outputs.

In summary, a results chain (or logic model) provides a depiction of the program theory or theory of change by showing a plausible causal relationship between the inputs and the intended outcomes. The five components of the results chain show each step of this causal relationship.

Figure 2.2 provides a more detailed schematic of what goes into a results chain diagram. Note that some results can be negative. For example, although an increase in manufacturing output could lead to economic improvements (positive), it can also lead to more pollution (negative).

FIGURE 2.2 A more detailed view of what goes into a results chain (logic model)

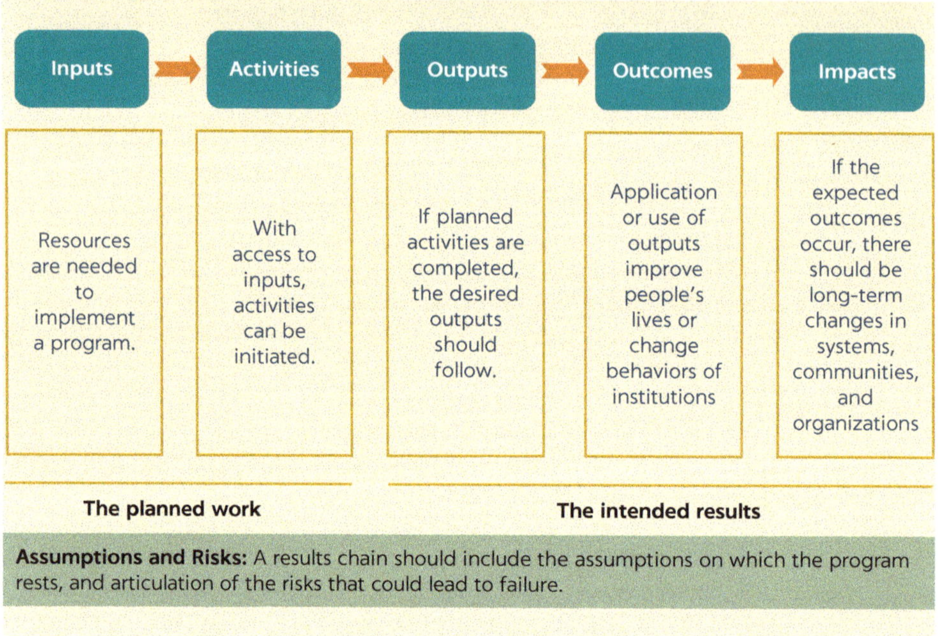

Source: Adapted, with permission, from W. K. Kellogg Foundation 2004.

Two examples of the types of information in a results chain are shown in figure 2.3. The top rectangle (with rounded corners) that spans the four boxes on the right is for an education program that changes the pedagogical methods and the textbooks used in secondary school. The bottom rectangle in those same boxes is for an immunization program that is administered through local health centers.

A few additional points are worth noting regarding results chains. First, in relatively simple projects and programs the impacts, which can also be called the higher-level outcomes, may be the same as the outcomes. That is, the results chain may have only four, instead of five, components. An example of this is a program that provides food to poor households; the primary objective of the program may simply be to provide food to poor households. It is also worth noting that one can unpack outcomes into more detailed causal steps. So instead of two or three successive outcomes, some evaluators might break down a causal chain into 5, 10, or even more (detailed) outcomes. This additional unpacking depends on the level of abstraction that the evaluator is seeking—and whether a simple or more detailed view is required.

A second, and more important, point is that the chain of causal events relies on assumptions and risks, which are commonly articulated in results chains. Quite simply, the program may not work as planned because of inaccurate or unconsidered (implicit) assumptions, or because unforeseen (or foreseen but assumed to be unlikely) negative events interfere with

FIGURE 2.3 Examples of a results chain's components: Education and health sectors

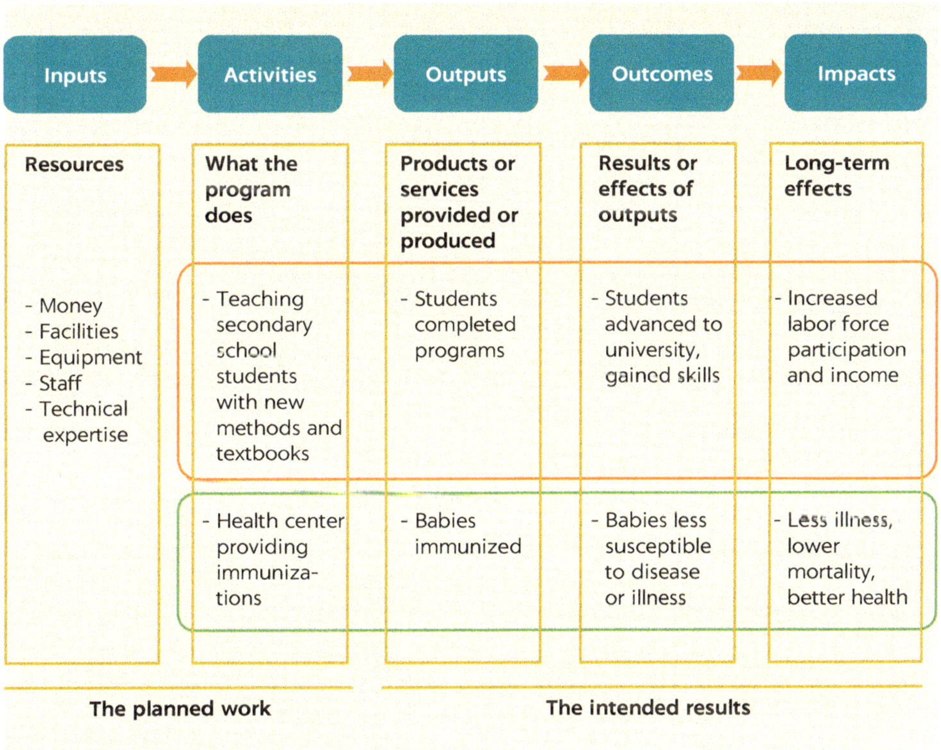

Source: Original figure for this publication.

the program. An example is a randomized controlled trial in China that provided free eyeglasses to primary school students with vision problems (see Glewwe, Park, and Zhao 2016). Unexpectedly, about one-third of parents (or in some cases the children) refused to accept the offer of free eyeglasses. While the reasons for these unexpected refusals are not known, a likely explanation is that many parents thought that wearing eyeglasses would exacerbate their children's vision problems.

Third, when comparing alternative programs (or projects or policies), developing results chains for each of them and discussing the underlying assumptions and risks of each one may be helpful. This exercise may be useful for deciding which program seems most likely to succeed.

A results chain from an actual program provides a useful example for how to construct such a chain. Recall the PROGRESA conditional cash transfer program that was implemented in Mexico in the late 1990s. Figure 2.4 provides a results chain for Mexico's PROGRESA program.

FIGURE 2.4 Example of a results chain: Mexico's PROGRESA program

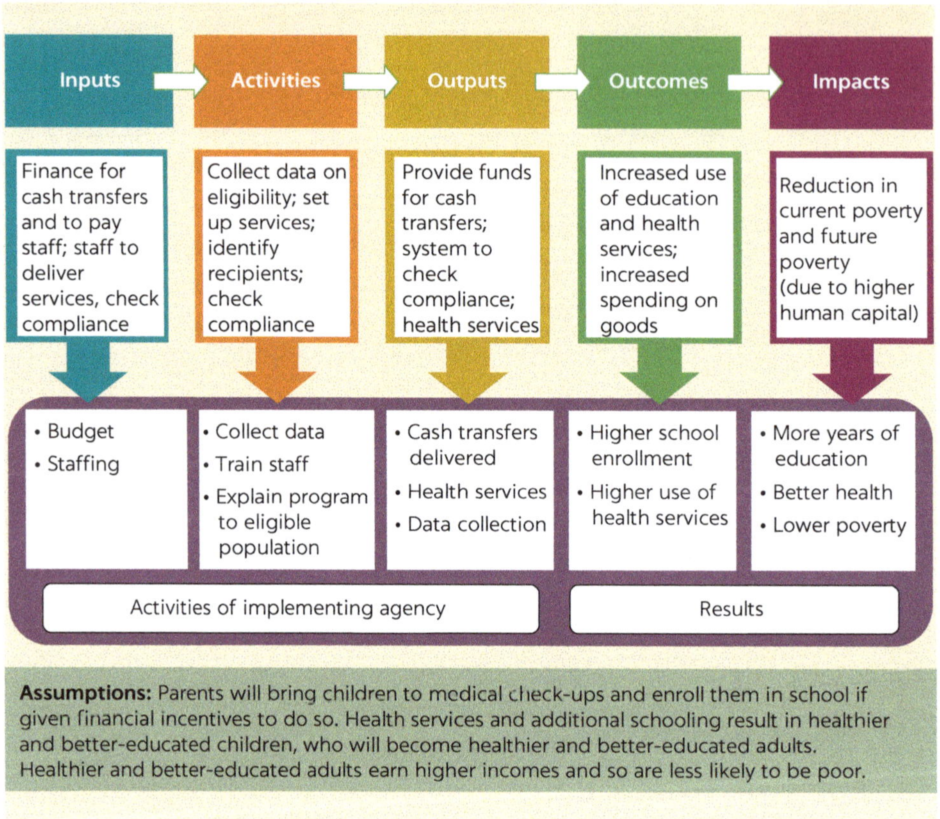

Source: Adapted from Gertler et al. 2011.

Figure 2.5 provides a more detailed example of a results chain for a regional vaccination program, showing the linkages across the component levels and the assumptions of the program. The reader is encouraged to fill out a similar results chain for a program that he or she is planning to evaluate.

Step 4. Formulating specific hypotheses for the impact evaluation

After a clear results chain has been developed, *specific hypotheses* can be developed regarding the impact of the program (or project or policy) on the outcome variables of interest. These hypotheses should be as detailed and specific as possible.

More precisely, every outcome that the program is expected to have an effect on, in both the short term and the long term, must be clearly defined. For example, Mexico's PROGRESA program was designed to increase school enrollment rates in the short run and

FIGURE 2.5 Example of a detailed, successive results chain: Regional vaccination program

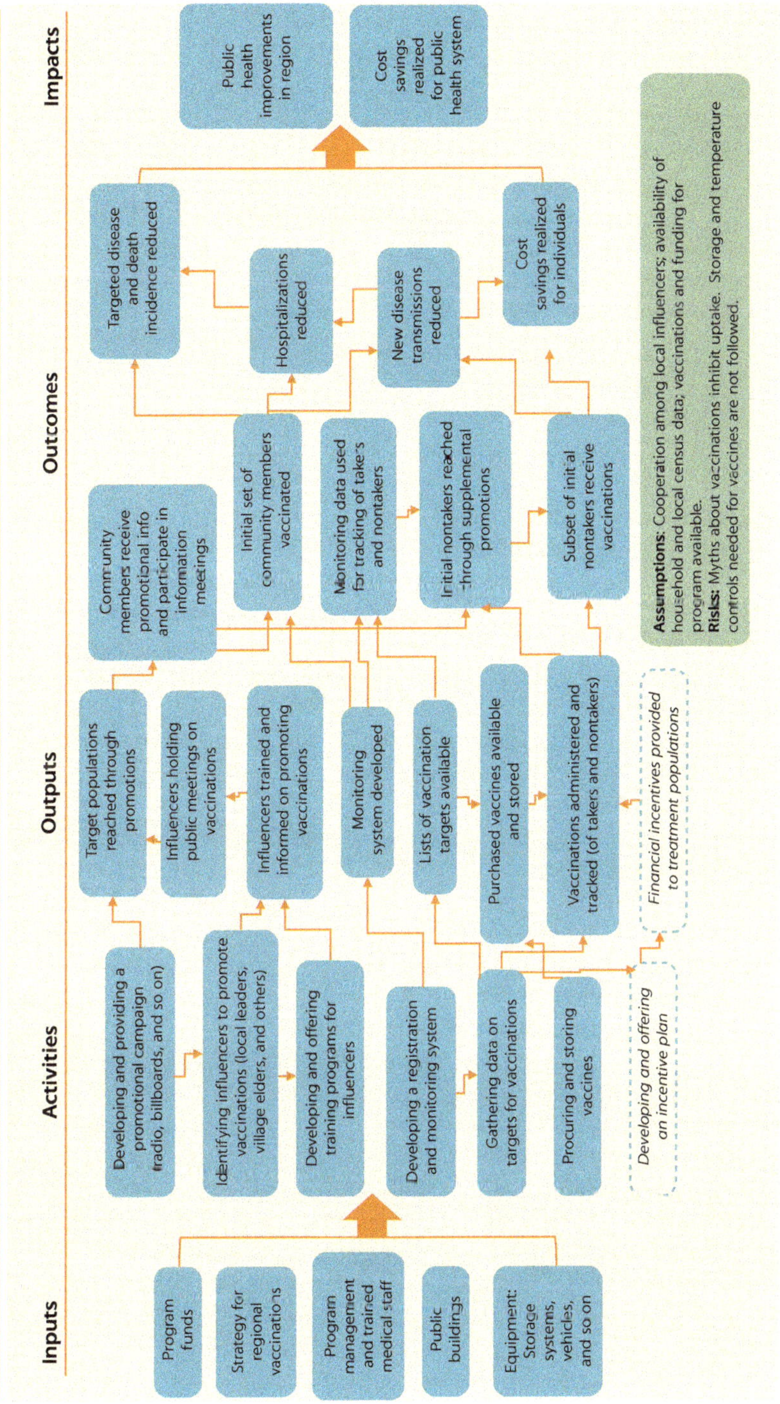

Source: Original figure for this publication.

raise completed years of schooling in the long run. As much as possible, unintended outcomes of the program should be included, including those that may be negative side effects of the program.

Two other aspects of the outcomes should be kept in mind. First, the timing of when the outcome is expected to appear should be specified. Some outcomes may change immediately while others appear only later, and both types should be measured. Second, different outcomes may be expected for different subpopulations of interest. In this case, the outcomes specified should also indicate which subpopulations are expected to be affected. For example, a program to increase the number of female teachers is likely to have a larger impact on the enrollment of girls than on the enrollment of boys.

Step 5. Selecting performance indicators for monitoring and evaluation

The last step is to select indicators for the outcomes that the program is intended to change. However, the outcome variables of interest may not be easy to measure. In addition to outcome variables, measuring progress in program implementation is also worthwhile. The acronym "SMART" provides useful guidance on how to select performance indicators. The five letters in SMART can be used to remember the characteristics that all performance indicators should have: Specific, Measurable, Achievable, Relevant, and Time-bound. This section explains these characteristics and provides specific examples to illustrate them.

First, a performance indicator should be *specific*; that is, it should provide relatively simple yet precise information that can be easily communicated by the provider, and easily understood by the user, of the information.

For example, consider a family planning program in a developing country where couples usually have more than two children. The outcome variable of interest is the reduction in the number of children in a typical family. The program sets up new clinics for women of child-bearing age and provides low-cost contraceptives and health education. Suppose that two possible indicators are proposed: (1) increased number of small families, and (2) increased number of one-child and two-child families. Which of these is more specific? Clearly, the second one is more specific because "small" is rather vague; that is, it is not very specific.

As a second example, consider a program that is intended to improve rural children's health status. Two different indicators are proposed: (1) the number of children who were ill in the past four weeks, and (2) the number of children who became healthier. Again, which of the following indicators is more specific? In this case, the first is more specific because it refers to a particular period.

Second, a performance indicator should be *measurable*; that is, an indicator that is relatively easy to measure should be selected for each outcome of interest.

Two examples provide a more concrete idea of this attribute. Consider a program that has been designed to improve rural elementary schools' physical facilities. Suppose that the evaluation team has proposed the following two indicator variables for this program: (1) percentage of schools that have physical facilities that are generally regarded as having low quality, and (2) percentage of schools that have leaking classrooms (or do not have electricity, or do not have a library). Which of these indicators is more measurable? The first is difficult to measure because low quality can be a subjective concept. In contrast, the second is more objective and stated more clearly, and thus it is more measurable. It is worth noting that more measurable indicators sometimes can be blunt instruments for the outcomes they are trying to capture—and this is a potential trade-off to keep in mind.

A second example is a program that aims to improve rural families' living standards. Again, two indicator variables are proposed: (1) the number of families that became wealthier, or (2) the increase in monthly consumption of nonfood items in the targeted families. Which of these two indicators is more measurable? In fact, wealth is relatively hard to measure. For example, the value of a home is often difficult to measure in rural areas of developing countries because many, if not most, households have built their dwellings themselves, so there are no "rental market" data that provide information on the value of a particular house. Indeed, many households would be unable to answer this question even if they were willing to provide the information. In contrast, it is relatively easy for households to answer a series of questions about spending on nonfood items in the past month, which can then be used to calculate total spending for nonfood consumption in the past month.

Performance indicators should also be *achievable*, the third characteristic in the SMART acronym. The basic idea is that it is reasonable to expect the program to have an effect on this indicator, and that this effect will occur over the period that the program is in place, as opposed to occurring only after the program and the data collection have ended.

One example of an achievable performance indicator concerns a school intervention program that provides free after-school tutoring services to poorly performing students in primary schools. Consider two possible indicators: (1) a 0.2-standard-deviation increase in the test scores of students on a standardized exam administered one year after the program started, and (2) a 10-percentage-point increase in the number of primary school students who eventually attend university. Which of these two indicators is more achievable? The first is more achievable because it is measured relatively soon after the program has started. In contrast, given that the program is for primary school students, the second indicator cannot be measured for at least six years after the program starts, and in almost all cases this is far too long to wait to see whether a program has had an effect—data collection almost certainly will have ended before it can be measured.

As a second example of this characteristic, suppose that a program offers free regular checkups for pregnant women from poor families. The purpose of the evaluation is to determine whether this program has an impact on the health of newborn children. Two possible indicators are proposed: (1) percentage of newborns with low birth weight (< 2,500 grams), and (2) percentage of children who, at age 4–24 months, have adequate iron, as indicated by a hemoglobin test.[2] The first is clearly more achievable because prenatal health care can be expected to affect birth weight, but it would have little or no effect on hemoglobin levels at age 4–24 months because those levels would be determined almost entirely by the child's health and diet after being born and thus is unlikely to be affected by any type of prenatal program to improve the health of pregnant women.

A fourth important characteristic of performance indicators is that they should be *relevant*; that is, they should reflect information that is important and likely to be used for either management or immediate analytical purposes. In particular, the indicator should measure an outcome that is likely to be affected by the program.

Two examples illustrate this principle. Consider again the program that offers free regular checkups for pregnant women from poor families. To evaluate the impact of this program on the health of newborn children, two indicators have been suggested: (1) the percentage of newborn children with a cleft lip, and (2) the percentage of newborn children with low birth weight (< 2,500 grams). Which of these indicators is more relevant? In this case, the second is more relevant because the program is likely to have an effect on birth weight. The other suggested indicator, children with a cleft lip, represents a birth defect that is unlikely to be affected by prenatal checkups.

A second example is a program that offers free school lunches to students in a developing country where malnutrition is prevalent. Consider two potential indicators: (1) weight-for-height *z*-score of students, and (2) students' time spent participating in sports after school (which may increase because of more nutrition intake). To evaluate this program, which indicator is more relevant? The first is much more relevant because providing free school lunches is likely to increase the weight of students. In contrast, the likelihood of increasing participation in sports is uncertain, and increasing that participation may not be a priority for the government.

The fifth desirable characteristic of performance indicators is that they be *time-bound.* More specifically, the indicator should track progress in the program's outcomes and impacts at a desired frequency for a set period. The following two examples illustrate this characteristic.

First, consider a conditional cash transfer program that provides cash to poor rural families in a developing country if the parents in these families take their infants to regular health checkups at local health facilities. Two indicators are under consideration: (1) whether a family took its infant to a health checkup at least four times during the infant's first six months of life, and (2) whether a family had its infant checked up at one month, two months, four months, and six months of age. Regarding the condition for receiving cash transfers, which indicator is more time-bound? In this case the second is more time-bound in the sense that it indicates exactly when the checkups should take place, illustrating whether the precise conditions for regular health checkups were satisfied.

The second example considers the same program but focuses on monitoring the process by which the cash payments are transferred to the parents. The following two indicators are proposed for the purposes of monitoring the cash payments: (1) whether an eligible household received cash transfers bimonthly for the first year of the program, and (2) whether a family received a certain amount of cash sometime during the first year of the program. Which indicator is more time-bound? In this case, the first is most time-bound because it focuses on when the payments were provided and thus indicates whether they were provided at the times that they should have been issued. In contrast, the second does not indicate the timing of the payments, therefore providing less useful information to determine whether the program's payments were made to families in accordance with the rules of the program.

Conclusion

Almost all impact evaluations seek to estimate the causal impact of a project, program, or policy on particular outcomes of interest. This is a difficult task, and the remaining chapters in this book explain how it can be done. However, before choosing the best methodology, what program is being evaluated and what the outcomes of interest are must be made clear. In addition, a theory of change should be developed to clarify the evaluation questions, and this theory of change should be expressed in the form of a results chain. After developing the theory of change, specific hypotheses can be formulated, and performance indicators can be chosen that best measure the outcomes of interest, which may include intermediate outcomes.

This chapter provides an overview of how to accomplish these goals, expressing the process using five steps that any organization should take to develop a testable theory of change for an impact evaluation. The order of the steps is not rigid; sometimes an earlier step must be revisited because of unforeseen problems that appear in a later step. Once these five steps are complete, which method or methods to use to estimate the impact of the program on the outcomes of interest can be considered. But before choosing a method, it is important to be clear about the fundamental problem that all impact evaluations face. This is discussed in the next chapter.

Notes

1. This program was originally called PROGRESA. Later its name was changed to Oportunidades, and still later its name was changed to Prospera. This book refers to it by its original name, PROGRESA.
2. Note that a body's iron store lasts for four to six months.

References

Adato, Michelle. 2000. "The Impact of PROGRESA on Community Social Relationships." Project Paper, International Food Policy Research Institute, Washington, DC.

Adato, Michelle, Benedicte de la Briere, Dubravka Mindek, and Agnes R. Quisumbing. 2000. "The Impact of PROGRESA on Women's Status and Intra-household Relations." Project Paper, International Food Policy Research Institute, Washington, DC.

Bamberger, Michael, and Linda Mabry. 2020. *RealWorld Evaluation: Working under Budget, Time, Data, and Political Constraints*, 3rd ed. Thousand Oaks, CA: Sage.

Behrman, Jere, and John Hoddinott. 2001. "An Evaluation of the Impact of PROGRESA on Pre-school Child Height." FCND Briefs 104, International Food Policy Research Institute, Washington, DC.

Behrman, Jere, Piyali Sengupta, and Petra Todd. 2000. "The Impact of PROGRESA on Achievement Test Scores in the First Year." Project Paper, International Food Policy Research Institute, Washington, DC.

Chen, Yuyu, Hongbin Li, and Lingsheng Meng. 2013. "Prenatal Sex Selection and Missing Girls in China: Evidence from the Diffusion of Diagnostic Ultrasound." *Journal of Human Resources* 48 (1): 36–70.

Chu, Junhong. 2001. "Prenatal Sex Determination and Sex-Selective Abortion in Rural Central China." *Population and Development Review* 27 (2): 259–81.

Duflo, Esther, Rema Hanna, and Stephen P. Ryan. 2012. "Incentives Work: Getting Teachers to Come to School." *American Economic Review* 102 (4): 1241–78.

Funnell, Sue C., and Patricia J. Rogers. 2011. *Purposeful Program Theory: Effective Use of Theories of Change and Logic Models*. San Francisco, CA: Jossey Bass.

Gertler, Paul. 2004. "Do Conditional Cash Transfers Improve Child Health? Evidence from PROGRESA's Control Randomized Experiment." *American Economic Review* 94 (2): 336–41.

Gertler, Paul, Sebastian Martinez, Patrick Premand, Laura Rawlings, and Christel Vermeersch. 2011. *Impact Evaluation in Practice*. Washington, DC: World Bank.

Glewwe, Paul, Albert Park, and Meng Zhao. 2016. "A Better Vision for Development: Eyeglasses and Academic Performance in Rural Primary Schools in China." *Journal of Development Economics* 122: 170–82.

Handa, Sudhanshu, Mari-Carmen Huerta, Raul Perez, and Beatriz Straffon. 2001. "Poverty, Inequality and Spillover in Mexico's Education, Health and Nutrition Program." Discussion Paper, International Food Policy Research Institute, Washington, DC.

Hoddinott, John, and Emmanuel Skoufias. 2004. "The Impact of PROGRESA on Food Consumption." *Economic Development and Cultural Change* 53 (1): 37–61.

Hoddinott, John, Emmanuel Skoufias, and Ryan Washburn. 2000. "The Impact of PROGRESA on Consumption." Project Paper, International Food Policy Research Institute, Washington, DC.

Parker, Susan, and Emmanuel Skoufias. 2000. "The Impact of PROGRESA on Work, Leisure and Time Allocation." Project Paper, International Food Policy Research Institute, Washington, DC.

Schultz, T. Paul. 2004. "School Subsidies for the Poor: Evaluating the Mexico PROGRESA Poverty Program." *Journal of Development Economics* 74 (1): 199–250.

Skoufias, Emmanuel, and Vincenzo Di Maro. 2008. "Conditional Cash Transfers, Adult Work Incentives, and Current Poverty." *Journal of Development Studies* 44 (7): 935–60.

Skoufias, Emmanuel, and Susan Parker. 2001. "Conditional Cash Transfers and Their Impact on Child Work and Schooling: Evidence from the PROGRESA Program in Mexico." *Economia* 2 (1): 45–96.

Teruel, Graciela, and Benjamin Davis. 2000. "An Evaluation of the Impact of PROGRESA Cash Payments on Private Inter-household Transfers." Project Paper, International Food Policy Research Institute, Washington, DC.

W. K. Kellogg Foundation. 2004. *Logic Model Development Guide*. Battle Creek, MI: W. K. Kellogg Foundation.

CHAPTER 3

The Evaluation Problem

Introduction

A rigorous evaluation of a project, program, or policy of interest requires that the question the evaluation is seeking to answer be unambiguously clear. Recall from chapter 2 that almost all impact evaluations seek to answer the following question:

- What is the causal impact of the program (or project or policy) on the outcomes of interest?

The desire to answer this question is called the *evaluation problem*. Answering the question requires that each aspect of the question be well-defined.

First, the *outcomes of interest* are the characteristics of the population—and perhaps of the communities in which the population lives—that the program is intended to change, as well as other characteristics of the population, or those communities, that could be changed by the program even though it may not have been the intention of the program to change those characteristics. In general, the impact of almost any program will be different for different people, so which people are being referred to when estimating a program impact needs to be clear.

Second, as chapter 2 explains, it is also essential to be clear about *which program is being evaluated*, including which version or versions for programs that have many variations. An example of this is Colombia's Gratuidad school fee reduction program, which changed its eligibility criteria.

Finally, one needs to be explicit about what is meant by the *causal impact* of a program. See box 3.1 for a summary of these requirements.

BOX 3.1 Requirements for answering the evaluation problem, "What is the causal impact of the program (or project or policy) on the outcomes of interest?"

1. Define the outcomes of interest—the characteristics of the population that the program is intended to change.
2. Be clear about which program is being evaluated.
3. Be explicit about what is meant by the causal impact of the program.

Chapter 2 discusses the first two issues noted above, concerning the *outcomes of interest* and the *need for clarity regarding the program being evaluated.* This chapter presents what is meant by the *causal impact* of the program. In doing so, it sets the stage for most of the later chapters in this book. However, before turning to the more rigorous presentation, the important point must be made that *correlations between a program and the outcomes of interest do not necessarily imply a causal relationship.* The next section makes this point, and is followed by three sections that explain the essence of the evaluation problem, define the gain from participating in the program, and discuss the most common parameters of interest. The final section provides a brief conclusion, as well as a question for a short discussion.

Correlation does not imply causation

When determining whether a program has had a causal impact on an outcome of interest, it is tempting to examine whether that outcome of interest differs between those who participated in the program and those who did not. For example, if a program is intended to reduce the incidence of malaria, whether the incidence of malaria is lower in the communities where the program was implemented than in the communities where it was not implemented might be checked. More generally, correlations are often sought between the variable that indicates whether a person or a community has participated in a program and the outcomes of interest that the program was designed to affect. In the example of the program to reduce malaria, a finding of lower malaria in areas where the program was implemented relative to the areas where the program was not implemented would generate a negative correlation between the program variable (which equals 1 in the communities with the program and 0 in the communities without the program) and the variable indicating the prevalence of malaria. Such a negative correlation may seem to be evidence that the program has in fact led to a reduction in the incidence of malaria.

Yet correlation between participation in a program and the outcomes of interest that the program is intended to change does not necessarily imply that the program has had a causal impact that changed those outcomes; *correlation does not imply causation.* To see why this could be the case, consider again the example of a program to reduce the incidence of malaria. Of course, it would make little sense to implement such a program in communities with little or no malaria; it should be implemented in areas where malaria is a serious problem. Even if the program is effective in reducing malaria, it may not reduce it to the point that its prevalence is as low as it is in communities with little or no malaria. Thus even if the program is successful, program participation and the incidence of malaria may still be positively correlated when the correlation includes communities where malaria is not a serious problem, which would suggest that the program has increased the incidence of malaria.

Misleading correlations can be generated not only by decisions about where to locate programs, but also by decisions made by people to participate in a program. An example of this type of problem is a job training program. Most people who already have well-paying jobs are not particularly interested in participating in job training programs, whereas people without jobs, or with low-paying jobs, are usually much more likely to participate in such programs because they hope that doing so will help them get well-paying jobs. Even if the program has a positive impact on the incomes of its participants, their incomes may still be lower than those of the individuals who choose not to participate in the program. Thus the correlation between participation in this program and income from employment could be negative even if the program itself has a positive impact on participants' incomes.

The general lesson from these two simple examples is that correlation does not necessarily imply causation. Other factors are likely to determine where a program is implemented and who chooses to participate in a program, which could have an effect on the correlations between program participation and the outcomes of interest in addition to the correlations that are due to the causal impacts of a program on the outcomes of interest. Now that this general point is clear, the following section discusses the evaluation problem.

Potential outcomes and the evaluation problem

To be as clear as possible, some basic notation is needed. To begin simply, this book focuses on a single outcome of interest, such as school enrollment or a health status indicator. If a program affects more than one outcome, the evaluation methods presented in this book can usually be applied to each outcome separately; for example, if a school health program affects both students' health and their academic performance, the program's effect on students' health can be estimated first, followed by an estimate of its impact on their academic performance.

Let Y denote the outcome of interest. If the program has a causal impact on Y, then in fact for any person there are two potential values of Y, the value that would occur if he or she were not "treated" by the program, which can be denoted as Y_0, and the value that would occur if he or she were treated, which can be denoted as Y_1:

$$Y_0 = \text{value of } Y \text{ if the person is } \textit{not} \text{ treated,}$$

$$Y_1 = \text{value of } Y \text{ if the person } \textit{is} \text{ treated.}$$

It is important to understand that both Y_0 and Y_1 are defined, and therefore exist, for all people. However, it is impossible to measure both Y_0 and Y_1 at the same time for the same person. For a person who has been treated, that is, who has participated in the program, Y_1 can be observed, but Y_0 cannot. Yet Y_0, the value of Y for this person if he or she had not been treated, is still defined and would have been observed if this person had not participated in the program. Similarly, for a person who has not been treated, that is, who has not participated in the program, Y_0 can be observed, but Y_1 cannot. Yet Y_1, the value of Y for this person if he or she had been treated, is still defined and would have been observed if this person had participated in the program.

Usually, the most important objective of impact evaluation is to estimate $Y_1 - Y_0$, which is the causal impact of the program. Although estimating $Y_1 - Y_0$ for an individual person is almost impossible, it may well be possible to estimate the average of $Y_1 - Y_0$ for some population or subpopulation of interest.

The main problem for impact evaluation is that, for each person, only Y_0 or Y_1, but not both, can be observed at any given time. This is the fundamental problem that impact evaluation methods attempt to solve. This conception of the evaluation problem is called the *potential outcomes framework*. It was first introduced by Fisher (1935) and Roy (1951). Early discussions appear in Quandt (1972) and Rubin (1978). It is often called the *Roy model* in economics or the *causal model* in statistics.

Observed outcomes and the gain from treatment

Given that the main problem of impact evaluation is the inability to observe both Y_0 and Y_1 at the same time for a given person or other unit of interest (such as a household, a small business, or a community), a useful starting point for developing methods that may allow the impacts of particular programs or policies to be estimated is to clarify what can be observed, and how those "observable" variables are related to Y_0 and Y_1. Two observable variables are the most important. The first is P, the variable that indicates whether a person participates in the program (is treated by the program). In the simplest case, P takes only two values:

$P = 0$: The individual *was not* treated (did not participate in the program),

$P = 1$: The individual *was* treated (did participate in the program).

In most evaluations P is observed, but in some cases program participation is not available for some or all observations in a particular data set. For example, when evaluating the impact on health outcomes of taking a new medicine, data may be available on who has been provided the medicine but not whether those individuals actually took it; this issue is related to the discussion of intention-to-treat effects in chapter 6. Unless otherwise indicated, this book assumes that P is observed for all observations in the data.

The other most important observed variable is the *observed value of* Y, which by definition is always observed. For the rest of this book, Y without a 0 or 1 subscript indicates the observed value of Y. The relationship between Y, which is always observed, and Y_0 and Y_1, which cannot both be observed for the same person at the same time, is that for a person with $P = 1$ it must be that $Y = Y_1$, and for a person with $P = 0$ it follows that $Y = Y_0$.

Mathematically, this implies the following relationship between Y_0, Y_1, P, and Y:

$$Y = PY_1 + (1 - P)Y_0.$$

For any individual, the *gain from treatment* is defined as the difference between Y_1 and Y_0, denoted by Δ:

$$\Delta = Y_1 - Y_0.$$

Because only one state is observed at any given time (that is, at any time for a given individual either Y_0 or Y_1 is observed, but not both), the gain from treatment (Δ) is not directly observed for any specific person. Estimating Δ can therefore be seen as a *missing data problem*. The evaluation literature has developed a variety of different approaches to solve this problem.

A final helpful term that is often used in impact evaluations (and was introduced in chapter 1) is the *counterfactual*, which can be defined as *the potential outcome (Y_0 or Y_1) that is not observed.* (Counterfactual means something that did not happen and thus is "counter to fact.") Thus the observed Y for a person who has participated in a program is that person's Y_1; therefore, the counterfactual for that person is his or her Y_0. Similarly, the observed Y for a person who has not participated in a program is that person's Y_0, so the counterfactual is his or her Y_1. Continuing with the example of evaluating the impact on health outcomes of taking a new medicine, for a person who has taken the new medicine his or her Y_1 is observed, whereas Y_0 (what would have happened if that person had not taken the new medicine) is the counterfactual. Similarly, for a person who has not taken the new medicine, his or her Y_0 is observed whereas Y_1 (what would have happened if that person had taken the new medicine) is the counterfactual.

Parameters of interest

As mentioned, it is almost impossible to estimate the impact of a project, program, or policy for a single individual because it is impossible to measure both Y_1 and Y_0 for the same individual at the same time. Thus almost all impact evaluations calculate some kind of average causal effect over a defined population. However, the impacts of a project, program, or policy are likely to be different for different people. Thus average impacts are likely to be different for different groups of people. These different averages are often called *parameters of interest*. The two most common parameters of interest used in impact evaluation are the following:

- The average gain from the program for all persons in the population:

  $$E[Y_1 - Y_0] = E[\Delta].$$

  This is commonly referred to as the *average impact of the treatment*, or *average treatment effect*, denoted by ATE. Note that E[...] denotes "expected value," which is the population mean (average value for the population being studied) of the expression in the brackets.

- The average gain from the program for all persons in the population who are program participants:

$$E[Y_1 - Y_0 | P = 1] = E[\Delta | P = 1].$$

  This is called the *average treatment effect on the treated*, and is denoted by ATT. The vertical bar inside the brackets indicates conditionality; that is, the term or terms to the left of the bar are evaluated only for the group defined by the expression to the right of the bar.

In fact, it is sometimes possible to go further by estimating ATE and ATT for a group of people with the same characteristics **X**, where **X** is a vector (group) of variables that are observed in the data being used for the evaluation. An example would be women between the ages of 30 and 40 who have finished secondary school. Then, for any group with the characteristics **X**, the following can be defined:

$$\text{ATE}(\mathbf{X}) \equiv E[Y_1 - Y_0 | \mathbf{X}] = E[\Delta | \mathbf{X}],$$
$$\text{ATT}(\mathbf{X}) \equiv E[Y_1 - Y_0 | P = 1, \mathbf{X}] = E[\Delta | P = 1, \mathbf{X}].$$

In words, ATE(**X**) is the average gain from the program that would be experienced by *all* persons with characteristics **X**, including both those who have participated and those who have not, and ATT(**X**) is the average gain experienced for the subset of individuals with characteristics **X** who actually participated in the program (that is, for whom $P = 1$).

Conclusion

Impact evaluations seek to answer the following question: *What is the causal impact of the program (or project or policy) on the outcomes of interest?* This chapter focuses on what is meant by causal impact, or effect of the treatment. In doing so it introduces the concept of *potential outcomes*; in particular, Y_1 is defined as the value of the outcome of interest if a person has participated in the program, and Y_0 is defined as the value of the outcome of interest if that person had not participated. For any person, the causal impact of the program is defined as $Y_1 - Y_0$. Unfortunately, for any given person (or other unit of analysis) only Y_1 or Y_0 can be observed at any time, so it is not possible to calculate the causal impact, $Y_1 - Y_0$, for that person. This can be viewed as a missing data problem. However, it may be possible to calculate an average value over a well-defined population.

This chapter also introduces the average treatment effect, ATE, and the average treatment effect on the treated, ATT. Many chapters in this book focus on methods that can be used to estimate ATE and ATT, and some also discuss methods for estimating ATE(**X**) and ATT(**X**) for subpopulations with specific characteristics denoted by **X**. However, before turning to those methods it is worthwhile to discuss two general concepts of validity of estimates that are relevant for all these estimation methods; this is addressed in chapter 4.

Question for discussion:

- Suppose that participants in the program tend to be the people who receive the greatest benefit from it. Which of the following would you expect?

$$\text{ATT} > \text{ATE},$$

$$\text{ATT} = \text{ATE},$$

$$\text{ATT} < \text{ATE}.$$

References

Fisher, R. A. 1935. *The Design of Experiments*. Edinburgh: Oliver and Boyd.

Quandt, Richard. 1972. "A New Approach to Estimating Switching Regressions." *Journal of the American Statistical Association* 67 (338): 306–10.

Roy, A. D. 1951. "Some Thoughts on the Distribution of Earnings." *Oxford Economic Papers* 3 (2): 135–46.

Rubin, Donald. 1978. "Bayesian Inference for Causal Effects: The Role of Randomization." *Annals of Statistics* 6 (1): 34–58.

CHAPTER 4

Validity: Internal, External, and Trade-Offs

Introduction

As discussed in previous chapters, impact evaluation is concerned with measuring the impact of a project, program, or policy on outcomes of interest. Many chapters of this book focus on methods for generating unbiased estimates of programs' causal effects—which is no small feat, for reasons outlined in chapter 3 on the evaluation problem. However, when selecting an evaluation approach, researchers will have to consider several aspects of validity, which are the focus of this chapter. Validity includes not only how accurately estimates reflect the effect of the program being evaluated, but also how likely it is that these results will provide accurate information on how similar programs would perform in different contexts at different times. Practically, this means that researchers are likely to face trade-offs between the extent to which they control the intervention (including who has access to it) and how representative the subjects and environment in the study are of real-world scenarios of interest. These trade-offs are between the internal validity and external validity of an evaluation, and are discussed in this chapter.

A study has strong *internal validity* if the researcher is able to demonstrate that an observed correlation between program participation and the outcomes of interest represents a causal relationship; in other words, the study has successfully addressed the evaluation problem as stated in chapter 3. A study has strong *external validity* if a causal effect found for that study's environment can be generalized to other populations, places, or times. That is, internal validity focuses on whether the study has successfully identified the causal effects that a program or policy has in the context in which the study was performed, whereas external validity focuses on whether the study's findings provide a reliable estimate of what similar programs' effects would be in other contexts. Both types of validity are relevant for policy decisions; internal validity is needed to decide whether a project, program, or policy is effective for the context in which it has been implemented, and external validity is needed for deciding whether the project, program, or policy is likely to be effective in other contexts.

There are other types of validity not covered in this book,[1] including a widely used typology developed by Cook and Campbell (1979) and later refined by Hedges (2017). For a further discussion of issues concerning validity and related topics, see Bamberger and Mabry (2020); Bates and Glennerster (2017); Chen, Donaldson, and Mark (2011); and Shadish, Cook, and Campbell (2001).

With this introduction to the topic, the rest of this chapter is organized as follows. The next section defines, and discusses, threats to internal validity. The following section does the same for external validity. The subsequent section then reviews the trade-offs in internal validity and external validity that are present in different evaluation methods, and the final section concludes with some general advice.

Internal validity

A study is considered to have strong internal validity if the study's estimated effects can be considered causal for the context in which the study was done. Establishing that a relationship is causal usually depends upon the researcher identifying a valid comparison group that can be used to construct a valid counterfactual. To guarantee strong internal validity, the researcher may wish to control the environment and the treatment used, such as in a laboratory experiment. This is in contrast to studies that rely on observational data (such as large-scale household surveys or census data), which must draw conclusions based on phenomena observed in uncontrolled environments. When internal validity is strong, the researcher is confident that the intervention—not alternative factors or forces—caused the observed differences between the treatment and comparison groups in the context covered by the study.

When conducting impact evaluations, the researcher must always think carefully about alternative explanations for an observed apparent impact. In doing so, although there could be other threats to consider, there are three main threats to internal validity that should be kept in mind (see also Roe and Just 2009). The first, and perhaps most obvious, is a *lack of temporal clarity*. A lack of temporal clarity is a situation in which the researcher cannot be sure whether the observed outcome occurred after the event that is believed to have caused the outcome. This presents a problem because the researcher cannot rule out reverse causality. For example, suppose that a researcher discovers that students who received textbooks last school year also had higher test scores. To claim that these textbooks caused the higher test scores observed at the end of that school year, the researcher must be sure, at a minimum, that the students actually had access to the textbooks before being tested. Without knowing the timing of the distribution of textbooks and of the exam, an alternative explanation could be that students who did well on entrance exams were offered textbooks as a reward for their good performance or to enrich their school experience; in this case, scoring well on a test caused the students to receive the textbooks, not the other way around. In the absence of information on the timing of interventions and outcomes, this type of scenario cannot be ruled out. One way to obtain such information is through careful monitoring of the implementation of the intervention.

A second type of threat to internal validity is *systematic differences between treatment and comparison groups*. Systematic differences between treatment and comparison groups can threaten the validity of the estimates of a program's effects if there are differences between the treatment and comparison groups other than that the former has received the treatment and the latter has not received it. This is also known as a *selection problem*, which means that individuals who receive the treatment are selected (or self-select) on the basis of some characteristic that is correlated with outcomes of interest. Consider again the textbooks example. Suppose the researcher knows the scores are from tests administered at the end of the school year, and knows which students received textbooks at the beginning of the school year, ruling out any problem caused by lack of temporal clarity. To determine that there are also no systematic differences between members of the treatment and comparison groups, the researcher must also determine whether the students who received the textbooks were selected to receive them on the basis of some characteristic correlated with end-of-year test scores. For example, if the most motivated students went out of their way to obtain textbooks, textbooks would be positively correlated with motivation, which is likely to be positively correlated with learning and test scores and would lead to overestimation of the impact of textbooks. On the other hand, if low-achieving students were given textbooks as a form of extra support, textbooks would be negatively correlated with test scores, which would lead to underestimation of textbooks' impact. Both of these scenarios represent a threat to internal validity because of a systematic difference between members of the treatment and control groups. This problem would be resolved if textbooks were distributed randomly, or if their distribution were based on some characteristic not correlated with test scores.

The third main threat to internal validity is the possibility that *concurrent events* may have an impact on the outcome of interest at the same time that the treatment in question may be affecting that outcome. In an uncontrolled environment, third factors may simultaneously influence both the treatment and the outcome being studied, leading to correlation between the treatment and the outcome that is not due to the causal impact of the treatment on the outcome. Consider again the example of an evaluation of the impact of receiving textbooks. If the researcher is unaware that students who received textbooks were also selected to receive tutoring, the researcher is likely to ascribe some or all of the effect of tutoring to the effect of the textbooks. Even if the researcher is aware that the students who received textbooks also received tutoring, it may not be possible to separately identify the effects of each intervention.

In general, threats to internal validity vary according to the evaluation method used. In other words, internal validity depends on the identification strategy. There are also other threats to internal validity, and chapters 6–17 discuss in great detail all of the threats to internal validity that apply to each of the evaluation methods presented in those chapters.

External validity

If the three main threats to internal validity can be ruled out, establishing causality is more likely. However, establishing causality does not necessarily mean that the researcher should invest time in the study. In addition to knowing that the treatment's causal effect can be identified, the results of the study need to be useful. In most cases, the results will be most valuable if it is reasonable to extrapolate that the treatment effect identified in the study provides a good indication of the effect if the same treatment were offered again—perhaps at a different time, in a different context, or with a different population. When the results from a study can be generalized to a different time, place, and/or population, the study is said to have strong external validity. Researchers should consider several common threats to external validity when designing an evaluation.

The most common threat to external validity may be the interaction between characteristics unique to the context in which an intervention takes place and the treatment. If the treatment effect varies depending on when, where, or with what population the intervention takes place, the results from one evaluation may not hold when the intervention is offered again but in a different context. For this reason, an important part of designing an impact evaluation is considering whether the participants in the study are a good representation of the likely future beneficiaries of the program being evaluated. One way to achieve this representativeness is to choose a random sample of the population of potential beneficiaries for the evaluation. Using a sample that is representative of the population at large enables the researcher to estimate the average treatment effect for that population and, if the sample is large enough, to conduct subgroup analysis to capture the intervention's treatment effects for different subgroups.

Drawing a large and representative sample is often easier said than done, however, and such a sample usually implies trade-offs. First, a larger sample size increases data collection costs because more interviews must be conducted. Using a randomly drawn, representative sample will also increase data collection costs because it increases travel costs for the data collection teams. Detailed recommendations on data collection are presented in chapter 19. Second, a large, widely dispersed sample is also more difficult to monitor, which becomes particularly important when implementing a randomized experiment in which it may be necessary to monitor participants' compliance with their assigned treatment; the importance of such monitoring is made clear in chapters 6–9.

Even after ensuring that the sample is similar to the overall eligible population in certain characteristics, such as geography, sex, and ethnic group, the sample may differ from the population in more subtle ways. Academic researchers often turn to the population to which they have easiest access—students. Enticing students to participate in research with offers of free pizza may be an efficient way to gather a sample on a college campus but may be at the expense of the external validity of the study if the treatment effect for college students differs from the treatment effect for the overall eligible population. Students are likely to be younger and more willing to try new things than the overall population. Similarly, seeking volunteers to spend a day participating in an experiment will generate results that are representative of those who have relatively more free time on their hands, but may not reflect the effects that would be observed for a population with full-time jobs.

A second threat to external validity arises when the treatment as it is offered when being evaluated differs from how it is offered otherwise. If the evaluation is undertaken in a highly controlled environment, such as in a lab or a highly controlled field experiment, the treatment is likely to be delivered as it was designed to be delivered. Consider the textbook example again. If the textbook distribution is part of an evaluation, the evaluators are likely to ensure that the books are delivered to all the intended recipients at the appropriate time.

In the absence of the evaluation, the distribution will follow the usual practice of the current distribution system; in practice, textbooks may arrive late, or in insufficient quantity. The effect of other interventions, such as training or educational interventions, may require sufficient intensity. It is easy to imagine a training program being implemented with high fidelity when offered as part of a careful evaluation, but with lower intensity otherwise. If that were the case, the treatment effect found by the careful evaluation would likely overestimate the treatment's effect under more general circumstances. Bold et al. (2018) find this result for an education program that was effective when implemented on a small scale in Western Kenya, but when implemented across all provinces of Kenya by the government, the program was completely ineffective.

Trade-offs and intermediate approaches

In practice, there are often trade-offs between evaluations that have strong internal validity and those that have strong external validity. Evaluations that perform well in one dimension of validity may not perform as well in the other dimension of validity. At one extreme, highly controlled lab experiments have strong internal validity. In a controlled environment, randomly assigning participants to a treatment or a control group and closely monitoring their outcomes to evaluate the effect of the treatment is easy. Although researchers who run lab experiments can identify with confidence the causal effect of interventions as conducted in their labs, they may be hard-pressed to convince policy makers to use scarce resources to implement the interventions on a larger scale without knowing how well they would perform in a less controlled environment, with a broader sample of the population. That is, such evaluations may have low external validity. At the same time, even though researchers who use data from nationally representative household surveys or census data may have more confidence that their data represent the population at large, they will face serious challenges in identifying a causal effect with observational data, as explained in detail in chapters 11–17 of this book.

Most researchers use strategies between these two extremes; finding the right balance depends on the budget for an evaluation and the specific characteristics of the intervention being evaluated. The importance of using a study sample that represents the overall eligible population varies by the type of intervention. When evaluating medical interventions, knowing someone's age and weight may be sufficient, whereas evaluations of job training programs, or other programs that depend heavily on factors such as education, motivation, and labor market characteristics, require careful consideration of the extent to which the sample is representative of the overall eligible population.

Some general approaches, roughly going from most controlled (which tend to have stronger internal validity and weaker external validity) to least controlled (which tend to have weaker internal validity and stronger external validity), are outlined below. Table 4.1 summarizes the general relationships between the three types of experiments described in the following paragraphs and the level of control the researcher has over the fidelity of

TABLE 4.1 Control over fidelity of implementation and internal and external validity, by experiment type

	RESEARCHER'S LEVEL OF CONTROL OVER FIDELITY OF IMPLEMENTATION	INTERNAL VALIDITY	EXTERNAL VALIDITY
Lab experiment	High	High	Low
Field experiment	Moderate	Moderate	Moderate
Natural experiment or quasi-experiment	None	Varied; often low	Varied; often high

Source: Glewwe and Todd 2019.
Note: These are broad generalizations about each type of experiment. In reality, there will be exceptions to each of the characteristics presented in this table.

experimental implementation, internal validity, and external validity. It is important to note, however, that there are important exceptions to each of these relationships.

Lab experiments. Lab experiments are conducted in highly controlled environments in which the researcher controls all factors except the effect of the intervention being studied. Because the researcher can ensure that members of the treatment and control groups are similar in all ways except their treatment status, results from lab experiments have strong internal validity. The potential trade-off is that because a laboratory environment is rarely similar to a naturally occurring environment, to determine external validity one must carefully consider the extent to which these results reflect what would happen in another context.

Field experiments. Field experiments are prospective studies in which the researcher controls the application of a treatment in an uncontrolled, real-world environment. Working with a clearly defined sample, certain individuals (or households or schools or communities) are randomly selected to receive a treatment, while others are randomly assigned to a comparison group that does not receive the treatment. Random assignment facilitates the clear identification of a treatment's causal effect, as in a lab experiment. Controlling the environment and individuals' actions in the field is more difficult than in the lab, however. For example, individuals may not comply with their treatment assignment. On the other hand, a field experiment offers stronger external validity than a lab experiment by operating in a natural environment that may closely resemble the environment in which the intervention would be offered in the future. In practice, field experiments' external validity varies widely depending on the sample used.

Glewwe, Kremer, and Moulin (2009) conducted a randomized experiment to evaluate the impact of providing textbooks to primary school students in Kenya. To the authors' surprise, they found that the average treatment effect on students' test scores was small and statistically insignificant. Subgroup analysis revealed that the books did have a significant positive effect for the most advanced students in the sample, suggesting that the material in the books was too challenging for the lower-performing students. Had the study sample included only relatively low-performing students, or only high-performing students, the authors could not have discovered this result. Their selection of a diverse student population gave this field experiment stronger external validity than it would have had with a more homogeneous sample.

The International Food Policy Research Institute, an international agricultural research organization based in Washington, DC, led the evaluation of the PROGRESA conditional cash transfer program in Mexico. This was one of the first of many large-scale field experiments of government programs in developing countries. The evaluation sample included more than 24,000 households in 506 communities distributed across seven states in Mexico. Skoufias (2005) found that students in communities that participated in the program were significantly more likely to enter secondary school after completing primary school. This study has an unusually high external validity because it is based on a remarkably large sample of communities from several different states in Mexico. Of course, one important disadvantage of this large and wide-ranging sample is that it resulted in extremely high data collection costs.

Natural experiments or quasi-experiments with large administrative data sets. In a natural experiment, the researcher exploits some exogenous variation that causes certain individuals to receive a treatment while other similar individuals do not. This source of variation could be the result of a clerical error that causes some individuals to be excluded from a program for which they are eligible, or could be a sudden change in policy. Because the context is a natural environment, natural experiments tend to have higher external validity and, depending on the nature of the source of variation, may have high internal validity as well.[2] Other natural experiments may use a regression discontinuity design (covered in chapter 14) to take advantage of a discrete cutoff that enables people on one side of the cutoff to participate in a program while excluding those on the other side of the cutoff. Such a regression discontinuity design would be possible, for example, if a test score cutoff is used to determine school or college admissions decisions or eligibility for scholarships.

An example of an evaluation based on a natural experiment is a study by Duflo (2001), who exploited the rapid construction of more than 61,000 primary schools in Indonesia in the 1970s to analyze the effects of increased access to education on educational attainment and earnings. She combined differences across regions in the numbers of schools constructed with differences across cohorts of students in exposure to the program that were induced by the timing of the program to estimate these effects with observational data. Because her analytical approach was convincing, this study has strong internal validity. Because her analysis relied on a large and representative data set, her study also has strong external validity, which enabled her to draw conclusions about the average impact of access to education for Indonesia as a whole.

Conclusion

This chapter provides an explanation of two important concepts of validity for impact evaluations. *Internal validity* refers to an evaluation's ability to estimate the causal impact of program participation on the outcomes of interest for the population on which the evaluation study was conducted. *External validity* means that the findings of an evaluation can be generalized from the study environment to other populations, places, and/or times. There could be a tension between these two concepts of validity if measures taken to improve internal validity weaken external validity, or vice versa, but there is no inherent reason that an increase in one necessarily implies a decrease in the other.

No general solution exists to increase both internal and external validity, and to minimize possible tensions between the two types of validity, because every evaluation is unique in (1) how the treatment effect is expected to vary in different contexts; (2) the budget available for a large, representative sample; (3) the diversity of the overall eligible population; and (4) the question that one is attempting to answer. Researchers will also face constraints on what evaluation methods are possible. Some interventions cannot be randomly assigned, much less implemented in a laboratory. In other instances, large observational data sets may be available, but estimating the causal effect of the policy or program in question will be difficult. The researcher's challenging task is to identify the situations in which it is possible to design an evaluation that has sufficient internal and external validity to generate information that will provide useful guidance for policy makers, who must make decisions about where to invest scarce resources for public programs, including whether to terminate or modify programs that rigorous evaluations indicate are not working.

Notes

1. Among the more common other types are construct validity, data analysis validity, and ecological validity. *Construct validity,* as described in Bamberger and Mabry (2020, 110), refers to "the adequacy of the constructs used to define processes, outcomes and impacts, contextual and intervening variables." In the context of evaluation, this determines the extent to which we can draw inferences from the instruments, practices, and settings that constitute a policy intervention, including adequately defining core concepts, integrating those concepts into a meaningful theory of change, and engaging with existing research. *Data analysis validity* gauges the extent to which the evaluation has paid attention to risks of bias (unreliable data, improper choice of methods, and so on), and whether the evaluation has addressed such risks. Finally, *ecological validity* assesses the extent to which the analysis and findings can be extended to real-life settings, as described in Andrade (2018).
2. The main concern regarding external validity of natural experiments is whether the impact of the program may differ in other contexts as a result of different characteristics of the population in those contexts relative to the population that experienced the natural experiment.

References

Andrade, Chittaranjan. 2018. "Internal, External, and Ecological Validity in Research Design, Conduct, and Evaluation." *Indian Journal of Psychological Medicine* 40 (5): 498–99.

Bamberger, Michael, and Linda Mabry. 2020. *RealWorld Evaluation: Working Under Budget, Time, Data, and Political Constraints*, third edition. Thousand Oaks, CA: Sage.

Bates, Mary Ann, and Rachel Glennerster. 2017. "The Generalizability Puzzle." *Stanford Social Innovation Review,* Winter 2017. https://ssir.org/articles/entry/the_generalizability_puzzle.

Bold, Tessa, Mwangi Kimenyi, Germano Mwabu, Alice Ng'ang'a, and Justin Sandefur. 2018. "Experimental Evidence on Scaling Up Education Reforms in Kenya." *Journal of Public Economics* 168 (December):1–20.

Chen, Huey, Stewart Donaldson, and Melvin Mark, eds. 2011. "Advancing Validity in Outcome Evaluation: Theory and Practice." Special issue, *New Directions for Evaluation* 130 (2011).

Cook, Thomas D., and D. T. Campbell. 1979. *Quasi-Experimentation: Design and Analysis Issues for Field Settings*. Boston: Houghton Mifflin.

Duflo, Esther. 2001. "Schooling and Labor Market Consequences of School Construction in Indonesia: Evidence from an Unusual Policy Experiment." *American Economic Review* 91 (4): 795–814.

Glewwe, Paul, Michael Kremer, and Sylvie Moulin. 2009. "Many Children Left Behind? Textbooks and Test Scores in Kenya." *American Economic Journal: Applied Economics* 1 (1): 112–35.

Glewwe, Paul, and Petra Todd. 2019. Course materials, "APEC 8212: Econometric Analysis II" and "ECON712: Graduate Topics Course in Program Evaluation Methods," University of Minnesota, Minneapolis–St. Paul, and University of Pennsylvania, Philadelphia.

Hedges, L. V. 2017. "Design of Empirical Research." In *Research Methods and Methodologies in Education, edited* by R. Coe, M. Waring, L. V. Hedges, and J. Arthur. Thousand Oaks, CA: Sage.

Roe, Brian, and David Just. 2009. "Internal and External Validity in Economics Research: Tradeoffs between Experiments, Field Experiments, Natural Experiments and Field Data." *American Journal of Agricultural Economics* 91 (5): 1266–71.

Shadish, William, Thomas Cook, and Donald Campbell. 2001. *Experimental and Quasi-Experimental Designs for Generalized Causal Inference*, second edition. Boston, MA: Cengage Learning.

Skoufias, Emmanuel. 2005. *PROGRESA and Its Impacts on the Welfare of Rural Households in Mexico.* Research Report 139. Washington, DC: International Food Policy Research Institute.

CHAPTER
5

Overview of Impact Evaluation Methods

Introduction

Up to this point the material covered in this book has been relatively nontechnical. The next 12 chapters of this book, chapters 6–17, present a detailed and mathematically rigorous description of impact evaluation methods. While this material is unavoidably technical, readers with modest to moderate mathematical and statistical skills are encouraged to see how far they can go in reading these chapters.

Many evaluation organizations are overseen or directed by managers whose technical skills may be limited or not up to date, so they may have difficulty understanding the mathematical and statistical details of the material covered in chapters 6–17. However, they can still be effective managers as long as they have a general understanding of the impact evaluation methods discussed. More generally, many nontechnical staff in evaluation agencies need not know the details of the material, yet a general understanding of different evaluation methods will be beneficial to their work.

This chapter offers a general understanding by providing a brief review of the impact evaluation methods discussed in detail in chapters 6–17. It begins with a discussion of randomized controlled trials (RCTs) and then turns to methods based on nonexperimental and quasi-experimental data. It concludes by summarizing which methods are most useful for different sets of circumstances.

Using randomized controlled trials to evaluate program impacts

In theory, and often in practice, the best way to estimate the impact of a program, project, or policy is to implement it in some areas and not in other areas and compare the outcomes of interest. If the areas in which the program, project, or policy is implemented are randomly chosen from a well-defined population, then such a comparison will provide an accurate estimate of the impact of the program if no other problems arise. This is the general approach of RCTs, and when RCTs can be feasibly implemented, they can provide unbiased and consistent estimates of impacts without any further assumptions. RCTs are discussed in detail in chapters 6–9, and the rest of this section summarizes the content of those chapters. Chapter 10 discusses ethical considerations, which apply both to RCTs and to other impact evaluation methods but are particularly important for RCTs. Thus that chapter is also summarized at the end of this section.

Overview of randomized controlled trials

RCTs are increasingly being used to evaluate program impacts in both developed and developing countries. Many conditional cash transfer programs, such as Mexico's PROGRESA (which is now called Oportunidades), have been evaluated using RCTs. Other well-known examples are described in Banerjee and Duflo (2011) and Glennerster and Takavarasha (2013).

As explained in chapter 6, in its simplest form, an RCT randomly assigns some members of the population to a treatment group, who then participate in the program, and randomly assigns other members of the population to a control group, who do not participate in the program. Random assignment of the treatment ensures that the treatment group and the control group are similar in all aspects except that only the former group receives the treatment. Therefore, any systematic differences in the outcomes of interest between the treatment group and the control group are solely due to the treatment, that is, to participation in the program. Indeed, the average program impact can be estimated by the difference between the treatment group and the control group in the mean of the outcomes of interest. This average program impact is often called the *average treatment effect* (ATE).[1]

In practice, it is not always possible to ensure that individuals follow their random assignment. The simplest case happens when no one in the control group is able to participate in the program, but some people who were randomly assigned to the program choose not to participate. This case is also explained in chapter 6. In this situation it is no longer possible to estimate the ATE, but as long as nonparticipants do not receive indirect benefits from the program, the impact of the program on those who did in fact participate can be estimated. This impact, which is called the *average treatment effect on the treated* (ATT), is not necessarily equal to the ATE because those who participate may differ from the general population under consideration.

The common occurrence that some people randomly assigned to the treatment group choose not to participate in the program has led some researchers to propose a different type of treatment effect: the average impact of the program among those offered the treatment. This is the *intention-to-treat effect* (ITT), defined as the impact of the program among those who were offered the opportunity to participate in the program, regardless of whether they actually participated.

ITT is a useful measure of program impact because it shows what will happen to the average value of the outcome of interest for the entire population that is offered the opportunity to participate in the program, not just for those who actually participate. ITT is also simple to calculate using observed data from an RCT, as explained in chapter 6. Quite simply, ITT can be calculated as the average value of the outcome of interest for those who were randomly offered the opportunity to participate in the program (the treatment group) minus the average value of the outcome of interest for those who were randomly not offered the opportunity to participate in the program (the control group).

Another potential problem with RCTs is that the impacts of some types of programs may spill over onto individuals who do not participate, which may not be a serious problem if the only nonparticipating individuals who are so affected are those who were in the treatment group. For example, suppose that mosquito bednets are offered to households in 100 randomly selected villages but are not offered in another 100 randomly selected villages. Perhaps some households in the 100 treatment villages do not accept the bednets. Those households may still benefit because the fact that other people did accept them may reduce their probability of getting malaria or another disease transmitted by mosquitoes. As long as this spillover does not affect anyone in the 100 control villages that did not receive bednets, it is still possible to estimate ITT, the average effect of the treatment on the households in the treatment villages, all of whom were offered the opportunity to participate in the program, including those who did not accept the nets but benefited from the spillovers. However, as explained in chapter 6, ATT can no longer be estimated, and even ITT cannot be estimated if spillovers affect the control villages as well.

In some cases, some of the individuals who were randomly assigned to the control group find a way to participate in the program, or in a very similar program. When this occurs, it is also likely that some individuals randomly assigned to the treatment group choose not to participate in the program. Under these circumstances, it is not possible to estimate ATE, ATT, or ITT. However, it is possible to estimate the impact of the treatment for a subset of the population, namely those people who comply with their random assignment, which is often referred to as the *local* average treatment effect (LATE). This approach is called *encouragement design* and is explained in the last section of chapter 6. It is implemented using an instrumental variables (IV) estimation method, which is a general method that can be used in a wide variety of settings. IV estimation is discussed further in this chapter in the section titled "Impact evaluations based on nonrandomized and quasi-experimental data."

RCTs can often be used to estimate ATE and ITT simply by comparing the means of the treatment and control groups, as explained previously. However, regression methods are also commonly used to estimate ATE, ITT, ATT, and LATE; this is explained in detail in chapter 7. There are three main benefits of using regression methods. First, regression methods are convenient for assessing the statistical significance of the different types of estimated treatment effects. Second, regression methods offer a useful method for controlling for other variables that have an impact on the outcome of interest, and doing so may increase the statistical precision of the estimated treatment effects. Third, regression methods are helpful for estimating the impact of a program on different subsets of the population, such as men versus women or rural versus urban populations, although such subpopulation estimates need to be interpreted with care because even if the true effect of the program on all subpopulations is zero, sooner or later, by statistical chance, an estimate for one (or more than one) subpopulation will be statistically significant.

The discussion of how to apply regression methods to analyze data from an RCT in chapter 7 begins with the simplest case, one in which all individuals comply with their random assignments: a simple regression can be used to estimate ATE. The chapter then considers how to use regression methods when some individuals in the treatment group choose not to participate in the program, which allows ITT to be estimated, assuming that no one in the control group obtains the treatment. If the further assumption is made that individuals in the treatment group who choose not to participate do not obtain any benefit from the participation of others in their treated communities, then it is also possible to estimate ATT. Note that this assumption may not hold in many cases; for example, if the treatment reduces the general prevalence of infectious diseases in the treated communities, then it may well benefit individuals in those communities who choose not to participate in the program.

Regression methods are also useful for analyzing data from an RCT when there are problems of sample attrition, that is, when some of the individuals who were in the treatment or control groups at the baseline data collection cannot be found when data are collected again from the same people after the program has been operating for a few months (or even a few years). The next section of chapter 7 explains how to check for sample attrition, and then how to conduct a *bounds analysis* if substantial sample attrition is found. Bounds analysis uses some plausible assumptions to obtain upper and lower bounds on treatment effects.

Finally, the last sections of chapter 7 provide further recommendations on how to apply regression methods to estimate treatment effects from data generated by RCTs. More specifically, these sections explain how to use regression methods to increase the statistical precision of the estimated treatment effects and then show what methods should be used to obtain the correct standard errors for the estimated treatment effects and other parameters. The chapter ends with advice and recommendations for using regression methods to analyze data from an RCT.

Potential problems with randomized controlled trials

If implemented correctly, RCTs can provide unbiased estimates of program impacts. However, in practice, implementing RCTs can be difficult, and many things can go wrong. Whereas chapters 6 and 7 discuss what to do when some of the individuals randomly assigned to the treatment group choose not to participate in the program, chapter 8 examines several other problems that are, in general, more difficult to solve. It also provides more detailed guidance on how to conduct an RCT to obtain high-quality impact evaluations.

The first section of chapter 8 discusses six common problems that arise in practice when conducting RCTs, along with suggestions for how to avoid them or at least minimize their impact. The first problem occurs when some people in the control group are able to get into the program, or into a similar program, which is often referred to as *contamination bias*. Chapter 8 begins by providing advice on how to prevent this from happening in the first place. When it does occur, one way to estimate program impacts is to use IV methods to estimate LATE, where random assignment is the instrumental variable. This econometric method is discussed in detail in chapter 15. Another, admittedly partial, solution to contamination bias would be to acknowledge the problem and revise the kind of program impact that can be estimated. For example, perhaps only a lower bound on the impact of the program can be estimated.

A second common problem is that some program participants may drop out before completing the program. If this dropping out were random it would not lead to bias in the estimates: the dropouts could simply be excluded from the estimation. But dropouts are usually not a random sample of the people assigned to the program, which can lead to bias. Several approaches can be used to minimize bias, or to obtain upper or lower bounds on the impact of the program. One example is to assume that the program impact on dropouts is less than the full effect they would have received if they had not dropped out, in which case comparing the treated (including dropouts) with the controls yields a *lower bound* estimate of the ATE. Another example is to assume that, on average, dropouts would have benefited less from the program than those who did not drop out; in this case excluding the dropouts from the estimate of the program effect would lead to an *upper bound* estimate of the ATE.

A third problem, which affects both RCTs and other, nonexperimental types of impact evaluation methods, is sample attrition. In almost any RCT evaluation, people in both the treatment group and the control group can drop out of the sample because of the research team's inability to locate them (for example, if they migrate) or if they refuse to participate in follow-up interviews. If the attrition within the treatment group or the control group is not random, biased estimates could result. When attrition occurs, which is almost always the case, at a minimum researchers should report attrition rates for both the treatment group and the control group. If these rates are not significantly different from each other, it is likely, though not certain, that there is little or no attrition bias. If the attrition rates are significantly different for the treatment and control groups, three main approaches are available: (1) attempt to track down the people, or a random subsample of the people, who drop out of the sample; (2) implement bounds analysis, as discussed in chapter 7; and (3) compare changes in outcomes before and after the treatment group participates in the program (apply difference-in-differences estimation). Each of these approaches is discussed in chapter 8.

A fourth complication is the general issue of conducting ethical research. This issue is especially important when analyzing the impact of a health intervention because it is generally accepted that it is unethical for a researcher who discovers that an individual has a treatable illness to withhold that information from that person. Indeed, many proponents of ethical standards would also say that a researcher who knows that an individual has a treatable illness and is able to provide the treatment has the ethical obligation to do so, and to do so without delay. Although these ethical obligations must be taken seriously, one consequence is that they complicate the implementation of RCTs, especially those for which the program being evaluated includes medical treatments. In particular, adhering to these ethical obligations will contaminate the control group because some members of that group are, at a minimum, informed of a medical problem that many of them were unaware of, or may even be offered the treatment, both of which could lead them to be treated. As discussed in chapter 8, no simple solution to this conundrum is available; many researchers work in organizations with institutional review boards, which can provide guidance on these issues.

In certain cases randomization may change how the program operates; for example, some people may not want to participate in an "experiment," or they may change their behavior if they know they are part of an experiment (for example, Hawthorne effects, which are discussed in chapter 8). This fifth type of problem is often referred to as *randomization bias*, in which bias can occur because those who choose not to participate are unlikely to be a random sample of the people selected to participate in the RCT. One way to minimize the bias that arises because participants know whether they are in a treatment group or a control group is to try to implement the program in such a way that participants do not know which group they are in. In many cases, however, concealing from participants whether they are in the treatment group or the control group is difficult or impossible. Chapter 8 discusses this issue in more detail.

A final problem faced by RCTs is that of spillover effects, which occur when the treatment impact can spill over onto the control group, especially if the control group is nearby. Spillovers can happen for evaluations of programs designed to reduce the incidence of an infectious disease or in evaluations of education programs that randomize access to the program within schools (which may lead to program impacts on the control group through peer effects). If spillovers are positive, the program impact will be underestimated, and if they are negative, the program effect will be overestimated. Perhaps the best remedy for addressing bias from spillovers is to implement random assignment at a level that is high or large enough to eliminate, or at least minimize, the possibility of spillovers. Further information is provided in chapter 8.

Other practical advice for implementing randomized controlled trials

Three general ways are used to randomly assign some individuals or groups to a treatment group and others to a control group: lotteries, gradual phase-in, and encouragement design. The advantages and disadvantages of each type of random assignment are discussed in detail in chapter 8.

Consider a lottery, which consists of randomly assigning some individuals or groups to the control group and the rest to one or more treatment groups. The understanding among potential participants is that those who are assigned to the control group will never be treated. Although unpopular in some situations, this method is used fairly frequently in RCTs.

In contrast to a lottery, a gradual phase-in is a randomization design in which all groups eventually are given the opportunity to participate in the program, but some are allowed to participate before others; that is, the order of treatment over time across the different groups is randomized. This method is also used frequently, and is perhaps the most commonly used method.

Finally, encouragement design randomization is used in cases in which it is not possible to exclude individuals from participating in the program. However, it is still possible to randomly provide incentives to participate in, or provide information about, a program that is to be evaluated. For example, individuals can be randomly selected to receive promotional advertising for a program, which should increase their probability of participating relative to individuals who do not receive that advertising. Another technique is to offer some individuals a lower price, or a larger reward, than others for participating.

When lotteries are feasible they are usually the best method for obtaining unbiased, consistent estimates of program effects. The main impediment to their use is that denying treatment indefinitely to the control group may be deemed unethical or politically unacceptable. However, if the benefits of the program are in doubt, this denial may be less of a problem. It could also be argued that if the program is proven to be effective, the government will implement it nationwide and at that point the control group will be able to participate, but comprehensive implementation could be years, or even decades, in the future.

In many RCTs, a decision must be made about whether randomization should be performed at the group level or the individual level. Randomizing at the individual level is usually preferred because it provides a larger effective sample size, as explained in chapter 9. However, sometimes there may be little choice. For example, many education interventions can be implemented only at the classroom or school level (for instance, class size reductions). More generally, in many cases objections can be raised to randomizing at the individual level because the treatment and control individuals may know and interact with each other, and it may be awkward that some benefit from the program while others do not.

Several other factors must be kept in mind when deciding whether to randomize at the individual level or the group level. First, if the decision is made to randomize at the group level, the researcher needs to decide both how many groups to have in the sample and how many individuals to sample from each group; if a large group size is chosen, then the overall sample size must be larger to achieve a given level of statistical precision relative to a sample design with smaller, but more numerous, groups. The factors to consider when making this decision are discussed in more detail in chapter 9. Second, if there are spillovers at the individual level, but not at the group level, then it is better to randomize at the group level. Third, group-level randomization may increase cooperation and should reduce any complications caused by interactions between control and treatment units.

Several other practices should, in general, also be followed when conducting RCTs. First, baseline data should be collected before the program is implemented. Second, assessing more than one program, or variants of a program, in a randomized experiment is often useful. Third, conducting multiple randomized experiments on the same sample is sometimes both convenient and cost-reducing. Fourth, in difficult situations, starting with a small pilot program is often best, allowing complications and problems that may be impossible to foresee to surface, and providing an opportunity to try possible remedies to these complications and problems before conducting a large-scale RCT. Finally, researchers must monitor how the program is being implemented (including implementation of the randomization) and how the data are being collected, including the baseline data collection. Many randomized trials have been aborted or have provided useless results when researchers delegated monitoring to local data collectors whose motivation to implement the RCT as planned was much lower than the motivation of the researchers. All of these issues are discussed in more detail in chapter 8.

Although some RCTs are conducted on a national scale, most are conducted on a much smaller scale. A general problem with RCTs conducted on a smaller scale is that whether the results apply to the entire country or to other countries is not clear. This is the problem of external validity, covered in chapter 4. No simple solutions to this problem are available;

however, chapter 8 provides further discussion of this issue and advice on how to increase external validity.

Sample size, sample design, and statistical power

One of the first questions faced when conducting an impact evaluation is, What sample size is large enough? Of course, a larger sample will increase statistical precision, but obtaining a larger sample size almost always results in an increase in costs. A better question to ask is,

> If the researcher wants, with a certain level of probability, to be able to reject the null hypothesis of zero treatment effect when the null hypothesis is false, what sample size is needed?

Chapter 9 provides detailed recommendations on how to answer this question.

The answer to this better question leads to an important statistical concept, which is the *power* of a statistical test. In particular, the power of a statistical test is the probability that the test will reject the null hypothesis when it is false. This is a desirable feature of a statistical test: if the null hypothesis is false we want the statistical test to reject that erroneous hypothesis, so the higher the probability that this will happen, the better the test is.

The power of a statistical test depends on four factors: (1) the sample size (higher sample sizes increase the power of a statistical test), (2) the significance level chosen to test the null hypothesis (the higher the significance level, for example, 99 percent instead of 95 percent, the less likely, by definition, that the null hypothesis will be rejected and thus the lower the power of the test), (3) the proportion of the sample that is in the treatment group (for simple cases 50 percent is optimal), and (4) the amount of variance in the outcome variable that is not due to the program ("noisy" data weaken the power of statistical tests to reject almost any hypothesis). These four factors, and other factors as well, are discussed in detail in chapter 9.

Another statistical concept introduced in chapter 9 is the *minimum detectable effect size* (MDE). If the impact of a program on an outcome of interest is denoted by β, MDE provides the smallest β that can be detected for a specific level of power (a specific probability, such as 80 percent or 90 percent, of rejecting the null hypothesis when it is false), a certain significance level (for example, 95 percent or 99 percent) of the statistical test, the sample size, the proportion of the sample that is in the treatment group, and the variance in the outcome variable that is not explained by the program. This formula is explained in chapter 9. One way to use this formula is to specify the MDE (β) and all factors that affect power except the sample size; the formula will yield the sample size required to detect, with a certain probability, that the specified value of β will be statistically significant, given the values specified for all of the other relevant factors (power of the test, significance level of the test, the proportion of the sample that is treated, and the unexplained variance in the outcome variable).

As is often the case, this formula must be adapted to situations that are more complex. Chapter 9 explains how to handle situations with multiple treatments; what to do when the error terms in the regression equation are correlated within groups, such as within schools or communities; and how to adjust the formula when some individuals do not follow their random assignment. It also explains how to stratify the sample to increase statistical precision. The chapter closes with some practical recommendations and further discussion of additional statistical issues.

Ethical considerations

Impact evaluations—RCTs in particular, but other evaluation methods also—nearly always involve working with people, and thus they conduct research on human subjects. Researchers have a responsibility to conduct impact evaluations in a way that ensures that the people involved in the evaluation are not harmed by that research and, more generally, that the evaluation is conducted in an ethical way.

Chapter 10 provides an overview of key ethical issues that arise when conducting impact evaluations. The principles of ethical research are drawn from two key documents: the Nuremberg Code and the Belmont Report (see chapter 10). The principles set forth in these documents provide a starting point, but the responsibility of the researcher is not limited to adhering to the recommendations in these documents. The researcher must also be aware of local dynamics in the area where the work is being conducted. Researchers are also responsible for identifying potential conflicts of interest that may generate incentives for them not to conduct rigorous, unbiased research. Chapter 10 provides practical guidance on how to ensure that research is conducted in an ethical manner.

In addition to participants' safety, it is also important to respect participants' privacy. Research participants who provide personal information through physical examinations, academic tests, household surveys, or other means have the right to expect that the information will not be shared outside the research team. Exposing personal information can have negative social repercussions for the participant if the data reveal that the participant engages in behavior that is disapproved of, has had poor (or strong) academic performance, or has some disease or disorder. Revealing personal information could also have economic consequences if it leads to job loss or business losses. Finally, spreading private information can have serious emotional costs from embarrassment, social repercussions, or economic consequences. Chapter 10 also provides information on how to minimize the risk that participants' personal information will fall into the wrong hands. The chapter closes with a discussion of how conflicts of interest can compromise the integrity of research. A conflict of interest arises whenever a researcher has a financial or personal interest that may compromise his or her ability to conduct and report research results in an unbiased manner.

Impact evaluations based on nonrandomized and quasi-experimental data

Although RCTs are often the best method for evaluating a project, program, or policy, in many cases they are not feasible. Data that are obtained from the real world and that do not come from an experiment are called *observational data, nonexperimental data,* or *nonrandomized data.* Participation in a program may be nonrandom in two ways:

1. The communities in which the programs exist are not randomly chosen.
2. In communities where the program exists, the participants in the program are not randomly assigned. They may have been nonrandomly selected by program administrators, or they may have self-selected into (decided for themselves to participate in) the program.

Fortunately, several evaluation methods can be used when the data do not come from a randomized experiment and the people who participate in programs may be different from those who do not participate. These methods are described in detail in chapters 11–17 of this book. This section provides a brief description of each of these methods; each subsection refers to a different chapter in the book.

Cross-sectional and before-after estimation

Chapter 11 discusses two types of nonexperimental methods that have minimal data requirements but also are likely to produce biased estimates of program impacts. These two methods are cross-sectional estimation and before-after estimation, both of which are implemented using ordinary least squares or other regression methods.

The cross-sectional estimator calculates a program's impact by comparing outcomes of participants and nonparticipants in the same period, after the program started.[2] Thus there are no baseline ("before") data. As chapter 3 explains, the fundamental problem for estimating the impact of the program on those who participated in it is that what would have happened had they not participated in the program cannot be observed. Recalling the notation of chapter 3, this means that Y_1 is observed for program participants, but Y_0 is not observed. Similarly, for program nonparticipants Y_0 is observed but Y_1 is not observed. For both types, the outcome that is not observed is called the *counterfactual.*

The main potential problem with using the simple cross-sectional regression estimator to estimate program impacts is one of selection bias. The individuals who participate in the program are likely to differ systematically from those who do not, and these differences may not be fully captured by observed variables. Thus there is a risk that these differences are being mistakenly included in the estimate of the program impact. The assumptions needed to justify a cross-sectional regression estimator are most likely to be satisfied when the data include a large amount of information on both participants and nonparticipants that can be used to control for differences between these two groups in any characteristics that both influence their outcomes and affect their program participation decisions.

But when the data available do not include key factors that determine program participation decisions, unobserved characteristics may plausibly be systematically related to participation and may also predict the outcome variable, which can lead to bias in estimation. For example, consider unobservable characteristics such as motivation and intellectual ability. These characteristics are likely to be correlated both with the outcome variable and with participation in or access to the treatment. More-motivated people may be more likely to participate in the program, *and* their motivation may enable them to obtain greater benefits from the program. In this situation the cross-sectional estimator would lead to overestimation of program impacts.

A final point about the cross-sectional estimator is that although it imposes strong, and perhaps erroneous, assumptions on the program participation process, it is commonly used in evaluation work because of its minimal data requirements.

The before-after estimator calculates a program's impact by comparing the outcomes of program participants measured after they have participated in the program with their outcomes measured before they participated in the program. More specifically, this estimate of the impact of a program on the outcome variable Y is based on a comparison of the average value of Y for a group of individuals before they participate in the program with the average value of Y for the same individuals after they participate in the program. Because all of these individuals are program participants, such an estimate is an estimate of the ATT; in general, there are no data on individuals who do not participate in the program so it is not possible to estimate the ATE for the population as a whole.

An advantage of the before-after estimation strategy is that it allows for the presence of person-specific unobservables that affect both the program participation decision and the outcome variables, Y_0 and Y_1, as long as these unobservables are fixed over time. In other words, the estimator allows, to some extent, for program participation decisions to be based on the anticipated gains from participation.

The main potential problem with applying the before-after estimator is that changes over time that have nothing to do with the impact of the program may be mistakenly included as part of the estimated program effect. There could be economy-wide effects influencing outcomes, such as earnings or employment, or regional weather shocks affecting outcomes such as land productivity. For health programs, an increase or decrease in the nationwide prevalence of some infectious disease could have occurred, or health outcomes could have generally improved over time because of gradual improvements in sanitation or sources of drinking water. For education interventions, improvements over time may happen that are not due to the program, such as increasing income or changes in school quality that are not part of the program.

Whether application of either the cross-sectional estimator or the before-after estimator is appropriate in a particular evaluation setting will depend on whether there is good reason to believe that the assumptions needed to justify the methods are satisfied. If the researcher has a rich set of covariates thought to capture all of the important aspects of participation decisions, so that the remaining unobserved factors that affect participation are unlikely to affect the outcome variables (Y_0 and Y_1), then the cross-sectional estimator could well provide consistent estimates of program impacts. Or there may be some contexts in which changes over time in the outcome of interest are not expected to be very important, in which case the before-after estimator could yield reliable estimates. However, these assumptions are unlikely to hold in many situations, leading many researchers to use difference-in-differences (DID) and within regression estimators, which address some of the limitations of the cross-sectional and before-after methods but have more demanding data requirements.

Difference-in-differences estimation and within estimation

Chapter 12 introduces two additional regression-based estimators, the DID estimator and the within estimator. The assumptions needed for unbiased and consistent estimation are not as strong as they are for the cross-sectional estimator and the before-after estimator, but these assumptions could still be violated. However, because the assumptions for these two types of estimators are not as restrictive as those for the cross-sectional and before-after estimators, many impact evaluations have used these methods, especially DID estimation.

The DID estimator, which can be denoted by Δ_{DID}, measures the impact of the program intervention using the difference between participants and nonparticipants in the before-after change in outcomes. In fact, this estimator combines the before-after and cross-sectional (participant and nonparticipant) estimators. In the simplest case, with no other variables to include in a regression setup, the DID estimator can be expressed as

$$\Delta_{DID} = \Delta_1 - \Delta_2 = (Y_{\text{participant, after}} - Y_{\text{participant, before}}) - (Y_{\text{nonparticipant, after}} - Y_{\text{nonparticipant, before}}),$$

where Y denotes the outcome variable, Δ_1 is the before-after estimator for participants, and Δ_2 is the before-after estimator for nonparticipants. Note also that if both "before" Y variables in Δ_{DID} are removed from this expression, this is a simple (without covariates) cross-sectional estimator. By combining both the cross-sectional and the before-after estimators, the DID estimator removes the influence of time-invariant factors that differ across participants and nonparticipants, such as land quality if Y is agricultural productivity, as well as the influence of any common time trend, for example, the occurrence of a drought (again if Y is agricultural productivity). The time-invariant factors that differ across the two groups are eliminated by the differences within the two sets of parentheses, and the common time trend is eliminated by the difference between these two differences.

It is worth noting, however, that DID estimation requires that all unobservables that are correlated with the participation decision be time-invariant; that is, although it does allow for unobservable variables that affect Y to change over time, these changes must be the same for program participants and nonparticipants. If these changes were different, DID estimation would mistakenly assign this differential change in these unobserved factors to changes in Y caused by the program, leading to biases in DID estimates of program impacts.

So-called within estimators identify program impacts from changes in outcomes within some group or unit, such as within a family, a school, or a village. The advantage of these estimators is that they can be estimated using data at only one point in time.[3] Their primary benefit in estimating program impacts is that they control for unobserved differences across the groups or units that may lead to biased estimates of program impacts; for example, families or villages that participate in a program may be those with particularly low outcomes, which would underestimate the impact of a program designed to increase those outcomes if the researcher simply compared the outcomes of program participants and program nonparticipants.

To see how they work, consider the following example: Suppose a program provides nutritious foods to children from poor families. Within poor families, some children receive the nutritious foods and some do not. A within estimator would compare the nutritional outcomes of siblings, some of whom participate in the program and some of whom do not. In this context, the assumption of within estimators is that within families, which child gets the program needs to be essentially random, after conditioning on the observed variables.

Overall, the within estimator allows bias to be reduced, relative to a cross-sectional estimator, when data are available for only one period and the observations belong to different groups, such as families, schools, or communities. However, the assumption that within groups, program participants and nonparticipants are essentially randomly assigned after controlling for observed variables is questionable in many circumstances. Thus within estimators are not widely used to evaluate program impacts; DID estimation is much more commonly used.

Matching methods

Matching methods are widely used to evaluate programs. They compare the outcomes of program participants with the outcomes of similar (matched) nonparticipants. They can be used to estimate ATE and ATT. This approach is discussed in detail in chapter 13.

A key advantage of matching estimators over other kinds of evaluation estimators is that they do not require specification of the functional form of the potential outcome equations (the equations for Y_1 and Y_0) and therefore are not susceptible to bias caused by misspecification of that functional form. For example, they do not require the assumption that outcomes are linear in observables. Traditional matching estimators pair each program participant with an observably similar nonparticipant and interpret the difference in their outcomes as the effect of the program intervention. More recently developed methods can match each program participant with more than one nonparticipant observation and use a weighting scheme to construct the match in a way that optimally trades off the bias and variance of the estimator.

There are two main variants of matching estimators: (1) cross-sectional matching estimators, which require data from only one period; and (2) DID matching estimators, which require panel data or repeated cross-section data.

Cross-sectional matching estimators allow for selection on unobservables, but only in a limited sense. For the most part, these estimators are applicable in contexts in which the researcher is relatively certain that the major determinants of program participation are accounted for in the observed variables, so that any remaining variation in who participates, and who does not participate, in a program is due to random factors. DID matching estimators identify treatment effects by comparing the change in outcomes for treated persons to the change in outcomes for matched, untreated persons, which allows selection into the program to be based on unobserved time-invariant characteristics of individuals.

Matching methods have been used in many types of impact evaluations. Some examples are presented in chapter 13, which focuses on a class of matching estimators called *propensity score matching* (PSM) estimators; these methods are relatively easy to implement and are commonly used. PSM methods offer different ways to match observations, including nearest neighbor matching, caliper matching, stratification (interval) matching, and nonparametric (for example, kernel or local linear) matching. Another benefit of PSM methods is that they provide a convenient way to exclude observations for which such matches cannot be found; this is known as excluding observations that do not belong to the "region of common support."

Other topics related to matching methods covered in this book (all in chapter 13) are (1) the advantages that matching methods have over ordinary least squares estimation, which is used for the methods discussed in chapters 11 and 12; (2) methods for combining matching with DID estimation; (3) how to model (specify) the propensity score function for PSM estimation; (4) evidence on the performance of matching estimation methods; (5) matching estimation that allows for choice-based sampling; and (6) calculation of standard errors for matching estimators. Multiple treatments and continuous treatments, both of which allow for different "doses" of the treatment, are not covered, but for readers who are interested, references are provided for those two topics.

Regression discontinuity methods

Sometimes a researcher knows something about the rules by which people become eligible for programs. For example, an eligibility rule may be in place based on the value of some characteristic of an individual, a family, or a community, for example, a poverty reduction program that is available only to households with low incomes, or a housing program available only to persons living in communities with a poverty index above a certain level.

In such situations, it may be possible to estimate the impact of the program using regression discontinuity (RD) methods, which are sometimes called regression discontinuity design methods. The RD method exploits information about a rule governing eligibility for, or assignment to, thc program of interest. Chapter 14 explains how RD methods can be used to evaluate the impacts of certain types of programs or policies. It begins by explaining the intuition behind this approach, and then provides a more rigorous explanation of the assumptions needed to apply RD estimation, for both the "sharp" case and the "fuzzy" case.

The defining characteristic of the RD estimation method is that the probability of participating in the program changes discontinuously as a function of one or more underlying continuous variables. For example, a university scholarship for academically strong students may require students to have a score of, say, 150 points or higher on a national examination. The basic assumption is that people who score just above or just below some cutoff value are similar in all respects except for whether they participated in the program. Continuing with the example, students who score 149 on the national examination are, on average, almost identical to those who score 150. Thus the difference in the average outcome between these two groups of students can be attributed to the program. In other words, the outcome of the nonparticipants whose eligibility scores are close to the cutoff can be used as the counterfactual for the participants whose eligibility scores are also close to, but on the other side of, the cutoff point. As long as people cannot manipulate their scores, program participation can be considered to be locally randomized.

Two main types of discontinuity design are considered in the literature. In the *sharp design* case, program participation is determined exactly by the value of a continuous variable that has a precise cutoff point. In this case, no other factors determine program participation. The *fuzzy design* case allows for factors other than the variable with the cutoff point to affect program participation, but it still requires the probability of participation to "jump" discontinuously when that variable crosses the cutoff point.

Several different types of RD estimation methods are presented in chapter 14. The first two methods, which are not computationally demanding, are the local means approach and the local linear regression approach. A final point about RD estimation, which in some cases may be an important limitation, is that it calculates the treatment effects only for observations that are quite close to the cutoff point. One implication is that if there is large variation in treatment effects across different subgroups in the population, then the treatment effect estimated by RD methods could be quite different from the treatment effect for groups in the population whose average value of the continuous variable is far from the cutoff point.

Instrumental variables methods and local average treatment effect

The estimation methods presented in chapters 7, 11, 12, and 13 require the assumption that, after conditioning on (controlling for) observed variables, an individual's program participation status is uncorrelated with unobserved factors that determine the outcome variables of interest (Y_1 and Y_0). However, in many, if not most, situations this assumption is unlikely to hold. Chapter 15 presents IV methods, which do not require this assumption.

IV estimation does, however, have another requirement—a variable that has predictive power for program participation but does not have a direct impact on Y_1 or Y_0. Unfortunately, finding such variables can be difficult. Even when such a variable can be found, it may still not be possible to estimate the ATE or the ATT. However, IV methods can still be used to estimate a local average treatment effect (LATE). Chapter 15 covers both general IV estimation and the special case of LATE estimation.

IV methods have two general uses in evaluation of programs, policies, or projects. First, for an RCT that has been contaminated because some of the individuals or groups randomly assigned to the treatment group chose not to participate in the program, or because some of the individuals or groups randomly assigned to the control group were somehow able to participate in the program, IV methods allow estimation of the LATE. Second, and more generally, IV methods permit estimation of treatment effects when there are problems of selection bias, that is, when individuals have at least some ability to choose whether to participate in the program. This second point applies not only to RCT evaluations but also to evaluations that are based on nonrandomized (nonexperimental) data.

However, some difficulties do arise with using IV methods to estimate program impacts. First, the instrumental variables must satisfy certain assumptions, and finding instrumental variables that do so can be difficult. For RCTs in which there is imperfect compliance, the most obvious instrumental variable for whether a person receives the treatment is random assignment, but even here the researcher must carefully consider whether the instrument is valid. Plausible instrumental variables can be even more difficult to find for evaluations based on nonexperimental data. The instrumental variables need to influence program participation decisions but not be correlated with the outcome measures (after conditioning on observed variables). Some researchers have used distance needed to travel to a program site or characteristics of a program itself, such as capacity constraints, as instruments for whether people participate, but the validity of such instrumental variables must be carefully considered rather than taken for granted.

Second, in general, estimation of ATE or ATT via IV requires assumptions that may not hold. However, a different set of assumptions, which may well be more plausible in many contexts, allow LATE—the impact of the program on those individuals whose participation is influenced by the instrumental variable—to be estimated. Whether any IV assumptions are plausible will, of course, depend on the specific program being evaluated and the proposed instrumental variables.

Control function methods

A major concern in evaluating program impacts is that people who participate in a program or are subject to some treatment may differ systematically from nonparticipants in possibly unobserved ways. Control function methods, also known as generalized residual methods, are a class of evaluation estimators that are designed to explicitly control for selection into the program based on unobservables. They are presented in chapter 16.

Control function estimators explicitly recognize that nonrandom selection into the program may give rise to biased estimates, and they attempt to obtain unbiased parameter estimates by explicitly modeling the participation decision. The main advantage of these methods is that they allow selection into the program to be based on time-varying unobservable variables. Their main disadvantage is that they usually require exclusion restrictions (variables that determine the participation decision but are uncorrelated with the outcome variable, which is very similar to the requirements for instrumental variables), functional form assumptions, or both. A combination of the two types of assumptions is usually the best approach.

Control function and matching methods were developed largely in separate literatures in econometrics and statistics, but both methods make use of propensity scores in implementation and therefore have some similarities. Conventional matching estimators can in some sense be viewed as a restricted form of control function estimation. If program participation depends on unobserved factors that also influence the outcome variables of interest, matching methods cannot be used. One alternative in this case is IV methods, while another is control function methods. The former has been used by economists for many decades. The latter is a relatively new approach, although it is becoming more popular.

Quantile regression methods

Most of the evaluation literature is concerned with mean (average) treatment effects. However, the distribution of treatment effects is also often of interest, for example, to assess the proportion of program participants who actually benefit from the program and the extent to which program effects vary across individual participants. Chapter 17 considers quantile treatment effect estimation, which provides information on the distribution of treatment effects. Although quantile estimation methods were developed decades ago, their application to impact evaluations is relatively recent.

The quantile treatment effect estimators described in chapter 17 offer a way to explore how treatment effects are distributed within the population, either overall (unconditionally) or conditional on the values of other variables. If program participation can be assumed to be uncorrelated with Y_1 and Y_0 after conditioning on (controlling for) some observed variables (selection on observables), then standard quantile regression methods can be applied. If program participation does not satisfy this condition (selection on unobservables), then instrumental variables are needed to estimate quantile treatment effects. Although their application to impact evaluation is relatively recent, quantile treatment effect estimators are likely to be used more frequently in the future, especially in situations in which the distribution of treatment effects is of particular interest.

Ex ante evaluation

A recent development in the evaluation of programs in developed and developing countries is the use of ex ante evaluations. Although not as commonly used as other methods, they may become more common in the future. Because of their recent appearance and their complexity, they are not covered in this book. This subsection, however, provides a brief description of this approach, along with references for the interested (and ambitious) reader.

Most program evaluation research is ex post evaluation, which is the evaluation of programs that have already been implemented. For example, matching and RD methods require data on a treated group as well as on a comparison group, and in particular require data on the treated group after its members have participated in the program. Thus the evaluation takes place after the program has been implemented. A limitation of these approaches is that they cannot be used to evaluate effects of programs before their implementation.

Ex ante evaluation is an approach for analyzing the effects of a program before its implementation. This approach is also valuable at the program design stage to help choose program parameters in an optimal way to achieve some desired impacts at minimum cost. Using an experimental approach to answer such program design questions would typically require implementing different versions of the program on different subpopulations (in a random way) to be able to compare the results, which for many social programs is prohibitively costly. Using an ex ante approach can avoid the high cost of implementing a variety of programs that are later found to be ineffective.

Ex ante assessment can also provide evidence on the range of program impacts that can be expected for different program parameters, and it can help predict program take-up rates. For example, in designing a conditional cash transfer program that provides monetary incentives for households to send their children to school, important issues are (1) to whom to target the transfers, (2) how large the transfers should be, (3) whether to vary the transfers by the age and gender of the child, (4) who will take up (participate in) the program, and (5) what will be the resulting impacts on schooling and educational outcomes. With predictions of take-up decisions, it is possible to estimate the costs of any particular program design. Even when ex post evaluation methods are thought to be more reliable for estimating the impacts of existing programs, ex ante evaluation tools still have a role in addressing the many questions that arise in the design and implementation of any social program.

Economists and other researchers have developed a variety of ex ante evaluation methods. The most common approach develops and estimates a parametric structural model to describe the decision-making processes of individuals or households, and incorporates into the model how individuals are affected by the introduction of the program. This structural modeling approach typically requires making functional form assumptions about individuals' utility functions and budget constraints, and about whether decisions are being made in a static or dynamic environment, and with or without uncertainty.

An example of this approach is in Todd and Wolpin (2006), who develop a dynamic model of households' decisions about whether to send their children to school, put them to work, or keep them at home. The authors use the model to analyze the effects of Mexico's PROGRESA conditional cash transfer program on schooling and on household fertility. Model parameters were estimated using data from the households that were randomly assigned to the control group and thus never received the program, which makes their analysis an ex ante evaluation. The authors conducted a model validation exercise that compares the predicted program effects obtained from the model to the experimentally estimated program effects obtained from the PROGRESA RCT. After finding that the model performed well in predicting average program impacts for different subgroups, the authors used the model to study several variations in the program design, such as changes in the transfer payment schedule and removal of the school attendance conditionality requirements.

The main disadvantage of the ex ante approach for evaluating programs is that, compared with the methods described in this book, it is more complicated. In particular, it requires a high level of statistical and computer programming skills, which is the main reason it is not used as frequently as many of the ex post methods described here, although its relative usage could change in the future. Another criticism is that it requires strong (and thus perhaps unrealistic) functional form assumptions. However, as described in Todd and Wolpin (2008), ex ante evaluations do not always require strong parametric functional form assumptions. The authors provide examples of approaches that can be implemented nonparametrically, depending on the type of problem at hand.

A small but growing literature uses ex ante evaluation tools to evaluate programs in developing countries. So far, the tools have been used to evaluate the impacts of education programs, pension programs, and microfinance programs. For a summary of a variety of applications of the ex ante evaluation approach in development economics, see Todd and Wolpin (2010). For a detailed discussion of how dynamic discrete choice models can be used for ex ante evaluation purposes, see Keane, Todd and Wolpin (2011).

Conclusion

Economists, statisticians, and others have developed several different methods for estimating the causal impacts of programs (or projects or policies) on social and economic outcomes of interest. Many researchers advocate the use of RCTs, and chapters 6–9 of this book provide a thorough exposition of their use. However, some researchers remain unconvinced of the merits of RCTs, and in many situations RCTs cannot be implemented, for example, for ethical considerations, as discussed in chapter 10. Thus chapters 11–17

TABLE 5.1 Overview of impact evaluation methods

METHOD	WHEN TO USE	THREATS OR DISADVANTAGES
Randomized evaluations	Can be used when individuals, households, or villages can be randomly assigned to treatment and control groups. Usually the experiment is designed at the same time that the program is being planned.	Noncompliance with the treatment assignment, nonrandom attrition, control group contamination, ethical objections
Difference in differences	Can be used when there are data before and after program implementation, for both participants and a comparison group, and both groups can be assumed to have a similar time trend for the outcome variable in the event of nonparticipation (similar time trend for Y_0).	Violation of the common time trend assumption
Propensity score matching	Can be used when large samples of high-quality data are available to construct a comparison group based on individuals' probability of program participation.	Nonrandom selection into the program caused by unobserved factors
Regression discontinuity	Can be used when program participation is determined in part by an eligibility rule based on a continuous variable, such as test scores or a poverty index.	Small sample size; results may not be generalizable
Instrumental variables	Can be used when noncompliance occurs for a randomized evaluation, or when nonrandomized data are available and there is an "instrument" that determines program participation but, conditional on observed variables, the instrument has no effect on the outcome variables, or when there is a randomized encouragement design or a fuzzy regression discontinuity design.	Weak instruments; estimates only local average treatment effects, which apply to different groups depending on the instrument used; invalid instruments
Control function methods	Can be used when program participation is determined by unobserved variables that also have direct impacts on the outcome variables.	Requires exclusion restrictions or functional form assumptions that may not hold
Quantile regressions	Can be used when there is interest in estimating not only average treatment effects but also the distribution of those treatment effects.	Computationally demanding; assumptions may not hold

Source: Original table for this publication.

present several different types of impact evaluation estimation methods that can be implemented for nonexperimental data.

Table 5.1 summarizes the pros and cons of both RCTs and nonexperimental methods, and indicates the type of data that are needed for each method. The best method for any particular impact evaluation will depend on which methods are feasible given the data that have been, or can be, collected and on which assumptions are most credible. These issues are explained in detail in chapters 6–17 of this book.

Notes

1. Recall that ATE and ATT are defined in chapter 3.
2. Data collected at one point in time are called cross-sectional data.
3. The before-after and DID estimators can also be viewed as within estimators, in which the variation exploited is the change over time "within" a given individual. In this book, the term "within estimator" refers to estimation methods that use data from only one time period.

References

Banerjee, Abhijit, and Esther Duflo. 2011. *Poor Economics: A Radical Rethinking of the Way to Fight Global Poverty*. New York: Public Affairs.

Glennerster, Rachel, and Kudzai Takavarasha. 2013. *Running Randomized Evaluations: A Practical Guide*. Princeton, NJ: Princeton University Press.

Keane, Michael P., Petra E. Todd, and Kenneth I. Wolpin. 2011. "The Structural Estimation of Behavioral Models: Discrete Choice Dynamic Programming Methods and Applications." In *Handbook of Labor Economics*, Volume 4, Part A, edited by Orley Ashenfelter and David Card, 331–461. Amsterdam: Elsevier.

Todd, Petra, and Kenneth Wolpin. 2006. "Assessing the Impact of a School Subsidy Program in Mexico: Using a Social Experiment to Validate a Dynamic Behavioral Model of Child Schooling and Fertility." *American Economic Review* 96 (5): 1384–417.

Todd, Petra, and Kenneth Wolpin. 2008. "Ex Ante Evaluation of Social Programs." *Annals of Economics and Statistics* 91/92 (July–December): 263–91.

Todd, Petra, and Kenneth Wolpin. 2010. "Structural Estimation and Policy Evaluation in Developing Countries." *Annual Review of Economics* 2 (1): 21–50.

PART II

Experimental Methods

CHAPTER 6

Introduction to Randomized Controlled Trials

Introduction

In general, impact evaluation is easiest when researchers can implement a *randomized controlled trial* (RCT). RCTs have become much more common in the past 20 years, and many economists and other researchers are enthusiastic proponents of RCTs. Although others are less enthusiastic, and some are even quite critical of RCTs, their increased popularity is unlikely to diminish in the foreseeable future.

This chapter provides an introduction to RCTs, which are also known as randomized evaluations, randomized trials, randomized experiments, or social experiments. Chapters 7, 8, and 9 provide more detailed guidance on how to implement RCTs and how to analyze the data obtained from RCTs.

Although the ideas behind RCTs are straightforward, in practice certain aspects of RCTs can become complicated. This chapter focuses on the basic ideas. Complications and practical recommendations are considered in later chapters. For a more detailed, yet also less technical, exposition on how to conduct RCTs, see Glennerster and Takavarasha (2013).

The basic idea of a randomized controlled trial

In its simplest form, an RCT randomly assigns some members of the population to a treatment group; these people then participate in the program, and using the notation from chapter 3 this is indicated by $P = 1$. The RCT randomly assigns other members of the population to a control group; they do not participate in the program, so for them $P = 0$. For simplicity, assume for now that random assignment is always followed: everyone who is randomly assigned to participate does participate, so that $P = 1$, and everyone who is randomly assigned not to participate in fact does not participate, so that $P = 0$. Later in this chapter (and in subsequent chapters) this assumption is relaxed.

Random assignment of treatment ensures that the treatment group and the control group are similar in all aspects except that only the former group receives the treatment. Therefore, any systematic differences in the outcomes of interest between the treatment group and the control group are solely due to the treatment. Indeed, the average program impact can be estimated by the difference between the treatment group and the control group in the mean of the outcome variable.

Figure 6.1 provides a visual depiction of a randomized evaluation. The process starts with the target population, which is usually the population that the program is intended to benefit. In some cases certain members of that population may be unable or unwilling to participate, so the analysis will be limited to *potential participants,* those who are able and willing to participate in the program. From these potential participants, a random sample, often called the *evaluation sample*, is drawn. Finally, a fraction of the individuals (or households or villages) in the evaluation sample are randomly assigned to the treatment group, while the others in that sample are assigned to the control group. The possibility that some individuals in the treatment group may not participate, designated as "No shows" in figure 6.1, is discussed later in this chapter.

To see how random assignment works, consider a hypothetical example. Suppose that a sample of 2,000 individuals is drawn from the population of potential program participants. Half of these individuals are randomly assigned (for example, using a lottery) to the treatment group, and the other half are assigned to the control group. Assume that of the original 2,000 people, 40 percent were women. Because the treatment and control groups were randomly assigned, of the 1,000 people assigned to treatment, approximately 40 percent will also be women. Similarly, if among the 2,000 people, 20 percent had a college degree,

FIGURE 6.1 Setting up a randomized evaluation

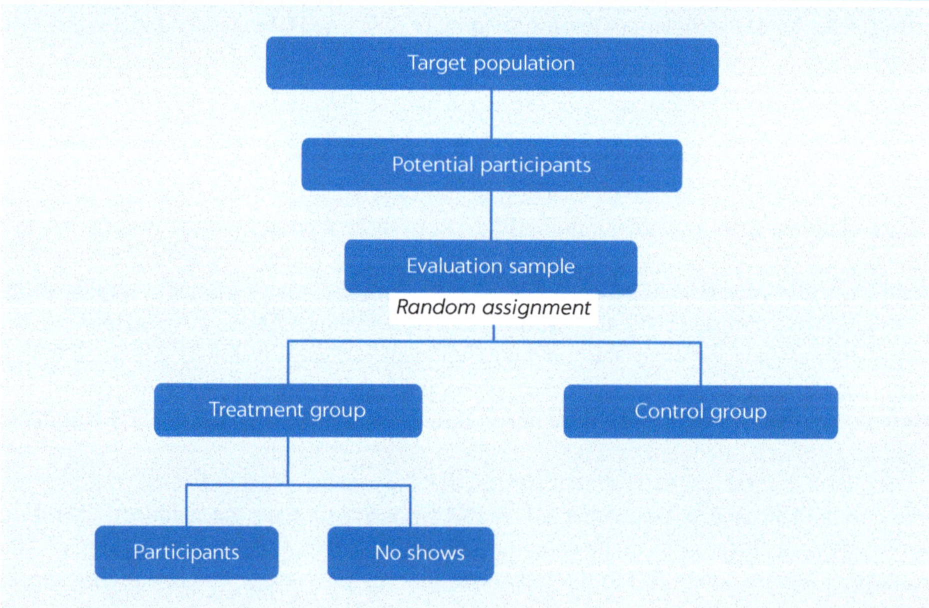

Source: Glewwe and Todd 2019.

then approximately 20 percent of both the treatment group and the control group should also have college degrees. A key point is that randomization implies that both observed characteristics (for example, sex and education) and unobserved characteristics (for example, motivation and preferences) are similar in both the treatment group and the control group. Figure 6.2 depicts how randomization leads to two groups with very similar characteristics.

The fact that the treatment and control groups are similar in all aspects except that the former is randomly assigned to be treated implies that any systematic difference in outcomes between the treatment and the control groups can be attributed to the program.

Of course, in an actual randomization the characteristics of the treatment and control groups will not be exactly the same. For example, table 6.1 is taken from the PROGRESA evaluation conducted in Mexico, which randomized 506 local communities into treatment and control groups. Table 6.1 shows that usually only small differences in community characteristics occur between the treatment and control communities, which is what one would expect given that the treatment has been randomly assigned.

How does randomization solve the evaluation problem?

Recall from chapter 3 that the two most commonly estimated parameters of interest are

1. Average gain for the entire population (average treatment effect, or ATE):

$$E[Y_1 - Y_0] = E[\Delta].$$

2. Average gain for program participants (average treatment effect for the treated, or ATT):

$$E[Y_1 - Y_0 | P = 1] = E[\Delta | P = 1].$$

The problem is that both Y_1 and Y_0 can never be observed for the same person at the same time. Instead, Y_1 is observed for those who participate in the program ($P = 1$) and Y_0 is observed for those who do not participate in the program ($P = 0$).

The essence of an RCT is that it randomly assigns some members of the population to the program (so that they have $P = 1$) and randomly assigns other members of the population to a control group (so that they have $P = 0$). To show more rigorously why random assignment can provide estimates of ATE and ATT, let R be the variable that denotes random assignment to treatment:

$R = 1$: Individual was randomly assigned to the treatment group,

$R = 0$: Individual was randomly assigned to the control group.

FIGURE 6.2 Characteristics of groups under randomized assignment

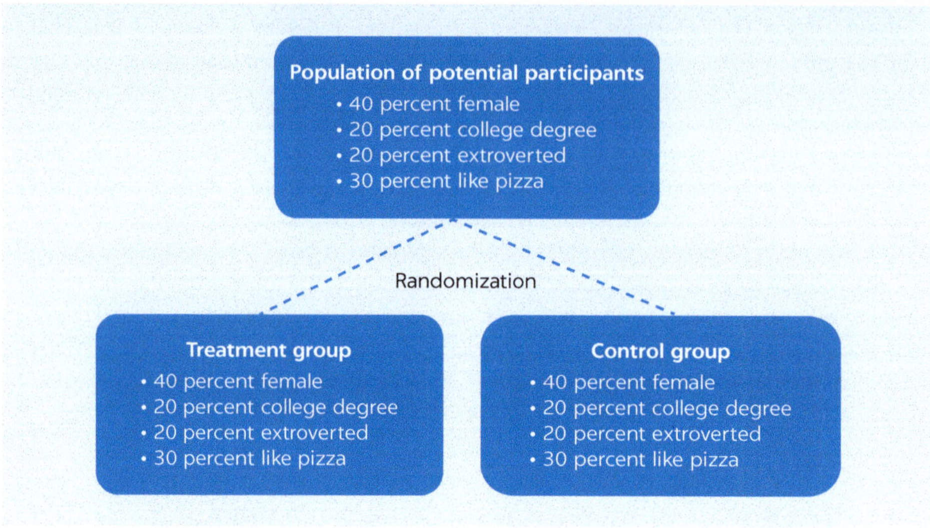

Source: Glewwe and Todd 2019.

TABLE 6.1 Selected characteristics of PROGRESA communities

	PROPORTION OF FACILITIES IN THE COMMUNITY		
PROPORTION OF COMMUNITIES WITH FACILITY	**ALL**	**CONTROL**	**TREATMENT**
Education facilities			
Preschool	0.82	0.83	0.82
Primary school	0.97	0.95	0.98
Telesecondary	0.17	0.25	0.13
Secondary school	0.01	0.01	0.01
High school	0.01	0.02	0.00
Heath facilities			
Health ministry clinic	0.10	0.13	0.08
Medical aids	0.60	0.62	0.58
Dispensary	0.07	0.09	0.06
Midwives	0.32	0.25	0.36
Traditional healers	0.12	0.12	0.13
Mobile health centers	0.75	0.76	0.74
Pregnancy supervision	0.28	0.26	0.29
Delivery supervision	0.25	0.24	0.25
Family planning	0.44	0.39	0.47

Source: Skoufias 2005.

In the simplest case, assume that all people assigned to the treatment group participate in the program, so that $R = 1$ implies $P = 1$, and that all people assigned to the control group do not participate, so that $R = 0$ implies $P = 0$. Then the ATE can be estimated as

$$\text{ATE} \equiv \text{E}[Y_1 - Y_0] = \text{E}[Y_1] - \text{E}[Y_0] = \text{E}[Y \mid R = 1] - \text{E}[Y \mid R = 0]. \tag{6.1}$$

That is, for all people for whom $R = 1$, the observed Y will be Y_1 because $R = 1$ implies $P = 1$. This group is a random sample of the population, which gives an unbiased estimate of $\text{E}[Y_1]$. That is, random assignment implies that $\text{E}[Y \mid R = 1] = \text{E}[Y_1]$. By the same logic, for all people randomly assigned to $R = 0$, the observed Y will be the Y_0, so $\text{E}[Y \mid R = 0]$ is an unbiased estimate of $\text{E}[Y_0]$. These two components allow ATE to be recovered because everyone offered the program participates and none of those who were not offered the program participates.

Another randomization method is often used in contexts in which a program already exists and people can choose whether to participate. For example, the objective may be to evaluate the effects of an existing job training program for which participation is voluntary. This alternative randomization method randomizes people into or out of the program after they have already applied and have been determined to be eligible for the program.

More specifically, for this method random assignment is implemented in two steps. First, people in the general population are made aware of the program, and some decide to participate in (apply for) the program. Second, among those who apply for the program, for whom by definition $P = 1$,[1] some are randomly selected to be admitted to the program ($R = 1$), and the rest are assigned to a control group ($R = 0$).

This method of randomization has two important characteristics. First, almost all the people who are randomly assigned to the treatment receive the treatment (or at least start the treatment) because they have already indicated that they want the treatment (and thus $P = 1$ for them). Second, assuming everyone assigned to the program is treated, as would be expected, this method estimates ATT, not ATE, because the randomization is applied only to the subpopulation that wants to participate (the subpopulation for whom $P = 1$).

What if some people assigned to the treatment group choose not to participate?

The rest of this chapter focuses on the first randomization method, the one in which the first step is to randomly assign people to the treatment group or the control group. A common complication with this method is that not everyone who is randomly assigned to the treatment group chooses to participate, raising the question of how to obtain unbiased estimates of ATE or ATT when this happens.

It turns out that it is still possible to estimate ATT, if it is assumed that all the people assigned to the control group do not participate in the treatment (in fact, this assumption can be relaxed, as will be explained in chapter 15 on instrumental variables methods and local average treatment effects). To see how this is possible, note first that in this situation there are *three types of people*:

1. People assigned to the control group; they provide an estimate of $E[Y_0] = E[Y \mid R = 0]$.
2. People assigned to the treatment group ($R = 1$) who choose to participate ($P = 1$); they provide an estimate of $E[Y_1 \mid P = 1] = E[Y \mid P = 1] = E[Y \mid P = 1, R = 1]$.[2]
3. People assigned to the treatment group ($R = 1$) who choose not to participate ($P = 0$); they provide an estimate of $E[Y_0 \mid P = 0] = E[Y \mid P = 0] = E[Y \mid P = 0, R = 1]$.[3]

These three types of people are depicted in figure 6.3.

Fortunately, the three expressions are sufficient to provide an estimate of ATT, which is expressed as $E[Y_1 - Y_0 \mid P = 1]$. How can this be done when all that is available are estimates of $E[Y_0]$, $E[Y_1 \mid P = 1]$, and $E[Y_0 \mid P = 0]$? Note first that $E[Y_1 \mid P = 1]$ is already half of what is needed. That is, $E[Y_1 - Y_0 \mid P = 1] = E[Y_1 \mid P = 1] - E[Y_0 \mid P = 1]$, so with an estimate in hand of $E[Y_1 \mid P = 1]$ what remains is to obtain the other half, $E[Y_0 \mid P = 1]$, which is often referred to as the *missing (or unobserved) counterfactual*.

The key to obtaining an estimate of $E[Y_0 \mid P = 1]$ is to use information on the fraction of the people who choose to participate in the program (treatment) when it is offered. To see how this works, let $\text{Prob}[P = 1]$ be the fraction of people who would participate if offered the opportunity to do so. The average value of Y_0, $E[Y_0]$, can be expressed as a weighted average over participants (those for whom $P = 1$) and nonparticipants (those for whom $P = 0$):[4]

$$E[Y_0] = E[Y_0 \mid P = 1] \times \text{Prob}[P = 1] + E[Y_0 \mid P = 0] \times \text{Prob}[P = 0].$$

FIGURE 6.3 Random assignment when some individuals choose not to participate

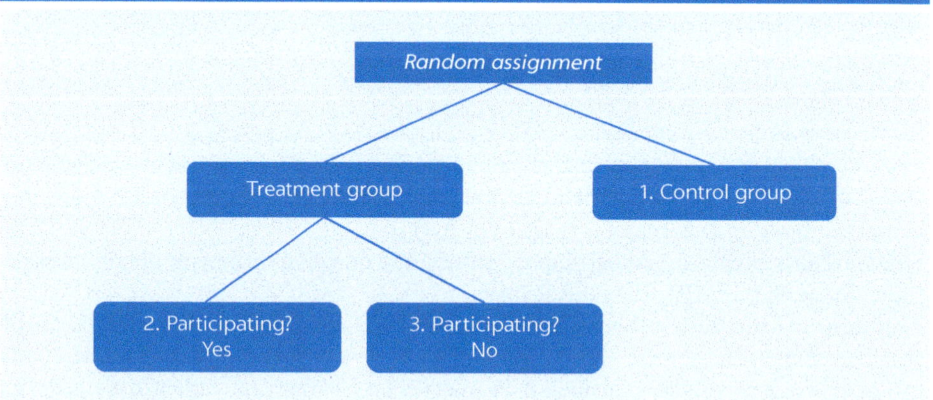

Source: Glewwe and Todd 2019.

Rearranging this yields the counterfactual for those who choose the treatment:

$$E\left[Y_0 \mid P=1\right] = \frac{E[Y_0] - E[Y_0 \mid P=0] \times \text{Prob}[P=0]}{\text{Prob}[P=1]}.$$

$\text{Prob}[P = 0]$, $\text{Prob}[P = 1]$, and $E[Y_0 | P = 0]$ can be estimated from the treatment group data, because randomization implies that $\text{Prob}[P = 1 \mid R = 1] = \text{Prob}[P = 1]$, $\text{Prob}[P = 0 \mid R = 1] = \text{Prob}[P = 0]$, and $E[Y_0 | P = 0, R = 1] = E[Y_0 | P = 0]$. The quantity $E[Y_0]$ can be obtained from the control group, because randomization implies that $E[Y_0 | R = 0] = E[Y_0]$.

Combining this with an estimate of $E[Y_1 | P = 1]$ yields a simple estimate of ATT:

$$\begin{aligned}
ATT &\equiv E\left[Y_1 - Y_0 \mid P=1\right] = E\left[Y_1 \mid P=1\right] - E\left[Y_0 \mid P=1\right] \\
&= E\left[Y \mid R=1, P=1\right] - \frac{E[Y_0] - E[Y_0 \mid P=0] \times \text{Prob}[P=0]}{\text{Prob}[P=1]} \\
&= \frac{E[Y \mid R=1, P=1] \times \text{Prob}[P=1] - E[Y \mid R=0] + E[Y \mid R=1, P=0] \times \text{Prob}[P=0]}{\text{Prob}[P=1 \mid R=1]} \quad (6.2) \\
&= \frac{E[Y \mid R=1] - E[Y \mid R=0]}{E[P \mid R=1]}.
\end{aligned}$$

The intuition for this estimate of ATT is as follows: The term $E[Y | R = 1] - E[Y | R = 0]$ is a weighted average of ATT ($= E[Y_1 - Y_0 | P = 1]$) and 0, where the weights are the proportion of the population for which $P = 1$ and the proportion of the population for which $P = 0$, because $E[Y | R = 1]$ is a weighted average of Y_1 for people with $P = 1$ and Y_0 for people with $P = 0$, and $E[Y | R = 0]$ is a weighted average of Y_0 for people with $P = 1$ and Y_0 for people with $P = 0$. Thus $E[Y | R = 1] - E[Y | R = 0]$ *underestimates* ATT (it equals ATT × $\text{Prob}[P = 1]$)[5] because it includes people for whom the program has no impact, who are those people who choose not to participate even when they are offered the opportunity to do so (these are the people for whom $P = 0$). The expression $E[P | R = 1]$, which equals $\text{Prob}[P = 1]$, corrects this underestimation by inflating $E[Y | R = 1] - E[Y | R = 0]$ (that is, by dividing ATT × $\text{Prob}[P = 1]$ by $\text{Prob}[P = 1]$) to obtain the ATT.

Finally, note that it is *not* possible to estimate ATE, even though half of it is already available, namely $E[Y_0]$. Intuitively, the problem is that the data do not have the value of Y_1 for any person who decides not to participate when offered the treatment. Thus Y_1 is never observed for a group of people in the population, so it is not possible to calculate the average of Y_1 over the whole population. More formally, one can write

$$E[Y_1] = E[Y_1 | P = 1] \times \text{Prob}[P = 1] + E[Y_1 | P = 0] \times \text{Prob}[P = 0].$$

Clearly, all four components are needed to calculate $E[Y_1]$, namely, $E[Y_1 | P = 1]$, $\text{Prob}[P = 1]$, $E[Y_1 | P = 0]$, and $\text{Prob}[P = 0]$. Of these four components, the one missing is $E[Y_1 | P = 0]$, which is the value of Y_1 for those people who choose not to participate in the program (for whom $P = 0$). Without that information $E[Y_1]$ cannot be estimated, and thus ATE, which equals $E[Y_1] - E[Y_0]$, cannot be estimated.

To make this technical discussion more intuitive, consider some simple examples of ATE and ATT. Suppose that there is a job training program that randomly assigns individuals to receive training. Half of these individuals are randomly assigned to the training, and the other half are randomly assigned not to receive training. Assume, for simplicity, that all individuals in the population will have an income of \$80 per day if they do not participate in the job training program. Assume also that the program is very effective for half of the population; they earn \$120 per day after completing the training (and thus $Y_1 - Y_0 = \$40$ per day). For the other half of the population, the training is less effective; they earn \$100 per day after completing the training (and thus $Y_1 - Y_0 = \$20$ per day). Now consider the following two examples.

Example A: Average treatment effect

Suppose that everyone assigned to the treatment group participates in the program and no one in the control group participates (that is, 100 percent compliance with random assignment). This is the ideal RCT case, and it can easily be estimated that ATE is \$30 per day. Table 6.2 shows how these estimates are calculated.

What is ATT in this scenario, and can it be estimated? It depends on how ATT is defined. If ATT is defined according to who actually participates, then ATT = ATE, meaning it can be estimated. Note, however, that this scenario assumes that all individuals assigned to the treatment group were "forced" to participate, which is how 100 percent compliance was obtained. However, some of them may not have participated if they had been given a choice. Instead, ATT could be defined as who would participate if given a choice, but if this definition of ATT is used, then ATT cannot be estimated under the scenario of 100 percent compliance with random assignment. In this example, some people gain \$20 and others gain \$40, and with perfect compliance the proportions of both groups who would

TABLE 6.2 Estimation of ATE with 100 percent compliance with random assignment

	TREATED (RECEIVES TRAINING) (1) $R = 1$	CONTROL (DOES NOT RECEIVE TRAINING) (2) $R = 0$	ATE (1) - (2)
Participate if, and only if, assigned to treatment	$P = R = 1$: $E[Y_1] = E[Y \mid P = 1]$ $= E[Y \mid R = 1]$ $= 0.5 \times \$120/\text{day} + 0.5 \times \$100/\text{day}$ $= \$110/\text{day}$	$P = R = 0$: $E[Y_0] = E[Y \mid P = 0]$ $= E[Y \mid R = 0]$ $= \$80/\text{day}$	$E[Y_1 - Y_0] =$ $E[Y \mid R = 1]$ $- E[Y \mid R = 0]$ $= \$110 - \$80$ $= \$30/\text{day}$ (ATE)

Source: Glewwe and Todd 2019.
Note: ATE = average treatment effect.

participate if given a choice cannot be estimated. These proportions are needed to calculate a weighted average of \$20 and \$40 for those who would participate if given a choice, so this second definition of ATT cannot be estimated for this example. These alternative definitions of ATT also raise the issue of whether forced participation is ethical; ethical issues are discussed in detail in chapter 10.

Next, consider a situation in which some individuals assigned to the treatment group choose not to participate. In this case, ATT can be estimated using the formula above from equation (6.2), which is shown again for convenience:

$$\text{ATT} = \frac{\text{E}[Y \mid R=1] - \text{E}[Y \mid R=0]}{\text{E}[P \mid R=1]}. \tag{6.2}$$

To see the intuition for this formula, consider a second example.

Example B: Average treatment effect on the treated

Suppose now that three-fourths of the population whose earnings increase by \$40 per day choose to participate in the program, while only one-fourth of the population whose earnings increase by \$20 per day choose to participate. Thus only half of the people assigned to the treatment group ($R = 1$) participate (continue to assume that no one in the control group participates). So the treatment group is divided into two subgroups: the "compliers" ($R = 1$ and $P = 1$) and the "noncompliers" ($R = 1$ and $P = 0$).

Recall that ATT measures the impact of the program on those who participate (the treated). In this scenario, the treated consist of three-fourths of those whose earnings increase by \$40 per day and one-fourth of those whose earnings increase by \$20 per day. Because these two groups are one-half of the total population, the program participants consist of one-fourth whose earnings increase by \$20 per day and three-fourths whose earnings increase by \$40 per day. A simple weighted average implies that ATT = \$35 (= 0.75 × \$40 + 0.25 × \$20).

The calculation of ATT in the previous paragraph is based on complete knowledge of the population, but it can also be calculated from observed information using equation (6.2) for ATT. First, the numerator can be calculated as follows:

$$\begin{aligned}
&\text{E}[Y \mid R=1] - \text{E}[Y \mid R=0] \\
&\quad = (0.5 \times (0.25 \times 80 + 0.75 \times 120)) + \\
&\quad\quad (0.5 \times (0.75 \times 80 + 0.25 \times 100)) - (0.5 \times 80 + 0.5 \times 80) \\
&\quad = 0.5 \times (20 + 90) + 0.5 \times (60 + 25) - 80 \\
&\quad = 55 + 42.5 - 80 = 17.5.
\end{aligned}$$

This value of 17.5 for the numerator is the impact of offering the program, averaged over those who accept the offer and those who decline the offer. The denominator in equation (6.2) for ATT, $\text{E}[P \mid R = 1]$, is equal to 0.5. Thus the estimate of ATT is 17.5/0.5 = \$35.

The intuition is that only half of the people in the treatment group get treated; the ATT formula accounts for this fact by inflating the term $E[Y \mid R = 1] - E[Y \mid R = 0]$ by dividing it by the share of the people in the treatment group who were indeed treated (that is, by dividing it by $E[P \mid R = 1] = 0.5$). This is shown in table 6.3; ATT is calculated only for those who participate (the bottom half of the table).

Note that $E[Y \mid R = 1] - E[Y \mid R = 0]$ no longer estimates ATE, because the impacts of the program on the noncompliers (had they participated) cannot be known. However, when the treatment group includes noncompliers, $E[Y \mid R = 1] - E[Y \mid R = 0]$ is the formula for the intention-to-treat effect, to which the discussion now turns.

Intention-to-treat effects

Because some people randomly assigned to the treatment group choose not to participate in the program, researchers have proposed a different type of treatment effect: the average impact of the program among those offered the treatment. This is the *intention-to-treat effect* (ITT). It is defined as follows:

$$\begin{aligned} ITT &\equiv E[Y_1 - Y_0 \mid P = 1] \times Prob[P = 1] + E[Y_0 - Y_0 \mid P = 0] \times Prob[P = 0] \\ &= E[Y_1 - Y_0 \mid P = 1] \times Prob[P = 1]. \end{aligned} \quad (6.3)$$

TABLE 6.3 Estimation of ATT when 50 percent of the treatment group are nonparticipants

	TREATED (OFFERED TRAINING) (1) $R = 1$	CONTROL (DO NOT RECEIVE TRAINING) (2) $R = 0$	ATT (1) - (2)
Do not participate even if offered the treatment (75 percent of those who gain \$20 and 25 percent of those who gain \$40)	$P = 0, R = 1$: $E[Y \mid P = 0, R = 1]$ = 0.75 × \$80 + 0.25 × \$80 = \$80.	$P = 0, R = 0$: $E[Y \mid P = 0, R = 0]$ = \$80 = 0.75 × \$80 + 0.25 × \$80 = \$80.	\$80 – \$80 = 0.
Participate if offered the treatment (25 percent of those who gain \$20 and 75 percent of those who gain \$40)	$P = 1, R = 1$: $E[Y \mid P = 1, R = 1]$ = 0.25 × \$100 + 0.75 × \$120 = \$25 + \$90 = \$115.	$P = 0, R = 0$: $E[Y \mid P = 0, R = 0]$ = 0.25 × \$80 + 0.75 × \$80 = \$20 + \$60 = \$80.	\$115 – \$80 = \$35

Source: Glewwe and Todd 2019.
Note: ATT = average treatment effect on the treated.

In words, ITT is the average impact of the program among those who were offered the opportunity to participate in the program, regardless of whether they actually participated. The first line in equation (6.3) shows that ITT is a weighted average of the impacts of the program on those who participate (for whom $P = 1$) and on those who do not participate (for whom $P = 0$). This definition assumes that Y_0 is unchanged for nonparticipants when others choose to participate, so the second term in the first line of equation (6.3) equals zero, which yields the second line in the definition.

In the context of a properly implemented RCT, those who were offered the opportunity to participate are those who were randomly assigned to the treatment group, that is, those for whom $R = 1$. Because R was randomly assigned, this definition of ITT applies to the population as a whole; that is, if another group were formed by randomly drawing from the population and assigning this group to the treatment, this group would have exactly the same ITT. In contrast, if the opportunity to participate in the program had not been randomly assigned, because the opportunity to participate in the program being evaluated was determined by some criteria other than random assignment, then ITT applies only to the group that actually was offered the opportunity to participate in the program, and not to the population as a whole. If another group had been offered the opportunity, ITT could be different for that group.[6]

ITT is a useful measure of program impact because it shows what will happen to the average value of Y for the entire population that is offered the opportunity to participate in the program, not just for those who actually participate. ITT is also easy to calculate using observed data from an RCT if it is possible to estimate ATT, that is, as long as no one in the control group (for whom $R = 0$) participates in the program. To see this, note that the definition of ATT given the above implies that ITT = ATT × Prob[$P = 1$], and recall that ATT can be estimated by dividing $E[Y \mid R = 1] - E[Y \mid R = 0]$ by Prob[$P = 1$]. This implies that ITT can be estimated as follows:

$$\text{ITT} = E[Y \mid R = 1] - E[Y \mid R = 0]. \tag{6.4}$$

This simple procedure for estimating ITT makes it appealing, and it is often used in impact evaluations. However, it is important to keep in mind that the above definition of ITT assumes that the program has no effect on nonparticipants. The next section considers the case in which such spillover effects may occur.

Intention-to-treat effects when effects spill over onto nonparticipants

The impacts of some types of programs can plausibly affect individuals who do not participate in the program. Such effects are often referred to as *spillover effects*; sometimes they are called *social effects* or *externalities*. Three examples are: (1) some individuals are treated for an infectious disease, which reduces the spread of that disease to untreated individuals; (2) some students in a classroom participate in a program that increases their learning, and their interactions with nonparticipating students also increase those students' learning; and (3) farmers who participate in an agricultural extension program learn about new crop production methods, and they provide some or all of this information to some of their neighbors who did not participate in the program.

Fortunately, the definition of ITT can readily be modified to allow for such spillover effects. The following definition, which is denoted as ITT(s), allows for such effects:

$$\text{ITT(s)} \equiv \text{E}[Y_1 - Y_0 | P = 1] \times \text{Prob}[P = 1] + \text{E}[Y_{0(s)} - Y_0 | P = 0] \times \text{Prob}[P = 0], \qquad (6.5)$$

where $Y_{0(s)}$ allows for spillovers onto individuals who do not participate in the program. Note that, unlike the case in which nonparticipants are unaffected, the second term does not equal zero, which also implies that ITT(s) $\neq$ ATT $\times$ Prob[P = 1].

Fortunately, ITT effects that account for spillovers can be easily estimated in the context of an RCT as long as it can be assumed that spillover effects do not occur for those individuals who are randomly assigned to the control group. This is a plausible assumption if random assignment is done at the community (or school) level and spillovers can be assumed to occur within communities (or schools) but not between them. This can be seen directly from the definition of ITT(s):

$$\begin{aligned} \text{ITT(s)} &\equiv \text{E}[Y_1 - Y_0 | P = 1] \times \text{Prob}[P = 1] + \text{E}[Y_{0(s)} - Y_0 | P = 0] \times \text{Prob}[P = 0] \qquad (6.6) \\ &= \text{E}[Y_1 | P = 1] \times \text{Prob}[P = 1] + \text{E}[Y_{0(s)} | P = 0] \times \text{Prob}[P = 0] \\ &\quad - (\text{E}[Y_0 | P = 1] \times \text{Prob}[P = 1] + \text{E}[Y_0 | P = 0] \times \text{Prob}[P = 0]) \\ &= \text{E}[Y_1 | P = 1, R = 1] \times \text{Prob}[P = 1 | R = 1] + \text{E}[Y_{0(s)} | P = 0, R = 1] \\ &\quad \times \text{Prob}[P = 0 | R = 1] - \text{E}[Y_0] \\ &= \text{E}[Y | P = 1, R = 1] \times \text{Prob}[P = 1 | R = 1] + \text{E}[Y | P = 0, R = 1] \\ &\quad \times \text{Prob}[P = 0 | R = 1] - \text{E}[Y | R = 0] \\ &= \text{E}[Y | R = 1] - \text{E}[Y | R = 0]. \end{aligned}$$

Note that this is exactly the same estimator of ITT as when no spillovers are present (equation (6.4)). Thus this estimator automatically accounts for spillovers onto individuals in the treatment group who choose not to participate, when those spillovers exist.

A final important point is that this estimator does not indicate whether such spillovers exist; to determine whether they exist, nonparticipants among those randomly assigned to the treatment group must be compared with the analogous individuals who were randomly assigned to the control group. In general, identifying precisely the individuals in the control group who would not have participated in the program had it been offered to them is quite difficult. Two possible approaches are to (1) ask those in the control group whether they would participate if given the opportunity, and (2) use the group that was offered the opportunity to participate (the treatment group) to estimate the factors that determine participation, and use the estimated parameters to predict which individuals in the control group would have participated if they had been given the opportunity. However, both of these methods may lead to misclassification of which individuals in the control group would have participated, which could lead to misleading estimates of whether spillover effects exist.

Encouragement designs

For many programs randomization may be impossible because no members of the population can be excluded from participating in the program. However, it may be possible to obtain an estimate of the impact of the program for a subset of the population by providing advertisements, other types of information, assistance in applying for the program, or even monetary incentives to a randomly selected subset of the population to increase program participation for that subgroup. As discussed in chapter 15, encouragement designs are essentially an instrumental variables estimation method.

Karlan and Zinman's (2008, 2009) studies on microfinance programs in South Africa are good examples of encouragement design evaluations. Special promotions and different loan products were randomly marketed to a bank's previous borrowers to measure the impacts of microfinance products on those borrowers' behavior and welfare. Another example is Devoto et al. (2012), who investigated the impacts of providing piped water to urban households in Morocco. In that study, the treatment group received detailed information about a piped water program as well as assistance with completing the application for the program.

A hypothetical example can be used to illustrate how encouragement design methods work. Suppose that, for some reason, RCTs are no longer feasible for evaluating a program, such as the job training program discussed previously. An encouragement design can be used instead, if it can be plausibly assumed that some eligible people do not participate because they do not have sufficient information about the program. If they had known more about the program, they would have participated. Similarly, if some individuals find the application process too complicated, or doubt that the benefits are worth the costs, they may choose to participate if they are given assistance for the application process or if they receive monetary incentives to participate in the program.

The most common encouragement design operates by providing more information about the program (for example, advertisements) to randomly selected subsets of the population to increase their participation rates. Assuming that participation is voluntary, there are three groups of people:

1. Those who never participate (regardless of the advertisement)
2. Those who always participate (regardless of the advertisement)
3. Those who participate only if encouraged (only if they receive the advertisement)

For an evaluation that randomly assigns some type of encouragement to participate, the average program impact can be estimated for a subset of the population, in this case for those who participate only if encouraged. Table 6.4 provides an example, in which $R = 1$ denotes the group that received the randomized encouragement and $R = 0$ denotes the group that was not encouraged.

The average program impact identified for people who participate only if encouraged (shown in the third row) is called the *local average treatment effect* (LATE); it is the average treatment effect that pertains to the complier subgroup (those who comply with

TABLE 6.4 Encouragement design (estimates local average treatment effect)

	(1) $R = 1$	(2) $R = 0$	DIFFERENCE BETWEEN (1) AND (2)
Never participate (20 percent)	$Y = Y_0$	$Y = Y_0$	0
Always participate (20 percent)	$Y = Y_1$	$Y = Y_1$	0
Participate only if encouraged (60 percent)	$Y = Y_1$	$Y = Y_0$	$Y_1 - Y_0$ (program impact)

Source: Glewwe and Todd 2019.

the encouragement). It is clearly not ATE, given that it does not include treatment effects for those who never participate or those who always participate (see the first and second rows). Nor is it ATT, because the average program impact on the always participators cannot be estimated (see second row). The general approach for estimating the LATE parameter, as well as the rationale for focusing on LATE, is presented in chapter 15.

Conclusion

This chapter introduces the basic concepts of RCTs and shows how RCTs can be used to estimate program impacts. The types of impacts that can be estimated depend on individuals' behavior in response to their random assignment. ATE can be estimated if every person or community complies with its random assignment. ATT can be estimated if everyone assigned to the control group does not participate but some in the treatment group do not participate, and the ITT can also be estimated in this situation.

Additional complications arise if individuals in the treatment group who choose not to participate are affected by the participation of others in the treatment group, that is, if spillovers exist, or if it is not possible to exclude individuals in the control group from participating in the program. If spillovers are possible, that is, if it is possible that Y_0 changes for some who were assigned to the treatment group but chose not to participate, then ITT estimates are still valid estimates of the average impact of being offered the treatment as long as the spillovers occur only among the individuals who were randomly assigned to the treatment group and do not affect those who were randomly assigned to the control group. Finally, encouragement designs can be used if it is not possible to exclude any members of the population from the program, in which case LATE can be estimated.

The next chapter discusses regression methods in the context of RCTs in more detail. The subsequent two chapters present practical recommendations for conducting RCTs and for choosing an appropriate sample design, respectively. Chapter 10 discusses ethical problems that can arise in research, both for RCTs and more generally. Finally, additional discussion of encouragement design methods is provided in chapter 15.

Notes

1. Strictly speaking, $P = 1$ indicates that these people would participate if given the opportunity. For this group of people, the subset who are randomly assigned to the control group (that is, have $R = 0$) will not actually participate in the program, and it could be argued that for them $P = 0$, rather than $P = 1$. Although new notation could have been devised that distinguishes between whether one would participate if given a choice and whether one actually participates, the decision was made not to do so for this book; the exposition should be clear without a more elaborate notation.
2. Because $R = 1$ is randomly assigned, it follows that $E[Y \mid P = 1] = E[Y \mid P = 1, R = 1]$. Similarly, for the third group $E[Y \mid P = 0] = E[Y \mid P = 0, R = 1]$.
3. This third group provides an estimate of $E[Y_0 \mid P = 0]$ only if there are no spillovers onto their outcomes that arise because some or all of the individuals assigned to the treatment group choose to participate in the program. This no-spillover assumption is made for the rest of this section; the section titled "Intention-to-treat effects when effects spill over onto nonparticipants" explains what can be estimated if this assumption does not hold.
4. Again, the conditioning on $P = 0$ for the term $E[Y_0 \mid P = 0]$ is conditioning on the participation decision that would be made when an individual has a choice, not the actual participation that occurs when that choice is constrained.
5. $E[Y \mid R = 1] - E[Y \mid R = 0]$
$$\begin{aligned} &= E[Y_1 \mid P = 1, R = 1] \times \text{Prob}[P = 1] + E[Y_0 \mid P = 0, R = 1] \times \text{Prob}[P = 0] \\ &\quad - \{E[Y_0 \mid P = 1, R = 0] \times \text{Prob}[P = 1] + E[Y_0 \mid P = 0, R = 0] \times \text{Prob}[P = 0]\} \\ &= E[Y_1 \mid P = 1] \times \text{Prob}[P = 1] + E[Y_0 \mid P = 0] \times \text{Prob}[P = 0] - \{E[Y_0 \mid P = 1] \times \text{Prob}[P = 1] \\ &\quad + E[Y_0 \mid P = 0] \times \text{Prob}[P = 0]\} \\ &= E[Y_1 - Y_0 \mid P = 1] \times \text{Prob}[P = 1] - 0 \times \text{Prob}[P = 0] \\ &= \text{ATT} \times \text{Prob}[P = 1]. \end{aligned}$$
6. Thus if ITT were defined more generally to apply to cases in which the opportunity to participate in the program was not strictly determined by random assignment, a variable O could be defined as the offer to participate in the program ($O = 1$ for those given that opportunity and $= 0$ for those not given that opportunity), and the definition of ITT would become $E[Y_1 - Y_0 \mid P = 1, O = 1] \times \text{Prob}[P = 1 \mid O = 1]$.

References

Devoto, Florencia, Esther Duflo, Pascaline Dupas, William Parienté, and Vincent Pons. 2012. "Happiness on Tap: Piped Water Adoption in Urban Morocco." *American Economic Journal: Economic Policy* 4 (4): 68–99.

Glennerster, Rachel, and Kudzai Takavarasha. 2013. *Running Randomized Evaluations: A Practical Guide.* Princeton, NJ: Princeton University Press.

Glewwe, Paul, and Petra Todd. 2019. Course materials, "APEC 8212: Econometric Analysis II" and "ECON 712: Graduate Topics Course in Program Evaluation Methods," University of Minnesota, Minneapolis–St. Paul, and University of Pennsylvania, Philadelphia.

Karlan, Dean, and Jonathan Zinman. 2008. "Credit Elasticities in Less-Developed Economies: Implications for Microfinance." *American Economic Review* 89 (3): 1040–68.

Karlan, Dean, and Jonathan Zinman. 2009. "Observing Unobservables: Identifying Information Asymmetries with a Consumer Credit Field Experiment." *Econometrica* 77 (6): 1993–2008.

Skoufias, Emmanuel. 2005. *PROGRESA and Its Impacts on the Welfare of Rural Households in Mexico.* Research Report 139. Washington, DC: International Food Policy Research Institute.

CHAPTER 7

Regression Methods for Randomized Controlled Trials

Introduction

The methods presented in chapter 6 for using randomized controlled trials (RCTs) to estimate average treatment effect (ATE), average treatment effect on the treated (ATT), and intention-to-treat effect (ITT) do not explain in detail how to estimate those effects. The most obvious approach is to estimate them as differences in means for different subgroups of the population. For example, in an RCT with perfect compliance, ATE can be estimated as the difference between the observed Y for the group that was randomly assigned to be treated and the observed Y for the group that was randomly assigned to the control group.

Although estimates of ATE, ATT, and ITT based on comparing means are intuitively simple to understand, calculating treatment effects using regression analysis is often helpful. There are three reasons for using regression analysis:

1. Regression analysis is a convenient way to test the statistical significance of estimated treatment effects.

2. Regression methods allow other variables that are unrelated to the treatment, but that can also affect Y, to be controlled for, which could increase the precision of the estimates of treatment effects.

3. Regression methods are convenient for estimating differences in average impacts across different subsets of the population, such as by sex or by age.

This chapter explains how relatively simple regression methods can be used to estimate ATE, ATT, and ITT using data from an RCT. Note that regression methods are presented in much more detail in part III of this book (chapters 11–17), which focuses on analysis of nonexperimental data. As will be seen, regression methods have many uses and, in general, almost all regression methods are suitable for both experimental and nonexperimental data. Yet many, if not most, analyses of RCTs use a small subset of the possible regression methods, so some basic regression methods that can be applied to experimental data generated from an RCT are reviewed here.

The rest of this chapter is organized as follows. The next section explains how to use regression methods for RCTs under ideal conditions, in particular when compliance with the random assignment is perfect. This will produce estimates of ATE. The following section examines how to use regression methods to estimate the impact of the program on those who participate in it, that is, ATT, when some of those randomly assigned to the treatment group do not participate in the program. The next section discusses the use of regression methods for addressing issues of sample attrition (inability to collect data from all of the participants in the RCT after the program is implemented), and is followed by a section that provides advice on how to increase precision in regression estimators. The subsequent section discusses methods for obtaining correct standard errors when the data are grouped and randomization is done at the group level, and the penultimate section provides final recommendations. The last section summarizes and provides concluding comments.

Estimating average treatment effects when no problems occur

In the ideal RCT, all individuals who were assigned to the treatment group ($R = 1$) participated in the program ($P = 1$), and all individuals who were assigned to the control group ($R = 0$) did not participate in the program ($P = 0$). In this case the observed value of Y is

$$Y = Y_0 + R(Y_1 - Y_0) = \mathrm{E}[Y_0] + R \times \mathrm{E}[Y_1 - Y_0] + \{Y_0 - \mathrm{E}[Y_0] + R \times (Y_1 - Y_0 - \mathrm{E}[Y_1 - Y_0])\}.$$

The expression to the the right of the second equality sign suggests that ATE can be estimated by simply regressing Y on a constant term and the randomized assignment variable R:

$$Y = \alpha + \beta R + u, \tag{7.1}$$

where $\alpha = \mathrm{E}[Y_0]$, $\beta = \mathrm{E}[Y_1 - Y_0]$, and u is $\{Y_0 - \mathrm{E}[Y_0] + R \times (Y_1 - Y_0 - \mathrm{E}[Y_1 - Y_0])\}$. Randomization implies that R is uncorrelated with u (it can easily be shown that $\mathrm{E}[u| R = 0] = \mathrm{E}[u| R = 1] = 0$), so the ordinary least squares (OLS) estimate of β is an unbiased and consistent estimate of $\mathrm{E}[Y_1 - Y_0]$, and thus of ATE.

More specifically, when perfect compliance holds, the constant term in equation (7.1), α, is an unbiased and consistent estimate of the mean of Y for the control group, and the sum of α and β is an unbiased and consistent estimate of the mean of Y for the treatment group. Thus α is an unbiased estimate of $\mathrm{E}[Y_0]$ and $\alpha + \beta$ is an unbiased estimate of $\mathrm{E}[Y_1]$, so the difference, β, is an unbiased and consistent estimate of ATE. Note that these regression estimates are exactly equal to the estimates that would be obtained by comparing the mean of Y for the observations randomly assigned to participate in the program to the mean of Y for the observations randomly assigned to the control group.

The simple regression in equation (7.1) may need modification for two main reasons. First, compliance may not be perfect, and problems of sample attrition may be present.

These problems are discussed in the next two sections. Second, even in the ideal case of perfect compliance and no sample attrition, modifying the regression equation may increase the statistical precision of the estimates, and a related issue is that when the data are grouped the formulas for the standard errors of the estimates must be modified to account for that grouping; these issues are discussed in later sections of this chapter.

Estimation when some in the treatment group are not treated

In practice, experiments often do not go completely according to plan. Perhaps the most common problem is that some individuals who were assigned to the treatment group decide not to participate. As chapter 6 explains, estimating ATE then becomes impossible. However, ATT and ITT can still be estimated easily using regression methods. Note that this chapter always assumes that none of the individuals randomly assigned to the control group was able to obtain treatment. If some individuals in the control group were able to participate in the program, then encouragement design methods can be used; the regression approach in this case involves estimation of the local average treatment effect, which is discussed in detail in chapter 15.

Estimating the average treatment effect on the treated

If some people who were assigned to participate in the program did not do so, but none of the people assigned to the nonparticipant group (control group) participated in the program, then $R = 1$ does not necessarily imply that $P = 1$, but it is still the case that $R = 0$ implies that $P = 0$. A simple OLS regression can be used to estimate ITT, as explained below, but not to estimate either ATE or ATT.

However, ATT can be estimated by using instrumental variable (IV) methods. This estimation is performed in two steps. The first step is to run an OLS regression of P on R and save the predicted values for P, which can be denoted by $\hat{P}$. More specifically, the first step is to estimate the following regression:

$$P = \alpha_P + \beta_P R + u_P,$$

where the P subscripts indicate that these coefficients are for a regression of P on R. The estimated coefficients from this regression can then be used to obtain the predicted values of P:

$$\hat{P} = \hat{\alpha}_P + \hat{\beta}_P R,$$

where $\hat{\alpha}_P$ and $\hat{\beta}_P$ are the OLS estimates of α and β, respectively.

The second step is to use these estimates of P, that is, to use $\hat{P}$, in the following regression to obtain an estimate of ATT:

$$Y = \alpha + \beta\hat{P} + u.$$

The estimate of β obtained from OLS estimation of this equation is a consistent estimate of ATT. Note, however, that the OLS standard errors for this estimate of β are not the correct standard errors. This approach, which regresses one variable on the predicted value of another variable, is called *instrumental variables (IV) estimation*; it will provide the correct standard errors for this estimate of β. IV estimation is presented in more detail in chapter 15.

Estimating intention-to-treat effects

It is also possible to estimate ITT when some people who were randomly assigned to the treatment group did not participate in the program, as long as none of those who were assigned to the control group obtained treatment. This estimation is accomplished by running the same OLS regression as in equation (7.1):

$$Y = \alpha + \beta R + u. \tag{7.2}$$

Again, randomization implies that R is uncorrelated with u, but in this situation it is not always the case that $P = R$. However, as long as no one in the control group obtained the treatment, the estimate of β from this regression will be an unbiased and consistent estimate of ITT, that is, the impact of offering the treatment. Intuitively, all the individuals randomly assigned to the treatment group were offered the treatment (and no one in the control group was offered, and thus none of them obtained, the treatment). Thus this regression estimates the average impact of being offered the treatment, which allows for the possibility that some who were offered the treatment chose not to take it. If everyone who was offered the treatment had accepted the offer, then ITT would be equal to ATE and so equation (7.2) would also estimate ATE.

Consequences of spillover effects

Thus far it has been assumed that the outcome variable Y of the individuals who do not obtain the treatment is unaffected by the fact that other individuals are treated. This is often called the *stable unit treatment value assumption* (SUTVA). In some cases this assumption is quite plausible but, as explained in the section titled "Intention-to-treat effects when effects spill over onto nonparticipants" in chapter 6, in other situations it is not.

If this assumption is not plausible, even if there is perfect compliance a simple OLS regression may not provide a consistent and unbiased estimate of ATE. The problem is that some individuals in the control group may have experienced a change in their outcomes from spillover effects resulting from participation in the program by the individuals in the treatment group, so the values of Y for the control group no longer provide an unbiased and consistent estimate of $E[Y_0]$. In addition, IV estimation may not yield a consistent estimate of ATT.

However, as discussed in the section titled "Intention-to-treat effects when effects spill over onto nonparticipants" in chapter 6, if such spillovers onto individuals who are not treated happen only to individuals who were offered the treatment and decided not to take it, then the ITT estimate in the subsection titled "Estimating intention-to-treat effects" is still a consistent estimate of the ITT effect. This is possible because it is assumed that spillovers do not affect the control group, so an unbiased and consistent estimate of $E[Y_0]$ can still be obtained. Take, for example, a campaign to provide treatment for an infectious disease in some randomly selected villages but not others. Everyone in the treatment villages is offered the treatment, but some refuse. It is plausible that spillovers from individuals who participated in the treatment onto those who did not will be confined to the village. If so, then the only people affected by those spillovers are people who were offered the treatment, and the people in the control villages are still a pure control group. An ITT estimate can be obtained using the OLS regression given in equation (7.2), which includes the spillover impact of the program onto the individuals offered the treatment but who declined to take it; this is denoted ITT(s) in chapter 6.

This approach raises the question of whether it is possible, if spillovers affect only people who were offered the treatment, to obtain a consistent estimate of ATT using the IV method discussed in the subsection in this chapter titled "Estimating the average treatment effect on the treated." Unfortunately, this is not the case. To see why, recall that the definition of ATT is $E[Y_1 - Y_0| P = 1]$. The observed values of Y for those in the treatment group who participate in the program provide a consistent estimate of $E[Y_1| P = 1]$, so what is needed is a consistent estimate of $E[Y_0| P = 1]$. When no spillovers occur, $E[Y_0| P = 1]$ could be estimated by noting the following:

$$E[Y_0] = E[Y_0| P = 1] \times \text{Prob}[P = 1] + E[Y_0| P = 0] \times \text{Prob}[P = 0].$$

As noted previously, the assumption of no spillovers onto the control group yields a consistent estimate of $E[Y_0]$, and consistent estimates of $\text{Prob}[P = 1]$ and $\text{Prob}[P = 0]$ can be obtained by observing the choices made by the individuals in the treatment group; so if a consistent estimate of $E[Y_0| P = 0]$ can be obtained, then a consistent estimate of $E[Y_0| P = 1]$ can be obtained, as explained in chapter 6. When spillover effects do not exist, a consistent estimate of $E[Y_0| P = 0]$ can be obtained from the observed values of Y for those in the treatment group who do not participate in the program, but those observed values do *not* consistently estimate $E[Y_0| P = 0]$ if spillovers exist, so IV methods, which essentially perform this calculation, do not provide a consistent estimate of ATT.

Complications caused by sample attrition

Another common problem that arises in randomized trials is sample attrition. Attrition occurs when, after the treatment and control groups have been randomly assigned and after the treatment group has participated in the program, data cannot be collected from every individual who was part of the random assignment. The potential problem with attrition is that the people who cannot be contacted differ in important ways from those who remain in the sample and, most important, that those in the treatment group who cannot be contacted are different from those in the control group who cannot be contacted.

A simple example of attrition bias

If the attrition within the treatment and control groups is not random, biased estimates could result. The following simple example provides the intuition for how this could happen.

Consider a program that provides free textbooks to primary school students in a country where the current practice is for parents to purchase textbooks for their children. Suppose that some low-performing students drop out of school and that the data are collected from schools, so it is not possible to obtain data on children who drop out. To see how this situation could affect the estimates of program impacts, consider the two cases in table 7.1 that, for simplicity, assume that there are only six students.

In this simple example, the three students in the control group are perfectly matched with the three students in the treatment group according to test scores before the intervention. It is clear that the ATE of this program is to increase test scores by 5 points; after the intervention the average score for the treatment group has increased to 65, while the average

TABLE 7.1 Effect of attrition on estimates of treatment effects

CASE 1: NO ATTRITION			
TEST SCORES BEFORE INTERVENTION		**TEST SCORES AFTER INTERVENTION**	
Treatment group	Control group	Treatment group	Control group
Student 1: 50	Student 2: 50	Student 1: 52	Student 2: 50
Student 3: 60	Student 4: 60	Student 3: 68	Student 4: 60
Student 5: 70	Student 6: 70	Student 5: 75	Student 6: 70
CASE 2: WITH ATTRITION (ONLY STUDENTS WITH SCORES > 50 REMAIN IN SCHOOL)			
TEST SCORES BEFORE INTERVENTION		**TEST SCORES AFTER INTERVENTION**	
Treatment group	Control group	Treatment group	Control group
Student 1: 50	Student 2: 50	Student 1: 52	Student 2: [absent]
Student 3: 60	Student 4: 60	Student 3: 68	Student 4: 60
Student 5: 70	Student 6: 70	Student 5: 75	Student 6: 70

Source: Glewwe and Todd 2019.

score for the control group remains at 60. In the first case there is no attrition from the sample, so ATE is easily calculated.

What will the estimate of ATE be if poorly performing students drop out? This is seen in the second case, in which the poorest performing student, Student 2, drops out of school and thus is not included in the calculation of the treatment effect. The estimate of Y_1 based on test scores after the intervention is still 65, but the estimate of Y_0 is also 65. Comparing these two estimates yields an average treatment effect of 0, which clearly underestimates the true effect.

Checking for attrition bias

Attrition can lead to bias in both straightforward and subtle ways. Fortunately, some simple things can be checked to make an initial assessment of whether attrition is likely to be a problem. The first item to check is whether the rate of attrition is the same in the treatment and control groups. If it is the same, then attrition bias is less likely, although it is still a possibility. If the rate of attrition is different, there may well be a problem of bias. To continue with the example in the previous paragraphs, if an RCT to evaluate the impact of a school improvement program shows an attrition rate of 20 percent in the control schools and 10 percent in the treatment schools, it is likely (assuming that the weakest students are most likely to drop out) that the 10-percentage-point difference means that, on average, the students who remain in the treatment schools are somewhat weaker students than those who remain in the control schools, which will lead to downward bias in estimates of the impact of the school improvement program.

To check whether the attrition rates are significantly different in the treatment and control schools, a dummy variable can be created indicating whether an individual who was part of the original random assignment was still in the sample after the program was implemented for the treatment group. This variable can be regressed on a constant term and the dummy variable R in a regression analogous to the regression in equation (7.1). If the coefficient on R is statistically significant, then the attrition rates are different, so bias caused by differential attrition could well be a problem.

Even if there is no significant difference in the attrition rates across the treatment and control groups, there is still potential for bias because those who left the treatment group may not be the same type of people as those who left the control group. For example, those who are no longer in the sample in the control group may be people who became upset because they were not selected to participate in the program and thought that the program would have been beneficial for them, while those no longer in the sample from the treatment group may be those who felt that the program did not work well for them and therefore refused to cooperate the next time data were collected. Thus determining whether those who dropped out are significantly different across the treatment and control groups is useful, even if the attrition rates are similar for these two groups.

If detailed data on the individuals in both the treatment and control groups had been examined before the program was implemented (which is strongly advised in chapter 8), whether the individuals who left the treatment group are significantly different from those who left the control group can be determined. This determination can be made by comparing variable means between those who left the treatment group and those who left the control group. Another option is to do the same for those who have not left, which will allow for a larger sample size. Such comparisons of means can be accomplished by a regression similar to that in equation (7.1)—regressing a variable on a constant term and the random assignment variable (R)—the coefficient on R indicates whether there is a significant difference.

Another method to check for attrition bias is to estimate whether attrition is completely random by regressing a dummy variable for attrition on baseline variables (variables with measurements before the program was implemented). This regression is performed separately for the treatment group and the control group. A result showing that no baseline variables have significant explanatory power suggests (but does not prove) that attrition is quite random and therefore does not lead to biased estimates of program impacts.

Bounds analysis

If there is reason to believe that attrition could lead to biased estimates, procedures often referred to as *bounds analysis* can be used to obtain upper and lower bounds of the true impact of the program. Relatively narrow bounds provide a reasonably informative idea of the impact of the program; wide bounds make it difficult to assess the impact of the program.

The simplest type of bounds analysis is as follows: Consider the case in which the attrition rate is 5 percent from the treatment group and 10 percent from the control group. Assume that the 5 percent in the treatment group would also have left the sample (experienced attrition) if they had been in the control group, so the potential bias comes from the 5 percent in the control group who would not have left the sample had they been in the treatment group. The problem is that it is not possible to determine which of the individuals in the treatment group who did not leave the sample would have left if they had been in the control group. To obtain an upper bound on the treatment effect, it can be assumed that this group is the 5 percent with the lowest (endline) values of Y_1 in the treatment group, and the impact of the treatment effect after dropping those individuals can be reestimated. Similarly, to obtain a lower bound on the treatment effect, it can be assumed that this group is the 5 percent with the highest values of Y_1 in the treatment group, and the impact of the treatment effect after dropping those individuals can be reestimated. This provides upper and lower bounds of the actual treatment effect.

More precise bounds can be obtained using a procedure proposed by Lee (2009). To see how this procedure works, two binary selection variables, denoted by S, need to be defined:

$$S_1 = 0 \text{ if attrition}, = 1 \text{ if no attrition, conditional on program participation } (P = 1),$$

$$S_0 = 0 \text{ if attrition}, = 1 \text{ if no attrition, conditional on program nonparticipation } (P = 0).$$

Just as everyone has a Y_1 and a Y_0, everyone also has an S_1 and an S_0, but S_1 is observed only if a person participates in the program, and S_0 is observed only if a person does not participate. Each of these S variables indicates whether a person is "selected" (remains in the sample), in which case the S variable equals one, or experiences attrition (is no longer in the sample), in which case the S variable equals zero. Observed selection, S, satisfies $S = P \times S_1 + (1 - P) \times S_0$.

To obtain bounds, Lee's method requires two assumptions. The first is that Y_1, Y_0, S_1, and S_0 are all independent of P, which will automatically be the case if all individuals follow their random assignment but may not hold if random assignment is not followed. The second assumption is that $S_1 \geq S_0$, which means that it is possible that some program participants who do not leave the sample (do not experience attrition) would have left if they had not participated, but it is never the case that a program participant who left the sample would not have left had he or she not participated. For many programs this assumption may be quite reasonable; some of those assigned to the control group may be disappointed at being unable to participate and therefore may not cooperate with subsequent data collection but would have cooperated had they been assigned to the treatment group and participated; but no one assigned to the treatment group who participated and later left would not have left the sample had he or she not participated.

The intuition behind Lee's bounds analysis is the following: The bounds are estimated for a variant of ATT, namely, the impact of the program on those in the treatment group who participate *and* would not leave whether they participated or not (those for whom $P = 1$ and $S_0 = 1$, who by the second assumption also have $S_1 = 1$). This treatment effect can be denoted as ATT($S_0 = 1$) and defined as ATT($S_0 = 1$) $\equiv$ E[$Y_1 - Y_0$| $P = 1$, $S_0 = 1$]. This can be estimated if E[Y_1| $P = 1$, $S_0 = 1$] and E[Y_0| $P = 1$, $S_0 = 1$] can be estimated. If the first assumption holds, as in an RCT with perfect compliance, then E[Y_0| $P = 1$, $S_0 = 1$] = E[Y_0| $P = 0$, $S_0 = 1$], which in turn can be estimated by E[Y| $P = 0$, $S_0 = 1$], which equals E[Y| $P = 0$, $S = 1$]. This can be estimated using data on the group in the lower right corner of table 7.2. The difficulty is estimation of E[Y_1| $P = 1$, $S_0 = 1$]. Among program participants for whom $S_1 = 1$, who are in the last two rows of column (1) of table 7.2, the data do not allow those for whom $S_0 = 1$ to be distinguished from those for whom $S_0 = 0$. To obtain a lower bound estimate of E[Y_1| $P = 1$, $S_0 = 1$], and thus a lower bound for ATT($S_0 = 1$), Lee (2009) assumes that, among program participants with $S_1 = 1$, those for whom $S_0 = 1$ are those who have the highest values of observed Y (highest values of Y_1), and he drops those individuals in his

TABLE 7.2 Observability of *Y* conditional on *P*, S_1, and S_0

	$P = 1$ (1)	$P = 0$ (2)
$S_1 = 0$, $S_0 = 0$	*Y* is not observed	*Y* is not observed
$S_1 = 1$, $S_0 = 0$	*Y* is observed	*Y* is not observed
$S_1 = 1$, $S_0 = 1$	*Y* is observed	*Y* is observed

Source: Glewwe and Todd 2019.

estimate of ATT(S_0 = 1). Similarly, to obtain an upper bound, he assumes that among program participants with S_1 = 1, those for whom S_0 = 1 are those who have the lowest values of observed Y, and he drops those from his calculations of ATT(S_0 = 1).

More formally, define p as the fraction of program participants who do not leave the sample but who would have left had they not participated in the program:

$$p = \frac{\text{Prob}[S = 1 \mid P = 1] - \text{Prob}[S = 1 \mid P = 0]}{\text{Prob}[S = 1 \mid P = 1]}.$$

Then the lower and upper bounds of ATT(S_0 = 1) can be estimated as follows:

$$\text{ATT}(S_0 = 1)^{LB} = \text{E}[Y| \, P = 1, S = 1, Y \leq Y_{(1-p)}] - \text{E}[Y| \, P = 0, S = 1],$$

$$\text{ATT}(S_0 = 1)^{UB} = \text{E}[Y| \, P = 1, S = 1, Y \geq Y_p] - \text{E}[Y| \, P = 0, S = 1],$$

where $Y_{(1-p)}$ is the value of Y among the nonleaving program participants for which p percent of the observations of Y are greater than that value, and Y_p is the value of Y among the nonleaving program participants for which p percent of the observations of Y are less than that value.

As long as the difference in the attrition rates between program participants and nonparticipants is a relatively small fraction of the total program participants who have not left, ATT(S_0 = 1)^{LB} and ATT(S_0 = 1)^{UB} should have similar values, which should yield tight bounds on ATT(S_0 = 1). These bounds can be made even tighter by including covariates in the calculations, but the calculations are somewhat more complicated (see Lee 2009). Finally, Lee (2009) also provides formulas to calculate the variances of ATT(S_0 = 1)^{LB} and ATT(S_0 = 1)^{UB}, which can be used to construct confidence intervals for the true value of ATT(S_0 = 1).

Methods for increasing precision of the estimates

The regression equations in the previous sections are simple in the sense that the outcome variable is regressed on a constant and only one other variable. However, more precise estimates can be obtained by including additional variables. This section provides advice on how to do so and what variables to add.

Adding control variables to the regression

In a simple regression model such as

$$Y = \alpha + \beta R + u,$$

the OLS estimate of β has a standard error equal to the square root of $\sigma^2/[N\bar{R}(1 - \bar{R})]$, where σ^2 is the variance of u, N is the sample size, and $\bar{R}$ is the mean (average) of R. As seen in chapter 9, the denominator is minimized when $\bar{R} = 0.5$, and of course the standard error can always be reduced by increasing the sample size N.

Another way to reduce the standard error is to reduce the variance of u, which can be accomplished by adding more variables to the regression that have explanatory power for Y.[1] Which variables have explanatory power will depend on what the outcome variable Y is. For example, if Y is an education outcome such as enrollment or a score on an academic test, parental education and household income (or wealth) are likely to have substantial explanatory power.

One variable that almost certainly has explanatory power for Y after the program has been implemented is the value of Y at baseline, that is, before the program started, which highlights the importance of collecting baseline data, as stressed in chapter 8. For example, children who are malnourished (for example, stunted) at baseline are also more likely to be malnourished when data are collected at a later date to assess the impact of a nutrition program; this is particularly true for variables that change slowly over time.

Finally, when adding variables to the regression to increase precision, two general recommendations should be kept in mind. First, it is essential that the added variables be characteristics that the program cannot affect.[2] If the program affects the control variables, then the impact of the program will operate via two pathways, a direct effect via the β coefficient and an indirect effect via any variable added to the regression that is affected by the program and measured after the program is implemented, which implies that β alone does not measure the total effect of the program. Variables that the program cannot affect would be any variable measured at baseline, as well as any variable that cannot be changed by the program, such as age or the formal education levels of individuals age 30 or older, regardless of when the variable was measured. If in doubt, it is usually best to leave the variable out, because a small gain in precision is unlikely to be worth the cost of possibly introducing bias. Second, even though the main results of interest may be those that include several additional variables that increase the precision of the estimates, reporting results that exclude such variables is also useful, because these results correspond to simple comparisons of means across the treatment and control groups.

Adding strata dummy variables

Another method for increasing statistical precision, and more important, for obtaining correct statistical tests, is to add dummy variables that indicate the strata used when drawing the sample. See Bruhn and McKenzie (2009) for a detailed explanation. As chapter 9 explains, in most cases randomization can lead to more precise estimates if the overall population sample is divided into subgroups, called strata, and then treatment and control groups are selected by randomly drawing within each stratum. For example, suppose that an RCT will be conducted in a geographic area that consists of five districts. The overall sample contains 5,000 individuals, from which half will be randomly assigned to the treatment group and half to the control group. The 5,000 individuals are spread across the five districts, which can be used as strata. That is, instead of drawing the treatment group by randomly selecting 2,500 people from the 5,000, it is better to divide the 5,000 people into groups according to the districts in which they live, and then within each district randomly assign half of the sample for that district to the treatment group. This process will ensure that, within each district, exactly half of the sample will be in the treatment group and exactly half will be in the control group.

When this stratification is used to select the sample, dummy variables should be added to the regression to increase the precision of the estimates. That is, for each stratum (each district in the example above) a variable is created for all individuals (both those in the treatment group and those in the control group) that equals one if the individual belongs to that stratum and equals zero if he or she belongs to another stratum. These dummy variables should be included in the regression analysis, and in general doing so will lead to increased statistical precision (smaller standard errors of estimated treatment effects).

A similar point is that sometimes randomization takes place by matching individuals with similar characteristics into pairs. For example, in a study sample of 1,000 people, similar people could be matched to each other so that there are 500 pairs. Within each pair, one is randomly assigned to the treatment group and the other is assigned to the control group. When randomization is performed in this way, regression analyses should include dummy variables for each pair; doing so will likely increase the precision of the estimates of the impact of the program.

Methods for obtaining correct standard errors

If randomization is carried out at the individual level, and if the population sample is a simple random sample from the entire population, there may be little reason to think that the error term (u) in the regression equation for any observation in the sample is correlated with the error term from another observation in the sample. In this case, the standard error formula from simple OLS estimation can be used to obtain the correct standard error of the OLS estimate of the program impact (as well as the correct standard errors for all other explanatory variables). However, there are often good reasons to expect that the error terms are correlated across observations, in which case the standard error formula must be adjusted to obtain correct standard errors. This section provides recommendations for the simplest cases. A more detailed exposition is provided in the section titled "Power and MDE [minimum detectable effect size] calculations in more complex settings" in chapter 9.

Most data collection is not a simple random sample from a population, but instead is a two- or three-stage process. For example, in a certain region of a country, 200 communities could be randomly drawn from the set of all communities in that region, and then within each of those communities 30 individuals could be randomly sampled. In such cases, it is quite likely that there are unobserved factors that are similar for individuals who live in the same community and that determine the outcome of interest (Y), which will lead to correlation in u for individuals in that community. For example, in an evaluation of a program to increase farm productivity, unobserved soil or weather conditions in a village may affect the crop production of all farming households in that village.

A common approach in regression estimation to account for correlation of the error terms of individuals who belong to the same group or community is to estimate the regression equation in a way that allows for group or community random effects. However, this estimation method has recently been criticized for being too restrictive. In particular, it implies that the correlation between the error terms of two people in the same community is identical for all possible pairs of people in that community, and it also requires that the extent of such within-community correlation be the same for all communities, as opposed to varying across communities. In response to this criticism, statisticians have developed robust formulas for standard errors of regression models that allow for correlation of the error term u within a community but do not require that the correlation be the same for each possible pair of people in the community, and do not require that the correlation structure within a community be the same for all communities. These "robust and clustered" standard errors can easily be implemented using standard software packages such as Stata. For a detailed discussion of these issues, see chapter 20 of Wooldridge (2010).

Unfortunately, a problem with the robust and clustered standard errors is that simulations suggest that they do not work well when the number of clusters, that is, the number of communities, is fewer than 50. They are perfectly valid methods when the number of clusters is very large (because they are based on asymptotic theory, which examines the properties of estimation methods as the number of clusters goes to infinity), but when the number of clusters is fewer than 50 they can yield poor approximations of the correct standard errors. One implication is that samples should be drawn so that there are at least 50 clusters. If this is not possible (or if the data have already been collected), work by Cameron, Gelbach, and Miller (2008) suggests that "wild bootstrapping" leads to valid estimates of statistical significance even with fewer than 50 clusters. For further discussion of these issues, and practical recommendations for estimation, see Cameron and Miller (2015).

Other useful advice and recommendations

This section provides additional advice for using regression methods to estimate program impacts from data obtained from an RCT.

Allowing program impacts to vary by population groups

The discussion thus far has focused on average treatment effects of a program, but this does not imply that the impact is the same for each person. Instead, the effect of the program is likely to vary across different types of people. An advantage of OLS and other regression methods is that they can easily estimate separate impacts for different groups of people. Consider an example of a program that could have different effects for men and women. For simplicity, assume an ideal RCT for which all those assigned to the treatment group participated in the program and all those who were assigned to the control group did not participate in the program. The following regression equation allows for separate effects by sex:

$$Y = \alpha + \beta R + \gamma Female + \delta R \times Female + u,$$

where *Female* is a dummy variable that indicates that the participant is a woman (equals one for women and zero for men). In this model, the impact of the program for men is estimated by β and the impact of the program for women is estimated by $\beta + \delta$. This approach can easily be extended to three or more groups, as well as to cases in which some of the people assigned to the treatment group choose not to participate in the program.

However, caution must be exercised in attempting to estimate treatment effects for a large number of groups by extending this method to many subpopulations of interest. To see the intuition, suppose program effects are estimated for 20 different subgroups. Even if the true impacts for all groups are exactly equal to zero, there is, at the 5 percent significance level, a 5 percent chance that a "significant" positive or negative impact will be found. Thus at least one of the subgroups will most likely have a statistically significant coefficient estimate (at the 5 percent level). The doubtful practice of trying many estimates until a statistically significant result is obtained is often referred to as *data mining*. For a forceful statement of this critique, see Deaton (2010).

Several approaches are available for dealing with this potentially serious problem. First, at a minimum, treatment effects for only a small number of subgroups, probably no more than three or four, should be estimated, and the rationale for why the treatment effect should vary for those subgroups, or why those subgroups are the most important ones to consider given the program being evaluated, should be clear. Second, results should be reported for all subgroups for which estimates were made, not just those with statistically significant results. Third, the researcher could commit before the intervention to examine only a specified set of subgroups. This approach is called a *pre-analysis plan*; it is often used in medical research but until recently has been rarely used in the social sciences. See chapter 8 for a discussion of, and recommendations for, pre-analysis plans. Fourth, statistical tests should be adjusted for the testing of multiple hypotheses; see chapter 9 for a discussion of methods used for multiple hypothesis testing.

Checking the validity of the randomization (balance checks)

The key advantage of a properly implemented RCT is that the treatment and control groups are essentially identical except that the treatment group participated in the program (or at least was offered the program) and the control group did not. Thus it is important to check whether this is indeed the case. This check requires only the baseline data and thus can be done even before the endline (postimplementation) data have been collected. This exercise is often referred to as *balance checks*.

Balance checks are quite simple to perform. Several key variables are regressed on a constant term and the randomization dummy variable (R) to check whether the coefficient on R is statistically significant. An obvious key variable of interest is the outcome variable (Y) measured before the program was implemented. Other basic individual characteristics, such as sex, age, education level, and occupation, may also be key variables. Finally, any variables that are thought to be closely related to the outcome variable should also be checked. Note that if a large number of variables are checked, it is possible that one or two are statistically significant for the reasons given in the previous subsection. Of course, if several key variables are statistically significant it is important to investigate whether the randomization was in fact correctly implemented; if individuals did not follow their random assignment, standard RCT methods cannot be used, but it may be possible to use IV estimation with random assignment as an instrument for actual program participation (see chapter 15 for a detailed discussion of IV methods).

Alternatively, a single regression can be used to check for balance by regressing R on the key variables to see whether any of them have explanatory power for R. This can be done using a probit model or a linear probability model (OLS). If the treatment and control groups are well balanced, the regression should yield no statistically significant effects. Of course, with a large number of variables in this regression, some may be significant by random chance; thus the best method for checking for balance is a joint test of the hypothesis that all of the regression coefficients equal zero. Note that if randomization were based on stratification or pairing of observations, this regression should include dummy variables indicating the strata or the pairs of observations; these variables are excluded from the joint test that all regression coefficients equal zero.

Estimation when there are multiple treatments

Sometimes it is useful to implement RCTs that evaluate several related programs at the same time. For example, an RCT that focused on education in the Indian state of Andhra Pradesh was implemented in 500 schools, 100 of which were randomly selected to be the control group and the other 400 of which were randomly assigned to four different treatments involving teacher contracts and teacher incentives (each treatment had 100 schools) (see Muralidharan and Sundararaman 2011). This approach is beneficial for two main reasons. First, the control group is used multiple times, which is efficient relative to a scheme in which each treatment group has its own control group of 100 schools, which would have required data collection from 800, rather than 500, schools. Second, it also allows for comparisons between the various treatment groups.[3]

Estimating treatment effects of multiple interventions in a single regression is straightforward. In the simplest case, there are only two treatments. Assume that compliance was perfect: for both treatments everyone who was randomly assigned to a treatment participated in that program, and none of those randomly assigned to the control group participated in either program. Let R_1 denote assignment to the first program and R_2 denote assignment to the second program. The regression to estimate is simply

$$Y = \alpha + \beta_1 R_1 + \beta_2 R_2 + u.$$

In this regression, the OLS estimate of β_1 is the estimated impact of the first program, the OLS estimate of β_2 is the estimated impact of the second program, and the OLS estimate of $\beta_1 - \beta_2$ provides an estimate of the difference in the impacts of the two programs. This procedure can easily be extended to three or more programs.

Conclusion

Evaluations based on RCTs allow ATE, ATT, and ITT to be estimated by comparing means across the treatment and control groups; however, regression analysis is often a convenient way to estimate these treatment effects. First, regression analysis can easily be used to test the statistical significance of estimated treatment effects. Second, regression methods allow other variables that are unrelated to the treatment but that can also affect Y to be controlled for, which is likely to increase the precision of the treatment effect estimates. Finally, regression methods are convenient for estimating differences in average impacts across different subsets of the population, or for different treatments.

This chapter explains how to use regression methods to estimate ATE, ATT, and ITT using data from an RCT. It first explains how to use simple regression methods for RCTs when participants fully comply with their random assignments. It then discusses how to use regression methods to estimate the impact of the program on those who participate when some of those randomly assigned to the treatment group choose not to participate. It also addresses issues of sample attrition. Advice is also provided on how to increase precision in regression estimators and how to obtain correct standard errors when the data are grouped and randomization is performed at the group level.

Note that regression methods are presented in much more detail in part III of this book (chapters 11–17), which focuses on analysis from nonexperimental data. As those chapters show, regression methods have many uses and, in general, there is a wide variety of regression methods that can be used for both experimental and nonexperimental data.

Notes

1. Technically, adding variables means that u itself will change, given that adding variables effectively removes some components of u. Even so, the main point is that adding variables to the regression generally reduces (and never increases) the variance of the error term in the regression.
2. Variables that can be affected by the program are sometimes referred to as *bad controls*.
3. See chapter 9 for a discussion of the issues involved in deciding what proportion of the overall sample to assign to the treatment group(s) and what proportion to assign to the control group.

References

Bruhn, Miriam, and David McKenzie. 2009. "In Pursuit of Balance: Randomization in Practice in Development Field Experiments." *American Economic Journal: Applied Economics* 1 (4): 200–32.

Cameron, Colin, Jonah Gelbach, and Douglas Miller. 2008. "Bootstrap-Based Improvements for Inference with Clustered Errors." *Review of Economics and Statistics* 90 (3): 414–27.

Cameron, Colin, and Douglas Miller. 2015. "A Practitioner's Guide to Cluster-Robust Inference." *Journal of Human Resources* 50 (2): 317–72.

Deaton, Angus. 2010. "Instruments, Randomization, and Learning about Development." *Journal of Economic Literature* 48 (2): 424–55.

Glewwe, Paul, and Petra Todd. 2019. Course materials, "APEC 8212: Econometric Analysis II" and "ECON 712: Graduate Topics Course in Program Evaluation Methods," University of Minnesota, Minneapolis–St. Paul, and University of Pennsylvania, Philadelphia.

Lee, David. 2009. "Training, Wages and Sample Selection: Estimating Sharp Bounds on Treatment Effects." *Review of Economic Studies* 76 (3): 1071–102.

Muralidharan, Karthik, and Venkatesh Sundararaman. 2011. "Teacher Performance Pay: Experimental Evidence from India." *Journal of Political Economy* 119 (1): 39–77.

Wooldridge, Jeffrey. 2010. *Econometric Analysis of Cross Section and Panel Data*, second edition. Cambridge, MA: MIT Press.

CHAPTER 8

Practical Advice for Implementing Randomized Evaluations

Introduction

In theory, the randomized controlled trial (RCT) method of impact evaluation introduced in chapter 6 is the gold standard for evaluating programs and policies. If implemented correctly, RCTs do provide accurate estimates of program impacts. In practice, however, implementing RCTs can be difficult. Many things can go wrong, and when they do RCTs may not provide accurate estimates of program impacts.

Chapter 6 discusses issues that arise when some of the individuals randomly assigned to the treatment group choose not to participate in the program. This chapter examines several other problems that are, in general, more difficult to address. It also provides more detailed advice on how to conduct an RCT to obtain high-quality impact evaluations.[1]

The rest of this chapter is organized as follows: the next section presents the most common problems that can arise, and what can be done to avoid them or to account for them when estimating program impacts. The following section discusses specific options for how to randomly assign individuals or groups to the treatment and control groups, highlighting the advantages and disadvantages of each option. Pre-analysis plans, which are intended to avoid data mining and are starting to be used in social science research, are discussed in the next section. The subsequent section provides some general practical advice for carrying out RCTs and is followed by a section that presents recommendations for increasing the external validity of the estimates. A final section concludes the chapter.

Potential problems with randomized experiments, and possible solutions

Unfortunately, many problems can arise in conducting randomized experiments. This section presents six common problems, along with suggestions for how to avoid them or how to modify the analysis to minimize their impact.

Contamination bias (some in the control group get the treatment)

Chapter 6 explains how to address the problem that occurs when some people in the treatment group decide not to participate in the program. A somewhat more difficult problem arises when some people in the control group are able to get into the program, or into a similar program. This is often referred to as *contamination bias*.

Contamination bias can occur for many reasons. First, some program administrators may feel that it is unfair for the program to withhold the treatment from the individuals who were randomly assigned to the control group. Second, some of the people assigned to the control group may find ways to gain admittance to the program. Third, other similar programs may be available, for example, job skills training programs or microfinance lenders, which some members of the control group choose to take advantage of. Finally, even if other, similar programs were not available at the start of the evaluation, organizations that offer such programs may be looking for areas where the program is not offered, and in doing so may introduce the program into the control group communities after the evaluation has begun.

The first recommendation for this problem, which is rather obvious, is to redouble efforts to exclude the individuals who are assigned to the control group from participating in the program. For example, training of program administrators should include an explanation of the research design, emphasizing that the evaluation will be compromised if some individuals in the control group are allowed to participate in the program. This training should also stress the need for program administrators to be alert to the possibility that members of the control group may attempt to participate in the program, and should provide practical advice for preventing this from happening. A second recommendation is to implement the evaluation in an area where similar programs do not exist to minimize the extent to which people who are assigned to the control group participate in another, similar program. A third recommendation is that organizations that offer similar programs should be informed of the study and asked not to introduce their programs, or at least to delay their implementation, in the control group areas. Finally, offering the members of the control group an opportunity to participate in the program at a later date may reduce the efforts of those individuals to try to get into the program; this raises the more general issue of what, if anything, should be done for members of the control group, which is discussed in the subsection titled "Ethical considerations."

Sometimes it is not possible to exclude all members of the control group from participating in the program. If this happens, one way to estimate program impacts is to use instrumental variables methods, where random assignment is the instrumental variable. This econometric method is discussed in detail in chapter 15.

A partial solution to the general problem of contamination bias may involve acknowledging the problem and then revising the type of program impact to be measured. For example, if some members of the control group participate in other programs, the estimated treatment effect can be redefined as the impact of enrolling in the program offered by the RCT, relative to either being enrolled in other, similar programs or not being enrolled in any program. In general, this type of program treatment effect will be smaller than the effect measured when no other programs are available, which will provide a lower bound on the impact of the program (relative to not participating in any program).

Dropouts from the program

Another common problem is that some program participants may drop out before completing the program. An example is a job skills training program. Participants may drop out of the program because they are dissatisfied with it or because they find a new outside opportunity, for example, a new job.

If this dropping out were random, it would not lead to bias in the estimates; the only problem would be a reduced sample size. Unfortunately, dropouts are usually not a random sample of the people assigned to the program, in which case this behavior can lead to bias. For example, dropouts may be those individuals whose eventual benefits from the program would be relatively low, in which case the estimated impact of the program would generally overestimate the average treatment effect (if dropouts are excluded from calculation of the average treatment effect).

Several approaches can be used to minimize bias, or to obtain upper or lower bounds on the impact of the program. If dropout occurs early, it may be reasonable to consider the dropouts as untreated. In this case, the approach used in chapter 6 to obtain an estimate of the average treatment effect on the treated (ATT) when some individuals assigned to the treatment group do not participate in the program can be applied. This approach can be implemented by applying instrumental variables methods, which are discussed in detail in chapter 15.

An alternative approach would be to define treatment as starting the program (and not necessarily completing it). In this case, dropping out is not a problem and the estimate can be defined as a type of intention-to-treat (ITT) estimate that allows for both not participating in the program and partial participation followed by dropping out.

A third general approach would be to make plausible assumptions that allow for estimating either upper or lower bounds of the impact of the program. An example is to assume that the program impact on dropouts is less than the full effect they would have received if they had not dropped out, in which case comparing the treated individuals (including dropouts) with the control individuals yields a lower bound estimate of the average treatment effect (ATE). Alternatively, another potentially plausible assumption is that the impact of the program on dropouts would have been smaller than average if they had completed the program (which is one reason why they dropped out). Under this assumption, comparing the treatment group (excluding dropouts) with the control group yields an upper bound estimate of ATE.

Note that these approaches for dealing with dropouts are not mutually exclusive. Estimates of ATE, ATT, and ITT, and in some cases upper or lower bounds of these treatment effects, can be presented under certain assumptions. Those who think that these assumptions are reasonable will then have at least one or two estimates of (or bounds on) at least one type of program effect.

Sample attrition

In almost all RCT evaluations, following both the people who were randomly assigned to the treatment group and those randomly assigned to the control group for a long time, as much as several years, would be beneficial. However, people in both groups can be lost from the sample because of the research team's inability to locate them (for example, if they migrate) or because they refuse to participate in follow-up interviews. Often, the people who were randomly assigned to treatment are more willing to continue to participate in data collection than the people in the control group, who were excluded from treatment. Chapter 7 discusses how to check for attrition bias and presents bounds analysis as one method for dealing with this problem. This subsection provides several other suggestions for addressing this sample attrition bias.

What can be done to minimize attrition bias? The first recommendation is that, at a minimum, researchers should report attrition rates for both the treatment group and the control group. If these rates are not significantly different from each other, it is likely, though not certain, that there is little or no attrition bias. For greater confidence, researchers should compare the observed characteristics of the dropouts in both groups; if they are similar, so that the types of people who are lost from the treatment and control group samples are similar, applying standard methods to those who did not drop out should yield unbiased estimates of the impact of the program.

On the other hand, if the attrition rates are significantly different between the treatment and control groups, three main approaches can be taken. First, the evaluation team should attempt to track people who leave the sample. If doing so is too expensive, the team should carefully track a small, randomly selected subsample of them and include this subsample (with appropriate weights) in the analysis. Second, bounds analysis, as discussed in chapter 7, can be implemented.

Third, for those who did not leave the sample, changes in outcomes before and after the treatment group participates in the program can be compared. Recall the second case in the discussion of table 7.1. Comparing the changes in test scores for the five students who did not drop out yields an estimated impact of 5 ($= ((2 + 8 + 5)/3 - (0 + 0)/2)$), which is equal to the actual ATE of 5, compared with the estimate of 0 ($= ((52 + 68 + 75)/3 - (60 + 70)/2)$) obtained by comparing those who did not leave using data collected only after the intervention. This difference-in-differences estimation technique, which can be applied to both RCTs and methods that can be used when program participation is not randomly assigned, is discussed in detail in chapter 12.

Ethical considerations

In some cases, especially situations involving testing the impact of providing a specific type of medical treatment, it is generally accepted that it is unethical for a researcher who discovers that an individual has a treatable illness to withhold that information from that person. Researchers have an ethical obligation to inform people when they diagnose an illness. Many proponents of ethical standards in research would go further and say that a researcher who knows that an individual has a treatable illness and is able to provide the treatment has the ethical obligation to treat the illness. This subsection provides an introduction to ethical considerations; a much more detailed exposition is provided in chapter 10.

Although the ethical obligations raised in the previous paragraph must be taken seriously, an unfortunate consequence is that they complicate the implementation of RCTs, especially those for which the program being evaluated includes medical treatments. The problem is that adhering to these ethical obligations will contaminate the control group given that some members of that group are, at a minimum, informed of a medical problem that many of them were unaware of (which may cause many of them to obtain treatment), or may even be treated (or at least offered the treatment).

This conundrum, which is faced by researchers and ethical review panels at virtually all major research institutions, has no simple solution. In some cases, a way to adhere to these ethical guidelines and still not provide treatment to the control group may be found. An example is an evaluation of the impact of providing deworming medicine on educational outcomes in Kenya (Miguel and Kremer 2004). The authors were able to adhere to the ethical guidelines and yet not treat the control group because the control group students were not diagnosed to see whether they had worms; because no diagnosis was performed on the control group, there was no ethical obligation to act on any diagnosis. After about two years, the control group students were diagnosed and treated, but the analysis was complicated by lack of knowledge about whether those in the control group who were later diagnosed with having worms had also had them two years earlier. Some may also argue that this approach, although technically not violating the ethical guideline, could be interpreted as violating the spirit of the guideline.

A final, more general ethical issue is whether, at some point, the control group should be offered the treatment or be compensated in another way if the treatment turns out to be extremely effective. If the treatment or other compensation is offered, should the researcher inform the control group at the outset of these possible future benefits? On one hand, informing them about possible future benefits should be avoided because doing so could affect the behavior of the control group during the course of the study. On the other hand, if they do not expect any future benefit they may be less likely to agree to participate in future data collection, leading to attrition problems.

Randomization bias

Another problem may be that randomization could change how the program operates. Some people may not want to participate if they think they will be part of an "experiment," or they may change their behavior (for example, Hawthorne effects, as discussed in the next paragraph). Similarly, program staff may work harder when they know that the program is being evaluated. These types of phenomena are referred to as *randomization bias* or *evaluation-driven effects*.

One example is *Hawthorne effects*, which occur when participants in the treatment group exert more effort because they want to support the program, or when program staff behave differently when they know the program is being monitored. Assessing the likelihood of these effects is difficult.[2] A similar example is *John Henry effects*, which occur when participants in the control group may exert more effort because they do not want to appear weak. In medical trials such problems are minimized by giving placebos, so that participants do not know whether they are in the treatment group or the control group, and by having double-blind designs so that even the administrators do not know which treatment they are administering, but this is difficult to do for most nonmedical randomized trials. However, even providing placebos may not completely remove bias; a *placebo effect* may occur, which is that the symptoms of people who receive a placebo could change because they think they are receiving a medical treatment, even though the placebo contains no medication of any kind.

What can be done to minimize randomization bias? In some cases the program may be implemented so that determining whether one is in the treatment group or in the control group is impossible. Although usually infeasible, if it is attempted then even the data collection team should not know who has been randomly assigned to each group. Other steps can also minimize this problem. The first would be to minimize interaction between the treatment group and the comparison group, which should reduce feelings of competition, anticipation, or demoralization in the two groups. This approach may be easier if randomization is at a higher level, such as the community level. Second, to reduce Hawthorne effects and John Henry effects, the staff in the organizations that are being evaluated should be assured that their jobs or incomes will not be affected by their work performance or the performance of the program. Third, the RCT could possibly be implemented such that the individuals in the control group are not aware that they are a control group, which should avoid John Henry effects.

Spillovers

A final problem when implementing RCTs is that in some cases the treatment impact spills over onto control group members, especially if the control group is nearby.[3] Spillovers can happen for programs to reduce infectious disease, air pollution mitigation interventions, and perhaps for other programs. Chapter 7 explains how spillovers can lead to bias in estimates of ATE (even with 100 percent compliance with the randomization) and ATT (even when using instrumental variables methods), although in some cases it may still be possible to obtain an unbiased estimate of ITT (see chapter 6). This subsection provides practical recommendations on what to do if spillovers are suspected.

The direction of bias from spillovers in estimates of program impacts depends on the nature of the spillovers. If spillovers are positive, that is, they can increase Y for the control group, the program impact will be underestimated. Spillovers reduce the gap in Y between the treatment group and the control group. Spillovers can also be negative. For example, if some low-income families are randomly offered the opportunity to move to a better neighborhood, and more motivated families are more likely to take up this offer, then the control group that is left behind is now in an environment with fewer motivated families, which may cause their outcomes to become worse, leading to overestimation of the program effect.

Perhaps the most important recommendation for addressing bias from spillovers is that random assignment should be done at a level that is high enough or large enough to eliminate, or at least minimize, the possibility of spillovers. For example, if spillovers are local in the sense that they affect only people in the same school or the same village, randomization should be done at that level (school or village level) to avoid bias. A second recommendation is to consider whether spillovers are more likely to be positive or negative. If they are positive, the true effect will be underestimated, establishing a lower bound on the true impact; if they are negative, the true effect will be overestimated, providing an upper bound of the true impact.

In many cases, estimating the extent of spillovers could be useful because it may have implications for when to implement, or how to design, the program in question. If spillovers are local, as described in the previous paragraph, they can be estimated by randomizing at both the community and the individual levels. Estimates based on the former randomization will not include spillovers, whereas estimates based on the latter randomization will include them, and the difference between these two estimates provides an estimate of the magnitude of the spillovers.

A more straightforward way to estimate spillovers is to compare the average value of observed Y for the individuals in the communities randomly assigned to be control communities with the average value of observed Y for the individuals in the treatment communities who were randomly assigned to be control individuals within those communities. Neither of these two groups was treated, but the latter group would have experienced any possible spillover effect, while the former group would not, so the difference between these two groups provides an unbiased estimate of the spillover effect. Of course, this approach works only if both communities and individuals comply with their random assignment. Miguel and Kremer's (2004) study of deworming in Kenya is a good example of practical issues that arise when estimating spillovers.

Practical advice for randomizing into treatment and control groups

This section provides recommendations for randomly assigning some individuals in the evaluation sample to the treatment group and the others to the control group. It begins by describing three general methods that can be used to randomize. It follows with advice on the level of randomization (group or individual), and then provides other advice on randomization.

Methods of randomization

Three general ways are used to randomly assign some individuals or groups to a treatment group and others to a control group: lotteries, gradual phase-in, and encouragement design. A lottery consists of randomly assigning some individuals or groups to the control group and the rest to one or more treatment groups. The understanding is that those who are assigned to the control group will never be treated, which in some situations may be unpopular. This method is used fairly frequently in RCTs.

A gradual phase-in is a randomization design in which all groups eventually are given the opportunity to participate in the program, but some are allowed to participate before others; that is, the order of treatment over time across the different groups is randomized. This method is used frequently and is perhaps the most commonly used method.

Finally, an encouragement design randomization is used in cases in which it is not possible to exclude individuals from participating in the program, yet it is still possible to randomly provide incentives to participate in, or provide information on, a program to be evaluated. For example, individuals can be randomly selected to receive promotional advertising for a program, which should increase their probability of participating relative to individuals who do not receive that advertising. Another example is offering some individuals a lower price, or a bigger reward, than others for participating.

Table 8.1 summarizes when to use each of these three methods, and the advantages and disadvantages of each method. Generally speaking, when feasible, lotteries are usually the best method for obtaining unbiased, consistent estimates of program effects. The main impediment to their use is that denying treatment indefinitely to the control group may be deemed unethical or politically unacceptable. If the program provides clear benefits to disadvantaged groups, obtaining ethical approval to assign some individuals, including some disadvantaged individuals, to the control group will be difficult. However, doing so may be less of a problem if the benefits of the program are in doubt. It could also be argued that if the program is proven to be effective, then the government will implement it

TABLE 8.1 Methods of randomization

METHOD	WHEN TO USE	ADVANTAGES	DISADVANTAGES
Lottery	1. Funds insufficient to treat all who are eligible 2. Ethically justified not to treat some	1. Accepted as fair 2. Easily understood 3. Can be done publicly 4. Control group will not change behavior in anticipation of future participation because they do not participate in the future	1. Control group may not cooperate 2. Differential attrition between treatment and control groups
Gradual phase-in	1. Program slowly expands over time 2. Everyone gets treated (eventually)	1. Easy to explain 2. Control group may be more likely to cooperate 3. Politically feasible	1. Control group's anticipation of future treatment may affect its behavior 2. Hard to measure long-term impact
Encouragement design	1. Program cannot exclude anyone	1. Can be used when exclusion is not possible	1. Applies only to those who respond to the incentive 2. Incentive may have no effect

Source: Glewwe and Todd 2019.

nationwide, at which point the control group will be able to participate; but this could be years, or even decades, in the future.

Another way to implement a lottery while at the same time allowing "the most deserving" to participate in the program is to divide the population of interest into three groups: the clearly deserving (all are treated), the somewhat deserving (treatment randomly determined by lottery), and the not deserving (excluded from program). In some cases, a not-deserving group is unnecessary, depending on the type of program. The essence of this approach is to randomize only for the somewhat-deserving group, which implies that the results of the RCT apply only to this group. This method is sometimes referred to as *randomization in a bubble*.

Randomization by gradual phase-in involves two distinct randomizations. First, the evaluation sample is randomly assigned to two or more groups, which ensures that the individuals in these groups are essentially the same. Second, the order in which these groups are offered the treatment is randomized. In practice, these two randomizations can be combined into a single randomization because the groups could be defined solely in terms of when they are allowed to participate in the program.

Finally, the encouragement design randomization method is implemented by randomly selecting individuals to be provided information on, or an incentive to participate in, a program. It is important that the encouragement (information or incentive) offered has no direct effect on the outcome variable of interest; the only effect should be indirect via the encouragement to participate in the program. An example is a study in South Africa by Karlan and Zinman (2009) that examines the impact of information and loan characteristics on borrowing behavior by randomizing both information and loan characteristics.

Level of randomization

In general, randomization could be performed at the group level or the individual level. Randomizing at the individual level is usually preferred because it provides a larger effective sample size. The statistical explanation for this is provided in chapter 9. Sometimes, however, there may be little choice. For example, many education interventions can occur only at the classroom or school level (for example, class size reductions). More generally, in many cases objections are raised to randomizing at the individual level because the treatment and control individuals may know and interact with each other, and the fact that some benefit from the program while others do not may lead to an awkward situation. Thus randomizing at the individual level, as opposed to the group level, has both advantages and disadvantages.

Several other factors should be kept in mind when deciding whether to randomize at the individual level or the group level. First, if group-level randomization is performed to attain a given level of statistical precision (power of a statistical test), how many groups to have in the sample and how many individuals to sample in each group must also be determined; a sample design with a small number of large groups requires a larger overall sample size to maintain a given power to reject the null hypothesis (of no effect) relative to a sample design with smaller, but more numerous, groups. Thus, for a given sample size, more statistical precision will be obtained by having many groups with fewer people in each group, as discussed in more detail in chapter 9.

Second, as discussed in the section titled "Potential problems with randomized experiments, and possible solutions," if spillovers occur at the individual level, but not at the group level, then randomization at the group level is better. Recall as well from the same section that it is possible to estimate the size of spillovers by randomizing at the group level and then at the individual level within the treated groups. Third, as mentioned, group-level randomization may increase cooperation and should reduce any complications caused by interactions between control group and treatment group individuals.

Other recommendations on randomization

Whether randomization is performed at the individual or group level, several other practices should, in general, be followed. First, assessing more than one program, or variants of a program, in a randomized experiment is often beneficial. For example, the individuals or communities could be divided into four groups, one control group and three different types of treatments. An example, from an evaluation of education interventions in India, is provided in chapter 7.

Second, conducting multiple randomized experiments on the same sample is sometimes convenient (and cost reducing). The researcher must ensure that the different treatments do not affect or interact with each other. An example is a series of studies carried out on the same 100 schools in Kenya. A study of textbooks was done for children in grades 3–8 in those schools (Glewwe, Kremer, and Moulin 2009). In the same schools, a separate preschool intervention was also evaluated. Because the operation of the preschools in these schools was essentially unrelated to the operation of grades 1–8 (different teachers, separate budgets, and so on), the risk that one intervention influenced the other was virtually nil.

A third variant of doing multiple studies with the same sample is a cross-cutting design. This is best explained with an example. In the textbooks study of the previous paragraph, the 100 schools were arranged in alphabetical order and assigned numbers 1 to 100. They were then divided into four groups by assigning schools 1, 5, 9, and so on to the first group; schools 2, 6, 10, and so on to the second group; schools 3, 7, 11, and so on to the third group; and schools 4, 8, 12, and so on to the fourth group. The fourth group served as the control group and the other groups implemented variants of the textbooks program. In addition, a study of teacher incentives was implemented at the same time for the same 100 schools. This was done by renumbering the schools in the first group to be schools 1–25 and those in second, third, and fourth groups to be schools 26–50, 51–75 and 76–100, respectively, and then assigning odd-numbered schools to the teacher incentive intervention and even-numbered schools to the control group for the teacher incentives intervention. Thus within each of the four groups for the textbooks study, half of the schools were assigned to the teacher incentives study treatment group and half were assigned to the teacher incentives study control group. These two interventions may possibly have had interaction effects (for example, the textbooks could have been most effective in schools in which incentives were provided for teachers), but that is not necessarily a problem; indeed, it may be worth investigating. (In fact, neither intervention in the 100 Kenyan schools had much effect, and there was no evidence of interaction effects.) Overall, such cross-cutting designs (also referred to as *factorial designs*) are likely to reduce costs (relative to conducting two separate, unrelated studies), and as long as the two (or more) randomizations are independently drawn neither study is likely to be compromised in any way.

The use of pre-analysis plans in impact evaluations

As mentioned in chapter 7, one potential danger when estimating treatment effects for a population of interest is estimating them for a large number of subpopulations of that population. Even if the program has no impact on any of these subgroups, estimates for large numbers of such groups will almost inevitably lead to statistically "significant" impacts that simply reflect random chance. For example, if the program effects are estimated for 20 different subgroups, one can expect that, on average, one of the subgroup estimates will be statistically significant at the 5 percent level, even when the true impacts are zero for all 20 subgroups. The doubtful practice of trying many estimates until a statistically significant result is obtained is often referred to as *data mining*.

Two other types of data mining should also be avoided. The first is to search for an outcome that could be affected by a program for the population as a whole. For example, if the program is to improve the quality of health clinics, the impact of the program on many different types of illnesses could be examined, or different types of use of health clinic services (or use of services from other types of health facilities) could be studied, until at last one outcome is "significant." The second is to try different statistical specifications until one of them finds a "significant" result. For example, when using regression methods many different sets of control variables, or different sets of interaction terms, or different transformations (such as logarithm or a dummy variable for exceeding a particular threshold) of the dependent variable could be tried. Of course, these three methods of mining the data until a significant result is obtained can be used together, such as trying different outcomes for different subpopulations.

Although data mining can occur for almost any type of impact evaluation, RCTs could be particularly prone to this problem, as argued by Deaton (2010). Pre-analysis plans (PAPs) are designed to avoid data mining by committing researchers, in writing, to a limited set of analyses before they begin to analyze the data.[4] The most rigorous PAP would be written, and registered, before any data are collected and before the program has been implemented. It would minimize the three types of data mining described above by specifying, at the beginning of the evaluation and in precise detail, (1) the population subgroups that will be examined, (2) the outcomes that will be considered, and (3) the statistical and econometric specifications to be used. This commits the research team to these subgroups, outcomes, and specifications, and in theory (though perhaps not in practice) prevents them from doing any analysis that includes other subgroups, outcomes, or specifications. More specifically, any analysis that goes beyond what is specified in the PAP is considered to be exploratory and as such those results are deemed to be less scientifically rigorous.

This section provides a relatively brief introduction to PAPs. More detailed discussions of PAPs can be found in Glennerster and Takavarasha (2013) and Olken (2015).

The benefits of pre-analysis plans

At first glance, many researchers will be reluctant to commit themselves to PAPs. Writing a PAP could take a fair amount of time and effort and, at least in theory, a PAP ties the researcher's hands if new insights are developed later, perhaps based on initial analysis of the data, that would require new subgroups, outcomes, or statistical specifications to pursue.

However, writing and registering PAPs confers several benefits. First, and most important, doing so can stop the researcher from, perhaps subconsciously, mining the data. Second, it will help determine what data to collect by forcing the researcher to think about how the program may bring about desired impacts on specific outcomes. It may even provide new ideas on how the program could be made more effective before it is implemented. Third, a strictly followed PAP can provide strong evidence that data mining did not occur, which may make it easier to publish the research. A related advantage is that journal referees and editors may decide that the existence of a PAP negates the need for a long series of robustness checks, which otherwise may be requested to reduce data mining, which could make publication easier and less time consuming.

Fourth, certain funders of research, for example, the International Initiative for Impact Evaluation (3ie), now require that PAPs be filed, in which case doing so will broaden the possible sources of research funding. Finally, PAPs may reduce conflicts with funders or program organizations, both of which may desire statistically significant results to show that the programs they operate and fund are effective. Funders and program organizations may pressure researchers to try new subgroups, outcome variables, and statistical specifications to find some evidence of the benefits of the program, and a PAP can be used by the researchers to persuade both entities that further action of this type, which is essentially data mining, should not be pursued. This advantage is best achieved by including both funders and program organizations in the writing of the PAP.

The disadvantages of using pre-analysis plans

Of course, PAPs also have disadvantages, as explained below, but first it is worth considering whether data mining is a serious problem. Studies have suggested that, at least for RCTs implemented by economists, data mining is not common. Evidence is summarized and discussed in Olken (2015) and Coffman and Niederle (2015). If data mining is rare, then the disadvantages described below may outweigh the main advantage of PAPs, which is to reduce data mining.

The first disadvantage of a PAP is that it takes time and effort to write, and fully specifying procedures and intent may be close to impossible. Suppose that the researcher wants not only to measure the impact of the program but also to understand why the program has (or does not have) an effect by considering "mechanism" variables. For example, consider the evaluation of a teacher incentive program in Kenya by Glewwe, Ilias, and Kremer (2010). The four main outcome variables were student test scores on two different sets of exams, students dropping out of school, and grade repetition. To understand why the program had little effect on student performance, the paper also examined the impact of the invention on (1) the formula used to reward teachers, (2) the probability of exam participation (separately for both sets of exams), (3) the probability of correctly answering multiple-choice questions, (4) the probability of correctly answering fill-in-the-blank questions (5) teacher attendance, (6) teacher presence in the classroom, (7) teacher use of a blackboard, (8) a measure of teacher energy, and (9) teacher assignment of homework. Together these constitute at least 13 different outcome variables of interest. A PAP would have required details regarding the specification of each of the 13 regressions (functional forms, control variables, and interaction terms) separately for different subgroups (boys vs. girls, different grades, and so on). Specifying all of this detail ahead of time suggests that the PAP could easily be more than 100 pages long.

The second disadvantage of writing, and strictly adhering to, a PAP is that doing so rules out analysis that was not foreseen at the outset of the evaluation but that gradually (or in some cases quickly) becomes apparent as the data are analyzed. Researchers learn from analyzing their data, but acting on this accumulated knowledge would not be allowed if a PAP were rigorously adhered to. Such additional analysis could be carried out, but it would have to be labeled explorations that are, strictly speaking, not statistically rigorous results. The Kenya teacher incentives study provides an example. The intervention did not increase student test scores on an exam that was not the basis of the incentives, but did increase test scores on the exam used to calculate the incentives. This outcome led to an investigation of what teachers can do to improve their students' test-taking techniques, one example of which is to encourage the students to guess on multiple-choice questions for which a student knows that at least one possible answer is unlikely to be correct. The study found evidence that students in the teacher incentive schools were more likely to answer multiple-choice questions, and answer them correctly. None of this was foreseen at the outset of the study.

A third disadvantage is that a very detailed PAP commits researchers to conducting many different sets of estimates that may not be useful. There is a temptation when writing the PAP to include many different subgroups, many outcome variables, and many specifications so as not to have an interesting result be labeled exploratory because it was not included in the PAP. At the analysis stage many of these estimates may be seen to be of little importance and thus not worth doing, but they must be done because they were specified in the PAP. Doing a large number of estimates—because they are specified in the PAP—for a program that turns out to be ineffective (which often happens in RCTs) may be a task of little interest or value that demands a large amount of researcher time.

A final disadvantage, which is related to the previous three but is more conjectural, is that requiring PAPs may provide an incentive for researchers to do relatively simple evaluations that have perhaps only one outcome variable and do not attempt to thoroughly investigate the mechanisms that led to the result for that outcome variable. Quite simply, if PAPs make more complex study designs more costly, researchers will conduct fewer such studies, and the knowledge that is produced by such studies would be delayed, or perhaps may never be produced.

Practical advice for pre-analysis plans

Researchers disagree on the value of PAPs, but even some skeptics agree that PAPs can be beneficial in certain circumstances. The debate about their value will continue, but at this point some practical suggestions can be offered.

First, for relatively simple studies, with perhaps one or two outcome variables and little interest in pursuing mechanisms, a PAP may be worth doing. In this situation, the costs may not be very large and the benefits outlined above, especially the benefit of minimizing data mining, may be worth the costs.

Second, for more complex studies there are several alternatives. The most obvious would simply be not to write a PAP because of the disadvantages cited earlier. Another would be to write a relatively simple PAP but to conduct not only the analyses specified in the PAP but also more exploratory analyses not included in the PAP. The latter analyses must be clearly labeled as exploratory, but the results may be sufficiently compelling that they could be included in the paper that includes the prespecified results. An example is a study of the expansion of health care insurance in Oregon by Finkelstein et al. (2012). Ultimately, journal referees and editors will determine the value of the exploratory analysis. A final approach would be a sort of sequential PAP, wherein the initial PAP lays out the simplest analyses to be done, after which a new PAP will be filed that is based on the results from the simple analyses. For example, the first PAP could be written before baseline data are collected. The research team could examine the baseline data (ideally, the data would not indicate which observations are in the treated group and which are in the control group) and then write a more thorough PAP that would be filed before the endline data are collected.

Third, if a PAP is prepared, it should be in collaboration with the funding and implementing organizations to avoid a situation in which those organizations pressure the research team to mine the data until a statistically significant result is obtained.

Finally, for researchers who are economists, the RCT should be registered in the American Economic Association's RCT registry, at the registry website: https://www.aeaweb.org/journals/policies/rct-registry. Note that registering a study does not require that a PAP be filed. The first purpose of the registry is to avoid publication bias, that is, the tendency for journals to publish only studies that find statistically significant results. A second, separate purpose is to provide a convenient location for economists and other researchers to file PAPs if they choose to do so.

More detailed practical guidance, further information, and somewhat opposing viewpoints regarding PAPs can be found in Christensen and Miguel (2018), Coffman and Niederle (2015), Glennerster and Takavarasha (2013), and Olken (2015).

Other practical advice

Researchers who have implemented RCTs in many different countries have learned from their experiences (both good and bad). This section describes several practices that are highly recommended when conducting RCTs to evaluate programs or policies.

Pilot program

In difficult situations small pilot programs are often the best starting point, allowing the researcher to learn about complications and problems that may be impossible to foresee. Although the relatively small amount of data collected will have fairly low statistical power, a pilot test will serve as a basis for a more successful large-scale intervention.

Conducting a pilot program confers two types of benefits. First, the evaluation team will almost certainly learn a substantial amount about both how to implement the program and how to collect the data. Second, the pilot program may convince wary participants and other interested parties (such as program administrators and government officials) that the randomized trial is neither harmful (and therefore not unethical) nor politically threatening, and that it could produce useful results.

Need to monitor implementation

Researchers must monitor how the program is being implemented (including the randomization) and how the data are being collected (including the baseline data). Many randomized trials have been aborted or have provided useless results when researchers delegated monitoring to local collaborators.

A Guatemala preschool study (Humpage 2012) is one example. After local collaborators described the experimental evaluation to teachers at participating schools, and after teachers agreed to participate, teachers failed to follow the plan. Teachers were expected to accept wait-listed students in the order of the randomized list that the researchers provided, but teachers instead selected students using their own criteria. Thus many students who had randomly been assigned to the bottom of the list (similar to being assigned to a control group) entered preschool while students randomly assigned to the top of the list (similar to a treatment group) were excluded. Researchers discovered this noncompliance when it was too late to intervene, and the research project had to be abandoned even after significant investments of time and financial resources had been made for the baseline data collection.

Thus researchers should be prepared to go to the field frequently to ensure that the randomized trial is being correctly implemented. After more experience has been gained by local collaborators, monitoring could be reduced, but it is better to err on the side of too much monitoring than not enough monitoring. Even quite competent local collaborators can do a poor job if they are not interested in the results of the evaluation.

Advantages of collecting baseline data

Baseline data are data that are collected before the program (treatment) is implemented. A common problem in evaluations of programs is delays in data collection, so that the first round of data is gathered after the program has already started, which greatly diminishes the usefulness of the baseline data. It is important that baseline data be gathered at a relatively early stage, ideally even before people are informed of the program, because informing them about future plans for a program may influence their current behavior.

Although it raises the cost of conducting the evaluation, collecting baseline data provides several advantages.[5] First, it generates useful control variables that, by definition, have not been affected by the treatment. These control variables can be used to increase the precision of the estimated impacts of the program. Second, these variables can also be used to check for interaction effects (effects of the program on population subgroups). Third, baseline data can be used to verify whether the treatment was really implemented in a random way (checking for balance). Finally, the evaluation team will likely acquire valuable experience and knowledge from collecting the baseline data, which will improve the quality of the data collected at later dates.

Increasing external validity

Although some RCTs are conducted on a national scale, most are conducted on a much smaller scale. A successfully implemented RCT will provide consistent and unbiased estimates of the impact of the program. Strictly speaking, this is true only for the population from which the sample was drawn for the evaluation; whether the results apply to the entire country or to other countries is not clear. There are no simple solutions to this problem; however, this section provides comments on this issue, as well as guidance on how to increase external validity.

One basic recommendation is that the sample on which the randomization is performed should always be drawn from a well-defined population to ensure the (internal) validity of the results for this population, even if it is a small fraction of the population of the entire country.

A general comment regarding external validity is that a program that was successful in a relatively small area may not have the same effect when it is scaled up to a national level even if the small area is representative of the country as a whole. The problem is that implementing the program on a national scale may have economy-wide implications, which are often referred to as *general equilibrium effects*. An example will make this point clearer. Consider a program that increases years of completed schooling among school-age children. Additional schooling should provide them with higher incomes when they become adults, but the program may not have as large an effect on income when it is scaled up to the national level because the increase in the educated labor force could reduce the wages of educated labor. In other words, once it becomes more common to be well educated, the relative advantage in wages for well-educated people is likely to decrease. Little can be done about this potential threat to external validity, but at a minimum such possibilities should be kept in mind when extrapolating the results from a small program to a nationwide program.

A final threat to external validity is a program that is difficult to implement on a nationwide scale. For example, it may be impossible to replicate on a national scale the high motivation of the implementers of a relatively small RCT. Ironically, this implies that those implementing the program for the randomized trial should be "average" (perhaps even unmotivated) personnel.

Conclusion

Although RCTs are very promising for evaluating a wide range of programs, many issues and difficulties can occur when implementing them. This chapter reviews the most common problems that arise, and provides suggestions for how to resolve them. In many cases the proposed resolutions work well, but this may not always be the case. The researcher may have to settle for an estimate that is not an ATE but instead is a different concept, such as ATT or ITT. In other cases only an upper or lower bound of a program's ATE (or some other type of treatment effect) can be estimated.

The main lesson is that much can be done at the planning and implementation stages to reduce the problems discussed in this chapter at the estimation stage. Examples are (1) taking steps to reduce the possibility that individuals assigned to the control group find a way to participate in the program, (2) reducing sample attrition from both the treatment group and the control group, and (3) choosing a level of randomization that will eliminate, or at least minimize, possible spillover effects.

This chapter also provides practical advice on how to assign individuals to the treatment and control groups, whether and how to commit to a pre-analysis plan, and how to increase external validity. Because RCTs are becoming common, further experience should provide other recommendations for how best to implement them, so researchers should try to keep abreast of new developments in RCT methodology and implementation. As mentioned, much more detailed recommendations are provided in Glennerster and Takavarasha (2013), and new books on RCTs are likely to appear in the years to come.

The issues raised in this chapter lead to perhaps the largest single question regarding RCTs (and more generally regarding almost all types of evaluations that collect new data), that of the size of the sample. This issue is taken up in detail in the following chapter.

Notes

1. See Glennerster and Takavarasha (2013) for a book-length treatment of how to implement RCTs, with a wide variety of practical advice.
2. The Hawthorne effect was first proposed in a study conducted in the 1920s of worker productivity in a factory near Chicago. Ironically, Levitt and List (2011) suggest that there was no Hawthorne effect at that plant.
3. Economists often refer to spillovers as externalities, or external effects. For clarity, this book always refers to them as spillovers.
4. Another method to avoid false inferences when testing multiple hypotheses is to adjust the statistical tests used, as discussed in the section titled "Further statistical issues" in chapter 9. Of course, this could be done in addition to preparing a PAP.
5. The first three of these advantages are discussed in more detail in chapter 7. Also, see McKenzie (2012) for statistical arguments about why it may be better to collect two (or more) rounds of data after the program has been implemented, rather than collecting one round of baseline data and one round of endline data. This argument is stronger the less correlated the outcome variable (Y) is over time, and the greater the degree of measurement error in that variable. Note, however, that this argument does not take into account the other advantages of collecting baseline data that are discussed in this paragraph.

References

Christensen, Garret, and Edward Miguel. 2018. "Transparency, Reproducibility and the Credibility of Economics Research." *Journal of Economic Literature* 56 (3): 920–80.

Coffman, Lucas, and Muriel Niederle. 2015. "Pre-Analysis Plans Have Limited Upside, Especially Where Replications Are Feasible." *Journal of Economic Perspectives* 29 (3): 81–97.

Deaton, Angus. 2010. "Instruments, Randomization, and Learning about Development." *Journal of Economic Literature* 48 (2): 424–55.

Finkelstein, Amy, Sarah Taubman, Bill Wright, Mira Bernstein, Jonathan Gruber, Joseph P. Newhouse, Heidi Allen, and Katherine Baicker. 2012. "The Oregon Health Insurance Experiment: Evidence from the First Year." *Quarterly Journal of Economics* 127 (3): 1057–106.

Glennerster, Rachel, and Kudzai Takavarasha. 2013. *Running Randomized Evaluations: A Practical Guide*. Princeton, NJ: Princeton University Press.

Glewwe, Paul, Nauman Ilias, and Michael Kremer. 2010. "Teacher Incentives." *American Economic Journal: Applied Economics* 2 (3): 205–27.

Glewwe, Paul, Michael Kremer, and Sylvie Moulin. 2009. "Many Children Left Behind? Textbooks and Test Scores in Kenya." *American Economic Journal: Applied Economics* 1 (1): 112–35.

Glewwe, Paul, and Petra Todd. 2019. Course materials, "APEC 8212: Econometric Analysis II" and "ECON 712: Graduate Topics Course in Program Evaluation Methods," University of Minnesota, Minneapolis–St. Paul, and University of Pennsylvania, Philadelphia.

Humpage, Sarah D. 2012. "When Are Field Experiments with Individual Assignment Too Risky? Lessons from a Center-Based Child Care Study in Guatemala." Technical Note IDB-TN-469, Inter-American Development Bank, Washington, DC.

Karlan, Dean, and Jonathan Zinman. 2009. "Observing Unobservables: Identifying Information Asymmetries with a Consumer Credit Field Experiment." *Econometrica* 77 (6): 1993–2008.

Levitt, Steven, and John List. 2011. "Was There Really a Hawthorne Effect at the Hawthorne Plant? An Analysis of the Original Illumination Experiments." *American Economic Journal: Applied Economics* 3 (1): 224–38.

McKenzie, David. 2012. "Beyond Baseline and Follow-Up: The Case for More T in Experiments." *Journal of Development Economics* 99 (2): 210–21.

Miguel, Edward, and Michael Kremer. 2004. "Worms: Identifying Impacts on Education and Health in the Presence of Treatment Externalities." *Econometrica* 72 (1): 159–217.

Olken, Benjamin. 2015. "Promises and Perils of Pre-Analysis Plans." *Journal of Economic Perspectives* 29 (3): 61–80.

CHAPTER 9

Sample Size, Sample Design, and Statistical Power

Introduction

One of the first questions faced when conducting an impact evaluation is,

- How large a sample size is needed?

A simple, but not very useful, answer is, As large as possible; that is, all else equal, a bigger sample will lead to more precise estimates. However, obtaining a larger sample size almost always implies an increase in costs. A better question is,

- If, for a specific level of probability, the researcher wants to be able to reject the null hypothesis of zero treatment effect when this null hypothesis is false, how large a sample size is needed?

This chapter provides advice for how to answer this question.

Statistical power as a criterion for choosing the sample design

To answer the "better" question, the starting point is to define the *significance level* and the *power* of a statistical test:

Definition: The ***significance level of a statistical test*** *is the probability of mistakenly rejecting the null hypothesis when it is true.*

Statisticians call this mistake a *Type I error*. Thus the significance level of a test is the probability of a Type I error.

The other type of mistake is failing to reject the null hypothesis when it is false. Statisticians call this a *Type II error*. This concept leads to the second definition:

Definition: The ***power of a statistical test*** *is the probability that the test will reject the null hypothesis when it is false.*

The power of a test corresponds to the probability of not committing a Type II error.

For impact evaluations, particularly in the context of randomized controlled trials (RCTs), the hypothesis test that is usually of most interest is a test of whether the treatment group mean equals the control group mean, which is a test for whether the average treatment effect is zero. One way to choose the sample design in an evaluation is to choose the treatment and control samples in such a way as to achieve a desired level of power (for example, 0.90) for testing a null hypothesis of interest (for example, the hypothesis that the difference in means is zero) for a given level of statistical significance (for example, 0.05).

A simple example may provide some intuition. Consider the estimation of the impact of an education program on students' test scores. Someone may decide that a program impact of 0.2 standard deviations (of the distribution of the students' test scores) is a big effect, and thus it is important that the sample size be large enough to ensure that if the true effect is this size or larger, there will be a high probability (for example, 90 percent) of rejecting the null hypothesis of no effect at, say, the 5 percent significance level. That is, the goal is to select a sample size that gives a specified amount of power; in this example, the power level is 0.90.

The power of a statistical test depends on the following four factors:

1. The *sample size*. The larger the sample, the more power the test has to reject the null hypothesis when it is false.
2. The *significance level* chosen to test the null hypothesis (the "size" of the test). Unfortunately, there is an unavoidable trade-off: the smaller the size of the test, the lower its power will be. In other words, the harder it is to reject the null hypothesis, the less likely that one will reject it when it is false. This is the trade-off between Type I errors (rejecting the null when it is true) and Type II errors (not rejecting the null when it is false) in statistics.
3. The *proportion* of the observations that are treated (the proportion of individuals in the sample who participate in the program).
4. The amount of *variance* in the outcome variable of interest that is not due to the program.

Other factors also affect power, as seen later in this chapter.

To see this more formally, consider the simplest way to estimate the impact of a program using ordinary least squares (OLS), which is by estimating the following regression:

$$Y = \alpha + \beta P + u,$$

where $P = 1$ for program participant observations and $P = 0$ for nonparticipants. Recall from chapter 7 that this regression equation can be used to estimate average treatment effects (ATE) for situations in which all of those assigned to the treatment group participate in the program and all of those assigned to the control group do not participate, and it can also be used to estimate intention-to-treat (ITT) effects for situations where only some of those assigned to the treatment group participate in the program, but all of those assigned to the control group do not participate.

If the unobserved component u can be assumed to be uncorrelated across individuals, then the variance of $\hat{\beta}_{OLS}$, which is the OLS estimate of β, is given by

$$\text{Var}(\hat{\beta}_{OLS}) = \frac{1}{\bar{P}(1-\bar{P})}\frac{\sigma^2}{N}, \tag{9.1}$$

where $\bar{P}$ is the proportion of the sample that participated (the sample mean, or average, of P), N is the total sample size, and σ^2 is the variance of u, which can also be expressed as Var(u). Although σ^2 is not directly observed, if the null hypothesis that the program has no effect is correct, then $\beta = 0$ and $\sigma^2 = \text{Var}(u) = \text{Var}(Y)$. If $\beta \neq 0$ then $\sigma^2 = \text{Var}(Y) - \beta^2\text{Var}(P)$, which is less than Var(Y).

This formula is not difficult to derive. Let N_0 denote the number of nonparticipants and N_1 the number of participants in the sample so that $N_0 + N_1 = N$. In the regression equation above, $Y = \alpha + \beta P + u$, the OLS estimate for β, which can be denoted by $\hat{\beta}_{OLS}$, is an unbiased estimate of the difference in means between the treatment group and the control group. This allows one to calculate the variance of $\hat{\beta}_{OLS}$ as follows:

$$\begin{aligned}\text{Var}(\hat{\beta}_{OLS}) &= \text{Var}\left(\frac{1}{N_1}\sum_{i=1}^{N_1} Y_{1i} - \frac{1}{N_0}\sum_{i=1}^{N_0} Y_{0i}\right) = \left(\frac{1}{N_1}\right)^2 N_1\text{Var}(Y_{1i}) + \left(\frac{1}{N_0}\right)^2 N_0\text{Var}(Y_{0i}) \\ &= \frac{\text{Var}(u)}{N_1} + \frac{\text{Var}(u)}{N_0} = \left(\frac{N}{N_1} + \frac{N}{N_0}\right)\frac{\sigma^2}{N} \\ &= \left(\frac{1}{\bar{P}} + \frac{1}{1-\bar{P}}\right)\frac{\sigma^2}{N} = \left(\frac{1}{\bar{P}(1-\bar{P})}\right)\frac{\sigma^2}{N}.\end{aligned}$$

Note that $\text{Var}(Y_1) = \text{Var}(u)$ because $P = 1$ if $Y = Y_1$; similarly, $\text{Var}(Y_0) = \text{Var}(u)$ because $P = 0$ if $Y = Y_0$.[1]

The formula for $\text{Var}(\hat{\beta}_{OLS})$ in equation (9.1) clearly depends on three of the four factors that determine the power of a statistical test, namely, the sample size (N), the proportion of the observations that are treated ($\bar{P}$), and the variance of the outcome variable that is not due to variation in program participation (σ^2). The fourth factor is the significance level of the test. Figure 9.1 shows how combining the significance level with the variance of $\hat{\beta}_{OLS}$ yields the power of a statistical test.[2]

The distribution on the left of figure 9.1 is the distribution of $\hat{\beta}_{OLS}$ under the null hypothesis (H_0) that the program has no effect ($\beta = 0$). For a given significance level for testing H_0 (denoted by α, for example, $\alpha = 0.05$), H_0 should be rejected if $\hat{\beta}_{OLS} > t_\alpha \times \text{SE}(\hat{\beta}_{OLS})$, where t_α is the critical value of the t-distribution at the α significance level, and $\text{SE}(\hat{\beta}_{OLS})$ is the standard error of $\hat{\beta}_{OLS}$ (that is, the square root of the variance of $\hat{\beta}_{OLS}$). This is a one-sided test; for a

FIGURE 9.1 The power of a statistical test

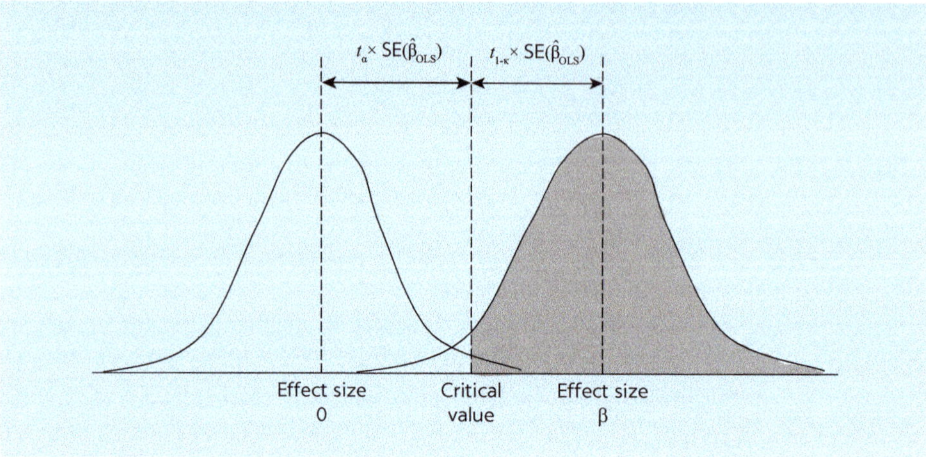

Source: Esther Duflo, Rachel Glennerster, and Michael Kremer, "Using Randomization in Development Economics Research: A Toolkit," chapter 15 in *Handbook of Development Economics*, vol. 4, edited by T. P. Schultz and J. Strauss, copyright Elsevier (2008).

two-sided test, replace t_α (for example, 1.645) with $t_{\alpha/2}$ (for example, 1.960). Note that the "α" for the significance level is not the same as the α in the regression equation ($Y = \alpha + \beta P + u$).

The distribution on the right of figure 9.1 is the distribution of $\hat{\beta}_{OLS}$ under the alternative hypothesis (H_1) of a positive effect, that is $\beta > 0$ (for example, $\beta = 0.2$). The power of the test of the null hypothesis (the probability that the null is rejected when it is false) is the shaded area under the curve to the right of the critical value.

Suppose that the researcher wants to achieve some level of power, denoted by κ (for example, 0.80), which implies that the goal is to reject the null hypothesis that $\beta = 0$ with probability κ when the null is false. Figure 9.1 demonstrates that this level of power can be achieved only if

$$\beta \geq (t_{1-\kappa} + t_\alpha) \times SE(\hat{\beta}_{OLS}).$$

Note for future reference that for a power of 0.80 the associated $t_{1-\kappa}$ ($t_{0.20}$) is 0.84, and for a power of 0.90 the associated $t_{1-\kappa}$ ($t_{0.10}$) is 1.28.

It follows that, for a given power (κ), a given significance level (α), a given sample size (N), and a given proportion of individuals treated ($\bar{P}$), the minimum value of β that can be detected, or the *minimum detectable effect size* (MDE), is

$$MDE = (t_{1-\kappa} + t_\alpha) \times SE(\hat{\beta}_{OLS}) = (t_{1-\kappa} + t_\alpha) \times \sqrt{\frac{1}{\bar{P}(1-\bar{P})}}\sqrt{\frac{\sigma^2}{N}}. \tag{9.2}$$

This is for a one-sided test; for a two-sided test replace α with α/2 (that is, replace t_α with $t_{\alpha/2}$).

Equation (9.2) can be used to answer the question posed at the beginning of this chapter regarding how large a sample size is needed. To obtain the answer, the following must be specified:

- The size of the effect to be detected (MDE). For example, if 0.2 standard deviations of the distribution of test scores is worth detecting for a particular program or policy, set MDE = 0.2 (and standardize Y so that its standard deviation = 1 by dividing it by its standard deviation).
- The size of the test for the null hypothesis (α). For example, should the null hypothesis be tested at the 1 percent level, the 5 percent level, or the 10 percent level?[3]
- The power of the test (κ). For example, is the goal an 80 percent probability or a 90 percent probability of rejecting the null hypothesis of no effect when the null is false?
- The proportion of the population that is treated ($\bar{P}$).
- The variance of u, the error term in the regression, which is denoted by σ^2.

Rearranging equation (9.2) yields the sample (N) needed to attain a particular value for MDE given the power (κ) and size (α) of the test, the proportion treated ($\bar{P}$), and the variance of u (σ^2):

$$N = \frac{(t_{1-\kappa} + t_\alpha)^2}{\text{MDE}^2} \times \frac{\sigma^2}{\bar{P}(1-\bar{P})}. \tag{9.3}$$

This clearly shows that an increase in power (κ), which increases $t_{1-\kappa}$, will increase the required sample size, as will a decrease in the significance level (α), which increases t_α. On the other hand, an increase in the MDE, that is, an increase in the size of an impact to be detected, reduces the sample size needed. Also, a reduction in the variance of u (σ^2) also reduces the required sample size.

Finally, the formula for N in equation (9.3) also provides useful advice about the optimal value of $\bar{P}$. For given values of α, κ, σ^2, and MDE, the sample size N is minimized by setting $\bar{P} = 0.5$ because $\bar{P}(1-\bar{P})$ is maximized at $\bar{P} = 0.5$.

However, an important qualification to the recommendation in the previous paragraph that the optimal choice of $\bar{P}$ is 0.5 is that this recommendation ignores the cost of the treatment. If the impact evaluation has a fixed budget, and the treatment is costly, the cost of the treatment must be weighed against the cost of collecting more data on the controls (cost of increasing N). More specifically, denote the fixed budget by B, the cost of collecting data for one more control observation by c_c, and the cost for treating (and collecting data on) one more treatment observation by c_t. It can be shown that minimizing N for a given MDE (or, alternatively, minimizing MDE for a given N) given this budget constraint implies the following optimal value for $\bar{P}$:[4]

$$\bar{P} = \frac{\sqrt{c_c}}{\sqrt{c_c} + \sqrt{c_t}}. \tag{9.4}$$

If the cost of obtaining control group observations and treatment group observations is equal (that is, $c_c = c_t$), then equation (9.4) implies that the sample should have equal numbers of treatment and control observations. Usually, however, the treatment is costly and increasing the size of the treatment group is more costly than increasing the size of the control group. In that case, it is optimal to set $\bar{P} < 0.5$, which indicates that it is optimal for the control group to be larger than the treatment group.

Example 1: MDE and sample size without clusters. Consider a cash transfer program (similar to the Mexican PROGRESA program described in chapter 6) that offers bimonthly cash benefits to poor rural households conditional on their children's school enrollment and health clinic visits. One outcome of interest is households' per capita food consumption, given that the ultimate goal of the program is to reduce poverty. The task is to determine the sample size needed to evaluate the program impact on food consumption. The government is of the opinion that a \$2 change in monthly per capita food consumption is worth detecting. Suppose that half of the eligible households will be assigned to the program, the randomization will be done by using a simple random sample (no clusters), and the standard deviation of per capita food consumption is \$8 (as determined by pilot studies).

The first task is to determine the sample size needed to detect, with 90 percent probability ($\kappa = 0.90$), an impact of \$2 that is statistically significant at the 5 percent level ($\alpha = 0.05/2 = 0.025$, assuming a two-sided hypothesis test). For illustration, it is useful to calculate the sample size needed for an MDE not only for a \$2 increase in monthly per capita food consumption, but also for \$1 and \$3. Table 9.1 summarizes the calculation results using equation (9.3), in which σ has been set to \$8 (so $\sigma^2 = \$64$).

If these samples seem too large, it may be useful to calculate the required sample size for a lower power of 0.8 (requiring only an 80 percent probability of detecting a significant effect). The required sample sizes are shown in table 9.2.

The calculations in tables 9.1 and 9.2 show two implications of using power calculations to select the sample size. First, the higher (more conservative) the power, the larger the sample size required. Second, the smaller the impact to be detected (smaller the MDE), the larger the sample size needed.

TABLE 9.1 Sample size required for various values of MDE, power = 0.9, no clusters

MDE	TREATMENT	CONTROL	TOTAL SAMPLE
\$1	1,344	1,344	2,688
\$2	336	336	672
\$3	150	150	300

Source: Adapted from Gertler et al. 2011.
Note: These calculations use $t_{0.90} = 1.28$ and $t_{0.975} = 1.96$. MDE = minimum detectable effect size.

TABLE 9.2 Sample size required for various values of MDE, power = 0.8, no clusters

MDE	TREATMENT	CONTROL	TOTAL SAMPLE
\$1	1,004	1,004	2,008
\$2	251	251	502
\$3	112	112	224

Source: Figures adapted from Gertler et al. 2011.
Note: These calculations use $t_{0.80} = 0.84$ and $t_{0.975} = 1.96$. MDE = minimum detectable effect size.

Power and MDE calculations in more complex settings

The discussion of statistical power and sample size in the previous section focuses on the simplest case. In many applications the situation is more complex, so the MDE formula, and related formulas, need to be adjusted. This section presents several important extensions.

Multiple treatments

As mentioned in chapter 7, some RCTs compare two or more programs with a single control group. Generalizations of the result in equation (9.4) provide useful guidance for this case. For example, suppose that the impacts of two programs, relative to no program at all, are to be compared, but there is no interest in comparing the relative impacts of the two programs. Suppose as well that equal weight is placed on evaluating each of the two programs. In this case, the *P*s for both treatments should be chosen to minimize the unweighted sum of the MDEs for both treatments, taking into account that the same control group is used for both treatments.

It can be shown that in this case it is optimal to divide the sample so that 25 percent of the individuals are randomly assigned to the first treatment, 25 percent are randomly assigned to the second treatment, and the remaining 50 percent constitute the control group. Intuitively, each control group observation is used twice, so each such observation is twice as valuable as any treatment group observation. More generally, the optimal allocation of the sample to two (out of possibly many) groups, *i* and *j*, satisfies

$$N_i/N_j = (\Sigma_{H_I}\, \omega_h / \Sigma_{H_J}\, \omega_h)\sqrt{c_j / c_i},$$

where ω_h is the "importance" weight for testing hypothesis *h*, and H_I (H_J) is the set of all hypotheses for group *i* (*j*). For instance, in the example above the importance weight for testing the hypothesis that the two programs have the same impact is zero, while the two hypotheses that each of the two programs has an impact of zero can be given a weight of one. Note that the control group can be group *i* or *j*, and that applying this formula to all pairs of groups will yield the optimal allocation of the total sample to each of the treatment groups and to the control group.

Correlated errors

In many applications, impact evaluations involve programs that are implemented at the group (village, school) level, so that in each group all people are either in the program (or at least offered the program) or not in the program (not offered the program). This complicates the calculation of the standard errors. Fortunately, methods to calculate standard errors in such situations have been worked out by statisticians and economists. The intuition here is that common shocks that affect *Y* (but have nothing to do with the program) affect all people in a group, which introduces correlation in the error terms across people in the same group.

To see how this modifies the MDE formula in equation (9.2), start with a regression equation that includes a group-level random effect (v_j) in the error term:

$$Y_{ij} = \alpha + \beta P_j + v_j + u_{ij},$$

where j is the group index and i is the individual index. To keep the discussion simple, assume the following:

- There are J groups or clusters, and each group has the same number, n, of observations.
- The variance of v_j, denoted by τ^2, is the same for all groups (all j), and v_j is independent across all groups.
- The variance of u_{ij} (σ^2) is the same for all i and j, and u_{ij} is independent across all observations.

Under these assumptions, the OLS estimate of β (still denoted by $\hat{\beta}_{OLS}$) is consistent, but its standard error is more complicated:

$$SE(\hat{\beta}_{OLS}) = \sqrt{\frac{1}{\bar{P}(1-\bar{P})}}\sqrt{\frac{n\tau^2+\sigma^2}{nJ}}.$$

If the program had been implemented at the individual level (instead of at the group level), and there is no source of correlation across individuals, the standard error of $\hat{\beta}_{OLS}$ would have been:

$$SE(\hat{\beta}_{OLS}) = \sqrt{\frac{1}{\bar{P}(1-\bar{P})}}\sqrt{\frac{\tau^2+\sigma^2}{nJ}},$$

which is smaller. The ratio of these two standard errors (given a fixed number of members per group) is called the *design effect*, which is given by:

$$D(\text{design effect}) = \sqrt{1+(n-1)\rho}, \text{ where } \rho = \tau^2/(\tau^2+\sigma^2).$$

Statisticians often refer to the groups as clusters, and the ρ term is called the *intracluster correlation*, which is the proportion of the overall variance of $v_j + u_{ij}$ that is caused by the variance across clusters (groups) due to the random effect v_j.[5]

Note that the design effect (D) is higher the more people there are in the group (n), and the higher the intracluster correlation (ρ). The result that n increases D implies that, for a given total sample size, it is better to have smaller, and thus more, groups.

The MDE equation (equation 9.2) changes when the program is implemented at the group level:[6]

$$MDE = (t_{1-\kappa}+t_{\alpha})\times\sqrt{\tau^2+\sigma^2}\sqrt{\frac{1}{\bar{P}(1-\bar{P})J}}\sqrt{\rho+\frac{1-\rho}{n}}. \quad (9.5)$$

Again, if a two-sided test is used, replace t_α with $t_{\alpha/2}$.

The formula for MDE in equation (9.5) indicates that an increase in J (the number of groups) reduces MDE by 1 over the square root of J. However, an increase in n (the number of observations per group) has a smaller effect because of the "ρ +" term under the square root sign. Thus, for example, if funds are available to double the overall sample, it is better to double the number of groups than to double the number in each group.[7]

Equation (9.5) can be rearranged to show the number required per group, n, for a given MDE and a given number of groups (J):

$$n = \frac{(t_{1-\kappa} + t_\alpha)^2(\tau^2 + \sigma^2)(1-\rho)}{\text{MDE}^2 \times \bar{P}(1-\bar{P})J - \rho(t_{1-\kappa} + t_\alpha)^2(\tau^2 + \sigma^2)}. \tag{9.6}$$

Similarly, the number of groups required (J) for a given MDE and a given number per group (n) can also be shown:

$$J = \frac{(t_{1-\kappa} + t_\alpha)^2(\tau^2 + \sigma^2)}{\text{MDE}^2 \times \bar{P}(1-\bar{P})} \times \left(\rho + \frac{1-\rho}{n}\right). \tag{9.7}$$

The following example illustrates how these formulas for MDE, n, and J can be used.

Example 2: MDE and sample size with clusters (groups). Consider again the conditional cash transfer example, but now assume that the program was implemented at the village level, which generates correlation across individuals in the same village (the same cluster). The new information needed to adjust the calculation of the sample sizes in table 9.1 is the *intracluster correlation* in per capita food consumption. Suppose that, from pilot studies, this number is estimated to be 0.04. Assume that there are only 100 villages available that can be used for the evaluation. With this new information, for different values of MDE one can use equation (9.6) to obtain n, the number of individuals needed per village, which when multiplied by the number of villages gives the total sample size. These calculations are shown in table 9.3.

The first thing to notice about table 9.3 is that given the available information, it is not possible to detect a $1 increase in per capita food consumption. (Applying equation (9.6) for n using J = 100 and MDE =1 yields a large negative number). At least 108 clusters will be needed, but even then the number of observations within each cluster will be extremely high (about 10,000). So, a large number of clusters is needed for an evaluation to have

TABLE 9.3 Sample size required for various values of MDE, power = 0.9, maximum clusters ≈ 100

MDE	NUMBER OF CLUSTERS (J)	UNITS PER CLUSTER (n)	TOTAL SAMPLE REQUIRED WITH CLUSTERS ($J \times n$)	TOTAL SAMPLE REQUIRED WITHOUT CLUSTERS
$1	not feasible	not feasible	not feasible	2,688
$2	99	9	891	672
$3	84	4	336	300

Source: Adapted from Gertler et al. 2011.
Note: MDE = minimum detectable effect size.

enough power to detect a relatively small program impact, regardless of the number of observations within each cluster.

The other main pattern of interest in table 9.3 is that, compared with sampling without clusters (the last column of table 9.3), the total sample required to attain a given MDE is higher. This is especially true for small values of MDE. Note that the number of clusters is not exactly equal to 100 because the formula would imply a non-integer value for n, which is not possible; thus the number of clusters is the largest value less than or equal to 100 for integer values of n.

A final point about the last column of table 9.3 is that one should not conclude that it is better not to have a clustered sample because that will reduce the sample size needed to attain a given value for the MDE. While this is technically correct, using a clustered sample design can lead to substantial reductions in the cost of collecting data, so a larger sample from a clustered sample design may cost much less than a smaller sample based on a sample design without clusters. See the discussion of table 9.5 below for further consideration of this point.

Table 9.4 shows the sample sizes per group when about 100 groups are used and the power (the probability of rejecting the null hypothesis when it is false) is reduced from 0.9 to 0.8. As expected, the required sample sizes decrease with the reduction in power, but they are still larger than those in table 9.2 for the case with no clusters. With this lower power, it is possible to attain an MDE of 1 with 100 groups, but doing so requires a very large number of observations per group (98).

A final use of the above formulas is to choose a particular MDE, for example, 2, and a given power, such as 0.9, and then calculate different combinations of total number of groups and number of persons per group that attain that MDE at that power. The choice of the optimal combination depends on the costs of data collection for these different combinations. An example of such calculations in given in table 9.5.

The main lesson from table 9.5 is that, for a given desired MDE and power, a small number of clusters, say, fewer than 50, will lead to a greatly increased total sample size. In general, the required total sample size, and in most cases data collection costs, are lower when there are a relatively larger number of clusters (100 or more) and a small number of

TABLE 9.4 Sample size required for various values of MDE, power = 0.8, maximum clusters ≈ 100

MDE	NUMBER OF CLUSTERS (J)	UNITS PER CLUSTER (n)	TOTAL SAMPLE REQUIRED WITH CLUSTERS ($J \times n$)	TOTAL SAMPLE REQUIRED WITHOUT CLUSTERS
$1	100	98	9,800	2,008
$2	100	6	600	502
$3	81	3	243	224

Source: Adapted from Gertler et al. 2011.
Note: MDE = minimum detectable effect size.

TABLE 9.5 Sample size required to detect a $2 minimum effect for various combinations of groups and individuals within each group, power = 0.9

MDE	NUMBER OF CLUSTERS (J)	UNITS PER CLUSTER (n)	TOTAL SAMPLE WITH CLUSTERS ($J \times n$)
$2	30	211	6,330
$2	60	20	1,200
$2	80	12	960
$2	100	9	900
$2	120	7	840
$2	135	6	810
$2	156	5	780

Source: Adapted from Gertler et al. 2011.
Note: MDE = minimum detectable effect size.

persons per cluster. However, at some point increasing the number of clusters and reducing the number of units per cluster may become inefficient from a cost perspective. For example, in table 9.5 the reduction in costs from reducing n from 6 to 5 may be less than the increase in costs from increasing the number of clusters from 135 to 156. The lowest-cost sample design will depend on the costs of additional units per cluster and the costs of additional clusters; returning to table 9.5, another column could be added, which would be the cost for the sample design in each row, and all else equal the design with the lowest cost should be selected.

Modifications for imperfect compliance in randomized trials

Recall from chapter 6 that, in some RCTs, some of the people assigned to be treated do not get the treatment, and some assigned to the control group obtain treatment. This situation can affect the MDE formula. To see what the implications are for choosing an adequate sample size, first, one must specify notation to indicate the extent of these two phenomena. This can be done by defining the following:

w = share of subjects assigned to the treatment group who actually get the treatment ("willing")
p = share of subjects assigned to the control group who actually get the treatment ("persisters")

In this case, the modified MDE formula (for the case of a simple random sample) becomes:

$$\text{MDE} = \left(t_{1-\kappa} + t_{\alpha}\right) \times \sqrt{\frac{1}{\bar{P}(1-\bar{P})}}\sqrt{\frac{\sigma^2}{N}}\frac{1}{w-p}. \qquad (9.8)$$

Clearly, the term $1/(w-p)$ is greater than 1 if either $w < 1$ or $p > 0$. Therefore, to attain a given MDE, a sample size larger than N (where N is the sample size needed to obtain that MDE when compliance is perfect) is required. Note, finally, that the adjustment factor $1/(w-p)$ is multiplied by the standard MDE formula for the case in which the sample design is not clustered (errors are not grouped); for the clustered sample design (grouped errors), imperfect compliance can be accommodated, if the rate is similar in all clusters (which should be true because clusters are randomly drawn), by multiplying the MDE formula for clustered samples by this same adjustment factor.

Control variables

In general, the precision of estimates of program impacts can be increased (which lowers MDE for a given N) by adding to the regression equation other variables that influence Y (but that are unaffected by the program). Ideally, these variables should be measured during the baseline survey because, as explained in chapter 7, their addition to the regression could lead to inconsistent estimates of program impact if they are measured after the program is implemented and they are affected by the program.

For the case in which P is randomly assigned in an RCT, the addition of covariates does not change the formula for $\text{Var}(\hat{\beta}_{OLS})$ given in equation (9.1). The reason is that the standard formula for that variance when using OLS, $\sigma^2(\mathbf{X'X})$, is block diagonal because P will be uncorrelated with all of the covariates (the variables in $\mathbf{X}$), which directly leads to the formula given in equation (9.1). Yet even though the formula for $\text{Var}(\hat{\beta}_{OLS})$ does not change, $\text{Var}(\hat{\beta}_{OLS})$ should be lower because the additional covariates should reduce the variance of u, that is, σ^2. The best way to obtain an estimate of σ^2 is to use baseline data (or data from a recent household survey) to regress the outcome variable on the covariates; standard statistical software will include an estimate of σ^2 under the conservative assumption that the program has no effect on the outcome variable (in effect, this regression constrains the coefficient on P to be zero).

In general, the more predictive power that the control variables have for Y, the greater the increase in the precision of the estimates of the program impact. A particularly good choice for a control variable is the Y variable measured at the baseline (before the program begins). For example, if the Y variable is test scores, test score data should be collected before the program is started. An example of how adding baseline test scores increases the precision of the estimates is provided in Glewwe, Park, and Zhao (2016); comparison of their Table 4 with their online Appendix Table A.4 shows, for example, that the standard error of the estimate of the impact of providing eyeglasses (averaged over all tests and both counties) decreased from 0.100 to 0.078, which turned a result that was statistically insignificant into a result that was significant at the 5 percent level.[8] More generally, whatever the Y variable is, baseline data that measure Y for both the treatment and control groups should be collected before the program is implemented.

Adjusting the above formulas for MDE, n, and J (equations (9.5), (9.6), and (9.7), respectively) is a straightforward process when estimating the regression equation ($Y_{ij} = \alpha + \beta P_j + v_j + u_{ij}$) with additional explanatory variables (additional covariates).

Quite simply, the variances of v_j and u_{ij} will change (usually will be reduced) when those variables are added to the regression and these new variances (new values of τ^2 and σ^2, respectively) are used instead of the corresponding variances without these additional variables.[9] (Note that these will change the estimate of ρ as well, since $\rho = \tau^2/(\tau^2 + \sigma^2)$.) In general, these variances are not known, so they need to be estimated based on household survey data that were collected earlier and that have both the Y variable and the additional control variables (and a variable that identifies the group when data are clustered).

Stratification (blocking)

Another useful method for increasing the precision of estimates of program impacts is to divide the overall population into a set of subpopulations (strata), and randomly draw treatment and control groups within each subpopulation. This is called *stratification* (or *blocking*). For example, if a program is implemented in several provinces or districts, each province or district can be made into a separate stratum. Stratification ensures that the treatment and control samples will be virtually identical for distributions of the strata variables. For example, if the population is divided into urban and rural areas, and in each of these two areas half of the sample is randomly assigned to the treatment groups and half is assigned to the control group, then the proportion of the treatment group that is rural will be exactly the same as the proportion of the control group that is rural. In general, any observed variable can be used as a strata variable, and two or more variables can be combined to have even more strata (for example, generating separate urban and rural strata within each province or district).

One rationale for stratifying before drawing the sample is that controlling for the strata variables ex post in the regression, which entails a loss of degrees of freedom, is not necessary. Nonetheless, researchers often include dummy variables indicating the strata in their regressions for estimating treatment effects; Bruhn and McKenzie (2009) present a strong case for doing so. For example, the regression would be as follows:

$$Y_{ij} = \alpha + \beta P_j + \gamma_1 M_{j1} + \gamma_2 M_{j2} + \ldots + \gamma_S M_{jS} + v_j + u_{ij},$$

where the M_{js}s are a set of S dummy variables indicating the strata of each observation, such as a set of dummy variables for districts or provinces.

For a more detailed discussion of stratification, see Cox and Reid (2000).

Practical issues regarding power calculations

Equations (9.2), (9.5), and (9.8) for MDE, and equations (9.3), (9.6) and (9.7) for N, n, and J, respectively, are called *power calculations*, and they can be used only if the information needed to use them is available. Unfortunately, the values of σ^2 or ρ are often unknown. However, if data from a recent household survey are available for the country or region in which the program to be evaluated will operate, estimates of, or at least bounds on, the values of σ^2 and ρ, might be obtained.

Turning to the value of σ^2, recall the basic regression equation $Y = \alpha + \beta P + u$. As long as P is randomly assigned, the following holds:

$$\begin{aligned}\text{Var}(Y) &= \beta^2\text{Var}(P) + \sigma^2 \\ &= \beta^2\bar{P}(1 - \bar{P}) + \sigma^2.\end{aligned}$$

This implies that $\sigma^2 \leq \text{Var}(Y)$, so Var($Y$) can serve as an upper bound for σ^2. Note in particular that under the null hypothesis that $\beta = 0$ it follows that $\sigma^2 = \text{Var}(Y)$. Thus in most cases the best estimate of σ^2 for the purpose of calculating MDE and performing related power calculations is Var(Y). If there are covariates that will be used in the regression model, and that are available in existing household survey data, then Y can be regressed on those covariates and a constant term, and the estimated variance of the error term in that regression can be an upper bound estimate of σ^2.

Obtaining an estimate of ρ using clustered data is potentially more difficult. In principle, estimates of the variances of both v_j and u_{ij} are needed. If household survey data for Y exist, Y could be regressed on a constant term, allowing for the random effects error structure presented in the subsection titled "Correlated errors" (assuming that the survey data also contain the "group" variable), to obtain estimates of τ^2 and σ^2. If such data are not available, a guess of 0.3 for ρ is probably a reasonably cautious estimate, although there is some chance that 0.3 is an underestimate. For test scores in schools, ρ can be high, ranging from 0.2 to over 0.5 (see Table 1 in Duflo, Glennerster, and Kremer 2008). For other Y variables ρ may be much closer to 0.

Another difficult issue is what effect size (value of β) is important for making policy decisions. One possible answer is that β should be large enough so that the intervention is cost-effective in some economic sense. This implies that low-cost interventions should have smaller effect sizes (smaller MDEs), and thus will require larger sample sizes to obtain estimates that are informative for policy decisions. An example of being cost-effective in an economic sense is an education intervention that increases students' test scores by a specific amount, which in turn increases future wages by some amount. Any benefits in higher wages that are less than the cost of the program are too small to be worth detecting, so a lower bound on β would be the value that implies increases in wages barely sufficient to pay for the program.

Alternatively, one could hold discussions with the policy makers who designed the program and need to decide whether the program is worthy of continued funding. In particular, in some cases policy makers may have an idea about what impact of the program is sufficiently large to continue funding it, or so small that it is not worth funding. This could depend on comparisons with other programs that are designed to achieve the same objective. This leads to issues of cost-benefit analysis and cost-effectiveness analysis, both of which are discussed in chapter 23.

Further statistical issues

This section presents two other issues to consider when analyzing data from an RCT. Both of these topics are still somewhat unresolved in the evaluation literature.

Multiple outcomes

Many evaluations have more than one *Y* variable of interest. For example, evaluations of education projects may include math, reading, and science tests. With many *Y* variables, even if the actual impact of the program on all of these variables is zero, there is a much higher than 5 percent chance of finding one that is "statistically significant at the 5 percent level" because there are many such variables. Figure 9.2 provides an intuitive (and humorous) example of what could happen if this issue is ignored.

More generally, the multiple hypothesis testing problem occurs when a large number of hypothesis tests are being conducted, either across multiple outcomes or multiple subgroups (or both), which can result in spurious statistical findings. This subsection describes some commonly used classic testing procedures, and then provides a summary of more recently developed methods for conducting multiple hypothesis testing. Note that even though many discussions of multiple hypothesis testing are within the context of RCTs, this issue is also a concern for evaluation methods that use nonrandomized research designs.

FIGURE 9.2 How to obtain "significant" results when a treatment has no impact

To begin, consider why a potential problem arises when multiple hypotheses are being tested. Suppose a researcher carries out 20 independent tests, each with a 5 percent statistical significance level, as in figure 9.2. The chance of a Type I error (rejecting the null hypothesis of no effect when it is true) in each of these tests is 5 percent. However, the chance of having at least one spurious nonzero impact in the set of 20 tests is

$$(1 - (0.95)^{20}) \times 100 = 64 \text{ percent.}$$

The probability of having at least one spurious impact is one minus the probability that none of the estimates is spurious. As the number of hypotheses being tested increases, the chance of observing at least one spurious "significant" impact becomes greater.

Multiple hypothesis testing procedures typically control for the probability of a Type I error in a group of tests by applying more stringent testing criteria (for example, significance levels), but the benefit of reducing the Type I error usually comes at the expense of increasing a Type II error, which reduces power. (Recall from the section titled "Statistical power as a criterion for choosing the sample design" that the power of a test is the probability of rejecting the null hypothesis when it is false.) In an evaluation context, a loss of power means that, when using multiple testing procedures, the likelihood that the tests will identify true differences between the treatment and control (comparison) groups is reduced.

Because of the potential for loss of power, there is controversy in the literature as to the usefulness of multiple testing procedures. For example, Cook and Farewell (1996) and Saville (1990) present arguments against multiple testing procedures, whereas Westfall et al. (1999) provide arguments in favor of these procedures. One additional critique leveled against these testing approaches is that additional parameters need to be determined in applying them, possibly making it easier for a researcher to manipulate test results in the direction of some favored hypothesis.

For what types of questions are multiple testing procedures warranted? Suppose a researcher has several outcome measures of interest and wishes to assess whether a specific program affected those outcomes. For example, in an evaluation of an educational program, the different outcomes may be test scores in math, reading, and science, as well as other outcomes such as school attendance. If the question of interest is whether the program affected a particular outcome, then there is no particular need for multiple hypothesis testing.

However, if the question of interest is whether the program had an effect on *any* of the outcomes, then the researcher should consider the use of multiple hypothesis testing. Similarly, suppose a researcher is interested in estimated program impacts for different subgroups, for example, subgroups defined by gender, age, or both. A question such as "Did the program affect younger and older groups in the same way?" could be addressed simply by including both groups in a regression analysis and testing for a significant interaction effect between the program variable and the age subgroup variable, as explained in the section titled "Other useful advice and recommendations" in chapter 7. On the other hand, a question such as "Did the program affect *either* the older *or* the younger subgroup?" would raise the need for multiple hypothesis testing because this type of hypothesis will involve multiple tests of statistical significance, that is, combining results from the separate hypotheses about the program impacts on the older and younger subgroups.

Suppose that treatment and control groups and data on N different outcome measures are available. Let μ_{Tj} denote the mean of outcome variable j for the treatment group, and let μ_{Cj} denote the mean of that outcome for the control group. Suppose that testing the null hypothesis (H_0) that $\mu_{Tj} = \mu_{Cj}$ for outcome j (the corresponding alternative hypothesis, H_A, is $\mu_{Tj} \neq \mu_{Cj}$) is the goal. A common testing procedure sets the statistical significance level, α, to 0.05 and rejects the null hypothesis if the p-value associated with the test statistic is less than 0.05.

Now suppose that tests on multiple outcomes $j = 1 \ldots N$ need to be carried out. The statistics literature considers two different metrics for controlling the rate of Type I errors:

1. The first is the *family-wise error rate* (FWER), which was first described by Tukey (1953). It is the probability that at least one null hypothesis is rejected when all null hypotheses are true:

$$FWER = 1 - (1 - \alpha)^N.$$

2. The second is the *false discovery rate* (FDR), which was introduced by Benjamini and Hochberg (1995). It is the expected fraction of all rejected null hypotheses that are false discoveries (fraction of rejected hypotheses that are Type I errors). More formally, of the N hypotheses that are tested, suppose that R reject the null hypothesis. Of these, suppose that S are correct rejections (the null hypothesis is false) and V are false rejections (the null hypothesis is correct). The FDR is then defined as

$$FDR = \mathrm{E}[V/(S + V)] = \mathrm{E}[V/R].$$

The FWER is an appropriate measure if the researcher's primary concern is to avoid mistakenly reporting any statistically significant findings. The FDR is appropriate if researchers are more interested in drawing inferences about the preponderance of evidence; that is, researchers might be willing to tolerate a certain fraction of false positives if the treatment effect has a statistically significant effect for a large number of outcomes.

Note that FDR is undefined if $R = 0$, that is, if none of the hypotheses is rejected. To allow for the possibility that $R = 0$, $V/(S + V)$ can be set equal to 0 if $R = 0$. This implies that the FDR can be defined as[10]

$$FDR = \mathrm{E}[V/R|\ R > 0] \times \mathrm{Prob}[R > 0].$$

It can be shown that the FWER and the FDR are equivalent if all the null hypotheses are true.[11] Otherwise, the FDR is less than the FWER.[12] This is consistent with the difference between these two statistics; the FDR is relatively small (closer to 0 than to 1) when several null hypotheses are rejected but most of these rejections are due to the null hypothesis being false, and the less common occurrence that a null hypothesis is mistakenly rejected (a Type I error) is judged to be not as worrisome as failing to reject several null hypotheses that are false (Type II errors), whereas in contrast the FWER could be much higher in the same situation because it focuses only on Type I errors (rejecting the null hypothesis when it is true) and ignores Type II errors. In this sense, the FDR is a less conservative indicator of false rejections of null hypotheses (Type I errors), but it has the advantage of leading to tests with greater power (less probability of Type II errors). Which test is most appropriate to use in any particular study will depend on the research questions of interest and on the study design. For example, if the cost of a false positive is very high, then the more conservative FWER might be preferred.

One method often used to minimize the FWER is the classic Bonferroni procedure. This procedure sets the statistical significance level for each of the individual tests at α/N, where N is the number of tests being conducted. This test can be applied to both discrete and continuous outcomes and in cases where test statistics are possibly dependent. The method also provides an easy way of obtaining adjusted confidence intervals simply by replacing α with α/N when constructing the confidence intervals. A drawback, though, is that this type of test is known to suffer from low power; this is the trade-off between Type I and Type II errors discussed in the section titled "Statistical power as a criterion for choosing the sample design," so this method reduces Type I errors at the cost of increasing Type II errors.

If interest instead centers on controlling the FDR, Benjamini and Hochberg (1995) propose a simple procedure, which assumes independence of the test statistics. First, for the J hypotheses to be tested, conduct J t-tests at the α level of significance. Second, order the p-values from smallest to largest, with a j subscript indicating the rank, so that $p_{(1)} \leq p_{(2)} \leq \ldots \leq p_{(J)}$. Third, define k as the largest j for which $p_{(j)} \leq j \times (\alpha/J)$. Fourth, all null hypotheses corresponding to $j \leq k$ can be rejected, but not for any null for which $j > k$. Also, if there is no j for which $p_{(j)} \leq j \times (\alpha/J)$ holds, then no null hypotheses can be rejected.

Benjamini and Yekutieli (2001) show how to control the FDR when the test statistics are not independent. Stepwise testing procedures for controlling the FDR are provided in Romano and Wolf (2005) and Romano and Shaikh (2006).

Schochet (2008) develops a set of general guidelines for addressing the problem of multiple hypothesis testing in an education research context. He recommends that (1) researchers limit the number of outcomes and subgroups that are of interest to a smaller set to reduce the chance of finding impacts when they do not exist, (2) protocols for multiple hypothesis testing be established before data analysis to reduce the possibility that tests could be manipulated, and (3) tests for similar outcomes be grouped together (for example, one test could be conducted for all test score outcomes and another for a school attendance outcome). These recommendations are similar to those made by advocates of pre-analysis plans, as explained in chapter 8.

The literature on multiple hypothesis testing is vast, and a thorough discussion is beyond the scope of this chapter. For example, Anderson (2008) and Kling, Leibman, and Katz (2007) provide two other approaches. Some useful summaries of the literature are provided in Heckman et al. (2010) and Schochet (2008). Some of the proposed methods use bootstrap and permutation procedures (see, for example, Westfall, Lin, and Young 1990; Westfall and Young 1993). Several of these methods are applied by Parker and Todd (2017) in their evaluation of the effects of Mexico's PROGRESA/Oportunidades conditional cash transfer program. They combine 787 different treatment effect estimates across multiple studies and multiple domains.

More on grouped data

Many statistical packages have the option to select robust estimates of the variance-covariance matrix of the OLS estimates for grouped (clustered) data. However, such robust estimates have recently been criticized. In particular, if the number of groups is 50 or fewer, these robust estimates may over-reject the null hypothesis, as demonstrated by Cameron, Gelbach, and Miller (2008).

The best solution is to have more than 50 groups. If this is not possible, one method that has recently been gaining acceptance is the "wild bootstrap," a variant of bootstrapping methods. This procedure is more complicated and is explained in detail in Cameron, Gelbach, and Miller (2008). Those authors find that the wild bootstrap generates fairly accurate *p*-values of statistical tests when the number of groups is well below 50. Another discussion of these issues can be found in Cameron and Miller (2015).

Conclusion

Many evaluations of projects, programs, or policies require the collection of new data, which can be expensive. This raises the question, How large a sample size is needed? This chapter starts by pointing out that this question by itself is not particularly useful. The following questions must be answered before the right sample size is chosen:

- How large a program effect is desired to be detected?
- With what probability should the null hypothesis be rejected when it is false?
- What level of significance should be used to test the null hypothesis?

This chapter shows how to use the answers to these questions, plus additional information about the variable of interest (in particular, its variance) and the type of sampling (in particular, whether the observations are grouped), to determine the sample size required to conduct an evaluation. In the simplest cases, relatively straightforward formulas can be applied, but many complications can arise, such as evaluations that involve two or more variations of the program, grouped errors, a high cost of implementing the program to the treatment group relative to the cost of collecting data from both the treatment and control groups, problems of noncompliance with random assignment, and the use of control variables.[13]

The formulas and recommendations in this chapter can be useful for planning a successful evaluation. Although not all the issues have been fully resolved, the information in this chapter should enable researchers to avoid the all-too-common mistake of drawing a sample that is far too small, or the less common mistake of drawing a sample that is much larger than necessary.

Notes

1. For Y_1, Var(Y_1) = Var($\alpha + \beta + u$) = Var(u), because α and β are constants. Similarly, Var(Y_0) = Var($\alpha + u$) = Var(u).
2. Figure 9.1, and much of the exposition, is from Duflo, Glennerster, and Kremer (2008),
3. Whether the test is one sided or two sided should also be clarified. The latter, which is more common, implies that α should be replaced with $\alpha/2$ in the MDE formula.
4. To see this, consider the expression for MDE. When costs can be ignored, the goal is to choose $\bar{P}$ to maximize $\bar{P}(1-\bar{P})$, which is 0.5. If costs are considered, $\bar{P}$ is related to N as follows: $B = \bar{P}Nc_t + (1-\bar{P})Nc_c$, where B is the budget available. This expression implies that $N = B/[\bar{P}c_t + (1-\bar{P})c_c]$. For both sides of equation (9.3), multiply by MDE^2 and divide by N; MDE is minimized by maximizing $\bar{P}(1-\bar{P})N$, which is $\bar{P}(1-\bar{P})]B/[\bar{P}c_t + (1-\bar{P})c_c]$. Differentiating this expression with respect to $\bar{P}$ leads to a fraction in which the numerator is $\bar{P}^2(c_c - c_t) - \bar{P}\,2c_c + c_c$. Setting this equal to zero requires the use of the quadratic formula, and gives the result that the optimal $\bar{P}$ is equal to $\sqrt{c_c}/\left(\sqrt{c_c} + \sqrt{c_t}\right)$.
5. This is called *intracluster correlation* because the less the total variance can be explained by the variance within clusters (the smaller σ^2 is relative to τ^2, which increases ρ), the more correlated are the within-cluster error terms.
6. Duflo, Glennerster, and Kremer (2008) contains a typo for this formula as given in equation (12) on page 3922; the term σ should be replaced by $\sqrt{\tau^2 + \sigma^2}$.
7. In the very unlikely situation of no intracluster correlation, so that the variance of v_j (τ^2) is zero, then equation (9.5) for MDE simplifies to equation (9.2) for MDE, and given the opportunity to double the sample size, doubling the number of groups (J) has the same effect on MDE as doubling the number of observations per group (n).
8. This example does not account for problems of inference caused by a small number of clusters, as discussed in the paper in detail, but the point still holds that adding baseline test scores often raises the precision of the estimates.
9. For further discussion, see Bloom (2005, 141–46).
10. That is, $E[V/R] = E[V/R|\ R > 0] \times \text{Prob}[R > 0] + 0 \times \text{Prob}[R = 0] = E[V/R|\ R > 0] \times \text{Prob}[R > 0]$.
11. In this case, $\text{Prob}[R > 0] = FWER$ and $E[V/R|\ R > 0] = 1$, so $FDR = \text{Prob}[R > 0] \times 1 = FWER$.
12. Because correct rejections are possible $E[V/R|\ R > 0] < 1$, so $FDR = \text{Prob}[R > 0] \times E[V/R|\ R > 0] < \text{Prob}[R > 0] \times 1 = FWER$.
13. For more complex situations, the software *Optimal Design* (https://sites.google.com/site/optimaldesignsoftware/) is very useful for carrying out power calculations.

References

Anderson, Michael L. 2008. "Multiple Inference and Gender Differences in the Effects of Early Intervention: A Reevaluation of the Abecedarian, Perry Preschool, and Early Training Projects." *Journal of the American Statistical Association* 103 (484): 1481–95.

Benjamini, Yoav, and Yosef Hochberg. 1995. "Controlling the False Discovery Rate: A New and Powerful Approach to Multiple Testing." *Journal of the Royal Statistical Society, Series B (Methodological)* 57 (1): 1289–300.

Benjamini, Yoav, and Daniel Yekutieli. 2001. "The Control of the False Discovery Rate in Multiple Testing under Dependency." *Annals of Statistics* 29 (4): 1165–88.

Bloom, Howard, ed. 2005. *Learning More from Social Experiments*. New York: Russell Sage Foundation.

Bruhn, Miriam, and David McKenzie. 2009. "In Pursuit of Balance: Randomization in Practice in Development Field Experiments." *American Economic Journal: Applied Economics* 1 (4): 200–32.

Cameron, Colin, Jonah Gelbach, and Douglas Miller. 2008. "Bootstrap-Based Improvements for Inference with Clustered Errors." *Review of Economics and Statistics* 90 (3): 414–27.

Cameron, Colin, and Douglas Miller. 2015. "A Practitioner's Guide to Cluster-Robust Inference." *Journal of Human Resources* 50 (2): 317–72.

Cook, Richard J., and Vern Farewell. 1996. "Multiplicity Considerations in the Design and Analysis of Clinical Trials." *Journal of the Royal Statistical Society, Series A (Statistics in Society)* 159 (1): 93–110.

Cox, David R., and Nancy Reid. 2000. *The Theory of the Design of Experiments*. London: Chapman and Hall.

Duflo, Esther, Rachel Glennerster, and Michael Kremer. 2008. "Using Randomization in Development Economics Research: A Toolkit." In *Handbook of Development Economics,* Vol. 4, edited by T. P. Schultz and J. Strauss. Amsterdam: Elsevier.

Gertler, Paul, Sebastian Martinez, Patrick Premand, Laura Rawlings, and Christel Vermeersch. 2011. *Impact Evaluation in Practice*. Washington, DC: World Bank.

Glewwe, Paul, Albert Park, and Meng Zhao. 2016. "A Better Vision for Development: Eyeglasses and Academic Performance in Rural Primary Schools in China." *Journal of Development Economics* 122 (September): 170–82.

Heckman, James J., Seong Hyeok Moon, Rodrigo Pinto, Peter A. Savelyev, and Adam Yavitz. 2010. "Analyzing Social Experiments as Implemented: A Reexamination of the Evidence from the HighScope Perry Preschool Program." *Quantitative Economics* 1 (1): 1–46.

Kling, Jeffrey, Jeffrey Liebman, and Lawrence Katz. 2007. "Experimental Analysis of Neighborhood Effects." *Econometrica* 75 (1): 83–119.

Parker, Susan W., and Petra E. Todd. 2017. "Conditional Cash Transfers: The Case of Progresa/Oportunidades." *Journal of Economic Literature* 55 (3): 866–915.

Romano, Joseph P., and Azeem M. Shaikh. 2006. "Stepup Procedures for Control of Generalizations of the Familywise Error Rate." *Annals of Statistics* 34 (4): 1850–73.

Romano, Joseph P., and Michael Wolf. 2005. "Stepwise Multiple Testing as Formalized Data Snooping." *Econometrica* 73 (4): 1237–82.

Saville, David J. 1990. "Multiple Comparison Procedures: The Practical Solution." *American Statistician* 44 (2): 174–80.

Schochet, Peter Z. 2008. "Guidelines for Multiple Testing in Impact Evaluations of Educational Interventions. Final Report." Mathematica Policy Research, Princeton, NJ. https://www.mathematica-mpr.com/our-publications-and-findings/publications/guidelines-for-multiple-testing-in-impact-evaluations-of-educational-interventions.

Tukey, John W. 1953. "The Problem of Multiple Comparisons." Unpublished, Princeton University, Princeton, NJ.

Westfall, Peter H., Youling Lin, and S. Stanley Young. 1990. "Resampling-Based Multiple Testing." In *Proceedings of the Fifteenth Annual SAS Users Group International,* 1359–64. Cary, NC: SAS Institute, Inc.

Westfall, P. H., R. Tobias, D. Rom, R. Wolfinger, and Y. Hochberg. 1999. *Multiple Comparisons and Multiple Tests Using SAS*. Cary, NC: SAS Institute, Inc.

Westfall, Peter H., and S. Stanley Young. 1993. *Resampling-Based Multiple Testing: Examples and Methods for P-Value Adjustment*. New York: John Wiley & Sons.

CHAPTER 10

Recommendations for Conducting Ethical Impact Evaluations

Sarah Humpage Liuzzi

Introduction

Impact evaluation nearly always involves working with people. Anyone who conducts an impact evaluation that involves people is, by definition, conducting human subjects research. The responsibility of a researcher who conducts impact evaluations is to ensure that the people who are involved in the evaluation in any capacity are not harmed by that research and, more generally, that the evaluation is conducted in an ethical way.[1]

Why should researchers be concerned about conducting ethical impact evaluations or, more generally, ethical research? Even researchers who are motivated purely by self-interest are better off if they conduct ethical research. Participants who feel that they have been harmed or treated unfairly by participating in an impact evaluation or a research project may be less motivated to cooperate with follow-up data collection or in subsequent evaluations or projects. Other researchers may be unwilling to collaborate with researchers who they believe conduct unethical work. Funders, fearing the negative publicity associated with unethical research practices, are unlikely to continue funding research that they suspect may be unethical, or to grant funding for new projects to researchers who have engaged in unethical research in the past. Academic journals may ask researchers to demonstrate that their research was approved by an institutional review board (IRB) or ethics board before considering publishing their work. Finally, in some cases researchers may be subject to legal action.[2]

This chapter provides an overview of key ethical issues that arise when conducting impact evaluations and, more generally, when conducting research on human subjects. The principles of ethical research are drawn from two key documents: the Nuremberg Code (U.S. Government Printing Office 1949) and the Belmont Report (U.S. Health and Human Services Office for Human Research Protection 1979). The principles set forth in these documents provide a starting point, but the responsibility of the researcher is not limited to adhering to the recommendations in these documents. It is also essential that the researcher be aware of local dynamics and legal requirements in the area where he or she is working, which may vary from the guidance provided in this chapter. Furthermore, the researcher is responsible for identifying potential conflicts of interest that may generate incentives for him or her not to conduct rigorous, unbiased research.

Two frameworks for conducting ethical evaluations and research

Guidelines for conducting ethical evaluations and research are motivated by a desire to ensure that people who participate in the evaluation or research are willing participants and are protected from harm as much as possible, and that any risks born by participants are minimized and balanced by the potential gains expected from the research. These ideas, represented by the principles of *respect for persons*, *beneficence,* and *justice*, are derived from two historical documents: the Nuremberg Code and the Belmont Report. This section reviews these documents' key contributions to the ethics of human subjects research.

The Nuremberg Code

The Nuremberg Code and the Belmont Report were created in the wake of human subjects research that was grossly unethical. Both represent efforts to learn from instances of exploitation to prevent similar episodes from occurring in the future. The lessons drawn from these documents also guide IRBs in their reviews of proposed and ongoing research.

The Nuremberg Code was written in the wake of the Nuremberg Trials, in which representatives of the Allied Forces tried surviving members of Nazi Germany's leadership for war crimes; these trials included trials against medical doctors for grossly unethical human experimentation. The trial proceedings included 10 key points that define legitimate

TABLE 10.1 The Nuremberg Code for ethical human subjects research

1. The voluntary consent of the human subject is absolutely essential; participants must understand their role in the research, and must not be coerced into participating.
2. The experiment should be expected to yield fruitful results for the good of society, which cannot be achieved reasonably through other means.
3. The research should be driven by existing knowledge of the problem under study, and the anticipated results should justify the performance of the experiment.
4. The experiment should avoid all unnecessary physical and mental suffering and injury.
5. No experiment should be conducted if there is reason to believe that death or a disabling injury will occur.
6. The degree of risk to be taken should never exceed that determined by the humanitarian importance of the problem to be solved by the experiment.
7. All appropriate measures should be taken to protect the experimental subjects against even remote possibilities of injury, disability or death.
8. The experiment should be conducted only by qualified persons.
9. All participants should be free to discontinue participation in the experiment at any time.
10. The researcher in charge must be prepared to terminate the experiment at any stage, if he or she has probable cause to believe that a continuation of the experiment is likely to result in injury, disability or death of any participant.

Source: U.S. Government Printing Office 1949.

human subjects research (see table 10.1). Although this code was developed to govern medical research, each of these points is relevant to human subjects research more generally.

The Belmont Report

The Tuskegee Syphilis Experiment is one of the most notorious examples of unethical research with human subjects. U.S. Public Health Service researchers recruited poor African-American sharecroppers in the U.S. state of Alabama to participate in the research, which took place from 1932 to 1972. Participants were not told that they were being studied; rather, they were told that they were receiving free medical care. Researchers tested participants for syphilis, but did not inform them if they tested positive for the disease, nor did they provide them with treatment when penicillin was found to be an effective cure in 1940. The 40-year long experiment finally ended when a whistleblower alerted the media to the study's activities in 1972. The U.S. government formally apologized and provided medical treatment to study participants and their families and paid reparations to surviving participants (Jones 2008).

The 1979 Belmont Report was written by the U.S. National Commission for the Protection of Human Subjects of Biomedical and Behavioral Research in response to revelations about the Tuskegee Syphilis Experiment. The Belmont Report states three principles of ethical research, which closely echo the ideas in the Nuremberg Code: respect for persons, beneficence, and justice. These principles and applications of the principles are presented in table 10.2.

TABLE 10.2 Principles and applications from the Belmont Report

ETHICAL PRINCIPLE	APPLICATION OF ETHICAL PRINCIPLE
Respect for persons. Individuals should be treated as autonomous agents, who are free to decide whether or not they will participate in research. Individuals with diminished autonomy (children, prisoners, individuals with diminished reasoning ability) are entitled to protection.	***Informed consent.*** Participants should receive information about what the research entails, the risks associated with participating, the purposes of the research, and an opportunity to ask questions. It is essential for the researcher to be sure that all participants comprehend this information, and that they have voluntarily agreed to participate without coercion.
Beneficence. Research should do no harm while maximizing benefits of the research and minimizing risks to participants.	***Assessment of risks and benefits.*** The researcher must make an attempt to systematically assess the risks and benefits to the research subjects and to society at large. If participants face significant risks, the importance of ensuring that participants understand these risks and participate voluntarily is increased.
Justice. Researchers should ensure the fair distribution of benefits and burden associated with their research. Those that bear the risks of research should reflect the populations expected to benefit from it.	***Selection of subjects.*** Researchers should not favor some individuals or groups for research that is likely to be beneficial to participants. Similarly, they should not target certain individuals or groups for high-risk research.

Source: U.S. Health and Human Services Office for Human Research Protections 1979.

To fulfill the respect for persons principle, researchers must treat participants as autonomous agents, which means that

- Prospective participants are free to make independent decisions about participating in the research,
- Their decisions are based on full information about their involvement in the research,
- They are free to discontinue participation at any point, and
- They are not coerced into participating.

Researchers can bring this principle into practice in at least two ways. First, the researcher must ensure that participants have understood all the information they need to make a fully informed decision to participate. Simply providing the information is not sufficient; the researcher must ensure that participants have understood the information. At a minimum, researchers must make information available using a language and terminology that the participants can understand, avoiding technical jargon. Importantly, this information should explain what participants can expect by participating, what risks and benefits are associated with participation, what the purpose of the study is, and where they can go to ask questions. Rather than simply asking potential participants to confirm that they have understood the information, researchers should ask specific questions about key components of the research to gauge potential participants' level of understanding.

The second way researchers can bring the respect for persons principle into practice is to record participants' agreement to participate once they are ready to decide. The researcher should create a record of agreement either by having a participant sign a written document or, if the participant does not read or write, by recording the participant making an oral statement of consent. The process of obtaining written or oral agreement from the participant after providing full information is called *obtaining informed consent*. Obtaining informed consent is an important part of human subjects research. Failing to obtain informed consent can cause problems for the researcher. If participants do not understand what is involved in the research, they may be more likely to drop out of the study. Furthermore, researchers may be called upon to demonstrate informed consent by an IRB or other authority, or by a journal or other outlet in which they would like to publish the results of their research.

In a few cases it may be appropriate not to reveal to research participants that they are participating in a study if participating in the study is not risky for participants, and if notifying participants would either interfere with the research or would be infeasible or costly. For example, public health researchers might evaluate alternative methods to remind patients to come to their appointments. Assuming none of the reminder methods is risky and none would make the study participants worse off, a researcher could ethically decide not to inform subjects that they are participating in research. Another example is research on corruption of politicians and other public servants, who may change their behavior if they learn that they are research subjects. Researchers should make this determination on a case-by-case basis, and conducting research without getting consent from participants should be done only if approved by an IRB or ethics board.

Upholding the second principle outlined in the Belmont Report, *beneficence*, means that researchers should never knowingly harm participants in their research, but should strive

TABLE 10.3 The Tuskegee Syphilis Experiment and the principles of ethical human subjects research

PRINCIPLE	VIOLATION IN THE TUSKEGEE SYPHILIS EXPERIMENT
Respect for persons	Participants' autonomy was not respected. Participants were not given the opportunity to offer informed consent. They were not informed that they were participating in research, or about the nature of the research. They were not informed when doctors diagnosed them with syphilis. Researchers also failed to respect participants' freedom to decide whether to participate.
Beneficence	Researchers did not have participants' best interests in mind. They did not offer participants who were sick with syphilis the treatment they knew would greatly improve their health, nor did they take care to keep participants from infecting others.
Justice	This research targeted a vulnerable population, who paid a high price for participating in the research. Those who would benefit from the research were those who might contract syphilis, a much broader population.

Source: Original table for this publication.

to maximize benefits for participants while minimizing risks. In practice, the researcher should take care to identify the risks born by participants, and determine whether the benefits to the participants and to society at large outweigh these risks. The researcher should also consider whether the research is necessary. If the research question can be answered without using human subjects, or if existing research has already addressed the same research question, pursuing the research may not be worthwhile.

The final principle, *justice*, refers to fairness in the selection of participants. The idea behind this principle is that the people who participate in the research should be a reflection of the population that is likely to benefit from the research. For example, researchers should not rely on disadvantaged participants for high-risk research that will benefit a broader population. Researchers can put this principle into practice by being careful to select participants that reflect the beneficiaries of their research. The Tuskegee Syphilis Experiment failed to uphold all three of these principles. The ways in which the experiment violated these principles are reviewed in table 10.3.

Confidentiality

Part of upholding the principle of beneficence is ensuring that research participants' privacy is respected. Research participants who provide personal information through physical examinations, academic tests, surveys, or other means have the right to expect that the information will not be shared outside the research team. Exposing personal information can have negative social repercussions for the participant if the data reveal that the participant engages in behavior that is disapproved of, has had poor (or strong) academic performance, or has a disease or disorder. Revealing personal information could also have economic consequences if it leads to job loss or business losses. Finally, spreading private information can have serious emotional costs from embarrassment, social repercussions, or economic consequences.

The researcher can take several concrete actions to minimize the risk that participants' personal information will fall into the wrong hands. As a first step, all project staff, including interviewers, data entry staff, and analysts, must be trained on the importance of data privacy, and on how to handle data properly. The project or agency should have procedures and policies in place to protect privacy. Paper-based surveys should be kept in a secure location at all times to prevent theft or loss. Electronic files should also be handled with care. Once data entry has been completed, data should be de-identified. To de-identify data, any identifying information that will not be used to conduct the analysis, such as respondents' names, addresses, phone numbers, and national identification (ID) numbers, should be removed and replaced with a study-specific ID number. A file that links the IDs to respondents' names should then be kept in a separate, secure location. This file should also be password protected. Finally, the number of people with access to personal data in hard copy or in electronic files should be limited.

Ethics of randomized controlled trials

Randomized controlled trials (RCTs) present unique ethical challenges because this method involves excluding a control group of individuals from receiving an intervention or treatment even though in many cases there is reason to believe that the treatment may be beneficial. As long as the randomization successfully created equivalent groups, the control group is, by definition, just as deserving of the intervention as the treatment group. Can a researcher managing an RCT still uphold the principles of respect for persons and beneficence while knowingly withholding something thought to be beneficial from research participants? The answer is, it depends. The researcher must answer this question on a case-by-case basis.

When determining whether an RCT is ethical, the researcher should consider whether the study upholds the three principles of respect for persons, beneficence, and justice. To fulfill the respect for persons principle, all participants should provide informed consent. This means that all participants understand that they are participating in a study, why the study is being conducted, and that whether they receive or do not receive the treatment will be determined randomly. When the study is an RCT, it is essential for all potential participants and program managers to understand that study participants may or may not receive treatment. Failing to clarify this is unfair to potential participants and also puts the study at risk.

To fulfill the principle of beneficence, the researcher must be sure that the research project will do no harm. If the treatment consists of a new service that is being introduced to the community for the sake of the RCT, it is difficult to argue that it could make the community worse off since some individuals receive something that they otherwise would not have access to while nothing is taken away from others in the community. Nonetheless, the researcher should take care to evaluate the dynamics of the study in participating communities, because the RCT may strain relationships between members of the treatment and control groups.

Finally, the principle of justice is upheld if the researcher ensures that research participants reflect the population that is likely to benefit from the research.

Consider, for example, a public preschool program with space for only 10 children. Because of limited space and strong interest, this program always turns some families away. Suppose individual preschool teachers are allowed to choose which families get the limited spots available. Under this scenario, 10 families that a given preschool teacher selects are able to use the preschool and all others are denied access because of the space constraint. Now suppose the government would like to implement an RCT to measure the effect of participating in this preschool program. Suppose as well that under this RCT, all interested families are told that they will be entered into a lottery along with other interested families and that all families will have an equal chance for their child to be enrolled in the preschool.

Has the RCT made families interested in preschool worse off? They are not guaranteed access to preschool, but they would not be guaranteed access in the absence of the study either. Whereas before, families were chosen subjectively by the teacher, under the RCT, all families have an equal chance of obtaining a place for their child. Has the RCT made any individual families worse off? Probably. Some families who might have been selected by the teacher in the absence of the study may be randomly assigned to the control group under an RCT. Although some families may become less likely to have access to preschool, others have improved odds. With the RCT, all families have equal probabilities of enrolling their child; this may actually be more fair than letting the teacher determine which children are enrolled.

In other cases, a researcher or organization may introduce a service just for the purpose of evaluating it; in the absence of the study, the service would not be offered. In this case, although individuals assigned to the control group will experience no change in access, individuals assigned to the treatment group will gain access. Although it may seem unfair to deny some people the service under study, it is important to remember that in cases in which the research project provides the service, no one would have received the service in the absence of the RCT. When funding permits, the researcher may choose to expand the service to the control group at the end of the study period. Strategies for implementing RCTs are covered in greater depth in chapters 6, 7, and 8. A more detailed discussion of ethical issues concerning RCTs can be found in Glennerster and Powers (2016).

Conflicts of interest

Thus far this chapter has focused on ensuring that research protects the well-being of potential research participants. In contrast, this subsection discusses how conflicts of interest can compromise the integrity of research. A conflict of interest arises whenever a researcher has a competing financial or personal interest that may compromise his or her ability to conduct research and report the results of that research in an unbiased manner. Conflicts of interest may arise because of competing financial, personal, professional, or academic interests. The following are a few examples:

- *Financial*. A researcher is charged with evaluating a product developed by a company where his wife is an executive. His wife may stand to gain financially if he finds the product to be effective.
- *Personal*. A researcher evaluates a program that her sister developed. Neither one stands to gain financially, but the researcher would like to find that her sister's program is effective.
- *Professional*. A researcher is competing with a coworker for a promotion. He has the opportunity to evaluate a project that his coworker implemented; the results of his evaluation will be part of his coworker's performance review.
- *Academic*. A researcher evaluates a program that she finds has significant effects with one statistical test, but not with several others. She believes that her research is more likely to be published if she reports only the significant results, even though most statistical tests show no effect.

In the first three examples, the researcher should declare his or her conflict of interest to a supervisor. Ideally, someone else would then be assigned to work on the project. In the fourth case, the researcher should state what statistical tests she ran and report the results rather than reporting only the tests with results that support her argument. Ideally, the researcher will identify which tests will be run before beginning the analysis to avoid data mining; such pre-analysis plans are often used, and sometimes required, in medical research.[3]

Especially in the public sector, researchers may be confronted by political conflicts of interest, often having more to do with a supervisor's interests than the researcher's own interests. For example, a minister of education may ask a staff person to conduct an evaluation of his flagship literacy program. The staff person may feel pressure to produce the positive results she knows the minister hopes to see. In some cases, a supervisor may even directly state that the results should show a positive effect.

Under extreme pressure from supervisors, the researcher may have limited options. In these cases, supervisors are not likely to request rigorous impact evaluations because results may be harder to manipulate with such methods. Nonetheless, the researcher can manage expectations by informing her supervisor of the possible outcomes of the research before beginning the work.

Ethical research in practice

Any impact evaluation should involve an ethical review. In some cases, for example, in research that involves analyzing existing data, an ethical review is likely to proceed quickly and lead to the conclusion that there are no ethical concerns (other than perhaps respecting data privacy). In other cases, such as RCTs with individual-level randomization, the ethical review is likely to be more involved. Most organizations have procedures in place for ethical reviews. Researchers should become familiar with the procedures in their organizations before beginning impact evaluations.

Universities and government offices usually have independent ethics committees or IRBs in place to provide independent assessments of the ethics of proposed research. After careful review of the proposed research, these boards may approve, request modifications to, or refuse to approve the proposed research. Conducting human subjects research in an institution that has a functioning IRB or ethics committee without that committee's approval is risky because these committees may order the research to be halted until it has been reviewed. To consider a submission, certain academic journals require IRB approval for human subjects research or will require a statement declaring why it was not necessary; two examples are the *American Economic Review* and the *American Economic Journal: Applied Economics*.

For some types of research, IRB or ethics committee approval is not necessary. This situation may vary by institution, but in general, the following types of research are exempt from IRB review:

- Research involving data in which individuals cannot be identified
- Research involving the use of data that are publicly available (unless the researcher can identify individuals in the data)
- Research conducted in commonly used educational settings, such as comparing two different instructional techniques or classroom management methods (unless test score data will be collected along with unique identifiers)
- Research involving educational tests or classroom observation (unless test score data will be collected along with unique identifiers)

Conclusion

This chapter provides an introduction, with recommendations, to conducting ethical impact evaluations. Ethical standards for medical research were established in response to extreme abuses during World War II and revelations of extremely unethical research in the United States from the 1930s to the 1970s. The Nuremburg Code and the Belmont Report are the founding documents for the conduct of ethical research, and this chapter provides specific recommendations for how to apply the principles in those documents to research on human subjects, and more specifically to the conduct of impact evaluations. Further guidance can be obtained from IRBs at universities and other research institutions.

After reading about the ethical concerns associated with conducting impact evaluations, researchers may be tempted to say that they are better safe than sorry, and decide not to conduct the research they had planned. Although risks may be associated with some types of research, the potential harm to society of not doing research could well be greater. Without research, the world would not have access to life-saving vaccines or medical care, nor would it understand that some social programs are highly effective while others are a waste of scarce public resources. Researchers, and the IRBs or ethics committees that supervise those researchers, have the important task of identifying the occasions when the potential benefit of learning from research outweighs the potential risks the research poses.

Notes

1. This book considers evaluations to be a particular type of research. Because almost all of the literature on ethical conduct applies to research more generally, this chapter covers general research ethics, not just ethical issues in conducting impact evaluations. However, virtually all of the material in this chapter fully applies to ethical conduct of impact evaluations, so that, in general, "research" can be replaced with "evaluations" in the rest of this chapter.
2. For example, the lawsuit filed after the Tuskegee Syphilis Experiment targeted individuals in addition to government agencies (Jones 2008). In another case, nearly 800 plaintiffs filed a lawsuit for nearly $1 billion against Johns Hopkins University for its role in unethical research in Guatemala in which researchers deliberately infected patients with sexually transmitted diseases, including syphilis and gonorrhea (Laughland 2015).
3. See chapter 8 for a discussion of, and advice on, pre-analysis plans.

References

Glennerster, Rachel, and Shawn Powers. 2016. "Balancing Risk and Benefit: Ethical Tradeoffs in Running Randomized Evaluations." In *The Oxford Handbook of Professional Economic Ethics,* edited by G. DeMartino and D. McCloskey, 367–401. New York: Oxford University Press.

Jones, James H. 2008. "The Tuskegee Syphilis Experiment." In *The Oxford Textbook of Clinical Research Ethics,* edited by Ezekiel J. Emanuel, Christine Grady, Robert A. Crouch, Reidar Lie, Franklin G. Miller, and David Wendler, 86–96. Oxford: Oxford University Press.

Laughland, Oliver. 2015. "Guatemalans Deliberately Infected with STDs Sue Johns Hopkins University for $1bn." *The Guardian*, April 3, 2015. https://web.archive.org/web/20150412134055/http://www.theguardian.com/us-news/2015/apr/02/johns-hopkins-lawsuit-deliberate-std-infections-Guatemala.

U.S. Government Printing Office. 1949. *Trials of War Criminals before the Nuremberg Military Tribunals under Control Council Law No. 10, Vol. 2, The Medical Case*, 181–82. Washington, DC: U.S. Government Printing Office. http://history.nih.gov/research/downloads/nuremberg.pdf. Accessed October 9, 2019.

U.S. Health and Human Services Office for Human Research Protections. 1979. "Ethical Principles and Guidelines for the Protection of Human Subjects of Research." Published April 18, 1979. http://www.hhs.gov/ohrp/humansubjects/guidance/belmont.html. Accessed October 9, 2019.

PART III

Nonexperimental Methods

CHAPTER 11

Regression Methods for Nonrandomized Data: Cross-Sectional and Before-After Estimators

Introduction

Earlier chapters consider how to conduct impact evaluations when the treatment, or at least the offer of the treatment, is randomly assigned. This chapter and the six subsequent chapters consider methods that can be applied when the data do not come from a randomized experiment and the people who participate in the program (or policy or project) may be different from those who do not participate. Data that are obtained from the real world and that do not come from an experiment are called *observational data*, *nonexperimental data*, or *nonrandomized data*.

Most randomized evaluations in developing countries have been conducted on new programs that did not exist before the randomized trial was undertaken. In contrast, impact evaluations that are not based on randomized trials almost always are conducted on programs that existed before the evaluation was planned or on programs for which randomization was deemed infeasible. There are two ways in which participation may be nonrandom:

1. The communities in which the programs exist are not randomly chosen.
2. In communities where the program exists, the participants in the program are not randomly assigned. They may have been nonrandomly selected by program administrators, or they may have decided for themselves to participate in (self-selected into) the program.

This chapter has two main objectives. The first is to introduce three basic estimation approaches—cross-sectional, before-after, and difference-in-differences (DID)—through several hypothetical examples. The second is to present key parameters of interest and to discuss the statistical and behavioral assumptions needed to estimate them for the cross-sectional estimator and the before-after estimator. Chapter 12 considers in more detail the DID estimator, as well as the within estimator.

Examples: Cross-sectional, before-after, and difference-in-differences estimators

To begin, consider three simple hypothetical examples that illustrate these estimators and their possible sources of bias.

Example 1: A cross-sectional estimator

The cross-sectional estimator calculates a program's impact by comparing outcomes of participants and nonparticipants in the same period, after the program started.[1] Consider a program that provides loans to poor farmers so that they can buy fertilizer to increase their maize production. Suppose that the only data available were collected one year after the program started, so there are no baseline (before the program started) data. One year after the program started, the farmers who enrolled in the program harvested an average of 1,100 kilograms of maize per hectare (kg/ha), while those who did not enroll harvested an average of 1,000 kg/ha. The cross-sectional estimator attributes this difference in yields to the program, so it calculates a program impact on maize yields of 100 (=1,100 – 1,000) kg/ha.[2] Is 100 kg/ha a plausible estimate of the program impact? Consider the following scenarios:

- *Scenario A*. More-productive farmers are more likely to obtain the loan, because they are more likely to be able to pay back the loan.
- *Scenario B*. Farmers who participate in the program reside in areas where the quality of land is relatively low, because such farmers need more fertilizer to compensate for lower land quality.

Questions for discussion:

- In Scenario A, is the cross-sectional estimator, which compares crop output for enrolled and nonenrolled farmers, biased? If so, what is the direction of the bias?
- In Scenario B, is the cross-sectional estimator biased? If so, what is the direction of the bias?

Example 2: A before-after estimator

The before-after estimator obtains a program's impact by comparing the outcomes of program participants measured after the program started with their outcomes measured before it started. Consider again the program that provides loans to poor farmers so that they can buy fertilizer to increase their maize production. In the year before the program started, the farmers who later enrolled in the program harvested an average of 1,000 kilograms of maize per hectare. One year after the program started, maize yields increased to 1,200 kg/ha. The before-after estimator assumes that all of this change in productivity over time is due to the program and thus assigns a program impact of 200 (=1,200 – 1,000) kg/ha. Is 200 kg/ha a plausible estimate of the program's impact? Consider two scenarios:

- *Scenario A*. Rainfall was normal during the year before the program started, but a drought occurred in the year the program was launched.
- *Scenario B*. A drought occurred in the year before the program started, but rainfall returned to normal during the year the program was launched.

Figure 11.1 illustrates these two scenarios.

As explained in chapter 3, the fundamental problem for estimating the impact of the program on those who participated in it is that the participating farmers' harvests had they not participated cannot be observed. Recalling the notation of chapter 3, this means that for farmers who participate in the program Y_1 is observed but Y_0 is not observed. Similarly, nonparticipating farmers' harvests had they participated cannot be observed; that is, Y_0 is observed, but Y_1 is not observed. For both participating and nonparticipating farmers, the harvest that is not observed is called the *counterfactual.* Turning to program participants, the before-after estimator essentially assumes that the missing counterfactual is equal to the harvest of those farmers before they participated in the program. This is labeled Counterfactual C in figure 11.1: the before-after estimator calculates the program impact as the distance from point C to point O in that figure.

FIGURE 11.1 The before-after estimator and three alternative counterfactuals

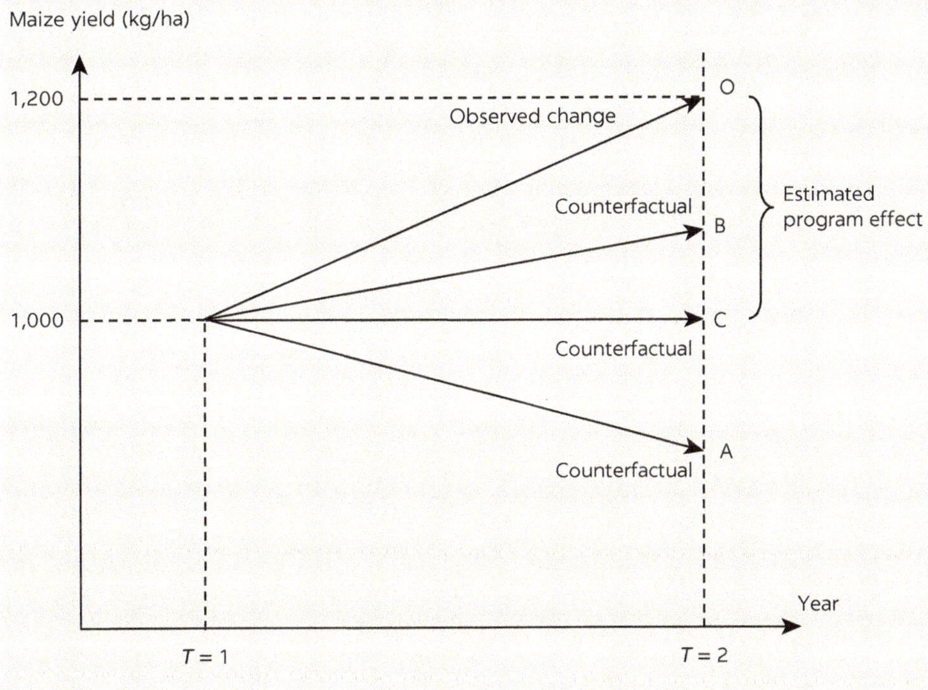

Source: Glewwe and Todd 2019.
Note: kg/ha = kilograms per hectare. See chapter text for description of counterfactuals.

A fundamental concern regarding the before-after estimator is whether the assumed counterfactual is correct. It is possible that the weather in the second period ($T = 2$) was worse than in the first period ($T = 1$), which corresponds to Scenario A, so that the correct counterfactual in figure 11.1 is Counterfactual A. It is also possible that the opposite occurred; that is, the weather in the second period was better than in the first period, which corresponds to Scenario B. If so, the correct counterfactual in figure 11.1 is Counterfactual B.

Questions for discussion:

- What is the direction of bias in the before-after estimator when the weather is worse in the second period than in the first period (for example, a drought occurs in the second period), that is, when Counterfactual A is the correct counterfactual?
- What is the direction of bias in the before-after estimator when the weather is better in the second period than in the first period (for example, a drought occurs in the first period), that is, when Counterfactual B is the correct counterfactual?

Example 3: A difference-in-differences estimator

Finally, consider one last time the loan program to help farmers buy fertilizer. A drought occurred the year before the program started, but rainfall was normal the year the program was launched. Assume that all farmers were affected by the drought and that all of them were affected in a similar way. Assume as well not only that data on maize yields were collected from a random sample of households one year after the program was launched, but also that data were collected from the same households on maize yields before the program was launched, and that both data sets include both participating and nonparticipating farmers. Suppose that, before the program started, the farmers who later enrolled in the program harvested 1,000 kilograms of maize per hectare, and that they harvested 1,150 kg/ha one year after the program started. The farmers who did not enroll in the program harvested 900 kg/ha before the program began, and 1,000 kg/ha one year after the program started. A DID estimator, which can be denoted by Δ_{DID}, combines the before-after and cross-sectional (enrolled-nonenrolled) estimators:

$$\Delta_{DID} = \Delta_1 - \Delta_0 = (Y_{\text{enrolled, after}} - Y_{\text{enrolled, before}}) - (Y_{\text{nonenrolled, after}} - Y_{\text{nonenrolled, before}}),$$

where Y denotes the outcome variable, kilograms of maize harvested per hectare. This yields an estimated impact of (1,150 – 1,000) – (1,000 – 900) = 50 kg/ha. The DID estimator, denoted by Δ_{DID}, removes the influence of time-invariant factors that differ across participants and nonparticipants, such as land quality, as well as the influence of any common time trend, for example, the occurrence of a drought. The time-invariant factors are removed in the Δ_1 and Δ_0 expressions, and the common trend over time is removed by subtracting Δ_0 from Δ_1.

Figure 11.2 illustrates the three estimators discussed thus far. In this figure, all three estimation methods are shown as follows:

- *Before-after.* The estimated effect is the vertical distance between points C and A, which can be expressed as C – A; this ignores any time trend in yields that affects all farmers.
- *Cross-sectional.* The estimated effect is the vertical distance between points C and D, which can be expressed as C – D; this ignores unobserved differences, such as differences in land quality, between the two groups of farmers (participants and nonparticipants).
- *DID.* Estimated effect = (C – A) – (D – B) = C – E; this accounts for both time trends and unobserved differences (that do not change over time) between the two groups.[3]

The rest of this chapter considers how to implement the cross-sectional and before-after estimators within a regression framework, where conditioning (control) variables are included to control for observable differences either between program participants and nonparticipants (cross-sectional estimator) or between time periods for program participants who are observed both before and after the program was implemented (before-after estimator).

FIGURE 11.2 The difference-in-differences estimator

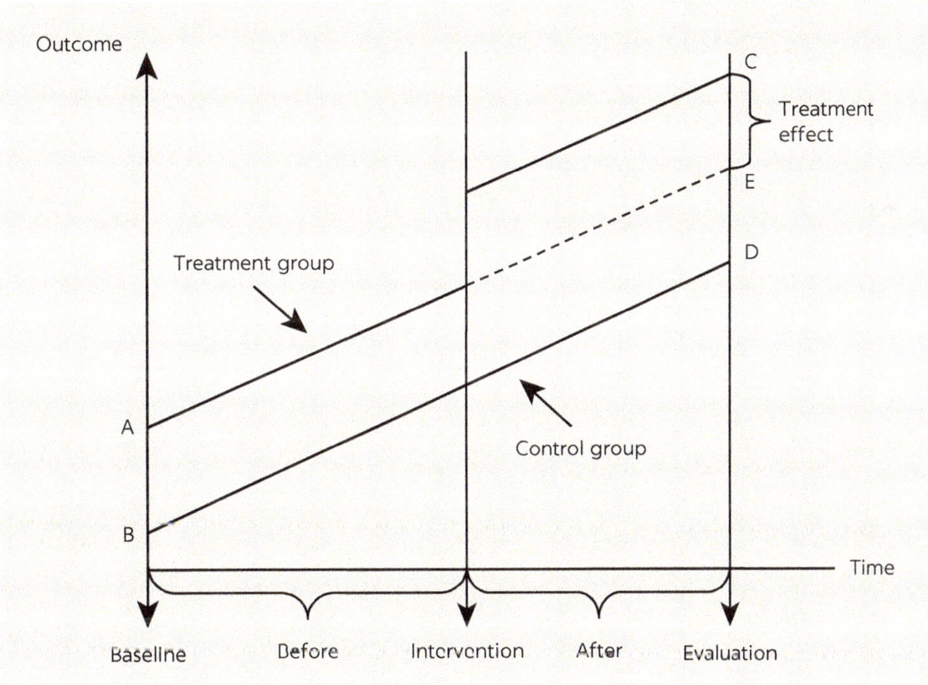

Source: Glewwe and Todd 2019.

Parameters of interest

Recall from chapter 3 the two most common parameters of interest for impact evaluation:

- *Average treatment effect (ATE)*. The average effect of the program for all persons in the population:

$$\text{ATE} \equiv \text{E}[Y_1 - Y_0] = \text{E}[\Delta].$$

- *Average effect of the treatment on the treated (ATT)*. The average effect of the program for program participants:

$$\text{ATT} \equiv \text{E}[Y_1 - Y_0 | P = 1] = \text{E}[\Delta | P = 1].$$

When data are available on observable characteristics (**X**), it is often possible to go further by estimating ATE and ATT for people with characteristics **X** (a vector of observable variables):

$$\text{ATE}(\mathbf{X}) \equiv \text{E}[Y_1 - Y_0 | \mathbf{X}] = \text{E}[\Delta | \mathbf{X}],$$
$$\text{ATT}(\mathbf{X}) \equiv \text{E}[Y_1 - Y_0 | P = 1, \mathbf{X}] = \text{E}[\Delta | P = 1, \mathbf{X}].$$

For example, **X** could simply be a variable that indicates male or female, so that ATE and ATT can be defined separately for men and women. More generally, there could be several variables, an example of which could be that **X** indicates men who are 30–39 years old and who live in rural areas.

If the individuals who participate in the program tend to be the ones who receive the greatest benefit from it, then one would expect ATT > ATE. To see why, assume that the impact of the program does not vary among women or among men, which implies that ATE(**X**) = ATT(**X**) when **X** indicates gender (women or men). If half of the population is women and the other half is men, and the impact of the program is higher for women ($200) than for men ($100) then ATE = $150 (= 0.5 × 200 + 0.5 × 100). However, women may be overrepresented in the participant population (those for whom $P = 1$) because they benefit more from the program. Suppose that three-fourths of the participants are women and only one-fourth are men. Then ATT = $175 (= 0.75 × 200 + 0.25 × 100), and thus ATT > ATE, even though ATE(**X**) = ATT(**X**) for all values of **X**.

The relationship between ATE and ATE(**X**) is that ATE is an average of ATE(**X**) over all possible values of **X**. If **X** consists of only continuous variables, then the relationship between ATE and ATE(**X**) is given by

$$\text{ATE} = \int \text{ATE}(\mathbf{X}) f(\mathbf{X})\, d\mathbf{X},$$

where $f(\mathbf{X})$ is the joint density of **X** (joint distribution of **X**).

Similarly, the relationship between ATT and ATT(**X**) is that ATT is an average of ATT(**X**) over all possible values of **X** for which at least some individuals participate in the program ($P = 1$). Again, if **X** contains only continuous variables, then the relationship between ATT and ATT(**X**) is

$$\text{ATT} = \int \text{ATT}(\mathbf{X})\, f(\mathbf{X} \mid P = 1)\, d\mathbf{X}$$

where $f(\mathbf{X} \mid P = 1)$ is the (conditional) joint density of **X** for program participants.

The following two sections consider two commonly used regression estimators: the cross-sectional estimator and the before-after estimator.

The cross-sectional estimator and sources of bias

The cross-sectional estimator uses data on a comparison group of nonparticipants to impute counterfactual outcomes for program participants. The data requirements of this estimator are minimal; one needs only data on participants ($P_{it} = 1$) and on nonparticipants ($P_{it} = 0$) at some period t after the participants enrolled in the program.[4] This notation is the same as in the previous section, except that it is modified to allow for an individual subscript i and a time subscript t:

Y_{1it} = value of Y for person i at time t if he or she participated in the program before time t
Y_{0it} = value of Y for person i at time t if he or she did not participate in the program before time t

As before, each person has both a Y_{1it} and a Y_{0it}, but only Y_{1it} is observed for those who are participants, and only Y_{0it} is observed for those who are nonparticipants.

The outcomes Y_{1it} and Y_{0it} could be measured at a particular time either during the course of a program or after an individual's participation in the program. The outcomes might also represent average values over some period, such as average earnings over the 18 months following the start of a job training program.

Let Y_{it} be the observed value of Y, which will be Y_{1it} for program participants and Y_{0it} for program nonparticipants. In general, for any group with characteristics **X**, the difference between the mean (average) of Y_{it} for that group's program participants ($P = 1$ group), for whom $Y_{it} = Y_{1it}$, and the mean of Y_{it} for that group's program nonparticipants ($P = 0$ group), for whom $Y_{it} = Y_{0it}$, will not provide a consistent (unbiased) estimate of either ATE(**X**) or ATT(**X**). To see how bias can come about, assume that for any person in the population the values of Y_{1it} (the value of Y at time t if person i participates in the program before time t) and Y_{0it} (the value of Y at time t if person i does not participate before time t) can be expressed as simple linear functions of the **X** variables for that person, plus an error term:

$$Y_{1it} = \mathbf{X}_i'\boldsymbol{\beta}_1 + U_{1it} \tag{11.1}$$

$$Y_{0it} = \mathbf{X}_i'\boldsymbol{\beta}_0 + U_{0it}. \tag{11.2}$$

These equations for Y_{1it} and Y_{0it} are *causal* relationships; they indicate how changes in the $\mathbf{X}_i$ variables change the values of Y_{1it} and Y_{0it}. Assume that $\text{E}[U_{1it}| \mathbf{X}_i] = \text{E}[U_{0it}| \mathbf{X}_i] = 0$, which is the conventional assumption that the unobserved components of outcomes are not correlated with the $\mathbf{X}_i$ variables (equivalently, the assumption can be written as $\text{E}[Y_{1it}| \mathbf{X}_i] = \mathbf{X}_i'\boldsymbol{\beta}_1$ and $\text{E}[Y_{0it}| \mathbf{X}_i] = \mathbf{X}_i'\boldsymbol{\beta}_0$).[5] For simplicity of notation, also assume that the $\mathbf{X}_i$ variables are not time-varying.[6] In most cases, $\mathbf{X}_i$ includes a constant term.

As explained in chapter 3, the observed value, Y_{it}, can be written as $Y_{it} = P_{it}Y_{1it} + (1 - P_{it})Y_{0it}$. Substituting equations (11.1) and (11.2) for Y_{0it} and Y_{1it} into this equation for Y_{it} allows Y_{it} to be expressed as

$$Y_{it} = P_{it}(\mathbf{X}_i'\boldsymbol{\beta}_1 + U_{1it}) + (1 - P_{it})(\mathbf{X}_i'\boldsymbol{\beta}_0 + U_{0it}).$$

Regrouping terms yields

$$Y_{it} = \mathbf{X}_i'\boldsymbol{\beta}_0 + P_{it}(\mathbf{X}_i'\boldsymbol{\beta}_1 - \mathbf{X}_i'\boldsymbol{\beta}_0) + \{U_{0it} + P_{it}(U_{1it} - U_{0it})\}. \tag{11.3}$$

What does this expression have to do with ATE($\mathbf{X}$) and ATT($\mathbf{X}$)? It is relatively easy to manipulate this expression to show what assumptions are needed to be able to use a cross-sectional regression estimator to estimate the ATE($\mathbf{X}$) or the ATT($\mathbf{X}$) parameters. Before doing so, it is useful to modify the notation slightly to indicate the ATE($\mathbf{X}$) and ATT($\mathbf{X}$) that pertain to individual *i*. For that individual, $\mathbf{X} = \mathbf{X}_i$, so the relevant ATE and ATT expressions can be denoted by ATE($\mathbf{X} = \mathbf{X}_i$) and ATT($\mathbf{X} = \mathbf{X}_i$). This notation, instead of ATE($\mathbf{X}_i$) and ATT($\mathbf{X}_i$), is used to indicate that these expressions apply to any person whose $\mathbf{X}$ variables are equal to $\mathbf{X}_i$, not just individual *i*. That is, ATE($\mathbf{X} = \mathbf{X}_i$) and ATT($\mathbf{X} = \mathbf{X}_i$) are averages over all individuals in the population for whom $\mathbf{X} = \mathbf{X}_i$.

The definition of ATE($\mathbf{X}$) implies that, whenever $\mathbf{X} = \mathbf{X}_i$, then ATE($\mathbf{X} = \mathbf{X}_i$) is defined as $\text{E}[Y_1 - Y_0| \mathbf{X} = \mathbf{X}_i]$. This conditional expectation applies to all members of the population for whom $\mathbf{X} = \mathbf{X}_i$, including individual *i*, which implies that $\text{ATE}(\mathbf{X} = \mathbf{X}_i) = \text{E}[Y_{1it} - Y_{0it}| \mathbf{X} = \mathbf{X}_i] = \text{E}[Y_{1it} - Y_{0it}| \mathbf{X}_i]$. Substituting equations (11.1) and (11.2) for Y_{1it} and Y_{0it} and rearranging terms yields an expression for ATE($\mathbf{X} = \mathbf{X}_i$) in terms of the components for those expressions:

$$\begin{aligned}
\text{ATE}(\mathbf{X} = \mathbf{X}_i) &= \text{E}[Y_{1it} - Y_{0it}| \mathbf{X} = \mathbf{X}_i] \\
&= \text{E}[Y_{1it} - Y_{0it}| \mathbf{X}_i] \\
&= \text{E}[(\mathbf{X}_i'\boldsymbol{\beta}_1 + U_{1it}) - (\mathbf{X}_i'\boldsymbol{\beta}_0 + U_{0it})| \mathbf{X}_i] \\
&= \text{E}[(\mathbf{X}_i'\boldsymbol{\beta}_1 - \mathbf{X}_i'\boldsymbol{\beta}_0)| \mathbf{X}_i] + \text{E}[U_{1it}| \mathbf{X}_i] - \text{E}[U_{0it}| \mathbf{X}_i] \\
&= (\mathbf{X}_i'\boldsymbol{\beta}_1 - \mathbf{X}_i'\boldsymbol{\beta}_0) \text{ (recall that } \text{E}[U_{1it}| \mathbf{X}_i] = \text{E}[U_{0it}| \mathbf{X}_i] = 0).
\end{aligned} \tag{11.4}$$

Equation (11.4) is valid for all values of $\mathbf{X}_i$, so it is the case that ATE($\mathbf{X}$) = ($\mathbf{X}'\boldsymbol{\beta}_1 - \mathbf{X}'\boldsymbol{\beta}_0$) for any $\mathbf{X}$. Thus, consistent (unbiased) estimates of ATE($\mathbf{X}$) can be obtained if consistent estimates of $\boldsymbol{\beta}_0$ and $\boldsymbol{\beta}_1$ can be obtained, so the question becomes,

> Under what assumptions can regression methods be used on cross-sectional data to consistently estimate $\boldsymbol{\beta}_0$ and $\boldsymbol{\beta}_1$?

The starting point to answer this question is to note that, given equation (11.4) for ATE($\mathbf{X} = \mathbf{X}_i$), equation (11.3) for Y_{it} can be written as

$$Y_{it} = \mathbf{X}_i'\boldsymbol{\beta}_0 + P_{it} \times \text{ATE}(\mathbf{X} = \mathbf{X}_i) + \{U_{0it} + P_{it}(U_{1it} - U_{0it})\}. \tag{11.5}$$

It can also be shown (by adding and subtracting the term $P_{it}\text{E}[U_{1it} - U_{0it}| \mathbf{X}_i, P_{it} = 1]$ and rearranging terms) that Y_{it} in equation (11.3) can also be written as a function of ATT($\mathbf{X} = \mathbf{X}_i$) as follows:[7]

$$Y_{it} = \mathbf{X}_i'\boldsymbol{\beta}_0 + P_{it} \times \text{ATT}(\mathbf{X} = \mathbf{X}_i) + \{U_{0it} + P_{it} \times (U_{1it} - U_{0it} - \text{E}[U_{1it} - U_{0it}| \mathbf{X}_i, P_{it} = 1])\}. \tag{11.6}$$

Equations (11.5) and (11.6) can be used to show the assumptions needed to apply ordinary least squares (OLS) to obtain estimates of ATE($\mathbf{X}$) or ATT($\mathbf{X}$).

Consider ATE($\mathbf{X}$). Equation (11.5) suggests that if Y_{it} is regressed on $\mathbf{X}_i$ and on P_{it} interacted with $\mathbf{X}_i$, the coefficients on those interaction terms can be used to obtain consistent estimates of ATE($\mathbf{X}$). More specifically, because ATE($\mathbf{X} = \mathbf{X}_i$) = ($\mathbf{X}_i'\boldsymbol{\beta}_1 - \mathbf{X}_i'\boldsymbol{\beta}_0$) = $\mathbf{X}_i'(\boldsymbol{\beta}_1 - \boldsymbol{\beta}_0)$, equation (11.5) can be written as $Y_{it} = \mathbf{X}_i'\boldsymbol{\beta}_0 + P_{it}\,\mathbf{X}_i'(\boldsymbol{\beta}_1 - \boldsymbol{\beta}_0) + \{U_{0it} + P_{it}(U_{1it} - U_{0it})\}$; this suggests a regression of Y_{it} on $\mathbf{X}_i$ and the interaction terms $P_{it}\mathbf{X}_i$ to obtain estimates of $\boldsymbol{\beta}_0$ and $\boldsymbol{\beta}_1 - \boldsymbol{\beta}_0$, the sum of which also provides an estimate of $\boldsymbol{\beta}_1$.

However, this OLS regression will yield unbiased and consistent estimates of $\boldsymbol{\beta}_0$ and $\boldsymbol{\beta}_1 - \boldsymbol{\beta}_0$, and thus of ATE($\mathbf{X}$), which equals $\mathbf{X}_i'(\boldsymbol{\beta}_1 - \boldsymbol{\beta}_0)$, only if the error term $\{U_{0it} + P_{it}(U_{1it} - U_{0it})\}$ is uncorrelated with both P_{it} and the included regressors $\mathbf{X}_i$. In other words, for this OLS regression to yield a consistent estimate of ATE($\mathbf{X}$), the following assumption must be made:

$$\text{E}[U_{0it} + P_{it}(U_{1it} - U_{0it})| \mathbf{X}_i, P_{it}] = 0.$$

This assumption is credible if people do not know their values of U_{0it} and U_{1it} (the factors not in the data that determine Y_1 and Y_0) when deciding whether to participate in the program. In that case, $\text{E}[U_{0it} + P_{it}(U_{1it} - U_{0it})| \mathbf{X}_i, P_{it}] = \text{E}[U_{0it} + P_{it}(U_{1it} - U_{0it})| \mathbf{X}_i] = 0$.[8]

This assumption can also be expressed in a different way. Because P_{it} is binary (has only the values 0 or 1), the required assumption can equivalently be written as[9]

$$\text{Prob}[P_{it} = 1| U_{0it}, U_{1it}, \mathbf{X}_i] = \text{Prob}[P_{it} = 1| \mathbf{X}_i].$$

This explicitly shows that U_{0it} and U_{1it} must not influence program participation decisions. This means that, of the factors that determine Y_{1it} and Y_{0it} in equations (11.1) and (11.2), only those that are observed ($\mathbf{X}_i$) should have predictive power for program participation. In other words, *all* factors that determine Y_{1it} and Y_{0it} *and* predict program participation must be observed in the data.

To use the same OLS regression to estimate ATT(**X**), equation (11.6) suggests that an OLS regression of Y_{it} on $\mathbf{X}_i$ and $P_{it} \times \mathbf{X}_i$ yields an estimate of the parameters that determine ATT(**X**) if the following assumption holds:[10]

$$E[U_{0it} + P_{it} \times (U_{1it} - U_{0it} - E[U_{1it} - U_{0it} | \mathbf{X}_i, P_{it} = 1]) | \mathbf{X}_i, P_{it}] = 0.$$

This assumption simplifies to $E[U_{0it} | \mathbf{X}_i, P_{it}] = 0$, which can be seen by considering the two possible values of P_{it}. If $P_{it} = 0$, this simplification is obvious. If $P_{it} = 1$, the expression $E[P_{it} \times (U_{1it} - U_{0it} - E[U_{1it} - U_{0it} | \mathbf{X}_i, P_{it} = 1]) | \mathbf{X}_i, P_{it}]$ becomes $E[(U_{1it} - U_{0it} - E[U_{1it} - U_{0it} | \mathbf{X}_i, P_{it} = 1]) | \mathbf{X}_i, P_{it} = 1]$; this equals $E[U_{1it} - U_{0it} | \mathbf{X}_i, P_{it} = 1] - E[U_{1it} - U_{0it} | \mathbf{X}_i, P_{it} = 1]$ and thus equals 0, so again the assumption becomes $E[U_{0it} | \mathbf{X}_i, P_{it}] = 0$.

Thus, to estimate ATT(**X**), the only assumption needed is that $E[U_{0it} | \mathbf{X}_i, P_{it}] = 0$. Equivalently, the required assumption can be written as

$$\text{Prob}[P_{it} = 1 | U_{0it}, \mathbf{X}_i] = \text{Prob}[P_{it} = 1 | \mathbf{X}_i],$$

which shows explicitly that to estimate ATT(**X**) using OLS, individuals' participation decisions cannot be based on U_{0it}. Recall that estimating ATE(**X**) by OLS requires a stronger assumption, that $E[U_{0it} + P_{it}(U_{1it} - U_{0it}) | \mathbf{X}_i, P_{it}] = 0$. This assumption is stronger because it also assumes something about U_{1it}; that is, that the part of the expected gain from participating in the program that is due to unobserved factors cannot be higher for participants than for nonparticipants, which implies that the expected gain for both groups equals 0.[11]

The intuition for why estimation of ATT(**X**) does not require making an assumption about U_{1it} is as follows: ATT(**X**) is the impact of the program (treatment) on the treated, that is, for the population with $P = 1$. For that population, Y_{1it} can be observed, so to estimate ATT(**X**) the only counterfactual needed is an estimate of Y_{0it}. Thus some assumptions about Y_{0it} are needed to estimate it, and because $Y_{0it} = \mathbf{X}_i'\boldsymbol{\beta}_0 + U_{0it}$, some assumptions about U_{0it} must be made. In contrast, to estimate ATE(**X**), values of Y_{1it} must be estimated for the members of the population who do not participate in the program, for whom $P_{it} = 0$. This requires some assumptions about Y_{1it}, and because $Y_{1it} = \mathbf{X}_i'\boldsymbol{\beta}_1 + U_{1it}$, some assumptions must be made about U_{1it} (in addition to making the assumptions about U_{0it}).

Heckman, Lalonde, and Smith (1999) provide a useful framework for understanding the different kinds of assumptions needed to estimate ATE(**X**) and ATT(**X**). They consider three scenarios, in order of increasing generality.

Scenario 1. Conditional on **X**, the program effect is the same for everyone ($U_{1it} = U_{0it}$).

Scenario 2. Conditional on **X**, the program effect varies across individuals ($U_{1it} \neq U_{0it}$), but even so, $U_{1it} - U_{0it}$ does not predict program participation.

Scenario 3. Conditional on **X**, the program effect varies across individuals, and $U_{1it} - U_{0it}$ predicts who participates in the program.

Together, these three scenarios cover all possible relationships between U_{1it}, U_{0it}, and program participation (P_{it}).

For Scenario 1, there is no treatment impact heterogeneity (no variation in the impact of the program) except for that due to variation in **X** ($\Delta_i = Y_{1i} - Y_{0i} = \mathbf{X}_i'\boldsymbol{\beta}_1 - \mathbf{X}_i'\boldsymbol{\beta}_0 + U_{1it} - U_{0it} = \mathbf{X}_i'\boldsymbol{\beta}_1 - \mathbf{X}_i'\boldsymbol{\beta}_0$). That is, everyone with the same observed characteristics (same $\mathbf{X}_i$) receives exactly the same impact from participation in the program. In contrast, Scenario 2 allows for impact heterogeneity beyond the heterogeneity due to variation in **X**, yet this additional heterogeneity from allowing U_{0it} to be different from U_{1it} operates only after the fact; it was not acted upon at the time individuals decided whether to participate in the program, presumably because they had no information at that time on how this additional heterogeneity would affect their program impact and so they could not act on that information. In other words, when they decided whether to participate in the program they had no information about themselves that would predict the program's impact on them other than the information contained in $\mathbf{X}_i$. (Strictly speaking, they did not know the $U_{1it} - U_{0it}$ component of their overall treatment effect when deciding whether to participate, so $U_{1it} - U_{0it}$ could not affect their decision to participate.) Under Scenario 3, individuals have information beyond that contained in **X** about what their future benefit from participating in the program will be, so they act on that information when they decide whether to participate.

Under Scenarios 1 or 2, ATE(**X**) = ATT(**X**). This can be seen by noting that ATE($\mathbf{X} = \mathbf{X}_i$) = ATT($\mathbf{X} = \mathbf{X}_i$) for any $\mathbf{X}_i$:

$$\begin{aligned}
\text{ATT}(\mathbf{X} = \mathbf{X}_i) &\equiv \text{E}[Y_{1it} - Y_{0it} | \mathbf{X} = \mathbf{X}_i, P_{it} = 1] \\
&= \text{E}[\mathbf{X}_i'\boldsymbol{\beta}_1 - \mathbf{X}_i'\boldsymbol{\beta}_0 + U_{1it} - U_{0it} | \mathbf{X}_i, P_{it} = 1] \\
&= \mathbf{X}_i'\boldsymbol{\beta}_1 - \mathbf{X}_i'\boldsymbol{\beta}_0 + \text{E}[U_{1it} - U_{0it} | \mathbf{X}_i, P_{it} = 1] \\
&= \text{ATE}(\mathbf{X} = \mathbf{X}_i) + \text{E}[U_{1it} - U_{0it} | \mathbf{X}_i, P_{it} = 1].
\end{aligned}$$

If Scenario 1 holds, the term $\text{E}[U_{1it} - U_{0it} | \mathbf{X}_i, P_{it} = 1]$ equals 0. It also equals 0 if Scenario 2 holds, because that scenario assumes that $\text{E}[U_{1it} - U_{0it} | \mathbf{X}_i, P_{it} = 1] = \text{E}[U_{1it} - U_{0it} | \mathbf{X}_i]$, which also equals zero. Thus ATT(**X**) = ATE(**X**) = $\mathbf{X}'\boldsymbol{\beta}_1 - \mathbf{X}'\boldsymbol{\beta}_0$ for both Scenario 1 and Scenario 2.

Under Scenarios 1 and 2, it is assumed that individuals do not use information on their future values of U_{0it} and U_{1it} when they are deciding whether to participate in the program. This assumption is most plausible when the major determinants of program participation are already accounted for by controlling for **X**. The assumptions that $U_{1it} = U_{0it}$ (Scenario 1) or alternatively that $\text{E}[U_{1it} - U_{0it} | \mathbf{X}_i, P_{it}] = 0$ (Scenario 2) do not necessarily imply that $\text{E}[U_{0it} | \mathbf{X}_i, P_{it}] = 0$, which is the assumption necessary for the OLS cross-sectional estimation to produce a consistent estimate of ATT(**X**). However, it is hard to imagine cases in which people select into programs on the basis of anticipated values of U_{1it} only, and not also on anticipated values of U_{0it}. Thus it would be reasonable to expect that when $E[U_{1it} - U_{0it}| \mathbf{X}_i, P_{it}] = 0$, it is also the case that $E[U_{0it}| \mathbf{X}_i, P_{it}] = 0$ and $E[U_{1it}| \mathbf{X}_i, P_{it}] = 0$, so the cross-sectional estimator generally yields consistent estimates of ATE(**X**) and ATT(**X**) under Scenarios 1 and 2 (indeed, under those scenarios ATE(**X**) = ATT(**X**)).

Scenario 3 assumes that individuals have information about their (future) values of U_{1it} and U_{0it} and that they use this information when they make their program participation decisions. This case is often referred to as *selection on unobservables*. Bias in estimating ATE(**X**) can arise if either $E[U_{0it}| \mathbf{X}_i, P_{it}] \neq 0$ or $E[U_{1it}| \mathbf{X}_i, P_{it}] \neq 0$. Bias in estimating ATT(**X**) arises only if $E[U_{0it}| \mathbf{X}_i, P] \neq 0$. In general, the cross-sectional regression estimator is not consistent under Scenario 3 and alternative evaluation methods need to be used.

To summarize, consistency of the cross-sectional regression estimator requires that the error term in the regression not be correlated with either **X** or *P*. This restriction is violated, and thus the cross-sectional regression estimator is biased and inconsistent, if people choose to participate in the program on the basis of their anticipated future gain from the program $U_{1it} - U_{0it}$ that is not captured by **X**. If the researcher has an extensive and rich set of control variables **X**, then the assumption that selection is on observables only may be satisfied. But when the data are missing key factors that determine program participation decisions, then it is plausible that there are unobservables that are systematically related to participation, which can lead to bias in estimation based on cross-sectional regressions.

For example, consider unobservable characteristics such as motivation, intellectual ability, or other advantages. These characteristics are likely to be correlated both with the outcome variable and with participation in or access to the treatment. For instance, more-motivated people may be more likely to participate in the program and their motivation may enable them to obtain greater benefit from the program.

More generally, any unobserved characteristics that lead to greater benefits (that is, greater $U_{1it} - U_{0it}$, which leads to greater $Y_{1it} - Y_{0it}$) are likely to increase the probability of participating in the program, in which case both Scenario 1 and Scenario 2 are unlikely to hold. These unobserved variables introduce potential bias into the treatment effect estimates. Whether the restrictions needed to justify application of a cross-sectional estimator are satisfied will depend in part on whether the data include a rich set of covariates **X** that capture the major determinants of the program participation decision. In that case, it might be plausible that selection is on observables and that the remaining variation in who participates after conditioning on **X** can be attributed to random factors that are uncorrelated with the outcomes (as required under Scenario 2). Even though the cross-sectional estimator imposes strong assumptions on the program participation process, the estimator is commonly used in evaluation work because of its minimal data requirements.

The before-after estimator

The before-after estimator of the impact of a program on the outcome variable *Y* is based on a comparison of the average value of *Y* for a group of individuals before they participate in the program with the average value of Y for the same individuals after they participate in the program. Because all of these individuals are program participants, such an estimate is an estimate of ATT; in general, there are no data on individuals who do not participate in the program so it is not possible to estimate ATE. This section explains how the before-after estimator is implemented and the assumptions needed to ensure that it provides a consistent (unbiased) estimate of ATT.

Suppose that panel data, that is, data collected from the same people for two or more periods, are available and that only program participants are in the data. For both of the potential outcomes (Y_{1it} and Y_{0it}), assume the same linear model (equations (11.1) and (11.2)) used in the previous section:

$$Y_{1it} = \mathbf{X}_{it}'\boldsymbol{\beta}_1 + U_{1it},$$
$$Y_{0it} = \mathbf{X}_{it}'\boldsymbol{\beta}_0 + U_{0it}.$$

Note, however, that the $\mathbf{X}_{it}$ variables may now be either fixed (for example, gender) or time varying (for example, age), but they are assumed to be unaffected by an individual's participation in the program. As in the previous sections, the error terms U_{1it} and U_{0it} are assumed to satisfy $\mathrm{E}[U_{1it}|\, \mathbf{X}_{it}] = \mathrm{E}[U_{0it}|\, \mathbf{X}_{it}] = 0$.

Suppose that the program intervention took place in period t_0. For $t < t_0$, none of the individuals had yet participated in the program, so Y_{0it} is observed, and $P_{it} = 0$. For $t > t_0$, Y_{1it} is observed, and $P_{it} = 1$.

Using equation (11.3), the observed outcome at any time t can be written as

$$Y_{it} = \mathbf{X}_{it}'\boldsymbol{\beta}_0 + P_{it}\Delta(\mathbf{X}_{it}) + U_{0it},$$

where P_{it} denotes having participated in the program and $\Delta(\mathbf{X}_{it}) = \mathbf{X}_{it}'\boldsymbol{\beta}_1 - \mathbf{X}_{it}'\boldsymbol{\beta}_0 + U_{1it} - U_{0it}$ is the treatment impact for individual i (note that this varies across i even for individuals with the same $\mathbf{X}_{it}$, due to $U_{1it} - U_{0it}$, and that it is not an average treatment effect).

Recall from chapter 3 that the evaluation problem can be viewed as a missing data problem; because each person is observed in only one of two potential states (treated or untreated) at any time, the missing state needs to be imputed. The before-after estimator addresses the missing data problem by using preprogram data to impute the missing counterfactual outcome.

Let t' and t'' denote two periods, the former before and the latter after the program intervention. The goal is to estimate the impact of the program on a person who participates between those two periods. In the notation of the panel data model, define the average treatment effect on a treated individual i at time t'', denoted by $\mathrm{ATT}(\mathbf{X} = \mathbf{X}_{it''})$, as

$$\mathrm{ATT}(\mathbf{X} = \mathbf{X}_{it''}) = \mathrm{E}[\Delta(\mathbf{X}_{it''})|\, P_{it''} = 1, P_{it'} = 0, \mathbf{X} = \mathbf{X}_{it''}],$$

where the conditioning on $P_{it''} = 1$ and $P_{it'} = 0$ indicates that the person had not yet participated in the program at time t' but had participated in the program by time t''.

The before-after estimator of the impact of the program on program participant i at time t'' is simply $Y_{it''} - Y_{it'}$, which can be written as follows:

$$Y_{it''} - Y_{it'} = \mathbf{X}_{it''}'\boldsymbol{\beta}_1 - \mathbf{X}_{it'}'\boldsymbol{\beta}_0 + U_{1it''} - U_{0it'}. \tag{11.7}$$

To show how OLS can be used to obtain an estimate of ATT($\mathbf{X} = \mathbf{X}_{it''}$), equation (11.7) can be rewritten as follows:

$$\begin{aligned}
Y_{it''} - Y_{it'} &= \mathbf{X}_{it''}'\boldsymbol{\beta}_1 - \mathbf{X}_{it'}'\boldsymbol{\beta}_0 + \mathrm{E}[\Delta(\mathbf{X}_{it''}) \mid P_{it''} = 1, P_{it'} = 0, \mathbf{X}_{it''}] \\
&\quad - \mathrm{E}[\Delta(\mathbf{X}_{it''}) \mid P_{it''} = 1, P_{it'} = 0, \mathbf{X}_{it''}] + U_{1it''} - U_{0it'} \\
&= \mathbf{X}_{it''}'\boldsymbol{\beta}_1 - \mathbf{X}_{it'}'\boldsymbol{\beta}_0 + \mathrm{ATT}(\mathbf{X} = \mathbf{X}_{it''}) \\
&\quad - \mathrm{E}[\mathbf{X}_{it''}'\boldsymbol{\beta}_1 - \mathbf{X}_{it''}'\boldsymbol{\beta}_0 + U_{1it''} - U_{0it''} \mid P_{it''} = 1, P_{it'} = 0, \mathbf{X}_{it''}] + U_{1it''} - U_{0it'} \\
&= \mathbf{X}_{it''}'\boldsymbol{\beta}_1 - \mathbf{X}_{it'}'\boldsymbol{\beta}_0 - \mathbf{X}_{it''}'\boldsymbol{\beta}_1 + \mathbf{X}_{it''}'\boldsymbol{\beta}_0 + \mathrm{ATT}(\mathbf{X} = \mathbf{X}_{it''}) \\
&\quad - \mathrm{E}[U_{1it''} - U_{0it''} \mid P_{it''} = 1, P_{it'} = 0, \mathbf{X}_{it''}] + U_{1it''} - U_{0it'} \\
&= (\mathbf{X}_{it''} - \mathbf{X}_{it'})'\boldsymbol{\beta}_0 + \mathrm{ATT}(\mathbf{X} = \mathbf{X}_{it''}) - \mathrm{E}[U_{1it''} - U_{0it''} \mid P_{it''} = 1, P_{it'} = 0, \mathbf{X}_{it''}] \\
&\quad + U_{1it''} - U_{0it''} + U_{0it''} - U_{0it'}.
\end{aligned}$$

The last expression implies that OLS can be used to estimate the following:

$$Y_{it''} - Y_{it'} = (\mathbf{X}_{it''} - \mathbf{X}_{it'})'\boldsymbol{\beta}_0 + \mathrm{ATT}(\mathbf{X} = \mathbf{X}_{it''}) + \varepsilon_{it''}, \tag{11.8}$$

where the residual term is

$$\varepsilon_{it''} = (U_{1it''} - U_{0it''} - \mathrm{E}[U_{1it''} - U_{0it''} \mid P_{it''} = 1, P_{it'} = 0, \mathbf{X}_{it''}]) + U_{0it''} - U_{0it'}. \tag{11.9}$$

Equation (11.8) suggests that the treatment impact can be obtained from a regression of the difference $Y_{it''} - Y_{it'}$ on $(\mathbf{X}_{it''} - \mathbf{X}_{it'})$ and also on $\mathbf{X}_{it''}$ in levels. The coefficients on $\mathbf{X}_{it''}$, along with the constant term, are estimates of $\boldsymbol{\beta}_1 - \boldsymbol{\beta}_0 + \mathrm{E}[U_{1it''} - U_{0it''} \mid P_{it''} = 1, P_{it'} = 0, \mathbf{X}_{it''}]$ and thus provide estimates of ATT($\mathbf{X} = \mathbf{X}_{it''}$).[12] Note that including the $(\mathbf{X}_{it''} - \mathbf{X}_{it'})$ variables in this regression controls for any time-varying $\mathbf{X}_{it}$ variables. If none of the regressors $\mathbf{X}_{it}$ is time varying, then the regression simplifies to a regression of $Y_{it''} - Y_{it'}$ on $\mathbf{X}_{it''}$ (because the term involving $\mathbf{X}_{it''} - \mathbf{X}_{it'}$ equals 0).

The main drawback of the before-after estimation strategy is that it assumes that $\boldsymbol{\beta}_1$ and $\boldsymbol{\beta}_0$ do not change over time, so it does not allow for estimation of time-specific intercepts. Thus the program effect estimates potentially conflate program impacts with time effects that would have arisen independently of the program. An important example is that the constant term in

β_0 may change over time, as shown in figure 11.2 for the case in which the only **X** variable is a vector of ones; the coefficient on this variable is the constant term, and the positive slope for the control group in that figure indicates that the constant term has increased over time.

Another assumption that is required when applying the before-after estimator to estimate ATT($\mathbf{X}_{it''}$) is that $E[\varepsilon_{it''} \mid P_{it''} = 1, P_{it'} = 0, \mathbf{X}_{it''}] = 0$. The term that appears in parentheses in equation (11.9) has a conditional mean of 0 by construction:

$$E[U_{1it''} - U_{0it''} - E[U_{1it''} - U_{0it''} \mid P_{it''} = 1, P_{it'} = 0, \mathbf{X}_{it''}] \mid P_{it''} = 1, P_{it'} = 0, \mathbf{X}_{it''}] = 0,$$

so the key assumption needed to ensure that $E[\varepsilon_{it''} \mid P_{it''} = 1, P_{it'} = 0, \mathbf{X}_{it''}] = 0$ is

$$E[U_{0it''} - U_{0it'} \mid P_{it''} = 1, P_{it'} = 0, \mathbf{X}_{it''}] = 0.$$

An interesting case in which this assumption is satisfied is when $U_{0it'}$ and $U_{0it''}$ can be decomposed into a fixed effect error structure:

$$U_{0it} = f_i + v_{it}, \text{ for } t = t', t'',$$

where f_i is fixed over time and v_{it} satisfies $E[v_{it''} - v_{it'} \mid P_{it''} = 1, P_{it'} = 0, \mathbf{X}_{it''}] = 0$. Intuitively, this assumption allows selection into the program to be based on unobservable characteristics that are time invariant (called f_i here), which could be correlated with $P_{it'}$ or $P_{it''}$. These fixed unobservables are "differenced out" of the expression $U_{0it''} - U_{0it'}$.

Thus, a before-after estimation strategy allows the presence of person-specific permanent unobservables that affect both the program participation decision and the outcome variables, Y_0 and Y_1, as long as these unobservables are fixed over time. In other words, the estimator allows, to some extent, for program participation decisions to be based on anticipated gains (as in Scenario 3); ATT(**X**) can be consistently estimated as long as the required condition on $U_{0it''} - U_{0it'}$ is satisfied. Essentially, the fixed effect error structure implies that past values of U_{0it} do not forecast future values of U_{0it} that may then be correlated with program participation decisions.[13]

The regression described above has one preprogram and one postprogram observation for each person and is estimated only for people who eventually participate in the program. The next chapter considers an extension of this framework to the case in which there are at least two periods of data available on both participants and nonparticipants and shows the advantages of having such data.

Conclusion

The main potential problem with using the simple cross-sectional regression estimator to estimate program impacts is one of selection bias. The individuals who participate in the program may differ systematically from those who do not in ways that are not fully captured by the included **X** covariates. Thus there is a risk that these differences are being mistakenly incorporated into the estimate of the program impact. The assumptions needed to justify a cross-sectional regression estimator are most likely to be satisfied when the data include rich information on **X** that can be used to control for differences in the observed characteristics of program participants and nonparticipants that are related to their outcomes and that may be driving their program participation decisions.

The main potential problem with applying the before-after estimator is that changes over time that have nothing to do with the impact of the program may be mistakenly included as part of the estimated program effect. Economy-wide effects could be affecting outcomes such as earnings or employment, or regional weather shocks could be affecting outcomes such as land productivity.

Whether application of either of these estimators is appropriate in a particular evaluation setting will depend on whether there is good reason to believe that the assumptions needed to justify the methods are satisfied. If the researcher has a rich set of covariates thought to capture the important aspects of participation decisions, so that the remaining unobserved factors are unlikely to be a source of concern, then the cross-sectional estimator could well provide consistent estimates of program impacts. Or there may be contexts in which time effects are not expected to be that important, in which case the before-after estimator could yield reliable estimates. However, in many situations these assumptions are unlikely to hold. The next chapter considers DID and within regression estimators, which address some of the limitations of the cross-sectional and before-after methods, but have the disadvantage that they entail more demanding data requirements.

Notes

1. Data collected in a relatively short period, during which each person, household, or other unit of observation is interviewed only once, are called cross-sectional data.
2. Later this chapter considers a regression-based cross-sectional estimator that controls for observable differences between program participants and nonparticipants that affect outcomes.
3. The DID estimator improves on the before-after estimator (C – A) by adjusting for the time trend common to all farmers (D – B) by subtracting (D – B) from (C – A). It improves upon the cross-sectional estimator (C – D) by subtracting the difference in the two types of farmers in the absence of the program (A – B) from the same difference after the program is in place (C – D); that is, it is calculated as (C – D) – (A – B), which equals (C – A) – (D – B).
4. While the data requirements are minimal, the cross-sectional estimator requires strong assumptions to produce unbiased estimates, as explained below.
5. If $E[U_{1it}| \mathbf{X}_i] \neq 0$ or $E[U_{0it}| \mathbf{X}_i] \neq 0$, ordinary least squares (OLS) estimates of $\boldsymbol{\beta}_1$ and $\boldsymbol{\beta}_0$ are biased, so other estimation methods such as instrumental variables (IV) must be used; such methods are explained in most econometrics textbooks and are not covered here; however, chapter 15 does discuss IV methods when $E[U_{1it}| P_{it}] \neq 0$ or $E[U_{0it}| P_{it}] \neq 0$.
6. In practice, time-varying **X** variables can be included, although this requires the assumption that the $\mathbf{X}_i$ variables are not affected by treatment (for example, age would be a valid time-varying variable).
7. This can be shown as follows: Define $ATT(\mathbf{X} = \mathbf{X}_i)$ as $E[Y_{1it} - Y_{0it}| \mathbf{X}_i, P_{it} = 1]$. Then

$$\begin{aligned}\text{ATT}(\mathbf{X} = \mathbf{X}_i) &= \text{E}[\mathbf{X}_i'\boldsymbol{\beta}_1 - \mathbf{X}_i'\boldsymbol{\beta}_0 + U_{1it} - U_{0it}|\ \mathbf{X}_i, P_{it} = 1] \\ &= \text{E}[\text{ATE}(\mathbf{X} = \mathbf{X}_i) + U_{1it} - U_{0it}|\ \mathbf{X}_i, P_{it} = 1] \\ &= \text{ATE}(\mathbf{X} = \mathbf{X}_i) + \text{E}[U_{1it} - U_{0it}|\ \mathbf{X}_i, P_{it} = 1] \\ &= \mathbf{X}_i'(\boldsymbol{\beta}_1 - \boldsymbol{\beta}_0) + \text{E}[U_{1it} - U_{0it}|\ \mathbf{X}_i, P_{it} = 1].\end{aligned}$$

8. This follows from the maintained assumption throughout that $\text{E}[U_{0it}|\ \mathbf{X}_i] = 0$ and $\text{E}[U_{1it}|\ \mathbf{X}_i] = 0$.
9. $\text{E}[U_{0it} + P_{it}(U_{1it} - U_{0it})|\ \mathbf{X}_i] = 0$ would be satisfied if $\text{E}[U_{0it}|\ \mathbf{X}_i, P_{it} = 0] = 0$ and $\text{E}[U_{1it}|\ \mathbf{X}_i, P_{it} = 1] = 0$. In other words, conditional on $\mathbf{X}$, P is uncorrelated with both U_0 and U_1. This conditional lack of correlation implies that $\text{E}[P_{it}|\ \mathbf{X}_i, U_{0it}, U_{1it} = \text{E}[P_{it}|\ \mathbf{X}_i]$. Because P_{it} is binary, $\text{E}[P_{it}|\ \mathbf{X}_i, U_{0it}, U_{1it}] = \text{Prob}[P_{it} = 1 \mid \mathbf{X}_i, U_{0it}, U_{1it}]$.
10. Unlike ATE($\mathbf{X}$), ATT($\mathbf{X}$) is not a simple function of $\boldsymbol{\beta}_0$, $\boldsymbol{\beta}_1$, and $\mathbf{X}$. Thus the coefficients on $\mathbf{X}$ and on the $P \times \mathbf{X}$ interaction terms will not be estimates of $\boldsymbol{\beta}_0$ and $\boldsymbol{\beta}_1$.
11. The assumption implies that, in addition to $\text{E}[U_{0it}|\ \mathbf{X}_i, P_{it}] = 0$, it is also the case that $\text{E}[P_{it}(U_{1it} - U_{0it})|\ \mathbf{X}_i, P_{it}] = 0$. For participants, $P_{it} = 1$, so $\text{E}[(U_{1it} - U_{0it})|\ \mathbf{X}_i] = 0$ for participants; their average unobserved gain is 0 for all values of $\mathbf{X}_i$. But the assumption that $\text{E}[U_{0it}|\ \mathbf{X}_i] = 0$ and $\text{E}[U_{1it}|\ \mathbf{X}_i] = 0$ implies that $\text{E}[U_{1it} - U_{0it}|\ \mathbf{X}_i] = 0$ for the population as a whole. Because it is true for the population as a whole and for participants, it must also be true for nonparticipants.
12. Recall that ATT($\mathbf{X}$) is not a simple function of $\boldsymbol{\beta}_0$, $\boldsymbol{\beta}_1$, and $\mathbf{X}$, and thus a flexible functional form for $\mathbf{X}_{it''}$ should be used, such as including squared terms and interaction terms between the different $\mathbf{X}_{it''}$ variables.
13. The fixed effect error structure might be relaxed by, for example, assuming a moving average process instead, but it would have to be assumed that the number of lags in the process is small enough so that past values of $U_{0it'}$, which are known to the individual, predict neither program participation $P_{it''}$ nor $U_{0it''}$.

References

Glewwe, Paul, and Petra Todd. 2019. Course materials, "APEC 8212: Econometric Analysis II" and "ECON 712: Graduate Topics Course in Program Evaluation Methods," University of Minnesota, Minneapolis–St. Paul, and University of Pennsylvania, Philadelphia.

Heckman, James, Robert Lalonde, and Jeffrey Smith. 1999. "The Economics and Econometrics of Active Labor Market Programs." *In Handbook of Labor Economics: Volume 3*, edited by Orley Ashenfelter and David Card. Amsterdam: North Holland.

CHAPTER 12

Regression Methods for Nonrandomized Data: The Difference-in-Differences Estimator and the Within Estimator

Introduction

Chapter 11 presents two relatively simple regression estimators, the cross-sectional estimator and the before-after estimator. It also shows that those two estimators make strong assumptions about the relationship between program participation and the outcomes that the program is intended to change, assumptions that may be violated in many situations, leading to biased and inconsistent estimates of program impacts.

This chapter elaborates on two additional regression-based estimators, the difference-in-differences (DID) estimator and the within estimator. The assumptions needed for unbiased and consistent estimation are not as strong, but they could still be violated. Many impact evaluations have used these methods, especially DID estimation. This chapter also presents four well-known studies that have applied the DID estimator, one of which also applies the within estimator, to estimate the impacts of various government programs in developing countries.

The difference-in-differences estimator

The DID estimator measures the impact of the program intervention by the difference between participants and nonparticipants in the change in the outcomes of interest over time. At the beginning of the period, neither the eventual participants nor the nonparticipants have participated in the program, but by the end of the period the participants have been in the program long enough for the program to have had an impact, whereas the nonparticipants have still not participated.

Estimation of average treatment effects on the treated

To see how the DID estimation method works, assume (as in chapter 11) that Y_1 and Y_0 are related to the observable variables $\mathbf{X}$ for individual i at time t as follows:

$$Y_{1it} = \mathbf{X}_{it}'\boldsymbol{\beta}_1 + U_{1it},$$
$$Y_{0it} = \mathbf{X}_{it}'\boldsymbol{\beta}_0 + U_{0it}.$$

As in chapter 11, these equations are assumed to be causal relationships, and it is also assumed that $\mathrm{E}[U_{1it}| \mathbf{X}_{it}] = 0$ and $\mathrm{E}[U_{0it}| \mathbf{X}_{it}] = 0$. The $\mathbf{X}_{it}$ vector usually includes a constant term, and it may also include one or more time-specific dummy variables, which indicate changes over time in the outcomes Y_1 and Y_0 that have nothing to do with the program being evaluated.

To begin, consider first the problem of estimating the program's average treatment effect on the treated (ATT), and the average impact for a treated individual i at time t for whom $\mathbf{X} = \mathbf{X}_{it}$, denoted by $\mathrm{ATT}(\mathbf{X} = \mathbf{X}_{it})$. Recall that the latter parameter of interest is defined as follows:

$$\mathrm{ATT}(\mathbf{X} = \mathbf{X}_{it}) \equiv \mathrm{E}[Y_{1it} - Y_{0it}| P_{it} = 1, \mathbf{X} = \mathbf{X}_{it}],$$

where conditioning on $P_{it} = 1$ restricts the sample to the treated (the program participants). Note that $\mathrm{ATT}(\mathbf{X} = \mathbf{X}_{it})$ is defined for a particular time, t. It is possible that if the program were implemented at a different time, or if the impact were measured at a later time (for example, several years after the program had been implemented), the impact would be different.

As in chapter 11, the value of $\mathrm{ATT}(\mathbf{X} = \mathbf{X}_{it})$ for a particular person i at time t is a function of that person's values of Y_1 and Y_0, so for that particular person the following relationship holds:

$$\begin{aligned}\mathrm{ATT}(\mathbf{X} = \mathbf{X}_{it}) &\equiv \mathrm{E}[Y_{1it} - Y_{0it}| P_{it} = 1, \mathbf{X} = \mathbf{X}_{it}] \\ &= \mathrm{E}[\mathbf{X}_{it}'\boldsymbol{\beta}_1 + U_{1it} - \mathbf{X}_{it}'\boldsymbol{\beta}_0 - U_{0it} \mid P_{it} = 1, \mathbf{X} = \mathbf{X}_{it}] \\ &= \mathrm{E}[\mathbf{X}_{it}'(\boldsymbol{\beta}_1 - \boldsymbol{\beta}_0) + U_{1it} - U_{0it} \mid P_{it} = 1, \mathbf{X} = \mathbf{X}_{it}] \\ &= \mathbf{X}_{it}'(\boldsymbol{\beta}_1 - \boldsymbol{\beta}_0) + \mathrm{E}[U_{1it} - U_{0it} \mid P_{it} = 1, \mathbf{X} = \mathbf{X}_{it}].\end{aligned} \tag{12.1}$$

Note that this expression implies that $\mathbf{X}_{it}'(\boldsymbol{\beta}_1 - \boldsymbol{\beta}_0) = \mathrm{ATT}(\mathbf{X} = \mathbf{X}_{it}) - \mathrm{E}[U_{1it} - U_{0it}| P_{it} = 1, \mathbf{X} = \mathbf{X}_{it}]$.

Using the same notation as in chapter 11, let t' denote a period before the program started and t'' be some period after it started. In addition, define a time-invariant indicator variable, I_i, that equals 1 for eventual participants (those for whom $P_{it'} = 0$ and $P_{it''} = 1$) and 0 for nonparticipants (for whom $P_{it'} = P_{it''} = 0$). Finally, it is useful to point out that Y_{1it} at period t'' can be expressed as

$$\begin{aligned}
Y_{1it''} &= Y_{0it''} + (Y_{1it''} - Y_{0it''}) \\
&= \mathbf{X}_{it''}'\boldsymbol{\beta}_0 + U_{0it''} + (\mathbf{X}_{it''}'\boldsymbol{\beta}_1 + U_{1it''} - \mathbf{X}_{it''}'\boldsymbol{\beta}_0 - U_{0it''}) \\
&= \mathbf{X}_{it''}'\boldsymbol{\beta}_0 + \mathbf{X}_{it''}'(\boldsymbol{\beta}_1 - \boldsymbol{\beta}_0) + U_{1it''} \\
&= \mathbf{X}_{it''}'\boldsymbol{\beta}_0 + \text{ATT}(\mathbf{X} = \mathbf{X}_{it''}) - \text{E}[U_{1it''} - U_{0it''} | P_{it''} = 1, P_{it'} = 0, \mathbf{X} = \mathbf{X}_{it''}] + U_{1it''} \\
&= \mathbf{X}_{it''}'\boldsymbol{\beta}_0 + \text{ATT}(\mathbf{X} = \mathbf{X}_{it''}) - \text{E}[U_{1it''} - U_{0it''} | P_{it''} = 1, P_{it'} = 0, \mathbf{X}_{it''}] + U_{1it''},
\end{aligned}$$

where the last line expresses the conditioning on $\mathbf{X} = \mathbf{X}_{it''}$ more compactly. For clarity, the condition $P_{it'} = 0$ is added to indicate that participants at time t'' had not yet participated at time t'.

With these preliminary derivations, the DID estimator can now be presented in a regression context. To begin, consider the change in the observed Y from time t' to time t'' for both participants and nonparticipants in the program that is being evaluated. For nonparticipants this change is

$$\begin{aligned}
Y_{it''} - Y_{it'} &= Y_{0it''} - Y_{0it'} \\
&= \mathbf{X}_{it''}'\boldsymbol{\beta}_0 + U_{0it''} - \mathbf{X}_{it'}'\boldsymbol{\beta}_0 - U_{0it'} \\
&= (\mathbf{X}_{it''} - \mathbf{X}_{it'})'\boldsymbol{\beta}_0 + U_{0it''} - U_{0it'}.
\end{aligned}$$

For participants, this change is

$$\begin{aligned}
Y_{it''} - Y_{it'} &= Y_{1it''} - Y_{0it'} \\
&= \mathbf{X}_{it''}'\boldsymbol{\beta}_0 + \text{ATT}(\mathbf{X} = \mathbf{X}_{it''}) - \text{E}[U_{1it''} - U_{0it''} | P_{it''} = 1, P_{it'} = 0, \mathbf{X}_{it''}] + U_{1it''} - \mathbf{X}_{it'}'\boldsymbol{\beta}_0 \\
&\quad - U_{0it'} \\
&= (\mathbf{X}_{it''} - \mathbf{X}_{it'})'\boldsymbol{\beta}_0 + \text{ATT}(\mathbf{X} = \mathbf{X}_{it''}) - \text{E}[U_{1it''} - U_{0it''} | P_{it''} = 1, P_{it'} = 0, \mathbf{X}_{it''}] + U_{1it''} \\
&\quad - U_{0it''}.
\end{aligned}$$

Combining program participants and nonparticipants into a single equation (with $I_i = 1$ if person i is a participant and $I_i = 0$ if he or she is not a participant) yields the following:

$$\begin{aligned}
Y_{it''} - Y_{it'} &= (\mathbf{X}_{it''} - \mathbf{X}_{it'})'\boldsymbol{\beta}_0 + I_i\{\text{ATT}(\mathbf{X} = \mathbf{X}_{it''}) - \text{E}[U_{1it''} - U_{0it''} | P_{it''} = 1, P_{it'} = 0, \mathbf{X}_{it''}] + U_{1it''} \\
&\quad - U_{0it''}\} + U_{0it''} - U_{0it'} \\
&= (\mathbf{X}_{it''} - \mathbf{X}_{it'})'\boldsymbol{\beta}_0 + I_i \times \text{ATT}(\mathbf{X} = \mathbf{X}_{it''}) + \varepsilon_{it''},
\end{aligned}$$

where $\varepsilon_{it''} = I_i(U_{1it''} - U_{0it''} - \mathrm{E}[U_{1it''} - U_{0it''} \mid P_{it''} = 1, P_{it'} = 0, \mathbf{X}_{it''}]) + U_{0it''} - U_{0it'}$.[1] Note that, for program participants ($I_i = 1$), the error term in this equation is identical to the error term obtained for the before-after estimator in chapter 11 (equation (11.9)). The I_i term is added to accommodate the inclusion of both participant and nonparticipant observations in the same regression; the nonparticipant observations are those for which $I_i = 0$.

This expression for $Y_{it''} - Y_{it'}$ suggests that a regression of $Y_{it''} - Y_{it'}$ on $(\mathbf{X}_{it''} - \mathbf{X}_{it'})$ and a general function of $\mathbf{X}_{it''}$ would yield an estimate of $\mathrm{ATT}(\mathbf{X} = \mathbf{X}_{it''})$. In particular, if it is assumed that $\mathrm{ATT}(\mathbf{X} = \mathbf{X}_{it''}) = \boldsymbol{\delta}'\mathbf{X}_{it''}$, then $I_i\mathrm{ATT}(\mathbf{X} = \mathbf{X}_{it''})$ corresponds to $\boldsymbol{\delta}'(I_i \times \mathbf{X}_{it''})$, which implies that $Y_{it''} - Y_{it'}$ can be regressed on $\mathbf{X}_{it''} - \mathbf{X}_{it'}$ and $I_i \times \mathbf{X}_{it''}$ to obtain an estimate of $\boldsymbol{\delta}$ (and $\boldsymbol{\beta}_0$), and thus an estimate of $\boldsymbol{\delta}'\mathbf{X}_{it''}$ (which equals $\mathrm{ATT}(\mathbf{X} = \mathbf{X}_{it''})$).

The DID estimator addresses an important shortcoming of the before-after estimator in that it allows the constant term in $\boldsymbol{\beta}_0$ to change over time (allows for time-specific intercepts); however, this change over time is assumed to be common across both groups in the population. That is, it can allow for a general change in Y_0 over time that affects both participants and nonparticipants in the same way, which is essentially the same as allowing for a common time trend as shown in figure 11.2. This can be done by specifying that one variable in $\mathbf{X}_{it}$ be a dummy variable that equals 0 at time t' and equals 1 at time t''. The coefficient in $\boldsymbol{\beta}_0$ that corresponds to this dummy variable equals this general change in Y_0 over time (that is, the change in the constant term in $\boldsymbol{\beta}_0$). Unlike the before-after estimator, the DID estimator is able to estimate this coefficient (technically, this time effect is identified separately from the treatment effect) because the nonparticipant observations (which are not used in the before-after estimator) provide the information needed to estimate it.

As with any regression estimation method, the DID estimator is unbiased and consistent only if the error term is uncorrelated with the variables in the regression equation, that is, only if $\mathrm{E}[\varepsilon_{it''} \mid I_i, \mathbf{X}_{it''}] = 0$. Note that I_i takes only two values, 0 and 1, so this condition can be checked for both of those values. For $I_i = 0$, it is clear from the definition of $\varepsilon_{it''}$ that $\mathrm{E}[\varepsilon_{it''} \mid I_i = 0, \mathbf{X}_{it''}] = \mathrm{E}[U_{0it''} - U_{0it'} \mid I_i = 0, \mathbf{X}_{it''}]$. It can also be shown that $\mathrm{E}[\varepsilon_{it''} \mid I_i = 1, \mathbf{X}_{it''}] = \mathrm{E}[U_{0it''} - U_{0it'} \mid I_i = 1, \mathbf{X}_{it''}]$. Thus, the estimator is unbiased and consistent if $\mathrm{E}[U_{0it''} - U_{0it'} \mid I_i, \mathbf{X}_{it''}] = 0$, which requires that program participants do not select into the program based on $U_{0it''} - U_{0it'}$, that is, based on anticipated changes in the unobservables corresponding to Y_0. Another way to see this is that $\mathrm{E}[U_{0it''} - U_{0it'} \mid I_i, \mathbf{X}_{it''}] = \mathrm{E}[U_{0it''} - U_{0it'} \mid \mathbf{X}_{it''}] = 0$ needs to be true, which makes it clear that, conditional on $\mathbf{X}_{it''}$, changes over time in the unobserved factors that affect Y_0 cannot differ for participants and nonparticipants; if they did differ, this would be a failure of the parallel trends assumption for Y_0.

Estimating average treatment effects

Estimation of average treatment effect (ATE) is similar but requires additional assumptions about program nonparticipants. Given the assumption above that Y_1 and Y_0 are linearly related to the observable variables $\mathbf{X}$ for individual i at time t, and recalling from chapter 11 (equation (11.4)) that the definition of ATE for a particular value of $\mathbf{X}$ allows $\mathrm{ATE}(\mathbf{X} = \mathbf{X}_{it})$ to be expressed as

$$\begin{aligned} \text{ATE}(\mathbf{X} = \mathbf{X}_{it}) &\equiv \text{E}[Y_{1it} - Y_{0it} | \mathbf{X} = \mathbf{X}_{it}] \\ &= \mathbf{X}_{it}'(\boldsymbol{\beta}_1 - \boldsymbol{\beta}_0) + \text{E}[U_{1it} - U_{0it} | \mathbf{X} = \mathbf{X}_{it}] \\ &= \mathbf{X}_{it}'(\boldsymbol{\beta}_1 - \boldsymbol{\beta}_0), \end{aligned}$$

where the last line follows from the assumption stated above, and maintained throughout this chapter, that $\text{E}[U_{1it} | \mathbf{X}_{it}] = 0$ and $\text{E}[U_{0it} | \mathbf{X}_{it}] = 0$.

The expression for $Y_{1it''}$ can be written in terms of $\text{ATE}(\mathbf{X} = \mathbf{X}_{it''})$ as

$$\begin{aligned} Y_{1it''} &= \mathbf{X}_{it''}'\boldsymbol{\beta}_0 + \mathbf{X}_{it''}'(\boldsymbol{\beta}_1 - \boldsymbol{\beta}_0) + U_{1it''} \\ &= \mathbf{X}_{it''}'\boldsymbol{\beta}_0 + \text{ATE}(\mathbf{X} = \mathbf{X}_{it''}) + U_{1it''}. \end{aligned}$$

Finally, note that changes in observed Y over time for participants are

$$\begin{aligned} Y_{it''} - Y_{it'} = Y_{1it''} - Y_{0it'} &= \mathbf{X}_{it''}'\boldsymbol{\beta}_0 + \text{ATE}(\mathbf{X} = \mathbf{X}_{it''}) + U_{1it''} - \mathbf{X}_{it'}'\boldsymbol{\beta}_0 - U_{0it'} \\ &= (\mathbf{X}_{it''} - \mathbf{X}_{it'})'\boldsymbol{\beta}_0 + \text{ATE}(\mathbf{X} = \mathbf{X}_{it''}) + U_{1it''} - U_{0it'}, \end{aligned}$$

and for nonparticipants are

$$Y_{it''} - Y_{it'} = Y_{0it''} - Y_{0it'} = (\mathbf{X}_{it''} - \mathbf{X}_{it'})'\boldsymbol{\beta}_0 + U_{0it''} - U_{0it'}.$$

Combining the observed Y for participants and nonparticipants gives the regression equation for estimating $\text{ATE}(\mathbf{X} = \mathbf{X}_{it''})$:

$$\begin{aligned} Y_{it''} - Y_{it'} &= (\mathbf{X}_{it''} - \mathbf{X}_{it'})'\boldsymbol{\beta}_0 + I_i \times \text{ATE}(\mathbf{X} = \mathbf{X}_{it''}) + U_{0it''} - U_{0it'} + I_i \times (U_{1it''} - U_{0it''}) \\ &= (\mathbf{X}_{it''} - \mathbf{X}_{it'})'\boldsymbol{\beta}_0 + I_i \times \text{ATE}(\mathbf{X} = \mathbf{X}_{it''}) + \varepsilon_{it''} \\ &= (\mathbf{X}_{it''} - \mathbf{X}_{it'})'\boldsymbol{\beta}_0 + I_i \times \mathbf{X}_{it''}(\boldsymbol{\beta}_1 - \boldsymbol{\beta}_0) + \varepsilon_{it''}, \end{aligned}$$

where $\varepsilon_{it''} = U_{0it''} - U_{0it'} + I_i \times (U_{1it''} - U_{0it''})$. An ordinary least squares (OLS) regression of $Y_{it''} - Y_{it'}$ on $\mathbf{X}_{it''} - \mathbf{X}_{it'}$ and $I_i \times \mathbf{X}_{it''}$ will yield unbiased and consistent estimates of $\boldsymbol{\beta}_0$ and $\boldsymbol{\beta}_1 - \boldsymbol{\beta}_0$, the latter of which can be used to calculate $\text{ATE}(\mathbf{X} = \mathbf{X}_{it''})$, *if* the conditional expectation of $\varepsilon_{it''}$ equals zero:

$$\text{E}[U_{0it''} - U_{0it'} + I_i \times (U_{1it''} - U_{0it''}) | I_i, \mathbf{X}_{it''}] = 0.$$

To see what this condition implies, it is helpful to check it separately for the cases in which $I_i = 1$ and $I_i = 0$. When $I_i = 0$ the condition becomes

$$\text{E}[U_{0it''} - U_{0it'} | I_i = 0, \mathbf{X}_{it''}] = 0.$$

This condition implies that $E[U_{0it''} - U_{0it'} | I_i = 1, \mathbf{X}_{it''}] = 0$,[2] so that the overall requirement for the $U_{0it''} - U_{0it'}$ component of $\varepsilon_{it''}$ is that

$$E[U_{0it''} - U_{0it'} | I_i, \mathbf{X}_{it''}] = 0.$$

As in the case of ATT, this condition implies that, conditional on $\mathbf{X}_{it''}$, unobserved factors that determine how Y_0 changes over time cannot differ for participants and nonparticipants; if they did the parallel trends assumption would not hold. Note also that the $\mathbf{X}_{it''}$ variables play two useful roles: first, they allow for a parallel trend for all observations by including a dummy variable that equals 1 only for the second period; and second, they allow participants and nonparticipants to have different observed trends over time by having different trends in the $\mathbf{X}_{it''}$ variables over time.

In addition, another assumption is needed for consistent and unbiased estimation of ATE. When $I_i = 1$, the condition that $E[U_{0it''} - U_{0it'} + I_i \times (U_{1it''} - U_{0it''}) | I_i, \mathbf{X}_{it''}] = 0$ also requires that

$$E[U_{1it''} - U_{0it''} | I_i = 1, \mathbf{X}_{it''}] = 0.$$

This means that, conditional on $\mathbf{X}_{it''}$, the expected gain from the program, $E[Y_{1it''} - Y_{0it''} | \mathbf{X}_{it''}]$, is the same for participants and nonparticipants.[3] This implies that ATE($\mathbf{X} = \mathbf{X}_{it''}$) is equal to ATT($\mathbf{X} = \mathbf{X}_{it''}$). In this way, the (conditional on $\mathbf{X}_{it''}$) counterfactual for nonparticipants can be inferred from the (conditional on $\mathbf{X}_{it''}$) gain for the participants. The intuition behind this additional assumption is that, conditional on $\mathbf{X}_{it''}$, the unobserved factors that contribute to the difference between Y_1 at time t'' and Y_0 at time t' cannot differ for participants and nonparticipants.

Estimation as a levels equation, and adding more periods

Returning to estimation of ATT, the DID estimator can also be specified as a levels equation rather than a differenced equation. Suppose in particular that Y_1 and Y_0 are defined so that any individual-specific but time-invariant component of the unobserved factors that determine Y_1 and Y_0 are represented by a term f_i. That is, for each individual i we have $Y_{1it} = \mathbf{X}_{it}'\boldsymbol{\beta}_1 + f_i + v_{1it}$ and $Y_{0it} = \mathbf{X}_{it}'\boldsymbol{\beta}_0 + f_i + v_{0it}$. This implies that the observed Y_{it} for any period is $Y_{it} = \mathbf{X}_{it}'\boldsymbol{\beta}_0 + P_{it} \times \mathbf{X}_{it}'(\boldsymbol{\beta}_1 - \boldsymbol{\beta}_0) + f_i + v_{0it} + P_{it} \times (v_{1it} - v_{0it})$. The definition of ATT($\mathbf{X} = \mathbf{X}_{it}$) in equation (12.1) means that this expression for Y_{it} can be written as

$$Y_{it} = \mathbf{X}_{it}'\boldsymbol{\beta}_0 + f_i + P_{it} \times \text{ATT}(\mathbf{X} = \mathbf{X}_{it}) + \varepsilon_{it} \text{ for } t = t', t'', \quad (12.2)$$

where $\varepsilon_{it} = v_{0it} + P_{it}(v_{1it} - v_{0it} - E[v_{1it} - v_{0it} | P_{it} = 1, \mathbf{X}_{it}])$. In this equation, f_i is an individual-level fixed effect, which can be estimated by including in the regression model an indicator (dummy) variable for each individual. As above, one variable in $\mathbf{X}_{it}$ must be a dummy variable that equals 0 at time t' and equals 1 at time t'', and the coefficient in $\boldsymbol{\beta}_0$ that corresponds to this variable measures this general change in Y_0 over time that applies to all individuals. This specification could also be estimated in deviation from (individual-specific) means form, in which case the fixed effect term would not need to be included because it would be differenced out.

If there are only two periods, then this level specification will produce exactly the same estimates of $\boldsymbol{\beta}_0$ and ATT($\mathbf{X} = \mathbf{X}_{it}$), the latter of which can be approximated by $\boldsymbol{\delta}'\mathbf{X}$, as in the differenced estimator for ATT (see the section "Estimation of average treatment effects on the treated"). The assumption required for unbiased and consistent estimates of $\boldsymbol{\beta}_0$ and $\boldsymbol{\delta}$ remains the same, $E[U_{0it''} - U_{0it'} | I_i, \mathbf{X}_{it''}] = 0$, which for the fixed effects error structure can be expressed as $E[v_{0it''} - v_{0it'} | I_i, \mathbf{X}_{it''}] = 0$.

Another useful characteristic of the DID estimator is that, with an additional assumption, it can be estimated using a level specification even if panel data are not available, but two cross-sectional data sets that include both participants and nonparticipants are available. Note, however, that such repeated cross-sectional data rule out the possibility of estimating fixed effects. This difference is important because the requirement that $E[\varepsilon_{it} | P_{it}, \mathbf{X}_{it}] = 0$ in this case imposes a stronger assumption on the error term than in the panel data case, namely, that $E[U_{0it} | P_{it}, \mathbf{X}_{it}] = 0$, where U_{0it} includes the unobserved individual factor f_i. This means that people cannot select into the program on the basis of any unobserved factors that determine Y_0, both those that change, and those that do not change, over time. This is in contrast to panel data, in which the time-invariant unobservables (denoted by f_i) are eliminated through differencing. On a more practical note, applying DID to two cross-sections is possible only if the individuals in the data at time t' who will participate at time t'' can be identified at time t', which may not be known for many types of programs.[4]

If data are available on the same individuals for three or more time periods, some of the restrictions required in the two-period case can be relaxed, or a more flexible functional form of the time trend can be used, when estimating program impacts. An example of the former is that three periods of data allow the parallel trends assumption to be dispensed with. To see how this works, suppose that there are data for participants and nonparticipants for two periods before the program started and one period after the program began; these three periods can be denoted, in chronological order, as t^0, t', and t''. The basic idea is to use the first two periods to estimate separate time trends for participants and nonparticipants, and deviations from that time trend in the third period for the participants (after allowing for time-period-specific shocks that affect both groups in the same way) are an estimate of the program impact.

More formally, the levels equation just discussed (equation (12.2)) can be modified to include separate time trends for participants and nonparticipants:

$$Y_{it} = \mathbf{X}_{it}'\boldsymbol{\beta}_0 + f_i + \tau_0 \times time + \tau_1 \times time \times I_i + P_{it} \times \text{ATT}(\mathbf{X} = \mathbf{X}_{it}) + \varepsilon_{it} \text{ for } t = t^0, t', t'', \quad (12.3)$$

where *time* is a variable that equals 0, 1, and 2 at periods t^0, t', and t'', respectively. Note that $\mathbf{X}_{it}$ must include a dummy variable for period t'' to allow for time-specific shocks that affect both program participants and program nonparticipants in the same way for that period.[5]

The intuition behind this method is seen in figure 12.1, for which there are two periods before, and one period after, the intervention. Note that the treatment and control group trends are not parallel. If there had not been a common shock and had not been an intervention, at time t'' the outcome variable for the treatment and control groups would have been at points E and F, respectively. These outcomes are not observed, but they can be calculated based on the slope information in the first two periods (calculated using points A and C for the treatment group and B and D for the control group, which yields the time trends τ_0 and τ_1 in equation (12.3)). The estimator assumes a common shock from period t' to period t'' for both the treatment and the control groups, which are shown as the difference between E and G for the treatment group and F and H for the control group; this corresponds to the dummy variable in $\mathbf{X}_{it}$ for period t''. Note that H is observed and F is calculated, so the distance from E to G can be calculated as the distance from F to H. Finally, the difference between the calculated G and the observed value for the treatment group, I, is the estimate of the treatment effect.

An analogous estimation procedure can be applied to situations in which there is one period before the program begins and two periods after it begins. This procedure does, however, require the assumption that the impact of the program be identical for both periods after the program begins; if this were not the case, it would not be possible to use those two periods to estimate the difference in the time trends between participants and nonparticipants.

FIGURE 12.1 Three periods, with nonparallel trends

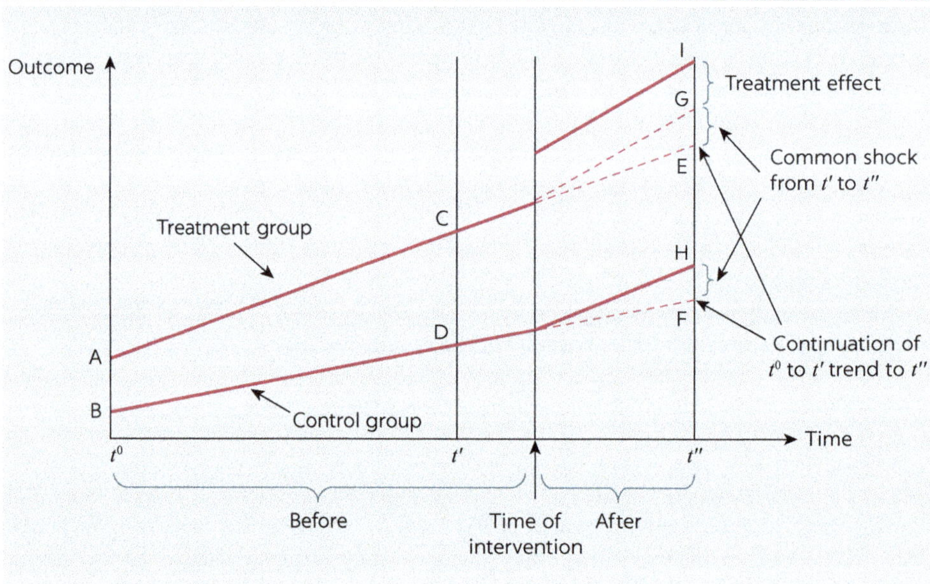

Source: Original figure for this publication.

Another alternative, if data with one period before the program began and two periods after it began are available, is to maintain the assumption of a common trend (though not necessarily linear) over all three periods, in the sense that a common shock can occur between the second and third periods), and to estimate how the impact of the program increases or decreases over time. In particular, equation (12.3) can be modified to include the same time trend for participants and nonparticipants but different impacts of the program in periods t' and t'':

$$Y_{it} = \mathbf{X}_{it}'\boldsymbol{\beta}_0 + f_i + \tau \times time + P_{1it} \times \text{ATT}(\mathbf{X} = \mathbf{X}_{it}) + P_{2it} \times \text{ATT}(\mathbf{X} = \mathbf{X}_{it}) + \varepsilon_{it} \text{ for } t = t^0, t', t'',$$

where P_{1it} equals 1 only for program participants, and only at time t', and P_{2it} equals 1 only for program participants, and only at time t''. As in equation (12.3), $\mathbf{X}_{it}$ must include a dummy variable for period t'' to allow for time-specific shocks that affect both program participants and program nonparticipants in the same way at that time.

The intuition for this estimation is shown in figure 12.2. From time t^0 to time t' the estimation of the treatment effect is the standard DID method, and the figure is essentially the same as figure 11.2. If the parallel trends assumption is maintained, it is also possible to estimate the treatment effect at time t'', even if a common shock affects both the treatment and control groups at time t''. The common shock assumption (combined with the parallel trends assumption) implies that H (which is not observed) can be estimated as I

FIGURE 12.2 Three periods, with parallel trends and time-varying impacts

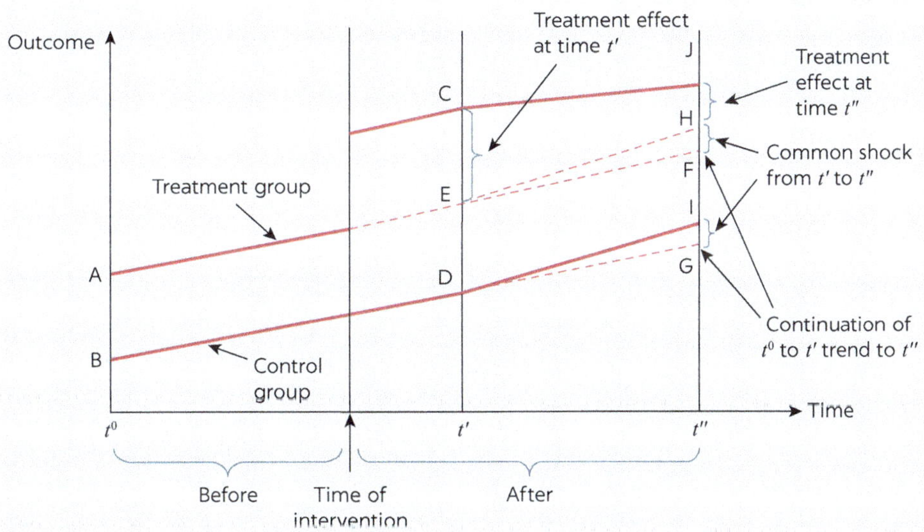

Source: Original figure for this publication.

(which is observed) plus the vertical distance from A to B. The distance between J (which is observed) and this estimate of H is the estimated treatment effect at time t''.

If four periods of data are available, with two periods before the program was implemented and two periods after its implementation, both nonparallel (but still linear) time trends could be allowed for, and different impacts of the program for the third and fourth periods could be estimated. More generally, an additional period can be put to one of three uses: allowing the time trend to differ between participants and nonparticipants, specifying a more flexible functional form (for example, quadratic) for a common time trend, or allowing the impact of the program to differ at different times. These alternative uses of additional periods could lead to different estimates of program impacts, so several different alternatives should be tried to check the robustness of the estimated program effects.

Synthetic control methods

Sometimes researchers seek to evaluate the effects of a particular program, or more generally a particular event or occurrence, using aggregate data. That is, they may wish to compare one or more units exposed to a program or event to one or more unexposed units. In some evaluations the data are available only at an aggregate level, such as state level, district level, or city level, and researchers apply a general method called a *comparative case study* approach. For example, Card (1990) studies the impact of the 1980 Mariel boatlift, a sudden influx of a large number of Cuban immigrants into Miami, using other southern U.S. cities as a comparison group. Another example is Abadie, Diamond, and Hainmueller (2010), who evaluate the impact of California's Proposition 99, a large-scale tobacco control program implemented in 1988. The comparison group in that study consisted of other states. A third example is Abadie and Gardeazabal (2003), who analyze the economic effects of a terrorist conflict in the Basque Country of Spain. The comparison group for this study was a combination of other regions in Spain.

To see how the synthetic control approach can be implemented, the following discussion presents the method of Abadie and Gardeazabal (2003), which was further elaborated by Abadie, Diamond, and Hainmueller (2010). This technique constructs a hypothetical control group from a weighted average of potential comparison group observations. The weights are generated such that pre-intervention outcomes and characteristics of the constructed control group are as similar as possible to those of the treated group.[6]

Suppose there are J regions, where it is assumed for expositional simplicity that only the first region was exposed to some intervention (program or event), so that the other $J - 1$ regions serve as potential controls. Let Y_{jt}^{N} denote the outcome that would be observed for region j at time t without the intervention, and let T_0 denote the number of pre-intervention periods (so that $t = 1, 2, \ldots T_0$ are the pre-intervention periods). Also, let Y_{jt}^{E} denote the outcome if region j is exposed to the intervention from period $T_0 + 1$ to t, where $T_0 + 1 \leq t \leq T$ (T is the last time period). The observed outcome for the region exposed to the intervention, which is region 1, can be written as

$$Y_{1t} = Y_{1t}^{N} + \alpha_{1t} D_{1t},$$

where

$$D_{1t} = 1 \text{ if } t > T_0$$
$$= 0 \text{ if } t \leq T_0.$$

The goal of the analysis is to estimate the effects of the intervention, namely, $\alpha_{1T_0+1}, \ldots, \alpha_{1T}$.

The synthetic control approach assumes a structure on the outcome equation that allows a weighted average of the groups that did not receive the intervention to serve as a control for the group that did receive the intervention. For example, Abadie, Diamond, and Hainmueller (2010) assume the following factor structure for any region j:

$$Y_{1j}^{N} = \gamma_t + \theta_t' \mathbf{Z}_j + \lambda_t' \mu_j + \varepsilon_{jt}, \tag{12.4}$$

where γ_t is a time period fixed effect, $\mathbf{Z}_j$ is a vector of observed covariates that do not change over time, $\boldsymbol{\mu}_j$ is a vector of unobserved covariates that do not change over time, and ε_{jt} is a random error term that is assumed to be uncorrelated with all the other variables.

In addition, Abadie, Diamond, and Hainmueller (2010) assume that the counterfactual outcome for region 1 can be represented as some weighted average over the outcomes of the $J - 1$ untreated regions. Any given set of weights represents a synthetic control. This can be expressed as follows:

$$Y_{1t}^{N} = \gamma_t + \theta_t' \sum_{j=2}^{J} w_j \mathbf{Z}_j + \lambda_t' \sum_{j=2}^{J} w_j \mu_j + \sum_{j=2}^{J} w_j \boldsymbol{\varepsilon}_{jt}. \tag{12.5}$$

The synthetic control approach finds optimal weights $w_j^*, j = 2, \ldots J$, which are restricted to be nonnegative and sum to one. One approach for choosing the weights is to minimize the distance between the outcome variables Y that are observed for the treated region (region 1) in periods before receiving the treatment (periods 1 to T_0) and the weighted average of the values for the J nontreated regions for the same periods. That is, the optimal weights (denoted by w_j^*) are chosen so that the following equalities hold:

$$Y_{11} = \sum_{j=2}^{J} w_j^* Y_{j1}, Y_{12} = \sum_{j=2}^{J} w_j^* Y_{j2}, \ldots Y_{1T_0} = \sum_{j=2}^{J} w_i^* Y_{iT_0}.$$

The weights should also do the same for the observables $\mathbf{Z}_1$:

$$\mathbf{Z}_1 - \sum_{j=2}^{J} w_j^* \mathbf{Z}_j.$$

If it is not possible to find weights such that these equalities hold exactly, then weights should be selected to minimize the differences between the quantities in each equation so that they hold approximately. Although imposing a similar condition on the unobservables $\boldsymbol{\mu}_j$ is not possible, Abadie, Diamond, and Hainmueller (2010) show that a synthetic control that satisfies the above conditions for a long set of pre-intervention outcomes will also fit the unobservable $\boldsymbol{\mu}_1$ vector. Abadie and Gardeazabal (2003) describe a minimum distance estimator that can be used to obtain the weights. In Abadie, Diamond, and Hainmueller (2010), a positive definite diagonal matrix was used as the weighting matrix to minimize the mean-squared prediction errors in the equations immediately above for $Y_{11}, Y_{12}, \ldots Y_{1T_0}$ and for $\mathbf{Z}_1$.

Under the assumption that ε_{jt} is independent across units and across time, and assuming that $\sum_{t=1}^{T_0} \boldsymbol{\lambda}_t \boldsymbol{\lambda}_t'$ is nonsingular, then Abadie, Diamond, and Hainmueller (2010) show (in an appendix to their paper) that

$$Y_{1t}^N - \sum\nolimits_{j=2}^{J} w_j^* Y_{jt}$$

will go to zero as the number of pre-intervention periods (T_0) increases. They therefore propose to estimate the treatment effect by

$$\hat{\alpha}_{1t} = Y_{1t} - \sum_{j=2}^{J} w_j^* Y_{jt}.$$

As described in Abadie, Diamond, and Hainmueller (2010), synthetic control methods under other types of structures can be applied on the outcome equation that are less restrictive than the above factor model shown in equations (12.4) and (12.5). Note that equation (12.5) for Y_{1t}^N could also be used to justify application of a DID (fixed effects) estimator if the assumption that λ_t is constant for all t is imposed. In that case, the unobserved $\boldsymbol{\mu}_j$ are eliminated by differencing. However, the factor model given above is more general than a fixed effects model.

In synthetic control studies, inference is often based on aggregate data, and the aggregate quantities may be known. The main source of uncertainty does not come from estimating the aggregate Y outcomes but rather from not knowing whether the constructed synthetic control group can reproduce the counterfactual of how the treated unit would have evolved over time in the absence of treatment (that is, model uncertainty). For this reason, Abadie and Gardeazabal (2003) suggest using a permutation-based placebo analysis to obtain measures of bias and variance for these types of estimators. Specifically, their leave-one-out approach applies the synthetic control method to every potential control observation in the sample. That is, one control observation is taken as the supposed intervention unit and the remaining $J-2$ comparison units are used as the pool of potential controls for which the set of weights is constructed. This is done repeatedly, cycling through the control observations until all are used. Because none of the controls actually received the intervention, the intervention effect is known to be zero. The distribution of these permutation-based estimators around zero can be used to estimate the bias and variance of the estimator.

To summarize the discussion on DID estimators, the main advantage of longitudinal (before-after or DID) estimators over cross-sectional methods is that they allow for unobservable determinants of program participation decisions that are potentially correlated with the outcome variables of interest. DID has the additional advantage over before-after estimation of not confounding general changes over time in Y_0 with the impact of the program. The latter advantage holds with repeated cross-sectional data, but the former does not.

However, the fixed effects error structure that is imposed to justify application of these estimators requires that all components of the unobservables that are correlated with the participation decision (P) be time invariant. This requirement does not allow for unobservable variables that both vary over time *and* are correlated with the observed variables. For example, if the outcome of interest is individuals' earnings, unobserved earnings shocks could be expected to be persistent, so that they make people more likely to participate in a social program (such as a public works program) and also affect future values of Y_0 (or Y_1). In this situation, program participation will be correlated with Y_0 or Y_1, even after conditioning on observed variables, and this correlation would not necessarily be removed by using the fixed effects error structure that underlies DID estimation.

Within estimators

So-called within estimators identify program impacts from changes in outcomes within some group, such as within a family, a school, or a community. The before-after and DID estimators can also be viewed as within estimators, in which the variation exploited is the change over time "within" a given individual. This section describes other kinds of within estimators, the general advantage of which is that they can be estimated using cross-sectional data (data collected at only one point in time).

Let Y_{0ijt} and Y_{1ijt} denote the outcomes for individual i, who is a member of group j, and is observed at time t. Recall that the group could be a community, a school, or even a family. The definition of ATT for the within estimator is exactly the same as for the DID estimator, except that the subscripts indicate that each individual i is one member (out of many) of a group j:

$$\text{ATT}(\mathbf{X} = \mathbf{X}_{ijt}) \equiv \text{E}[Y_{1t} - Y_{0t} | P_{ijt} = 1, \mathbf{X} = \mathbf{X}_{ijt}]. \tag{12.6}$$

To see how $\text{ATT}(\mathbf{X} = \mathbf{X}_{ijt})$ can be estimated using regression methods, define Y_0 and Y_1 as they were defined for the DID estimator, except indicate that individual i belongs to group j and allow the unobserved terms U_0 and U_1 to be the sum of two components:

$$Y_{1ijt} = \mathbf{X}_{ijt}'\boldsymbol{\beta}_1 + U_{1ijt} = \mathbf{X}_{ijt}'\boldsymbol{\beta}_1 + \theta_{jt} + v_{1ijt},$$
$$Y_{0ijt} = \mathbf{X}_{ijt}'\boldsymbol{\beta}_0 + U_{0ijt} = \mathbf{X}_{ijt}'\boldsymbol{\beta}_0 + \theta_{jt} + v_{0ijt},$$

where $U_{1ijt} = \theta_{jt} + v_{1ijt}$ and $U_{0ijt} = \theta_{jt} + v_{0ijt}$. That is, the unobserved components of Y_1 and Y_0 can be divided into two parts, the first of which is the same for all members of group j and is also the same for both U_1 and U_0. This first part, denoted by θ_{jt}, is often referred to as a *group fixed effect.*

Inserting these expressions for an individual i in group j into equation (12.6) for $\text{ATT}(\mathbf{X} = \mathbf{X}_{ijt})$ yields an expression that is very useful for regression estimation:

$$\begin{aligned}\text{ATT}(\mathbf{X} = \mathbf{X}_{ijt}) &\equiv \text{E}[Y_{1ijt} - Y_{0ijt} \mid P_{ijt} = 1, \mathbf{X} = \mathbf{X}_{ijt}]\\ &= \text{E}[\mathbf{X}_{ijt}'\boldsymbol{\beta}_1 + \theta_{jt} + v_{1ijt} - \mathbf{X}_{ijt}'\boldsymbol{\beta}_0 - \theta_{jt} - v_{0ijt} \mid P_{ijt} = 1, \mathbf{X} = \mathbf{X}_{ijt}]\\ &= \text{E}[\mathbf{X}_{ijt}'(\boldsymbol{\beta}_1 - \boldsymbol{\beta}_0) + v_{1ijt} - v_{0ijt} \mid P_{ijt} = 1, \mathbf{X} = \mathbf{X}_{ijt}]\\ &= \mathbf{X}_{ijt}'(\boldsymbol{\beta}_1 - \boldsymbol{\beta}_0) + \text{E}[v_{1ijt} - v_{0ijt} \mid P_{ijt} = 1, \mathbf{X} = \mathbf{X}_{ijt}].\end{aligned}$$

Note that the common group effect, θ_{jt}, plays no role in ATT because it affects Y_1 and Y_0 equally, so the difference between Y_1 and Y_0 is unaffected by θ_{jt}, although it is still possible that θ_{jt} affects program participation (for example, it may make participation more common in some groups, such as some communities, than in other groups).

Finally, as in the DID case, it is useful for regression analysis to point out that Y_{1ijt} for any individual i can be expressed as

$$\begin{aligned}Y_{1ijt} &= Y_{0ijt} + (Y_{1ijt} - Y_{0ijt})\\ &= \mathbf{X}_{ijt}'\boldsymbol{\beta}_0 + \theta_{jt} + v_{0ijt} + (\mathbf{X}_{ijt}'\boldsymbol{\beta}_1 + \theta_{jt} + v_{1ijt} - \mathbf{X}_{ijt}'\boldsymbol{\beta}_0 - \theta_{jt} - v_{0ijt})\\ &= \mathbf{X}_{ijt}'\boldsymbol{\beta}_0 + \theta_{jt} + \mathbf{X}_{ijt}'(\boldsymbol{\beta}_1 - \boldsymbol{\beta}_0) + v_{1ijt}\\ &= \mathbf{X}_{ijt}'\boldsymbol{\beta}_0 + \theta_{jt} + \text{ATT}(\mathbf{X} = \mathbf{X}_{ijt}) - \text{E}[v_{1ijt} - v_{0ijt} \mid P_{ijt} = 1, \mathbf{X} = \mathbf{X}_{ijt}] + v_{1ijt}\\ &= \mathbf{X}_{ijt}'\boldsymbol{\beta}_0 + \text{ATT}(\mathbf{X} = \mathbf{X}_{ijt}) - \text{E}[v_{1ijt} - v_{0ijt} \mid P_{ijt} = 1, \mathbf{X}_{ijt}] + \theta_{jt} + v_{1ijt}.\end{aligned}$$

These expressions allow the observed value of Y for person i in group j at time t to be written as

$$\begin{aligned}Y_{ijt} &= Y_{0ijt} + P_{ijt} \times (Y_{1ijt} - Y_{0ijt})\\ &= \mathbf{X}_{ijt}'\boldsymbol{\beta}_0 + \theta_{jt} + v_{0ijt} + P_{ijt} \times \{\mathbf{X}_{ijt}'\boldsymbol{\beta}_0 + \text{ATT}(\mathbf{X} = \mathbf{X}_{ijt}) - \text{E}[v_{1ijt} - v_{0ijt} \mid P_{ijt} = 1, \mathbf{X}_{ijt}]\\ &\quad + \theta_{jt} + v_{1ijt} - \mathbf{X}_{ijt}'\boldsymbol{\beta}_0 - \theta_{jt} - v_{0ijt})\}\\ &= \mathbf{X}_{ijt}'\boldsymbol{\beta}_0 + \theta_{jt} + v_{0ijt} + P_{ijt} \times \{\text{ATT}(\mathbf{X} = \mathbf{X}_{ijt}) - \text{E}[v_{1ijt} - v_{0ijt} \mid P_{ijt} = 1, \mathbf{X}_{ijt}] + v_{1ijt} - v_{0ijt})\}\\ &= \mathbf{X}_{ijt}'\boldsymbol{\beta}_0 + P_{ijt} \times \text{ATT}(\mathbf{X}_{ijt}) + \varepsilon_{ijt},\end{aligned}$$

where $\varepsilon_{ijt} = \theta_{jt} + v_{0ijt} - P_{ijt} \times \{\text{E}[v_{1ijt} - v_{0ijt} \mid P_{ijt} = 1, \mathbf{X}_{ijt}] - v_{1ijt} + v_{0ijt})\}$.

The within estimator essentially compares the observed values of two people in the same group, such as two people in the same community, school, or family. That is, the regression equation can be depicted as the difference in observed values of Y for two persons, i and i', in group j:

$$\begin{aligned}
Y_{ijt} - Y_{i'jt} &= (\mathbf{X}_{ijt}' - \mathbf{X}_{i'jt}')\boldsymbol{\beta}_0 + P_{ijt} \times \text{ATT}(\mathbf{X}_{ijt}) - P_{i'jt} \times \text{ATT}(\mathbf{X}_{i'jt}) + (\varepsilon_{ijt} - \varepsilon_{i'jt}) \\
&= (\mathbf{X}_{ijt}' - \mathbf{X}_{i'jt}')\boldsymbol{\beta}_0 + P_{ijt} \times \text{ATT}(\mathbf{X}_{ijt}) - P_{i'jt} \times \text{ATT}(\mathbf{X}_{i'jt}) \\
&\quad + (\theta_{jt} + v_{0ijt} - P_{ijt} \times \{\text{E}[v_{1ijt} - v_{0ijt} \mid P_{ijt} = 1, \mathbf{X}_{ijt}] - v_{1ijt} + v_{0ijt}\}) \\
&\quad - (\theta_{jt} + v_{0i'jt} - P_{i'jt} \times \{\text{E}[v_{1i'jt} - v_{0i'jt} \mid P_{i'jt} = 1, \mathbf{X}_{ijt}] - v_{1i'jt} + v_{0i'jt}\}) \\
&= (\mathbf{X}_{ijt}' - \mathbf{X}_{i'jt}')\boldsymbol{\beta}_0 + P_{ijt} \times \text{ATT}(\mathbf{X}_{ijt}) - P_{i'jt} \times \text{ATT}(\mathbf{X}_{i'jt}) \\
&\quad - v_{0ijt} + P_{ijt} \times \{\text{E}[v_{1ijt} - v_{0ijt} \mid P_{ijt} = 1, \mathbf{X}_{ijt}] - v_{1ijt} + v_{0ijt}\} \\
&\quad - v_{0i'jt} + P_{i'jt} \times \{\text{E}[v_{1i'jt} - v_{0i'jt} \mid P_{i'jt} = 1, \mathbf{X}_{i'jt}] - v_{1i'jt} + v_{0i'jt}\}). \qquad (12.7)
\end{aligned}$$

This expression for $Y_{ijt} - Y_{i'jt}$ suggests that a regression of $Y_{ijt} - Y_{i'jt}$ on $(\mathbf{X}_{ijt} - \mathbf{X}_{i'jt})$ and $P_{ijt} \times \text{ATT}(\mathbf{X}_{ijt})$ and $P_{i'jt} \times \text{ATT}(\mathbf{X}_{i'jt})$, where $\text{ATT}(\mathbf{X})$ is a general function of $\mathbf{X}$, would yield an estimate of $\text{ATT}(\mathbf{X})$. In particular, the expressions $\text{ATT}(\mathbf{X}_{ijt})$ and $\text{ATT}(\mathbf{X}_{i'jt})$ could be specified as $\boldsymbol{\delta}'\mathbf{X}_{ijt}$ and $\boldsymbol{\delta}'\mathbf{X}_{i'jt}$, respectively, so $P_{ijt} \times \text{ATT}(\mathbf{X}_{ijt})$ and $P_{i'jt} \times \text{ATT}(\mathbf{X}_{i'jt})$ could be specified as $\boldsymbol{\delta}'(P_{ijt} \times \mathbf{X}_{ijt})$ and $\boldsymbol{\delta}'(P_{i'jt} \times \mathbf{X}_{i'jt})$, respectively; then $Y_{ijt} - Y_{i'jt}$ can be regressed on $\mathbf{X}_{ijt} - \mathbf{X}_{i'jt}$ and $(P_{ijt} \times \mathbf{X}_{ijt} - P_{i'jt} \times \mathbf{X}_{i'jt})$ to obtain an estimate of $\boldsymbol{\delta}$ (and $\boldsymbol{\beta}_0$), and thus an estimate of $\text{ATT}(\mathbf{X})$ by $\boldsymbol{\delta}'\mathbf{X}$.

For this OLS estimator of $\text{ATT}(\mathbf{X})$ to be consistent and unbiased requires that the expectation of the unobserved component in the regression in equation (12.7) with respect to the variables in the regression equation ($\mathbf{X}_{ijt}$, $\mathbf{X}_{i'jt}$, P_{ijt}, and $P_{i'jt}$) equals 0. That is, it requires

$$\begin{aligned}
&\text{E}[v_{0ijt} - P_{ijt} \times \{\text{E}[v_{1ijt} - v_{0ijt} \mid P_{ijt} = 1, \mathbf{X}_{ijt}] - v_{1ijt} + v_{0ijt}\} \\
&\quad - v_{0i'jt} + P_{i'jt} \times \{\text{E}[v_{1i'jt} - v_{0i'jt} \mid P_{i'jt} = 1, \mathbf{X}_{i'jt}] - v_{1i'jt} + v_{0i'jt}\}) \mid \mathbf{X}_{ijt}, \mathbf{X}_{i'jt}, P_{ijt}, P_{i'jt}] = 0.
\end{aligned}$$

Fortunately, this assumption can be expressed in a form that is both simpler and more intuitive:[7]

$$\begin{aligned}
&\text{E}[v_{0ijt} - P_{ijt} \times \{\text{E}[v_{1ijt} - v_{0ijt} \mid P_{ijt} = 1, \mathbf{X}_{ijt}] - v_{1ijt} + v_{0ijt}\} \\
&\quad - v_{0i'jt} + P_{i'jt} \times \{\text{E}[v_{1i'jt} - v_{0i'jt} \mid P_{i'jt} = 1, \mathbf{X}_{i'jt}] - v_{1i'jt} + v_{0i'jt}\}) \mid \mathbf{X}_{ijt}, \mathbf{X}_{i'jt}, P_{ijt}, P_{i'jt}] \\
&\quad = \text{E}[v_{0ijt} \mid \mathbf{X}_{ijt}, \mathbf{X}_{i'jt}, P_{ijt}, P_{i'jt}] - \text{E}[v_{1ijt} - v_{0ijt} \mid P_{ijt} = 1, \mathbf{X}_{ijt}] + \text{E}[v_{1ijt} - v_{0ijt} \mid \mathbf{X}_{ijt}, \mathbf{X}_{i'jt}, P_{ijt} = 1, \\
&\quad\quad P_{i'jt}] \\
&\quad\quad - \text{E}[v_{0i'jt} \mid \mathbf{X}_{ijt}, \mathbf{X}_{i'jt}, P_{ijt}, P_{i'jt}] + \text{E}[v_{1i'jt} - v_{0i'jt} \mid P_{i'jt} = 1, \mathbf{X}_{i'jt}] - \text{E}[v_{1i'jt} - v_{0i'jt} \mid \mathbf{X}_{ijt}, \mathbf{X}_{i'jt}, P_{ijt}, \\
&\quad\quad P_{i'jt} = 1] \\
&\quad = \text{E}[v_{0ijt} \mid \mathbf{X}_{ijt}, \mathbf{X}_{i'jt}, P_{ijt}, P_{i'jt}] - \text{E}[v_{1ijt} - v_{0ijt} \mid P_{ijt} = 1, \mathbf{X}_{ijt}] + \text{E}[v_{1ijt} - v_{0ijt} \mid \mathbf{X}_{ijt}, P_{ijt} = 1] \\
&\quad\quad - \text{E}[v_{0i'jt} \mid \mathbf{X}_{ijt}, \mathbf{X}_{i'jt}, P_{ijt}, P_{i'jt}] + \text{E}[v_{1i'jt} - v_{0i'jt} \mid P_{i'jt} = 1, \mathbf{X}_{i'jt}] - \text{E}[v_{1i'jt} - v_{0i'jt} \mid \mathbf{X}_{i'jt}, P_{i'jt} = 1] \\
&\quad = \text{E}[v_{0ijt} \mid \mathbf{X}_{ijt}, \mathbf{X}_{i'jt}, P_{ijt}, P_{i'jt}] - \text{E}[v_{0i'jt} \mid \mathbf{X}_{ijt}, \mathbf{X}_{i'jt}, P_{ijt}, P_{i'jt}] - 0.
\end{aligned}$$

This assumption implies that, within a particular group, the unobserved factors that determine Y_{0ijt} are not correlated with the participation decisions of either person (recall the assumption made above that the **X** variables are assumed to be uncorrelated with U_0, so they are uncorrelated with v_0). That is, v_0 does not influence which individual in the group gets the treatment. Note that the term θ_j may still influence selection into treatment.

For example, suppose there is a program that provides nutritious foods to children from poor families. Within poor families, some children receive the nutritious foods and some do not. A within estimator might compare the nutritional outcomes of siblings, some of whom participate in the program and some of whom do not. The assumption that v_{0ijt} does not influence which child gets the treatment is a requirement that the child-specific component of nutritional status (the component that excludes θ_j, that is, the component that is not common across children from the same family) not be a determinant of whether the child is in the program. Within families, which child gets the program needs to be essentially random, after conditioning on the observed variables ($\mathbf{X}_{ijt}$ and $\mathbf{X}_{i'jt}$).

In summary, the within estimator allows the researcher to reduce bias, relative to a cross-sectional estimator, when data are available for only one time period and the observations belong to different groups, such as families, schools, or communities. A few issues should be kept in mind when applying this estimator. First, because the within estimator relies on comparing the outcomes of treated and untreated persons, the approach implicitly assumes that there are no spillover effects from treating one individual onto other individuals within the same group. In general, the larger the group the more plausible this assumption is. For example, the influence of one child on another child is more likely if the two children are in the same family compared with a situation in which they are in the same school but in different families; similarly, spillover effects are more likely for two children in the same school in a given community than for two children in two different schools in the same community.

Second, as with the before-after and DID estimation approaches, the within estimator allows treatment to be selective across groups; that is, it allows $E[\varepsilon_{ijt} | P_{ijt}, \mathbf{X}_{ijt}] \neq 0$, because treatment selection can be based on the unobserved heterogeneity term θ_j (heterogeneity shared among individuals within a group).

Third, when the variation being exploited for identification of the treatment effect is variation within a family, community, or school at a single time, then the within estimator can be implemented with a single cross-section of data.

Applications of difference-in-differences and within estimators

This section considers some applications of the DID and within estimators, including the following:

- An evaluation of the impact of a family planning and health counseling program on child outcomes in the Philippines (Rosenzweig and Wolpin 1986)
- A study of the effect of school construction on education, and of education on wages, in Indonesia (Duflo 2001)
- An evaluation of the impact of school meals on child nutrition in the Philippines (Jacoby 2002)
- A study of the impact of flip charts on student academic performance in Kenya (Glewwe et al. 2004)

Rosenzweig and Wolpin (1986)

One of the earliest applications of both the within estimator and the DID estimator is by Rosenzweig and Wolpin (1986). They evaluated the impact of a family planning and health counseling program on child outcomes in 20 barrios (villages) in the Philippines. The program focused on the health of children age five or younger. Survey data were collected in 1975 and 1979 from 240 randomly selected households residing in these barrios on the age, height, and weight of every family member. Information was also obtained in 1979 from each of the barrios on the dates of introduction of rural health clinics and family planning clinics financed by the national government. To estimate the effects of the facilities on child health, Rosenzweig and Wolpin used a sample of 274 children (defined as those under age 18 in 1979) in 85 households for whom height and weight information was collected in both years of the survey.

The main estimation issue is the statistical problems created by nonrandom program placement, that is, the possibility that the placement of programs may depend on the outcome variable of interest. A program that is targeted to areas with poor health outcomes will appear to be ineffective if the health outcomes in areas with that program are compared with the health outcomes in areas without that program.

For estimation, Rosenzweig and Wolpin (1986) used the following regression model:

$$H^a_{ijt} = \beta x^a_{ij} + \mu_i + \mu_j + \varepsilon_{ijt},$$

where

H^a_{ijt} = health (height, weight) for child i, at age a, living in village j at time t,
x^a_{ij} = length of time that the child was exposed to the program,
μ_i = time-invariant, child-specific unobserved health endowment,
μ_j = unobserved time-invariant community- (village-)level effect,
ε_{ijt} = time-varying, child-specific random term, assumed to be uncorrelated with x^a_{ij}.

Consider first the estimation with only community fixed effects (μ_j) and without child fixed effects (μ_i). Community fixed effects allow different communities to have different initial health endowments, which may be correlated with the length of time the program has been in the community. This is an application of the within estimator; the coefficient β is estimated on the basis of variation in exposure *within* communities, which depends on variation in exposure caused by children being of different ages (for example, older children had little or no exposure, whereas younger children had more exposure, during their first five years of life). Note that the within estimation method allows allocation of the program to be selective on unobserved characteristics at the community level, but not at the individual level. When child fixed effects (μ_i) are added, two or more periods are needed (otherwise each observation for data from only one time period would be perfectly predicted by the child fixed effect μ_i); adding child fixed effects to this estimation leads to the DID estimator, because it compares changes in health outcomes for children who were exposed to the program to changes for children who were not exposed.[8]

Rosenzweig and Wolpin (1986) compared results using different estimators: simple OLS regression (not controlling for either μ_i or μ_j); OLS regression controlling for community fixed effects (controlling for μ_j but not for μ_i), which is within estimation; and first-differenced regressions (controlling for both μ_i and μ_j), which is DID estimation. As seen in table 12.1, the differences in estimated program exposure effects across the specifications are striking for both health measures. For example, in the height regressions (panel a of table 12.1), both the cross-sectional and community fixed effects estimates (within estimation) of health and family planning clinic effects are generally negative, with standard errors that are at least as large as the point estimates. The child fixed effect (DID) estimates, however, indicate that exposure to health and family planning clinics increases height, with the family planning effect statistically significant at conventional levels and the health clinic effect marginally significant.

In summary, when Rosenzweig and Wolpin (1986) used within estimation, their estimates yielded the unexpected result that health clinics and family planning clinics have negative impacts on children's health. In contrast, their DID estimates indicate that the height of a child who had access to a health clinic would be 5 percent higher than that of an otherwise similar child without access to such a clinic, while exposure to a family planning clinic increases height by 7 percent. The weight regressions yield similar results.

TABLE 12.1 Main results from Rosenzweig and Wolpin (1986)

VARIABLE	OLS	FIXED EFFECT	
	CROSS-SECTION	COMMUNITY (BARRIO)	CHILD
a. Log of standardized height			
Rural health clinic exposure	−0.005	−0.021	0.051
	(0.53)	(0.40)	(1.21)
Family planning clinic exposure	−0.013	−0.009	0.071
	(1.12)	(0.27)	(3.32)
R^2	0.034	0.170	0.066
b. Log of standardized weight			
Rural health clinic exposure	−0.031	−0.162	0.099
	(1.35)	(1.20)	(1.52)
Family planning clinic exposure	0.026	0.080	0.121
	(0.87)	(0.90)	(2.76)
R^2	0.034	0.140	0.050
Degrees of freedom	268	249	272

Source: Rosenzweig and Wolpin 1986, Table 3.
Note: Figures in parentheses are *t*-statistics. The R^2 in the last two columns are from first-differenced estimation. OLS = ordinary least squares.

Duflo (2001)

A study by Duflo (2001) uses a DID estimator to evaluate the effects of a school construction program in Indonesia on education, and the effect of education (years of schooling) on wages. In 1973, the Indonesian government launched a major school construction program, the Sekolah Dasar INPRES program. Between 1973–74 and 1978–79, more than 61,000 primary schools were constructed, an average of two schools per 1,000 children ages 5 to 14 in 1971. Enrollment rates among children ages 7 to 12 increased from 69 percent in 1973 to 83 percent by 1978. This was in contrast to the absence of capital expenditure and a decline in enrollment in the early 1970s. Duflo exploited this policy change to estimate the impacts of this school construction program on education and earnings.

The major estimation issue is that the placement of schools was not random. The construction of new schools was, in part, locally financed: more schools were built in more-affluent communities. Individuals from those communities usually enjoy better outcomes even without any intervention, so it is difficult to draw reliable inferences from cross-sectional comparisons of communities with and without the new schools. In other words, local economic conditions may be omitted variables in a cross-sectional OLS regression, yielding biased and inconsistent estimates of the program impact.

To address this estimation problem, Duflo used a DID estimator. Note that exposure to the school construction program varied by region and by year. Thus the education of individuals who were young when the program began was more affected by the school building program than was the education of older individuals. Also, the program's effect should be stronger in regions where larger numbers of schools were built.

Duflo's (2001) identification strategy compares the differences in the outcomes of older and younger individuals in regions where the school construction program was most active with the same difference in regions where that program was less active. The first comparison (between outcomes of different cohorts of individuals in the same region) controls for (removes) the influences of local economic conditions, and the second comparison (between "active" and "less active" regions) estimates the impact of the school construction program in a way that differences out nationwide general trends in enrollment.

Table 12.2 illustrates Duflo's (2001) identification strategy by presenting means of years of education and (the log of) wages for different population groups. Children who were ages 2 to 6 in 1974 were young enough to benefit from the program, but only those in areas with a high level of building new primary schools received a large "dose" of the program. In contrast, children ages 12 to 17 in 1974 were too old to benefit from the new primary schools. In the areas where the program was most intense, the eventual mean years of education of children ages 2 to 6 in 1974 was 0.47 years higher than for children who were 12 to 17 in 1974 (8.49 – 8.02). In the areas where the program was least intense, the eventual mean years of education of children ages 2 to 6 in 1974 was only 0.36 years higher than for children who were 12 to 17 in 1974 (9.76 – 9.40). The difference in these two differences is about 0.12, which implies that this is the effect of the program. A similar calculation for log wages shows an impact of 0.026, which is a 2.6 percent increase in wages.

A comparison of the older cohort with an even older cohort (both of which should not have been affected by the program) is shown in panel b of table 12.2. The difference in the differences of these two cohorts is much smaller and thus very close to zero, which is what

TABLE 12.2 Results from Duflo (2001)

	YEARS OF EDUCATION			LOG(WAGES)		
	LEVEL OF PROGRAM IN REGION OF BIRTH			LEVEL OF PROGRAM IN REGION OF BIRTH		
	HIGH	LOW	DIFFERENCE	HIGH	LOW	DIFFERENCE
a. Experiment of interest						
Ages 2 to 6 in 1974	8.49	9.76	−1.27	6.61	6.73	−0.12
	(0.04)	(0.04)	(0.06)	(0.01)	(0.01)	(0.01)
Ages 12 to 17 in 1974	8.02	9.40	−1.39	6.87	7.02	−0.15
	(0.05)	(0.04)	(0.07)	(0.01)	(0.01)	(0.01)
Difference	0.47	0.36	0.12	−0.26	−0.29	0.026
	(0.07)	(0.04)	(0.09)	(0.01)	(0.01)	(0.015)
b. Control experiment						
Ages 12 to 17 in 1974	8.02	9.40	−1.39	6.87	7.02	−0.15
	(0.05)	(0.04)	(0.07)	(0.01)	(0.01)	(0.01)
Ages 18 to 24 in 1974	7.70	9.12	−1.42	6.92	7.08	−0.16
	(0.06)	(0.04)	(0.07)	(0.01)	(0.01)	(0.01)
Difference	0.32	0.28	0.034	0.056	0.063	0.007
	(0.08)	(0.06)	(0.098)	(0.013)	(0.010)	(0.016)

Source: Duflo 2001, Table 3.
Note: Standard errors shown in parentheses.

would be expected given that the program should not have had any effect on either of these cohorts. A larger difference, for example, similar to the difference in panel a, would have indicated that something else, not the school construction program, was the cause of the estimated program effects found in panel a.

Duflo (2001) presents regression estimates in Table 4 of her paper. These estimates suggest that each new school constructed per 1,000 children resulted in an increase of 0.12 to 0.19 years of education, and a 1.5 to 2.7 percent increase in earnings for the first cohort of children fully exposed to the program. This implies that the economic returns to education range from 6.8 to 10.6 percent. These estimates of economic returns to education were obtained using instrumental variables methods, which are discussed in chapter 15 of this book.

Jacoby (2002)

Jacoby (2002) studies whether public transfers targeted toward children "stick" to them, as opposed to the transfers being diluted by intrahousehold reallocation of food at home away from the child and toward other household members. This sticking of transfers is sometimes called the *flypaper effect*. More specifically, Jacoby (2002) examines the impact of a school feeding program in the Philippines using data on 3,189 children in 159 schools. He uses a DID strategy that compares interday (school day vs. non–school day) calorie differentials across program participants and nonparticipants. The analysis assumes that the only reason the calorie intake of program participants varies across school and non–school days, relative to nonparticipants, is because of the school feeding program.[9]

To estimate the impact of the school feeding program on calorie consumption, Jacoby (2002) estimates the following equation:[10]

$$C_{is}^{T} = \alpha_{P} C_{is}^{P} \times D_{s}^{P} \times D_{is}^{A} + \alpha_{A} D_{is}^{A} + f_{s} + u_{is},$$

where

C_{is}^{T} = total daily calorie intake for child i in school s,

C_{is}^{P} = calories consumed by child i in school s from the calories provided by the program,

D_{s}^{P} = an indicator for whether the school offers a feeding program,

D_{is}^{A} = an indicator that calorie data for child i in school s is for a school day,

f_{s} = a school fixed effect, and

u_{is} = unobserved child-specific determinants of calorie intake.

If parents do not give their children who participate in the program fewer calories at home, then the coefficient on α_P should equal 1, which indicates that there is a flypaper effect (the calories provided at school stick to the child).

Jacoby's empirical results suggest that there is a flypaper effect; there is very little evidence of reallocation of targeted transfers away from children, except for weak evidence of calorie reallocation in the poorest families. That is, the child's calorie consumption rises roughly one for one with feeding program calories. This is seen in table 12.3, which shows that, for a variety of estimation methods, the estimates of α_P are very close to 1.[11]

Glewwe et al. (2004)

As a final word of caution, Glewwe et al. (2004) question the reliability of the DID estimation approach in an evaluation of the effectiveness of an educational intervention in Kenya that provided schools with flip charts (charts bound together that can be put on an easel or hung on a wall; figure 12.3 provides an example) to use as teaching aids in certain subjects.

One of the goals of the Glewwe et al. (2004) study was to compare the estimates obtained from a nonexperimental DID estimation approach to those obtained from a randomized controlled trial. The DID estimator compares changes over time in test scores in flip chart and non–flip chart subjects within the schools that received the intervention. The experiment

TABLE 12.3 Main results from Jacoby (2002)

	IMPACT OF PROGRAM ON TOTAL DAILY CALORIES		
SPECIFICATION (N = 3,189)	$\hat{\alpha}_P$	$\hat{\alpha}_A$	p-VALUE
OLS	1.104	61.1	0.000
	(0.134)	(21.9)	
2SLS	1.153	38.9	0.739
	(0.460)	(39.0)	
2SLS with day-of-interview dummies	1.082	65.6	0.616
	(0.464)	(66.0)	

Source: Jacoby 2002, Table 1.
Note: Standard errors in parentheses. The OLS p-value is for the hypothesis that all the control variables are statistically insignificant. The p-value for the first set of 2SLS estimates is for the hypothesis that C_{is}^{P} is exogenous. The p-value for the second set of 2SLS estimates is for the hypothesis that day-of-interview dummies are jointly insignificant. OLS = ordinary least squares; 2SLS = two-stage least squares.

FIGURE 12.3 A mathematics flip chart of the type evaluated by Glewwe et al. (2004)

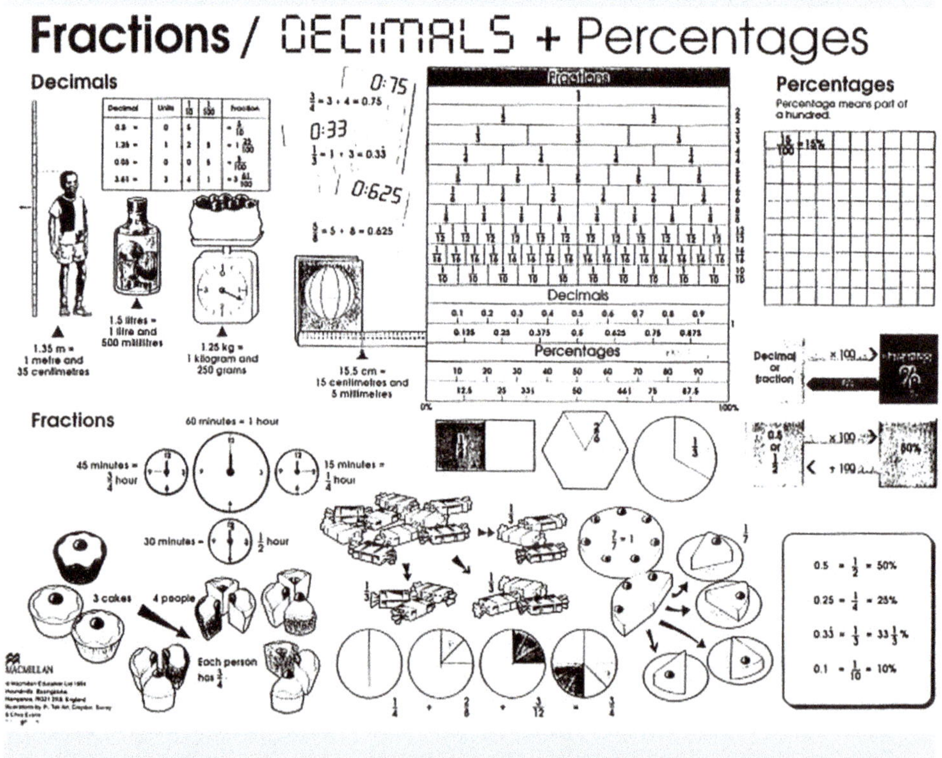

Source: Glewwe et al. 2004.
Note: Reprinted from *Journal of Development Economics*, volume 74, issue 1, Paul Glewwe, Michael Kremer, Sylvie Moulin, and Eric Zitzewitz, "Retrospective vs. Prospective Analyses of School Inputs: The Case of Flip Charts in Kenya," pages 251–268, copyright 2004), with permission from Elsevier. Further permission required for reuse.

TABLE 12.4 OLS and difference-in-differences estimates from Glewwe et al. (2004)

Dependent variable: Normalized test score

SPECIFICATION	(1)	(2)	(3)	(4)
	LEVEL ESTIMATES		DIFFERENCE-IN-DIFFERENCES	
School random effects	Yes	Yes	Yes	Yes
School × subject random effects	No	No	No	Yes
Schools	79	79	79	79
Pupils	4,998	4,998	4,998	4,998
Grades included	6–8	6–8	6–8	6–8
Subjects included	Science, math, home science	Science, math, home science	All	All
Flip chart variables				
Number of flip charts in school	0.205***	0.076*	0.154***	0.157***
(divided by four)	(0.064)	(0.041)	(0.057)	(0.056)
Charts × flip chart subject			0.049**	0.040*
(Science, math, home science)			(0.021)	(0.024)

Source: Glewwe et al. 2004.
Note: Columns (1), (3), and (4) control for school inputs (textbooks, teacher training); column (2) controls for student scores on non-flip chart subjects. Science includes agriculture, and home science includes business education. Statistical significance at the 10%, 5%, and 1% levels is indicated by one, two and three asterisks, respectively.

randomly allocated the schooling intervention (flip charts) to a subset of schools and compares the schools that did and did not receive the intervention.

As seen in table 12.4, the DID estimates in columns (3) and (4) are statistically significant, which suggests that flip charts increase student learning. However, results from a randomized controlled trial, which are shown in table 12.5, indicate no learning effect of flip charts. Glewwe et al. (2004) conclude that DID estimates can be unreliable.

Conclusion

This chapter presents in detail two additional regression-based estimators, the DID estimator and the within estimator. The assumptions needed for unbiased and consistent estimation are not as strong as the assumptions needed for the cross-sectional and before-after estimators discussed in chapter 11, but it is still possible that they could be violated.

When data are available for only one period and the observations belong to different groups, such as families, schools, or communities, the within estimator allows bias to be reduced, relative to a cross-sectional estimator. However, several things must be kept in

TABLE 12.5 Estimates from a randomized controlled trial (Glewwe et al. 2004)

Dependent variable: Normalized test score

	CONTROL FOR PAST PERFORMANCE	FLIP CHART SCHOOL COEFFICIENT	FLIP CHART SCHOOL STANDARD ERROR	OBSERVATIONS
a. Flip chart subjects				
Science	No	0.0005	0.0752	20,446
	Yes	−0.0007	0.0591	
Math	No	−0.0201	0.0600	20,441
	Yes	−0.0212	0.0486	
Home science	No	−0.0295	0.0728	20,434
	Yes	−0.0276	0.0559	
Geography, history, civics, religious education	No	0.0018	0.0714	20,450
	Yes	−0.0012	0.0553	
b. Non-flip chart subjects				
English	No	0.0038	0.0737	20,433
	Yes	−0.0100	0.0576	
KiSwahili	No	0.0110	0.0790	20,448
	Yes	0.0146	0.0737	
Arts, crafts, music	No	−0.0679	0.0758	20,417
	Yes	−0.0723	0.0589	

Source: Glewwe et al. 2004.
Note: Regressions include school and school × year random effects and test fixed effects. Past performance controls are school-average performance on a July 1996 practice exam. Science includes agriculture, and home science includes business education.

mind when applying this estimator. First, because it relies on comparing the outcomes of treated and untreated persons, the approach implicitly assumes that there are no spillover effects from treating one individual onto other individuals within the same group, which could be a doubtful assumption in many contexts. Second, as with the before-after and DID estimation approaches, the within estimator allows treatment to be selective across groups; that is, treatment selection can be based on the unobserved heterogeneity term θ_j (heterogeneity shared among individuals within a group). Third, when the variation being exploited for identification of the treatment effect is variation within a family, school, or community at a single time, then the within estimator can be implemented with a single cross-section of data.

If data for two or more periods for the same individuals are available, DID estimation can be used. The main advantage of longitudinal (before-after or DID) estimators over cross-sectional methods is that they permit unobservable determinants of program participation decisions that are potentially correlated with outcomes. DID has the additional advantage over before-after estimation of not confounding general changes over time in Y_0 with the impact of the program. The latter advantage holds with repeated cross-sectional data, but the former does not. However, the fixed effects error structure that is imposed to justify application of DID estimators requires that all components of the unobservables that are correlated with the participation decision be time invariant, which does not allow for unobservable variables that both vary over time and are correlated with the observed variables. An example is a program designed to increase individuals' earnings; unobserved negative earnings shocks might be present that make people more likely to participate in a social program (such as a public works program) *and* persist over time, which would not necessarily be captured by a fixed effects error structure.

The regression-based estimators discussed in chapter 11 and this chapter have been used by economists for decades. Another approach, which was developed in the statistics literature, is the use of matching methods, which has become more common in recent years among researchers who evaluate programs in both developed and developing countries. This method is introduced in the following chapter.

Notes

1. Note that $I_i = P_{it''}$ for any individual i. The use of one or the other depends on which is more clear or intuitive in the particular context.
2. $E[U_{0it''} - U_{0it'} | \mathbf{X}_{it''}] = E[U_{0it''} - U_{0it'} | I_i = 0, \mathbf{X}_{it''}] \times Prob[I_i = 0] + E[U_{0it''} - U_{0it'} | I_i = 1, \mathbf{X}_{it''}] \times Prob[I_i = 1]$. The assumption that $E[U_{0it''} - U_{0it'} | \mathbf{X}_{it''}] = 0$, combined with $E[U_{0it''} - U_{0it'} | I_i = 0, \mathbf{X}_{it''}] = 0$, implies $E[U_{0it''} - U_{0it'} | I_i = 1, \mathbf{X}_{it''}] = 0$.
3. The expected gain for participants conditional on $\mathbf{X}_{it''}$ is $E[Y_{1it''} - Y_{0it''} | I_i=1, \mathbf{X}_{it''}] = E[\mathbf{X}_{it''}(\boldsymbol{\beta}_1 - \boldsymbol{\beta}_0) + U_{1it''} - U_{0it''} | I_i=1, \mathbf{X}_{it''}] = \mathbf{X}_{it''}(\boldsymbol{\beta}_1 - \boldsymbol{\beta}_0) + E[U_{1it''} - U_{0it''} | I_i = 1, \mathbf{X}_{it''}] = \mathbf{X}_{it''}(\boldsymbol{\beta}_1 - \boldsymbol{\beta}_0)$. Recall that $E[U_{1it''} - U_{0it''} | \mathbf{X}_{it''}] = 0$, and note $E[U_{1it''} - U_{0it''} | \mathbf{X}_{it''}] = E[U_{1it''} - U_{0it''} | I_i = 0, \mathbf{X}_{it''}] \times Prob[I_i = 0 | \mathbf{X}_{it''}] + E[U_{1it''} - U_{0it''} | I_i = 1, \mathbf{X}_{it''}] \times Prob[I_i = 1 | \mathbf{X}_{it''}]$, which implies that $E[U_{1it''} - U_{0it''} | I_i = 0, \mathbf{X}_{it''}] = 0$, and thus, for nonparticipants as well, that $E[Y_{1it''} - Y_{0it''} | I_i = 0, \mathbf{X}_{it''}] = \mathbf{X}_{it''}(\boldsymbol{\beta}_1 - \boldsymbol{\beta}_0)$.
4. Groups that appear in multiple cross-sections, where some groups receive treatment and others do not (such as age cohorts), could be defined. Then an error components structure can be defined in terms of that group, that is, a group-level fixed effect. This would allow program selection to be based on some group-level unobservables, generalizing somewhat the assumptions stated in the text. For related discussion, see Deaton (1985).
5. Technically, a dummy variable for period t' to account for a common shock in that period cannot be added because the trends for the treatment and control groups from time t^0 to time t' already include that shock.
6. The approach builds on the idea, suggested by Heckman and Hotz (1989), of using preprogram exogeneity tests to choose from among competing estimators.
7. The first equality holds by using the law of iterated expectations and the fact that the P terms drop out when $P = 0$. The second equality assumes the "stable unit treatment value" assumption; that is, it assumes that one person's idiosyncratic gains do not depend on the values of $\mathbf{X}$, or the participation decision, of any other person. In particular, the following assumptions are made: $E[v_{1ijt} - v_{0ijt} | \mathbf{X}_{ijt}, \mathbf{X}_{i'jt}, P_{ijt} = 1, P_{i'jt}] = E[v_{1ijt} - v_{0ijt} | \mathbf{X}_{ijt}, P_{ijt} = 1]$ and $E[v_{1i'jt} - v_{0i'jt} | \mathbf{X}_{ijt}, \mathbf{X}_{i'jt}, P_{ijt}, P_{i'jt} = 1] = E[v_{1i'jt} - v_{0i'jt} | \mathbf{X}_{i'jt}, P_{i'jt} = 1]$.

8. In general, when child fixed effects are added it is no longer possible to estimate community fixed effects because the latter are, in effect, included in each child's fixed effect. However, Rosenzweig and Wolpin (1986) were able to estimate both community and individual fixed effects by using observations on families that migrated across communities.
9. As Jacoby (2002) notes, a potential threat to the validity of his DID strategy is that the program might be targeted toward poorer households, and poor children may spend more time working when not in school and therefore have higher calorie consumption, which would tend to bias the estimates against finding a flypaper effect.
10. Jacoby adds another variable to the interaction term associated with α_p, a dummy variable indicating whether the child chooses to participate in the program. For simplicity, it is assumed here that all eligible children participate.
11. There are several other complications that could cause bias in the estimates, such as the possibility that C_{is}^{P} is endogenous. See Jacoby (2002) for a detailed discussion of these issues.

References

Abadie, Alberto, Alexis Diamond, and Jens Hainmueller. 2010. "Synthetic Control Methods for Comparative Case Studies: Estimating the Effect of California's Tobacco Control Program." *Journal of the American Statistical Association* 105 (490): 493–505.

Abadie, Alberto, and Javier Gardeazabal. 2003. "The Economic Costs of Conflict: A Case Study of the Basque Country." *American Economic Review* 93 (1): 112–32.

Card, David. 1990. "The Impact of the Mariel Boatlift on the Miami Labor Market." *Industrial and Labor Relations Review* 43 (2): 245–57.

Deaton, Angus. 1985. "Panel Data from Times Series of Cross Sections." *Journal of Econometrics* 30 (1): 109–26.

Duflo, Esther. 2001. "Schooling and Labor Market Consequences of School Construction in Indonesia: Evidence from an Unusual Policy Experiment." *American Economic Review* 91 (4): 795–813.

Glewwe, Paul, Michael Kremer, Sylvie Moulin, and Eric Zitzewitz. 2004. "Retrospective vs. Prospective Analyses of School Inputs: The Case of Flip Charts in Kenya." *Journal of Development Economics* 74 (1): 251–68.

Heckman, James J., and V. Joseph Hotz. 1989. "Choosing among Alternative Nonexperimental Methods for Estimating the Impact of Social Programs." *Journal of the American Statistical Association* 84 (408): 862–74.

Jacoby, Hanan. 2002. "Is There an Intrahousehold Flypaper Effect? Evidence from a School Feeding Program." *Economic Journal* 112 (476): 196–221.

Rosenzweig, Mark, and Kenneth Wolpin. 1986. "Evaluating the Effects of Optimally Distributed Public Programs." *American Economic Review* 76 (3): 470–82

CHAPTER 13

Matching Methods

Introduction

Matching is a widely used evaluation method that compares the outcomes of program participants with the outcomes of similar, matched nonparticipants. It can be used to estimate the average treatment effect on the treated (ATT) and the average treatment effect (ATE). Some of the earliest applications of matching to evaluate economic development programs were World Bank evaluations of antipoverty programs (for example, Jalan and Ravallion 2003a, 2003b).

Economists and other researchers have long used ordinary least squares (OLS) regressions and, in some respects, have been slow to adapt to matching methods. They correctly note that conventional matching methods, similarly to OLS regressions, control for observable differences between treated and untreated observations but do nothing to correct for unobserved differences. Even so, matching methods have three advantages over standard OLS regressions in how they control for observed variables.

The first advantage is that matching estimators do not require researchers to specify a functional form of the outcome equations (the equations for Y_0 and Y_1), and therefore they are not susceptible to bias caused by misspecification along that dimension. For example, matching estimators do not require the assumption that outcomes be linear in observables, which is usually assumed in the regression-based estimation methods discussed in chapters 11 and 12. However, matching methods do require a researcher to make some functional form assumptions when estimating the probability of program participation (propensity score) function.[1] A second advantage of matching estimators is that, by imposing a common support condition, they use only observations on program nonparticipants that are similar to treatment-group (program participant) observations, and thus they effectively exclude or downweight observations that are not observably similar. In contrast, OLS regressions, as commonly implemented, do not omit or assign lower weight to comparison-group observations that are dissimilar to treatment-group observations. The third advantage is that matching emulates some features of randomized experiments by aligning the distribution of the observables in the matched comparison group to be the same as the distribution of those observables in the treatment group.

Thus, even though conventional cross-sectional matching estimators do not address the problem of unobserved differences between program participants and nonparticipants, they do have some advantages over OLS regression within the class of methods that control only for observable differences between treated and untreated observations.

Traditional matching estimators pair each program participant with an observably similar nonparticipant and interpret the difference in their outcomes as the effect of the program intervention (see, for example, Rosenbaum and Rubin 1983). More recently developed methods pair program participants with more than one nonparticipant and use a weighting scheme to construct the match in a way that optimally trades off the bias and variance of the estimator.

There are two main variants of matching estimators:

1. Cross-sectional estimators, which require data from only one postintervention period
2. Difference-in-differences (DID) matching estimators, which require panel data or repeated cross-sectional data obtained both before and after the time of the intervention

Cross-sectional matching estimators allow for selection on unobservables, but only in a very limited sense, described below. For the most part, these estimators are applicable in contexts in which the researcher is relatively certain that the major determinants of program participation are accounted for and that most or all of the remaining variation in who participates in a program is due to random factors. Similar to the DID estimation methods discussed in chapter 12, DID matching estimators identify treatment effects by comparing the change in outcomes for treated persons to the change in outcomes for matched, untreated persons. DID matching estimators allow selection into the program to be based on unobserved time-invariant characteristics of individuals.

Matching methods have been used in many types of impact evaluations, some examples of which are presented in this chapter. This chapter covers both cross-sectional matching and DID matching. The focus throughout is on a class of matching estimators called *propensity score matching* (PSM) estimators because these methods are relatively easy to implement and so are commonly used. PSM methods have been extended to the case of multiple discrete treatments and to the case of continuous treatments, in which there is a treatment "dose." These methods are beyond the scope of this chapter; for discussions of such methods, see, among others, Frölich (2004), Imbens (1999), and Lechner (2001). For discussions of other (non-PSM) matching estimators, see, for example, Cochran and Rubin (1973), Rubin (1980, 1984), and Todd (2008).

Two simple examples

The fundamental idea of matching is to use statistical techniques to construct an artificial control group by identifying for every treated observation an untreated observation that has similar observable characteristics. In this way, the estimation method creates a comparison group for which the joint distribution of observables is the same as that of the treated group. It is useful to begin with two examples to see how matching works.

Example 1: Exact matching. Consider a financial aid program that awards scholarships to university students from poor families. The award decisions are made in two steps:

> *Step 1.* Only students whose grade point average (GPA) and family income are in a certain range (such as GPA > 3.2, family income ≤ \$30,000) are eligible for the program.
> *Step 2.* Final recipients of the scholarship are chosen from the pool of eligible recipients according to criteria that include not only observable factors, such as gender, GPA, and family income, but also unobservable factors, such as which administrator was evaluating the application.

Table 13.1 illustrates how exact matching works. Matching assumes that, conditional on a set of observed characteristics (in this example, sex, years of college, GPA, and family income), whether a person received a scholarship was essentially random and, in particular, random with respect to outcomes of interest (Y_0 and Y_1). In this example, each row in the two panels of table 13.1 represents a student. The left panel is for students who were awarded financial aid, and the right panel is for students who were not awarded financial aid. Here, three pairs of students are matched exactly by their observed characteristics (the ones with same color shading).

If conditioning on a large set of characteristics is required, it may be quite difficult to apply exact matching. This is sometimes called the *curse of dimensionality problem*. In the above example, when all four matching variables are used, most students cannot be matched.

Example 2: Propensity score matching. PSM resolves the dimensionality problem, under the assumption that conditional on a set of observed characteristics (**Z**), program participation (P) is independent of the potential outcomes with (Y_1) and without (Y_0) the treatment.[2] More specifically, if that assumption holds, Rosenbaum and Rubin (1983) show that if the researcher conditions on the probability that a person participates in the program on the basis of observed characteristics (**Z**), which is called the *propensity score* ($\Pr(\mathbf{Z}) = \text{Prob}[P = 1 | \mathbf{Z}]$), this person's participation decision (P) is also independent of the potential outcomes (Y_1 and Y_0). The practical implication is that, instead of trying to match each participant to a nonparticipant by matching exactly for all observed characteristics **Z**, each participant can simply be matched to nonparticipants with the same (or similar) propensity score, $\text{Prob}[P = 1 | \mathbf{Z}]$. This resolves the dimensionality problem, because now only one variable needs to be matched.[3]

Because propensity scores are predicted probabilities that have a continuous range (support) between 0 and 1, the matching is sometimes done by dividing this support into several smaller intervals, such as (0, 0.1], (0.1, 0.2], (0.2, 0.3], . . ., (0.9, 1.0), and declaring that a match consists of being in the same interval. Other matching methods are discussed later in this chapter.

Table 13.2 illustrates the propensity score interval matching method.

TABLE 13.1 Exact matching

AWARDED FINANCIAL AID (PARTICIPANTS)				NOT AWARDED FINANCIAL AID (NONPARTICIPANTS)			
SEX	YEARS OF COLLEGE	GPA	FAMILY INCOME	SEX	YEARS OF COLLEGE	GPA	FAMILY INCOME
F	2	3.6	$20,000~$30,000	M	3	3.8	> $60,000
F	1	3.8	$10,000~$20,000	F	1	4.0	< $10,000
M	2	3.7	$20,000~$30,000	M	1	3.5	$20,000~$30,000
F	1	3.5	$10,000~$20,000	F	2	3.0	$10,000~$20,000
F	3	3.6	< $10,000	F	2	3.6	$20,000~$30,000
F	1	4.0	< $10,000	M	2	3.7	$20,000~$30,000
F	2	3.6	$10,000~$20,000	M	1	3.7	$20,000~$30,000
M	1	3.4	<$10,000	F	2	3.2	$30,000~$40,000

Source: Original table for this publication.
Note: F = female; GPA = grade point average; M = male.

TABLE 13.2 Propensity score matching

PARTICIPANTS					NONPARTICIPANTS				
SEX	YEARS IN COLLEGE	GPA	FAMILY INCOME	Pr(Z)	SEX	YEARS IN COLLEGE	GPA	FAMILY INCOME	Pr(Z)
F	2	3.5	$20,000–$30,000	0.65	M	3	3.3	> $60,000	0.20
F	1	3.8	$10,000–$20,000	0.95	F	1	3.7	$10,000–$20,000	0.85
M	2	3.7	$20,000–$30,000	0.83	M	1	3.5	$20,000–$30,000	0.63
F	1	3.5	$10,000–$20,000	0.45	F	2	3.0	$10,000–$20,000	0.10
F	3	3.6	< $10,000	0.82	F	2	3.6	$20,000–$30,000	0.67
F	1	4.0	< $10,000	0.99	M	2	3.6	$20,000–$30,000	0.75
F	2	3.6	$10,000–$20,000	0.75	F	2	3.6	$40,000–$50,000	0.61
M	1	3.4	<$10,000	0.48	F	2	3.8	$30,000~$40,000	0.44

Source: Original table for this publication.
Note: Pr(**Z**) = Prob[P = 1| **Z**]. F = female; GPA = grade point average; M = male.

Two points about table 13.2 should be noted. First, more participants can be matched than in the previous table, but some participants may still not have any matches (the rows with no shading) from among the group of nonparticipants; more precisely, the two participants with the highest propensity scores could not be matched to anyone in the nonparticipant group. Matching can be done only for individuals whose propensity scores lie within

FIGURE 13.1 Propensity scores and the area of common support

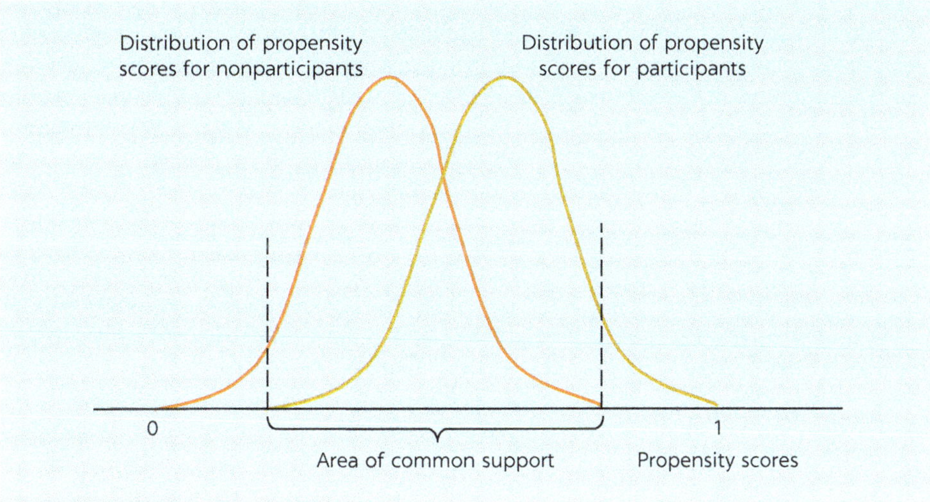

Source: Original figure for this publication.

the common support, which is the values of the propensity scores for which there are observations in the data for both the participants and the nonparticipants. Figure 13.1 illustrates the areas of common support.

The second point to note about table 13.2 is that for some participants, there may be several nonparticipants with similar propensity scores (for example, the three rows in the right panel with propensity scores between 0.61 and 0.67). A participant can be matched to either a single nonparticipant (the closest propensity score match) or to several nonparticipants with similar propensity scores, as discussed later in this chapter.

Matching can be performed with or without replacement. A disadvantage of matching without replacement is that the final estimate will then typically depend on the initial ordering in which the treated observations were matched. If matching is performed with replacement, it is good to check whether a few observations are being used repeatedly for the matches, because then the final estimates may hinge on those few observations. Imposing a common support condition, as explained later in this chapter, will help guard against this possibility.

To estimate the ATT or ATT($\mathbf{Z}$) of the program, the matching estimator first computes the average differences between the outcomes (observed values of Y) of individual participants and their matched nonparticipants, which yields the program impacts for each set of matched participants and nonparticipants. The mean of these individual differences, then, yields the estimated ATT. The mean over a particular set of the treated individuals—those with a given set of characteristics $\mathbf{Z}$ provides the estimate of ATT($\mathbf{Z}$).[4]

Keeping this basic idea of PSM in mind, the next section presents the technical assumptions required to justify the application of matching methods.

Cross-sectional matching

The simplest and most common applications of matching estimators are those implemented using cross-sectional data sets. Cross-sectional matching estimators require the assumption that a set of observed characteristics, denoted by **Z**, exists such that the outcome variables Y_0 and Y_1 are independent of program participation conditional on **Z**. An additional assumption is that the distribution of the **Z** variables is unaffected by the treatment.

The assumptions required for cross-sectional matching

The most important assumption for cross-sectional matching is that both potential outcomes (Y_0 and Y_1) be statistically independent of an individual's participation status, denoted by P, after conditioning on **Z**:

$$(Y_0, Y_1) \perp\!\!\!\perp P \mid \mathbf{Z}. \tag{13.1}$$

where the $\perp\!\!\!\perp$ symbol indicates statistical independence. This assumption is sometimes called *strong ignorability* or strict ignorability. Two equivalent ways of writing this assumption are

$$\text{Prob}[P = 1 \mid Y_0, Y_1, \mathbf{Z}] = \text{Prob}[P = 1 \mid \mathbf{Z}], \text{ and}$$
$$\text{F}(Y_0, Y_1 \mid \mathbf{Z}, P) = \text{F}(Y_0, Y_1 \mid \mathbf{Z}),$$

where $\text{F}(Y_0, Y_1, \mid \mathbf{Z}, P)$ denotes the conditional joint cumulative distribution function. Note that this second equivalent way to express equation (13.1) directly implies that $\text{E}[Y_0 \mid \mathbf{Z}, P] = \text{E}[Y_0 \mid \mathbf{Z}]$ and $\text{E}[Y_1 \mid \mathbf{Z}, P] = \text{E}[Y_1 \mid \mathbf{Z}]$.

The independence assumption implies that, for a group of people with the same values of the **Z** variables, P is uncorrelated with both Y_0 and Y_1. The most important implication of this assumption is that, conditional on **Z**, P is uncorrelated with the gain from the program, $Y_1 - Y_0$, which suggests that people do not select into the program on the basis of their anticipated gain, other than that part of the gain that can be captured by the observable **Z** variables.

Matching methods also require the assumption that, for all **Z**, the probabilities of participating ($P = 1$) and of not participating ($P = 0$) in the program are both positive:

$$0 < \text{Prob}[P = 1 \mid \mathbf{Z}] < 1. \tag{13.2}$$

This second assumption is required so that matches for $P = 0$ and $P = 1$ observations can be found. The intuition for this assumption is that if there are participants for whom treatment status is always 1 or 0, then it is not possible to find a match based on Prob[P = 1| **Z**]. For example, if for a certain value of **Z** it is the case that Prob[P = 1| **Z**] = 1 (all the observations with this value of **Z** are program participants), then there are no observations for Y_0 for those individuals with that value of **Z.** These individuals are considered to be outside the region of common support.

If the above two assumptions are satisfied, then the problem of determining mean program impacts can be solved by substituting the Y_0 distribution observed for the matched nonparticipant group (for whom $P = 0$) for the unobserved Y_0 distribution for program participants (for whom $P = 1$). The outcomes observed for the nonparticipants serve as a counterfactual for the individuals with whom they have been matched on the basis of their propensity score.

If the only interest is in estimating the impact of the program on those who participate, that is, if only ATT or ATT(**Z**) needs to be estimated, then the two assumptions in equations (13.1) and (13.2) can be weakened somewhat to become the following assumptions:

$$Y_0 \perp\!\!\!\perp P \mid \mathbf{Z} \text{ and } \text{Prob}[P = 1 \mid \mathbf{Z}] < 1.$$

Intuitively, if the only interest is in ATT or ATT(**Z**), then all the values of Y_1 that are needed are available because the interest here is only on program participants. Thus the only requirement is that P be uncorrelated with Y_0, which enables the needed Y_0 counterfactuals to be obtained. Also, complete statistical independence is not needed; the only requirement is that the mean of Y_0 conditional on **Z** does not depend on P.

The assumption that $Y_0 \perp\!\!\!\perp P \mid \mathbf{Z}$ implies that $E[Y_0 \mid \mathbf{Z}, P = 1] = E[Y_0 \mid \mathbf{Z}, P = 0]$, which means that, after conditioning on **Z**, the (conditional) mean of Y_0 does not depend on P. An important consequence of this is that it rules out selection into the program based directly on anticipated values of Y_0 that are not explained by the **Z** variables. However, no restriction is being imposed on Y_1, so individuals may select into the program on the basis of anticipated levels of Y_1. This allows for the possibility that some unobservables affect program participation decisions. However, assuming that individuals select into the program on the basis of anticipated values of Y_1 but not on the basis of anticipated values of Y_0 is generally not realistic; participation is primarily determined by the gain from doing so, which is $Y_1 - Y_0$, so the anticipated values of both Y_1 and Y_0 should influence participation.

Finally, the assumption that 0 < Prob[P = 1| **Z**] is not necessary. This condition is needed only to ensure that some Y_1 observations can be found to match with nonparticipants for whom the researcher wants to estimate treatment effects. The condition is not required if the main parameter of interest is ATT or ATT(**Z**), because these parameters of interest focus only on the participants.

Under the conditional independence assumptions or under the weaker conditional mean assumption, the overall mean impact of the program on program participants (which integrates ATT(**Z**) over the distribution of **Z** for program participants) can be written as

$$\begin{aligned} \text{ATT} &\equiv \text{E}[Y_1 - Y_0 \mid P = 1] = \text{E}[Y_1 \mid P = 1] - \text{E}_{\mathbf{Z} \mid P=1}[\text{E}[Y_0 \mid P = 1, \mathbf{Z}]] \\ &= \text{E}[Y_1 \mid P = 1] - \text{E}_{\mathbf{Z} \mid P=1}[\text{E}[Y_0 \mid P = 0, \mathbf{Z}]], \end{aligned}$$

where the second term can be estimated from the mean outcomes of the matched (on **Z**) nonparticipant group. The notation $\text{E}_{\mathbf{Z} \mid P=1}$ denotes that the expectation is taken with respect to the $f(\mathbf{Z} \mid P = 1)$ density; intuitively, the weighted average of observed Y is based on the distribution of **Z** for those people who participate in the program. More formally, this notation is defined as follows:

$$\text{E}_{\mathbf{Z} \mid P=1}[\text{E}_{Y \mid P=0,\mathbf{Z}}[Y_0 \mid P = 0, \mathbf{Z}]] = \int_z \int_y y f(y \mid P = 0, z)\, dy\, f(z \mid P = 1)\, dz.$$

Reducing the dimensionality of the matching problem

As noted above, matching can be difficult to implement when the set of conditioning variables **Z** is large. Rosenbaum and Rubin (1983) provide a useful theorem for reducing the dimension of the conditioning problem. In particular, they note that applying the law of iterated expectations to the random variables Y and **Z**, and to the discrete random variable P, yields the following relationship:

$$\text{E}[P \mid Y, \text{Prob}[P = 1 \mid \mathbf{Z}]] = \text{E}[\text{E}[P \mid Y, \mathbf{Z}] \mid Y, \text{Prob}[P = 1 \mid \mathbf{Z}]].$$

The most important implication of this result is the following:

$$\text{E}[P \mid Y, \mathbf{Z}] = \text{E}[P \mid \mathbf{Z}] \Rightarrow \text{E}[P \mid Y, \text{Prob}[P = 1 \mid \mathbf{Z}]] = \text{E}[P \mid \text{Prob}[P = 1 \mid \mathbf{Z}]].$$

That is, Rosenbaum and Rubin's (1983) theorem shows that when Y outcomes are independent of program participation, conditional on **Z**, they are also independent of participation conditional on the probability of participation, $\text{Prob}[P = 1 \mid \mathbf{Z}]$. The practical benefit of this theorem is that the analysis does not need to match on **Z**, which could involve a large number of variables. Instead, the analysis needs to match only on $\text{Prob}[P = 1 \mid \mathbf{Z}]$, a single variable that summarizes the influence of **Z** on the probability of participating.

The expression $\text{Prob}[P = 1 \mid \mathbf{Z}]$ is often called the *propensity score*, and it is denoted by Pr(**Z**). In impact evaluation terms, this is the probability of receiving the treatment being evaluated, given a set of characteristics denoted by **Z**. Because of this dimensionality reduction benefit, much of the literature on matching focuses on PSM methods.

Using the Rosenbaum and Rubin (1983) theorem, the matching procedure can be implemented in two steps:

1. The propensity score $\Pr(\mathbf{Z}) = \text{Prob}[P = 1 | \mathbf{Z}]$ is estimated, usually using a parametric binary discrete choice model such as a logit or probit model.

2. Individuals are matched on the basis of their first-stage estimated probabilities of participation, denoted by $\widehat{\Pr}(\mathbf{Z})$. The match does not have to be exact. As explained previously, and in more detail below, matches can be made if the estimated propensity scores are close enough.

Implementation of propensity score matching estimators

Statisticians and economists have developed a variety of matching estimators based on the propensity score. This section discusses some of the most commonly applied matching estimators. It then discusses how to choose the region of common support and how to implement matching estimators by reweighting the data.

Four types of matching estimators

This subsection presents four of the most common types of matching estimators. For notational simplicity, let Pr denote $\widehat{\Pr}(\mathbf{Z})$.[5]

A typical cross-sectional matching estimator for the ATT takes the form:

$$\widehat{\text{ATT}}_{\text{M}} = \frac{1}{n_1} \sum_{i \in I_1 \cap S_P} (Y_{1i} - \hat{\text{E}}[Y_{0i} | P = 1, \Pr_i]), \tag{13.3}$$

where

$$\hat{\text{E}}[Y_{0i} | P = 1, \Pr_i] = \sum_{j \in I_0} W_{ij} Y_{0j}.$$

In this expression, I_1 denotes the set of program participants, I_0 is the set of nonparticipants, S_p is the region of common support (the region over which matches can be found, which is discussed more below), n_1 is the number of people in the set $I_1 \cap S_p$, and W_{ij} are weights for every individual in the nonparticipant group.

In equation (13.3), the Y_1 of participant i is matched to a counterfactual that is constructed by a weighted average of the Y_0's of similar (matched) nonparticipants. The weights (W_{ij}) depend on the distance between $\Pr_i$ and $\Pr_j$, with larger weights assigned to observations for which $\Pr_j$ is closer to $\Pr_i$. Another concept used in matching estimation is a "neighborhood," which can be denoted by $C(\Pr_i)$ for each i in the participant sample. The neighbors of person i are nonparticipants ($j \in I_0$) whose propensity scores (Pr_j) are in the neighborhood of (are close to) the propensity score of person i (Pr_i).

Matching can also be used to find the average effect of treatment on the untreated by finding matches for each untreated observation. That is, rather than finding one or more untreated observations to match to each treated person, one or more treated observations are found to match to each untreated person. The ATT and the average effect of treatment on the untreated can then be combined (by taking a weighted average) to get the overall ATE.

A variety of matching estimators are described in the following discussion. They differ primarily in two ways: (1) how the neighborhood is defined, and (2) how the weights W_{ij} are constructed.

Nearest neighbor matching. Traditional nearest neighbor matching, which is also called *pairwise matching*, can be defined by setting the neighborhood function to be

$$C\left(\mathrm{Pr}_i\right) = \min_j |\mathrm{Pr}_i - \mathrm{Pr}_j|,\ j \in I_0,$$

where $|\mathrm{Pr}_i - \mathrm{Pr}_j|$ is the distance (in this case the simple difference) between Pr_i and Pr_j. That is, the nonparticipant whose Pr_j is closest to Pr_i is selected as the match. The nearest neighbor matching estimator is often used because of its ease of implementation.

Caliper matching. Caliper matching (Cochran and Rubin 1973) is a variation of nearest neighbor matching that attempts to avoid bad matches (those for which Pr_j is far from Pr_i) by imposing a limit on the maximum distance $|\mathrm{Pr}_i - \mathrm{Pr}_j|$ allowed. That is, the nearest neighbor match for person i is selected only if, in addition, $|\mathrm{Pr}_i - \mathrm{Pr}_j| < \varepsilon_c$, where ε_c is a specified "tolerance" (limit). Thus, for caliper matching, the neighborhood is defined as $C(\mathrm{Pr}_i) = \{\mathrm{Pr}_j \mid |\mathrm{Pr}_i - \mathrm{Pr}_j| < \varepsilon_c\}$. Treated persons for whom no matches can be found (that is, no values of $|\mathrm{Pr}_i - \mathrm{Pr}_j|$ are within the caliper) are excluded from the analysis. Caliper matching is one way to impose the common support requirement that there be both treated and untreated persons with very similar propensity score values.

A drawback of caliper matching is that it is difficult to know ahead of time what value for the tolerance level (ε_c) is reasonable. A choice that is too small could lead to too many matches being excluded, and a choice that is too large could lead to bad matches that are not necessarily comparable because Pr_i and Pr_j are not close enough to being almost the same.

Stratification or interval matching. Another simple variant of matching is stratification or interval matching. It is implemented in three steps:

1. The common support of the propensity scores (the Pr's) is partitioned into a set of intervals.

2. Within each interval, a separate impact is calculated by calculating the difference between the mean of observed Y for participants ($P = 1$) and the mean of observed Y for nonparticipants ($P = 0$).

3. A weighted average of the interval impact estimates, using the fraction of the $P = 1$ population in each interval for the weights, provides an overall estimate of ATT.

Implementing this method requires a decision about how wide the intervals should be. Dehejia and Wahba (1999) implement interval matching using intervals that are selected so that the mean values of the estimated Pr_i's and Pr_j's are not statistically different from each other within each interval.

Nonparametric methods: Kernel matching and local linear matching. More recently developed matching estimators construct a match for each program participant using a weighted average over multiple persons in the nonparticipant group rather than a single nearest neighbor. The main advantage of averaging over multiple persons to construct the match is a reduction in the variance of the estimated matched outcome, which may come at the expense of higher bias. Choosing the number of observations to include in the local averaging entails a bias-variance trade-off.

Nonparametric matching methods include the nonparametric kernel matching estimator and local linear regression matching methods. Consider, for example, the nonparametric kernel matching estimator, which is given by

$$\widehat{\text{ATT}}_{\text{KM}} = \frac{1}{n_1} \sum_{i \in I_1 \cap S_P} \left\{ Y_{1i} - \sum_{j \in I_0} Y_{0j} W_{ij} \right\} = \frac{1}{n_1} \sum_{i \in I_1 \cap S_P} \left\{ Y_{1i} - \frac{\sum_{j \in I_0} Y_{0j} G\left(\frac{\text{Pr}_j - \text{Pr}_i}{a_n} \right)}{\sum_{k \in I_0} G\left(\frac{\text{Pr}_k - \text{Pr}_i}{a_n} \right)} \right\}, \tag{13.4}$$

where $G(\cdot)$ is a kernel function[6] and a_n is a bandwidth parameter. Note that the weights, W_{ij}, are equal to $G\left(\frac{\text{Pr}_j - \text{Pr}_i}{a_n} \right) \Big/ \sum_{k \in I_0} G\left(\frac{\text{Pr}_k - \text{Pr}_i}{a_n} \right)$. For a kernel function bounded between -1 and 1, the neighborhood is $C(\text{Pr}_i) = \{|(\text{Pr}_i - \text{Pr}_j)/a_n| \leq 1\}$. Under standard conditions on bandwidth and the kernel function, the ratio in the brackets of equation (13.4) is a consistent estimator of $E[Y_0| P = 1, \text{Pr}_i]$.

Heckman, Ichimura, and Todd (1997) propose a generalized version of kernel matching, called *local linear matching*. This estimator replaces the expression for W_{ij} in equation (13.4) with the following (local linear) weighting function:

$$W_{ij} = \frac{G_{ij} \sum_{k \in I_0} G_{ik} \left(\text{Pr}_k - \text{Pr}_i \right)^2 - G_{ij} \left(\text{Pr}_j - \text{Pr}_i \right) \sum_{k \in I_0} G_{ik} \left(\text{Pr}_k - \text{Pr}_i \right)}{\sum_{j \in I_0} G_{jk} \sum_{k \in I_0} G_{ik} \left(\text{Pr}_k - \text{Pr}_i \right)^2 - \sum_{j \in I_0} G_{ij} \left(\text{Pr}_j - \text{Pr}_i \right) \sum_{k \in I_0} G_{ik} \left(\text{Pr}_k - \text{Pr}_i \right)}, \tag{13.5}$$

As demonstrated in research by Fan (1992), local linear estimation has some advantages over standard kernel estimation, including a faster rate of convergence near boundary points and greater robustness to different data design densities. In general, local linear regression tends to perform better than kernel estimation near boundary points and in cases in which the nonparticipant observations on P tend to fall on one side of the participant observations. Heckman, Ichimura, and Todd (1997) study the performance of local linear regression matching estimators and find that they perform better than simple nearest neighbor methods.

Determining the overlap support region

To implement the matching estimator, the region of common support S_P needs to be determined. In theory, as the sample size gets large, all propensity scores that are greater than zero and less than one should be in the common support region because there is a positive probability of observing treated and untreated persons. However, a finite sample may contain values of Pr that are between zero and one for which no good matches can be found. This leads to an empirical failure of the support requirement.

One simple way to determine the support region is to plot a histogram of the propensity score distribution for the $P = 1$ and $P = 0$ groups and to visually search for regions of P that do not have common support. Heckman, Ichimura, and Todd (1997) propose a more systematic approach that makes use of kernel density estimation methods to check directly where the density of Pr is positive for both the $P = 1$ and $P = 0$ distributions. The common support region can be estimated by

$$\hat{S}_P = \{\text{Pr} : \hat{f}\,(\text{Pr} \mid P = 1) > 0 \text{ and } \hat{f}\,(\text{Pr} \mid P = 0) > 0\},$$

where $\hat{f}\,(\text{Pr}|\ P = 1)$ and $\hat{f}\,(\text{Pr}|\ P = 0)$ are nonparametric density estimators given by

$$\hat{f}\,(\text{Pr} \mid P = d) \;=\; \frac{1}{(n_d a_n)} \sum_{k \in I_d} G\left(\frac{\text{Pr}_k - \text{Pr}}{a_n}\right), d = 0,\ 1,$$

and where a_n is a bandwidth parameter. In words, the region of common support ($\hat{S}_p$) is the values of Pr for which the values of Pr estimated from the data are greater than zero for both the participants ($P = 1$) and the nonparticipants ($P = 0$); that is, the values of Pr for which the data contain both participants and nonparticipants.

To ensure that the densities are strictly positive (that is, exceed 0 by a certain amount), Heckman, Ichimura, and Todd (1997) use a "trimming level" q. That is, after excluding any Pr points for which the estimated density is 0, they also exclude a small percentage

(q percent) of the remaining Pr points for which the estimated density is positive but extremely low. The set of eligible matches is given by

$$\hat{S}_p = \{\text{Pr} : \hat{f}(\text{Pr}|\ P = 1) > c_q \text{ and } \hat{f}\ (\text{Pr}|\ P = 0) > c_q\},$$

where c_q is the density cutoff level that satisfies

$$\sup_{c_q} \frac{1}{2J} \sum_{i \in \bar{I}_1} \left\{ 1\left(\hat{f}\left(\text{Pr}|P=1\right) < c_q\right) + 1\left(\hat{f}\left(\text{Pr}|P=0\right) < c_q\right) \right\} \le q,$$

where $\bar{I}_1$ is the set of observations for which both $\hat{f}(\text{Pr}|\ P = 1) > 0$ and $\hat{f}(\text{Pr}|\ P = 0) > 0$, and J is the number of observations in the set $\bar{I}_1$, and "sup" indicates that this is the largest value of c_q for which the summation term is $\le q$. That is, c_q is set so that q percent of the observations are trimmed (excluded) because either $\hat{f}\ (\text{Pr}|\ P = 1)$ or $\hat{f}\ (\text{Pr}|\ P = 0)$ is less than c_q. Thus matches are constructed only for the program participants for whom the propensity scores lie in $\hat{S}_p$. The value of c_q is chosen so that all estimated densities that are zero are excluded *and* a small percentage (q) of positive densities are *also* excluded.

Implementing matching estimators by reweighting the data

The matching estimators discussed thus far in this chapter are ones that are most commonly used. However, the literature has developed some alternative, more efficient estimators, some of which are implemented through reweighting of the data rather than through explicit matching of nonparticipants to participants. Examples of this approach are Hahn (1998) and Hirano, Imbens, and Ridder (2003). This section briefly explains how to implement the Hirano, Imbens, and Ridder (2003) estimator.

To see how to implement the matching estimator as a weighted estimator, consider the definition of the ATE parameter:

$$\text{ATE} \equiv \text{E}[Y_1 - Y_0]\ .$$

As usual, the observed outcome, Y, can be expressed as $Y = PY_1 + (1 - P)Y_0$.

Following Hirano, Imbens, and Ridder (2003), and noting that $PY_1 = PY$, yields the following method for expressing $\mathrm{E}[Y_1]$ in terms of a weight that is the inverse of the propensity score (Pr):

$$\begin{aligned}
\mathrm{E}\left[\frac{PY}{\mathrm{Pr}}\right] &= \mathrm{E}\left[\frac{PY_1}{\mathrm{Pr}}\right] = \mathrm{E}\left[\mathrm{E}\left[\frac{PY_1}{\mathrm{Pr}} \mid \mathbf{Z}\right]\right] \\
&= \mathrm{E}\left[\frac{\mathrm{E}[P \mid \mathbf{Z}] \times \mathrm{E}[Y_1 \mid \mathbf{Z}]}{\mathrm{Pr}}\right] \\
&= \mathrm{E}\left[\frac{\mathrm{Pr} \times \mathrm{E}[Y_1 \mid \mathbf{Z}]}{\mathrm{Pr}}\right] = E_{\mathbf{Z}}\left[E\left[Y_1 \mid \mathbf{Z}\right]\right] \\
&= E\left[Y_1\right].
\end{aligned} \tag{13.6}$$

Analogous calculations can be used to show that

$$\mathrm{E}\left[\frac{(1-P)Y}{1-\mathrm{Pr}}\right] = E\left[Y_0\right]. \tag{13.7}$$

Equations (13.6) and (13.7) for $\mathrm{E}[Y_1]$ and $\mathrm{E}[Y_0]$ imply that ATE can be estimated as

$$\widehat{\mathrm{ATE}}_{\mathrm{IPW}} = (1/\mathrm{N})\sum_{i=1}^{N}\left[\frac{P_iY_i}{\mathrm{Pr}_i} - \frac{(1-P_i)Y_i}{1-\mathrm{Pr}_i}\right],$$

where the subscript IPW indicates inverse propensity score weighting.

Difference-in-differences matching

Matching estimators assume that the outcome variables (Y_0 and Y_1) are independent of program participation after conditioning on observables. However, for a variety of reasons, systematic differences between participant and nonparticipant outcomes may be present, even after conditioning on observables. Such differences may arise, for example, because of program selection on unmeasured characteristics (such as motivation) or because of systematic differences in the levels of outcome variables across the different communities in which the participants and nonparticipants reside. A DID matching strategy, as proposed in Heckman, Ichimura, and Todd (1997, 1998), allows program participation to be based on unobservables as long as the unobservables do not vary over time. This approach is analogous to the standard DID regression estimator presented in chapter 12, but it reweights the participant and nonparticipant observations according to the weighting functions implied by specific matching estimators.

To see how this works, start with the following independence assumption:

$$(\Delta Y_0, \Delta Y_1) \perp\!\!\!\perp P \mid \mathbf{Z}, \tag{13.8}$$

where $\Delta Y_0 = Y_{0t''} - Y_{0t'}$; $\Delta Y_1 = Y_{1t''} - Y_{0t'}$; t' and t'' are periods before and after the program enrollment date, respectively; and $\perp\!\!\!\perp$ indicates statistical independence. This is a key assumption of the DID matching approach. Intuitively, it means that although P may predict Y_0 and Y_1 after conditioning on the observed variables in $\mathbf{Z}$, it does not help predict *changes* in the values of Y_0 (that is, $Y_{0t''} - Y_{0t'}$) or Y_1 (that is, $Y_{1t''} - Y_{0t'}$) conditional on $\mathbf{Z}$. Thus, for example, individuals cannot select into the program on the basis of anticipated changes in Y_0 (that is, on the basis of the anticipation of $Y_{0t''} - Y_{0t'}$). DID matching allows for selection into the program to be based on any time-invariant unobservables that affect $Y_{0t''}$ and $Y_{0t'}$ (or $Y_{1t''}$ and $Y_{0t'}$) in the same way; these unobservables would be eliminated by taking the difference $Y_{0t''} - Y_{0t'}$ (or $Y_{1t''} - Y_{0t'}$).

As with the cross-sectional matching estimator, the Rosenbaum and Rubin (1983) theorem can be applied to show that the previous conditional independence assumption (equation (13.8)) implies that

$$(\Delta Y_0, \Delta Y_1) \perp\!\!\!\perp P \mid \text{Prob}[P = 1 \mid \mathbf{Z}].$$

The DID matching estimator also requires the same support condition needed for standard (cross-sectional) matching estimation:

$$0 < \text{Prob}[P = 1 \mid \mathbf{Z}] < 1.$$

If interest centers on the ATT or ATT($\mathbf{Z}$) parameter, then the independence assumption required for matching needs to be assumed only for ΔY_0, and the common support condition needed is only that $\text{Prob}[P = 1 \mid \mathbf{Z}] < 1$. The intuition for the weaker assumption is that ATT focuses only on those who obtain the treatment, for whom Y_1 is known, so there is no need to assume anything about Y_1 for individuals whose Y_1 is not observed. Also, values of $\mathbf{Z}$ for which $\text{Prob}[P = 1 \mid \mathbf{Z}] = 0$ do not need to be excluded; those $\mathbf{Z}$ values would be excluded automatically because, by definition, participant observations could not have those values of $\mathbf{Z}$. However, if interest includes ATE or ATE($\mathbf{Z}$), then the previous two assumptions—the conditional independence assumption and the support condition—cannot be weakened; intuitively, in this case the impact of the program for everyone, including individuals who currently are not participating, needs to be considered. For nonparticipants, some assumptions are needed about Y_1 because it is not observed. Also, matches can be found only for individuals with $\mathbf{Z}$ values for which the probability of participating is greater than 0 and less than 1.

As with cross-sectional matching, nonparametric weighting can be used to construct matches. More explicitly, the local linear DID estimator of the ATT is given by

$$\widehat{\text{ATT}}_{\text{KDM}} = \frac{1}{n_1} \sum_{i \in I_1 \cap S_p} \left\{ \left(Y_{1t''i} - Y_{0t'i} \right) - \sum_{j \in I_0 \cap S_p} W_{ij} \left(Y_{0t''j} - Y_{0t'j} \right) \right\},$$

where n_1 is the number of program participants in the sample and the weights, W_{ij}, are the local linear weights defined in equation (13.5).

Angelucci and Attanasio (2013) provide an example of the use of a DID matching estimator on data from a developing country. They estimate the impact of Mexico's Oportunidades conditional cash transfer program on food consumption in urban areas of Mexico. (Unlike in rural areas, Oportunidades was not implemented in urban areas as part of a randomized control trial.) They compare their estimates of that program's impact on food consumption in urban areas with standard estimates of food demand patterns (Engel curves) obtained using data from households that were not affected by the program. They find that their estimates of the impact of the program are inconsistent with their estimates of food demand obtained using standard economic models of demand patterns. They conclude that this discrepancy is likely due to the fact that the Oportunidades program gives the cash transfers to women in the household, which changes those women's bargaining position and thus changes households' food consumption patterns in a way that is not accounted for by standard models of the demand for food.

Another study that uses the DID matching estimator is that of Galiani, Gertler, and Schargrodsky (2005), who analyze the impact of privatization of water services on child mortality. The study uses variation in ownership of water provision services across time and space that was generated by the privatization process in Argentina in the 1990s. The authors use a DID PSM estimator to account for nonrandomness in which localities privatized at which time. They find that child mortality fell 8 percent in the areas that privatized and that the effect was even larger, 26 percent, in poor areas. In contrast to their finding that privatization is associated with reductions in deaths from infectious and parasitic diseases, they find no association between privatization and child mortality from causes unrelated to water.

Additional topics for matching methods

This section presents several important considerations when using matching estimation methods. It begins with a discussion of how to model the participation decision, followed by using balance tests to check the propensity score specification. It then discusses methods to use when a choice-based sample is available, and how to calculate standard errors for matching estimators.

Modeling the program participation decision

An important decision when implementing either cross-sectional or DID PSM estimators is the choice of the set of conditioning variables used to estimate the propensity score (the **Z** variables). Unfortunately, there is no statistical procedure for choosing a particular set **Z** to satisfy the identifying assumptions required to justify application of matching. Somewhat surprisingly, the set **Z** that satisfies the required matching conditions is not necessarily the one with the largest possible number of variables. It turns out that augmenting a set that satisfies the conditions could lead to a violation of the conditions. Indeed, Heckman and Navarro-Lozano (2004) provide some examples in which augmenting the conditioning set makes matching perform less well. Adding more conditioning variables could also reduce the proportion of observations that satisfy the common support requirement. Thus the choice of which variables to include in the propensity score specification should be made after careful consideration of the factors that may enter into the participation decision.

Example: The decision to participate in a U.S. job training program. Heckman, Lalonde, and Smith (1999) present a simple economic model of the decision to participate in a job training program that can serve as a guide when considering which variables to include in a propensity score specification, particularly in job training–related applications. The model is the following:

- Individuals have the option of participating in training in period k, and if they do they have to forgo earnings during that training period.
- For all t prior to k, we observe Y_{0t}, $t = 1 \ldots k - 1$. For $t = k$, we observe Y_{0k} for nonparticipants and neither Y_{0k} nor Y_{1k} for participants. For all t after k, we observe one of two potential outcomes, either Y_{0t} (for nonparticipants) or Y_{1t} (for participants).
- To participate in training, individuals must apply and be accepted, and there may be several decision makers who determine which applicants get the training.
- Finally, assume that participation decisions are based on maximizing future earnings:

$$P = 1 \text{ if } \mathrm{E}\left[\sum_{j=1}^{T-k}\frac{Y_{1,k+j}}{(1+r)^j} - C - \sum_{j=0}^{T-k}\frac{Y_{0,k+j}}{(1+r)^j} \mid I_k\right] \geq 0, \text{ else } P=0,$$

where

- $\mathrm{E}\left[\sum_{j=1}^{T-k}\frac{Y_{1,k+j}}{(1+r)^j}\right]$ = the expected earnings stream starting at time $k+1$ if the individual participates (T is the last time period of work before retirement);
- C = direct cost of training;
- $\sum_{j=0}^{T-k}\frac{Y_{0,k+j}}{(1+r)^j}$ = the expected earnings stream starting at time k if the individual does not participate; and
- I_k = information at time k used to form expectations about future earnings.

This simple decision model has some interesting implications for who participates in training programs:

- Past earnings are irrelevant to the participation decision, except for their value in predicting future earnings. Thus they enter only through I_k.
- Persons with lower forgone earnings or lower costs are more likely to participate in the program, so that people will tend to participate when their opportunity costs are low. For example, unemployed persons should be more likely to participate in training than employed persons.
- Older persons are less likely to participate because they have a shorter period over which to reap the rewards of training.
- The decision to take training is correlated with future earnings only through its correlation with expected future earnings.

To see the implications for estimating the propensity score function, suppose that costs C are known to the individual but are unknown to the researcher. For the individual, the above participation decision can be expressed as

$$P = 1 \text{ if } \mathrm{E}\left[\sum_{j=1}^{T-k}\frac{Y_{1,k+j}}{(1+r)^j} - \sum_{j=1}^{T-k}\frac{Y_{0,k+j}}{(1+r)^j} \mid I_k\right] \geq C + Y_{0k}. \tag{13.9}$$

In words, this means that the individual will choose to participate if the expected gains in future earnings from program participation are at least as great as the direct cost of participating in the training and the cost of forgone earnings, represented by the term $C + Y_{0k}$.

Let $\mathrm{H}(\mathbf{Z})$ be the expected future benefits (the expectation to the left of $\geq$ in equation (13.9)), where the $\mathbf{Z}$ variables are the variables in the information set (I_k), as discussed further below. Let $v = C + Y_{0k}$. Then equation (13.9) implies that $P = 1$ if $\mathrm{H}(\mathbf{Z}) \geq v$, which in turn implies that $\mathrm{Prob}[P = 1| \mathbf{Z}] = \mathrm{Prob}[\mathrm{H}(\mathbf{Z}) \geq v]$. Placing a distributional assumption on v yields a discrete choice model. For example, if v follows a logistic distribution, then

$$\mathrm{Prob}\left[P = 1 \mid \mathbf{Z}\right] = \mathrm{Prob}\left[\mathrm{H}(\mathbf{Z}) \geq v\right] = \frac{e^{(\mathrm{H}(\mathbf{Z})-\mu_v)/\sigma_v}}{1+e^{(\mathrm{H}(\mathbf{Z})-\mu_v)/\sigma_v}}, \tag{logit}$$

where μ_v is the mean of v and σ_v is the standard deviation of v. Alternatively, if v follows a normal distribution, then

$$\mathrm{Prob}\left[P = 1 \mid \mathbf{Z}\right] = \mathrm{Prob}\left[\mathrm{H}(\mathbf{Z}) \geq v\right] = \Phi\left(\frac{H(\mathbf{Z}) - \mu_v}{\sigma_v}\right). \tag{probit}$$

The variables to include in the participation model (the $\mathbf{Z}$ variables) should be those that might be used in forming expectations about program gains (the difference between earnings with and without participation), as suggested by the model. Also, variables that capture aspects of program costs might be included. If program administrators also play a role in determining who participates, then the decision model should also take into consideration the factors governing their decisions.

To guide in the selection of **Z**, there is some accumulated empirical evidence on how the performance of matching estimators depends on the choice of **Z** in particular applications. For example, Heckman et al. (1998), Heckman, Ichimura, and Todd (1997), and Lechner (2001) show that the variables that are included in the estimation of the propensity score can have a substantial effect on the estimator's performance. These papers find that biases tended to be more substantial when a limited number of conditioning variables were used. They also selected the set **Z** to maximize the percentage of people correctly classified by treatment status under the model, although there is no theoretical justification for this procedure.

Using balancing tests to check the propensity score specification

Rosenbaum and Rubin (1983) present a result that is useful for determining the specification of the propensity score model for a given set of **Z** variables, in particular, which interactions and higher order terms to include. They note that because P is discrete, the following holds:

$$\mathbf{Z} \perp\!\!\!\perp \mathbf{P} \mid \text{Prob}[P = 1 \mid \mathbf{Z}],$$

or equivalently:

$$\text{E}[P \mid \mathbf{Z}, \text{Prob}[P = 1 \mid \mathbf{Z}]] = \text{E}[P \mid \text{Prob}[P = 1 \mid \mathbf{Z}]].$$

The basic intuition is that after conditioning on Prob[$P = 1| \mathbf{Z}$], additional conditioning on **Z** does not provide new information about P. Thus, dependence of P on **Z** even after conditioning on the estimated values of Prob[$P = 1| \mathbf{Z}$] suggests misspecification in the model used to estimate Prob[$P = 1| \mathbf{Z}$]. The independence condition holds for any **Z**, including sets of **Z** that do not satisfy the conditional independence condition required to justify matching. Therefore, this result provides no information about which variables should be included in **Z**. However, it can be used to develop specification tests for Prob[$P = 1|\mathbf{Z}$], such as whether interaction terms for the **Z** variables are needed.

Specification tests based on the above conditional dependence result typically check whether there are differences in **Z** between the $P = 1$ and $P = 0$ groups after conditioning on Prob[$P = 1| \mathbf{Z}$], which can be denoted by Pr(**Z**). They are called *balancing tests*, and they are similar to the balance tests used in checking the validity of randomized experiments, except that the tests are performed conditional on values of Pr(**Z**). Various testing approaches have been proposed in the literature. Eichler and Lechner (2002) modify a test suggested by Rosenbaum and Rubin (1985) that is based on standardized differences between the treatment and matched comparison-group samples in terms of means of each variable in **Z**, squares of each variable in **Z**, and first-order interaction terms between each pair of variables in **Z**.[7] An overall test would be a joint test of differences in the means of all of these terms; this test can also be carried out within a regression framework, as explained below. If the joint hypothesis that all of the differences in means equal zero is rejected, then more interaction or squared terms, or both, need to be added to Pr(**Z**).

Alternatively, Dehejia and Wahba (1999) divide the observations into strata based on estimated propensity scores. These strata are chosen so that there are no statistically significant differences in the mean of the estimated propensity scores between the participant group and nonparticipant group observations within each strata, though how the initial strata are chosen and how they are refined if statistically significant differences are found is not made precise. The problem of choosing the strata in implementing the balancing test is analogous to the problem of choosing the strata in implementing the interval matching estimator described in the previous section entitled "Implementation of propensity score matching estimators." A common practice is to use five strata (for example, quintiles of the propensity score). Within each stratum, *t*-tests are used to test for mean differences in each **Z** variable between the experimental and comparison-group observations.

Smith and Todd (2005) propose another way of implementing the balancing test by regressing each element of the set **Z**, denoted by Z_k, on a power series expansion in Pr(**Z**) and on interactions of P with each element of that power series,

$$
\begin{aligned}
Z_k = \alpha &+ \beta_1 \mathrm{Pr}(\mathbf{Z}) + \beta_2 \mathrm{Pr}(\mathbf{Z})^2 + \beta_3 \mathrm{Pr}(\mathbf{Z})^3 + \ldots + \beta_j \mathrm{Pr}(\mathbf{Z})^j \\
&+ \gamma_1 \mathrm{Pr}(\mathbf{Z})P + \gamma_2 \mathrm{Pr}(\mathbf{Z})^2 P + \gamma_3 \mathrm{Pr}(\mathbf{Z})^3 P + \ldots + \gamma_j \mathrm{Pr}(\mathbf{Z})^j P + \nu,
\end{aligned}
$$

followed by a test of whether the estimated γ's are jointly significantly different from zero. When significant differences are found for particular variables, higher-order and interaction terms in those variables are added to the propensity score model and the testing procedure is repeated, until such differences no longer emerge. In this way, the specification for the propensity score is iteratively refined.

Accommodating choice-based sampling

Data samples used in evaluating the impacts of programs are often choice based, with program participants being oversampled relative to their frequency in the population. Under choice-based sampling, weights are required to consistently estimate the probabilities of program participation, Pr(**Z**), where the weights correspond to the ratio of the proportion of program participants in the population relative to the proportion in the sample. Manski and Lerman (1977) provide a detailed discussion of weighting for logistic regressions.

The true population proportions needed to construct the weights usually cannot be obtained from the sample at hand and therefore must be derived from some other sources. When the weights are known, the Manski and Lerman (1977) procedure can be implemented to estimate propensity scores consistently. Heckman and Todd (2009) show that, in the case in which the choice-based sampling weights are unknown and the propensity score is estimated ignoring the choice-based sampling weights, matching methods can still be applied. The odds ratio, Pr(**Z**)/(1 – Pr(**Z**)), estimated using a logistic model ignoring the choice-based sampling is a scalar multiple of the true odds ratio, which is itself a monotonic transformation of the true propensity scores.

Under certain conditions, matching can proceed on the basis of the odds ratio (or on the log odds ratio) obtained without accounting for choice-based sampling. In particular, with nearest neighbor matching, whether matching is performed on the odds ratio or on the propensity scores (estimated ignoring choice-based sampling) does not matter, because the ranking of the observations is the same and the same neighbors will be selected either way. Thus, failure to account for choice-based sampling will not affect nearest neighbor point estimates. However, failure to account for choice-based sampling will matter for the kernel or the local linear matching methods discussed earlier in this chapter, because those methods take into account the absolute distance between, and not just the ranking of, the propensity scores ($\Pr(P = 1|\mathbf{Z})$) for different observations.

Calculating the standard errors of matching estimators

The distribution theory for cross-sectional and DID kernel and local linear matching estimators is derived in Heckman, Ichimura, and Todd (1998). However, calculating the asymptotic standard errors can be cumbersome, which has led many researchers to calculate standard errors for matching estimators by using bootstrap (resampling) methods. See Efron and Tibshirani (1993) and Cameron and Trivedi (2005).

However, Abadie and Imbens (2008) show that standard bootstrap methods are invalid for assessing the variability of nearest neighbor estimators, where the bandwidth varies with the distance to the nearest neighbor. Those authors present alternative standard error formulas that can be used to assess the variability of nearest neighbor matching estimators, and they make software available to implement their method. Regular bootstrap standard errors are, however, valid for kernel or local linear matching estimators that use fixed bandwidths.

Empirical applications of matching estimators

Matching methods have been used to estimate program impacts in both developed and developing countries. This section begins with an example from a developing country: the impact of providing piped water on child health. It then summarizes some recent studies from developed countries.

Piped water and child health in India

Jalan and Ravallion (2003a) use cross-sectional matching to evaluate the effect of having access to piped water on the prevalence and duration of diarrhea among children younger than age five in rural India. Their analysis provides an example of cross-sectional matching.

Background. India accounts for more child deaths from unsafe water than any other country. Expanding access to piped water should improve child health in India by replacing contaminated water sources with clean water sources. However, whether greater access to piped water actually improves child health status, and the extent to which it does so, is an empirical question. For example, improper storage of piped water in the home could lead to its contamination, which may reduce or even nullify any benefits. Ideally, the potential health benefits from piped water would be compared with the health benefits of alternative uses of the funds used to pay for piped water, such as the provision of child nutrition programs or the delivery of medical care.

Empirical strategy. The provision of piped water in any country is not random. For example, better-educated parents, who presumably are more likely to understand health benefits from having piped water, are more likely to obtain access to piped water. Thus a simple cross-sectional estimator comparing child health status between households that have piped water and those that do not is likely to yield upwardly biased results of the impact of piped water because those estimates would attribute other child health gains from having educated parents (for example, higher household incomes) to the effect of having piped water.

To deal with this selection problem, Jalan and Ravallion (2003a) apply PSM methods. In particular, they find households with and without access to piped water that otherwise have very similar observable characteristics. They also examine whether any gains of having piped water vary by household income and by the education level of the child's mother.

Data. Jalan and Ravallion (2003a) use data from a large survey conducted in 1993–94 by India's National Council of Applied Economic Research that include data on the health and education status of 33,000 rural households living in 1,765 villages from 16 states in India. This sample includes 9,000 households with piped water and 24,000 without piped water. This large data set allows Jalan and Ravallion (2003a) to use PSM at both the individual and the village levels. About 7 percent (650) of the treatment households (those with piped water) were excluded during matching because their propensity scores were outside the area of common support. Figure 13.2 displays the distributions of propensity scores for households with and without piped water. The propensity score estimates are not surprising. Households living in villages with larger populations, a high school, a paved road, a bus stop, a telephone, a bank, and a market were more likely to have piped water. The probability of scheduled tribe (but not scheduled caste) households having access to piped water was lower relative to the nonminority population. Christian households were more likely to have access. Households living in brick and cement houses, having electricity, and with more land were also more likely to have piped water.

Results. Jalan and Ravallion (2003a) find that having piped water reduced diarrheal disease; its prevalence would be 21 percent higher and its duration 29 percent longer without piped water. However, these impacts do not apply to low-income households unless the woman in the household has more than a primary school education. In fact, Jalan and Ravallion (2003a) find that the health impacts of piped water are larger and more

FIGURE 13.2 Propensity scores for households with and without piped water

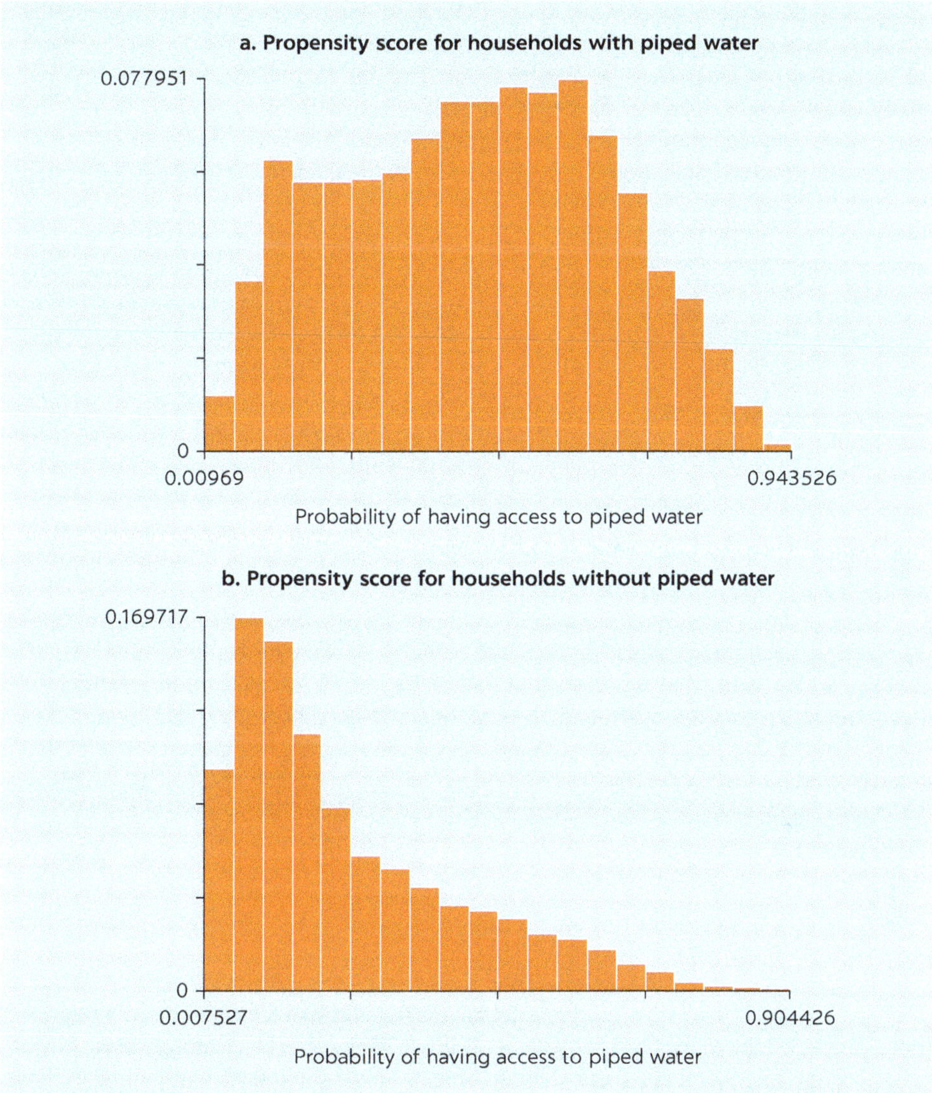

Source: Jalan and Ravallion 2003a.

Note: Reprinted from *Journal of Econometrics*, volume 112, Issue 1, Jyotsna Jalan and Martin Ravallion, "Does Piped Water Reduce Diarrhea for Children in Rural India?" pages 153–173, copyright 2003), with permission from Elsevier. Further permission required for reuse.

significant in households with better-educated women. They conclude that their study illustrates the need to combine infrastructure investments, such as piped water, with programs that increase education and reduce poverty.

Evidence on the performance of matching estimators

A few studies evaluate the performance of matching estimators by comparing them with randomized experiments. An example is Heckman, Ichimura, and Todd (1997), who used experimental data from the U.S. National Job Training and Partnership Act experiment combined with nonexperimental data on eligible nonparticipants, who were people living in the same geographic areas as program participants and who qualified for the program but did not apply for it. They also used data from the Survey of Income and Program Participation to obtain data on individuals who were qualified for the program but did not apply. These people did not live in the same geographic areas, and they were interviewed using a different survey questionnaire. The study concludes that matching estimators used to evaluate job training programs perform best when the treatment and control groups live in the same geographic area. Smith and Todd (2005) also study the performance of matching estimators when different survey questionnaires are used to collect data from the comparison and treatment groups and the groups reside in different geographic areas; they find that matching estimators performed poorly.[8] These studies also indicate that DID matching methods are more reliable than cross-sectional matching methods, particularly when treatments and controls are mismatched either geographically or in the survey questionnaires used. Different labor markets or different survey questionnaires might plausibly lead to level differences in outcomes between the treatment and control groups, which are adequately controlled for by DID matching estimators.

Overall, the accumulated empirical evidence shows that the success of matching approaches for impact evaluation depends strongly on the data being of relatively high quality, in the sense that the data contain the important variables that are thought to determine program participation decisions. This implies that the remaining, unobserved variables affecting program participation can be considered to influence participation in a fairly random way, conditional on the observed variables. When some important variables are unobservable, then DID matching can perform better than cross-sectional matching.[9]

Conclusion

Matching methods have been used to evaluate the impacts of a wide variety of programs in both developed and developing countries. Economists have been relatively slow to adopt them, often citing the problem that they do little or nothing to reduce bias caused by unobserved differences between program participants and nonparticipants. However, even given this limitation, matching methods have some advantages over standard OLS estimates of program impact.

PSM provides a convenient method for matching observations in the control group to the program participant observations. When the underlying ignorability assumption holds, matching methods are worthwhile and, in general, yield consistent (unbiased) estimates of program impacts. Unfortunately, when this assumption does not hold, which is difficult to check directly, estimates of program impacts based on matching methods may be inconsistent (biased). On a more optimistic note, matching methods can be combined with DID estimation to minimize problems of bias. They tend to be most reliable in replicating results from randomized controlled trials when the data are of high quality.

Notes

1. If the probability of participation, usually denoted by Prob[P = 1|**Z**], were estimated completely nonparametrically, then the estimation problem would again be of high dimension and there would be no dimensionality reduction from matching on the propensity score instead of matching directly on **Z**. For this reason, the propensity score function is usually assumed to be parametric or semiparametric. See Heckman, Ichimura, and Todd (1998) for a full discussion.
2. In previous chapters observed variables were denoted by **X**. In this chapter they are denoted by **Z** because this is the standard notation used in the matching literature.
3. Another implicit assumption is that the propensity score can be estimated using a parametric or semiparametric model. If the propensity score were estimated fully nonparametrically, then estimation of Pr(**Z**) would be a high-dimensional estimation problem that would still be subject to the dimensionality problem. See Ichimura and Todd (2007) for further details.
4. ATT(**Z**) is the same as ATT(**X**) in chapter 12 because both **Z** and **X** are observed variables. This chapter uses **Z** instead of **X** because the **Z** notation is commonly used in both theoretical papers on, and empirical studies that use, matching estimators.
5. Note that Pr is not the same as *P*; Pr is the estimated probability that *P* = 1, conditional on **Z**.
6. A kernel function is a function that is symmetric around zero and integrates to a value of one.
7. The **Z** variables in the propensity score function Pr(**Z**) do not have all of these terms. That is, this test is applicable to any specification of Pr(**Z**) that is based on an index function that is linear in **Z**, or has some squared and interaction terms, but not the full set of those terms that are used in this test.
8. There was a debate in the literature about the performance of matching estimators in this context. An earlier study by Dehejia and Wahba (1999) concludes that matching estimators performed well, even in the situation in which treatment- and comparison-group observations reside in different areas and data are collected using different survey instruments. However, Smith and Todd (2005) reanalyzed the same data and found that Dehejia and Wahba (1999) imposed sample restrictions that effectively omitted about 40 percent of the observations. When these observations were included, matching estimators performed poorly and did not dominate the performance of other types of estimators.
9. Heckman, Ichimura, and Todd (1997) and Smith and Todd (2005) implement both cross-sectional matching and DID matching. They find that DID matching performs better and to some extent compensates for level differences in outcomes that could arise from differences in local labor markets or from variables being measured by different survey instruments.

References

Abadie, Alberto, and Guido Imbens. 2008. "On the Failure of the Bootstrap for Matching Estimators." *Econometrica* 76 (6): 1537–57.

Angelucci, Manuela, and Orazio Attanasio. 2013. "The Demand for Food of Poor Mexican Households: Understanding Policy Impacts Using Structural Models." *American Economic Journal: Economic Policy* 5 (1): 146–78.

Cameron, Colin, and Pravin Trivedi. 2005. *Microeconometrics: Methods and Applications*. New York: Cambridge University Press.

Cochran, William, and Donald Rubin. 1973. "Controlling Bias in Observational Studies." *Sankhya* 35 (4): 417–46.

Dehejia, Rajeev, and Sadek Wahba. 1999. "Causal Effects in Nonexperimental Studies: Reevaluating the Evaluation of Training Programs." *Journal of the American Statistical Association* 94 (448): 1053–62.

Efron, Bradley, and Robert Tibshirani. 1993. *An Introduction to the Bootstrap*. New York: Chapman and Hall.

Eichler, Martin, and Michael Lechner. 2002. "An Evaluation of Public Employment Programmes in the East German State of Sachsen-Anhalt." *Labour Economics* 9 (2): 143–86.

Fan, Jianqing. 1992. "Design-Adaptive Nonparametric Regression." *Journal of the American Statistical Association* 87 (420): 998–1004.

Frölich, Markus. 2004. "Programme Evaluation with Multiple Treatments." *Journal of Economic Surveys* 18 (2): 181–224.

Galiani, Sebastian, Paul Gertler, and Ernesto Schargrodsky. 2005. "Water for Life: The Impact of the Privatization of Water Services on Child Mortality." *Journal of Political Economy* 113 (1): 83–120.

Hahn, Jinyong. 1998. "On the Role of the Propensity Score in Efficient Semiparametric Estimation of Average Treatment Effects." *Econometrica* 66 (2): 315–31.

Heckman, James, Hidehiko Ichimura, Jeffrey Smith, and Petra Todd. 1998. "Characterizing Selection Bias Using Experimental Data." *Econometrica* 66 (5): 1017–98.

Heckman, James, Hidehiko Ichimura, and Petra Todd. 1997. "Matching as an Econometric Evaluation Estimator: Evidence from Evaluating a Job Training Program." *Review of Economic Studies* 64 (4): 605–54.

Heckman, James, Hidehiko Ichimura, and Petra Todd. 1998. "Matching as an Econometric Evaluation Estimator." *Review of Economic Studies* 65 (2): 261–94.

Heckman, James, Robert Lalonde, and Jeffrey Smith. 1999. "The Economics and Econometrics of Active Labor Market Programs." In *Handbook of Labor Economics*, Vol. 3A, edited by Orley Ashenfelter and David Card, 1865–2097. Amsterdam: North Holland.

Heckman, James, and Salvador Navarro-Lozano. 2004. "Using Matching, Instrumental Variables, and Control Functions to Estimate Economic Choice Models." *Review of Economics and Statistics* 86 (1): 30–57.

Heckman, James, and Petra Todd. 2009. "A Note on Adapting Propensity Score Matching and Selection Models to Choice Based Samples." *Econometrics Journal* 12 (S1): S230–34.

Hirano, Keisuke, Guido Imbens, and Gert Ridder. 2003. "Efficient Estimation of Average Treatment Effects Using the Estimated Propensity Score." *Econometrica* 71 (4): 1161–89.

Ichimura, Hidehiko, and Petra Todd. 2007. "Implementing Nonparametric and Semiparametric Estimators." In *Handbook of Econometrics*, Vol. 6B, edited by J. Heckman and E. Leamer. Amsterdam: North-Holland.

Imbens, Guido. 1999. "The Role of the Propensity Score in Estimating Dose-Response Functions." NBER Working Paper 237, National Bureau of Economic Research, Cambridge, MA.

Jalan, Jyotsna, and Martin Ravallion. 2003a. "Does Piped Water Reduce Diarrhea for Children in Rural India." *Journal of Econometrics* 112 (1): 153–73.

Jalan, Jyotsna, and Martin Ravallion. 2003b. "Estimating the Benefit Incidence of an Antipoverty Program by Propensity Score Matching." *Journal of Business and Economic Statistics* 21 (1): 19–30.

Lechner, Michael. 2001. "Identification and Estimation of Causal Effects of Multiple Treatments under the Conditional Independence Assumption." In *Econometric Evaluation of Labour Market Policies*, ZEW Economic Studies, Vol. 13, edited by Michael Lechner and Friedhelm Pfeiffer, 43–58. New York: Physica-Verlag.

Manski, Charles, and Steven Lerman. 1977. "The Estimation of Choice Probabilities from Choice-Based Samples." *Econometrica* 45 (8): 1977–88.

Rosenbaum, Paul, and Donald Rubin. 1983. "The Central Role of the Propensity Score in Observational Studies for Causal Effects." *Biometrika* 70 (1): 41–55.

Rosenbaum, Paul, and Donald Rubin. 1985. "Constructing a Control Group Using Multivariate Matched Sampling Methods That Incorporate the Propensity Score." *American Statistician* 39 (1): 33–38.

Rubin, Donald. 1980. "Bias Reduction Using Mahalanobis' Metric Matching." *Biometrics* 36 (2): 295–98.

Rubin, Donald. 1984. "Reducing Bias in Observational Studies Using Subclassification on the Propensity Score." *Journal of the American Statistical Association* 79 (387): 516–24.

Smith, Jeffrey, and Petra Todd. 2005. "Does Matching Address Lalonde's Critique of Nonexperimental Estimators?" *Journal of Econometrics* 125 (1–2): 305–53.

Todd, Petra. 2008. "Matching Estimators." In *The New Palgrave Dictionary of Economics,* 2nd edition, edited by S. Durlauf and L. Blume. New York: Palgrave Macmillan.

CHAPTER 14

Regression Discontinuity Methods

Introduction

A researcher often knows something about the rules by which people become eligible for programs. For instance, an eligibility rule may be based on the value of some characteristic of an individual, a family, or a community. An example would be a poverty program that is available only to households with low incomes, or a housing program available only to persons living in communities with a poverty index above a certain level.

In such situations, it may be possible to estimate the impact of the program using regression discontinuity (RD) methods, which are sometimes called regression discontinuity design (RDD) methods. The RD method exploits information about a rule governing assignment to a program. This chapter explains how RD methods can be used to evaluate the impacts of certain types of programs or policies. It begins by explaining the intuition for this approach and then provides a more rigorous explanation of the assumptions needed to apply RD estimation, for both the "sharp" case and the "fuzzy" case. The chapter ends by presenting three examples of such estimation.

Intuition for regression discontinuity methods

Suppose that the program under consideration is an education intervention (for example, a scholarship) that is available only for students whose initial test scores are above some threshold, denoted by z_0. Figure 14.1 plots the relationship between the final test (posttest) score and the initial test (pretest) score. A comparison of scores around the cutoff point, denoted by z_0, suggests that the program raised the scores of students who received it, particularly if the program represents the most plausible explanation for the "jump" in the posttest score observed at point z_0.

The RD evaluation approach was first proposed by Thistlethwaite and Campbell (1960). They used U.S. data to estimate the effect that receiving a National Merit Scholarship Award has on students' success in obtaining additional college scholarships and on their career aspirations. The National Merit awards are given if an individual's score on a specific test exceeds a threshold, just as in the above example, so the cutoff point can be used to study the effects of receiving the award for the subgroup of people near the cutoff point.

FIGURE 14.1 The intuition for regression discontinuity estimation

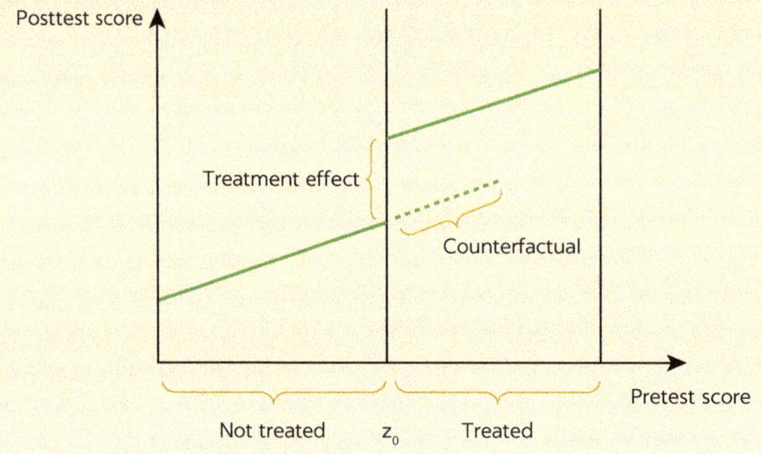

Source: Original figure for this publication.

Statisticians have developed and refined RD methods in subsequent decades. Trochim (1984) provides a detailed exposition of parametric and semiparametric RD methods that were developed in the statistics literature from the early 1960s to the mid-1980s. Economists developed an interest in RD estimation, and its use to evaluate programs, starting in the 1990s. Van der Klaauw (2002) presents a rigorous treatment of identification and estimation in a semiparametric model under a constant treatment effect assumption, while Hahn, Todd, and van der Klaauw (2001) allow for variable treatment effects and use relatively weak assumptions on the distribution of outcome variables. Lee and Lemieux (2010) summarize a variety of RD estimation approaches and review empirical applications.

As shown later in this chapter, the defining characteristic of the RD estimation method is that the probability of receiving treatment changes discontinuously (that is, with a jump) as a function of one or more underlying variables. The basic assumption is that people who score just above or just below some cutoff value are similar in all respects except for the treatment. Thus the difference in the average outcome between these two groups of people can be attributed to the treatment. In other words, the outcome of the untreated people whose eligibility scores are close to the cutoff can be used as the *counterfactual* for the treated people whose eligibility scores are close to the cutoff point. As long as people cannot manipulate their scores, the treatment can be considered to be locally randomized (Lee and Lemieux 2010).

Identification of treatment effects under "sharp" and "fuzzy" data

This section provides a more detailed exposition of the RD method. The discussion follows most closely the exposition in Hahn, Todd, and van der Klaauw (2001).

Suppose that the goal of an evaluation is to determine, for some person i, the effect of a binary treatment variable P_i (participation in the program) on an outcome Y_i. As in previous chapters, the model for the observed outcome of person i, Y_i, can be written as

$$Y_i = Y_{0i} + P_i \times (Y_{1i} - Y_{0i}) = Y_{0i} + P_i \times \Delta_i,$$

where $\Delta_i \equiv Y_{1i} - Y_{0i}$, and the subscript i is added to Δ to emphasize that the treatment effect can vary by i.

Two main types of discontinuity designs are considered in the literature:

1. *Sharp design.* The treatment P_i depends in a deterministic way on a variable Z_i:

$$P_i = f(Z_i),$$

where Z_i (an observable variable) varies over a continuum of values. The function $f(Z_i)$ changes discontinuously at a known point z_0, from a value of zero to the value of one. In other words, $f(Z_i) = 0$ if $Z_i \leq z_0$ and $f(Z_i) = 1$ if $Z_i > z_0$.

2. *Fuzzy design.* The treatment P_i is a random variable given (conditional on) Z_i, meaning that factors other than Z_i also influence program participation, P_i. The expected value of P_i conditional on Z_i equals the probability that P_i is equal to 1 conditional on Z_i:

$$\mathrm{E}[P_i \mid Z_i] = \mathrm{Prob}[P_i = 1 \mid Z_i] \equiv f(Z_i).$$

Under a fuzzy RD design, the conditional probability $\mathrm{Prob}[P_i = 1 \mid Z_i]$ is discontinuous at z_0, a known point.

The rest of this section explains more formally how knowing that the probability of receiving treatment changes discontinuously as a function of an underlying variable can be used to obtain an unbiased estimate of the impact of a program on Y_i under these two types of designs.

The sharp regression discontinuity design

To simplify the exposition, consider a specific example of a sharp discontinuity design. Person i is treated (participates in the program) if Z_i crosses a threshold z_0:[1]

$$\begin{aligned} P_i &= 1 \text{ if } Z_i > z_0 \\ &= 0 \text{ if } Z_i \leq z_0. \end{aligned}$$

The variable Z may be correlated with the outcome variables Y_1 and Y_0, so the assignment process is not necessarily random with respect to outcomes. A simple comparison of outcomes between persons who received and did not receive the treatment will generally be a biased estimator of the impact of the program. In particular, there is no reason to expect that, in general, people with Z_i values above the threshold are comparable to those with Z_i values below the threshold.

However, there may be reason to believe that people with Z_i values close to the threshold, z_0, are similar, particularly if people do not know the rule that assigns treatment around z_0, or if it is difficult for people to change their Z values. For example, people may apply to a program for which there is a threshold determining who gets into the program, but people do not necessarily have knowledge of this threshold when they apply or, even if they know the threshold, they may not have the ability to manipulate their Z variables. In that case, people just above the threshold z_0 can reasonably be expected to be comparable to those just below, and the design may be viewed as "almost experimental" near z_0. For this reason, the RD design is sometimes referred to as a *quasi-experimental* design. (See the section titled "Checking the validity of a regression discontinuity design" for a detailed discussion of situations in which the assumption that people just above and just below the threshold z_0 are comparable could be violated, and how to check for such violations.)

To be precise, let $e > 0$ denote an arbitrarily small number. Comparing conditional means for people who received and did not receive treatment gives

$$\begin{aligned}
&\mathrm{E}[Y_i | Z_i = z_0 + e] - \mathrm{E}[Y_i | Z_i = z_0 - e] \\
&\quad = \mathrm{E}[Y_{1i} | Z_i = z_0 + e] - \mathrm{E}[Y_{0i} | Z_i = z_0 - e] \\
&\quad = \mathrm{E}[Y_{1i} | Z_i = z_0 + e] - \mathrm{E}[Y_{0i} | Z_i = z_0 + e] + \mathrm{E}[Y_{0i} | Z_i = z_0 + e] - \mathrm{E}[Y_{0i} | Z_i = z_0 - e] \\
&\quad = \mathrm{E}[\Delta_i | Z_i = z_0 + e] + \mathrm{E}[Y_{0i} | Z_i = z_0 + e] - \mathrm{E}[Y_{0i} | Z_i = z_0 - e].
\end{aligned}$$

If people near z_0 are similar, $\mathrm{E}[Y_{0i} | Z_i = z_0 + e]$ can be expected to be approximately equal to $\mathrm{E}[Y_{0i} | Z_i = z_0 - e]$. This intuition motivates the following assumptions:

Assumption RD-1. $\mathrm{E}[Y_{0i} | Z_i = Z]$ is continuous in Z at z_0.

Assumption RD-2. The limit of $[\Delta_i | Z_i = z_0 + e]$ as e approaches zero is well defined.

Under assumptions RD-1 and RD-2, it is easy to see that

$$\lim_{e \to 0^+} \{\mathrm{E}[Y_i | Z_i = z_0 + e] - \mathrm{E}[Y_i | Z_i = z_0 - e]\} = \mathrm{E}[\Delta_i | Z_i = z_0].$$

By comparing persons arbitrarily close to the point z_0 who did and did not receive treatment, one can, in the limit, identify $\mathrm{E}[\Delta_i | Z_i = z_0]$, which is the average treatment effect for people with values of Z_i at the point of discontinuity z_0. Assumptions RD-1 and RD-2 are sufficient for identification. Note that assumption RD-1 specifies that there is no nonrandom program selectivity near the cutoff value; that is, there is no jump in Y_0 at the cutoff point caused by, for example, people with particular values of Y_0 adjusting their value of Z to move it above or below the cutoff point.

The key limitation of the RD design is that it estimates treatment effects only for persons whose Z values are near the cutoff point. Thus, in general, RD methods cannot estimate the average treatment effect (ATE) or the average treatment effect on the treated (ATT) (and cannot estimate ATE(**X**) or ATT(**X**)) because they focus on a subset of the population of interest. On the other hand, sometimes treatment effects near the cutoff points are precisely the points of interest, for example, if the policy change being considered is to move the cutoff point. Also, if much of the data lie near the cutoff value, then the ATE near the cutoff is generally of greater interest than when the cutoff value pertains to very few people.

The fuzzy regression discontinuity design

The fuzzy design differs from the sharp design in that the treatment assignment is not a deterministic function of Z_i because there are other variables that determine assignment to treatment. The common feature that the fuzzy design shares with the sharp design is that the probability of receiving treatment (the propensity score), $\text{Prob}[P_i = 1|\, Z_i]$, viewed as a function of Z_i, is discontinuous at some known point, z_0. For the fuzzy design, this assumption can be stated as follows:

Assumption RD-3. $\text{Prob}[P_i = 1|\, Z_i = Z]$ is discontinuous at $Z = z_0$.

As shown in Hahn, Todd, and van der Klaauw (2001), mean treatment effects can be identified even under a fuzzy design.

Consider next what treatment parameter is identified by the fuzzy RD design under alternative assumptions that can be made on the degree to which program impacts are heterogeneous.

Common treatment effects. Suppose that the treatment effect is the same for all individuals and equals Δ. The mean difference in outcomes for persons slightly above and slightly below the discontinuity point z_0 is

$$
\begin{aligned}
&\text{E}[Y_i|\, Z_i = z_0 + e] - \text{E}[Y_i|\, Z_i = z_0 - e] \\
&\quad = \text{E}[Y_{1i}|\, Z_i = z_0 + e] \times \text{Prob}[P_i = 1|\, Z_i = z_0 + e] \\
&\quad\quad + \text{E}[Y_{0i}|\, Z_i = z_0 + e] \times \text{Prob}[P_i = 0|\, Z_i = z_0 + e] \\
&\quad\quad - \{\text{E}[Y_{1i}|\, Z_i = z_0 - e] \times \text{Prob}[P_i = 1|\, Z_i = z_0 - e] \\
&\quad\quad + \text{E}[Y_{0i}|\, Z_i = z_0 - e] \times \text{Prob}[P_i = 0|\, Z_i = z_0 - e]\} \\
&\quad = \text{E}[Y_{1i}|\, Z_i = z_0 + e] \times \text{E}[P_i|\, Z_i = z_0 + e] + \text{E}[Y_{0i}|\, Z_i = z_0 + e] \times (1 - \text{E}[P_i|\, Z_i = z_0 + e]) \\
&\quad\quad - \{\text{E}[Y_{1i}|\, Z_i = z_0 - e] \times \text{E}[P_i|\, Z_i = z_0 - e] + \text{E}[Y_{0i}|\, Z_i - z_0 - e] \\
&\quad\quad \times (1 - \text{E}[P_i|\, Z_i = z_0 - e])\} \\
&\quad = \text{E}[Y_{1i} - Y_{0i}|\, Z_i = z_0 + e] \times \text{E}[P_i|\, Z_i = z_0 + e] \\
&\quad\quad - \text{E}[Y_{1i} - Y_{0i}|\, Z_i = z_0 - e] \times \text{E}[P_i|\, Z_i = z_0 - e] \\
&\quad\quad + \text{E}[Y_{0i}|\, Z_i = z_0 + e] - \text{E}[Y_{0i}|\, Z_i = z_0 - e] \\
&\quad = \Delta \times \{\text{E}[P_i|\, Z_i = z_0 + e] - \text{E}[P_i|\, Z_i = z_0 - e]\} + \text{E}[Y_{0i}|\, Z_i = z_0 + e] - \text{E}[Y_{0i}|\, Z_i = z_0 - e].
\end{aligned}
$$

Assumption RD-1 implies that $\lim_{e \to 0^+} \{E[Y_{0i}| Z_i = z_0 + e] - E[Y_{0i}| Z_i = z_0 - e]\} = 0$. This in turn implies that

$$\begin{aligned} &\lim_{e\to 0^+}\{E[Y_i \mid Z_i = z_0 + e] - E[Y_i \mid Z_i = z_0 - e]\} \\ &\quad = \Delta \times \lim_{e\to 0^+}\{E[P_i \mid Z_i = z_0 + e] - E[P_i \mid Z_i = z_0 - e]\}. \end{aligned} \tag{14.1}$$

Equation (14.1) implies that Δ can consistently be estimated (identified) by the ratio

$$\hat{\Delta}_{FRD} = \frac{\lim_{e\to 0^+} E[Y_i \mid Z_i = z_0 + e] - \lim_{e\to 0^+} E[Y_i \mid Z_i = z_0 - e]}{\lim_{e\to 0^+} E[P_i \mid Z_i = z_0 + e] - \lim_{e\to 0^+} E[P_i \mid Z_i = z_0 - e]}. \tag{14.2}$$

The denominator is nonzero, because assumption RD-3 implies that $E[P_i = 1| Z_i = Z]$ (the propensity score) is discontinuous at $Z = z_0$.

Variable treatment effects. Now consider the more realistic assumption that treatment effects are heterogeneous (vary over the population). In addition to assumptions RD-1, RD-2, and RD-3, assume

Assumption RD-4. P_i is independent of Δ_i conditional on Z_i near z_0: $P_i \perp\!\!\!\perp \Delta_i| Z_i = z_0$.

This assumption implies that individuals are assumed not to select into the program on the basis of anticipated program gains, at least not near the cutoff z_0. Under assumptions RD-1, RD-2, RD-3, and RD-4, equation (14.2) for $\hat{\Delta}_{FRD}$ provides a consistent estimate of (identifies) the *average* treatment effect (ATE) near the cutoff point, $E[\Delta_i| Z_i = z_0]$.

In addition to these two cases, Hahn, Todd, and van der Klaauw (2001) also consider another assumption (which replaces assumption RD-4) that can be made on the nature of impact heterogeneity, in which the RD estimate can have a local average treatment effect (LATE) interpretation (LATE methods are discussed in chapter 15). In that case, the RD estimator gives the average effect of the program for the people induced to participate by being on one side of the cutoff rather than the other (the so-called complier group).

Checking the validity of a regression discontinuity design

The key assumption of RD estimators is that people around the cutoff value are comparable. When using an RD estimator, this assumption should be verified, to the extent possible. One way to do so is to examine the distribution of observed baseline covariates around the cutoff value. A common practice is to report the mean of the baseline characteristics within some interval around the cutoff value and to test whether the means for the observations slightly above the cutoff value are statistically significantly different from the means of the observations that are slightly below the cutoff value. This can be done by applying the sharp RD estimation methods, discussed below, using the baseline characteristics as the Y variable.

Baseline covariates that are not comparable just around the cutoff could indicate that some people near the cutoff are altering their Z_i to affect their participation outcomes. For example, if the criterion for getting into a program is a score on a test, some people may be able to take the test repeatedly until they get a passing score. The people who took the test repeatedly until they passed it may be on average more motivated than the others, violating the assumption that people just above and below the cutoff are comparable. Another example is provided by Urquiola and Verhoogen (2009), who present a model of household and school administrator behavior in a school system with a maximum class size that suggests that total enrollment (in all classrooms) in a given grade will jump on either side of the class-size threshold (and at multiples of that threshold), and they find evidence from Chile that is consistent with this behavior.

The Hahn, Todd, and van der Klaauw estimation method

This section describes a simple RD estimation approach proposed in Hahn, Todd, and van der Klaauw (2001). For both the sharp and fuzzy designs, the following ratio identifies the treatment effect at $Z = z_0$:

$$\hat{\Delta}_{\text{FRD}} = \frac{\hat{Y}^{+} - \hat{Y}^{-}}{\hat{P}^{+} - \hat{P}^{-}},$$

where $\hat{Y}^{+} = \lim_{e \to 0^{+}} \{\text{E}[Y_i \mid Z_i = z_0 + e], \hat{Y}^{-} = \lim_{e \to 0^{+}} \{\text{E}[Y_i \mid Z_i = z_0 - e], \hat{P}^{+} = \lim_{e \to 0^{+}} \{\text{E}[P_i \mid Z_i = z_0 + e],$ and $\hat{P}^{-} = \lim_{e \to 0^{+}} \{\text{E}[P_i \mid Z_i = z_0 - e]$. Given consistent estimators of the four one-sided limits in that ratio, the treatment effect can be consistently estimated. For the sharp design, the probability of receiving treatment goes from zero to one. Therefore, the denominator equals one and only the numerator needs to be estimated. The following discussion describes the estimation for the fuzzy design, in which all four limits need to be estimated; estimation for the sharp design requires estimation of only the two limits in the numerator.

Local means approach

One simple nonparametric estimator estimates the limits by taking averages over the Y_i values and the P_i values within a specified distance of the boundary points. The distance is called a *bandwidth*. Given bandwidths above and below the cutoff point (h_+ and h_-, respectively), the limits can be estimated by the following equations:

$$\hat{Y}^{+} = \frac{\sum_{i=1}^{n} Y_i \times 1(z_0 < Z_i < z_0 + h_+)}{\sum_{i=1}^{n} 1(z_0 < Z_i < z_0 + h_+)} \qquad \hat{Y}^{-} = \frac{\sum_{i=1}^{n} Y_i \times 1(z_0 - h_- < Z_i < z_0)}{\sum_{i=1}^{n} 1(z_0 - h_- < Z_i < z_0)}$$

$$\hat{P}^{+} = \frac{\sum_{i=1}^{n} P_i \times 1(z_0 < Z_i < z_0 + h_+)}{\sum_{i=1}^{n} 1(z_0 < Z_i < z_0 + h_+)} \qquad \hat{P}^{-} = \frac{\sum_{i=1}^{n} P_i \times 1(z_0 - h_- < Z_i < z_0)}{\sum_{i=1}^{n} 1(z_0 - h_- < Z_i < z_0)}$$

The 1( ) function is an indicator function, which equals 1 if the expression is true and 0 otherwise. It is clear that each of these four terms represents a simple mean of either Y or P for the observations that are sufficiently close to the cutoff point z_0. This approach of simple averaging on either side of the cutoff is equivalent to performing a nonparametric kernel regression, using a uniform kernel function.

Local linear regression approach

The RD estimator can also be implemented using local linear regression methods, as discussed in Hahn, Todd, and van der Klaauw (2001), which in theory perform better than kernel averaging methods at boundary points (see Fan 1992). Local linear methods fit separate linear regressions on the right side and the left side of the cutoff value, which reduces bias at boundary points relative to simple averaging. In effect, these methods use a weighting scheme to construct weighted averages (the weights are described in chapter 13 on matching estimators). These methods are not discussed in detail here because they are not commonly used in RD applications.

Choosing the bandwidth and getting standard errors

How should the bandwidths (h_+ and h_-) that control how many observations on either side of the cutoff are used in the estimation be chosen? Hahn, Todd, and van der Klaauw (1999) use leave-one-out cross-validation to select the optimal bandwidth of the RD estimator. Imbens and Kalyanaraman (2012) developed a data-dependent optimal plug-in bandwidth estimator for the RD estimator based on the local linear regression approach (and also provide Matlab software that can be used to implement it).

Standard errors can be obtained using bootstrap methods. These methods construct so-called bootstrap samples, which are data subsamples (with replacement) of the original observations. RD estimates are obtained for each of the bootstrap samples. If 100 percent resampling is used, then standard errors can be estimated from the empirical variance over the bootstrap estimates (excluding the estimate that is based on the original data set).

For example, obtain 1,000 bootstrap samples, where each is obtained by sampling, with replacement, from the original data until a (bootstrap) sample with the same number of observations as in the original data is achieved. Calculate the RD estimate for each bootstrap sample. Calculate the variance of these 1,000 RD estimates. The square root of that calculated variance is the standard error of the original RD estimate. For a discussion of bootstrap methods, see Efron and Tibshirani (1993) and Cameron and Trivedi (2005).

Alternative estimation approaches

Lee and Lemieux (2010) describe simpler parametric RD estimators that appeared in the earlier RD literature. Some methods estimate a single regression that includes observations both below and above the cutoff, with an indicator variable for receiving treatment. For example, for the sharp design, a simple way of estimating the effect of the program is as follows:

$$Y = \alpha + \tau P + \mathbf{X}'\boldsymbol{\beta} + \varepsilon.$$

This approach imposes a specific functional form for the outcome in the absence of the program: Y is assumed to be a linear function of the **X** variables. Note that this method of estimating the program impact makes use of all the data in the estimation, rather than just the data near the cutoff value. Using more data can provide a more precise estimate for the case in which the functional forms assumptions are correct, but this benefit has to be weighed against the risk of model misspecification. The local average methods described previously were nonparametric and did not require any functional form assumptions for the outcome equation. Even if this simple regression-based estimation strategy were adopted, it is worthwhile to check whether the estimated impact would differ substantially if the estimate were obtained using only the observations near the cutoff.

An alternative estimation approach proposed by van der Klaauw (2002) for the sharp RD design is to assume (in addition to continuity) a flexible parametric specification for $g(\mathbf{X}) = \mathrm{E}[Y_{0i}| \mathbf{X}_i]$ and to add this as a control function to the regression of Y_i on P_i.[2] For the fuzzy design, van der Klaauw proposes a similar approach, except that P_i in the control function–augmented regression equation is replaced by a first-stage estimate of $\mathrm{E}[P_i| Z_i]$, which can be estimated either by linear regression or nonparametrically.

Examples of regression discontinuity methods

The most common application of RD methods has been the evaluation of the effects of educational interventions in the United States. The RD approach has been used only occasionally to evaluate social programs in developing country settings. Three examples of recent applications follow.[3]

Example 1: Teacher incentives and student performance in Israel (Lavy 2009)

Many developed and developing countries have implemented teacher incentive programs that link teachers' pay to their students' performance. Lavy (2009) uses an RD estimator to evaluate the effects of a teacher incentive program on student performance in Israeli high schools.

Background. In early December 2000, the Israeli Ministry of Education launched a new teachers' bonus experiment in 49 Israeli high schools. The program introduced a rank-order tournament (among teachers of Arabic, English, Hebrew, and mathematics in Israel) that rewarded teachers with cash bonuses for improving their students' performance on high school matriculation exams. Among comprehensive high schools, only those whose most recent school-level matriculation rates were equal to or lower than the national mean (45 percent) were eligible.

Methodology. One of the methods used by Lavy (2009) is an RD method that exploits the sharp discontinuity in the treatment assignment rule (that is, schools are eligible only if their most recent matriculation rates are less than 45 percent). More specifically, Lavy (2009) compares the postintervention student test scores between marginal participants (treated schools with matriculation rates in the 40–45 percent range) and marginal nonparticipants (untreated schools with matriculation rates in the 46–52 percent range).

Results. Table 14.1 summarizes the results from the study. The RD results show that the teacher incentive program significantly increased the proportion of students in the treatment group who took the matriculation exam, as well as the pass rates and the average scores on that exam. The impact on the mathematics exam was larger, and had higher statistical significance, than the impact on the English exam.

Example 2: Chile's 900 schools program (Chay, McEwan, and Urquiola 2005)

Chay, McEwan, and Urquiola (2005) use an RD design to evaluate the effects of Chile's 900 schools program (called the P-900 program), which gave additional resources to low-performing, publicly funded schools. A school's participation in that program was determined by its mean test score in 1988. A school was treated if its mean score fell below a cutoff value in its region. Treated schools received infrastructure improvements, instructional materials, teacher training, and resources for tutoring low-achieving students.

Methodological issues. The impact of the P-900 program is of interest in its own right, but the study's authors' goal was to show that the estimated impact of such a program might be misleading using conventional estimators (for example, difference-in-differences [DID]). The main problem was due to testing noise, which creates a so-called mean-reversion problem. For example, some schools had very low scores in the baseline year (1988) simply because they experienced an unlucky circumstance or a bad draw of students in that year. They are unlikely to experience a bad draw again in the evaluation year (1990), so their postintervention test scores will tend to rise. A before-after estimator or a DID estimator will tend to overestimate the program impact on students' test scores. Chay, McEwan, and Urquiola (2005) show that conventional estimators yield significant impacts, even when using data collected before the P-900 program was implemented.

TABLE 14.1 Impact of teacher incentives on student performance in Israel

	MATH		ENGLISH	
	LIMITED SET OF CONTROLS	FULL SET OF CONTROLS	LIMITED SET OF CONTROLS	FULL SET OF CONTROLS
Proportion tested				
Control group mean	0.767		0.826	
Treatment effect	0.072	0.055	0.053	0.048
	(0.034)	(0.029)	(0.022)	(0.018)
	[0.049]	[0.040]	[0.032]	[0.026]
Pass rate				
Control group mean	0.602		0.745	
Treatment effect	0.111	0.088	0.039	0.033
	(0.037)	(0.028)	(0.029)	(0.022)
	[0.052]	[0.040]	[0.041]	[0.031]
Average score				
Control group mean	51.2		55.2	
Treatment effect	6.7	5.8	3.0	2.7
	(2.4)	(1.8)	(1.9)	(1.4)
	[3.4]	[2.6]	[2.6]	[2.0]

Source: Lavy 2009.

Note: Reprinted from *American Economic Review*, volume 99, issue 5 (December), Victor Lavy, "Performance Pay and Teachers' Effort, Productivity, and Grading Ethics," pages 1979–2011, copyright American Economic Association, 2009; reproduced with permission of the *American Economic Review*. Further permission required for reuse. "Limited set of controls" columns include schools' one-year lagged matriculation rate and students' attempted credit units. "Full set of controls" columns include those two variables as well as sets of dummy variables for number of siblings and father's and mother's education, a dummy for Asian-African ethnic background, immigration status, gender dummy, the average score of students' attempted credit units, overall credit units awarded, and credit units awarded for the subject in question only. All models include school fixed effects. There are no results for Arabic or Hebrew because school participation in the experiment was not required for those subjects. Standard errors in parentheses are clustered at the school-year level, and standard errors in brackets are clustered at the school level (combining across years in each school).

Empirical strategy. The authors show that an RD design solves the mean-reversion problem, and thus provides consistent estimates of the program impact. As long as any mean-reversion effect is smooth around the test score cutoff, it can be absorbed into a smooth function of pre-intervention scores (the study tried three different functional forms). The discrete nature of the program participation rule can be used to produce consistent estimates of the program impact.

Results. Using data collected from more than 4,600 schools, Chay, McEwan, and Urquiola (2005) find that the P-900 program had statistically significant positive effects on students' test scores, but these estimates were not as large as the DID estimates of the program's impacts. They show that the P-900 program resulted in no test score gains from

1988 to 1990, the end of the first year of its operation, but that it did increase 1992 test scores over 1988 test scores by about 0.2 standard deviations (of the distribution of the test score variables). In contrast, conventional DID estimates suggest that the program increased 1992 test scores over 1988 test scores by 0.4–0.7 standard deviations.

Example 3: The performance of regression discontinuity methods (Buddelmeyer and Skoufias 2004)

Buddelmeyer and Skoufias (2004) study the performance of RD methods using data from Mexico's PROGRESA program. Specifically, they compare program impacts estimated using RD methods with those obtained using randomized controlled trial (RCT) methods (which are widely considered to be the most reliable impact evaluation methods). Thus they use the experimental estimates as the benchmark for checking the performance of the RD estimator.

Background. Recall from chapter 6 that, in the original PROGRESA evaluation, 506 poor villages in Mexico were randomly divided into 320 treatment villages and 186 control villages. Within each treatment village, only families that were eligible for the program according to an eligibility index (the so-called discriminant score) were allowed to participate. The index was derived from poverty criteria, such as whether the family had a dirt floor or a bathroom in their home. Most families deemed eligible for the program chose to participate in it. The interaction between the treatment assignment and the eligibility index divides PROGRESA households into four subgroups, as shown in table 14.2.

TABLE 14.2 Distribution of PROGRESA sample (all households) into treatment and control villages

HOUSEHOLD ELIGIBILITY STATUS	DISCRIMINANT SCORE (*PUNTAJE*)	LOCALITY WHERE PROGRESA WAS FIRST IMPLEMENTED (TREATMENT LOCALITY) ($R = 1$)	LOCALITY WHERE PROGRESA WAS IMPLEMENTED LATER (CONTROL LOCALITY) ($R = 0$)
Not eligible for PROGRESA benefits ($E = 0$)	High (above threshold)	**C** $E = 0, R = 1$	**D** $E = 0, R = 0$
Eligible for PROGRESA benefits ($E = 1$)	Low (below threshold)	**A** $E = 1, R = 1$	**B** $E = 1, R = 0$

Source: Buddelmeyer and Skoufias 2004.
Note: The discriminant score is an index derived from poverty criteria, such as whether the family had a dirt floor or a bathroom in their home.

Methodology. The fact that households' participation was determined by their discriminant score allowed Buddelmeyer and Skoufias (2004) to use an RD approach. Most of the households in their sample had eligibility scores near the cutoff values (about 50), making the sample near the cutoff an interesting subsample to study. Moreover, the criteria for eligibility were not made public, alleviating concerns that households may have manipulated their poverty status to become eligible for the program.

Because families with eligibility index values just above and just below the cutoff are very similar, Buddelmeyer and Skoufias (2004) calculate program impacts (for the households near the cutoff) by comparing households living in treated communities with scores just above (Group C in table 14.2) and below (Group A) the cutoff. They use data collected in rounds 1 (baseline), 3 (the first postintervention round), and 5 (the third postintervention round) in their analysis. They could have also evaluated the performance of the RD estimator by comparing groups B and D near the cutoff values, in which case the RD estimator should have yielded a value of zero.

Results. Buddelmeyer and Skoufias (2004) find that the estimates based on the RD method are quite close to those derived from RCT methods using the round 5 data. But this is not the case for the round 3 data (see table 14.3). They then check several potential problems that might have undermined the performance of the RD method when using the round 3 data, such as the choice of bandwidth and spillover effects (given that Group C also resides in treatment villages). They conclude that Group C is not a good comparison group because the intervention likely altered the behavior of some of the ineligible households in treatment villages.

Buddelmeyer and Skoufias (2004) then use noneligible households in the control villages (Group D) as another comparison group, because this group is unlikely to be subject to spillover effects. This time, they find that the estimated program impacts using the RD approach and the RCT methods are extremely similar (see table 14.4). This finding lends credibility to the RD approach, and it also highlights the importance of finding a good comparison group when conducting any impact evaluation.

Conclusion

Some programs have specific rules that determine which people are eligible for them. Examples of this are eligibility rules based on the value of some individual, family, or community characteristic. In such situations, it may be possible to estimate the impact of the program using RD methods.

RD methods can provide estimates of the impacts of certain types of programs or policies that, under certain conditions, approximate an RCT. In particular, they can be used in cases in which eligibility is determined by a continuous variable for which there is a cutoff point that separates those who are eligible from those who are not. Until recently, these methods were used mainly in the context of evaluating effects of education interventions in the United States, but now they are increasingly being used to analyze both education and noneducation programs in developing countries.

TABLE 14.3 Estimates of program impact, by round, for boys 12–16 years old

	EXPERIMENTAL ESTIMATES			RD ESTIMATES	
	DOUBLE DIFFERENCES	CROSS-SECTIONAL DIFFERENCES	CROSS-SECTIONAL DIFFERENCES 50	EPANECHNIKOV KERNEL	QUARTIC KERNEL
Schooling					
Round 1	n.a.	0.013	−0.001	−0.031	−0.016
		(0.018)	(0.028)	(0.029)	(0.031)
Round 3	0.050***	0.064***	0.071**	0.010	0.008
	(0.017)	(0.019)	(0.028)	(0.031)	(0.034)
Round 5	0.048**	0.061***	0.099***	0.066**	0.072**
	(0.030)	(0.019)	(0.030)	(0.030)	(0.032)
Work					
Round 1	n.a.	0.018	0.007	−0.004	−0.016
		(0.019)	(0.029)	(0.029)	(0.032)
Round 3	−0.037	−0.018	−0.007	0.002	−0.004
	(0.023)	(0.017)	(0.029)	(0.026)	(0.028)
Round 5	−0.046*	−0.028	−0.037	−0.030	−0.029
	(0.025)	(0.017)	(0.025)	(0.026)	(0.028)

Source: Buddelmeyer and Skoufias 2004.

Note: Double differences = difference-in-differences estimator using data from all three rounds. Cross-sectional differences = cross-sectional difference between treatment and control villages. Cross-sectional differences 50 = cross-sectional difference method applied to households whose eligibility indexes are within the (−50, 50) interval around the eligibility cutoff. Treatment group for experimental and RD estimates: beneficiary households in treated villages (Group A). Comparison group for experimental estimates: eligible households in control villages (Group B). Comparison group for RD: noneligible households in treated villages (Group C). n.a. = not applicable; RD = regression discontinuity.

* significant at 10 percent level; ** significant at 5 percent level; *** significant at 1 percent level

TABLE 14.4 Estimates of program impact using noneligible households in control villages as a comparison group

	(1)	(2)	(3)	(4)	(5)	(6)
	EXPERIMENTAL RESULTS			RD ESTIMATES		
	DOUBLE DIFFERENCES	CROSS-SECTIONAL DIFFERENCES	CROSS-SECTIONAL DIFFERENCES 50	UNIFORM KERNEL	TRIANGULAR KERNEL	GAUSSIAN KERNEL
Schooling: Boys 12–16 years old						
Round 3	0.068***	0.066**	0.161***	0.094***	0.105***	0.086***
	(0.018)	(0.025)	(0.033)	(0.029)	(0.032)	(0.023)
Round 5	0.060**	0.059**	0.097**	0.147***	0.139***	0.107***
	(0.031)	(0.025)	(0.033)	(0.027)	(0.030)	(0.022)
Schooling: Girls 12–16 years old						
Round 3	0.070***	0.059**	0.142***	0.117***	0.132***	0.108***
	(0.017)	(0.025)	(0.043)	(0.029)	(0.033)	(0.023)
Round 5	0.105***	0.094**	0.149***	0.112***	0.131***	0.108***
	(0.020)	(0.026)	(0.046)	(0.032)	(0.037)	(0.024)

Source: Buddelmeyer and Skoufias 2004.

Note: Double differences = difference-in-differences estimator using data from all three rounds. Cross-sectional differences = cross-sectional difference between treatment and control villages. Cross-sectional differences 50 = cross-sectional difference method applied to households whose eligibility indexes are within the (−50, 50) interval around the eligibility cutoff. Treatment group: beneficiary households in treatment villages (Group A). Comparison group: Noneligible households in control villages (Group D). RD = regression discontinuity.

* significant at 10 percent level; ** significant at 5 percent level; *** significant at 1 percent level

Notes

1. For some programs, eligibility occurs if Z_i is less than z_0. The following exposition can be easily modified for this situation, where $P_i = 1$ if $Z_i < z_0$ and $P_i = 0$ if $Z_i \geq z_0$. In both cases, the program impact is measured by the difference in Y_i between those whose Z_i is just above z_0 and those whose Z_i is just below z_0.
2. The control function approach is presented in detail in chapter 16.
3. A fourth application is a study of the impact of school quality on student learning in Kenya by Lucas and Mbiti (2014).

References

Buddelmeyer, Hielke, and Emmanuel Skoufias. 2004. "An Evaluation of the Performance of Regression Discontinuity Design on Progresa." Policy Research Working Paper 3386, World Bank, Washington, DC.

Cameron, Colin, and Pravin Trivedi. 2005. *Microeconometrics: Methods and Applications*. New York: Cambridge University Press.

Chay, Kenneth, Patrick McEwan, and Miguel Urquiola. 2005. "The Central Role of Noise in Evaluating Interventions That Use Test Scores to Rank Schools." *American Economic Review* 95 (4): 1237–58.

Efron, Bradley, and Robert Tibshirani. 1993. *An Introduction to the Bootstrap*. New York: Chapman and Hall.

Fan, J. 1992. "Design-Adaptive Nonparametric Regression." *Journal of the American Statistical Association* 87 (420): 998–1004.

Hahn, Jinyong, Petra Todd, and Wilbert van der Klaauw. 1999. "Evaluating the Effect of an Antidiscrimination Law Using a Regression Discontinuity Design." NBER Working Paper 7131, National Bureau of Economic Research, Cambridge, MA.

Hahn, Jinyong, Petra Todd, and Wilbert van der Klaauw. 2001. "Identification and Estimation of Treatment Effects with a Regression-Discontinuity Design." *Econometrica* 69 (1): 201–09.

Imbens, Guido W., and Karthik Kalyanaraman. 2012. "Optimal Bandwidth Choice for the Regression Discontinuity Estimator." *Review of Economic Studies* 79 (3): 933–59.

Lavy, Victor. 2009. "Performance Pay and Teachers' Effort, Productivity, and Grading Ethics." *American Economic Review* 99 (5): 1979–2011.

Lee, David, and Thomas Lemieux. 2010. "Regression Discontinuity Design in Economics." *Journal of Economic Literature* 48 (2): 281–355.

Lucas, Adrienne, and Isaac Mbiti. 2014. "Effects of School Quality on Student Achievement: Discontinuity Evidence from Kenya." *American Economic Journal: Applied Economics* 6 (3): 234–63.

Thistlethwaite, Donald L., and Donald T. Campbell. 1960. "Regression-Discontinuity Analysis: An Alternative to the Ex Post Facto Experiment." *Journal of Educational Psychology* 51 (6): 309–17.

Trochim, William M. K. 1984. *Research Design for Program Evaluation: The Regression-Discontinuity Approach*. Beverly Hills: Sage Publications.

Urquiola, Miguel, and Eric Verhoogen. 2009. "Class-Size Caps, Sorting, and the Regression-Discontinuity Design." *American Economic Review* 99 (1): 179–215.

van der Klaauw, Wilbert. 2002. "Estimating the Effect of Financial Aid Offers on College Enrollment: A Regression Discontinuity Approach." *International Economic Review* 43 (4): 1249–87.

CHAPTER 15

Instrumental Variables Estimation and Local Average Treatment Effects

Introduction

The regression estimation methods presented in previous chapters (chapters 7, 11, and 12) require two types of assumptions:

1. Functional form assumptions on the relationship between Y_1 and $\mathbf{X}$, or between Y_0 and $\mathbf{X}$, such as $Y_1 = \mathbf{X}'\boldsymbol{\beta}_1 + U_1$ or $Y_0 = \mathbf{X}'\boldsymbol{\beta}_0 + U_0$
2. Lack of correlation between the program participation variable (P) and one or both error terms (U_1 and U_0), after conditioning on $\mathbf{X}$, an example of which (see chapter 11) is $\mathrm{E}[U_0 + P(U_1 - U_0)| \mathbf{X}, P] = 0$, which is required to estimate the average impact of the treatment on the treated (ATT($\mathbf{X}$))

Chapter 13 presents matching methods, which do not require the first assumption but do require the second assumption. This chapter presents instrumental variables (IV) methods, which do not require the second assumption but in almost all applications require the first assumption.[1]

Although IV estimation does not require the second assumption, it does have another requirement, namely, a variable that has predictive power for participation (P) but does not have a direct impact on Y_1 or Y_0. Unfortunately, it is difficult to find such variables. Even when such a variable is available, it may still not be possible to estimate the average treatment effect (ATE) or the average treatment effect on the treated (ATT). However, IV methods can still be used to estimate a local average treatment effect (LATE). This chapter covers both general IV estimation and the special case of LATE estimation.

Two uses of instrumental variables estimation for impact evaluation analysis

To estimate the impacts of programs or policies, IV estimation is used in two general ways. First, IV methods can be used to address the problem of noncompliers in randomized controlled trials (RCTs). To see how, suppose that some people assigned to the treatment group in an RCT choose not to participate (they can be called "never takers"), and that some people assigned to the control group find a way to participate in the program, or in a very similar program ("always takers"). In general, estimating ATE for the whole population is not possible because the program impact on people who are never takers or always takers cannot be estimated; there are no counterfactuals available for these two groups of people.

Table 15.1 illustrates why it is not possible to estimate ATE for the population as a whole. Because Y_1 can never be observed for the never takers (the first group) and Y_0 can never be observed for the always takers (the third group), it is not possible to estimate the impact of the program for those two groups. However, it may be possible to estimate the impact of the program on the people who follow their random assignment (the second group), who can be called "compliers."[2]

Clearly, the estimated impact on the compliers is not the ATE. Nor is it the ATT, because the always takers are part of the treated group, and it is not possible to estimate program impacts for them. Yet table 15.1 suggests the possibility of estimating something else, the *average treatment effect for the compliers*, or the LATE, and it turns out that IV methods can be used to do so.

How can a program's LATE be estimated? Recall from chapter 6 that, in an RCT, the intention-to-treat effect (ITT) can always be estimated by $E[Y \mid R = 1] - E[Y \mid R = 0]$ as long as none of the individuals randomly assigned to the control group finds a way to participate in the program (and as long as there are no spillovers onto the control group). But, as explained in chapter 6, the ITT is not equal to the treatment effect on the compliers (unless strong assumptions are imposed) because ITT estimates include noncompliers. The intuition for the IV approach is that it uses the treatment assignment to obtain an estimate of the proportion of compliers in the treatment group (which includes both compliers and always takers), and then uses this estimated proportion to adjust the ITT to obtain an estimate of LATE. This is similar to the explanation in chapter 6 for how to obtain an estimate of ATT from an estimate of ITT for the case in which no one in the control group is treated, that is, there are no always takers in the control group.

The second, and more general, use of IV estimation is to avoid problems of selection bias in nonexperimental settings. The goal of impact evaluations is to estimate the causal impact of the program. But selection bias can lead to situations in which the difference in

TABLE 15.1 Observed value of the outcome variable (Y) for three different groups in a randomized controlled trial

	(1) $R = 1$	(2) $R = 0$	(1) - (2)
(1) Never participate (never takers)	$Y = Y_0$	$Y = Y_0$	0
(2) Participate only if assigned to treatment (compliers)	$Y = Y_1$	$Y = Y_0$	$Y_1 - Y_0$
(3) Always participate (always takers)	$Y = Y_1$	$Y = Y_1$	0

Source: Original table for this publication.

outcomes between a program's participants and its nonparticipants is not solely due to the program, but instead also reflects other differences between these two groups. If certain conditions hold, IV methods can be used to remove selection bias from regression-based estimates of program impacts.

The intuition for why IV estimation can reduce selection bias is as follows: The variation in program participation (P) in the eligible population comes from two sources: one is random factors that have little or nothing to do with program impacts, and the other is nonrandom selectivity. Selectivity can arise, for example, if some people do not participate because they think the program effect on them is small. Instrumental variables, which can be denoted by $\mathbf{Z}$, extract the random variation from P (by regressing P on $\mathbf{Z}$) and use only this extracted random part of P to estimate the program's impacts. This is done in two steps:

1. Regress P on $\mathbf{Z}$ and the baseline covariates (that is, the $\mathbf{X}$ variables), and save the fitted value (denoted by $\hat{P}$) from this regression (recall that fitted values are the predicted values of the left-hand-side variable, based on the regression model's estimates).

2. Regress the observed outcome Y on $\hat{P}$ and the baseline covariates used in the first step; the estimated coefficient for $\hat{P}$ is the IV estimate of the program impact.

These two steps can be rapidly implemented using almost any statistical software package.

In nonexperimental settings, finding a credible instrumental variable is usually difficult; in particular, it is difficult to find an instrumental variable that has predictive power for program participation (P) but does *not* have a direct impact on Y_1 or Y_0. However, if the evaluation is based on an RCT, a natural candidate for predicting P (the identifying instrumental variable) is the random assignment of treatment (R), which should have predictive power for participation but, because it is random by definition, should have no direct impact on Y_1 and Y_0. The rest of this chapter presents a more rigorous discussion of the IV approach, which can be used to estimate program impacts in both experimental and nonexperimental settings.[3]

Instrumental variables estimation of ATE and ATT

Recall that ATE ≡ $E[Y_1 - Y_0]$ and that ATT ≡ $E[Y_1 - Y_0 | P = 1]$. This section explains the assumptions needed to estimate ATE and ATT using IV methods.[4] It turns out that the assumptions needed to estimate ATE and ATT are fairly strong, so the following section introduces the LATE, which requires much weaker assumptions.

Assumptions needed to estimate ATE and ATE(X) by IV methods

It is quite likely that the impact of any program on $Y_1 - Y_0$ will vary over members of the population. A key problem for estimating program effects arises when individuals' unobservable characteristics that contribute to this variation are correlated with participation, P, which is likely to be the case. When using IV methods to estimate ATE, the error term in the regression equation for Y is allowed to be correlated with the participation decision (P), but the instrumental variable must not predict the variation in gains from participation caused by unobserved variables. This is now explained in more detail.

To see the assumptions needed to estimate ATE, and ATE(**X**), using IV methods, assume that Y_1 and Y_0 for individual i take the following linear functional form:

$$Y_1 = \mathbf{X}'\boldsymbol{\beta}_1 + U_1, \tag{15.1}$$

$$Y_0 = \mathbf{X}'\boldsymbol{\beta}_0 + U_0, \tag{15.2}$$

where $\mathrm{E}[U_1] = \mathrm{E}[U_0] = 0$ and $\mathrm{E}[U_1| \mathbf{X}] = \mathrm{E}[U_0| \mathbf{X}] = 0$. As in chapters 11 and 12, these equations for Y_1 and Y_0 are causal relationships; they indicate how changes in the **X** variables change the values of Y_1 and Y_0. These expressions for Y_1 and Y_0 also imply that ATE and ATE(**X**) can be expressed as follows:

$$\mathrm{ATE} \equiv \mathrm{E}[Y_1 - Y_0] = \mathrm{E}[\mathbf{X}'\boldsymbol{\beta}_1 + U_1 - \mathbf{X}'\boldsymbol{\beta}_0 - U_0] = \mathrm{E}[\mathbf{X}]'(\boldsymbol{\beta}_1 - \boldsymbol{\beta}_0),$$

$$\mathrm{ATE}(\mathbf{X}) \equiv \mathrm{E}[Y_1 - Y_0| \mathbf{X}] = \mathrm{E}[\mathbf{X}'\boldsymbol{\beta}_1 + U_1 - \mathbf{X}'\boldsymbol{\beta}_0 - U_0| \mathbf{X}] = \mathbf{X}'(\boldsymbol{\beta}_1 - \boldsymbol{\beta}_0).$$

Consider the use of regression methods to estimate ATE(**X**).[5] Equations (15.1) and (15.2) for Y_1 and Y_0 imply that observed Y can be expressed as

$$\begin{aligned} Y &= Y_0 + P(Y_1 - Y_0) \\ &= \mathbf{X}'\boldsymbol{\beta}_0 + U_0 + P(\mathbf{X}'\boldsymbol{\beta}_1 + U_1 - \mathbf{X}'\boldsymbol{\beta}_0 - U_0) \\ &= \mathbf{X}'\boldsymbol{\beta}_0 + P\mathbf{X}'(\boldsymbol{\beta}_1 - \boldsymbol{\beta}_0) + \{U_0 + P(U_1 - U_0)\} \\ &= \mathbf{X}'\boldsymbol{\beta}_0 + P \times \mathrm{ATE}(\mathbf{X}) + \{U_0 + P(U_1 - U_0)\}. \end{aligned} \tag{15.3}$$

Equation (15.3) for Y suggests that ATE(**X**) could be estimated by regressing Y on the variables in **X** (which typically includes a constant term) and the interaction terms contained in P**X** (which includes P because **X** includes a constant term). In such a regression, the coefficients on the P**X** interaction terms would be an unbiased and consistent estimate of $\boldsymbol{\beta}_1 - \boldsymbol{\beta}_0$, which for any **X** can be used to calculate ATE(**X**), which equals $\mathbf{X}'(\boldsymbol{\beta}_1 - \boldsymbol{\beta}_0)$, if the error term $U_0 + P(U_1 - U_0)$ is uncorrelated with all of these regressors (**X** and P**X**).

However, there is a problem, or more specifically three problems. Even though U_1 and U_0 are assumed not to be correlated with **X**, the error term $U_0 + P(U_1 - U_0)$ is likely to be correlated with P, for three reasons. First, the error term $U_0 + P(U_1 - U_0)$ contains P, so it is likely to be correlated with P. Second, P is likely to be correlated with $U_1 - U_0$, because the larger $U_1 - U_0$ is, the larger is the gain to participating in the program (the larger is $Y_1 - Y_0$), so the more likely it will be that $P = 1$. Third, P is likely to be correlated with

U_0 because the smaller U_0 is, the larger is $U_1 - U_0$ and thus the larger is the gain to participating in the program (and thus the more likely it is that $P = 1$).

One approach to resolving this selection bias problem is to use IV methods. At a minimum, one or more instruments are needed, which can be denoted by **Z**, that have predictive power for P but are uncorrelated with U_1 or U_0. If such instruments can be found, they can be used as the instruments for P, and their interactions with the **X** variables can be used as instruments for P**X**.

Unfortunately, there is still a problem. Although these instruments are assumed to be uncorrelated with U_1 and U_0, so that $E[U_0| \mathbf{X}, \mathbf{Z}] = 0$ and $E[U_1| \mathbf{X}, \mathbf{Z}] = 0$, they could still be correlated with $P(U_1 - U_0)$ if they have predictive power for P. As Heckman (1997) shows, this is possible even if **Z** were randomly assigned. A simple example shows that $P(U_1 - U_0)$ is correlated with **Z** even if **Z** is randomly assigned. For simplicity, assume that Z is a single variable and that there is no variation in the **X** variables, so that they can be ignored. Z is randomly assigned, so $E[U_1 - U_0| \mathbf{Z}] = 0$. Assume that $U_1 - U_0$ has only three values, all with probability of ⅓: −3, 1, and 2. Clearly, $E[U_1 - U_0] = 0$. Assume that when $Z = 0$ then $P = 1$ if $U_1 - U_0 = 2$, but otherwise $P = 0$. Assume also that if $Z = 1$ then $P = 1$ if $U_1 - U_0 = 2$ or 1, but $P = 0$ if $U_1 - U_0 = -3$. That is, Z has an effect on P if $U_1 - U_0 = 1$ but not if $U_1 - U_0 = 2$ or −3. It is straightforward to show that $E[P(U_1 - U_0)| Z = 0] = ⅔$, but $E[P(U_1 - U_0)| Z = 1] = 1$, so $E[P(U_1 - U_0)| \mathbf{Z}] \neq 0$, and thus $P(U_1 - U_0)$ is correlated with **Z**.

One way to avoid this correlation between the overall error term $U_0 + P(U_1 - U_0)$ and the **Z** variables is to assume that $U_1 = U_0$, which removes $P(U_1 - U_0)$ from the regression equation. However, this restriction is improbable. In particular, the basic equations for Y_1 and Y_0 allow the observed variables (**X**) to have different impacts on outcomes in the treated and untreated states, because $\boldsymbol{\beta}_1$ is allowed to be different from $\boldsymbol{\beta}_0$, so why should one assume that the unobserved variables have the same impacts in the two states?

A somewhat more plausible argument that allows IV estimation to yield consistent estimates of ATE(**X**) is to assume that $E[U_0 + P(U_1 - U_0)| \mathbf{X}, \mathbf{Z}] = 0$. We also need to assume that $\text{Prob}[P = 1| \mathbf{X}, \mathbf{Z}] \neq \text{Prob}[P = 1| \mathbf{X}]$; this is the standard assumption that the instrumental variables have predictive power for P after conditioning on the variables that determine Y_1 and Y_0, but the first assumption, that $E[U_0 + P(U_1 - U_0)| \mathbf{X}, \mathbf{Z}] = 0$, deserves more scrutiny. This assumption is equivalent to condition (C-1-a) in Heckman (1997).

The assumption that $E[U_0 + P(U_1 - U_0)| \mathbf{X}, \mathbf{Z}] = 0$ does not require that $U_1 = U_0$. One possible scenario is that the decision to participate, P, is made before U_1 and U_0 are known, in which case P and $U_1 - U_0$ are independent, which implies that $E[P(U_1 - U_0)| \mathbf{X}, \mathbf{Z}] = E[P| \mathbf{X}, \mathbf{Z}] \times E[U_1 - U_0 | \mathbf{X}, \mathbf{Z}]$, which equals 0 because $E[U_1 - U_0 | \mathbf{X}, \mathbf{Z}] = 0$.[6] Whether this assumption is credible depends on the variables in **X** and **Z**, on what the error terms U_1 and U_0 represent, and on the factors that determine P. But it should be kept in mind that, as shown above, this condition may not be satisfied even when the **Z** variable is randomly assigned.

To see why these assumptions are sufficient to identify the ATE(**X**) parameter, take the expectation of the outcome equation for Y conditional on two different values of **Z** ($\mathbf{Z}_0$ and $\mathbf{Z}_1$) and a specific value of **X**:

$$\mathrm{E}[Y|\,\mathbf{X}, \mathbf{Z} = \mathbf{Z}_0] = \mathbf{X}'\boldsymbol{\beta} + \mathrm{E}[P|\,\mathbf{X}, \mathbf{Z} = \mathbf{Z}_0] \times \mathrm{ATE}(\mathbf{X}) + \mathrm{E}[U_0 + P(U_1 - U_0)|\,\mathbf{X}, \mathbf{Z} = \mathbf{Z}_0], \quad (15.4)$$

$$\mathrm{E}[Y|\,\mathbf{X}, \mathbf{Z} = \mathbf{Z}_1] = \mathbf{X}'\boldsymbol{\beta} + \mathrm{E}[P|\,\mathbf{X}, \mathbf{Z} = \mathbf{Z}_1] \times \mathrm{ATE}(\mathbf{X}) + \mathrm{E}[U_0 + P(U_1 - U_0)|\,\mathbf{X}, \mathbf{Z} = \mathbf{Z}_1]. \quad (15.5)$$

Subtracting equation (15.5) from equation (15.4) and imposing the assumptions that $\mathrm{E}[U_0|\,\mathbf{X}, \mathbf{Z}] = 0$ and that $\mathrm{E}[P(U_1 - U_0)|\,\mathbf{X}, \mathbf{Z} = \mathbf{Z}_0] = \mathrm{E}[P(U_1 - U_0)|\,\mathbf{X}, \mathbf{Z} = \mathbf{Z}_1] = 0$ yields the following expression for ATE(**X**):

$$\mathrm{ATE}(\mathbf{X}) = \frac{\mathrm{E}\left[Y|\mathbf{X}, \mathbf{Z} = \mathbf{Z}_1\right] - \mathrm{E}\left[Y|\mathbf{X}, \mathbf{Z} = \mathbf{Z}_0\right]}{\mathrm{E}\left[P|\mathbf{X}, \mathbf{Z} = \mathbf{Z}_1\right] - \mathrm{E}\left[P|\mathbf{X}, \mathbf{Z} = \mathbf{Z}_0\right]}$$

$$= \frac{\mathrm{E}[Y|\mathbf{X}, \mathbf{Z} = \mathbf{Z}_1] - E[Y|\mathbf{X}, \mathbf{Z} = \mathbf{Z}_0]}{\Pr[P = 1|\mathbf{X}, \mathbf{Z} = \mathbf{Z}_1] - \Pr[P = 1|\mathbf{X}, \mathbf{Z} = \mathbf{Z}_0]}. \quad (15.6)$$

In practice, standard IV regression methods, with **Z** serving as a set of instruments for P (and interactions of the **X** and **Z** variables serving as instruments for the interactions between the **X** variables and P), can be used to estimate the equation $Y = \mathbf{X}'\boldsymbol{\beta}_0 + P \times \mathrm{ATE}(\mathbf{X}) + \{U_0 + P(U_1 - U_0)\}$ to obtain this estimate of ATE(**X**).

A final point is how to obtain an estimate of ATE, as opposed to ATE(**X**). Obtaining this estimate is straightforward because $\mathrm{ATE}(\mathbf{X}) = \mathbf{X}'(\boldsymbol{\beta}_1 - \boldsymbol{\beta}_0)$, which implies that $\mathrm{ATE} = \mathrm{E}[\mathbf{X}]'(\boldsymbol{\beta}_1 - \boldsymbol{\beta}_0)$. One disadvantage is that the calculation of the standard error of this estimate of ATE is not so straightforward. To calculate the standard error of this estimate of ATE, redefine both Y and the **X** variables as deviations from their means. That is, using the fact that $\mathrm{E}[Y_0] = \mathrm{E}[\mathbf{X}]'\boldsymbol{\beta}_0$ and $\mathrm{E}[Y_1] = \mathrm{E}[\mathbf{X}]'\boldsymbol{\beta}_1$, the equation $Y = \mathbf{X}'\boldsymbol{\beta}_0 + U_0 + P(\mathbf{X}'\boldsymbol{\beta}_1 + U_1 - \mathbf{X}'\boldsymbol{\beta}_0 - U_0)$ can be rewritten as

$$\begin{aligned} Y = {} & \mathrm{E}[Y_0] + (\mathbf{X} - \mathrm{E}[\mathbf{X}])'\boldsymbol{\beta}_0 + U_0 + P \times \{[\mathrm{E}[Y_1] + (\mathbf{X} - \mathrm{E}[\mathbf{X}])'\boldsymbol{\beta}_1 + U_1] \\ & - [\mathrm{E}[Y_0] + (\mathbf{X} - \mathrm{E}[\mathbf{X}])'\boldsymbol{\beta}_0 + U_0]\} \\ = {} & \mathrm{E}[Y_0] + (\mathbf{X} - \mathrm{E}[\mathbf{X}])'\boldsymbol{\beta}_0 + P \times \mathrm{ATE} + P(\mathbf{X} - \mathrm{E}[\mathbf{X}])'(\boldsymbol{\beta}_1 - \boldsymbol{\beta}_0) + \{U_0 + P(U_1 - U_0)\} \\ = {} & \mathbf{X}'\boldsymbol{\beta}_0 + P \times \mathrm{ATE} + P(\mathbf{X} - \mathrm{E}[\mathbf{X}])'(\boldsymbol{\beta}_1 - \boldsymbol{\beta}_0) + \{U_0 + P(U_1 - U_0)\}. \end{aligned} \quad (15.7)$$

Equation (15.7) implies that a regression of Y on $\mathbf{X}$ (which includes a constant), P, and $P(\mathbf{X} - \mathrm{E}[\mathbf{X}])$ will yield an estimate of ATE, namely, the coefficient on P. It also yields an estimate of $(\boldsymbol{\beta}_1 - \boldsymbol{\beta}_0)$, which is the coefficient corresponding to $P(\mathbf{X} - \mathrm{E}[\mathbf{X}])$ and can be used to estimate ATE($\mathbf{X}$) for any $\mathbf{X}$. Finally, note that the error term is identical to the one in equation (15.3), so all of the estimation issues discussed above apply to this regression as well.

Assumptions needed to estimate ATT and ATT(X) by IV methods

Using slightly different assumptions, the impact of the program (treatment) on those who participated in the program (ATT) can also be estimated. Recalling that $Y_1 = \mathbf{X}'\boldsymbol{\beta}_1 + U_1$ and $Y_0 = \mathbf{X}'\boldsymbol{\beta}_0 + U_0$, and the assumptions that $\mathrm{E}[U_1] = \mathrm{E}[U_0] = 0$ and $\mathrm{E}[U_1 | \mathbf{X}] = \mathrm{E}[U_0 | \mathbf{X}] = 0$, ATT and ATT($\mathbf{X}$) can be expressed as follows:

$$\begin{aligned}
\mathrm{ATT} \equiv \mathrm{E}[Y_1 - Y_0 | P = 1] &= \mathrm{E}[\mathbf{X}'\boldsymbol{\beta}_1 + U_1 - \mathbf{X}'\boldsymbol{\beta}_0 - U_0 | P = 1] \\
&= \mathrm{E}[\mathbf{X} \mid P = 1]'(\boldsymbol{\beta}_1 - \boldsymbol{\beta}_0) + \mathrm{E}[U_1 - U_0 | P = 1], \text{ and} \\
\mathrm{ATT}(\mathbf{X}) \equiv \mathrm{E}[Y_1 - Y_0 | \mathbf{X}, P = 1] &= \mathrm{E}[\mathbf{X}'\boldsymbol{\beta}_1 + U_1 - \mathbf{X}'\boldsymbol{\beta}_0 - U_0 | \mathbf{X}, P = 1] \\
&= \mathbf{X}'(\boldsymbol{\beta}_1 - \boldsymbol{\beta}_0) + \mathrm{E}[U_1 - U_0 | \mathbf{X}, P = 1].
\end{aligned} \tag{15.8}$$

Consider the use of regression methods to estimate ATT($\mathbf{X}$).[7] These expressions for Y_1 and Y_0, and rearranging equation (15.8) as $\mathbf{X}'(\boldsymbol{\beta}_1 - \boldsymbol{\beta}_0) = \mathrm{ATT}(\mathbf{X}) - \mathrm{E}[U_1 - U_0 | \mathbf{X}, P = 1]$, allow the observed Y to be written as

$$\begin{aligned}
Y &= Y_0 + P(Y_1 - Y_0) \\
&= \mathbf{X}'\boldsymbol{\beta}_0 + U_0 + P(\mathbf{X}'\boldsymbol{\beta}_1 + U_1 - \mathbf{X}'\boldsymbol{\beta}_0 - U_0) \\
&= \mathbf{X}'\boldsymbol{\beta}_0 + P\mathbf{X}'(\boldsymbol{\beta}_1 - \boldsymbol{\beta}_0) + \{U_0 + P(U_1 - U_0)\} \\
&= \mathbf{X}'\boldsymbol{\beta}_0 + P \times \{\mathrm{ATT}(\mathbf{X}) - \mathrm{E}[U_1 - U_0 | \mathbf{X}, P = 1]\} + \{U_0 + P(U_1 - U_0)\} \\
&= \mathbf{X}'\boldsymbol{\beta}_0 + P \times \mathrm{ATT}(\mathbf{X}) + \{U_0 + P \times [(U_1 - U_0) - \mathrm{E}[U_1 - U_0 | \mathbf{X}, P = 1]]\}.
\end{aligned}$$

The last line suggests that, to estimate ATT($\mathbf{X}$), Y can be regressed on $\mathbf{X}$ (which includes a constant term) and on interaction terms between P and functions of $\mathbf{X}$; the remaining terms in the { } brackets are the error term in this regression.[8] P could well be correlated with that error term, so $\mathbf{Z}$ variables are needed as instruments for P. Assume that the $\mathbf{Z}$ variables satisfy the standard assumption that $\mathrm{E}[U_0 | \mathbf{X}, \mathbf{Z}] = \mathrm{E}[U_1 | \mathbf{X}, \mathbf{Z}] = 0$; as with ATE($\mathbf{X}$), that alone does not ensure consistent estimates of ATT($\mathbf{X}$). The regression approach suggested above will produce consistent estimates of ATT($\mathbf{X}$) only if that error term is uncorrelated with $\mathbf{Z}$ after conditioning on $\mathbf{X}$:

$$\mathrm{E}[\{U_0 + P(U_1 - U_0) - P \times \mathrm{E}[U_1 - U_0 | \mathbf{X}, P = 1]\} | \mathbf{X}, \mathbf{Z}] = 0. \tag{15.9}$$

For the **Z** variables to be valid instruments, they must have predictive power for P *and* equation (15.9) must equal zero. In fact, equation (15.9) equals zero if two assumptions hold. The first is that $\mathrm{E}[U_0| \mathbf{X}, \mathbf{Z}] = 0$, which has already been assumed and is standard. The second is that $\mathrm{E}[\{P(U_1 - U_0) - P \times \mathrm{E}[U_1 - U_0| \mathbf{X}, P = 1]\}| \mathbf{X}, \mathbf{Z}] = 0$. Clearly, if $P = 0$, this expression equals zero. So the real issue is the case in which $P = 1$. Thus, the requirement becomes

$$\begin{aligned}&\mathrm{E}[\{(U_1 - U_0) - \mathrm{E}[U_1 - U_0| \mathbf{X}, P = 1]\}| \mathbf{X}, \mathbf{Z}, P = 1]\\&= \mathrm{E}[U_1 - U_0| \mathbf{X}, \mathbf{Z}, P = 1] - \mathrm{E}[U_1 - U_0| \mathbf{X}, P = 1] = 0.\end{aligned}$$

Again, the rather unrealistic assumption that $U_1 = U_0$ ensures that this assumption holds. More plausibly, one can invoke the general assumption that $\mathrm{E}[U_1 - U_0| \mathbf{X}, \mathbf{Z}, P = 1] = \mathrm{E}[U_1 - U_0| \mathbf{X}, P = 1]$. The requirement is that, for program participants, **Z** can have no predictive power for the unobserved gain from the program after conditioning on **X**. The discussion in the subsection titled "Assumptions needed to estimate ATE and ATE(**X**) by IV methods" of the plausibility of this assumption applies here as well, although in this case the discussion pertains only to program participants, whereas in that subsection it pertains to both participants and nonparticipants.

Finally, consider the use of regression methods to estimate ATT without conditioning on **X**. As in the case of ATE, one option is to obtain an estimate of ATT by averaging ATT(**X**) over all observations for which $P = 1$, using sampling weights if the survey data are not self-weighted. The other option, similar to the method suggested in the subsection titled "Assumptions needed to estimate ATE and ATE(**X**) by IV methods" to estimate ATE using a regression, is to express observed Y in terms of a regression equation, recalling that ATT $= \mathrm{E}[\mathbf{X}| P = 1]'(\boldsymbol{\beta}_1 - \boldsymbol{\beta}_0) + \mathrm{E}[U_1 - U_0| P = 1]$:

$$\begin{aligned}Y &= Y_0 + P(Y_1 - Y_0)\\&= \mathbf{X}'\boldsymbol{\beta}_0 + P\mathbf{X}'(\boldsymbol{\beta}_1 - \boldsymbol{\beta}_0) + \{U_0 + P(U_1 - U_0)\}\\&= \mathbf{X}'\boldsymbol{\beta}_0 + U_0 + P \times \{\mathrm{ATT} - \mathrm{E}[\mathbf{X}| P = 1]'(\boldsymbol{\beta}_1 - \boldsymbol{\beta}_0) - \mathrm{E}[U_1 - U_0| P = 1]\\&\quad + \mathbf{X}'(\boldsymbol{\beta}_1 - \boldsymbol{\beta}_0) + (U_1 - U_0)\}\\&= \mathbf{X}'\boldsymbol{\beta}_0 + P \times \mathrm{ATT} + P(\mathbf{X} - \mathrm{E}[\mathbf{X}| P = 1])'(\boldsymbol{\beta}_1 - \boldsymbol{\beta}_0) + \{U_0 + P(U_1 - U_0)\\&\quad - P \times \mathrm{E}[U_1 - U_0| P = 1]\}.\end{aligned}$$

This suggests that an IV regression of observed Y on **X**, P, and P interacted with $\mathbf{X} - \mathrm{E}[\mathbf{X}| P = 1]$ (using the **Z** variables as instruments for P and the **Z** variables interacted with $\mathbf{X} - \mathrm{E}[\mathbf{X}| P = 1]$ as instruments for P interacted with $\mathbf{X} - \mathrm{E}[\mathbf{X}| P = 1]$) will yield an estimate of ATT, which is the coefficient on P. Of course, this estimate will be consistent only if, conditional on **X**, the error term in the regression equations is uncorrelated with **Z**, which will be the case if $\mathrm{E}[\{U_0 + P(U_1 - U_0) - P\mathrm{E}[U_1 - U_0| P = 1]\}| \mathbf{X}, \mathbf{Z}] = 0$. The initial U_0 term is not a problem because $\mathrm{E}[U_0| \mathbf{X}, \mathbf{Z}]$ is assumed to be 0. There is also no problem with the rest of the error term if $P = 0$ because it is also zero. When $P = 1$, the rest of the error term is $(U_1 - U_0) - \mathrm{E}[U_1 - U_0| P = 1]$, and this is required to be uncorrelated with **Z** conditional on **X**: E[{($U_1 - U_0$) – E[$U_1 - U_0$| P = 1]}| **X**, **Z**, P = 1] = E[{($U_1 - U_0$) – E[$U_1 - U_0$| P = 1]}| **X**, P = 1]. By the law of iterated expectations, this is E[$U_1 - U_0$| **X**, **Z**, P = 1] – E[$U_1 - U_0$| P = 1] = E[$U_1 - U_0$| **X**, P = 1] – E[$U_1 - U_0$| P = 1], which is further simplified to E[$U_1 - U_0$| **X**, **Z**, P = 1] = E[$U_1 - U_0$| **X**, P = 1]. Thus the intuition for the condition that the error term not be correlated with **Z** conditional on **X** is that, conditional on **X**, **Z** has no predictive power for $U_1 - U_0$ (the unobserved gain from program participation) for program participants.

Using IV methods to estimate local average treatment effects

Imbens and Angrist (1994) introduced another kind of treatment effect that differs from both ATE and ATT, called local average treatment effect (LATE). LATE's advantage is that the assumptions required are less restrictive than those used in IV estimation of ATE and ATT. However, LATE's disadvantage is that it is the average treatment effect for a particular subgroup within the general population, those that the instrumental variable induces to participate in the program. This will become clearer later in the discussion.

To begin, let Z be an instrumental variable that has predictive power for the decision to participate (P). Assume that Z is a single variable, as opposed to a set of variables. Assume also that Z takes only two values, 0 and 1.

Next, some new notation is needed. Define P_0 and P_1 as

$$P_0 = \text{value of } P \text{ if } Z = 0,$$

$$P_1 = \text{value of } P \text{ if } Z = 1.$$

Recall that everyone in the population has a Y_0 and a Y_1. Similarly, everyone also has a P_0 and a P_1. These definitions imply that the observed value of P can be expressed as

$$P = (1 - Z)P_0 + ZP_1 = P_0 + Z(P_1 - P_0).$$

Thus P equals P_0 if $Z = 0$ and equals P_1 if $Z = 1$. Finally, plugging this expression for P into $Y = Y_0 + P(Y_1 - Y_0)$ gives

$$Y = Y_0 + P_0(Y_1 - Y_0) + Z(P_1 - P_0)(Y_1 - Y_0).$$

A key assumption of estimation of LATE is that the instrument Z is independent of Y_0, Y_1, P_0, and P_1:[9]

$$(Y_0, Y_1, P_0, P_1) \perp\!\!\!\perp Z.$$

At first it may seem strange to assert this for P_0 and P_1, since IV estimation requires that Z has an effect on (has predictive power for) P. However, this effect of Z on P does not necessarily mean that Z cannot be independent of P_0 and P_1. Quite simply, by definition changing Z from 0 to 1 changes P from P_0 to P_1, but this does not mean that Z is correlated with either P_0 or P_1. For example, in the context of a randomized trial, random assignment of the offer of the program can be used as Z, but because this is random it is not correlated with P_0 or P_1, which represent what a person would decide without the offer and with the offer, respectively, even though Z is correlated with P.

The above assumption for Z also implies that Z has no relationship with either Y_0 or Y_1. Although this is often plausible, it may not be true, even if Z is randomly generated as part of an RCT. An example is the Colombia private school vouchers paper (Angrist et al. 2002), which is further discussed later in this chapter. Although vouchers were randomly assigned, the program stipulated that a student repeating a grade was no longer eligible to receive a voucher. Thus it is possible that the private schools were more likely to promote those students who randomly received vouchers and used them to attend those schools (relative to students in those schools who did not receive vouchers), because if a student with a voucher were not promoted the voucher would end and the school may then lose a tuition-paying student. That is, if Y_1 is students' current grade in school among students in private schools (students for whom $P = 1$), that variable could be higher for students who participated in the program (attended a private school) because they were randomly provided a voucher ($Z = 1$) relative to students who participated in the program (attended a private school) even though they were not provided a voucher ($Z = 0$); quite simply, private schools have an incentive to give higher grades to students with vouchers to keep these students enrolled in their schools.

To see how LATE estimation works, consider four possible types (T) of people:

1. Never takers (denoted by $T = n$) $P_0 = P_1 = 0$
2. Compliers (denoted by $T = c$) $P_0 = 0, P_1 = 1$
3. Defiers (denoted by $T = d$) $P_0 = 1, P_1 = 0$
4. Always takers (denoted by $T = a$) $P_0 = P_1 = 1$

Defiers are perhaps irrational. Assuming that there are no defiers, table 15.2 shows how the observed values of P and Z correspond to the three other types of people. Note that in the data, some always takers (those with $P = 1$ and $Z = 0$) are clearly identified, while others (those with $P = 1$ and $Z = 1$) cannot be identified because they are mixed together with some compliers. A similar point holds for never takers. In contrast, the data do not allow any of the compliers to be identified with certainty; the best an analyst can do is identify the two groups in which there are some compliers, namely, the group for which $P = 1$ and $Z = 1$ and the group for which $P = 0$ and $Z = 0$.

The assumption that there are no defiers, which is called the *monotonicity assumption*, is key for obtaining IV estimates of treatment effects.

Next, consider what type of treatment effect can be estimated in this situation, which can be done in two steps. First, from the observed data (and the assumptions made) proportions

TABLE 15.2 Correspondence of *P* and *Z* to never takers, compliers, and always takers

	Z = 0	Z = 1
P = 0	Never taker or complier	Never taker
P = 1	Always taker	Always taker or complier

Source: Original table for this publication.

of the population that are compliers, always takers, and never takers can be estimated. To start, consider the people for whom $Z = 0$. For these people, the proportion who are always takers is observed. Because Z is assumed to be independent of P_0 and P_1, and these two variables determine who is an always taker, Z is uncorrelated with the proportion of the population who are always takers (which can be denoted by P_a), so we have

$$P_a = \text{Prob}[P = 1 | Z = 0].$$

By similar reasoning the proportion of never takers can be obtained:

$$P_n = \text{Prob}[P = 0 | Z = 1].$$

Finally, those who remain must be the compliers:

$$P_c = 1 - P_a - P_n.$$

The second step uses the distribution of Y for different values of P and Z to obtain the average treatment effect for compliers. This is done as follows:

1. Estimate $f(Y | P = 0, T = n)$ for the subpopulation for which $Z = 1$ and $P = 0$. This is the distribution of Y_0 for never takers.
2. Consider the distribution of Y_0 for people with $Z = 0$ and $P = 0$. This distribution of Y_0 is a mixture that combines never takers with compliers. Statistically, it is a weighted average of the two distributions, with weights being the proportions of these types in the total population (P_n and P_c). This information can be used to back out the distribution of Y_0 for compliers, which can be expressed as

$$f(Y | P = 0, T = c) = f(Y_0 | P = 0, T = c).$$

3. Repeating this for always takers, then bringing in compliers, yields

$$f(Y \mid P = 1, T = c) = f(Y_1 \mid P = 1, T = c).$$

Finally, the means of these two (conditional) distributions for the compliers can be calculated to obtain

$$\begin{aligned} \text{LATE} &= \text{E}[Y_1 - Y_0 \mid P_0 = 0, P_1 = 1] \\ &= \text{E}[Y_1 - Y_0 \mid T = c]. \end{aligned}$$

This process may appear rather complicated. Fortunately, there is a much easier way to estimate LATE, as shown by Imbens and Angrist (1994), which is simply to use Z as an instrumental variable for P, that is,[10]

$$\text{LATE} = \frac{\text{E}[Y|Z=1] - \text{E}[Y|Z=0]}{\text{E}[P|Z=1] - \text{E}[P|Z=0]} = \frac{\text{E}[Y \times (Z - \text{E}[Z])]}{\text{E}[P \times (Z - \text{E}[Z])]}.$$

Note that this is the same as equation (15.6) for ATE($\mathbf{X}$), except that here there is no conditioning on $\mathbf{X}$, and Z can take only two values, 0 or 1.

In the case of an RCT with imperfect compliance of the form in which some individuals assigned to the treatment group choose not to participate in the program (but assuming that none of the individuals assigned to the control group find a way to participate), LATE is equivalent to the ITT divided by the probability of being treated for those assigned to the treatment group. That is, in this case $\text{E}[P| Z = 0] = 0$, so LATE = ATT. Finally, note that if most people are compliers, a bounds approach that uses this estimate of LATE can be used to obtain bounds for an estimate of ATE (see pp. 59–60 of Imbens and Wooldridge 2009).

Example: School vouchers in Colombia

Angrist et al. (2002) study the impacts of a voucher program in Colombia, the Programa de Ampliación de Cobertura de la Educación Secundaria (PACES) program, using both an ITT approach and an IV approach. The Colombian government established the PACES program in late 1991 as part of a wider decentralization effort and as an attempt to expand private provision of public services. The PACES program provided more than 125,000 students with vouchers covering slightly more than half the cost of attending private secondary school. Because the PACES budget was limited, the vouchers were allocated via a lottery.

Angrist et al. (2002) took advantage of this randomly assigned treatment to estimate the effect of the voucher program on educational and social outcomes. However, the simple comparison between outcomes of lottery winners and losers does not generate a consistent estimate of ATE (although it is an estimate of a particular type of ITT) because there was some noncompliance with the assignment of treatment. Only about 90 percent of lottery winners used the voucher or any other type of scholarship, while 24 percent of lottery losers received scholarships from other sources. Angrist et al. (2002) therefore use lottery status (win or lose) as an instrument for scholarship receipt in an IV setup.

Angrist et al.'s (2002) ITT estimates[11] indicate that lottery winners were 10 percent more likely to complete the eighth grade and scored, on average, 0.2 standard deviations higher on standardized tests three years after the initial lottery. The IV regressions generate LATE estimates of the impact of the voucher program on eighth grade completion and test scores that are roughly 50 percent higher than the ITT of winning the lottery. This is not surprising because, in this case, LATE is equal to ITT divided by $E[P \mid Z = 1] - E[P \mid Z = 0]$, and the difference between $E[P \mid Z = 1]$ and $E[P \mid Z = 0]$ was equal to about two-thirds $(0.90 - 0.24)$.

Conclusion

IV methods have two general uses for the evaluation of programs, projects, or policies. First, for an RCT that has been contaminated because some of the individuals or groups randomly assigned to the treatment group choose not to be treated, or because some of the individuals or groups randomly assigned to the control group were somehow able to be treated, IV methods allow LATE to be estimated. Second, and more generally, IV methods provide a way to estimate treatment effects when there are problems of selection bias, that is, when individuals have at least some ability to choose whether to participate in the program. This second point applies not only to RCT evaluations but also to evaluations that are based on nonrandomized (nonexperimental) data.

However, some difficulties arise with using IV methods to estimate program impacts. First, the instrumental variables must satisfy certain assumptions and thus it may be hard to find credible instrumental variables. For RCTs in which there is imperfect compliance, the most obvious instrumental variable for whether a person receives treatment is random assignment, but even here whether the instrument is valid must be carefully considered. Alternatively, if excluding individuals from participating in the program is not possible, researchers can artificially generate instruments by, for example, randomizing monetary vouchers or price discounts to encourage program take-up; this is the encouragement design approach discussed in chapter 6, examples of which are found in Dupas (2014), Karlan and Zinman (2008, 2009), and Thornton (2008).

Plausible instrumental variables can be difficult to find for evaluations based on nonexperimental data. The instrumental variables need to influence program participation decisions but cannot be correlated with the outcome measures after conditioning on the observed variables. Researchers have sometimes used travel distance to a program site or characteristics of a program itself, such as capacity constraints, as instruments for whether people participate. A study by Schultz and Tanzel (1997) analyzes the effect of disability on productivity (as measured by labor supply and wages) using local food prices and health services as instruments for disability days.

Second, in general, estimation of ATE or ATT via instrumental variables requires assumptions that may not hold. However, a different set of assumptions, which may be plausible in at least some contexts, allow LATE, which is the impact of the program on those individuals whose participation is influenced by the instrumental variable, to be estimated. Whether any of the IV assumptions are plausible will, of course, depend on the specific program being evaluated and the proposed instrumental variables.

Notes

1. In recent years economists and statisticians have developed nonparametric IV methods, which require neither assumption (see, among others, Horowitz 2011). However, these methods are rarely used because they are difficult to implement.
2. A fourth possible group would be "defiers," who do not participate if assigned to the treatment group but do participate if assigned to the control group. Such people are likely to be rare and so can be ignored in most settings; see the section titled "Using IV methods to estimate local average treatment effects" for further discussion.
3. In practice, the advantage of an evaluation based on an experimental design is that the random assignment variable (R) is usually a valid instrument (for the purpose of estimating LATE, as explained below, but not necessarily for estimating ATE or ATT). In a nonexperimental setting it is often difficult to find a credible instrumental variable, so finding such a variable is the biggest challenge to using IV methods to estimate program impacts in this setting.
4. This discussion is based on Heckman (1997).
5. Regression methods to estimate the ATE are presented at the end of this subsection.
6. Here is another way to express this assumption. Note that both $\mathrm{E}[U_0| \mathbf{X}, \mathbf{Z}]$ and $\mathrm{E}[U_0| \mathbf{X}]$ are already assumed to be zero, so the issue is with the $P(U_1 - U_0)$ term. P takes only two values, so $\mathrm{E}[P(U_1 - U_0)| \mathbf{X}, \mathbf{Z}] = \mathrm{E}[1 \times (U_1 - U_0)| \mathbf{X}, \mathbf{Z}, P = 1] \times \mathrm{Prob}[P = 1| \mathbf{X}, \mathbf{Z}] + \mathrm{E}[0 \times (U_1 - U_0)| \mathbf{X}, \mathbf{Z}, P = 1] \times \mathrm{Prob}[P = 0| \mathbf{X}, \mathbf{Z}] = \mathrm{E}[(U_1 - U_0)| \mathbf{X}, \mathbf{Z}, P = 1] \times \mathrm{Prob}[P = 1| \mathbf{X}, \mathbf{Z}]$. This implies that the assumption can be expressed as $\mathrm{E}[(U_1 - U_0)| \mathbf{X}, \mathbf{Z}, P = 1] \times \mathrm{Prob}[P = 1| \mathbf{X}, \mathbf{Z}] = 0$. Since $\mathbf{Z}$ has explanatory power for P, it is not possible for $\mathrm{Prob}[P = 1| \mathbf{X}, \mathbf{Z}] = 0$. Thus, this assumption can be expressed as $\mathrm{E}[(U_1 - U_0)| \mathbf{X}, \mathbf{Z}, P = 1]$; in words, conditional on **X**, **Z** does not have predictive power for the unobserved gain of the participants.
7. Regression methods to estimate ATT are presented at the end of this subsection.
8. Notice that when regression methods were used to estimate ATE(**X**), the linear assumptions regarding the impact of **X** on Y_1 and Y_0 implied that $\mathrm{ATE}(\mathbf{X}) = \mathbf{X}'(\boldsymbol{\beta}_1 - \boldsymbol{\beta}_0)$, and thus that $P \times \mathrm{ATE}(\mathbf{X}) = P \times \mathbf{X}'(\boldsymbol{\beta}_1 - \boldsymbol{\beta}_0)$, so that the regression simply included $P \times \mathbf{X}$ to estimate ATE(**X**). In contrast, the expression for ATT(**X**) is not a simple linear function of **X**, so the approach taken here is to allow ATT(**X**) to be a more flexible function of **X**, which implies that $P \times \mathrm{ATT}(\mathbf{X})$ is approximated by interactions of P with a more flexible function of **X**.
9. This assumption is for the simplest case, in which there are no other variables, denoted by **X**, that determine Y_0 and Y_1. In the more general case in which such variables are included, the required assumption becomes $(Y_0, Y_1, P_0, P_1) \perp\!\!\!\perp Z \mid \mathbf{X}$, which in many contexts may be more plausible.
10. That the second ratio is equal to the first can be seen by considering the numerator in the second term. That is, $\mathrm{E}[Y \times (Z - \mathrm{E}[Z]) = \mathrm{E}[YZ] - \mathrm{E}[Y]\mathrm{E}[Z] = \mathrm{E}[Y| Z = 0] \times \mathrm{Prob}[Z = 0] \times 0 + \mathrm{E}[Y| Z = 1] \times \mathrm{Prob}[Z = 1] \times 1 - (\mathrm{E}[Y| Z = 0] \times \mathrm{Prob}[Z = 0] + \mathrm{E}[Y| Z = 1] \times \mathrm{Prob}[Z = 1]) \times \mathrm{E}[Z] = \mathrm{E}[Y| Z = 1] \times \mathrm{E}[Z] - (\mathrm{E}[Y| Z = 0] \times (1 - \mathrm{E}[Z]) + \mathrm{E}[Y| Z = 1] \times \mathrm{E}[Z]) \times \mathrm{E}[Z] = \mathrm{E}[Z]\{(1 - \mathrm{E}[Z]) \times \mathrm{E}[Y| Z = 1] - (1 - \mathrm{E}[Z]) \times \mathrm{E}[Y| Z = 0]\} = (\mathrm{E}[Z] - \mathrm{E}[Z]^2)(\mathrm{E}[Y| Z = 1] - \mathrm{E}[Y| Z = 0])$. Similarly, one can show that the denominator is $(\mathrm{E}[Z] - \mathrm{E}[Z]^2)(\mathrm{E}[P| Z = 1] - \mathrm{E}[P| Z = 0])$; this yields the first ratio.
11. These estimates are ITT estimates if ITT is defined as the impact of offering this particular program (PACES), given that no one in the control group was able to participate in this program. In contrast, they are *not* ITT estimates of the impact of participating in any scholarship program, because 24 percent of those randomly assigned to the control group were able to participate in another scholarship program. See chapter 7 for an explanation of why ITT cannot be estimated when some in the control group are able to participate in the program.

References

Angrist, Joshua, Eric Bettinger, Erik Bloom, Elizabeth King, and Michael Kremer. 2002. "Vouchers for Private Schooling in Colombia: Evidence from a Randomized Natural Experiment." *American Economic Review* 92 (5): 1535–58.

Dupas, Pascaline. 2014. "Short-Run Subsidies and Long-Run Adoption of New Health Products: Evidence from a Field Experiment." *Econometrica* 82 (1): 197–228.

Heckman, James. 1997. "Instrumental Variables: A Study of Implicit Behavioral Assumptions Used in Making Program Evaluations." *Journal of Human Resources* 32 (3): 441–62.

Horowitz, Joel. 2011. "Applied Nonparametric Instrumental Variables Estimation." *Econometrica* 79 (2): 347–94.

Imbens, Guido, and Joshua Angrist. 1994. "Identification and Estimation of Local Average Treatment Effects." *Econometrica* 62 (2): 467–75.

Imbens, Guido, and Jeffrey Wooldridge. 2009. "Recent Developments in the Econometrics of Program Evaluation." *Journal of Economic Literature* 47 (1): 5–87.

Karlan, Dean, and Jonathan Zinman. 2008. "Credit Elasticities in Less-Developed Economies: Implications for Microfinance." *American Economic Review* 89 (3): 1040–68.

Karlan, Dean, and Jonathan Zinman. 2009. "Observing Unobservables: Identifying Information Asymmetries with a Consumer Credit Field Experiment." *Econometrica* 77 (6): 1993–2008.

Schultz, T. Paul, and Aysit Tansel. 1997. "Wage and Labor Supply Effects of Illness in Côte d'Ivoire and Ghana: Instrumental Variable Estimates for Days Disabled." *Journal of Development Economics* 53 (2): 251–86.

Thornton, Rebecca. 2008. "The Demand for, and Impact of, Learning HIV Status." *American Economic Review* 98 (5): 1829–63.

CHAPTER 16

Control Function Methods

Introduction

As noted in earlier chapters, a major concern in evaluating the effects of treatments is that people who participate in a program or are subject to some treatment may differ systematically from nonparticipants in possibly unobserved ways. A class of evaluation estimators designed to explicitly control for selection based on unobservables is *control function methods*, also known as generalized residual methods. These methods were first proposed as a solution to the evaluation problem by Heckman and Robb (1985) and are related to the selection bias correction methods developed by Heckman (1979, 1980). Early applications were to estimate female labor force participation decisions and to model the determinants of occupational choice (Heckman and Honoré 1990; Roy 1951).

Control function estimators explicitly recognize that nonrandom selection into the program may give rise to an endogeneity problem; the problem is that nonrandom selection could cause participation in the program to be correlated with unobserved factors that influence the outcome variable. Control function estimators aim to obtain unbiased parameter estimates by modeling the source of the endogeneity. The main advantage of these methods is that they allow selection into the program to be based on time-varying unobservable variables. Their main disadvantage is that they usually require exclusion restrictions (similar to those for instrumental variables [IV] estimation), functional form assumptions, or both.

This chapter is organized as follows. The next section introduces the basic idea behind the control function methodology; it is followed by a section that presents methods for estimating control functions and shows how they can be applied to estimate program effects. Several ways to obtain standard errors for estimates based on the control function approach are then explained. Control function methods are then compared with matching methods. Because the discussion through these sections focuses on estimation of average treatment effects on the treated (ATT), the subsequent section explains how control function methods can be used to estimate average treatment effects (ATE), which apply to the population as a whole. The penultimate section provides an example of the application of this method, and the final section concludes.

The basic idea of the control function approach

To see how the control function method works, the starting point is the same model for Y that was used in chapters 11, 12, and 15, which assumes that $Y_0 = \mathbf{X}'\boldsymbol{\beta}_0 + U_0$ and $Y_1 = \mathbf{X}'\boldsymbol{\beta}_1 + U_1$ are relationships that show the causal impact of $\mathbf{X}$, U_0, and U_1 on Y_0 and Y_1. As in those chapters, the observed value of the outcome variable of interest is

$$\begin{aligned} Y &= Y_0 + P \times (Y_1 - Y_0) \\ &= \mathbf{X}'\boldsymbol{\beta}_0 + U_0 + P \times \{\mathbf{X}'(\boldsymbol{\beta}_1 - \boldsymbol{\beta}_0) + (U_1 - U_0)\}. \end{aligned} \tag{16.1}$$

This section and the following three sections focus on estimation of ATT. In particular, they focus on estimating ATT conditional on the values of the observed variables in the vector $\mathbf{X}$—the ATT($\mathbf{X}$) function—and they also show how this function can be used to estimate ATT without conditioning on $\mathbf{X}$ (by averaging over all program participants). An explanation is also provided of how to adapt the method to estimate both the ATE($\mathbf{X}$) function and ATE without conditioning on $\mathbf{X}$.

To begin, equation (16.1) for the observed outcomes of Y can be written in terms of the ATT($\mathbf{X}$) function by adding and subtracting the term $P \times \mathrm{E}[U_1 - U_0| \mathbf{X}, P = 1]$:

$$\begin{aligned} Y &= \mathbf{X}'\boldsymbol{\beta}_0 + U_0 + P \times \{\mathbf{X}'(\boldsymbol{\beta}_1 - \boldsymbol{\beta}_0) + \mathrm{E}[U_1 - U_0| \mathbf{X}, P = 1] - \mathrm{E}[U_1 - U_0| \mathbf{X}, P = 1] + (U_1 - U_0)\} \\ &= \mathbf{X}'\boldsymbol{\beta}_0 + P \times \mathrm{ATT}(\mathbf{X}) + \varepsilon, \end{aligned}$$

where

$$\mathrm{ATT}(\mathbf{X}) = \mathrm{E}[Y_1 - Y_0| \mathbf{X}, P = 1] = \mathbf{X}'\boldsymbol{\beta}_1 - \mathbf{X}'\boldsymbol{\beta}_0 + \mathrm{E}[U_1 - U_0| \mathbf{X}, P = 1]$$

is the parameter (function) of interest and the error term ε is

$$\varepsilon = U_0 + P \times (U_1 - U_0 - \mathrm{E}[U_1 - U_0| \mathbf{X}, P = 1]).$$

Any method that uses a standard ordinary least squares (OLS) regression to estimate $Y = \mathbf{X}'\boldsymbol{\beta}_0 + P \times \mathrm{ATT}(\mathbf{X}) + \varepsilon$ must consider whether ε is correlated with P and $\mathbf{X}$. In particular, OLS estimates will be biased if this error term is correlated with the regressors, that is, if $\mathrm{E}[\varepsilon| \mathbf{X}, P] \neq 0$.

If $P = 0$, then $\varepsilon = U_0$ and $\mathrm{E}[\varepsilon| \mathbf{X}, P = 0] = \mathrm{E}[U_0| \mathbf{X}, P = 0]$. Similarly, if $P = 1$, application of the law of iterated expectations demonstrates that $\mathrm{E}[\varepsilon| \mathbf{X}, P = 1] = \mathrm{E}[U_0| \mathbf{X}, P = 1]$. Thus the general issue that must be considered is whether $\mathrm{E}[U_0| \mathbf{X}, P] \neq 0$. Because the decision to participate may be influenced by the potential outcomes (Y_0 and Y_1), it is plausible that $\mathrm{E}[U_0| \mathbf{X}, P] \neq 0$. For example, U_0 is likely to be correlated with P because people select into the program in part on the basis of their anticipated values of Y_0, which are determined in part by U_0. (Note, however, that it is still assumed that U_0 is uncorrelated with $\mathbf{X}$.)

Heckman (1979) shows that this endogeneity problem can be interpreted as a problem of omitted variable bias. To see this, note that the expression

$$\mathrm{E}[U_0 | \mathbf{X}, P] = P \times \mathrm{E}[U_0 | \mathbf{X}, P = 1] + (1 - P) \times \mathrm{E}[U_0 | \mathbf{X}, P = 0]$$

implies that equation (16.1) for Y can be rewritten as

$$\begin{aligned} Y &= \mathbf{X}'\boldsymbol{\beta}_0 + P \times \mathrm{ATT}(\mathbf{X}) + \mathrm{E}[U_0 | \mathbf{X}, P = 0] + P \times (\mathrm{E}[U_0 | \mathbf{X}, P = 1] - \mathrm{E}[U_0 | \mathbf{X}, P = 0]) \\ &\quad - \mathrm{E}[U_0 | \mathbf{X}, P] + \varepsilon \\ &= \mathbf{X}'\boldsymbol{\beta}_0 + P \times \mathrm{ATT}(\mathbf{X}) + K_0(\mathbf{X}) + P \times [K_1(\mathbf{X}) - K_0(\mathbf{X})] + \omega, \end{aligned} \tag{16.2}$$

where

$$\begin{aligned} K_0(\mathbf{X}) &= \mathrm{E}[U_0 | \mathbf{X}, P = 0], \\ K_1(\mathbf{X}) &= \mathrm{E}[U_0 | \mathbf{X}, P = 1], \text{ and} \\ \omega &= U_0 - \mathrm{E}[U_0 | \mathbf{X}, P] + P \times \{U_1 - U_0 - \mathrm{E}[U_1 - U_0 | \mathbf{X}, P = 1]\}. \end{aligned}$$

When the $K_1(\mathbf{X})$ and $K_0(\mathbf{X})$ are included in the regression, then, by construction, the error term ω will satisfy the orthogonality condition $\mathrm{E}[\omega | \mathbf{X}, P] = 0$.

The functions $K_1(\mathbf{X})$ and $K_0(\mathbf{X})$ are called *control functions*. When these functions are known, at least up to some finite number of parameters, they can be included in the regression model to control for endogeneity, and then regression methods can be applied to obtain consistent estimates of ATT(**X**), the average program impacts for the treated conditional on **X**. Alternative methods for estimating control functions are described in the next section.

A final point is that after estimating ATT(**X**), it is a straightforward process to obtain an estimator for the overall ATT parameter, which is defined as

$$\mathrm{ATT} \equiv \int_{-\infty}^{\infty} \mathrm{ATT}(\mathbf{X}) f(\mathbf{X} | P = 1) d\mathbf{X}.$$

In practice, this is calculated as the sample average of ATT(**X**) over all the treated observations:

$$\mathrm{ATT} = \frac{1}{n_1} \sum_{i=1}^{n_1} \mathrm{ATT}(\mathbf{X}_i),$$

where n_1 is the number of treated observations.

Methods for estimating control functions

If no restrictions are placed on ATT(**X**), K_1(**X**), or K_0(**X**), then ATT(**X**) cannot be separately identified from the control functions, because all are functions of **X**. Thus some identifying restrictions are needed. Different types of control function estimators in the literature impose different kinds of restrictions.

The restrictions can be either functional form restrictions, or exclusion restrictions, or both. In this context, exclusion restrictions are requirements that one or more variables that determine the participation process (that is, the choice of P) be excluded from the outcome equations for Y_0 and Y_1. For example, the distance between an individual's residence and a program site may be a determinant of program participation, but the outcomes Y_0 and Y_1 may not directly depend on this distance. The excluded variables generate variation in the control functions (K_1(**X**) and K_0(**X**)) that is independent of ATT(**X**).

Usually, a combination of functional form and exclusion restrictions is imposed to be able to separate the estimated treatment effect from the control function. In principle, it is possible to separately identify the treatment effect on the basis of functional form assumptions alone, with no exclusion restrictions. However, this approach to identification relies heavily on potentially arbitrary modeling assumptions to be able to distinguish the control functions from the treatment effects. On the other hand, identification based on exclusion restrictions alone, without imposing functional form assumptions on the control function, does not allow the treatment effect to be estimated separately from the constant term in the control function. This can be seen in equation (16.2) for the observed value of Y; both ATT(**X**) and K_1(**X**) − K_0(**X**) are interacted with P, and even if one variable in K_1(**X**) − K_0(**X**) is not in ATT(**X**), nonparametric approximations of both will each have a constant term, and without functional form assumptions it will not be possible to distinguish between the constant term in ATT(**X**) and the constant term in [K_1(**X**) − K_0(**X**)].[1] Thus a combination of both restrictions is usually the best approach.

Ideally, functional form restrictions are not arbitrary but are based on some type of reasoning. For example, Heckman and Robb (1986) derive particular functional form restrictions on K_1(**X**) and K_0(**X**) by constructing an economic model of the participation process. Participation (P) is assumed to depend on a set of characteristics **Z** through an index, $h(\mathbf{Z}'\gamma)$, and on some unobservable characteristics V, as follows:

$$
\begin{aligned}
P &= 1 \text{ if } h(\mathbf{Z}'\gamma) + V > 0, \\
&= 0 \text{ if } h(\mathbf{Z}'\gamma) + V \leq 0,
\end{aligned}
$$

where $h(\mathbf{Z}'\gamma) + V$ represents the net utility from participating in the program (that is, the utility of participating in the program minus the utility from not participating in the program), which may depend on both observed and unobserved variables.

This model implies that the function $K_1(\mathbf{X}) = \mathrm{E}[U_0| \mathbf{X}, P = 1]$ can be written as

$$\begin{aligned}\mathrm{E}[U_0| \mathbf{X}, P = 1] &= \mathrm{E}[U_0| \mathbf{X}, h(\mathbf{Z}'\gamma) + V > 0] \\ &= \frac{\int_{-h(\mathbf{Z}'\gamma)}^{\infty}\int_{-\infty}^{\infty} U_0 f(U_0, V \mid \mathbf{X})\, dU_0\, dV}{\int_{-h(\mathbf{Z}'\gamma)}^{\infty}\int_{-\infty}^{\infty} f(U_0, V \mid \mathbf{X})\, dU_0\, dV},\end{aligned} \tag{16.3}$$

where $f(U_0, V \mid \mathbf{X})$ is the conditional joint density of the unobservables U_0 and V. Note also that the definition of the $h(\mathbf{Z}'\gamma)$ function implies that the conditional probability of participation, $\mathrm{Prob}[P = 1| \mathbf{Z}]$, can be written as a function of the index $\mathbf{Z}'\gamma$:

$$\begin{aligned}\mathrm{Prob}[P = 1| \mathbf{Z}] &= \mathrm{Prob}[V > -h(\mathbf{Z}'\gamma)] \\ &= 1 - F_V(-h(\mathbf{Z}'\gamma)),\end{aligned}$$

where $F_V(\cdot)$is the marginal cumulative distribution function of V.

Let $F(U_0, V \mid \mathbf{X})$ be the cumulative distribution function for the joint density $f(U_0, V| \mathbf{X})$. Assume that it is continuous with full support on R^2 (the two-dimensional Euclidean space) and assume also that $F_V(\cdot)$ is invertible. Then the index $\mathbf{Z}'\gamma$ can be written as a function of the conditional probability of participation:

$$h(\mathbf{Z}'\gamma) = -F_V^{-1}(1 - \mathrm{Prob}[P = 1| \mathbf{Z}]).$$

Heckman and Robb (1986) note that the additional assumption that the joint distribution of the unobservables, U_0 and V, does not depend on $\mathbf{X}$, which can be expressed as

$$f(U_0, V \mid \mathbf{X}) = f(U_0, V),$$

implies that $\mathrm{E}[U_0| \mathbf{X}, P = 1]$ can be written solely as a function of the probability of participating in the program, $\mathrm{Prob}[P = 1| \mathbf{Z}]$:

$$\mathrm{E}[U_0| \mathbf{X}, P = 1] = \mathrm{E}[U_0| P = 1, \mathrm{Pr}(\mathbf{Z})] = K_1(\mathrm{Pr}(\mathbf{Z})),$$

$$\mathrm{E}[U_0| \mathbf{X}, P = 0] = \mathrm{E}[U_0| P = 0, \mathrm{Pr}(\mathbf{Z})] = K_0(\mathrm{Pr}(\mathbf{Z})),$$

where $\mathrm{Pr}(\mathbf{Z}) = \mathrm{Prob}[P = 1| \mathbf{Z}]$. To see why this is the case, substitute $f(U_0, V)$ for $f(U_0, V \mid \mathbf{X})$ in equation (16.3) for the conditional mean $\mathrm{E}[U_0| \mathbf{X}, P = 1]$; it is clear that this expression is a function only of Pr(**Z**) because the values of both integrals are functions of $h(\mathbf{Z}'\gamma)$ alone and $h(\mathbf{Z}'\gamma) = -F_V^{-1}(1 - \text{Prob}[P = 1|\ \mathbf{Z}]) = -F_V^{-1}(1 - \Pr(\mathbf{Z}))$. This result—that a linear index of **Z** is sufficient to represent the bias control function, that is, that $K_0(\Pr(\mathbf{Z})) = h_0(\mathbf{Z}'\gamma)$ and $K_1(\Pr(\mathbf{Z})) = h_1(\mathbf{Z}'\gamma)$—is called an *index sufficiency assumption*.[2]

Most formulations of the control function method (for example, Heckman 1979) assume that U_0 and V are jointly normally distributed, which implies a parametric form for $K_1(\Pr(\mathbf{Z}))$ and $K_0(\Pr(\mathbf{Z}))$.[3] If the density of U_0 and V is assumed to be jointly normal, then the control functions take the form

$$\text{E}[U_0 \mid \mathbf{X}, P = 1] = K_1\left(\Pr\left(\mathbf{Z}\right)\right) = \frac{\sigma_{U_0,V}}{\sigma_V^2} \times \frac{\phi\left(-h\left(\mathbf{Z}'\gamma\right)\right)}{1 - \Phi\left(-h\left(\mathbf{Z}'\gamma\right)\right)},$$

$$\text{E}[U_0 \mid \mathbf{X}, P = 0] = K_0\left(\Pr\left(\mathbf{Z}\right)\right) = \frac{\sigma_{U_0,V}}{\sigma_V^2} \times \frac{-\phi\left(-h\left(\mathbf{Z}'\gamma\right)\right)}{\Phi\left(-h\left(\mathbf{Z}'\gamma\right)\right)},$$

where $\sigma_{U_0,V}$ is the covariance of U_0 and V, and σ_V^2 is the variance of V.

The control function bias correction method can be implemented in two stages:

1. Estimate a model of program participation to obtain an estimate of $h(\mathbf{Z}'\gamma)$, which can be denoted as $h(\mathbf{Z}'\gamma)$.

2. Construct $\lambda_1(\mathbf{Z}'\hat{\gamma}) = \dfrac{\phi(-h(\mathbf{Z}'\hat{\gamma}))}{1 - \Phi(-h(\mathbf{Z}'\hat{\gamma}))}$ and $\lambda_0(\mathbf{Z}'\hat{\gamma}) = \dfrac{-\phi(-h(\mathbf{Z}'\hat{\gamma}))}{\Phi(-h(\mathbf{Z}'\hat{\gamma}))}$

   and include them in the outcome equation to control for bias when estimating that equation:

$$Y = \mathbf{X}'\beta_0 + P \times \text{ATT}(\mathbf{X}) + \rho_0(1 - P)\lambda_0(\mathbf{Z}'\hat{\gamma}) + \rho_1 P\lambda_1(\mathbf{Z}'\hat{\gamma}) + \omega, \qquad (16.4)$$

where ρ_0 and ρ_1 are coefficients to be estimated and, as in the section titled "The basic idea of the control function approach," $\omega = U_0 - \text{E}[U_0|\ \mathbf{X}, P] + P \times \{U_1 - U_0 - \text{E}[U_1 - U_0|\ \mathbf{X}, P = 1]\}$. Note that both ρ_0 and ρ_1 equal $\sigma_{U_0,V} / \sigma_V^2$; that is, the joint normality assumption implies that $\rho_0 = \rho_1$. If the estimated values of ρ_0 and ρ_1 are significantly different from each other, then that assumption—or some other underlying assumption—is incorrect, so another, perhaps more general, estimation approach is needed.

This outcome equation (equation (16.4)) can be estimated by regressing Y on the following regressors: **X**, P, interaction terms between P and **X**, $(1 - P)\lambda_0(\mathbf{Z}'\hat{\gamma})$, and $P\lambda_1(\mathbf{Z}'\hat{\gamma})$. The coefficient on P, and more generally the coefficients on interaction terms between P and **X**, provide estimates of ATT(**X**) for specific values of the **X** variables (for example, by gender, race, age group, education group). In the case where ATT(**X**) is constrained to be the same for all values of **X**, the regression model would contain both **X** and P as regressors, but not interactions of P with the **X** variables.

Variations of control function methods have been developed that do not assume joint normality (see, for example, Andrews and Schafgans 1998; Heckman 1990; Heckman and Navarro 2004). For example, one approach proposed in Heckman (1990) approximates the control functions by a power series in Pr(**Z**). In the context of the treatment effects model, though, using a power series approximation leads to an identification problem, because it is not generally possible to separately identify the constant term of the power series approximation from the treatment effect. This occurs because the treatment effect $P \times$ ATT(**X**) would include P (because ATT(**X**) would include a constant term), but so would the power series (which would be $P \times (\text{constant} + \alpha_1(\mathbf{Z}'\hat{\gamma}) + \alpha_2(\mathbf{Z}'\hat{\gamma})^2 + \ldots)$).

Heckman (1990) shows that if there are some individuals for whom Pr(**Z**) = 1, then these individuals can be used to secure identification of the K_1(Pr(**Z**)) function, and thus identification of the ATT(**X**) function, using the power series approach described in the previous paragraph. Such individuals have **Z** values that imply that they would always select into the program, so for them it follows that $E[U_0| \mathbf{X}, P = 1] = 0$.[4] The idea is to use the subset of people for whom Pr(**Z**) is very close to 1 (and thus for whom there is no selection problem) to identify the coefficients associated with P. This identification approach is called *identification at infinity*, because it focuses on people for whom $h(\mathbf{Z}'\gamma)$ is close to infinity, leading them to always participate in the program. Similarly, individuals for whom Pr(**Z**) = 0 can be used to secure identification of coefficients associated with $(1 - P)$ in the regression equation for Y (equation (16.4)); for this group, $E[U_0| \mathbf{X}, P = 0] = 0$. The usefulness of this limiting method of securing identification of model intercept parameters depends in part on how many people have estimated Pr(**Z**) values that are close to zero or one. In addition, nonparametric identification of the parameters associated with the control function terms (the power series terms, for example) requires that $\mathbf{Z}'\hat{\gamma}$ varies distinctly from **X**. This usually requires that there be a continuous variable that is included in **Z** but is not in **X**, that is, a variable that affects program participation but does not affect treatment effects.[5] See Andrews and Schafgans (1998) for further discussion of how to implement this type of estimator.

Standard error calculations for control function estimation methods

Calculation of the standard errors in a regression that includes a control function involves one slight complication, which is that the model includes an estimated regressor (because the control function is a function of Pr(**Z**), which was estimated) and the first-stage estimation of Pr(**Z**) needs to be taken into account. There are several ways to do this. One is to use the delta method, as originally applied in Heckman (1979) in the context in which the error terms are assumed to be jointly normally distributed.[6] Heckman et al. (1998) apply the delta method to derive asymptotic standard error formulas for a semiparametric partially linear control function model, in which the control function is estimated nonparametrically as a function of Pr(**Z**). This type of model is also discussed in Ichimura and Todd (2007).

Programming asymptotic standard error formulas can be cumbersome, so an easier approach to implement may be to obtain standard errors using bootstrap methods. There are a variety of bootstrap approaches, but the following is a convenient one. First, generate B bootstrap samples (for example, $B = 1{,}000$), each of which samples observations with replacement from the original data. When drawing the bootstrap sample, stratify the original sample into treatment and control groups and draw (with replacement) from each of those groups bootstrap samples with the same number of observations as in the original groups. Because sampling is done with replacement, some observations may be sampled more than once in any particular bootstrap sample, and other observations may not be in that sample at all. Second, within each of the bootstrap samples, estimate the model for Pr(**Z**) along with the outcome model. Third, compute the empirical variance of the estimated regression coefficients across all of the bootstrap samples, the square roots of which are the bootstrap standard errors. The actual parameter estimates are those based on the original sample.

Comparing control functions to matching methods and instrumental variables

Control function and matching methods were developed largely in separate literatures in econometrics and statistics, but the two methods both make use of propensity scores in implementation and so are related.

Conventional matching estimators can in some sense be viewed as a restricted form of a control function estimator. To see why, recall that traditional cross-sectional matching methods assume that selection is on observables (once observable variables are controlled for, P is uncorrelated with Y_1 and Y_0). Using the model for the outcome variable Y given in equation (16.4), the assumption that justifies matching outcomes on the basis of some set of characteristics **X** is

$$\mathrm{E}[Y_0 | \mathbf{X}, P = 1] = \mathrm{E}[Y_0 | \mathbf{X}, P = 0].$$

Recalling that $Y_0 = \mathbf{X}'\boldsymbol{\beta}_0 + U_0$, this assumption implies that

$$\mathrm{E}[U_0 | \mathbf{X}, P = 1] = \mathrm{E}[U_0 | \mathbf{X}, P = 0].$$

Under the control function approach, this assumption is equivalent to assuming that the control functions are equal for both the $P = 0$ and $P = 1$ groups:

$$K_1(\Pr(\mathbf{Z})) = K_0(\Pr(\mathbf{Z})),$$

in which case the model for outcomes in equation (16.2) can be written as

$$Y = \mathbf{X}'\boldsymbol{\beta} + P \times \text{ATT}(\mathbf{X}) + K_0(\Pr(\mathbf{Z})) + U_0 - \text{E}[U_0| \mathbf{X}, P] \\ + P \times \{U_1 - U_0 - \text{E}[U_1 - U_0| \mathbf{X}, \text{P} = 1]\}. \tag{16.5}$$

In the control function literature, this special case is referred as *selection on observables* (see Heckman and Robb 1985). The model in which U_0 and V are jointly normally distributed is consistent with this assumption only if $\sigma_{U_0,V} = 0$, which means that there is no bias caused by selection on unobservables.

The important point here is that when $K_1(\Pr(\mathbf{Z})) = K_0(\Pr(\mathbf{Z}))$ there are no identification problems, because the treatment effects (ATT($\mathbf{X}$)) now can be separately identified from the control function terms. As seen in equation (16.5), the treatment effects appear in the regression interacted with P, whereas the control function term ($K_0(\Pr(\mathbf{Z}))$) is not interacted with P. For example, if $K_0(\Pr(\mathbf{Z}))$ in equation (16.5) is approximated by a power series, the constant term in that series is, in contrast to the situation in the section titled "Methods for estimating control functions," not multiplied by P, and thus the coefficient on the product of the constant term in ATT($\mathbf{X}$) and P is identified. More generally, the assumption of matching estimators that P is uncorrelated with Y_0 after conditioning on $\mathbf{X}$ implies that there is no need for a control function to remove bias caused by P being correlated with Y_0 conditional on $\mathbf{X}$ (that is, being correlated with U_0). Thus $K_0(\Pr(\mathbf{Z}))$ can also be dropped from equation (16.5).

Thus assuming that selection is based on observables makes the evaluation problem simpler. However, this is a strong restriction that may not be satisfied. Heckman et al. (1998) devise a semiparametric statistical test for the equality of the estimated control functions, and they reject the restriction using data on a group of program applicants to a job training program who were randomly assigned to the control group combined with data on people who chose not to apply. They find that selection on unobservables is an important feature of their data.

Comparing the control function approach to IV estimation is also worthwhile. IV methods do not require any functional form assumptions for the error term in either the equation predicting program participation or the equation measuring the impact of the program; however, this approach does require an exclusion restriction, that is, a variable that predicts program participation but has no direct effect on the outcomes of interest (Y). In contrast, the control function approach does not require an exclusion restriction, but without an exclusion restriction it generally requires functional form assumptions for the error terms of both equations.[7] In practice, most researchers recommend that applications of the control function approach also use an exclusion restriction. Thus the real difference between these two approaches is the following: Almost all applications of the control function approach to estimate treatment effects require a distributional assumption for the error terms in the participation equation and in the outcome equation; this requirement enables ATT and ATE to be estimated. In contrast, IV methods do not require any distribution assumption for the error terms in the participation equation or the outcome equation, but this robustness comes at the cost of being able to estimate only the local average treatment effect (LATE), not ATT or ATE.

Adapting the control function approach for estimating ATE(X) and ATE

The discussion thus far has focused on estimating ATT. Some evaluations may also want estimates of ATE, which includes not only those who participate in the program but also those who do not participate. This section explains how to extend the control function approach to obtain estimates of average treatment effects that are functions of the **X** variables, that is, ATE(**X**). It also briefly explains how to estimate ATE without conditioning on **X** (which in effect averages ATE(**X**) over the entire population).

To begin, the observed values of Y in terms of the ATE(**X**) parameter, which equals $\mathbf{X}'(\boldsymbol{\beta}_1 - \boldsymbol{\beta}_0)$, can be expressed as

$$Y = \mathbf{X}'\boldsymbol{\beta}_0 + P \times \{\mathbf{X}'(\boldsymbol{\beta}_1 - \boldsymbol{\beta}_0)\} + (1 - P) \times U_0 + P \times U_1 .$$

The starting point for using the control function approach is to add and subtract the following two terms: $(1 - P) \times \mathrm{E}[U_0| \mathbf{X}, P = 0]$ and $P \times \mathrm{E}[U_1| \mathbf{X}, P = 1]$. This yields

$$Y = \mathbf{X}'\boldsymbol{\beta}_0 + P \times \mathrm{ATE}(\mathbf{X}) + (1 - P) \times \kappa_0(\mathbf{X}) + P \times \kappa_1(\mathbf{X}) + \omega, \tag{16.6}$$

where

$$\kappa_0(\mathbf{X}) = \mathrm{E}[U_0| \mathbf{X}, P = 0],$$

$$\kappa_1(\mathbf{X}) = \mathrm{E}[U_1| \mathbf{X}, P = 1], \text{ and}$$

$$\omega = (1 - P)\{U_0 - \mathrm{E}[U_0| \mathbf{X}, P{=}0]\} + P \times \{U_1 - \mathrm{E}[U_1| \mathbf{X}, P = 1]\}.$$

Note that $\kappa_1(\mathbf{X})$ is not the same control function as $K_1(\mathrm{Pr}(\mathbf{Z}))$ in the section titled "Methods for estimating control functions," because the former equals $\mathrm{E}[U_1| \mathbf{X}, P = 1]$ and the latter equals $\mathrm{E}[U_0| \mathbf{X}, P = 1]$. However, $\kappa_0(\mathbf{X})$ is equal to $K_0(\mathrm{Pr}(\mathbf{Z}))$, since both are equal to $\mathrm{E}[U_0| \mathbf{X}, P = 0]$.

Under the previous index sufficiency assumptions on U_0 and by making analogous assumptions on U_1, the control functions $\kappa_1(\mathbf{X})$ and $\kappa_0(\mathbf{X})$ can be written solely as a function of the probability of participating in the program, $\mathrm{Pr}(\mathbf{Z})$, that is, as $\kappa_1(\mathrm{Pr}(\mathbf{Z}))$ and $\kappa_0(\mathrm{Pr}(\mathbf{Z}))$, as done previously in the model for the ATT(**X**) parameter. In the case in which all the error terms (U_0, V) are assumed to be jointly normally distributed and (U_1, V) are also assumed to be jointly normally distributed, $\mathrm{E}[U_1| \mathbf{X}, P = 1]$ and $\mathrm{E}[U_0| \mathbf{X}, P = 0]$ can be expressed as

$$\mathrm{E}[U_1 \mid \mathbf{X}, P = 1] = \kappa_1\left(\Pr\left(\mathbf{Z}\right)\right) = \frac{\sigma_{U_1V}}{\sigma_V^2} \times \frac{\phi\left(-h\left(\mathbf{Z}'\gamma\right)\right)}{1-\Phi\left(-h\left(\mathbf{Z}'\gamma\right)\right)},$$

$$\mathrm{E}[U_0 \mid \mathbf{X}, P = 0] = \kappa_0\left(\Pr\left(\mathbf{Z}\right)\right) = \frac{\sigma_{U_0V}}{\sigma_V^2} \times \frac{-\phi\left(-h\left(\mathbf{Z}'\gamma\right)\right)}{\Phi\left(-h\left(\mathbf{Z}'\gamma\right)\right)}.$$

The expressions for $\kappa_1(\Pr(\mathbf{Z}))$ and $\kappa_0(\Pr(\mathbf{Z}))$, when added to equation (16.6) for Y, allow unbiased estimates of $\boldsymbol{\beta}_1$ and $\boldsymbol{\beta}_0$ to be obtained, which can then be used to calculate ATE($\mathbf{X}$), which equals $\mathbf{X}'(\boldsymbol{\beta}_1 - \boldsymbol{\beta}_0)$. This is true not only when (U_0, V) and (U_1, V) are assumed to be jointly normally distributed, but also more generally. The overall ATE parameter can be obtained by averaging over all the ATE($\mathbf{X}$) estimates for all the individuals in the sample (assuming the data represent a random sample of individuals).

An application: The performance of public and private schools in Chile

Sapelli and Vial (2002) use a control function model to analyze the performance of private and public schools in Chile in raising second grade students' test scores, taking into account nonrandom selection of children into different types of schools. They use the modeling framework described previously, in which the error term is assumed to be normally distributed, and they estimate both the ATE and ATT parameters. The covariates included in both the outcome and school choice equations are income group, mother's and father's education, and a dummy variable indicating that the child comes from an indigenous family. In addition, the school choice model includes as exclusion restrictions the number of municipal and private subsidized schools per square kilometer, and the ratio of the number of students in private subsidized schools divided by the number of students in either municipal or private subsidized schools, by geographical area.

Sapelli and Vial (2002) find evidence of a small and slightly negative ATE and a substantial ATT. More specifically, OLS estimates that do not include control function terms to control for selection into private schools suggest that the ATE over the entire population of enrolling in a private school is an increase in the student's language test score of about 0.20 (9.6/47.6) standard deviations of the distribution of that test score. However, when control function methods are applied, the estimate of ATE becomes slightly negative (−0.05 standard deviations). However, for the students who choose to attend private schools, the estimated impact (which is an estimate of ATT) is positive and relatively large (0.14 standard deviations). This suggests that private schools are most effective for the types of children who attend them.

Conclusion

When randomized controlled trials cannot be used to estimate program impacts, many different types of estimators can be applied to nonexperimental data. An important issue when applying the various methods is whether they assume that program participation could depend on unobserved factors. If this is possible, matching methods cannot be used. One alternative in this case is IV methods, and another is control function methods. IV methods have been used by economists for many decades, but control function methods are a relatively new approach, and this chapter provides a brief introduction.

Control function methods remove bias caused by selection on unobservables by explicitly modeling the selection process and how it relates to the observed outcomes. The major challenge in applying these methods for estimating program impacts is separately identifying the intercept of the control function from the treatment effect. As previously described, identification can usually be achieved through a combination of functional form restrictions, exclusion restrictions, and identification at infinity assumptions.

Notes

1. Many applications of the control function approach, which was first proposed by Heckman (1979), are not evaluations of programs, such as controlling for sample selection when estimating the determinants of women's wages. In this case, the control function is not interacted with any other variable. Although it is still true that the constant term in a nonparametric approximation of the control function cannot be distinguished from the constant term in the equation of interest, such as the determinants of women's wages, the constant term in that equation is usually not of particular interest. In such applications, exclusion restrictions alone are generally sufficient to identify the parameters of interest.
2. Note that three assumptions were used to obtain this result: (1) participation depends on $\mathbf{Z}$ via a function of a linear index of $\mathbf{Z}$, $h(\mathbf{Z}'\gamma)$; (2) the function $F_V(\cdot)$ is invertible; and (3) $f(U_0, V|\mathbf{X}) = f(U_0, V)$.
3. In many applications, including Heckman (1979), who first proposed the control function approach, the $h(\cdot)$ function is usually assumed to be linear, so that $h(\mathbf{Z}'\gamma)$ simply equals $\mathbf{Z}'\gamma$.
4. For these individuals $\text{Prob}[P = 1|\ \mathbf{Z}] = 1$, which implies that $1 - F_V(-h(\mathbf{Z}'\gamma)) = 1$ and thus that $F_V(-h(\mathbf{Z}'\gamma)) = 0$, which occurs only if $h(\mathbf{Z}'\gamma)$ approaches infinity. For the case in which U_0 and V are jointly normally distributed, $E[U_0 \mid \mathbf{X}, P = 1] = (\sigma_{U_0V} / \sigma_V^2) \times [\phi(-h(\mathbf{Z}'\gamma)) / [1 - \Phi(-h(\mathbf{Z}'\gamma))]]$. As $\mathbf{Z}'\gamma$ approaches infinity, $\phi(-h(\mathbf{Z}'\gamma))$ approaches 0 and $1 - \Phi(-h(\mathbf{Z}'\gamma))$ approaches 1, so $E[U_0|\ \mathbf{X}, P = 1] = 0$ for any value of σ_{U_0V}. For more general assumptions of the joint distribution of U_0 and V, it can still be shown that $E[U_0|\ \mathbf{X}, P = 1] = 0$.
5. For example, distances that individuals need to travel to get to the program site could be such a valid exclusion restriction.
6. See Greene (2012,1083–84) and Wooldridge (2010, 47) for explanations of the delta method.
7. One exception to this functional form assumption requirement would be to estimate the participation equation using a semiparametric method, such as the Klein and Spady (1993) method, but this would not allow the intercept term in the outcome equation to be separately identified from the intercept in the control function, which means that the treatment effect would not be identified. The only option would then be the "identification at infinity" approach of Heckman (1990) that was discussed in the section titled "Methods for estimating control functions," which is rarely used. For further discussion on the implementation and limitations of that method, see Andrews and Schafgans (1998).

References

Andrews, Donald, and Marcia Schafgans. 1998. "Semiparametric Estimation of the Intercept of a Sample Selection Model." *Review of Economic Studies* 65 (3): 497–518.

Greene, William. 2012. *Econometric Analysis, Seventh Edition.* Upper Saddle River, NJ: Prentice Hall.

Heckman, James. 1979. "Sample Selection Bias as a Specification Error." *Econometrica* 47 (1): 153–61.

Heckman, James. 1980. "Addendum to Sample Selection Bias as Specification Error." In *Evaluation Studies Review Annual*, edited by E. Stromsdorfer and G. Frakas. San Francisco: Sage.

Heckman, James. 1990. "Varieties of Selection Bias." *American Economic Review* 80 (2): 313–18.

Heckman, James, and Bo Honoré. 1990. "The Empirical Content of the Roy Model." *Econometrica* 58 (5): 1121–49.

Heckman, James, Hidehiko Ichimura, Jeffrey Smith, and Petra Todd. 1998. "Characterizing Selection Bias Using Experimental Data." *Econometrica* 66 (5): 1017–98.

Heckman, James, and Salvador Navarro. 2004. "Using Matching, Instrumental Variables, and Control Functions to Estimate Economic Choice Models." *Review of Economics and Statistics* 86 (1): 30–57.

Heckman, James, and Richard Robb. 1985. "Alternative Methods for Evaluating the Impact of Interventions." In *Longitudinal Analysis of Labor Market Data*, edited by James Heckman and Burton Singer, 156–264. Cambridge: Cambridge University Press.

Heckman, James, and Richard Robb. 1986. "Alternative Methods for Solving the Problem of Selection Bias in Evaluating the Impact of Treatments on Outcomes." In *Drawing Inferences from Self-Selected Samples*, edited by H. Wainer, 63–108. New York: Springer-Verlag.

Ichimura, Hideko, and Petra Todd. 2007. "Implementing Nonparametric and Semiparametric Estimators." In *Handbook of Econometrics*, Vol. 6B, edited by J. Heckman and E. Leamer. Amsterdam: Elsevier.

Klein, Roger, and Richard Spady. 1993. "An Efficient Semiparametric Estimator for Binary Response Models." *Econometrica* 61 (2): 387–421.

Roy, Andrew D. 1951. "Some Thoughts on the Distribution of Earnings." *Oxford Economic Papers* 3 (2): 135–46.

Sapelli, Claudio, and Bernardita Vial. 2002. "The Performance of Private and Public Schools in the Chilean Voucher System." *Cuardenos do Economía* 39 (118): 423–54.

Wooldridge, Jeffrey. 2010. *Econometric Analysis of Cross Section and Panel Data*, 2nd edition. Cambridge, MA: MIT Press.

CHAPTER 17

Quantile Treatment Effects

Introduction

Most of the evaluation literature is concerned with mean treatment effects. However, the distribution of treatment effects is also often of interest. For example, a program may have a positive average treatment effect (ATE), but for some members of the population the impact of the program (Δ, that is, $Y_1 - Y_0$) could be negative, and it may be important to know the proportion of the population for whom Δ is negative. Even if a program generates positive benefits for everyone, a program that provides greater benefits at the lower tail of the distribution of Y_0 may be considered more valuable. More generally, there are many cases in which it would be beneficial to know the distribution of Δ to investigate the heterogeneity of the treatment effects, and the extent to which this heterogeneity varies according to individuals' characteristics (which can be denoted by $\mathbf{X}$).

This chapter considers the class of *quantile treatment effect* (QTE) estimators. It draws in part on a survey by Fröhlich and Melly (2010) that reviews five types of QTE estimators:

1. Conditional QTE when the treatment is exogenous conditional on a set of observed variables, denoted by $\mathbf{X}$
2. Conditional QTE when the treatment is endogenous even after conditioning on a set of $\mathbf{X}$ variables, and a binary instrumental variable Z is available
3. Unconditional QTE with random treatment assignment (that is, a randomized controlled trial)
4. Unconditional QTE when the treatment is exogenous conditional on a set of $\mathbf{X}$ variables
5. Unconditional QTE when the treatment is endogenous

This chapter discusses in detail only the first four types of QTE estimators, the last type has only recently been developed and is just beginning to be applied.

The basic idea of quantile regression, with an example

For an idea of how quantile regression methods may be used for evaluating program impacts, one can start, as in previous chapters, with the equation for the observed outcome (Y):

$$Y = PY_1 + (1 - P)Y_0,$$

where P is an indicator for program participation, Y_1 is the value of Y for a person if he or she participates in the program, and Y_0 is the value of Y for the same person if he or she does not participate in the program. As previously noted, the treatment effect, $\Delta = Y_1 - Y_0$, is not directly observed for anyone, even in a randomized experiment. Also, in almost all cases the treatment effect will vary over the population, so that there is a distribution of treatment effects. As explained in detail later in this chapter, estimating the distribution of treatment effects requires additional assumptions beyond those necessary to estimate average treatment effects, such as ATE(**X**) or the average impact of the treatment on the treated, ATT(**X**).

To get an idea of what is meant by distribution of treatment effects, consider figure 17.1. It shows the standard case of a simple linear regression with only one **X** variable (denoted by X) and, more important, with homoskedasticity; that is, the variance of Y (conditional on X) does not depend on the value of X. The regression line $E[Y \mid X] = \alpha + \beta X$ shows the expected values of Y conditional on X, and the three bell-shaped curves illustrate the conditional densities of the Y variable given X (imagine that the curves are rising

FIGURE 17.1 Linear regression with homoskedasticity

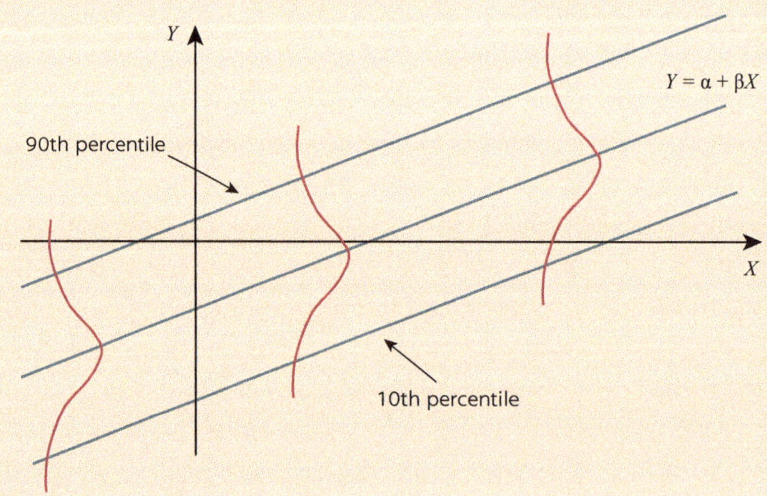

Source: Adapted from Deaton (2018, 80).

perpendicularly from the figure). The three straight lines are the quantile regression lines that connect the points on the 10th, the 50th, and the 90th percentiles of the distribution of Y for each given value of X. These different percentiles are referred to as *quantiles*.

These bell-shaped curves are also the conditional densities of the error term ε in the regression equation $Y = \alpha + \beta X + \varepsilon$, because all of the variation in Y conditional on X is coming from the variation in ε. When the distribution of this error term (the deviation from the conditional mean of Y) is symmetric, as in figure 17.1, the conditional mean (or regression function) is simply the 50th percentile line. In the homoskedasticity case, the quantile regression lines are parallel; all regression lines shown have the same slope, β.

Next, figure 17.2 shows an example with heteroskedasticity using data from rural Pakistan; heteroskedasticity is defined as a regression model where the variance of Y (conditional on X) can be determined by the value of X. It shows a food Engel curve (Y = budget share for food, and X = log of per capita expenditure) for 9,119 households interviewed in the 1984–85 Household Income and Expenditure Survey of Pakistan. Notice two characteristics of the distribution of income effects on food consumption. First, the slopes of the three quantile regression lines are all negative, but the βs (the slopes) differ for the different quantiles. Second, the 10th and 90th percentiles of the conditional distribution are much further apart among wealthier than among poorer households, indicating that although wealthier households devote a smaller proportion of their budgets to food, they exhibit more dispersion in the share of their budgets spent on food (more dispersion of tastes). Quantile regression estimators attempt to measure this dispersion in the conditional distribution of Y by estimating different β coefficients for the different percentiles, or quantiles, of that conditional distribution.

FIGURE 17.2 Food Engel curve under heteroskedasticity

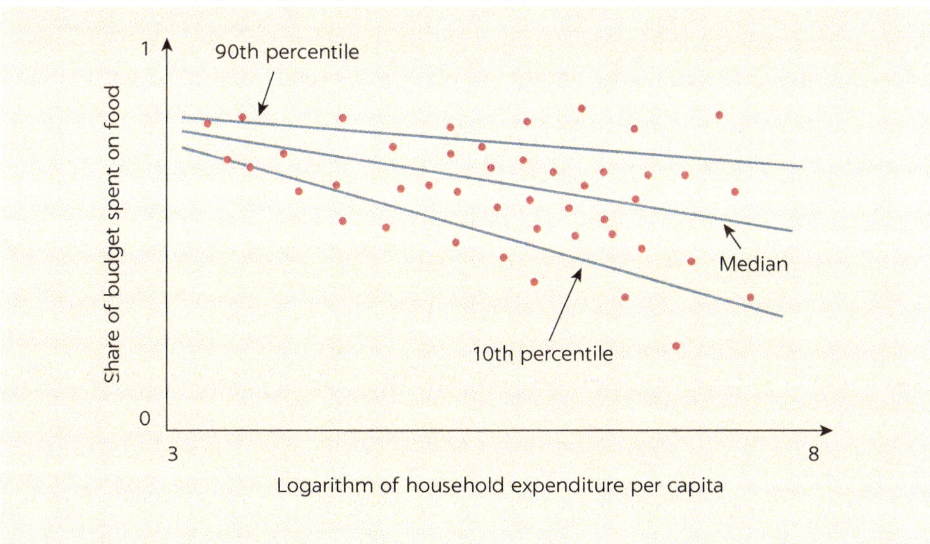

Source: Adapted from Deaton (2018, 81).

For some estimation methods, such as instrumental variables (IV) estimation (chapter 15) and the control function approach (chapter 16), estimation of the ATE usually proceeds by first estimating a conditional (on **X**) average treatment effect under a particular assumption (such as selection on observables) and then integrating over the distribution of the **X** variables. Unfortunately, this approach does not work for quantile estimation because the mean of the quantile is not equal to the quantile of the mean. The literature on quantile estimation has developed different approaches, described later in this chapter, for estimating both conditional and unconditional QTEs.

The rest of this chapter explains in more detail how to apply quantile regression methods to evaluate the distribution of program impacts.

Conditional and unconditional quantile treatment effect estimators

Quantile regression methods can be applied in several different ways to calculate the distribution of treatment effects. The most important distinction between the different methods is the distinction between conditional and unconditional estimation methods, because these two types focus on different parameters of interest:

- *Conditional QTE estimators* focus on features of the distribution of the treatment effect conditional on **X**.
- *Unconditional QTE estimators* focus on features of the distribution of the treatment impact without conditioning on **X**.

Within these two general types, alternative QTE estimators make different types of identifying assumptions.

To clarify the difference between these two types of QTE estimators, note that an individual can be high in the unconditional (marginal) distribution of Δ, while at the same time being low in the conditional distribution of Δ. This is possible if that person has values of **X** that are associated with a large value of Δ but, relative to other people with those values of **X**, he or she has a low Δ. For example, suppose the following describes the pattern of treatment effects for different people with respect to a variable X that takes only two values, 1 or 2:

Person 1	$\Delta = 1.5$	$X = 1$
Person 2	$\Delta = 2.0$	$X = 1$
Person 3	$\Delta = 2.5$	$X = 1$
Person 4	$\Delta = 3.0$	$X = 2$
Person 5	$\Delta = 3.5$	$X = 2$
Person 6	$\Delta = 4.0$	$X = 2$

Person 4 has a relatively high Δ unconditionally, but conditional on $X = 2$ he or she has a low Δ.

In the unconditional case, and assuming that an individual's rank in the Y_0 and Y_1 distributions remains the same, the QTE can be easily visualized. Figure 17.3 shows that the unconditional QTE corresponds, for any fixed percentile, to the horizontal distance between two cumulative distribution functions, the first of which is the cumulative distribution of Y_0 and the second of which is the cumulative distribution of Y_1; note that this depiction assumes no change in individuals' ranks in the distributions, so the same person is at any given quantile in the two distributions. For impact evaluations, this provides information on the distribution of program impacts, not just the average impact.

To define the conditional QTE estimators, this chapter assumes a parametric model for outcomes. As discussed by Fröhlich and Melly (2010), parametric conditional QTE estimators converge at the parametric ($\sqrt{n}$) rate. Nonparametric unconditional QTE estimators also converge at a $\sqrt{n}$ rate, but they are less often used than parametric estimators in applied work. Nonparametric conditional QTE estimators converge at a slower rate.

Conditional quantile treatment effect estimators

This section examines QTE estimators that condition on a set of observable variables, denoted by **X**. The first subsection considers the case in which program participation can

FIGURE 17.3 Unconditional quantile treatment effects (assuming no change in ranks)

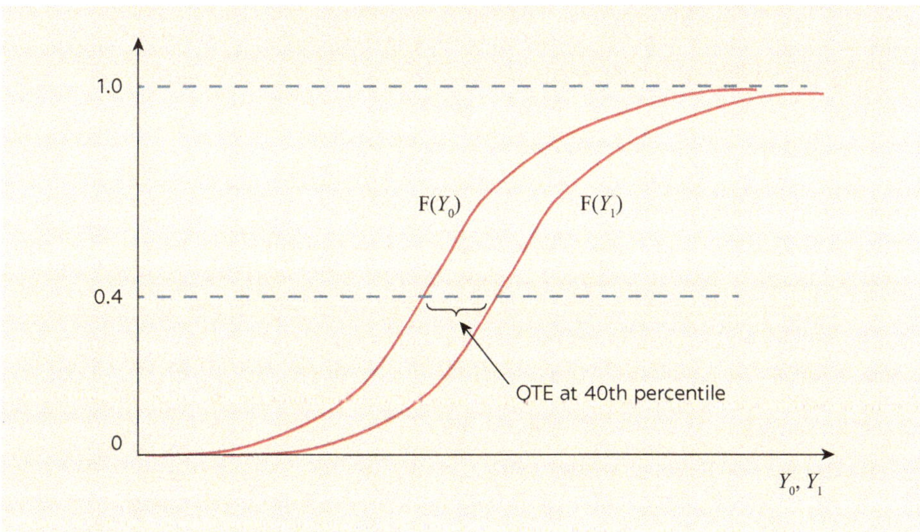

Source: Original figure for this publication.
Note: QTE = quantile treatment effect.

be assumed to be exogenous. The second subsection presents methods that can be applied when program participation is endogenous. QTE estimators that do not condition on other variables are discussed in the section titled "Unconditional quantile treatment effect estimators."

Conditional QTE when treatment (participation) is exogenous

Most applications of conditional QTE estimators estimate the distribution of treatment effects under the assumption that treatment (participation) is exogenous conditional on a set of observables **X**. This assumption is sometimes called an *unconfoundedness* assumption. (Recall that this selection-on-observables assumption is also often made for matching estimators and cross-sectional regression estimators.) Assume that the model for Y can be written as a linear function of **X** and P, but now the coefficients on **X** and P are allowed to vary by quantile as in the usual quantile regression framework, just as the slopes β in figure 17.2 were allowed to be different for different quantiles.

The maintained parametric assumption on potential outcomes is that Y_1 and Y_0 take an additive form. For a median regression, this can be expressed as

$$Y_P = \mathbf{X}'\boldsymbol{\beta}^{0.5} + P\delta^{0.5} + \varepsilon^{0.5}, \ P = 0, 1, \tag{17.1}$$

where the 0.5 superscripts for $\boldsymbol{\beta}$, δ, and ε indicate that this is a median regression. Note that both $\boldsymbol{\beta}^{0.5}$ and the unobservable $\varepsilon^{0.5}$ are assumed to be the same for the two potential outcome states. The assumption that $\varepsilon^{0.5}$ is the same implies rank invariance, that is, that an individual's rank in the distribution of Y_P conditional on **X** does not depend on treatment status P. This is a strong assumption, and it is required for most QTE estimation methods; it is relaxed for one estimation method discussed later in this section.

This equation for the (conditional) median of Y_P can also be expressed as

$$Q^{0.5}(Y_P| \mathbf{X}) = \mathbf{X}'\boldsymbol{\beta}^{0.5} + P\delta^{0.5}, \ P = 0, 1, \tag{17.2}$$

where the $Q^{0.5}(Y_P| \mathbf{X})$ notation indicates that the median value of Y_P, conditional on **X** and P, is given by $\mathbf{X}'\boldsymbol{\beta}^{0.5} + P\delta^{0.5}$. The $Q^{0.5}(\cdot \mid \mathbf{X})$ expression is essentially a function that calculates the median of the first argument (in this case Y_P) conditional on **X**; equation (17.2) for $Q^{0.5}(Y_P| \mathbf{X})$ was obtained by applying this function to equation (17.1) for the median of Y_P, which implies that the conditional median of $\varepsilon^{0.5}$ is 0, that is, $Q^{0.5}(\varepsilon^{0.5}| \mathbf{X}) = 0$. This is analogous to taking the conditional expectation of both sides of this regression equation; as long as the conditional median and the conditional mean of $\varepsilon^{0.5}$ are equal,[1] which implies that they both equal 0, then $E[Y_P| \mathbf{X}] = \mathbf{X}'\boldsymbol{\beta}^{0.5} + P\delta^{0.5}$, and thus $Q^{0.5}(Y_P| \mathbf{X}) = E[Y_P| \mathbf{X}]$.

Although the conditional median of Y_P may be of particular interest, it is only one feature of the conditional distribution of Y, and to study the overall conditional distribution of Y_P this additivity assumption must be generalized to other quantiles. Generalizing the functional form assumption in equations (17.1) and (17.2) to other quantiles can be expressed as

$$Q^{\tau}(Y_P|\,\mathbf{X}) = \mathbf{X}'\boldsymbol{\beta}^{\tau} + P\delta^{\tau},\ P = 0,\ 1.$$

The superscript τ refers to the quantile of the Y_P distribution, and δ^{τ} is the conditional QTE; for median regression $\tau = 0.5$. Intuitively, $Q^{\tau}(Y_P|\,\mathbf{X})$ is the value of Y_P for which $(\tau \times 100)$ percent of the density of Y_P, conditional on $\mathbf{X}$, is below, and $((1-\tau) \times 100)$ percent of the density of Y_P, conditional on $\mathbf{X}$, is above.

Just as the regression equation $Y_P = \mathbf{X}'\boldsymbol{\beta}^{0.5} + P\delta^{0.5} + \varepsilon^{0.5}$ corresponds to the equation $Q^{0.5}(Y_P|\,\mathbf{X}) = \mathbf{X}'\boldsymbol{\beta}^{0.5} + P\delta^{0.5}$ for the median of Y_P conditional on $\mathbf{X}$, there is also a regression equation $Y_P = \mathbf{X}'\boldsymbol{\beta}^{\tau} + P\delta^{\tau} + \varepsilon^{\tau}$ that corresponds to the equation $Q^{\tau}(Y_P|\,\mathbf{X}) = \mathbf{X}'\boldsymbol{\beta}^{\tau} + P\delta^{\tau}$ for the τth quantile of (the distribution of) Y_P conditional on $\mathbf{X}$.[2] Moreover, just as there is a different $\boldsymbol{\beta}^{\tau}$ for each value of τ, there is also a different δ^{τ} for each value of τ. The different values of $\boldsymbol{\beta}^{\tau}$ and δ^{τ} can be seen in figure 17.4, which is for the special case of only one $\mathbf{X}$ variable.

Figure 17.4 illustrates that the impacts of the $\mathbf{X}$ variable at different quantiles (that is, the values for $\boldsymbol{\beta}$) differ for each quantile (different values of τ), yet they are the same for $Q^{\tau}(Y_1|\,\mathbf{X})$ and $Q^{\tau}(Y_0|\,\mathbf{X})$ for any given quantile. Note also that the treatment effects can vary by quantile; in figure 17.4 the treatment effect at the 90th conditional quantile, $\delta^{0.9}$, is larger than the effect at the 50th conditional quantile, $\delta^{0.5}$, which in turn is larger than the effect at the 10th conditional quantile, $\delta^{0.1}$. However, it could also be that the treatment effects are larger at lower quintiles, so that $\delta^{0.1} > \delta^{0.5} > \delta^{0.9}$; note that this would cause the lines for $Q^{\tau}(Y_1|\,\mathbf{X})$ to cross in figure 17.4.[3]

FIGURE 17.4 Conditional quantile treatment effects (under the additivity assumption)

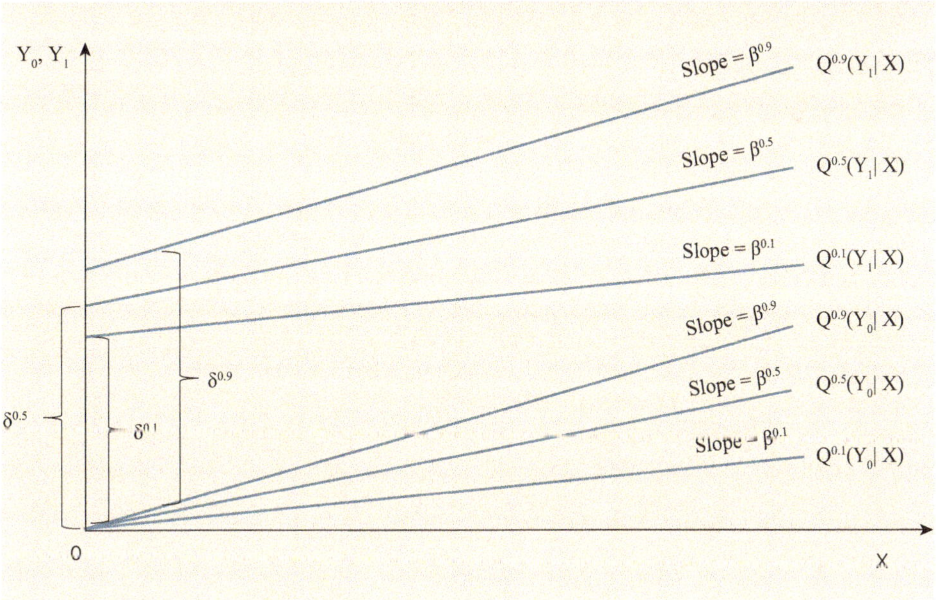

Source: Original figure for this publication.

A final point is that there is also a different ε^τ for each value of τ. Having a different ε for each τ may seem strange, but one way to see the intuition is to compare the distribution of Y_P conditional on $\mathbf{X}$ to its expectation for the standard linear regression model $Y_P = \mathbf{X}'\boldsymbol{\beta} + P\delta + \varepsilon$; because there is only one $\boldsymbol{\beta}$ there can be a single ε that is defined to be the difference between a given value of Y_P conditional on $\mathbf{X}$ and its expectation, $E[Y_P| \mathbf{X}] = \mathbf{X}'\boldsymbol{\beta} + P\delta$. Indeed, the only way to depict the conditional distribution of Y_P in a standard regression model is to specify the distribution for ε. In contrast, for quantile regression the difference between a given value of Y_P conditional on $\mathbf{X}$ and τth quantile for Y_P conditional on $\mathbf{X}$ is different for each τ, so for each τ there is a distinct error term ε^τ.

This specification for $Q^\tau(Y_P| \mathbf{X})$ has two implicit assumptions that are worth noting. The first assumption is that the impact of the $\mathbf{X}$ variables on the conditional distribution of Y_P, that is, on $Q^\tau(Y_P| \mathbf{X})$, is the same for both Y_1 and Y_0; in other words, the coefficient on $\mathbf{X}$ is simply $\boldsymbol{\beta}^\tau$ instead of $\boldsymbol{\beta}_1^\tau$ for Y_1 and $\boldsymbol{\beta}_0^\tau$ for Y_0. Thus, the conditional QTE, that is, δ^τ, is independent of the value of $\mathbf{X}$ (is the same for all $\mathbf{X}$), which is a restriction that is commonly made. In terms of figure 17.4, $\delta^{0.1}$, $\delta^{0.5}$, and $\delta^{0.9}$ are the same for all values of $\mathbf{X}$; this would not hold if the various $\boldsymbol{\beta}^\tau$ terms were different for Y_1 and Y_0. This is in contrast with some estimation methods in other chapters of this book, such as difference-in-differences estimation (chapter 12), IV estimation (chapter 15), and control function methods (chapter 16), which do not assume that $\boldsymbol{\beta}_0 = \boldsymbol{\beta}_1$, and more generally allow for the impact of the treatment to vary with $\mathbf{X}$.

The second assumption is that participation in the program (treatment) is exogenous with respect to outcomes conditional on a set of observables. This can be expressed as

$$Y_P \perp\!\!\!\perp P \mid \mathbf{X},$$

or equivalently, as

$$\varepsilon^\tau \perp\!\!\!\perp P \mid \mathbf{X} \text{ for all } \tau.$$

Whether this assumption is reasonable will depend upon the program, the $\mathbf{X}$ variables, and the unobserved variables included in the residuals ε^τ. This assumption implies rank invariance: conditional on $\mathbf{X}$, individuals have the same rank in the distributions of Y_0 and Y_1.[4] A weaker assumption that is sometimes made in the literature on QTE estimation is rank similarity, which is an assumption that an individual's rank is not necessarily the same for Y_0 and Y_1 but has the same probability distribution in these two treatment states, which implies that the expected rank, conditional on $\mathbf{X}$, is the same in both states.

Under these assumptions, the conditional QTE can be estimated using the standard quantile regression estimator introduced in Koenker and Bassett (1978). This can be implemented in Stata using the "qreg" command. As shown in Koenker and Bassett (1978), these estimators are the solution to the following minimization problem:

$$\left(\hat{\beta}^\tau, \hat{\delta}^\tau\right) = \underset{\beta,\delta}{\arg\min} \sum_{i=1}^{n} \rho_\tau\left(Y_i - \mathbf{X}_i'\beta - P_i\delta\right),$$

where $\rho_\tau(v) = v \times (\tau - 1[v < 0])$.[5] For example, if $\tau = 0.5$, then $\rho_\tau(v) = 0.5v$ when $v > 0$ and $= 0.5 \times (-v)$ when $v < 0$ (and $= 0$ when $v = 0$). Thus $\rho_{0.5}(v) = 0.5 \times |v|$, so it symmetrically weights positive and negative residuals. When $\tau = 0.5$ this is a median regression.[6]

Conditional QTE when treatment (participation) is endogenous

Sometimes the above assumption that ε^τ is independent of P conditional on **X**, which is often referred to as *selection on observables*, is doubtful. If treatment assignment is endogenous, but an instrumental variable is available, then there are a few estimators in the literature that can be applied. This subsection presents two approaches. The first requires either rank invariance or rank similarity, but does not require any additional functional form assumption. The second does not require either rank assumption but does require a functional form assumption.

Methods that assume rank invariance or rank similarity. Chernozhukov and Hansen (2005) develop an approach for identifying QTE that makes a rank invariance assumption (or a weaker rank similarity assumption), allows for endogeneity in treatment assignment, and does not impose functional form assumptions for the effect of **X** and P on Y_P. The authors define a quantile treatment response function $q(P, \mathbf{X}, \tau)$ that represents the potential outcomes Y_0 and Y_1 when $P = 0$ or $P = 1$, conditional on **X**, where τ is the τth quantile.[7] That is, the relationship between this function and Y_0 and Y_1 is

$q(0, \mathbf{X}, \tau)$ = value of the τth quantile of the distribution of Y_0, conditional on **X**, and

$q(1, \mathbf{X}, \tau)$ = value of the τth quantile of the distribution of Y_1, conditional on **X**.

For example, suppose that P represents whether a person has participated in a job training program and that $q(P, \mathbf{X}, \tau)$ is the earnings function, which describes the earnings in the labor market of an individual with ($P = 1$) or without ($P = 0$) training, who has characteristics **X** and ability τ. Then the impact of the training on the earnings of a person with characteristics **X** at the τth quantile of the ability distribution would be $q(1, \mathbf{X}, \tau) - q(0, \mathbf{X}, \tau)$. The earnings function may vary for different levels of τ if there are heterogeneous effects of training that vary with an individual's ability. The rank invariance assumption implies that individuals who had high earnings in the absence of training also have high earnings with training. That is, the ranks of earnings are preserved with or without training, conditional on **X**.

The method developed by Chernozhukov and Hansen (2005) to estimate QTEs when P is endogenous makes the following assumptions, where Z is a binary instrumental variable:

1. Conditional on **X**, for both $P = 0$ and $P = 1$, $Y_P = q(P, \mathbf{X}, U_P)$, where $q(P, \mathbf{X}, U_P)$ is strictly increasing in U_P (strict monotonicity) and U_P (called a rank variable) is uniformly distributed on the unit interval ($U_P \sim \mathrm{U}(0,1)$).[8]
2. For all P, U_P is independent of Z conditional on **X**.

3. $P = \delta(Z, \mathbf{X}, V)$ is the selection mechanism, where V is an unobserved random variable.

4a. Rank invariance: $U_0 = U_1 \mid \mathbf{X}, Z$,

or

4b. Rank similarity: U_0 and U_1 have the same distribution conditional on V.

5. P, $\mathbf{X}$, Z, and $Y = q(P, \mathbf{X}, U_P)$ are observed variables.

Chernozhukov and Hansen (2005) show that the above assumptions are sufficient for identification of the model's parameters because they imply the following conditional moment restriction:

$$\text{Prob}(Y \leq q(P, \mathbf{X}, \tau) \mid \mathbf{X}, Z) = \tau.$$

They also show that some implications of these assumptions can be tested. For example, it is possible to test whether the τth quantile of Y_0 (or Y_1) conditional on $Z = Z_0$ and $\mathbf{X}$ equals the τth quantile conditional on $Z = Z_1$. Chernozhukov and Hansen (2005) provide references to papers that develop estimation methods based on IV quantile restrictions.

Methods that do not assume rank invariance. If the rank invariance assumption is doubtful, then it is possible to apply the local QTE estimator (LQTE) of Abadie, Angrist, and Imbens (2002). This method incorporates more flexible heterogeneity in that it allows an individual's rank to be different in the Y_0 and the Y_1 distributions. However, similar to the local average treatment effect (LATE) estimator, the LQTE estimator of Abadie, Angrist, and Imbens (2002) recovers QTEs only for the subset of the population who are compliers.

To implement this method, assume that there is a binary instrumental variable, Z; that is, Z is assumed to take only two values, 0 or 1. Define two potential treatment indicators, P_0 and P_1, which indicate the value that P would take (for a particular person) when Z equals 0 or 1, respectively. Just as Y_0 and Y_1 exist for all people (even though only one of these is observed), so do P_0 and P_1. This is the same assumption used for LATE estimation, as explained in chapter 15. The IV quantile regression estimator (IVQTE) of Abadie, Angrist, and Imbens (2002) requires the following assumptions for consistent estimation:[9]

$$(Y_0, Y_1, P_1, P_0) \perp\!\!\!\perp Z \mid \mathbf{X},$$

$$0 < \text{Prob}[Z = 1 \mid \mathbf{X}] < 1,$$

$$\text{E}[P_0 \mid \mathbf{X}] \neq \text{E}[P_1 \mid \mathbf{X}], \text{ and}$$

$$\text{Prob}[P_1 \geq P_0 \mid \mathbf{X}] = 1.$$

The first assumption is that, conditional on $\mathbf{X}$, the potential outcomes (Y_0, Y_1, P_1, P_0) are not directly affected by the instrument Z, which means that Z has no effect on Y except through its effect on P, and thus comparisons of Y for different predicted values of P (as predicted by Z) identify the causal effect of the program via the instrument Z. Although at first it may seem strange that Z is independent of P_1 and P_0 given its effect on P, it is not; see the explanation of this point in the discussion of LATE estimation in chapter 15. The second assumption is that Z varies conditional on $\mathbf{X}$; if it did not vary, it would have no explanatory power for P conditional on $\mathbf{X}$ and thus would not be a useful instrumental variable. The third assumption is that the instrument influences participation status for at least some members of the population (conditional on $\mathbf{X}$); that is, when $Z = 1$ then $P = P_1$ and when $Z = 0$ then $P = P_0$, and this variation in Z should lead to variation in P. Finally, consider the fourth assumption. As with the LATE IV estimator discussed in chapter 15, the population can be divided into four types of people. Those for whom $P_1 > P_0$ are referred to as "compliers," because they are induced by a change in the value of the instrument to obtain the treatment. People for whom $P_1 = P_0 = 1$ are "always takers," and people with $P_1 = P_0 = 0$ are "never takers." The last assumption implies that there are no people who would have treatment status $P = 1$ when $Z = 0$ but would have $P = 0$ when $Z = 1$. In the language of Abadie, Angrist, and Imbens (2002), this means that there are assumed to be no "defiers."

Assuming the same linear model for outcomes used above, $Y = \mathbf{X}'\boldsymbol{\beta}^{\tau} + P\delta^{\tau} + \varepsilon^{\tau}$, the conditional QTE can be estimated by a weighted quantile regression:

$$(\hat{\beta}^{\tau}_{IV}, \hat{\delta}^{\tau}_{IV}) = \arg\min_{\beta,\delta} \sum_{i=1}^{n} W_i \rho_{\tau}(Y_i - \mathbf{X}_i{'}\beta - P_i\delta),$$

where

$$W_i = 1 - \frac{P_i(1-Z_i)}{1-\text{Prob}[Z=1\,|\,\mathbf{X}_i]} - \frac{(1-P_i)Z_i}{\text{Prob}[Z=1\,|\,\mathbf{X}_i]} \text{ and } \rho_{\tau}(v) = v(\tau - 1[v<0]).$$

Implementation of this method requires an initial estimator of Prob[$Z = 1|\, \mathbf{X}$] to construct the weights, which can be done using a standard probit regression.

As Abadie, Angrist, and Imbens (2002) note, and as Fröhlich and Melly (2010) discuss, this problem is not convex because some weights are negative and some positive. For this reason, Abadie, Angrist, and Imbens (2002) suggest the use of alternative weights:

$$W_i^{+} = \text{E}[W_i \,|\, Y_i, P_i, \mathbf{X}_i],$$

which they prove are always positive. The weights are unknown and must also be estimated. Fröhlich and Melly (2010, 431–44) discuss how to use the "ivqte" command in Stata to implement this estimator and to estimate the weights.

Unconditional quantile treatment effect estimators

Researchers are often interested in the relationship between outcomes and participation status without fixing values of other covariates. This section examines QTE estimators that do not condition on other observable variables. The unconditional QTE is the correct estimation method to use when the object of interest is the unconditional distribution of the treatment effects. This section first considers the case in which program participation can be assumed to be exogenous (as would be true for a randomized experiment) or exogenous conditional on some observables, and later briefly discusses estimation methods that can be used when program participation is endogenous. As explained below, conditioning on an additional set of control variables may be necessary for identification, even if the goal is to obtain an unconditional QTE.

Unconditional QTE with random treatment (participation) assignment

When treatment (program participation) is exogenous, for example, a randomized controlled trial in which all participants comply with their random assignment, implementing an unconditional QTE estimator is straightforward. The unconditional QTE, which does not condition on any covariates, is defined as

$$\Delta^{\tau} = Q^{\tau}(Y_1) - Q^{\tau}(Y_0),$$

where $Q^{\tau}(Y_P)$ is the τth quantile of the Y_P distribution ($P = 0$ or 1). For example, if $\tau = 0.75$, $Q^{0.75}(Y_1)$ is the value in the Y_1 distribution for which 25 percent of the values of the distribution of Y_1 are greater than that value, and 75 percent of the values of the distribution of Y_1 are smaller than that value.

For this simple estimator to give quantiles of the distribution of the impact of the program (distribution of Δ), an additional assumption is required: the ranking of each individual in the Y_1 distribution is identical to his or her ranking in the Y_0 distribution. More precisely, it must be assumed that someone at the τth quantile of the Y_0 distribution is also at the *same* quantile of the Y_1 distribution. This is a strong assumption; however, it is commonly made because it is impossible to directly determine the joint density of Y_1 and Y_0 from the data.[10]

If the assumption that each individual's rank is the same in both the Y_0 and the Y_1 distributions is not imposed, Heckman, Smith, and Clements (1997) note that all possible permutations of the ranks can be considered, and a collection of possible treatment effect distributions can be formed. There would be 100! possible different permutationally generated treatment effect distributions.[11] The two extremes would be perfect positive dependence (one-to-one matching in the Y_0 and Y_1 ranks) and perfect negative dependence (highest ranked Y_1 is the lowest ranked Y_0, second-highest ranked Y_1 is the second-lowest ranked Y_0, and so on). Allowing for all possible ranks generally leads to large bounds on the conceivable distribution of treatment effects, which in practice is not very useful. For this reason, Heckman, Smith, and Clements (1997) suggest instead restricting the space of possible distributions by allowing for a certain amount of slippage from the perfect positive dependence case, as measured by an indicator of rank correlation (such as Kendall's τ or Spearman's ρ). They discuss how models of the way people decide to participate in programs can be used to motivate assumptions on the rank correlations.

Under the assumption of perfect dependence (rank invariance), the unconditional QTE estimator can be implemented by directly calculating the quantiles of the Y_1 and Y_0 distributions. That is, Δ^τ can be estimated by $Q^\tau(Y_1) - Q^\tau(Y_0)$.[12] Note that, technically speaking, the unconditional QTE is a special case of the (parametric) conditional QTE, because the unconditional parametric QTE model is equivalent to the conditional QTE model with no covariates (no **X** variables). One advantage of using unconditional QTE estimators relative to conditional QTE estimators is that they are fully nonparametric (because there are no **X** variables for which to specify a parametric functional form) but can still be estimated at a $\sqrt{n}$ convergence rate.

Although covariates are not included in the definition of the unconditional QTE with exogenous treatment assignment, they are sometimes used in estimation. See Fröhlich and Melly (2010) for a more detailed discussion.

Unconditional QTE when treatment (participation) is exogenous conditional on X

For situations in which program participation was not determined by random assignment, direct calculation of the quantiles of the Y_1 and Y_0 distributions are quite unlikely to provide consistent estimates of QTEs. However, it may still be possible to estimate unconditional QTEs if certain assumptions hold. There are two possible approaches.

Firpo (2007), Fröhlich (2007), and Melly (2006) consider estimation of unconditional QTE for the case in which (1) the treatment is exogenous conditional on observables **X** (selection on observables); and (2) the support condition is satisfied. Formally, these two assumptions are

$$(Y_0, Y_1) \perp\!\!\!\perp P \mid \mathbf{X},$$

$$0 < \text{Prob}[P = 1 \mid \mathbf{X}] < 1.$$

Note that these are the same assumptions required for the consistency of conventional cross-sectional matching estimators, as explained in chapter 13.

Under these two assumptions, Frölich and Melly (2010) propose the following estimator of the unconditional QTE:

$$\left(\hat{\alpha}^\tau, \hat{\Delta}^\tau\right) = \underset{\alpha,\Delta}{\arg\min} = \sum_{i=1}^{n} W_i^F \rho_\tau\left(Y_i - \alpha - P_i\Delta\right),$$

where

$$W_i^F = 1 - \frac{P_i}{\text{Prob}[P_i = 1 \mid \mathbf{X}_i]} - \frac{1 - P_i}{1 - \text{Prob}[P_i = 1 \mid \mathbf{X}_i]}.$$

These weights are equal to the inverse of the probability of participating, or the propensity score. Thus implementation requires obtaining a preliminary estimate of the propensity score.

Unconditional QTE when treatment (participation) is endogenous

The assumption that treatment (participation) is exogenous conditional on some observed variables may not hold. In this case, participation is endogenous, and IV methods can be used to estimate the unconditional QTE. Frölich and Melly (2010, 446) conjecture that "it seems likely that it is valid" for more recently developed quantile regression methods. Proving the validity of bootstrap methods for different QTE estimators is an active area of current research.

Standard errors

Calculation of analytical standard errors for QTE estimators can be difficult. Partly for this reason, bootstrap methods are often used. However, the validity of the bootstrap has thus far been shown only for the standard quantile regression, and not for more recently developed quantile regression estimators such as IV quantile regression estimators. On a more optimistic note, Frölich and Melly (2010) conjecture that "it seems likely that it is valid" for more recently developed quantile regression methods.

Correct analytical variances have been derived for some QTE estimators. As described in Frölich and Melly (2010), the Stata "ivqte" command can be used to implement these analytical variance estimators for conditional exogenous QTEs, conditional endogenous QTEs, unconditional exogenous QTEs, and unconditional endogenous QTEs. These analytical expressions usually involve nonparametric estimation of a density and a choice regarding the bandwidth and kernel function. More generally, see Frölich and Melly (2010) for an extensive discussion of how to implement the various QTE estimators, and how to obtain the standard errors of those estimators, using Stata.

Examples of applications

One interesting application of quantile regressions is the Schultz and Mwabu (1998) study on how South African labor unions affect the distribution of wages. Labor unions are an important economic and political force in South Africa, and estimates indicate that union membership grew from 400,000 in 1985 to 1,205,612 in 1993, the latter figure representing 37 percent of workers that year. This union share of the labor force is quite high for a country with a relatively low income level. Yet wage inequality is higher in South Africa than in almost any other country in the world. Schultz and Mwabu (1996) explore how South African unions affect the distribution of economic welfare. More specifically, they use quantile regressions to estimate the impact of being a union member on wages, and how this impact varied by the (conditional) distribution of wages. Their estimation focuses on conditional QTEs, in which union participation is assumed to be exogenous conditional on a set of explanatory variables denoted by $\mathbf{X}$.

Schultz and Mwabu (1998) use nationally representative data collected in 1993 from 9,000 households. Their quantile regressions (table 17.1) show that, among African (black) workers, union membership increases wages by 145 percent ($e^{0.895} - 1$) at the 10th percentile of the (conditional) wage distribution but by only 11 percent ($e^{0.107} - 1$) at the 90th percentile. Among white workers, union membership raises wages by 21 percent at the 10th percentile but reduces them by 24 percent at the 90th percentile; for white workers at the 50th percentile wages decreased by 11 percent (table 17.2).

TABLE 17.1 Quantile regression estimates of the wage function controlling for union membership: African men (absolute values of bootstrap t-ratios in parentheses)

	WAGE QUANTILES			
EXPLANATORY VARIABLE	.10	.50	.90	MEAN (OLS)
a. Education and Experience Variables				
Years of Primary Education	.085	.075	.033	.074
	(5.56)	(7.59)	(3.14)	(9.74)
Years of Secondary Education	.143	.142	.169	.160
	(6.67)	(11.2)	(13.6)	(14.9)
Years of Higher Education	.300	.322	.274	.293
	(7.14)	(8.45)	(6.56)	(10.2)
Potential Job Experience in Years	.049	.053	.049	.049
	(3.68)	(8.25)	(4.20)	(9.27)
Potential Job Experience Squared (x 10^{-2})	-.0720	-.0687	-.0638	-.0655
	(3.73)	(5.67)	(3.34)	(7.19)
b. Location and Union Variables				
Rural Area (1 = Rural Residence)	-.437	-.298	-.237	-.357
	(5.62)	(9.00)	(9.20)	(11.1)
Union Status (1 = Union Member)	.895	.446	.107	.468
	(13.9)	(13.1)	(1.84)	(14.7)
Constant Term	-.800	.180	1.291	.219
	(.418)	(2.05)	(7.58)	(2.41)
Pseudo R^2	.321	.217	.215	.399
Sample Size		2,364		

Source: Schultz and Mwabu 1998.

Note: Reprinted from T. Paul Schultz and Germano Mwabu, "Labor Unions and the Distribution of Wages and Employment in South Africa," *Industrial and Labor Relations Review*, volume 51, issue 4 (July), pages 680–703, copyright 1998 by *Industrial and Labor Relations Review*; reprinted by permission of SAGE Publications, Inc. Further permission required for reuse. OLS = ordinary least squares.

TABLE 17.2 Quantile regression estimates of the wage function controlling for union membership: White men (absolute values of bootstrap t-ratios in parentheses)

	WAGE QUANTILES			
EXPLANATORY VARIABLE	.10	.50	.90	MEAN (OLS)
a. Education and Experience Variables				
Years of Primary Education	.016	–.056	–.036	–.011
	(.06)	(1.82)	(.52)	(.45)
Years of Secondary Education	.242	.090	.007	.084
	(4.18)	(1.92)	(.25)	(3.01)
Years of Higher Education	.098	.126	.183	.150
	(3.56)	(6.15)	(6.23)	(8.34)
Potential job Experience in Years	.126	.078	.091	.103
	(6.61)	(6.74)	(4.91)	(10.9)
Potential Job Experience Squared (x $1(10^{-2})$)	–.250	–.130	–.149	–.187
	(5.15)	(4.71)	(3.80)	(8.89)
b. Location and Union Variables				
Rural Area (1 = Rural Residence)	–.057	–.178	–361	–.294
	(.06)	(1.81)	(2.41)	(2.62)
Union Status (1 = Union Member)	.188	–.112	–.270	–.051
	(1.88)	(2.33)	(3.32)	(.75)
Constant Term	104	2.344	3.032	1.823
	(.06)	(16.0)	(5.84)	(11.2)
Pseudo R^2	.261	.171	.160	.276
Sample Size		653		

Source: Schultz and Mwabu 1998.
Note: Reprinted from T. Paul Schultz and Germano Mwabu, "Labor Unions and the Distribution of Wages and Employment in South Africa," *Industrial and Labor Relations Review*, volume 51, issue 4 (July), pages 680–703, copyright 1998 by *Industrial and Labor Relations Review*; reprinted by permission of SAGE Publications, Inc. Further permission required for reuse. OLS = ordinary least squares.

Schultz and Mwabu (1998) also examine the possibility that the union effects presented in tables 17.1 and 17.2 may have captured some interindustry wage effects (for example, some industries pay higher wages, and workers cannot easily move across industries). Controlling for nine industry groups, their quantile regressions (not shown here) confirm that a substantial part of the effect of union membership can be explained by industry categories, which perhaps reflects the influence of Industrial Councils or the spillover of administered wages by industry. The union log wage advantage, controlling for industry, ranges from 41 percent ($e^{0.345} - 1$) for the lowest decile to 1 percent ($e^{0.005} - 1$) for the top decile among African men, and from 15 percent to −22 percent for white men at the bottom and top deciles, respectively.

Another interesting, and more recent, application of QTE estimators is Schiele and Schmitz (2016), who analyze the effects of job loss on health using data from the German Socioeconomic Panel. They examine how job loss affects physical and mental health for individuals located at different parts of the health distribution, taking into account the endogeneity of job loss and using Firpo's (2007) estimation approach. Their analysis controls for education, work experience, occupational position, gross labor income, and unemployment experience, and they also report estimates that do not control for these covariates. They find significant effects of job loss on physical health but only for individuals in the middle and lower parts of the health distribution.

Conclusion

Although most evaluations of program impacts focus on mean (average) treatment effects, the full distribution of treatment effects is often also of interest. The QTE estimators described in this chapter offer a way to explore the way treatment effects are distributed within the population, either overall (unconditionally) or conditional on the values of other variables, which can be denoted by **X**. If the treatment (program participation) can be assumed to be exogenous conditional on some **X** variables (selection on observables), then standard quantile regression methods can be applied. If treatment is plausibly endogenous (selection on unobservables), then instrumental variables are needed to estimate QTEs.

QTE estimation is relatively new, and several papers have extended its application to more complex situations. For example, Powell (2020) develops a generalized QTE model that divides the covariates into what he calls treatment variables and control variables, where the treatment variables are included in the structural quantile function and the control variables are used to aid in identification. The estimated QTEs are conditional on the treatment variables and unconditional on the control variables. The framework allows for treatment participation to be endogenous. Powell (2020) applies the method to study the effect of teacher incentives on teacher attendance and student achievement in India, using data from the Duflo, Hanna, and Ryan (2012) study. Other recent studies have extended QTE to regression discontinuity settings, for example, see Frandsen, Frölich, and Melly (2012).

Notes

1. This would be the case if the distribution of $\varepsilon^{0.5}$ (conditional on **X**) is symmetric.
2. This implies that $Q^{\tau}(\varepsilon^{\tau}| \mathbf{X}) = 0$ for all τ. To see the intuition, consider $Y_p = \mathbf{X}'\boldsymbol{\beta}^{0.9} + P\delta^{0.9} + \varepsilon^{0.9}$. This must hold for all values of Y_p conditional on **X**. Because $\mathbf{X}'\boldsymbol{\beta}^{0.9} + P\delta^{0.9}$ in effect focuses on the upper tail of Y_p conditional on **X**, for 90 percent of the values of Y_p conditional on **X** the following will hold: $Y_p < \mathbf{X}'\boldsymbol{\beta}^{0.9} + P\delta^{0.9}$. This in turn implies that $Y_p = \mathbf{X}'\boldsymbol{\beta}^{0.9} + P\delta^{0.9} + \varepsilon^{0.9} < \mathbf{X}'\boldsymbol{\beta}^{0.9} + P\delta^{0.9}$, so for 90 percent of the values of Y_p it is the case that $\varepsilon^{0.9} < 0$. That is why $Q^{0.9}(\varepsilon^{0.9}| \mathbf{X}) = 0$.

3. Another consequence of the case in which $\delta^{0.1} > \delta^{0.5} > \delta^{0.9}$ is that it is not possible for the rank invariance assumption to hold if the constant term for $Q^{\tau}(Y_0| \mathbf{X})$ is the same for all quantiles, which is the case shown in figure 17.4.
4. One condition that implies rank invariance is that individuals' ε^{τ} are the same regardless of whether $P = 1$ or 0, but rank invariance does not imply (does not require) that these residuals are the same for $P = 0$ or 1.
5. $1[v < 0]$ is the indicator function, which in this case equals 1 when $v < 0$ and equals 0 when $v \geq 0$.
6. Median regression is sometimes used as an alternative to ordinary least squares to reduce the sensitivity of the estimated parameters to outliers; this is done in a wide variety of contexts and is not limited to impact evaluations.
7. Chernozhukov and Hansen's (2005) method assumes a continuous outcome and either a discrete or a continuous treatment. The discussion here is the approach for a discrete (binary) treatment.
8. U_P plays the same role as $\varepsilon^{0.5}$ in $Y_P = \mathbf{X}'\boldsymbol{\beta}^{0.5} + P\delta^{0.5} + \varepsilon^{0.5}$, that is, it allows for variation in Y_P conditional on $\mathbf{X}$ and P. Note, however, that U_P is different from $\varepsilon^{0.5}$ in that it can be different for $P = 1$ and $P = 0$, whereas $\varepsilon^{0.5}$ is the same for $P = 1$ and $P = 0$.
9. These assumptions are essentially the same as those required for LATE IV estimation, as discussed in chapter 15.
10. A somewhat indirect way to test this assumption would be to compare the rankings for the treated group before and after they are treated; if there is no measurement error in Y_1 and Y_0, then the rankings should be identical.
11. The mathematical notation 100! (known as "factorial") is equal to $100 \times 99 \times 98 \times \ldots \times 3 \times 2 \times 1$. The number 100 simply indicates that there are 100 percentiles, from 1 to 100.
12. If the number of observations for Y_1 and Y_0 are the same, as may be the case in a randomized controlled trial, then Δ^{τ} can be estimated using Stata by matching by rank across the two distributions and then using the "qreg" command to regress $Y_1 - Y_0$ on a constant term.

References

Abadie, Alberto, Joshua Angrist, and Guido Imbens. 2002. "Instrumental Variables Estimates of the Effect of Subsidized Training on the Quantiles of Trainee Earnings." *Econometrica* 70 (1): 91–117.

Chernozhukov, Victor, and Christian Hansen. 2005. "An IV Model of Quantile Treatment Effects." *Econometrica* 73 (1): 245–61.

Deaton, Angus. 2018. *The Analysis of Household Surveys: A Microeconomic Approach. Reissue Edition with a New Preface*. Washington, DC: World Bank. doi:10.1596/978-1-4648-1331-3. License: Creative Commons Attribution CC BY 3.0 IGO.

Duflo, Esther, Rema Hanna, and Stephen Ryan. 2012. "Incentives Work: Getting Teachers to Come to School." *American Economic Review* 102 (4): 1241–78.

Firpo, Sergio. 2007. "Efficient Semiparametric Estimation of Quantile Treatment Effects." *Econometrica* 75 (1): 259–76.

Frandsen, Brigham, Markus Frölich, and Blaise Melly. 2012. "Quantile Treatment Effects in the Regression Discontinuity Design." *Journal of Econometrics* 168 (2): 382–95.

Frölich, Markus. 2007. "Nonparametric IV Estimation of Local Average Treatment Effects with Covariates." *Journal of Econometrics* 139 (1): 35–75.

Frölich, Markus, and Blaise Melly. 2010. "Estimation of Quantile Treatment Effects with Stata." *Stata Journal* 19 (3): 423–57.

Heckman, James, Jeffrey Smith, and Nancy Clements. 1997. "Making the Most Out of Social Experiments: Accounting for Heterogeneity in Program Impacts." *Review of Economic Studies* 64 (4): 487–535.

Koenker, Roger, and Gilbert Bassett. 1978. "Regression Quantiles." *Econometrica* 46 (1): 33–50.

Melly, Blaise. 2006. "Estimation of Counterfactual Distributions Using Quantile Regression." Discussion paper, Universität St. Gallen. http://www.alexandria.unisg.ch/Publikationen/22644.

Powell, David. 2020. "Quantile Treatment Effects in the Presence of Covariates." *Review of Economics and Statistics* 102 (5): 994–1005.

Schiele, Valentin, and Hendrik Schmitz. 2016. "Quantile Treatment Effects of Job Loss on Health." *Journal of Health Economics* 49 (C): 59–69.

Schultz, T. Paul, and Germano Mwabu. 1998. "Labor Unions and the Distribution of Wages and Employment in South Africa." *Industrial and Labor Relations Review* 51 (4): 680–703.

PART IV

Data Collection and Project Management

CHAPTER 18

Designing Questionnaires and Other Data Collection Instruments

Introduction

Although some types of impact evaluations can be implemented using administrative data or other data that have already been collected, most require new data collection. New data collection usually involves gathering data from one or more of the following sources:

- Households, and the individuals within them
- Service providers (schools, health clinics, microfinance institutions, and so on)
- Community leaders
- Private enterprises

Collection of new data is an important—and time-consuming—process. In many impact evaluations, the cost of new data collection is the most expensive component of the evaluation. Most important, errors in data collection can undermine an entire evaluation, and many kinds of errors are possible.

Data collection can be divided into three distinct components:

1. Designing the survey questionnaires

2. Collecting the data

3. Managing the data after it is collected

This chapter and the following two chapters discuss each of these topics. The focus of this chapter is questionnaire design, including both paper questionnaires and electronic questionnaires that are installed into tablets or other electronic devices. As with data collection as a whole, questionnaires to collect data must be carefully designed because there are many types of potential errors, and serious errors can render the data useless for the purpose of conducting an impact evaluation. Even seemingly small errors can greatly reduce the quality of an impact evaluation. This chapter provides an introduction to this topic. For more detailed recommendations, see Grosh and Glewwe (2000). More recent recommendations on specific topics can be found at the World Bank's Living Standards Measurement Study website: http://surveys.worldbank.org/lsms.

General principles and recommendations

This section provides some general principles and recommendations for designing effective survey questionnaires. The following sections provide more detailed guidance on several specific topics.[1]

Who should participate in questionnaire development?

Perhaps the first decision to be made regarding the development of questionnaires and other survey instruments is who should participate in their development. Much can be gained by including a variety of individuals and groups because there are many details to keep track of, and the more people contributing to this effort the more likely that some important details will not be overlooked. The following sets of people are the most important groups to include in the process of designing survey questionnaires:

- The research team that will eventually use the data
- The managers and supervisors of those who will collect the data
- The persons responsible for the data entry system
- One or more administrative staff members from the agency that implements the program that is being evaluated

Designing household survey questionnaires typically involves a large number of meetings. The most frequent meetings are for those who have been assigned to design the questionnaire, but other meetings are needed to get feedback from all four sets of people listed above. Even though it may seem faster, or more efficient, to send drafts of questionnaires to people to get their comments in writing, in reality such requests are often given low priority, so it is best to have meetings with the above groups to ensure that they give the draft questionnaires their full attention.

Need to field test (pilot test)

Before collecting data using a questionnaire (or any other type of survey instrument), the questionnaire must be field tested, which is perhaps the most important task in questionnaire development. Indeed, it is good practice to do two field tests, once for the original draft questionnaire and once for the revised draft questionnaire (revised on the basis of the first field test).

A field test (sometimes called a pilot test, or a pretest) is simply the process of testing the draft questionnaire on a large number of households (or service providers, or communities, or firms) of the type for which the questionnaire will be used. Some specific suggestions include the following:

- Administer the field test to at least 50 households, and better yet to 100–200. If the unit of observation is a service provider, community, or firm, the field test should include at least 10 of these, and 20 or 30 would be even better.[2]

- Make sure to include all types of households (or service providers, or communities, or firms) that will be in the sample (for example, both urban and rural, different regions and agricultural zones, and so on).
- Use both average or slightly above average interviewers and experienced interviewers. Using average interviewers will reveal how well the questionnaire performs when administered by those who will conduct the actual survey, while the feedback of experienced interviewers can be invaluable for refining a survey instrument to be best suited for the target population.

More detailed advice on how to conduct a field test can be found in Grosh and Muñoz (1996).

Translation into local languages (and back translation)

In many cases, the team developing the questionnaire will work in a language that is different from the ones that the interviews will be conducted in. Whenever this is the case, having a good translation from the team language (often an international language, such as English, French, or Spanish) to the local language is critical. Ideally, the team should include local team members in the design and planning of the survey, given that they know the language and local context, and can review plans, questionnaires, and other survey instruments.

The best way to check whether the translation into the local language is good is to have the translated questionnaire translated back into the language that the team designing the questionnaire is working in (the team language), which as noted is often an international language. The back translation should be performed by someone hired especially for this task who has no knowledge of the research plan or the program being evaluated, and has no connection to the research team. This person should be fluent in both languages (the one that the questionnaire is in and the one that the questionnaire development team is using) and should have experience translating from the local language into the language used by the team.

In almost all cases, comparison of the original team questionnaire with the back-translated questionnaire will yield many instances in which the meaning has changed. These discrepancies should be checked carefully to see whether there are problems with the version of the questionnaire in the local language(s). In fact, it is quite likely that this is the source of the discrepancies. Although this may seem to be an onerous task, it is extremely important given that bad translations could have negative effects on the quality of the data collected and thus on the quality of the overall evaluation. A final point is that back translations must be done for all languages into which the questionnaire is translated.

General advice on the design of questionnaires

Questionnaires can be designed in many ways that increase the probability of obtaining complete and accurate data. This section provides several recommendations.

Design the questionnaire to make the interview easier for respondents

In many, if not most, developing countries, a large proportion of survey respondents are not highly educated. In addition, they have no particular motivation to provide accurate information. Most survey respondents will try to provide accurate information, however, and they can be helped by a questionnaire that has been designed to lighten the burden on them. The following recommendations are specific suggestions for how to make the interview easier for respondents.

The questions must be easy to understand. Questions addressed to survey respondents should be relatively short, and as much as possible, use simple vocabulary. Respondents should be able to answer questions using units that are most natural to them. For example, when asked how often they participate in some activity of interest, allow them to answer in terms of days, weeks, months, or years instead of requiring them to answer, say, only in months. The method for recording the answers should allow for this type of flexibility.

Start by asking less sensitive questions, and save the most sensitive questions for the end of the interview. Many questions asked of respondents are not particularly sensitive, whereas others, such as those related to savings, fertility, or attitudes toward the government, can be very sensitive. In general, questionnaires should begin with less sensitive questions, which will allow the interviewer to develop some trust or rapport with the respondent. Once that trust has been established, the respondent is more likely to provide accurate answers for later, more sensitive questions. Reserve the most sensitive questions for the end of the questionnaire; if the respondent becomes uncooperative and stops the interview, then data will already have been collected for the less sensitive questions.[3]

Avoid long questionnaires. Researchers are often tempted to collect a large amount of data from household members or other respondents. One reason for this is that interviewers often spend more time traveling from one interview to the next than they spend conducting interviews, so an increase in interview time from adding more questions may not result in a large increase in interviewers' work time. However, asking more questions can come at a cost:

- Answers may become less accurate because of respondent (and interviewer) fatigue.
- Long interviews may irritate respondents, reducing their cooperation.

Thus additional questions should be carefully checked; if their usefulness is doubtful, they should be dropped. The optimal interview time for a given respondent will depend on the context. Individuals in urban areas, and relatively wealthy individuals, usually will grant at most one hour of their time for an interview. In contrast, individuals who live in rural areas, or who are relatively poor, may be willing to be interviewed for two or three hours.

Essential information ("metadata") that should be collected

Almost any questionnaire needs to include additional data that are, strictly speaking, not questions asked of survey respondents. These data include the following:

- Date of the interview
- Location of the interview (province, district, village, respondent address)
- Information on who conducted the interview

- Identification of which individuals answered the questions
- Information on how well the interview went, for example, the cooperativeness of the respondents and whether any questions confused the respondents
- If no interview occurred, the reason why (for example, refusal, respondent not found)

For much of this information, code numbers can be developed that will make metadata collection go more smoothly, for example, codes for provinces, districts, villages, schools, health clinics, households, and interviewers, and even respondents within the household.

Finally, if no interview occurs, in most cases it should be possible to collect some basic data from knowledgeable people (neighbors, relatives, local officials, others), which will help in assessing whether the sample of households (or service providers, or communities, or firms) that completed the interview is representative of the sample that was intended to be interviewed.

Recommendations for formatting questionnaires

A well-formatted questionnaire can greatly improve the work of the interviewers, and more generally, improve the quality and accuracy of the data collected. The following general recommendations for formatting a questionnaire (whether a paper questionnaire or an electronic questionnaire on a digital device) have proven to be worthwhile in a wide variety of settings. When possible, the team should also consult an expert on survey design who can review the ways the questions are asked, the response codes, and other survey details.

Write out the exact questions. The best way to ensure that the data collected are accurate is for each question to be written out explicitly, and to train interviewers to use that wording when they conduct the interviews. Scott and others (1988) show that errors increase by 7–20 times when questions are not written out.

Have precoded answers. Most questions asked of respondents have a small number of possible answers. Each possible answer should be given a code number, and those code numbers should appear next to the question. Roughly speaking, if the number of possible answers is 10 or fewer, codes can be placed immediately below or next to the question. If the number is much larger than 10 (for example, occupation codes or province where born), then the codes should appear at the bottom of the questionnaire page, or on a facing page.

Use skip codes (skip patterns). In many questionnaires, the answer to one question determines which question is asked next. For example, a respondent should be asked about his or her current work if the respondent has first replied "yes" to the question "Are you currently working?" To ensure that irrelevant questions are not asked, skip codes can be used that inform the interviewer to proceed to a later question (or set of questions) if a certain response is given to the current question. An example of instructions for doing this is, "IF THE ANSWER IS NO, GO TO QUESTION 4" or, more succinctly: "IF NO, → Q.4."

Use consistent formatting. Code numbers for certain common answers to questions should be the same throughout the questionnaire. Two examples of consistent formatting are the following:

- Always use "1" for "YES" and "2" for "NO."
- Time units: minute = 1, hour = 2, day = 3, week = 4, month = 5, year = 6.

Another useful formatting rule is to distinguish between questions that are read to the respondent and instructions to the interviewer. The latter could always be in upper case or in bold.

Example 1 illustrates the above recommendations. First, all of the questions are written out in full. Second, all of the questions have a small number of possible answers, all of which are assigned numeric codes that can be written in the boxes provided for that purpose. Third, the first two questions have instructions on how to skip questions in the event of a "NO" response from the respondent. Finally, commonly used codes are used consistently. In particular, a "YES" response is always coded as 1 and a "NO" response is always coded as 2 (note that this could have been done differently, such as coding a "NO" response as 0, but the important point is to be consistent throughout the questionnaire).

Example 1: Questions on Housing

1. Is this dwelling owned by a member of your household?

   YES 1
   NO .... 2 » QUESTION 7

2. Do you have legal title to the dwelling or any document that shows ownership?
   YES 1
   NO .... 2 » QUESTION 4

3. What type of title is it?
   FULL LEGAL TITLE, REGISTERED 1
   LEGAL TITLE, UNREGISTERED................ 2
   PURCHASE RECEIPT.................................. 3
   OTHER...(SPECIFY ____________)........... 4

4. If you make installment payments for your dwelling, what is the amount of the installment?

   WRITE ZERO IF THE HOUSEHOLD DOES NOT MAKE INSTALLMENT PAYMENTS

   AMOUNT (UNITS OF CURRENCY)

   TIME UNIT

TIME UNITS	DAY 3	MONTH.............. 5	HALF YEAR ... 7
	WEEK................. 4	QUARTER.......... 6	YEAR............... 8

Household questionnaires

Most data collection for conducting evaluations gathers information from individuals or households, often using a household questionnaire. Entire books have been written on how to design household questionnaires. For detailed suggestions, see, among others, Grosh and Glewwe (2000). This section provides some basic recommendations for how to design household questionnaires that should be applicable to a wide range of evaluations.

First, nearly all household questionnaires are designed to obtain a list of household members, suggesting that a definition of the household members is needed. A common definition is a group of people who eat meals together and pool their income, but there may be good reasons for using another definition, such as a legal definition, in specific circumstances.

Second, a common practice when collecting data from households is to collect all of the information on all household members from a single respondent. However, this practice is not recommended because it often leads to inaccurate data. Instead, getting different types of information from the individuals in a given household who are the most knowledgeable on the different topics is a better approach. Thus the interview will often require the participation of more than one household member, for example, all adult household members.

Third, for many types of analyses, data on household income or expenditure are useful. Collecting this information is difficult, however, because there are many types of income and expenditure, which households often forget. Much more detailed guidance on how to collect income and expenditure information is provided by Bardasi et al. (2011), Beegle et al. (2012), Deaton and Grosh (2000), Gibson et al. (2015), and McKay (2000).

Fourth, for many impact evaluation studies it is often beneficial, and in some cases essential, to interview the household more than once, for example, both before and after the program is implemented. Locating previously interviewed households is often difficult, even after only one or two years, so the first survey should collect information that would help in finding households in later years. The following recommendations are useful:

- Record addresses of dwellings in as much detail as possible, and photograph the dwelling (if the photograph can be taken without violating privacy or other restrictions).
- In each community, construct detailed maps of the community, and identify where the surveyed households are on the map.
- Use global positioning system (GPS) equipment to record the precise longitude and latitude (and perhaps elevation) of the location of the household.
- Request phone numbers of all household members who have mobile or landline phones.
- Ask household members for the names of people in the community who would be most likely to know their whereabouts if they were to move to a different community (and get the phone numbers of those community members).

Service provider questionnaires

Many impact evaluations focus on programs that are closely tied to government or private schools, health clinics, banks, and other providers of social services, which usually implies that collecting data on those service providers is essential. Indeed, in many evaluations of education programs the main source of data is schools, and the basic unit of sampling is the school, not the household.

Providing general advice on how to collect data from service providers is difficult because they vary greatly by the type of service they provide. See the chapters on education and health in Grosh and Glewwe (2000) for specific advice on school and health clinic questionnaires, respectively. The following subsection provides some general advice, and the subsequent subsections focus on school and health facility questionnaires.

General observations

Many impact evaluations cover two or three different kinds of service providers (for example, schools with the new program and schools without the new program). For many purposes, knowing which service providers are of which type is sufficient. However, to understand the results, collecting additional information on all types of service providers to verify (monitor) whether those with the new program really are different from those without the program is useful.

For schools, health clinics, and perhaps other service providers, it is often informative for trained observers to watch teachers, doctors, and others perform their duties. School inspectors do this in many school systems, so school principals and teachers are accustomed to it. See Das and Leonard (2008) for recommendations on how to observe health care providers.

Finally, see Amin, Das, and Goldstein (2008) for a collection of studies on how to collect data from service providers in developing countries.

School questionnaires

This subsection provides basic information on how to design school questionnaires. For more detailed advice, see Glewwe (2000). Additional recommendations can be found in Beegle (2008).[4]

Data on school fees are often necessary, but collecting the data is not a simple task. First, there may be many types of fees, some of which may be "under the table." Also, in some countries poor students may obtain exemptions, either official or unofficial, from paying fees, highlighting the need for extensive field testing of any questionnaire, but especially school questionnaires, to ensure that the desired information is obtained. Sensitive information, such as questions about fees that may contradict government policies, should be asked at the end of the questionnaire. Alternatively, sensitive information may be more readily obtained from households than from the schools or other facilities.

Another type of worthwhile information to collect using school questionnaires is a list of current teachers, and some basic information on them, including their age, sex, highest level of schooling, highest degree obtained, and years of experience as a teacher (both at the current school and over an entire career). Obtaining information on the subjects they teach, and the grades they teach, to better match them with students, is also important. If the school has a large number of teachers (such as 12 or more), then it may be best to randomly sample two or three teachers per grade.

When school questionnaires are used in conjunction with household questionnaires, matching the child to the school that he or she attends is critical. It may not be the closest school, or the main school in the community where the child lives. Unique school codes should be developed and recorded on both the household questionnaire (for children currently enrolled in school) and the school questionnaire. These codes should indicate not only the school but also the community in which the school is located.

Health facility questionnaires

Many, if not most, evaluations of health programs that are administered through local health facilities should collect data from those facilities. This subsection provides general guidance. For more detailed suggestions see Gertler, Rose, and Glewwe (2000). Additional information can be found in Beegle (2008) and Das and Leonard (2008).

In many cases, obtaining information from facilities that are not participating in the program being evaluated is also helpful. For example, a program may operate through public (government-operated) facilities, but information from nearby private facilities might also be worthwhile because the impact of the program may vary depending on the extent of competition from those private facilities.

In almost all cases, prices for each type of general service offered by a health facility are important. If possible, prices for medications should be separated from prices for services. Many prices may be unofficial, and in this case the best source for these prices may be people who have recently been to the facility. Another price to obtain is travel times to communities served by the clinic, given that travel time may have a major impact on who visits the clinic.

Measuring the quality of care is difficult (Das and Leonard 2008; Gertler, Rose, and Glewwe 2000). However, some general advice can be given. To assess clinic quality, several types of information should be collected. First, the health facility questionnaire should obtain information on the medications available at the clinic. In addition to finding out what medications are typically available, asking how many are actually in stock on the day of the visit is important. Second, the health facility questionnaire should request information on the types of medical equipment available at the clinic. It is also important to ask whether the equipment actually works. Third, information should be collected on which types of common medical procedures are offered by the clinic, and whether they are available on the day of the visit. Finally, the health facility questionnaire should include questions on the hours of operation, not only the official hours, but also how many hours the facility has actually been open for each of the past seven days.

Community (and price) questionnaires

Community questionnaires are often useful for obtaining general information about the communities in which households live. In some settings, communities are well defined, for example, in many rural areas. In other situations, they are harder to define, for example, in most urban areas. For detailed recommendations, see Frankenberg (2000). This section provides general guidance.

The first recommendation is to realize that the real community for households may not be the same as the official community as defined by political or geographical boundaries. This difference can be ascertained by discussions with local leaders and knowledgeable individuals. Official boundaries can change from one year to the next, but the boundaries of a "real" community are often more stable.

A second general recommendation is that often the best way to collect community data is to have a meeting of community leaders and officials (local government leaders, teachers, health service providers, and traditional leaders). All questions are asked at the meeting, and the person or persons who are best able to provide the answers can respond. In some cases, separately collecting information from a subgroup, especially if that subgroup is disadvantaged in some sense, is the best approach. For example, the best way to collect information of special relevance to women may be to have a meeting of women's leaders that does not include male leaders.

Finally, price data are best gathered at markets. Whenever possible, prices should be collected from more than one vender. Each item must be specifically defined and should be commonly found throughout the area under study. For example, do not just ask for the "price of rice" but ask for a particular, very common type of rice, and specify as much as possible the quality of that rice. The expertise of local research team members and other local experts should be fully used when choosing the items to include in the price questionnaire.

Other data collection instruments

In many impact evaluations, outcomes of interest cannot be obtained using questionnaires and must be collected more directly. Three common examples are cognitive skills of students, health status, and individuals' personality traits and related variables. This section describes all three types of information and then briefly reviews methods for measuring them.

Testing to measure cognitive skills

Many evaluations of education programs attempt to measure the impact of those programs on student learning. In addition, some evaluations may test the skills of children who are not in school, or even of adults (for example, to evaluate an adult literacy program). The following discussion provides some general advice. See Burdett (2016) for a review of many of the issues involved.

When evaluating the impact of an education program on student learning, test scores for students may be available from schools; at first glance, using such scores appears to be a convenient and low-cost option for measuring student learning, but substantial caution is warranted. For example, different schools may use different tests that are not comparable across schools. Another problem is that nationwide tests may be too difficult for the population in question, such as poor students in rural areas, so most of the scores obtained from such students may be little more than guessing on the part of those students.

Given the above, it may be useful to administer a test as part of the evaluation. Many tests have been developed that have good psychometric properties, such as the Peabody Picture Vocabulary Test. If an appropriate existing test cannot be found, designing a new test may be the best approach; in such cases, hiring a local or international expert for this work is often desirable. If an expert cannot be hired, engaging local teachers or education officials to design a test may be reasonable, but they are almost always less skilled than experts.

Almost all education evaluations seek to test students' reading and mathematics skills. Other subjects, such as science, may also be worthy of analysis, depending on the aims of the program being evaluated.

Ideally, it is best to test students in their schools. Children who are not in school should be persuaded to return to school for testing. If not possible, another quiet place (for example, a community center) might be found. Testing in homes can be difficult, but if there are no alternatives, testing at home is usually better than not testing at all.

Health indicators

Individuals' health status can be measured in several ways. Indirect measures, which are responses to questions, are the easiest to implement but are not always reliable. More direct measurements are more difficult to implement but have increased reliability. This subsection reviews the most common methods. See Alderman (2000) and Gertler, Rose, and Glewwe (2000) for further information.

The easiest (and perhaps least reliable) method for measuring health status is to ask questions on activities of daily living. Examples of such questions are (1) "Can you walk 5 kilometers?" and (2) "Can you carry a load of 20 kilograms?" These are most often used for relatively elderly people, such as individuals who are age 40 and older.

Anthropometric measures (height, weight, arm circumference) are somewhat harder to gather but are collected in many surveys. Standardized measures of height-for-age are useful indicators of chronic (cumulative) malnutrition in children, and standardized weight-for-height is an indicator of the current nutritional status of children. Body mass index (defined as weight in kilograms divided by the square of height in meters) is an indicator of both inadequate nutrition and obesity in adults. For further discussion of these health indicators, see Alderman (2000).

Even more ambitiously, invasive data collection methods include drawing blood samples (for example, pinprick to test for anemia or vitamin A deficiency), obtaining hair clippings (to measure zinc), and using special equipment to measure lung capacity. Trained health professionals must be used to collect this type of data, and such data collection can raise serious ethical issues, as discussed in chapter 10. If feasible and affordable, an intensive study of the impact of a health program could involve administering full health exams to study participants.

Measuring personality traits and related variables

Recent efforts to understand why programs do not work as expected have involved attempts to collect data on individuals' personality traits and related variables, also referred to as noncognitive, socioemotional, or psychosocial skills. Examples of such variables are trust, cooperation, agreeableness, depression, optimism, and aspirations. Economists also would like to measure variables such as risk aversion and time preferences (discount rates). The following discussion summarizes the most commonly used methods for measuring these variables and provides references to much more detailed treatments of them.

Some measures of psychosocial variables are relatively simple to use and require that a respondent answer only 10–12 questions. Such measurements could be collected as part of a household questionnaire or as a separate questionnaire for an individual respondent (with one or more such respondents per household). Two prominent examples are the Rosenberg (1965) self-esteem scale and the Center for Epidemiological Studies Depression (CES-D) Scale (Radloff 1977). The self-esteem scale consists of 10 statements about the respondent's current psychological state, and the respondent is asked to express agreement on a four-point Likert scale (strongly agree, agree, disagree, and strongly disagree). The CES-D consists of 12 statements, such as, "I felt that everything that I did was an effort"; the respondent is asked, for a reference period of the past week, to express the frequency of such feelings on a four-point scale (never, once in a while, sometimes, and frequently).

A more general questionnaire-based assessment is the 44-question inventory that measures the big-five psychological traits (openness, conscientiousness, extraversion, agreeableness, and neuroticism), which are also referred to as personality traits. This set of questions, and their links to the five psychological traits, is provided by John and Srivistava (1999). Finally, another good source for measuring psychological or personality traits is the World Values Survey (Inglehart et al. 2014), the questionnaire for which can be downloaded from http://www.worldvaluessurvey.org/WVSDocumentationWV6.jsp. For example, this survey contains small sets of questions that measure trust, social values, ethical values, and religious values.

Economists have increasingly attempted to measure fundamental constructs such as time preferences and risk aversion. Questionnaires have been developed to measure these constructs, but another way to measure them is to conduct "experiments" with individuals, which are often referred to as artefactual field experiments. For example, a person could be presented with a set of lotteries, including one that involves no risk at all, and asked which one he or she would like to choose. After making the choice, the lottery is played and the person receives an amount of money (or some desired good) that depends on the outcome of the lottery. This approach is used to increase the accuracy of these measurements, because the individual's choice will determine an outcome of interest to that individual (in contrast to using a questionnaire, for which there are no consequences to the response given). There is a large and growing literature on measuring these concepts. Further discussion of methods used by economists can be found in the two volumes edited by Bernheim, DellaVigna, and Laibson (2018).

Measuring female empowerment

Gender disparities are an important issue in developing countries, and such disparities have attracted increasing attention in recent years. Underlying many of these disparities is a lack of empowerment of both women and girls. In recent years, researchers have developed tools to measure women's and girls' empowerment. One example is the guide developed by the Abdul Latif Jameel Poverty Action Lab (J-PAL) at the Massachusetts Institute of Technology, which is available at https://www.povertyactionlab.org/sites/default/files/resources/practical-guide-to-measuring-womens-and-girls-empowerment-in-impact-evaluations.pdf.

Paper questionnaires versus computer-assisted personal interviewing

Many statistical agencies and other data collection organizations have moved from traditional paper questionnaires to laptop computers, tablets, personal digital assistants (PDAs), and other electronic devices to enter respondents' answers to questions directly into an electronic format. This is often called computer-assisted personal interviewing (CAPI). CAPI data collection has both advantages and disadvantages, as summarized in the following paragraphs.

The four main advantages of using CAPI data collection are the following:

1. The data entry program used by the laptop or digital device can find errors and inconsistencies in the data during the interview, so those problems can be corrected during the interview by asking the respondent to explain unusual or inconsistent answers.
2. The data can be sent in to headquarters quickly and, more generally, the time required to create complete data sets is reduced because there is no need for a separate data entry step. This will hasten the day when the analysis of those data sets can begin.
3. The data collection agency does not need a large storeroom to deposit paper questionnaires so that they can be checked in the future when likely errors are found in the data.
4. Backing up the data electronically shortly after the interview is conducted reduces the likelihood that questionnaires, and thus the information in them, are lost, which has happened in data collection efforts using paper questionnaires.

Of course, CAPI data collection has disadvantages as well:

1. The electronic equipment may break down and stop the process; in general, interviewers should have a few spare paper questionnaires to use in the event this happens. Note that the quality and durability of the equipment used for CAPI data collection increases nearly every year.
2. The cost may be high, although costs typically fall relatively steeply each year.

3. Respondents may not like technology that they are not familiar with, especially if it "beeps" when they give answers that may have errors; also, interviewers may have less eye contact with respondents if they spend more time looking at the laptop or tablet screens, which could reduce respondents' cooperation.
4. In some areas, theft may be a problem, and interviewers may not feel safe carrying expensive laptops, tablets, PDAs, and similar devices.

Several evaluations of the advantages and disadvantages of CAPI data collection have been written, some of which include references to specific software and hardware. Examples are Caeyers, Chalmers, and De Weerdt (2010) and Shaw et al. (2011).

Conclusion

Evaluations of programs, projects, and policies often require the collection of new data, which usually involves the use of questionnaires of various types. Although designing questionnaires may seem rather mundane, careful attention to detail, and thorough field testing, can be decisive in determining whether an evaluation is successful or unsuccessful. The entire evaluation team needs to be involved in this process to avoid serious problems that could compromise the entire evaluation.

This chapter provides a brief introduction to the design of these questionnaires. Although the general recommendations provided in this chapter can be helpful, the references provided must be consulted to ensure a well-designed set of questionnaires. Much can, and should, be learned from the experiences of others.

Notes

1. One type of questionnaire not covered in this chapter is firm questionnaires. For designing surveys of various types, with a focus on surveys of firms, see Iarossi (2006).
2. Further discussion on this topic, from the perspective of educational research, can be found in Johanson and Brooks (2010).
3. Chapter 19 provides recommendations on how to conduct interviews when the questionnaire contains sensitive questions.
4. Education research has increasingly collected classroom observation data. For recent advances, see the World Bank's Teach initiative (https://www.worldbank.org/en/topic/education/brief/teach-helping-countries-track-and-improve-teaching-quality) and the Measures of Effective Teaching project at the Bill & Melinda Gates Foundation (https://k12education.gatesfoundation.org/resource/#?initiative=measures-of-effective-teaching).

References

Alderman, Harold. 2000. "Anthropometry." In *Designing Household Survey Questionnaires for Developing Countries: Lessons from 15 Years of the Living Standards Measurement Study,* Vol. 1, edited by M. Grosh and P. Glewwe, 251–72. New York: Oxford University Press.

Amin, Samia, Jishnu Das, and Markus Goldstein, eds. 2008. *Are You Being Served? New Tools for Measuring Service Delivery.* Washington, DC: World Bank.

Bardasi, Elena, Kathleen Beegle, Andrew Dillon, and Pieter Serneels. 2011. "Do Labor Statistics Depend on How and to Whom the Questions Are Asked? Results from a Survey Experiment in Tanzania." *World Bank Economic Review* 25 (3): 418–47.

Beegle, Kathleen. 2008. "Health Facility and School Surveys in the Indonesia Family Life Survey." In *Are You Being Served? New Tools for Measuring Service Delivery,* edited by Samia Amin, Jishnu Das, and Markus Goldstein, 343–64. Washington, DC: World Bank.

Beegle, Kathleen, Joachim De Weerdt, Jed Friedman, and John Gibson. 2012. "Methods of Household Consumption Measurement through Surveys: Experimental Results from Tanzania." *Journal of Development Economics* 98 (1): 3–18.

Bernheim, Douglas, Stefano DellaVigna, and David Laibson. 2018. *Handbook of Behavioral Economics,* Vols. 1 and 2. Amsterdam: Elsevier.

Burdett, Newman. 2016. "The Good, the Bad and the Ugly—Testing as Part of the Education Ecosystem." RISE Working Paper 16/010. https://www.riseprogramme.org/publications/rise-working-paper-16010-good-bad-and-ugly-testing-key-part-education-ecosystem.

Caeyers, Bet, Neil Chalmers, and Joachim De Weerdt. 2010. "A Comparison of CAPI and PAPI through a Randomized Field Experiment." World Bank, Washington, DC. http://siteresources.worldbank.org/INTLSMS/Resources/3358986-1199367264546/Caeyers_Chalmers_DeWeerdt_CAPIvsPAPI.pdf.

Das, Jishnu, and Kenneth Leonard. 2008. "Use of Vignettes to Measure the Quality of Health Care." In *Are You Being Served? New Tools for Measuring Service Delivery,* edited by Samia Amin, Jishnu Das, and Markus Goldstein, 299–310. Washington, DC: World Bank.

Deaton, Angus, and Margaret Grosh. 2000. "Consumption." In *Designing Household Survey Questionnaires for Developing Countries: Lessons from 15 Years of the Living Standards Measurement Study,* Vol. 1, edited by M. Grosh and P. Glewwe, 91–134. New York: Oxford University Press.

Frankenberg, Elizabeth. 2000. "Community and Price Data." In *Designing Household Survey Questionnaires for Developing Countries: Lessons from 15 Years of the Living Standards Measurement Study,* Vol. 1, edited by M. Grosh and P. Glewwe, 315–38. New York: Oxford University Press.

Gertler, Paul, Elaina Rose, and Paul Glewwe. 2000. "Health." In *Designing Household Survey Questionnaires for Developing Countries: Lessons from 15 Years of the Living Standards Measurement Study,* Vol. 1, edited by M. Grosh and P. Glewwe, 177–215. New York: Oxford University Press.

Gibson, John, Kathleen Beegle, Joachim De Weerdt, and Jed Friedman. 2015. "What Does Variation in Survey Design Reveal about the Nature of Measurement Errors in Household Consumption?" *Oxford Bulletin of Economics and Statistics* 77 (3): 466–74.

Glewwe, Paul. 2000. "Education." In *Designing Household Survey Questionnaires for Developing Countries: Lessons from 15 Years of the Living Standards Measurement Study,* Vol. 1, edited by M. Grosh and P. Glewwe, 143–75. New York: Oxford University Press.

Grosh, Margaret, and Paul Glewwe, eds. 2000. *Designing Household Survey Questionnaires for Developing Countries: Lessons from 15 Years of the Living Standards Measurement Study.* New York: Oxford University Press for the World Bank.

Grosh, Margaret, and Juan Muñoz. 1996. "A Manual for Planning and Implementing the Living Standards Measurement Study Survey." Living Standards Measurement Study Working Paper 126, World Bank, Washington, DC.

Iarossi, Giuseppe. 2006. *The Power of Survey Design: A User's Guide for Managing Surveys, Interpreting Results, and Influencing Respondents*. Washington, DC: World Bank.

Inglehart, R., C. Haerpfer, A. Moreno, C. Welzel, K. Kizilova, J. Diez-Medrano, M. Lagos, P. Norris, E. Ponarin, and B. Puranen, et al., eds. 2014. *World Values Survey: Round Six*. Country-Pooled Datafile Version. JD Systems Institute, Madrid. www.worldvaluessurvey.org/WVSDocumentationWV6.jsp.

Johanson, George, and Gordon Brooks. 2010. "Initial Scale Development: Sample Size for Pilot Studies." *Educational and Psychological Measurement* 70 (3): 394–400.

John, Oliver, and Sanjay Srivastava. 1999. "The Big-Five Trait Taxonomy: History, Measurement, and Theoretical Perspectives." in *Handbook of Personality: Theory and Research*, Vol. 2, edited by L. A. Pervin and O. P. John, 102–38. New York: Guilford Press.

McKay, Andrew. 2000. "Should the Survey Measure Total Household Income?" In *Designing Household Survey Questionnaires for Developing Countries: Lessons from 15 Years of the Living Standards Measurement Study*, Vol. 2, edited by M. Grosh and P. Glewwe, 83–104. New York: Oxford University Press.

Radloff, Lenore. 1977. "The CES-D Scale: A Self-Report Depression Scale for Research in the General Population." *Applied Psychological Measurement* 1: 385–401.

Rosenberg, Morris. 1965. *Society and the Adolescent Self-Image*. Princeton, NJ: Princeton University Press.

Scott, Christopher, Martin Vaessen, Sidiki Coulibaly, and Jane Verrall. 1988. "Verbatim Questionnaires versus Field Translation or Schedules: An Experimental Study." *International Statistical Review* 56 (3): 259–78.

Shaw, Arthur, Lena Nguyen, Ulrike Nischan, and Herschel Sy. 2011. "Comparative Assessment of Software Programs for the Development of Computer-Assisted Personal Interview (CAPI) Applications." The IRIS Center, University of Maryland, College Park, MD. http://siteresources.worldbank.org/INTSURAGRI/Resources/7420178-1294259038276/CAPI.Software.Assessment.Main.Report.pdf.

CHAPTER 19

Data Collection and Data Management

Introduction

Most impact evaluations collect new data to compare program participants to individuals who have not participated in the program. Data collection and data management are important tasks that should not be delegated to a group that has no particular interest in the evaluation. These two tasks are complicated, and thus require particular attention to many details. This chapter provides recommendations on both data collection and data management. Further advice is provided in Muñoz (2005).

There are two general goals for data collection and data management, which may at times conflict:

1. *Timeliness*. The data must be collected and analyzed relatively quickly because policy makers are waiting for the results.
2. *Quality*. The data must be accurate and useful for the planned evaluation.

Clearly, there is an inherent trade-off between these two goals, but careful data collection and data management will ensure that a situation is not created in which better decisions could have increased both the timeliness and quality of the data. The rest of this chapter uses the chronological order of the data collection process to provide specific recommendations for how to increase both the timeliness and the quality of the data.

The steps involved in data collection and data management

The overall process of collecting and managing data can be divided into five chronological steps:

1. Establish procedures for collecting and managing the data.
2. Collect the data (including monitoring of data quality).
3. Check data quality.
4. Create data files for analysis and dissemination.
5. Establish a system to store, revise, and disseminate the data.

Although data collection and management can vary widely given that the programs, projects, or policies being evaluated can vary along many dimensions, virtually all evaluations will require each of these five steps.

The rest of this chapter discusses each of these steps in more detail. Although most of the chapter focuses on the collection of new data, much of the guidance also applies to evaluations that are based on existing data. Indeed, many impact evaluations combine new data with existing data, such as administrative data.[1] The chapter also assumes that surveys (of households, service providers, community leaders, and so on) will be the primary method used to collect new data for impact evaluations. Yet there are also more qualitative approaches for collecting new data, such as focus groups and direct observations. Such methods are discussed in chapter 22.

Establish procedures for collecting and managing the data

The first task in data collection and management is to put together a plan that describes how the data will be collected and managed. This task can be divided into several distinct components.

Choose a data manager

In general, the first decision is to choose a data manager for the impact evaluation. As explained in chapter 20, the overall impact evaluation needs to establish a team that will work on the evaluation, and one of the key positions is that of data manager. The ideal person for this job would be someone with general data management experience and with knowledge of or experience with the types of surveys used for the evaluation (such as household, service provider, community, or firm surveys).

In some situations, having two data co-managers could be beneficial, one being a high-level official from the organization managing the research project, and the other an outsider with experience in collecting and managing data for the purpose of conducting impact evaluations.

Draw the sample

Once the population has been chosen for the impact evaluation, a sample of households or other entities (for example, schools or communities) must be drawn. For randomized controlled trials, drawing the sample for data collection can be combined with random assignment of the treatment. For example, from a population of 5,000 schools, 100 can be randomly drawn to be assigned to the program and another 100 can be randomly drawn to serve as the control schools.

For nonexperimental evaluations that do not involve randomized controlled trials, a sample of households (or schools or communities) must also be drawn. If either the treated or the control households are relatively rare (are a small percentage of the general population), it may be necessary to oversample the "rare" group to ensure that there are adequate numbers of people who are treated and untreated. When participation in treatment is a choice and the sampling is based on that choice, the sampling yields a *choice-based sample*, which is a special type of stratified sampling. For a discussion of stratified and choice-based sampling, see chapter 13 and Amemiya (1985, 319–38).

Link new data collection with any existing data that will be used

In some impact evaluations, linking newly collected data with existing data already collected by the government or some other organization is beneficial. For example, some countries (such as Brazil) undertake a school census every year that includes useful information on all schools in the country. A very different example is geospatial rainfall and other weather data that are collected over many years via satellite observations. The first step in linking existing data to new data is to obtain permission to use the existing data. In some cases, obtaining such permission is difficult, so it cannot be assumed that such permission will be obtained.

Perhaps the main issue, after permission to use the data has been granted, is matching the existing data to the new data. In many, but not all, cases, some kind of code can be used for matching. For example, there may be unique school codes in the existing data, and the same codes should be used for the newly collected data. In some countries each individual may have a unique national identity number (for example, a social security number in the United States) that can be used to link new to existing data, so, if possible, collecting the national identity number in the household questionnaire will be useful.[2]

Organize a system of data entry

In general, the last step before data collection is to train interviewers, focusing on the specifics of the new questionnaire. During this final training it is almost inevitable that some errors will be found in the questionnaire that will have to be corrected. Therefore, the final version of the questionnaire should be printed in large quantities only after the training. However, even before the questionnaire has been finalized, the general system for entering the data can be established.

A general recommendation for data entry is that it should be done as soon as possible after the interviews have been completed. Indeed, if interviewers use laptop computers or smaller electronic devices such as tablets to conduct the interviews, data entry is automatically done at the time of interview. Rapid data entry allows the data entry software to find errors in time for interviewers to return to respondents to correct those errors.

However, data are often still collected using paper questionnaires, so data entry takes place after the paper questionnaires have been filled out. In such cases, a system should be set up that ensures that data entry will be done within at most a few days after the interview.

With either type of questionnaire (paper or electronic), a data entry program is needed for storing the data electronically and, more important, for checking the internal consistency of the data. Some specific recommendations regarding data entry software are the following:

- Several software programs are available. For an overview of the issues involved, with links to different computer-assisted personal interviewing software packages, see World Bank (2011).
- The software should check for internal consistency and "beep" (or send some other signal) when inconsistencies are found. If an inconsistency is found during the interview, the interviewer can re-ask questions to resolve the inconsistency. If data are entered after the interview, ideally there would be time to return to the household to resolve any inconsistencies.
- Four kinds of data checks should be conducted: (1) range checks, (2) checks against reference tables (for example, anthropometric data),[3] (3) checks that skip codes are correctly followed, and (4) checks for mutually inconsistent data.
- The draft program should be checked during the field test and the training.

Train interviewers and supervisors

Once the questionnaire has been finalized and all other preparations have been made, interviewers and supervisors should be trained in the use of the questionnaires and other survey instruments. Training should occur immediately before the data collection is scheduled to start, although (as mentioned previously) it is quite likely that some errors will be found in the questionnaires during the training, so some minor adjustments will probably need to be made and new questionnaires will need to be prepared (and the data entry program must be finalized) before the data collection can start.

General guidance on interviewer and supervisor training includes the following:

- Interviewers must understand the informational goal of each question or set of questions.
- All field team members must clearly understand the data collection goals.
- All field team members must clearly understand the intervention (if an experiment, they should know how the randomization was performed and what the control group can expect).
- If respondents are to receive financial incentives, it is crucial that they be made clear to all involved; one option is to announce them publicly.
- To ensure cooperation by households, the data collection team should
  - Train all team members to be polite and respectful;
  - Use mass media or local media to publicize the need for households and individuals to cooperate with data collection, if appropriate;
  - Obtain cooperation from local authorities;
  - Consider giving monetary or material incentives for households' cooperation (though this should be done carefully);
  - Use appropriate interviewers for particular circumstances, for example, female interviewers to ask women about family planning and fertility questions; and

- Find ways to provide privacy for sensitive topics such as attitudes toward the government or domestic violence, for instance, by conducting the interview in an outdoor area away from others or in a nearby school classroom not in use.

Collect the data (including monitoring of data quality)

Once the procedures have been established for collecting the data, the interviewers and supervisors have been trained, and the questionnaire and data entry program have been finalized, the survey teams can begin collecting the data. The data collection procedures will vary according to the program being evaluated, but some general points can be made.

Fieldwork schedule

The pilot test should provide an accurate estimate of how long it will take to collect data from a typical household (or school, or community, or firm). For the sample size chosen, this time estimate can be used to determine how many interviewers and other team members are needed, and how much time they will spend in the field.

It is also important to account for transportation, both cost and time. In many, if not most, data collection efforts, field staff spend more time moving from one area to another (and arranging accommodations and introducing themselves to local officials) than they do actually interviewing respondents.

Some other points to keep in mind regarding the fieldwork schedule are the following:

- Data should be collected at approximately the same time for the treatment group and the comparison group, especially in rural areas where work and other activities (for example, school attendance) vary according to agricultural seasons.
- Ideally, there should be a supervisor for every three to four interviewers. Supervisors should do some or all the following:
    - Observe several interviews to check that interviewers are following the established protocol.
    - Check completed questionnaires (either paper or electronic files) to ensure that they are complete, and completed correctly (for example, skip codes should be followed).
    - Randomly reinterview households to ensure that basic information is accurate (for example, all household members are included in the questionnaire).
- Top management for the evaluation should also conduct unannounced supervisory visits, to check not only the work of the interviewers but also the work of the supervisors.
- All data files should be backed up immediately after data entry, to avoid losing days or weeks of work, which may require reinterviews of survey respondents.

Methods for checking data quality in the field

To ensure that the information being collected is accurate, a variety of data quality checks should be implemented while the data are being collected. Many of these checks are specific to the type of data being collected, but several general recommendations apply in almost all circumstances. The following provides such general advice for ensuring data quality during fieldwork:

- If paper questionnaires are used, the data from those questionnaires should be recorded using the data entry program as soon as possible after the interview has been completed. The interviewer should return to the household as quickly as possible to resolve errors and inconsistencies detected by the data entry program.
- Errors will sometimes be found in the questionnaire, the data entry program, or both. New instructions for modifying the questionnaire should be provided as soon as possible to all data collection teams, and a corrected data entry program should also be quickly sent to all teams.
- All problems with data quality that cannot be resolved in the field should be immediately reported to top management.

Further advice on improving fieldwork, and more generally improving the implementation of impact evaluations, can be found in Karlan and Appel (2016). The authors present several common types of problems that can cause impact evaluations to fail, and then present six detailed case studies of evaluations that failed. More can often be learned from others' failures than from their successes.

Further checks of data quality after the fieldwork

After all data have been collected, researchers can begin to prepare the data for analysis. Before the data are analyzed, further checks should be conducted that are difficult or impossible to conduct in the field. As with data checks conducted in the field, many data quality checks after the fieldwork has been completed are specific to the type of data being collected. However, it is still possible to provide some general recommendations:

- Check for duplicate households (or schools, or communities, or firms) as indicated by identification (ID) codes; it is surprising how often duplicates are found.
- Key variables—such as income, total expenditure, quantities of food consumed, prices (including prices calculated by dividing expenditure by quantity), test scores, and health indicators—should be checked for unusually large or small values. Paper questionnaires can be checked for data entry errors, and interviewers can be contacted for clarification of unusual values for variables of interest.
- If previous data were collected from the same households (or schools or communities), they should be matched and consistency checks should be conducted to ensure that the matches are correct. For example, the ages of household members should increase by the number of years between the two periods of data collection, and the sex of, and relationships between, household members should not change over time.

- Summary statistics of key variables (income, school enrollment, disease prevalence, and so on) can be compared with other sources, such as administrative data.
- Important constructed variables (for example, total income or expenditure) should be created and compared with the same variables collected in previous surveys.
- All changes to the data should be documented, and original (uncorrected) data files should be kept if later researchers want to try different methods to handle data problems.

Create data files for analysis and dissemination

As part of the data quality checks conducted after the fieldwork is done, the first step is to assign the data from each household (or health clinic, community, or firm) to files organized by type of data. For example, many household questionnaires are divided into sections that cover different topics, such as the household roster (list of household members with basic demographic information), education, health, employment, and income. For data analysis, a separate data file for each household is not very useful. Instead, files should be created that contain data on the household roster for all households, education for all households, and so on. The data can be merged using community and household ID codes to conduct analysis.

Once the data files have been rearranged in this way, and the quality of the data has been thoroughly (but quickly) checked, the following steps are needed to prepare the data for analysis:

- Some widely used variables should be created from the data, such as total income, total expenditure, *z*-scores of anthropometric measurements, and various types of aggregate scores (for example, latent values derived from item response theory) on academic tests.
- The different thematic data sets must all have ID codes so that they can be merged with other data sets. For example, health and education data are usually individual specific, so such data from a household questionnaire should have not only the household ID number but also the individual ID numbers.
- The "levels" of data sets can also differ. Some data may be at the individual level, whereas other data are at the household level or community level. In a survey of 2,000 households with 10,000 individuals, there is no need for household-level data to have 10,000 observations; 2,000 observations (one per household) contain all the needed information, and household-level data can always be merged with individual-level data using household ID codes.
- Data from other sources, such as administrative data, should be combined with the newly collected data to enrich and expand the possible analysis. The ID codes from these other data sets may need to be modified to match those in the newly collected data.
- It may be convenient to make the data available in several different formats, such as SAS files, Stata files, and others. However, this may be unnecessary given that software is available that quickly transforms data from one type to another.

- A document should be written that explains how the data sets were created and any modifications that were made. The document should contain any code numbers that are not in the survey questionnaires and should explain how any summary variables (for example, total income, total expenditures) were created. In the long run, creating this document early on will reduce the time spent answering questions from data users.
- All data files should be backed up at regular intervals, even weekly, to avoid losing months of work to a hardware malfunction or other storage problem.

Establish a system to store, revise, and disseminate the data

Evaluations of the impact of programs, policies, or projects fall within the general field of social science research. Advances in information technology and influences from other fields of research (such as the physical and biological sciences, and in particular medicine) have led to an increase in the importance of transparency and replicability of empirical results in the social sciences. An important aspect of this improvement in social science research is the need to store, revise, and disseminate data, including data collected by impact evaluations.

In general, the organization undertaking the impact evaluation should take responsibility for storing the data, revising it (as researchers point out deficiencies in or problems with the data), and disseminating it to interested researchers. In some cases, the organization that implements the evaluation is not expected to continue indefinitely, in which case the data could be transferred to another organization (university or research institute, or government evaluation unit) that is expected to exist in perpetuity.

Of course, the details of data storage will depend on the type of program being evaluated and the kinds of data that were collected. However, the following observations and general advice should apply in a wide variety of circumstances:

- Many funding organizations now require researchers to make all data collected publicly available.
- All information that could identify survey respondents (names, addresses, national ID codes) should be removed. In some cases, the names of schools, health clinics, and local communities may also have to be removed. Variables that are removed because they identify the people from whom the data were collected can be replaced by ID codes that contain no particular information and have no use other than to identify the individuals and allow them to be matched across different data sets. The evaluation team should take care not to overlook this step.
- To defray costs and reduce frivolous requests for data, modest charges could be set for providing the data to outside researchers.
- To publicize the availability of the data, a research dissemination conference could be organized, with a large amount of publicity directed toward national and international researchers as well as the general public.
- Training courses could be set up to teach local researchers how to use the data. Local universities could incorporate the data into their research methods classes.

- If the questionnaires are in local languages, they should be translated into major international languages (English, French, Spanish, or perhaps Arabic, Russian, or Chinese), which will make them available to more users.

Conclusion

Many impact evaluations collect new data to evaluate the effectiveness of the program or policy that is being evaluated. Although it is tempting to delegate the admittedly tedious data collection and data management tasks to a group that is not particularly interested in the evaluation, researchers and evaluation teams should not give in to this temptation. Because these two tasks are complicated, they require extremely close attention, including attention to many details. This chapter provides guidance on the best ways to organize both data collection and data management. Additional recommendations can be found in Muñoz (2005).

The two general goals for data collection—timeliness and high-quality data—will sooner or later come into conflict. There is an inherent trade-off between these two goals, but careful data collection and data management will ensure that one goal is not unnecessarily sacrificed for the other. The exact point at which it is worthwhile to give less weight to one goal in return for more progress on the other is a matter of judgment and will depend in part on the needs of the organization that operates the program being evaluated.

Notes

1. See Feeney et al. (2018) for advice on using administrative data in the context of a randomized evaluation.
2. Of course, these national identifying numbers must be excluded from the data that are disseminated for public use, as explained in the last section of this chapter.
3. Anthropometric data are physical measurements of individuals, such as height, weight, upper-arm circumference, and skinfold thickness.

References

Amemiya, Takeshi. 1985. *Advanced Econometrics.* Cambridge, MA: Harvard University Press.

Feeney, Laura, Jason Bauman, Julia Chabrier, Geeti Mehra, and Michelle Woodford. 2018. "Using Administrative Data for Randomized Evaluations." J-PAL North America, Cambridge, MA. https://www.povertyactionlab.org/sites/default/files/resources/Admin_Data_Guide.pdf.

Karlan, Dean, and Jacob Appel. 2016. *Failing in the Field: What We Can Learn When Field Research Goes Wrong.* Princeton, NJ. Princeton University Press.

Muñoz, Juan. 2005. "A Guide for Data Management of Household Surveys." In *Household Sample Surveys in Developing and Transition Countries,* 305–332. Department of Economic and Social Affairs. Statistics Division. New York: United Nations. http://unstats.un.org/unsd/hhsurveys/pdf/Household_surveys.pdf.

World Bank. 2011. *Comparative Assessment of Software Programs for the Development of Computer-Assisted Personal Interview (CAPI) Applications.* LSMS Guidebook. Washington, DC: World Bank Group. https://hubs.worldbank.org/docs/imagebank/pages/docprofile.aspx?nodeid=31957645.

CHAPTER 20

Survey Management

Introduction

Most impact evaluations require new data collection, and the most common type of such data collection is a household survey. Other types of surveys are also possible, such as surveys of firms, health clinics, schools, or communities. Implementing a survey requires a variety of skills and a great deal of logistical coordination, and those with little experience in doing such work have a marked tendency to underestimate the complexity of, and thus to allocate inadequate time for, planning the implementation of the survey. Even those with more experience implementing surveys sometimes still underestimate the time and effort required.

This chapter provides an introduction to issues involved in planning and managing a survey to collect new data for conducting an impact evaluation. Because the most common type of data collection is a household survey, the emphasis is on that type of survey, but much of the advice provided in this chapter is also applicable to other types of surveys. Note that this chapter can provide only an introduction. More detailed advice can be found in Amin, Das, and Goldstein (2008), Glewwe (2005), Grosh and Muñoz (1996), and Muñoz (2005).

The following topics are discussed in this chapter: First, issues concerning budgeting and developing an overall plan of activities are reviewed. Then general advice on human resources management is presented, followed by a discussion of logistical coordination, with an emphasis on acquisition and delivery of equipment and on transportation arrangements. An introduction to community relations is provided, followed by a section that shows how errors in data collection have caused problems in actual evaluations of programs. A final section provides a brief summary and conclusion.

Budgeting and developing an overall plan of activities

The first two steps in planning an impact evaluation are to work out a budget and to develop an overall plan of activities. This section discusses both of these steps.

Budgeting

A budget consists of a list of all the materials and activities required to implement the survey and estimates of the costs of each of the items on this list. The necessary materials and activities may vary, but most of them are found in the vast majority of surveys.

This section presents the most common costs associated with conducting a survey, especially household surveys.

Personnel. A useful place to begin when determining the budget for a survey is the costs of all the personnel who are needed to implement it. A typical survey will require most or all of the following types of personnel and associated costs:

- Management (will vary by survey but often includes an overall survey manager, a data manager, and a field manager)
- Team supervisors
- Interviewers (also called enumerators)
- Data entry personnel
- Drivers
- Specialized data collection personnel (for example, for educational testing, health assessments, or anthropometric measurements)
- Accident insurance for field staff
- Training costs (rental space for meetings, accommodations, food)

How many are needed, how long they are needed, and how much they should be paid must be determined for each type of personnel. In addition, how much training will be needed for each type of personnel, so that they are prepared to perform work of sufficient quality to ensure the success of the particular survey, must be calculated. Unusual surveys and complex surveys will require relatively intensive training.

Transportation. Many evaluations require data to be collected in locations that are far from where survey personnel live and may require them to travel from one place to the next many times over the course of the survey. Thus transportation costs can often be a major component in the budget for a survey. If vehicles are purchased or rented to provide transportation, the total costs usually consist of the direct vehicle costs, fuel and maintenance, and insurance.

In some cases, public transportation may meet all transportation needs, in which case the only cost is purchase of tickets for buses, trains, ferries, airplanes, and other modes of transit. Transportation could also be a combination of public transport and purchased or rented vehicles. The exact choice will depend on the specific circumstances, and perhaps on the budget.

Equipment and supplies. Almost every household survey will make use of several different types of materials that must be included in the survey budget. The following are the most commonly required items:

- Copies of the survey questionnaires (if paper questionnaires are used)
- Other data collection items (for example, equipment to measure height and weight)
- Tablets or other handheld devices to enter data during an interview (if used)
- Laptop computers for use in the field to enter and check data
- Computers at the central office
- Data entry software
- Cell phones, and credit for calls made by the field staff and central office
- Cash, food, or other goods for use as compensation for respondents
- Cost of community meetings if held in conjunction with fieldwork (rental space, food, and so on)

The team management must first decide how many of each of these items are needed, including an allowance for extras to serve as backups in case some are lost or break down. Perhaps the very first decision is whether to use paper questionnaires or to use a digital version on laptop computers, tablets, or some other type of electronic equipment. Even if a decision is made to use electronic questionnaires, a few paper questionnaires should be kept on hand to overcome equipment problems or a lack of electricity. Pilot testing will help the survey team make this decision.

Unforeseen expenses. Even the best budget planning cannot foresee some costs that may arise during the course of the survey. Thus it is advisable to add a contingency category for such unforeseen expenses. Past experience in the country may provide guidance about how large this contingency amount should be, but if there is little experience to draw on a useful rule of thumb would be to add 10 percent to the overall budget to cover such unanticipated costs.

Overall plan of activities

Once the budget has been established, the next step is to develop an overall plan of activities. This step must come before any personnel are hired. After the survey manager is hired, a more detailed plan of activities, and a more detailed budget, can be developed. In many cases, development of the overall plan of activities will require the budget to be revised, so that the budget and overall plan of activities are developed iteratively.

The overall plan of activities should include the following:

- *Personnel.* Who is needed, and with what qualifications?
- *Training.* What training does each type of personnel need? How long will the training take?
- *Transportation.* What mode of transportation will be used that is safe, efficient, and cost-effective?
- *Timeline.* How long will it take to implement the survey? What is the best time of year to implement the survey? Will a follow-up survey be done later?
- *Revised budget.* Is the plan within the available budget?

Timeline. The hypothetical timeline for survey activities in table 20.1 provides a guide for thinking about how to develop an overall plan of activities. Note that this is only one example of the timing of activities needed to implement a survey; actual survey times can vary widely. Table 20.2 provides another type of timeline for a study that gradually phased in new health record software for three nongovernmental organizations.

Budget. A budget needs to be drawn up that includes the cost of all activities. Budgets vary enormously depending on the type of program and the evaluation method. It is always useful to check with country counterparts to obtain the in-country norms regarding the costs for travel, remuneration, translation, and other expenses. Table 20.3 provides an example of how to organize a budget. For each item in the budget, the number of units is specified along with the type of unit and the cost per unit. This exercise is performed separately for each of four stages of the evaluation (the number of stages may vary).

TABLE 20.1 Hypothetical timeline for survey activities

MONTH	TASKS	QUESTIONS TO CONSIDER
1–2	Prepare draft survey questionnaires	*Are other types of data collection instruments, such as achievement tests, needed?* *How much time is needed for an average interview?*
2	Draw up a budget and an approximate timeline	*What is more important: fewer interviewers and high supervision over many months, or using many interviewers to perform this task quickly?*
2	Hire a survey manager	
3	Revise budget and plan with survey manager	
3	Recruit, train some interviewers	
4	Pilot the survey in one or more communities. If in multiple languages, pilot the survey in each language.	*Did the survey go well? Did respondents understand the questions? What can be improved?*
4	Revise survey and training methods	
4	Hire and train remaining interviewers	*Should respondents be compensated for their time? If yes, by money or in-kind payments?*
5	Contact community leaders before team's arrival	
5–6	Visit and conduct interviews in communities	
5–6	If baseline, collect information for future contact	
5–6	Follow up for households missed by current survey	
5–7	Enter data (as soon as possible after interviews)	
7	Clean data	
7	Evaluate data collection experience	*What can be improved for follow-up data collection (if another wave of data collection will be done)?*

Source: Original table for this publication.

TABLE 20.2 Hypothetical timeline for survey activities, with visual depiction

Activity	2010					2011						2012	
		April	May	June	July	Aug.	Sep.	Oct.	Nov.	Dec.	Jan.	Feb.	Mar.
Agreements with Ministry of Health, NGOs	■												
Finalization of intervention design	■												
Software development	■												
Software installation, 1st NGO		■											
Training, 1st NGO		■											
Pilot implementation, 1st NGO			■	■	■	■	■	■	■	■			
Software installation, 2nd NGO			■										
Training, 2nd NGO			■										
Pilot implementation, 2nd NGO				■	■	■	■	■	■	■			
Software installation, 3rd NGO				■									
Training, 3rd NGO				■									
Pilot implementation, 3rd NGO					■	■	■	■	■	■	■		
Baseline health worker survey, 1st NGO		■											
Baseline health worker survey, 2nd NGO			■										
Baseline health worker survey, 3rd NGO				■									
Household surveys, 1st NGO area										■			
Household surveys, 2nd NGO area										■			
Household surveys, 3rd NGO area											■		
Analysis of monitoring data				■	■	■	■	■	■	■	■	■	■
Final analysis											■	■	■
Write evaluation paper								■	■	■	■	■	■

Source: Original table for this publication.
Note: NGO = nongovernmental organization.

TABLE 20.3 Example of a budget

	PREPARATION STAGE				INITIAL DATA COLLECTION STAGE			
	UNIT	COST PER UNIT (US$)	NUMBER OF UNITS	TOTAL COST (US$)	UNIT	COST PER UNIT (US$)	NUMBER OF UNITS	TOTAL COST (US$)
a. Salaries of local staff	Weeks	7,500	2	15,000	Weeks	7,500	2	15,000
b. Consultant fees								
Senior consultant (1)	Days	450	15	6,750	Days			
Mid-level consultant (2)	Days	350	10	3,500	Days	350	10	3,500
Research assistant or field coordinator	Days				Days	188	130	24,440
c. Travel and subsistence								
Staff: International airfare	Trips	3,350	1	3,350	Trips	3,350	1	3,350
Staff: Hotel and per diem	Days	150	5	750	Days	150	5	750
Consultants: International airfare	Trips	3,500	2	7,000	Trips	3,500	2	7,000
Consultants: Hotel and per diem	Days	150	20	3,000	Days	150	20	3,000
Field coordinator: International airfare	Trips				Trips	1,350	1	1,350
Field coordinator: Hotel and per diem	Days				Days			
d. Data collection								
Data type 1: Consent					School	120	100	12,000
Data type 2: Education outcomes					Child	14	3,000	42,000
Data type 3: Health outcomes					Child	24	3,000	72,000
Total cost per stage				**39,350**				**184,390**

continued on next page

TABLE 20.3 Example of a budget *(continued)*

	FOLLOW-UP DATA STAGE I				FOLLOW-UP DATA STAGE II			
	UNIT	COST PER UNIT (US$)	NUMBER OF UNITS	TOTAL COST (US$)	UNIT	COST PER UNIT (US$)	NUMBER OF UNITS	TOTAL COST (US$)
a. Salaries of local staff	Weeks	7,500	2	15,000	Weeks	7,500	2	15,000
b. Consultant fees								
Senior consultant (1)	Days	450	15	6,750	Days	450	10	4,500
Mid-level consultant (2)	Days	350	20	7,000	Days	350	10	3,500
Research assistant or field coordinator	Days	188	100	18,800	Days	188	130	24,440
c. Travel and subsistence								
Staff: International airfare	Trips	3,350	2	6,700	Trips	3,350	2	6,700
Staff: Hotel and per diem	Days	150	10	1,500	Days	150	10	1,500
Consultants: International airfare	Trips	3,500	2	7,000	Trips	3,500	2	7,000
Consultants: Hotel and per diem	Days	150	20	3,000	Days	150	20	3,000
Field coordinator: International airfare	Trips	1,350	1	1,350	Trips	1,350	1	1,350
Field coordinator: Hotel and per diem	Days	150	3	450	Days	150	3	450
d. Data collection								
Data type 1: Consent								
Data type 2: Education outcomes	Child	14	3,000	42,000	Child	14	3,000	42,000
Data type 3: Health outcomes	Child	24	3,000	72,000	Child	24	3,000	72,000

continued on next page

TABLE 20.3 Example of a budget *(continued)*

	FOLLOW-UP DATA STAGE I				FOLLOW-UP DATA STAGE II			
	UNIT	COST PER UNIT (US$)	NUMBER OF UNITS	TOTAL COST (US$)	UNIT	COST PER UNIT (US$)	NUMBER OF UNITS	TOTAL COST (US$)
e. Other								
Workshops						20,000	2	40,000
Dissemination and reporting						5,000	3	15,000
Total cost per stage				**181,550**				**236,440**
Total budgeted costs								**641,730**
Contingency costs (of 10%)								**64,173**
Total evaluation costs								**705,903**

Source: Original table for this publication.

Human resources (personnel) management

The composition of the survey staff for any evaluation will vary by the type of program being evaluated and by the evaluation methodology. Two general issues faced for almost any evaluation are the number of staff needed, which depends in part on how quickly the data are to be collected, and what to do when some staff quit or are let go in the middle of the data collection effort.

The number of staff needed depends on the answer to the following question: Is it more important to finish data collection quickly or to have highly trained personnel who are supervised closely? If the data need to be collected quickly, the evaluation team will need to hire a large number of data collection personnel, but if speed is less important than data quality, the team should hire a small number of data collection personnel and train them more intensively (and supervise them more closely). This choice depends on time pressure and the complexity of the data collection. For all staff needed, it will be important to have job descriptions prepared, along with a plan for advertising and recruitment, and to start the recruitment process early.

Turning to the issue of staff attrition, almost any data collection effort will experience at least some turnover of its fieldworkers, either because the work is demanding or because some workers perform poorly and need to be replaced. One approach is to hire more staff to participate in training than will be needed for the evaluation and to make a final selection of the best staff after training. If staff quit or perform poorly, the evaluation team can then replace them with some of the people who participated in the training but were not selected at the end of the training.

The rest of this section explains in detail what types of personnel are needed, including their qualifications and the tasks for which they will be responsible, and then provides some additional advice regarding personnel.

Qualifications and responsibilities of survey personnel

The following discussion describes the types of survey personnel that are typically needed for almost any type of evaluation. For each type, the qualifications, as well as the tasks that they are expected to perform, are described.

Survey manager. Virtually every evaluation that will collect new data will require a survey manager. In general, this person should be a social scientist, a statistician, or a specialist who works on the type of program being evaluated, such as a health or education specialist. The survey manager should have a graduate degree or at least a college (bachelor's) degree. This is a senior position. The survey manager has substantial decision-making authority and should be involved in every step of the survey design. He or she should regularly communicate with the research team and the field team.

Data manager. Usually, a second person is needed to focus on management of the data collected by the evaluation. This person should have strong data management experience, as well as statistical skills and computer skills. This is also a senior position. The data manager chooses the software to use for data entry, writes the data entry manuals, and manages the data entry operators. He or she also prepares the data sets for analysis and may produce some basic tables with results.

Field manager. Having a separate manager who oversees the actual collection of data in the field is also generally recommended. The field manager should have strong management experience, preferably in managing surveys. He or she should also have good computer skills. The field manager is in charge of all field procedures, including training field staff, managing local communication, and developing sampling procedures.

Field supervisors. Data collection personnel are often organized into small teams that work in different areas. Each team should have its own field supervisor who manages the work responsibilities assigned to that team. Desirable qualifications for this position include experience managing people and the ability to pay attention to a wide variety of details. A secondary education is also a minimum requirement. Field supervisors do much of the same work as the field manager, but at the team level. They serve as liaisons between individual interviewers and the field manager.

Interviewers. The individuals who collect data from respondents or from other sources are the interviewers, who are sometimes referred to as enumerators. In general, they should have a secondary education, but more education is not necessarily an advantage because the rate of turnover tends to be higher among people who are more highly educated. In addition to administering the survey questionnaires, the interviewers' responsibilities include establishing initial contact with households and other individuals who provide data (for example, teachers, health care professionals), selecting individual respondents, and ensuring completion of the survey.

Specialists. Sometimes special types of data are collected, which may require certain types of personnel. For example, evaluations of health programs may require the collection of indicators of health, such as height, weight, and even a blood sample. Another example, which is relevant for evaluations of education programs, is the administration of tests to individuals to measure their knowledge and skills. Although specialists to perform these tasks should have a secondary education, a medical or other degree may not be necessary because in many cases these individuals can be trained to collect this type of data. Of course, their responsibilities will vary depending on the specific project.

Data entry operators. If interviewers use paper questionnaires, data entry staff will be needed to transfer the information from the completed paper questionnaires into electronic files. They are responsible for inputting all survey data. These data entry operators need to have only basic computer literacy; they can be trained in a relatively short time (for example, one week) to learn how to use the specific data entry software. Data entry operators may enter data from paper questionnaires using a laptop or another mobile device in the field, or may receive completed paper questionnaires at an office and input data there. They are expected to identify potential errors in the data, and in the data entry software, and to notify the field team as soon as possible when any potential errors are found.

Further considerations regarding personnel

Several issues regarding the composition of survey staff merit additional attention. The first relates to the gender of the staff. Depending on the cultural requirements of each area and security considerations, it may be important to consider whether the interviewers should be male, female, or a mix. In some cultures, women are discouraged from talking to males who are strangers, which suggests that female interviewers may be needed to interview female survey respondents. On the other hand, security situations might put women in more danger than men, which may indicate a need to reduce or dispense with female interviewers in those areas. In most cases, national statistical agencies with experience in making these types of decisions can be called upon for guidance.

A second, similar point regarding composition of survey staff is the religious, ethnic, and linguistic characteristics of the respondents. Ideally, interviewers should be fluent in the language of the respondents, and in countries with multiple languages the survey staff should be chosen to cover as many languages as possible. Language issues aside, to gain the confidence of the respondents it may also be helpful for interviewers to belong to the same religious or ethnic group as the respondents.

Third, depending on the scale of the project and the qualifications of specific staff members, it may be possible to combine roles. For example, one person could be both the data manager and the field manager (if he or she is qualified for both positions). Another example is that, for each survey team, one interviewer or other team member may also be able to take on the role of team supervisor. This person could be someone whose data collection responsibilities are less time-consuming, such as a specialist or the field data entry person.

Training

Training serves two distinct purposes. The first is to train survey team members on how to implement the survey instruments correctly and consistently. The second is to determine which trainees are the most qualified to do the actual fieldwork. (Recall that it is usually advisable to train more individuals than are needed to have a reserve of trained people to call on if some survey personnel leave before the data collection is finished).

Training is a complex activity, but in most cases it includes the following components:

- *Orientation.* All personnel must understand the overall purpose of the evaluation, especially if it is a randomized evaluation. Every team member should be able to clearly explain the evaluation activities in a way that provides a consistent message to anyone who expresses interest in the evaluation.
- *Role playing.* Every interviewer trainee should have a chance to practice implementing the survey and to be critiqued.
- *Evaluating.* Training is an important opportunity to evaluate interviewers before sending them into the field. Evaluating and grading each potential interviewer on a variety of criteria can be very useful, including for the selection of those who will carry out the actual fieldwork.

Logistical coordination

Although it may seem straightforward, keeping track of logistics for a large-scale survey can be complex, and logistics are a key element of a survey's success. It is important to ensure the following, at a minimum:

- Vehicles must be in good working order and have adequate fuel supplies.
- Specific plans must be made for accommodations in the field.
- A system must be set up to ensure adequate supplies of work-related materials (copies of the survey questionnaires and other required forms).
- A cushion of time and personnel should be available in case team members become ill or injured, or other unforeseen events occur.
- Smooth communication channels (via phone, email, phone applications such as WhatsApp or Slack) must be put in place between supervisors and other members of the team. File sharing tools, such as Google Docs, Microsoft OneDrive, or team websites, can also help teams communicate and share information.

One aspect of logistics that deserves special attention is security. In some areas, fieldwork is a risky activity. Before going into the field, obtaining up-to-date information on local security concerns is worthwhile, including the following:

- *Transportation.* Is it safe to use local public transportation (considering risk of traffic accidents as well as crime)? Are field personnel exposing themselves to increased risks if they carry equipment such as laptops and tablets? Discussions with, and possibly hiring of, local professional drivers can be useful to increase the security of transportation arrangements.
- *Crime.* Is it risky for field staff to travel into remote areas or at night? Is it possible to work with local partners who are able to mitigate such risks?
- *Accommodations.* Are accommodations available that are reasonably safe for survey team members?
- *Gender-based crime.* Are women at higher risk than men in survey areas? If so, how can this risk be reduced?

Community relations

Almost all impact evaluations involve collecting data from local communities, and survey personnel need to develop good relationships with both the leaders and the general population in those communities to ensure that the work goes smoothly. This section provides some general suggestions for developing and maintaining good relationships with the local community.

First, before visiting the community, a letter or some other type of message should be sent to local leaders telling them of the nature of the data collection, the overall purpose of the activity, and the approximate dates. It is helpful if this letter is accompanied by a general letter from a government official stating that the government supports this data collection effort and requests that local community leaders assist the survey teams in carrying out their work. National statistical agencies usually have experience with this and should have letters that have proven to be effective.

Second, when arriving in the community, the survey team should first go to local leaders before making any other contact with community members. At that time, additional information on the data collection and, more generally, on the impact evaluation should be provided to community leaders. These community leaders can then be asked to explain to survey respondents that they support this activity and to ask the respondents to cooperate with the data collection.

Third, to ensure cooperation, survey personnel need to treat everyone in the community with respect. If the fieldworkers are recruiting individuals to participate in the study, it is important that they not pressure hesitant individuals to participate. In particular, to conduct ethical research informed consent must be obtained from study participants. This means that study participants should be informed that they are part of a study, and the data collection team should explain clearly to them the type of data being collected from them and how the researchers will use these data. Fieldworkers should provide this information in a clear and culturally appropriate way to ensure that participants have an accurate understanding of their role in the study. See chapter 10 for further discussion of how to treat study participants ethically.

Finally, in some situations providing token gifts to local leaders and to households may be helpful. National statistical agencies often have standard protocols for whether this is appropriate, and in general they should be followed. These gifts, however, should not be of significant value because that may create pressure on households to participate that otherwise do not want to participate.

Lessons from unfortunate experiences

This section provides four real world examples of how failure to follow the guidelines provided in this chapter led to serious problems with evaluations.

China eyeglasses study and the need to inform the team. Glewwe, Park, and Zhao (2016) conducted a randomized controlled trial that examined the effect of having access to eyeglasses on educational outcomes for primary school students in China. Not all of the money in the budget for purchasing eyeglasses for the treatment group was spent. In a few townships, the unspent funds were used to buy eyeglasses for students in the control group. This obviously contaminated the control group, which should not have been given eyeglasses until after the study was completed. Because of this, 40 percent of the sample was lost, which probably could have been avoided if every member of the research team understood the importance of the experimental design.

Food stamps in Jamaica. As part of the 1988 Jamaica Survey of Living Conditions, respondents were asked if they had received food stamps in the past month.[1] Many food stamp recipients indicated that they had not. It was later discovered that this was because food stamps are distributed every two months. This type of error would likely have been discovered by careful piloting of the survey instrument.

Preschool study in Guatemala. In an evaluation of a preschool program in Guatemala, survey teams explained to families whose children were on a waiting list for preschool that the children who would be able to attend preschool the following year would be determined randomly by a lottery. They were also informed that families that were not selected would be compensated with a bag of food for the time they spent responding to the survey. Many families misinterpreted the message and expected ongoing financial benefits. When these benefits did not materialize, families suspected preschool teachers had stolen the goods. Frustrated by the experience, preschool teachers stopped collaborating with the study, demonstrating the importance of clear communication with survey teams and between survey teams and study participants. For further information, see Humpage (2012).

Matching students and schools in Vietnam. In the 2006 Vietnam Household Living Standards Survey, which collected detailed information on education, the household survey questionnaire did not collect information from students on where their school was located, because it was assumed that all children would attend schools in their own communes. This proved not to be true: many secondary school students attended schools that were not located in their communes. Thus for many students it was not possible to match child data to school data because it was not clear whether the school code for those children referred to a school in their commune or to a school in a neighboring commune.

Conclusion

This chapter provides an overview of how to plan and manage a survey to collect new data for the purpose of conducting an impact evaluation. The most common type of data collection for impact evaluation is a household survey, so most of the discussion focuses on how to conduct such a survey. However, most of the advice in this chapter can be applied to other types of surveys and data collection efforts. Even so, this chapter is only an introduction to this topic. More detailed advice can be found in the references.

Once data have been collected and analyzed, the next task for the evaluation team is to disseminate the results and, hopefully, to influence policy makers. These issues are taken up in the next chapter.

Note

1. See https://microdata.worldbank.org/index.php/catalog/2317/related-materials for information on this household survey questionnaire.

References

Amin, Samia, Jishnu Das, and Marcus Goldstein, eds. 2008. *Are You Being Served? New Tools for Measuring Service Delivery.* Washington, DC: World Bank.

Glewwe, Paul. 2005. "Overview of the Implementation of Household Surveys in Developing Countries." In *Household Sample Surveys in Developing and Transition Countries,* 53–66. Department of Economic and Social Affairs. Statistics Division. New York: United Nations. http://unstats.un.org/unsd/hhsurveys/pdf/Household_surveys.pdf.

Glewwe, Paul, Albert Park, and Meng Zhao. 2016. "A Better Vision for Development: Eyeglasses and Academic Performance in Rural Primary Schools in China." *Journal of Development Economics* 122 (September): 170–82.

Grosh, Margaret, and Juan Muñoz. 1996. "A Manual for Planning and Implementing the Living Standards Measurement Study Survey." Living Standards Measurement Study Working Paper 126, World Bank, Washington, DC. http://documents.worldbank.org/curated/en/1996/05/438573/manual-planning-implementing-living-standards-measurement-study-survey.

Humpage, Sarah. 2012. "When Are Field Experiments with Individual Assignment Too Risky? Lessons from a Center-Based Child Care Study in Guatemala." Technical Note IDB-TN-469, Inter-American Development Bank, Washington, DC.

Muñoz, Juan. 2005. "A Guide for Data Management of Household Surveys." In *Household Sample Surveys in Developing and Transition Countries,* 305–32. Department of Economic and Social Affairs. Statistics Division. New York: United Nations. http://unstats.un.org/unsd/hhsurveys/pdf/Household_surveys.pdf.

PART V

Related Topics

CHAPTER 21

Dissemination of Results and Working with Policy Makers

Introduction

The ultimate goal of impact evaluation is to improve government policies. Once one or more rigorous impact evaluations have been conducted, the results need to be disseminated to a wide variety of interested parties who will act on them. Perhaps the most important audience for impact evaluation results is government policy makers. They are the ones who need to be convinced that policy changes suggested by impact evaluations are worth doing.

This chapter provides an overview of the issues regarding how to disseminate results and how to work with policy makers to ensure that improved policies, based on rigorous impact evaluations, are actually implemented. It begins with a discussion of which products need to be delivered by the impact evaluation team, and then provides advice on how those products should be disseminated. It ends with some general guidance on how to work with policy makers.

What products should the impact evaluation deliver?

The following products are usually provided by the impact evaluation team to interested parties:

- Impact evaluation plan
- Baseline report
- Preliminary results report
- Final results report
- Specialized policy briefs
- Data sets

Each of these is explained in more detail in the rest of this section.

Impact evaluation plan

Before beginning the actual evaluation, the impact evaluation team needs to develop a plan for conducting the evaluation. This plan should be sent to all interested parties to see whether they are in agreement with it. The two most important parties to obtain approval from are the government agency most closely tied to the program being evaluated and the funding agency (if funding comes from a source other than the implementing agency). Much of the content of this plan is discussed in earlier chapters, in particular chapters 2, 18, 19, and 20. However, a draft outline will prove useful. Table 21.1 presents a draft outline, adapted from Gertler et al. (2011), which should serve as a good starting point for developing an impact evaluation plan.

Baseline report

As discussed in several earlier chapters, baseline data are often collected from both individuals (or service providers, or communities, or firms) who participate in the program and those who do not participate. After the baseline data are collected, it may be necessary to wait for one or two years before any follow-up data are collected. This time should be spent examining the baseline data to get a better idea of the conditions faced by the population in question, and checking whether certain assumptions of the impact evaluation plan do in fact hold.

There are two main objectives of the baseline report: (1) to describe baseline (preprogram) characteristics and outcomes of the population of interest, and (2) to check whether the evaluation plan will in fact work. The suggested outline in table 21.2, also from Gertler et al. (2011), is a good starting point for preparing a baseline report.

TABLE 21.1 Suggested outline for an impact evaluation plan

1. Introduction
2. Description of the intervention
3. Objectives of the evaluation (hypotheses, theory of change, policy questions, key outcome indicators)
4. Evaluation design (which may include a pre-analysis plan, as discussed in chapter 8)
5. Sampling and data (including power calculations, as explained in chapter 9)
6. Data collection plan (including baseline and follow-up surveys)
7. Products to be delivered (the topic of this chapter)
8. Dissemination plan for results (also a topic of this chapter)
9. Important ethical considerations
10. Timeline
11. Budget and funding
12. Composition of evaluation team

Source: Adapted from Gertler et al. 2011.

TABLE 21.2 Suggested outline for a baseline report

1. Introduction
2. Description of the intervention (including whether it has changed)
3. Objectives of the evaluation (usually the same as in the impact evaluation plan)
4. Evaluation design (including any changes in response to new information since the impact evaluation plan was written)
5. Sampling and data (including what data have been collected thus far)
6. Validation of evaluation design (for example, checking for balance in the randomized controlled trial, or for continuity of the variable that determines eligibility in a regression discontinuity design)
7. Descriptive statistics from baseline data (the largest section of the report)
8. Recommendations for any changes to the impact evaluation plan

Source: Adapted from Gertler et al. 2011.

Preliminary results report

In many situations, interested parties would like to know the results as soon as possible. In such cases, preliminary results might be provided relatively quickly. Such results will have some or all of the following characteristics:

- The methods used are relatively simple.
- Only the first round of follow-up data has been collected.
- Data may not be available yet for the full sample (in which case extreme care must be taken in determining whether the data available are representative).
- Some variables that require a large amount of time to construct are not yet available.

If the evaluation is a randomized controlled trial, this report should also provide information on the extent to which the treatment and control groups comply with their treatment assignments. For randomized controlled trials, it is absolutely crucial to monitor and report, and to the extent possible take measures to reduce, noncompliance; this should be done as early as possible.

The outline of the preliminary results report will be similar to that of the final report, which is presented next, although the preliminary results it contains are generally not as comprehensive as the results provided in the final report.

Final results report

The main purpose of the final results report is to present all the evaluation results, which ideally will address all of the policy questions that were to be answered by the impact evaluation. Of course, the final report should be based on a valid strategy for estimating causal impacts, which needs to be explained clearly in the report (with technical material put into a technical appendix).

The final report should include the following:

- A clear description of the intervention that is being evaluated, including both the original plan for implementation and how it was actually implemented
- A description of the original evaluation plan, including a description of the purpose of the program and the main policy questions
- A complete description of the sampling plan, including any problems that arose in practice, and a description of the data actually collected
- A detailed presentation of the results and their implications for the key policy questions

Table 21.3 provides a suggested outline for the final report, which should serve as a starting point for most types of final reports. This suggested outline should be modified to fit the specific intervention and the specific evaluation method.

Specialized policy briefs

The final report is likely to be at least 50 pages long, and 100–200 page reports are quite common. Although this length provides a thorough evaluation of the intervention, it will also greatly reduce the number of people who actually read the report. To maximize readership of the results of the evaluation, shorter policy briefs should be written that omit detail (which can be found in the final report, and that report should be referenced in the policy brief) but provide the overall conclusions in an easy-to-read format. For simple interventions, one brief may be sufficient, but for more complex interventions (for example, those that compare several different policies or programs) multiple briefs (for example, one for each policy or one for each of the major outcomes of interest) may be useful.

TABLE 21.3 Suggested outline for a final report

1. Introduction
2. Description of the intervention (both design and actual implementation)
3. Objectives of the evaluation (policy questions, hypotheses, key outcomes)
4. Evaluation design (both the original plan and how it was actually implemented)
5. Sampling (including power calculations) and data (both the plan and what was actually collected, with detailed discussions of deviations from the plan)
6. Validation of the evaluation design (same as in baseline report)
7. Complete results (the largest section of the report)
8. Robustness checks (alternative estimators, checks of statistical assumptions)
9. Conclusions and policy recommendations

Source: Adapted from Gertler et al. 2011.

Effective policy briefs typically have the following three characteristics:

1. Short (2–3 pages, or small brochures)
2. Colorful, with bright graphics, data visualizations, and photographs of the program in action
3. Readable, with no specialized jargon or technical details

Examples of policy briefs can be found on the websites of major international organizations, such as the World Bank, and of research organizations that specialize in impact evaluations, such as the Abdul Latif Jameel Poverty Action Lab (J-PAL).

Data sets

A final important product is the data sets used in the analysis. These should be made public so that additional data analysis can be conducted by interested parties and so that skeptics can see for themselves where the results come from.

In addition to the data sets themselves, the following accompanying materials should be provided:

- A user's guide document that explains the sampling scheme, how the data were collected, how the final data sets were created, and how to merge one data set with another. This may also include a codebook describing variables.
- The software programs used to generate the results, including the programs used to create the tables in the final report (and in any other reports).
- The original survey instruments (which in some cases could be used in place of a codebook).
- A table with some key descriptive statistics.

Providing these materials along with the data set will make it easier for interested parties to replicate the results and potentially provide new results. If the accompanying materials are well written, they will also reduce inquiries on how to use the data.

Dissemination of the findings

Dissemination of the results from an impact evaluation should take many different forms, depending on the audience. Dissemination plans should be developed early in the impact evaluation process. *Do not wait until the end!*

Working with communications and knowledge management experts will help shape the reports and outreach plans to better match the different audiences. These experts will be able to contribute to a range of tasks, including the writing and editing of the reports, the shaping of the main messages from the results, the data visualizations to communicate some of the findings, and different ways to communicate the conclusions to optimize reach and influence.

Most impact evaluations have multiple audiences. The following audiences are the most common:

- Policy makers
- Civil society (nongovernmental groups interested in the outcomes that the program seeks to have an impact on)
- The media
- Bilateral and international aid organizations
- Academic audiences
- Beneficiaries of the intervention, or the affected populations

Different audiences will be interested in different types of dissemination products. For example, policy makers will be interested in the preliminary report, the final report, and the various policy briefs. In contrast, civil society organizations and the media will tend to limit their attention to the policy briefs. Bilateral and international aid organizations will be interested in final reports and policy briefs, and academic audiences will be interested in the final reports, but also in the data and the associated accompanying materials.

Finally, the results of an impact evaluation can be disseminated in many ways, which can vary according to the particular audiences. The most common forms are the following:

- Policy maker conferences, which are usually held in a relevant government ministry. Others involved in impact evaluations may also be invited to comment.
- Research conferences, which are relatively technical and held at prominent universities or research institutions.
- Publication in scholarly journals or relevant professional publications.
- Exposure through the popular media, such as newspaper stories, radio or television interviews, or social media, such as Twitter.
- Publication online: ministry website or a research organization website or blog. In general, all policy briefs and reports should be made available online.

Working with policy makers

The ultimate aim of impact evaluations is to improve government policies, so it is important that the evaluation team develop a strong working relationship with policy makers to ensure that the results lead to improved policies. The following discussion provides suggestions for working with policy makers.

The first recommendation is to start building relationships with policy makers at the very beginning of the evaluation process. Indeed, relationships should be established before almost anything else is done. One simple way to begin is to meet with government officials to ask for more information about how the program actually works or is intended to work. In these early meetings, policy makers may indicate what information would be most useful to them and what policy decisions they will face. This knowledge is worthwhile to researchers because they may not always know which policies the government may be open to changing and which other policies the government may be completely unwilling to change.

A second suggestion is that the evaluation team itself should include policy makers, or at least government officials selected by key policy makers. However, their inclusion needs to be done carefully. Although policy maker participation is valuable, it is also important for the research team to maintain independence and be wary of political motivations that may be behind attempts to influence the research questions or results.

A third recommendation for working with policy makers is that agreements should be established, early in the process, on how the results will be disseminated. A particularly important issue is how to report results in the event that the program does not appear to be effective. By definition, any evaluation will be unlikely to detect effects that are smaller than the evaluation design's minimum detectable effect size (see chapter 9 for a thorough discussion of this topic). The evaluation team's description of how it will present insignificant or significantly negative estimated impacts may be reassuring to the relevant policy makers.

This chapter closes with two examples of how to disseminate results and work with policy makers. The first focuses on a specific intervention: providing deworming medicine to primary-school-age students. In 2004, Miguel and Kremer (2004) published a paper reporting the results of a randomized evaluation of a school deworming program. They found that the program reduced the absenteeism rate by one-quarter, and it also improved child health. Furthermore, the program had significant spillover effects because both untreated children in treatment schools and children in neighboring schools benefited from the intervention.[1] This intervention was also more cost-effective than alternative strategies for boosting student attendance. Motivated by their findings, the authors have collaborated with others to promote this policy in developing countries, starting a nonprofit called Deworm the World (https://www.evidenceaction.org/dewormtheworld/). This nonprofit's mission is to promote school-based deworming programs.

A second example pertains more to disseminating research results to policy makers. Researchers from the Jameel Poverty Action Lab (J-PAL, www.povertyactionlab.org) at the Massachusetts Institute for Technology have promoted information from their affiliates' research through online documents they call "Policy Insights." These documents present the results from various studies in an accessible and visually appealing format. One example is an online document on the benefits of providing insecticide-treated bednets free of charge.[2] These documents synthesize research results in such a way that the audience can learn from a large number of studies without reading each one. They present the findings of the studies, as well as practical policy implications.

Conclusion

The final objective of any impact evaluation is to improve government policies. Even a well-executed evaluation could be deemed to have failed if governments and other relevant parties do not incorporate the results of the evaluations when they formulate their policies. Thus researchers need to convince policy makers of the usefulness of their results.

This chapter provides basic recommendations for researchers for disseminating their results and work to policy makers to ensure that improved policies, as determined by rigorous impact evaluations, are in fact implemented. More specifically, this chapter explains the types of products that the impact evaluation team should produce and how those products should be disseminated. It concludes with general advice on working with policy makers.

Notes

1. Two papers by epidemiologists (Aiken et al. 2015; Davey et al. 2015) have raised questions concerning some of the findings in Miguel and Kremer (2004). Hicks, Kremer, and Miguel (2015) respond to these criticisms, and Hargreaves et al. (2015) comment on their response.
2. See the J-PAL website at https://doi.org/10.31485/pi.2270.2018.

References

Aiken, Alexander M., Calum Davey, James R. Hargreaves, and Richard J. Hayes. 2015. "Re-analysis of Health and Educational Impacts of a School-Based Deworming Programme in Western Kenya: A Pure Replication." *International Journal of Epidemiology* 44 (5): 1572–80.

Davey, Calum, Alexander M. Aiken, Richard J. Hayes, and James R. Hargreaves. 2015."Re-analysis of Health and Educational Impacts of a School-Based Deworming Programme in Western Kenya: A Statistical Replication of a Cluster Quasi-Randomized Stepped-Wedge Trial." *International Journal of Epidemiology* 44 (5): 1581–92.

Gertler, Paul, Sebastian Martinez, Patrick Premand, Laura Rawlings, and Christel Vermeersch. 2011. *Impact Evaluation in Practice*. Washington, DC: World Bank.

Hargreaves, James R., Alexander M. Aiken, Calum Davey, and Richard J. Hayes. 2015. "Authors' Response To: Deworming Externalities and School Impacts in Kenya." *International Journal of Epidemiology* 44 (5): 1596–99.

Hicks, Joan Hamory, Michael Kremer, and Edward Miguel. 2015. "Commentary: Deworming Externalities and Schooling Impacts in Kenya: A Comment on Aiken et al. (2015) and Davey et al. (2015)." *International Journal of Epidemiology* 44 (5): 1593–96.

Miguel, Edward, and Michael Kremer. 2004. "Worms: Identifying Impacts on Education and Health in the Presence of Treatment Externalities." *Econometrica* 72 (1): 159–217.

CHAPTER 22

Qualitative Approaches, Data, and Analysis in Impact Evaluations

Joan DeJaeghere

Introduction

International organizations, scholars, and practitioners have repeatedly called for expanding the approaches and methods used in impact evaluation. Qualitative research that uses rigorous and relevant approaches, methods, and analysis can be as useful as quantitative designs and data, whether experimental, quasi-experimental, or nonexperimental, to understand different impacts of interventions. This chapter discusses how qualitative research can be combined with quantitative analyses, both by conducting mixed-methods evaluations or in stand-alone studies.

For this chapter, qualitative approaches are ways in which researchers and evaluators attempt to understand and explain phenomena, such as educational programs, by analyzing rich and detailed data that reveal meanings, contexts, and processes. Qualitative researchers use different assumptions, stances, methods, and analyses than quantitative researchers, and there are many variations of qualitative approaches, data, and analysis. This chapter also uses the commonly accepted term *mixed methods*, which generally refers to the combination of different methods of data collection, such as surveys, interviews, and observations. However, *mixed designs* is a more appropriate—though less used—term, because the evaluations referred to in this chapter generally combine designs, such as randomized controlled trials (RCTs) and case studies, or quasi-experimental designs using survey data with longitudinal interviews, which entails not only mixing methods (types of data collection) but also mixing designs and analyses (research methodologies).

This chapter is organized as follows: The next section explains the different ways that qualitative research can contribute to impact evaluations and reviews reasons for several challenges in using qualitative research in such evaluations. It is followed by a section that sets out two different perspectives, interpretive and realist, that lead to different qualitative approaches. Next comes a discussion of different purposes and designs of qualitative research that are used to answer different types of questions in impact evaluations. The subsequent section briefly summarizes the most common types of methods used and data collected by qualitative researchers. The following section discusses several frequently used approaches: case-based, qualitative longitudinal, and theory-based qualitative studies.

Two studies are summarized to show how these approaches can be used, alone or together, for different exploratory or explanatory purposes. The final section presents practical suggestions for designing, gathering, and analyzing qualitative data within the context of conducting mixed-methods impact evaluations. There is not enough space in this chapter to cover the details of different methodologies or methods for analysis; however, references to good empirical examples are given throughout. For more discussion of these topics, see DeJaeghere et al. (2019).

Contributions and challenges in using qualitative research in impact evaluations

Although evaluations based on well-implemented RCTs or other experimental and quasi-experimental designs can show whether an intervention, such as an education program, has had an impact on program participants, these analyses are limited in their explanations for the results, or in being able to capture the complexity of some phenomena under study. There are various reasons for using qualitative research, both for general exploratory or quasi-experimental studies and for impact assessment, including the following:

- Some phenomena simply do not lend themselves to quasi-experiments because they are too complex, or their long-term effects are not easily discernible (or too costly to measure) through a quasi-experimental study.
- Some phenomena of interest may not be ready for an intervention and examination of impact, and thus a more exploratory analysis may be needed.
- Some interventions and their effects are not amenable to or ethically feasible for randomization and the identification of a comparison group, or they may involve too few participants.
- Experimental studies answer one important yet narrow causal question: What is the average net effect of an intervention on a particular outcome of interest? Qualitative studies can offer further explanations, causal or inferential, for understanding why and how the effects happened.
- Qualitative studies can enhance the generalizability (external validity) of causal claims produced through quasi-experiments, or provide explanations for why the claims may not hold for other contexts and populations.
- Qualitative studies can be used to identify both positive and negative unintended effects of an intervention.

Even though qualitative research and data can make these important contributions to our understanding of interventions and their effects, it is less clear among researchers, evaluators, and practitioners precisely *how* to integrate qualitative methods and data into impact evaluations. The fundamental question is, How can effective mixed-methods designs be implemented so that each type of data and analysis adds to the explanation of impacts? Too often, evaluations include both quantitative and qualitative data, but they are analyzed separately with little or no integration of these two methodological approaches (Garbarino and Holland 2009). In contrast, Bamberger (2015), Bamberger, Rao, and Woolcock (2010), and Greene and Caracelli (2003) offer examples of how mixed-methods designs integrate qualitative and quantitative methods and data at different phases of the research—in the design, in the data collection, and in the analysis.

Despite many efforts to undertake mixed-methods evaluations, combining qualitative and quantitative designs and data to explain program impacts is challenging. These challenges occur at each of the three different stages of the research: design, implementation and data gathering, and analysis and use. There are at least three reasons for these challenges:

1. Difficulties in framing the purpose and questions as a mixed-methods design because researchers and evaluators think of designs only from within their practiced approaches, which can result in a mismatch between research questions and data

2. Lack of clarity on whether and how to combine different types of qualitative and quantitative data at both the data-gathering and analysis stages so that the data can provide comprehensive answers to the evaluation questions, which can lead to underutilization of both types of data

3. Lack of understanding of the purposes and credibility of qualitative research on the part of policy makers and practitioners, which can lead to misinterpretation of the findings

The first reason for these challenges arises at the framing or design stage of the research, suggesting a need for greater clarity regarding the distinction between using mixed-methods research designs versus simply gathering mixed-methods data. Evaluators often gather data without sufficient thought as to how different types of data relate to the overall purpose and the questions to be answered. For example, if quantitative survey data (based on closed-ended questions) and qualitative interviews (semistructured or unstructured interviews with open-ended questions) are both used to gather data, researchers and evaluators need to decide whether these methods, and their respective data, answer similar evaluation questions—which implies that both forms of data should be used to triangulate findings—or whether the data answer different evaluation questions.

These issues need to be addressed in the early stages of the evaluation design. However, evaluation questions are often written within the framework of one approach, or by evaluators trained in a particular perspective (for example, quasi-experimental designs), and then the way in which the evaluation question is framed does not easily allow for other methods and data to be used. Consider, for example, this question: *Did the program intervention have different effects on young women and men?* Evaluators from a quantitative perspective (meaning an empiricist perspective on causality and attribution) might assume that this question is best answered with survey data analyzed through different types of statistical estimation methods, such as structural equation modeling or difference-in-differences estimation. From a qualitative perspective, this question could also be answered through data from open-ended and in-depth interviews using qualitative comparative analysis or process tracing to explain differences and effects. But often researchers or evaluators from these different perspectives who work together on a team may not fully understand each other's perspectives, and how such data could answer the questions of differential effects. In addition, simply collecting qualitative data from interviews, without a design plan of how the data need to be analyzed to answer the question, is ineffective. Yet many evaluations simply "add" qualitative data to a quantitative evaluation without a design and analysis plan. Therefore, a mixed-methods design not only refers to the types of quantitative and qualitative data collected but also considers the purposes for which the data will be used and how they will be analyzed (see Pawson 2002; Ragin 2014). Although this seems logical and indisputable, many evaluations have not been designed to include both quantitative and qualitative data to answer specific evaluation questions, and little thought has been given to how the analyses, particularly of qualitative data, would answer the questions.

The second set of challenges that hinders using a combination of quantitative and qualitative data in impact evaluations occurs at the data collection, analysis, and interpretation phases. It is important to know whether qualitative and quantitative data will be used to answer similar questions or different questions, which affects the timing of data collection and the analysis processes. There are at least two common approaches here: (1) the question can be answered by both quantitative and qualitative data, and the data are gathered and analyzed concurrently; or (2) there are different questions, and the timing and analysis of different data will depend on which questions are answered with quantitative data and which with qualitative data.

Taking the same main evaluation question as above—*Did the program intervention have different effects on young women and men?*—different types of data could be collected and analyzed concurrently to find an answer. For example, surveys may use questions linked directly to the intended outcomes, such as whether the program increased employment for young women and men. The questionnaire may define employment as whether, and how much, income was earned in the past month. Open-ended qualitative interviews, in contrast, have a less restricted definition of the intended outcome because the questions allow for more nuance and do not preclude other possible outcomes. In this example, a qualitative interview might discern whether the employment was casual (for a short time) or whether it provided a long-run source of earnings (with a contract, and so on). Although a quantitative survey could ask about these additional forms of employment, it may not adequately capture the various subtleties of the intended outcome. By using both quantitative data and qualitative data, and triangulating them, a richer and more nuanced understanding of the outcomes can be achieved.

We could also ask another related evaluation question, such as: *Why did the program have different effects?* Or: *What were the mechanisms that caused different effects?* In this case, qualitative data may be collected concurrently or sequentially along with the quantitative data, but they would not be used necessarily to triangulate directly with the data points of the quantitative survey. Rather, the qualitative data would be used to clarify and deepen the analysis of the quantitative data. If the program did have different effects, then one design might be to conduct a sequential qualitative comparative study of a select group of women and a select group of men for whom there were different effects. This sort of design might search for the contributions a program made, or did not make, in terms of its effects, and the data could be a retrospective perspective of participants (see box 22.1 for an example). Another option is for qualitative data to be collected concurrently with quantitative data, and the kind of qualitative data collected would focus on various mechanisms that, based on a theory of change or emergent factors, are related to different effects.

Finally, at the data interpretation and use stage, qualitative data are often misinterpreted or underutilized because policy makers misunderstand the validity and robustness of qualitative research. For example, qualitative data are often presented as "additional" quotes or stories about the program implementation or effects, leading some policy makers to regard the data as anecdotal and questioning the strength of conclusions. Two related problems occur in the interpretation of qualitative results: (1) policy makers (or others who read the reports) often interpret qualitative findings within the parameters of quantitative designs—for example, they may question the generalizability of the findings, when generalizability to a population is not the intent of qualitative research; and (2) qualitative researchers and evaluators often do not use or clearly articulate a systematic approach to analysis, and therefore do not show how they have come to the claims they make. The section on qualitative analysis later in this chapter suggests that researchers and evaluators need to be clearer about how their data are analyzed, and also how the results can be effectively presented to policy makers so that they understand the rigor of the analysis.

In sum, to use qualitative methods and data effectively, researchers and evaluators need to understand the different purposes for using qualitative designs, and how they can contribute to the overall objectives of the evaluation.

Different purposes and types of qualitative approaches

The literature on mixed methods has long debated whether and how qualitative approaches can be used with quantitative designs in evaluations (Bamberger 2015; Greene and Caracelli 2003; Leeuw and Vaessen 2009; Pawson and Tilley 1997; Tashakkori and Teddlie 1998). This scholarship has generally provided two perspectives on the relationship between qualitative and quantitative methods: the *interpretive* perspective and the *realist* perspective. The interpretive perspective takes the position that quantitative and qualitative data are generally situated in different paradigms (empiricist and interpretive, respectively), and therefore they cannot be combined; rather, they are used to answer different research or evaluation questions. In contrast, the realist perspective claims that these paradigms are not as distinct as some portray, and therefore a mixed-methods approach can be used at the different phases of design, data collection, and analysis. This second perspective assumes that objective and subjective realities exist, and different types of data are needed to understand complex interventions and their outcomes (Greene and Caracelli 2003; Maxwell 2012; Pawson 2013) (see table 22.1 for differences between these two perspectives).

The interpretive perspective regards qualitative data as subjective, seeking to discern specific meanings and deeper understandings of the phenomena in local contexts. This perspective assumes that all meanings of social phenomena are constructed by individuals, that cause and effect cannot be determined, and that social phenomena can be

TABLE 22.1 Comparison of interpretive and realist perspectives

	INTERPRETIVE (EXPLORATORY)	REALIST (EXPLANATORY)
Relationship between qualitative and quantitative data	Quantitative and qualitative data are from two different paradigms and cannot be compared. These two types of data are used to answer two different sets of research questions.	Quantitative and qualitative data are not necessarily from two distinct paradigms. Thus they can be combined (that is, mixed methods can be used) to answer the same research questions.
Perspective of reality and how we can understand and explain it	We understand reality as constructed through our perceptions and standpoints. Qualitative data capture these perceptions and meanings of participants.	The social world we study exists independently of our perceptions, and we also construct how that real world affects us. Qualitative and quantitative data can be combined to explain reality and our constructions of it.
Possibility of explaining causal relationships	It is impossible to explain causal effects and relationships.	The purpose of analysis is explanatory, and it is possible to explain causality—in this case meaning the processes and mechanisms by which outcomes occur.
Role of theory in analysis	Qualitative data play an important role in developing theory that is specific to the phenomenon being investigated. Social phenomena can be understood only within a specific social context, and therefore, theories are used as a heuristic for other contexts rather than to test their generalizability.	Theory should be used to understand and identify both causal mechanisms and contextual factors.
Types of methodologies and research designs used	• Case-based approaches, including single and multiple sites (ethnography) • Qualitative longitudinal designs that use ethnographic methods	• Case-based approaches and longitudinal designs using a theory to identify process relationships • Analysis processes include contribution analysis, process tracing, and qualitative comparative analysis

Source: Original table for this publication.

understood only within a specific context and cannot be generalized from one setting to another (Guba and Lincoln 1989). Evaluators using this approach usually regard the purpose of qualitative methods and data in impact evaluations as answering different questions than those addressed by quantitative (both experimental and nonexperimental) methods. Additionally, from this perspective, the design is usually sequential, with qualitative either used before or after the main quantitative approach to help explore phenomena that the quantitative analysis was unable to study. Evaluators often use qualitative data to capture local meanings to inform the development of constructs and questions for the collection of quantitative data. For instance, qualitative data may precede the collection of survey data in an RCT. But this use of qualitative data is quite limited. An interpretive approach can also be used to analyze cases either to identify diverse and unintended outcomes that might result from the intervention in a specific context or to examine contextual factors that may affect implementation and impact. Usually, interpretive analyses of qualitative data (for example, ethnographies, or designs using general qualitative data, such as interviews) are used to build theory rather than to offer causal analytical claims (Ragin 2014).

The second perspective, in which quantitative and qualitative data are combined to explain multiple impacts, draws on a realist approach to evaluation (Pawson 2002; Greene and Caracelli 2003). The purpose of these data is to be explanatory—analyses are conducted to explain underlying factors and contexts related to how and why a program was, or was not, effective. Realism assumes that events and experiences in our social world are complex and contextual. At the same time, by applying a rigorous methodology and analysis to complex and contextual data, evaluators can investigate underlying mechanisms and structures that exist (objective) and also understand how social actors make many decisions and take action on the basis of what they know, or think they know (subjective), to achieve a diversity of program outcomes (Bhaskar 2008).

The guiding questions of realist informed evaluations are, What works for whom? What works in which circumstances? And, why did it work? (Pawson 2013, 87–88; Westhorpe 2014, 9; see also annex 22A). From this perspective, the task of an evaluation is to open up the black box of interventions to understand the mechanisms, or the inputs and processes, within specific contexts that, based on an underlying theory of change of the intervention and the implementers, will cause particular outcomes to occur. But mechanisms do not operate autonomously; they are triggered by a long chain of social actors who affect and create change when they implement the interventions. Thus data must also be analyzed for how these social actors introduce differing interpretations of the intervention components (Pawson 2013). Mechanisms that cause outcomes are not always visible, nor are they easily discernible through previously defined factors as is often assumed in quantitative research. Rather, mechanisms are investigated by examining the various institutional and program factors that emerge in contexts, and how actors act on them to produce outcomes (Westhorpe 2014). For example, a program offers resources, but whether these resources produce the desired (or unintended) impacts depends on the actions of the social actors—both those who implement the program and those who are affected by it. An intervention can work as intended only if all the social actors behave in a way assumed by the program's theory of change (Pawson 2013, 90).

From a realist and causal analytic perspective, evaluations seek to show patterns of outcomes, or how results are, or are not, achieved for selected groups, in particular times and places (contexts). The aim is to analyze both quantitative and qualitative data to explain the multiple causal mechanisms within institutions and programs that, when activated by social actors, cause a result to occur (Pawson 2013, 87). Thus, realist evaluations use theory (either that of the program, related literature, or emergent theory) to identify mechanisms and contextual factors that explain the transformational relations between interventions and outcomes within their contextual factors (Stern 2015).

Pawson (2013) cautions, however, that many evaluations intending to use realist approaches for explaining causality may not succeed because they (1) do not pay enough attention to explanations of mechanisms that inform different or multiple impacts; (2) do not use multiple methods, but rather rely on single sources of data or methods; or (3) do not investigate context, mechanisms, and outcomes within a theoretical framework. Having a well-defined theory of mechanisms and outcomes, as discussed in detail in chapter 2, focuses the analysis process so that better explanations can be achieved. In addition, having clearly defined outcomes with different forms of data, qualitative and quantitative, will help reveal patterns in intended and unintended outcomes. Finally, determining different mechanisms that affect outcomes within specific contexts requires analyzing these relationships and their interconnections, not simply cataloging them. There are different analysis approaches, including Pawson's approach to realist evaluations, process tracing, and contribution analyses, that can be used to explain the mechanisms and processes that affect outcomes. These types of analysis are introduced briefly below and references to recent studies are provided, but the details of analyses cannot be explained in this chapter.

Table 22.2 summarizes different purposes of (column (1)) and the associated questions (column (2)) for impact evaluations, referring to both relevant quantitative and qualitative approaches (column (3)); the kind of mixed-methods research designs that can be used for these purposes and questions (column (4)); and the types of qualitative analyses that can be used, both exploratory and interpretive, and explanatory and realist (column (5)). For example, in the first row, the main evaluative purpose is to assign attribution of a given effect to the program being evaluated, which is done primarily through an RCT design. For this purpose, qualitative data are most often used in an exploratory way to guide the development of the survey questions to ensure that they are well matched to local characteristics and meanings.

In the second row, a different evaluative purpose is to understand the *contribution* of the program to achieving diverse impacts, many of which may be unexpected. Distinct from attribution, evaluating the contribution of a program to achieving impacts aims to link program components to various impacts through a theory of change by analyzing data to investigate which program components appear to contribute to the outcomes of interest, without assigning direct attribution. Depending on the credibility of the data and of the analysis, stronger or weaker claims are made about the relationship between the components of the program and the impacts. To answer this evaluative question, qualitative data can be used concurrently with quantitative quasi-experimental designs to draw conclusions about relationships. The primary purpose of this evaluative question is to show the

TABLE 22.2 Evaluation purposes, questions, approaches, designs, and types of analyses

EVALUATION PURPOSE	EVALUATION QUESTIONS	EXAMPLES OF QUANTITATIVE AND QUALITATIVE APPROACHES	MIXED-METHODS DESIGNS	QUALITATIVE ANALYSES
Attribute impact to intervention	To what extent can impact be attributed to the intervention or program?	Classic experimental—randomized controlled trial Interpretive qualitative cases (ethnographic or participatory)	Qualitative and quantitative are sequential, with quantitative methods dominant and qualitative used primarily to inform development of quantitative survey questionnaire (construct validity of items)	Exploratory—analyzed for semantic meanings and themes to inform quantitative analysis
Understand the *contribution* of the program; multiple and d fferent impacts	Did the intervention or program make a difference? • What different impacts did it have? And did the impacts last or change? • Which impacts were unintended, but positive? Which were negative?	Quasi-experimental quantitative designs (difference-in-differences) Qualitative case-based approaches, including comparative cases or theory-based cases (to identify different impacts) Qualitative longitudinal approaches	Quantitative and qualitative are concurrent (or sequential) and equivalent, for example, survey using difference-in-differences design, accompanied by qualitative case studies or a qualitative longitudinal study	Exploratory and explanatory—emergent or existing theory of change Qualitative comparative analyses and contribution analyses • Longitudinal data analysis to examine other impacts (unintended and intended) at different periods

continued on next page

TABLE 22.2 Evaluation purposes, questions, approaches, designs, and types of analyses *(continued)*

EVALUATION PURPOSE	EVALUATION QUESTIONS	EXAMPLES OF QUANTITATIVE AND QUALITATIVE APPROACHES	MIXED-METHODS DESIGNS	QUALITATIVE ANALYSES
Understand *how* the program achieved its impacts	Which combination of contextual factors, implementation factors, and individual participant factors mattered? When and for whom?	Quantitative survey of process variables (with structural equation modeling or regression analysis of factors in a theory of change) Theory-based qualitative studies, including case-based or longitudinal designs	Qualitative dominant design (alongside experimental or quasi-experimental)	Explanatory—emergent or existing theory of change Process tracing Realist evaluation of context, mechanisms, and outcomes
Understand why the program worked in specific contexts, and whether it will in others	*Why* did the intervention or program work in this context? Will it work in other contexts?	Theory-based models Qualitative comparative cases (of different contexts)	Qualitative-dominant design	Exploratory and explanatory Interpretive ethnographic cases Qualitative comparative analysis Process tracing

Sources: Adapted from Stern 2015, 11, 22; and Pawson 2002.

contributions to different impacts, but these analyses do not yet explain the processes behind achieving these impacts.

The question in the third row attempts to explain how the program achieved impacts. For this question, qualitative methods and data are best. Similarly, the purpose in the fourth row is to explain why a program did or did not have impacts in specific contexts, and whether it will have external validity. Here again, qualitative methods and data can be valuable for revealing context-specific factors and program implementation factors that help explain why impacts occur, or do not occur.

Before discussing examples of different approaches to qualitative designs that can be used for both exploratory and explanatory purposes, the next section briefly summarizes the main methods for gathering qualitative data. Then, the discussion turns to how case-based and qualitative longitudinal approaches can be combined (or not) with theory-based approaches to answer the different evaluation questions presented in table 22.2.

The most common methods for collecting qualitative data

Qualitative researchers collect a wide variety of data to conduct many different types of analysis. There is not enough space in this chapter to provide a comprehensive description of the different types of data collection methods used by qualitative researchers; however, a brief description of the most commonly used methods, and the type of data they collect, is useful for those who are unfamiliar with qualitative research methods. This section provides relatively brief descriptions of the three most common methods.

Perhaps the most common qualitative data collection method is *open-ended interviews*. These are verbal (and nonverbal) recordings, transcriptions, or both based on open-ended questions posed in a conversation. The interview questions may be semistructured, that is, based on a set of questions that add structure to the interview but allow for probes and clarifications, or unstructured, consisting of one or two opening questions, after which the interviewer follows the responses to ask additional questions related to the phenomenon under study. The questions and responses during the interviews include respondents' experiences, perceptions, opinions, feelings, and knowledge.

Interviews can be with individuals or with groups; they can be unstructured, semi-structured, or structured; and they can be conducted once or many times. A specific form of group interview is a *focus group*. Small group interviews and focus groups are generally used for different purposes. Small group interviews may be undertaken when an individual interview is not appropriate, or when they help facilitate conversation. Focus groups are a planned group discussion designed to obtain perceptions on a clearly defined topic. Individual responses prompt responses from others, which can reveal different perspectives. The analysis of focus groups is usually on the overall group ideas, consensus, or differences, rather than individual perspectives and experiences. The use of interview data in reports and articles consists of actual, verbatim quotations that are usually explained within a context of the respondents' role, status, or life experiences.

A much different type of qualitative data is *documents and other textual data*. These consist of both written and digital materials, including program or organization documents, official publications and reports, and personal written works of participants, including educational tasks, written exams or essays, diaries, and stories. These data from participants can be collected using participatory methods, such as drawings and mappings, or other written tools, such as story-boarding and comics.

For example, story-boarding and comics are useful ways to collect the ideas of children and youth, who are often less inclined to talk in an interview. These methods ask participants to draw out or write out a story, either alone or in a group, that relates to the phenomena or question under study. Text data are increasingly being captured through digital means (from cell phones and computers, through social media and direct, one-to-one communication). The use of these data in reports consists of excerpts or representations of these texts, with an explanation of their context, including how and why the participant engaged with the data-gathering method.

The last of these three most common methods for collecting qualitative data consists of *direct observations and collection of other visual data*. This approach consists of recordings and images of activities, behaviors, actions, interpersonal interactions, and processes as they are observed. These data may take the form of written field notes with rich descriptions, or drawings, images, and photos, including video recordings. Representations of these data in reports include detailed descriptions and visuals that illustrate the actions and interactions, the contexts of the gathering of the data, and explanations of the observed setting.

All these types of data can be used within the different designs for data collection and analysis that are discussed below, including case studies, theory-based approaches, and longitudinal studies. In addition, these designs and methods can be combined, such as undertaking a theory-based approach within a longitudinal design (over several years), using documents, interviews, and observations. The types of data used in these designs vary in the time required for data collection, the depth of interaction in the field, and the processes for analysis.

Exploratory and explanatory qualitative approaches

As discussed previously, qualitative studies can be used in impact evaluations for both exploratory and explanatory purposes. This section provides three different approaches that can be designed for these different purposes. Case-based approaches can be used for exploratory purposes, and a rigorous analysis of case-based qualitative data can provide evidence of emergent theories that can be tested further. Case-based approaches can also use a theory for explanatory purposes, in which case the sampling, data gathering, and analysis would be oriented toward explaining the theory of change in achieving the outcomes. Similarly, qualitative longitudinal studies could be exploratory, and a rigorous analysis of factors and mechanism over time can be used to develop new theories; or they can focus on a specific theory to be tested through the data collection and analysis. Theory-based approaches are used in both of the designs above, or alone, to test a theory and outcomes.

Case-based approaches and analyses

Cases can be sites where the intervention is implemented, or individuals who are the intended beneficiaries. Each case is considered as a holistic and complex entity when gathering data and undertaking analyses. Therefore, a combination of methods, including interviews, focus groups, observations, and documents, are used to provide a broad array of data that can be analyzed to understand what combinations of factors affect the intervention's impact in specific contexts.

Cases can be used for either exploratory or explanatory purposes. Exploratory purposes tend to use interpretive analyses of the intervention mechanisms, the context, or the outcomes. A small number of cases are generally used in this type of analysis, which aims to explain these cases holistically and contextually with rich qualitative data. Exploratory cases tend to be used sequentially in mixed-methods designs, meaning that the qualitative case study is undertaken separately either before or after one or more forms of quantitative data analysis are used. Cases that gather data before the intervention might be analyzed to understand the context. Cases that gather data after the intervention, along with other forms of quantitative data, might be used to help explain how the intervention achieved, or did not achieve, its intended impacts. If the mixed-methods design includes cases conducted after the intervention, the cases may not provide sufficient data about the intervention to examine a combination of conditions and factors that produced impacts, and therefore researchers are unable to rule out other conditions and factors that might have affected the impact during the intervention. Still, sequential designs that draw on ethnographic techniques can gather data from multiple sources and often use more in-depth data to examine the intervention holistically and to inform theory building (rather than testing theory).

Case-based designs used for explanatory purposes usually are combined with theory-based approaches, using a theory of change or an emergent theory. These designs are structured, and the data may sometimes be quantified (such as fuzzy sets analysis in comparative qualitative analysis, as in Trujillo and Woulfin 2014). Three common approaches to analyzing data for explanatory purposes are (1) contribution analysis, used to explain a combination of conditions or factors *within* cases that contribute to impacts; (2) qualitative comparative analyses, used to explain similar or different patterns of impacts *across* many cases; and (3) process tracing, used to explain the causal mechanisms toward the intended or theorized outcomes. Contribution analysis seeks to explain a combination of conditions and factors that contribute to impacts, so it tends to use a small number of cases (Stern 2015). A larger number of cases should be used when applying comparative analysis to study similar or different impacts across many sites or groups. Process tracing also examines the conditions and mechanisms that achieve impact but requires an additional data and analysis step that examines confirmatory evidence that the mechanisms caused the outcomes. Case-based designs that are founded on theory and used for explanatory purposes are best developed concurrently with the quantitative approaches so that data are gathered throughout the intervention (from baseline to endline). A concurrent design also allows for identification of emergent mechanisms and contextual factors that influence impacts over time. For further discussion and explanation of how to conduct contribution analysis and process tracing, see Befani and Mayne (2014), Byrne and Ragin (2009), and the Process Tracing guide developed by Oxfam (n.d.). For further details on qualitative comparative analysis, see Befani (2013), Ragin (2014), and Rihoux (2006).

An example of a case-based approach that compares impacts between individuals and sites is provided in box 22.1. This case-based evaluation included both sites and individuals exposed to the intervention and sites and individuals that did not experience the program. The intervention focused on youth employment as an outcome of participating in the program. The qualitative data were collected at the same time as the endline quantitative survey data for the purpose of explaining differences in outcomes among different types of participants, and between participants and nonparticipants, based on emergent findings (rather than a specific theory of change). No baseline qualitative data were collected, although baseline quantitative data were collected. Two main types of qualitative data were collected: interviews and focus groups. The analysis was thematic, comparing outcomes between groups and the implementation across the sites. By making comparisons between groups, the study attempts to be explanatory, although because of limitations in data (no baseline) and the analysis, it is primarily exploratory. Data gathered before and after the intervention and more in-depth analyses, guided by an explicit theory, would be needed to explain the differences between groups with more certainty.

BOX 22.1 Case studies and comparative qualitative analysis: Example of Akazi Kanoze Youth Livelihoods Project (Alcid 2014)

A randomized controlled trial (RCT) was implemented to answer the following question:

Did employability and livelihood outcomes improve as a result of the Akazi Kanoze program?

The RCT randomly assigned 300 rural youths to participate in a nine-month program that included work readiness, technical training, and an internship. Another 300 youths had also applied but were not selected to participate in the program; they were randomly assigned to the control group. Baseline data were collected on the 300 youths who participated in the program (the last cohort) and the associated control group, and the endline data were collected six months after the training was completed.

The case studies of multiple sites and groups of participants, with interview and focus group data collected only at the endline, were designed to answer questions that were not explained by the quantitative data collected as part of the RCT design. The interview data were collected to gather holistic case studies of individuals who had participated in the program even in districts where the RCT did not occur, because the RCT was not representative of the larger program, which trained 21,000 youths in 19 rural and urban districts in Rwanda. In addition, focus groups of employed and unemployed youths in one district were designed to gather more in-depth data about how and why the program worked, or did not work.

There were three main questions for the qualitative component of the study. The first question examined the role of contextual factors that affected youth employment

continued on next page

BOX 22.1 Case studies and comparative qualitative analysis: Example of Akazi Kanoze Youth Livelihoods Project (Alcid 2014) *(continued)*

opportunities (or pathways to employment), and it focused on understanding what differentiated youth who were employed from those who were not employed. The second question sought to explain program processes that contributed to outcomes. The third question describes other outcomes that youth might have gained, including increasing their employability even if not employed, especially given that the quantitative data found a decrease in employment overall.

1. What pathways to employment have Akazi Kanoze youths used to seek better economic opportunities? Have they been successful in their attempts?
2. From the perspective of Akazi Kanoze youths, what are the most useful skills that they acquired during the program, and how have they applied these skills?
3. From the perspective of the Akazi Kanoze youths, how has the program changed their lives and improved their employability?

The qualitative methods included individual interviews with 9 youths who participated in the program in six districts, urban and rural, where the program was implemented. These 9 graduates were not randomly selected; the program staff selected them to include employed and self-employed youth. In addition, 13 youths, 9 of whom participated in the program and 4 of whom did not participate, who reported that they were unemployed at endline, were also interviewed four months after endline data collection to explore the unexpected drop in employment at endline, especially in one of the two districts where the RCT took place. These individual interviews were designed to explore possible unobserved and contextual factors behind the changes in reported employment at endline and the researcher's hypothesis that youth employment was transient and could have already changed in a few months. In addition, one of the two districts in the RCT was chosen as a case study to examine how and why the program worked, or did not work. Focus groups were used to collect data in this district from 19 (9 male and 10 female) youths who had participated in the program and 17 (9 male and 8 female) youths who had not participated. Thus the qualitative data were used to make comparisons between groups on the basis of livelihood outcomes.

Analyses

Qualitative data were analyzed thematically, searching for patterns between those in the program and those not in the program, and those who were employed and those who were not.

A key finding of the quantitative data from the RCT is that the proportion of youth employed *decreased* at the time of endline relative to the base level, though the percentage decline for the intervention group was less than that of the control group. This decrease in percentage of employed youth was mostly among those who were self-employed. The reasons for this drop in employment for both the control group and the intervention group could not be explained using the quantitative survey data, though from qualitative data there was some suggestion that this decrease might be in part

continued on next page

BOX 22.1 Case studies and comparative qualitative analysis: Example of Akazi Kanoze Youth Livelihoods Project (Alcid 2014) *(continued)*

because youth were often employed intermittently, and some might have been between jobs at the time of the survey. In addition, the analysis of survey data found that youth in both groups switched from employment to unemployment, and vice versa, at the same rate. For example, 70 percent of the youths were involved in a different type of work at the endline than at baseline. Alcid (2014) argues, on the basis of qualitative data, that the youths who participated in the program were able to find new employment faster, using their employability skills and networks. Survey data were not collected on why or how long they were out of work, though interview data with the unemployed group provided some insight. For example, some youths reported being unemployed but that they were continuing their training; others who had been unemployed at the time of the endline reported having work when interviewed later.

Quantitative and qualitative data were collected at the endline to triangulate some findings, such as why youths did not have or find work. Qualitative interviews were also used to obtain additional reasons for their unemployment that were not collected as part of the quantitative survey. The qualitative interviews provide further understanding of both positive and negative outcomes from the intervention, though the lack of multiple points of data both throughout the intervention and afterward make it difficult to draw strong conclusions. It is clear from follow-up interviews with those who were unemployed that their employment has great variability, and collecting data for a longer period would have been useful to provide an understanding of this variability.

The qualitative data also suggested the existence of problems with the fidelity of program implementation in certain areas; implementation was not well monitored. Three different local organizations implemented the training, and qualitative interviews revealed that youths had varying experiences, particularly in their technical training, based on the strength of the implementing organization. In addition, after realizing that there were differences in program implementation, the evaluation team collected interview data from the implementing partners and local youth center officials after collecting the youth data. For example, the implementing organization in one rural district did not have sufficient resources to do the technical training; it drew on local trainers, and the quality of training was variable. Additional monitoring data during the program would have been useful to reveal some of these implementation differences. Contributing to the understanding of why the program worked, or did not work, is a common use of qualitative data, but to add the question of fidelity of implementation to its design, quantitative and qualitative data are needed on the different implementation processes across the program sites.

Qualitative longitudinal approaches and analyses

Qualitative longitudinal designs are another approach that, while not often included in many evaluation guides, can be quite useful for explaining outcomes over time, and how the impacts of an intervention become permanent or lose potency over time.

Qualitative longitudinal analyses can be particularly worthwhile in educational interventions and other types of social programs because the duration of time between an intervention and its impacts is often unknown, or is longer than the short duration of most quantitative impact evaluations. Educational impacts are often cumulative; on the other hand, however, some may fade out over time.

Whereas some qualitative longitudinal analyses can be exploratory and descriptive with regard to changes over time, explanatory analyses can also be undertaken to show which events, factors, and other intervening conditions affected and shaped the outcomes (Saldana 2003, 2015). Longitudinal analytical questions consider which outcomes change over time, and what the particular rhythms of change are. For example, one can ask, Are the changes consistently positive, negative, or do they fluctuate? And why do these changes in outcomes occur in these patterns over time? There is insufficient space in this chapter to go into the details of qualitative longitudinal analyses; the reader is encouraged to consult Saldana (2015) for further explanation of longitudinal analysis processes.

Box 22.2 provides an example of a mixed-methods design that included a survey used to collect quantitative data before and after a program (used in a propensity score matching analysis) as well as qualitative (and quantitative) longitudinal data. This evaluation is primarily a sequential mixed-methods design, using the quantitative survey data to estimate training effects of youth livelihood programs, while qualitative interviews and quantitative demographic data were analyzed over five years to show long-term outcomes, how they changed, and how some unintended outcomes emerged. In addition, the design included comparisons across different programs and country contexts, and also of different types of program participants (for example, men and women). The analysis used a theory of change based on the program design, and it also identified emergent mechanisms and outcomes over time (see Pellowski Wiger, DeJaeghere, and Chapman 2015).

BOX 22.2 Longitudinal and theory-based design and analysis: Example of Learn, Earn, and Save Initiative of Youth Livelihoods Programs in Tanzania and Uganda

The question that guided the quantitative data collection and analysis of the short-term outcomes of training was the following:

1. *Over the course of the training, did the youths learn the knowledge, skills, and attitudes that the program designers intended that they learn?*

To answer this question, the survey was designed to measure the specific intended knowledge, skills, and attitudes that the programs taught participants.

More specifically, for the propensity score matching analysis that was conducted, the evaluation asked:

2. *Did the training have different effects on the knowledge, skills, and attitudes of the youths who participated and did not participate in the livelihoods program?*

continued on next page

BOX 22.2 Longitudinal and theory-based design and analysis: Example of Learn, Earn, and Save Initiative of Youth Livelihoods Programs in Tanzania and Uganda *(continued)*

Quantitative data for these questions were collected before and after the training for different cohorts who participated in the training at different times. Then, to determine the overall effects of the program, a propensity score matching design and analysis was used to compare the change in knowledge, skills, and attitudes of the participants in the training program with the same changes of those who did not participate. The data (discussed below) represent the first cohort of 244 participants and 232 nonparticipants from a specific program implemented in both Tanzania and Uganda.

The question that guided the data collection and analysis of the *long-term* outcomes of the program was the following:

3. *How did the program change the trajectory of youths' livelihoods over five years, and what were the mediating factors affecting these trajectories?*

Qualitative data (and some quantitative data) were collected every year for five years from 43 youths (20 from Tanzania and 23 from Uganda; the original sample included 30 each, but some could not be interviewed for all five years). In addition, interviews were conducted with program implementers and community stakeholders every year for the same five years. The data included in-depth qualitative interviews, adapted each year to probe emerging themes, and quantitative demographic data. The gathering and analysis of data were guided by the program's theory of change as well as by theories that accounted for individual, household, community, program, and macro-context factors or mechanisms that could affect the impact of these youths' training on their valued livelihood outcomes.[a] The theories used included a capability approach, which theorizes that contextual conditions, such as one's geographic location, affect individuals' valued livelihood outcomes differentially (DeJaeghere and Baxter 2014). In addition, a review of the literature on youth livelihood programs revealed a set of other contextual and programmatic factors that could influence the achievement of outcomes (Pellowski Wiger et al. 2015). In this study, these livelihood outcomes included quantitative data about earnings, savings, and individual and family well-being; they also included qualitative data to explore these outcomes, what the youths valued about their earnings and savings, and how they valued other notions of well-being from work, such as being able to care for family members. Although this evaluation was not initially designed as a realist evaluation, the main principles and concepts of realist evaluations, meaning analyses that aim to identify mechanisms within contexts that affect outcomes, was applied retrospectively. (See Tikly [2015] for a discussion of realism and the capability approach; see also DeJaeghere, Morris, and Bamattre [2019] for an example of how the qualitative data and quantitative data analyses revealed different short- and long-term outcomes, and mechanisms that affected outcomes.)

Analyses

The propensity score matching analysis revealed that the program had significant and strong effects on participants' knowledge, skills, and attitudes, although the impact of

continued on next page

BOX 22.2 Longitudinal and theory-based design and analysis: Example of Learn, Earn, and Save Initiative of Youth Livelihoods Programs in Tanzania and Uganda *(continued)*

the program in Uganda was different from that in Tanzania (Krause, McCarthy, and Chapman 2016). For example, responses to questions about concrete skills, such as knowing how to apply for a savings account, showed significant gains from the program, with a mean of 1.31 (on a scale of 1–4) for the group that did not yet have training, and 2.68, or 105 percent higher, for the participants who participated in the training in Tanzania. In Uganda, nonparticipants had a mean score of 2.41, and those who participated in the training had a score of 3.03, or only 25.6 percent higher. The much larger percentage gains for youths in Tanzania were due in part to nonparticipants' much lower initial levels. In addition, in both countries a number of items in the survey had a ceiling effect, so change resulting from the program was not well captured by the survey. An analysis by gender also revealed that the program had different effects on men's and women's reported outcomes. From these analyses, the report concluded that there were significant effects on youths' skills and knowledge related to employment and financial literacy in both countries, though the effects varied by country and gender (Bamattre and Morris 2016).

Qualitative longitudinal and quantitative demographic data were used to find out how these skills affected youths' livelihood trajectories after completing the program (see Pellowski Wiger, DeJaeghere, and Chapman 2015). For example, interviews with a subsample of the youths from Tanzania and Uganda who participated in a similar program for developing their livelihoods and self-employment revealed that they had different experiences in applying for and using savings accounts across these two countries. Over the five years, a greater percentage of the youths interviewed in Uganda had bank accounts and used them for saving, while a greater percentage of youths in Tanzania used community savings groups. Despite reporting increased knowledge about applying for savings accounts following the program, this knowledge did not necessarily translate into having savings accounts. Multiple mechanisms influenced these different outcomes, including proximity to banks, trust in banks, costs of using banks, and the alternative ease of use of, and trust in, community groups. The authors hypothesized that fees for bank accounts would be a factor affecting their use, particularly for youths whose earnings were unstable and uncertain, which often was the case. These data also revealed that community savings groups can be a better mechanism for accessing larger loans because they tend to have lower interest rates than banks (Bamattre and Morris 2016).

This example illustrates how different types of data and analyses were used to answer different questions. The data also show how long-term impacts are different from the immediate posttraining impacts, and that knowledge learned and behaviors enacted during the program may take different forms in the years following the program. Finally, the processes, mechanisms, and context that affected outcomes can be analyzed using these longitudinal data.

a. "Valued livelihood outcomes" were determined by asking the individuals in the study what they valued.

Theory-based approaches and analyses

Theory-based approaches use an explicit theory of change and identified outcomes, and theory-based analyses aim to identify causal processes and mechanisms. Thus these approaches are found within the realist perspective and are explanatory. A theory-based approach focuses on causal analysis and explanations for how and why a program worked in specific contexts (Pawson 2002), and therefore the theory may be emergent, or it may be described and tested beforehand, as in process tracing analysis. As stated previously, theory-based approaches are often combined with case-based and qualitative longitudinal studies. However, theory-based designs seek to identify and confirm theories, and are not limited to specifically defined "cases," that is, sites or sets of individuals that must have a boundary to define them as a case.

Theory-based designs can also help disentangle multiple causal chains when program components, processes, and outcomes are interlinked. For example, Pawson (2013) provides an example of a motor and sensory program aimed at improving impairments in young children that included occupational therapy, the regular curriculum, parent participation in some activities, and training for teachers. The mechanisms that trigger outcomes and the contexts in which they operate need to be unpacked for each of these strategies. Examining the different mechanisms—curriculum, teacher training, parents' role, and so on—of a complex program requires different types of data, but all forms of data need to be analyzed in relation to desired outcomes, how these different mechanisms are predicted to affect outcomes, and then how the mechanisms actually do affect outcomes. This approach requires developing the causal model (related to the program but also based on past research and theory) to guide the evaluation design, and then examining the data empirically to identify whether the theorized mechanisms affect the outcome within the context (see also White 2009).

Practical suggestions for designing, gathering, and analyzing qualitative data

Evaluations often focus on identifying the sources and types of data. However, as argued in the previous sections, the design of the evaluation and analyses of the data are as critically important as the methods used to gather data for the overarching goal of answering the evaluation questions. This section provides practical guidance for collecting and analyzing qualitative data in a mixed-methods evaluation design. The first subsection begins by providing advice on activities that should take place before data are collected. The second subsection contains practical suggestions for actual data collection, and the third subsection provides recommendations for analyzing the data.

Before collecting data

Before qualitative data are collected, several activities must be undertaken, the most important of which are selecting the data collection methods and training the team members who will gather the data. As with quantitative survey data collection, qualitative researchers must be rigorously trained. In qualitative research, the researcher (evaluator) uses the interview questions or observation tool to elicit and gather detailed data that are both focused and useful for answering the research questions. In addition, the researcher's own assumptions and interpretations affect how data are collected and analyzed, and researchers need to be aware of these assumptions. Therefore, training is essential to ensure the project team understands the research questions and what they aim to answer, as well as how the specific methods—interviews, documents or texts, or observations—allow the questions to be answered.

Ensure the research team understands the key purpose and aims of the research. Similar to quantitative data, gathering large amounts of qualitative data requires having a team of researchers. Each member of the team needs to fully understand the questions that guide the data collection, and the questions should be reiterated often and kept in mind as data are being gathered. In addition, researchers often assume that the purpose of an evaluation is to determine whether the program had an impact, but not necessarily to answer other questions. Thus, all members of a research team need to recognize that the evaluation questions include gaining an understanding of unintended impacts, variation in impacts, and how impacts occurred. Ideally, a team conducting qualitative data gathering would have experience with conducting interviews, observations, or focus groups, and asking questions in an open-ended way that seeks responses and stories, and not "answers."

Ensure that the team understands that gathering qualitative data aims to help the researchers understand and explain the phenomena underlying the evaluation questions, not just answer questions or fill in boxes. It is critical that the team of researchers be trained in the specific types of qualitative data collection methods that they will use. Many may be accustomed to collecting quantitative data as in a household survey or other type of survey. Therefore, when conducting an interview, for example, they must be taught how to administer open-ended questions to gather meaningful data in a conversation, not only as a question and answer. This conversation includes knowing when and how to probe for clarification, deeper understanding, or additional responses. With written data and observations, the team members need to know what to look for to answer the evaluation questions.

Review the interview or observation protocol thoroughly, and practice or pilot its use. As in a quantitative survey, the researchers need to understand the key concepts used in questions and what data are sought from each question. Chapter 18 addresses this issue for quantitative methods. Interviewers also need to understand that they play a critical role in how the participant responds to the questions, and that the goal is to elicit deeper explanations, not just simple answers. Critical to gathering qualitative data is knowing when to ask additional questions or probes that help clarify meaning, elicit further explanation, or challenge assumptions. For example, in an evaluation about an intervention to support girls' completion of schooling and reduction in early marriage, the researcher may ask whether the girl is married or plans to be married soon. If the girl answers yes, the researcher cannot simply infer that being married necessarily means that she will not complete school. The interviewer needs to probe for how marriage affects her educational participation and plans. This additional questioning allows for assumptions and interpretations of data to be assessed with the participant. Therefore, researchers need to practice administering probing questions and knowing when they may need to follow up on particular answers with additional questions.

Conduct translation and back-translation of the protocols. Translation is critical because it shapes the responses that the researchers will get, and their meanings. For example, in one of the interview protocols for the Learn, Earn and Save Initiative (described in box 22.2), the researchers asked about influences on girls and boys in the community. When this question was translated into Swahili, it referred to and elicited only negative aspects, though the question aimed to understand both positive and negative influences. In a different example, the concept "education" was translated into *elimu*, which refers to formal schooling, while many youths who participated in the interviews were in nonformal education programs, or *mafunzo*, which is related to vocational and nonformal programs. Therefore, translation by one researcher and back-translation by another, both fluent in both languages, is important to check meanings of terms used.

Data gathering

Data gathering and analysis are iterative processes—what is learned while gathering the data informs how they are analyzed; in turn, the analysis of each set of data allows for additional questions to be asked in future rounds of data collection. Therefore, the process of gathering the data should not be separated from the analysis of the data, and involving all members of the research team in both processes is important. The first step in this iterative process is still to gather data, and this subsection provides recommendations on how to do so.

Ensure confidentiality and consent of all participants, and check their understanding of the purpose of the research. Because qualitative data are based on direct quotes or actions of the participants, confidentiality and consent are critical. Reiterating that the data are confidential also helps reduce socially desirable responses, such as telling a narrative they think the evaluator wants to hear, particularly about the program.

Use data for meaningful purposes for the participants and their community, not in extractive ways. Qualitative data have the potential not only to help researchers understand local perspectives and frameworks, but also to be educative. The data-gathering process should be used in ways that further the participants' and communities' interests and needs as much as those of the researchers (Garbarino and Holland 2009). The data-gathering process can be used for individual or community reflective purposes, and the sharing of the data with the community can be worthwhile for their own concerns. Of course, from the perspective of an RCT, sharing data can affect the intervention; but even for an RCT the gathering of data can cause a change in perspective or reflection and thus affect how the participants as social actors take up, implement, or respond to the intervention. When and how to share the data will depend on the design and timeline of the RCT, and more broadly of any other type of quantitative evaluation.

Conduct rigorous oversight of the data-gathering process. A lead team member should be responsible for organizing the schedules for all interviews, observations, and other types of data collection. The lead team member should also ensure that all data are recorded, uploaded, and backed up while at the site. In addition, reviewing selected samples of data during the interview or observation process can help identify problems and improve the quality, reliability, and validity of the data.

Keep complete audio or digital recordings and write memos while in the field. All qualitative data, including written documents that may be gathered, should be digitized to ensure data are not lost and to ease analysis. In addition, memos of interviews, observations, and even debriefing and analysis meetings should be copied, digitally scanned or recorded, and included in data files. Memos may be related to one specific source or type of data, as in a summary of key themes and context for an interview or observation. They may also be summaries of key themes across data sources at the end of a day or completion of work at a site. These memos can serve as a first point of analysis.

Ensure appropriate translation and transcription of data. Research and evaluation teams need to account for the time and cost of translation (if needed) and transcription of the data they collect. Both an original digital copy of interviews and observations and their transcriptions should be saved so that if any questions arise about the transcription, they can be reviewed by listening to or viewing the original interview or observation. There are many different approaches to transcription (ranging from not at all, given that digital data can be analyzed without transcription, to summaries, to full transcriptions, including nonverbal communication noted during the interview). The team should decide on the form of transcription and translation that is necessary for a rigorous and thorough analysis. For example, a thorough transcription would be important for longitudinal data that show change over time and related mechanisms that triggered change.

Data analysis

The final stage is data analysis, although as mentioned previously data collection and data analysis are iterative processes. This subsection provides advice on analyzing qualitative data. There is not enough room to go into detail about specific analysis processes, so additional references are provided. Some of these analysis processes are described in greater detail in DeJaeghere et al. (2019).

Analyze all data in line with the purposes of the research questions. Qualitative data can be overwhelming when starting the analysis process. To avoid being unnerved, the researcher must focus on the questions, the theory of change, or emerging hypotheses. For example, if the purpose is to show different impacts among different groups and what caused them, then the data need to be analyzed using cross-case qualitative analyses using the theory of change, and comparing themes both within sites and across sites. Once the data are analyzed thoroughly (and cross-checked by other researchers), a report on the findings should be written to answer the questions, showing the different impacts, causal mechanisms, and comparisons. Because qualitative data are extensive, researchers too often present limited amounts of data, running the risk of not answering the questions thoroughly. Still, good choices about the type and amount of data presented need to be made. Short vignettes, displays of qualitative data, and key quotes can all be used.

Computer-assisted qualitative data analysis software (CAQDAS) can be used to manage and analyze large and mixed-methods data sets. CAQDAS offers a range of functions to researchers for organizing, analyzing, and storing text-based data (generated from project documents, interviews, focus groups, open-ended surveys, video recordings, articles, social media, and so on). Among other features, CAQDAS software can assist researchers with storing and managing data, linking multiple sources of data over time, building a coding framework, linking codes and coded data, categorizing and ordering codes and coded data, comparing and retrieving coded data, and visualizing and mapping data. CAQDAS allows for various types of coding and analysis, such as quantifying qualitative data or linking qualitative data to participant survey data.

CAQDAS packages also allow multiple researchers to code and analyze data, which can improve the consistency and transparency of analysis, providing a useful platform for efficiently coding relevant references to saturation. Importantly, CAQDAS packages do not replace qualitative researchers; rather, they assist skilled researchers in more consistently and reliably coding and interpreting qualitative data. Advances in machine-assisted content analysis permit the automation of specific data collection and classification tasks, but they must still be supported by researcher inputs at all stages of design and implementation. For instance, to enhance intercoder reliability, evaluation teams should compare the classification or interpretation of data across two or more independent coders, examining potential differences when researchers independently process data using the same coding scheme. CAQDAS can be a useful tool for conducting these tests of reliability, offering a platform with which to compare and resolve differences in interpretation and coding.

In addition, CAQDAS allows for triangulating evidence across multiple sources and for synthesizing across a large and potentially unwieldy corpus of data. For instance, data from surveys can be linked with interview data, such that analyses can be conducted more easily across distinct groups. See Vaessen, Lemire, and Befani (2020) and the CAQDAS Networking Project at the University of Surrey (https://www.surrey.ac.uk/computer-assisted-qualitative-data-analysis) for more information on CAQDAS uses, good practices, and software packages.

Describe and illustrate the analysis process. Many evaluation reports fail to describe the analysis processes thoroughly, often because those processes are quite complex. Explaining the analysis process helps readers understand the rigor of the analysis and the reliability of the data for making the claims that are made. As discussed previously, the evaluation report should clearly describe how analysis processes, such as contribution analysis, process tracing, qualitative longitudinal analysis, or qualitative comparative analyses, are undertaken. For examples of empirical studies using process tracing, see Bamanyaki and Holvoet (2016) and Dryden-Peterson and Mulimbi (2017); and for contribution analysis, see Delahais and Toulemonde (2012), Leeuw (2012), and Vaessen and Raimondo (2012). For explanations and use of qualitative comparative analysis, see Blackman, Wistow, and Byrne (2013) and Trujillo and Woulfin (2014). Examples of qualitative longitudinal approaches and analysis can be found in Goldberg et al. (2003).

Discuss key findings with the quantitative research team, and report both types of data according to the research design. Mixed-methods designs for evaluating an intervention can be most effective in providing an understanding of the impacts if the findings across the different methods are shared. These findings can be used to prompt further analysis as well as different designs and questions for subsequent data collections. Sharing and writing about both quantitative and qualitative findings should follow the purposes of the evaluation. If the evaluation design used quantitative findings to answer one question and qualitative findings to answer another, the report should clearly reflect the approach; these findings should be regarded as complementary. If the evaluation questions aimed to use both qualitative and quantitative findings to answer the same question, then researchers should triangulate the data to understand whether the findings are similar or different. Differences among the data should prompt questions by the researchers about why the findings are contradictory. The contradictory findings should be reported, and possible explanations for these contradictions should be given.

Conclusion

This chapter discusses how qualitative approaches, methods, and analyses can be used in mixed-methods impact evaluation designs. Two different perspectives on the use of qualitative approaches are discussed: The first is the interpretive perspective, which uses qualitative approaches and data to explore a phenomenon that cannot be easily understood or explained using quantitative data or does not yet have a well-established theory for explanatory purposes. The second is the realist perspective, which uses qualitative data in a causal analytic way to explain different impacts and the various conditions and mechanisms that influenced the impacts. Table 22.2 shows different purposes and evaluation questions and how different approaches and designs can be used to answer different evaluation questions. A brief summary of different types of methods for collecting qualitative data is provided in the section titled "The most common methods for collecting qualitative data."

Three main qualitative designs used in impact evaluations are explained—case-based, qualitative longitudinal, and theory-based. These designs are not mutually exclusive, so they can be combined. The chapter also provides two examples of mixed-methods evaluations using a case-based approach for exploratory purposes and a qualitative longitudinal approach for explanatory purposes. These examples illustrate how quantitative and qualitative methods can be combined in different ways, for example, with one approach being more dominant and another complementary, and data can be sequentially or concurrently collected and analyzed. The discussion of these designs illustrates some of the challenges in mixed-methods evaluation, as well as some of its shortcomings, particularly if designs and data analysis are not thoroughly thought through.

The last section offers practical suggestions for designing, gathering, and analyzing different types of qualitative data. This chapter cannot discuss in any depth the many different ways to gather and analyze qualitative data. The reader should refer to other sources and studies cited to understand and use these approaches. In summary, this chapter offers a guide for researchers and evaluators to consider how to use qualitative approaches and designs in mixed-methods impact evaluations.

Annex 22A Questions for realist evaluations

These questions are adapted from Westhorpe (2014, 9).

- For whom does the intervention work and not work, and why? (Note that this question does not ask who the intended beneficiaries of this program are. It asks, within the intended beneficiaries, for which subgroups is it more or less effective.)
- What influenced whether subgroups participated?
- What were the outcomes (expected and unexpected) for the various subgroups?
- To what extent does it work, or not work, for different groups or in different contexts?
- How strong are the impacts for different subgroups or in different contexts?
- Did the expected mechanisms operate? For whom? And were there unexpected mechanisms that affected outcomes?
- What features of the context prevented anticipated mechanisms from operating as expected?
- What were the critical aspects of implementation, program staffing, or organizational context that influenced how the program operated?
- What were the critical features of culture, belief systems, population group, history, and so on that influenced whether or which mechanisms operated?

References

Alcid, Annie. 2014. "A Randomized Controlled Trial of Akazi Kanozi Youth in Rural Rwanda." EDC and USAID, Washington, DC.

Bamanyaki, Patricia A., and Nathalie Holvoet. 2016. "Integrating Theory-Based Evaluation and Process Tracing in the Evaluation of Civil Society Gender Budget Initiatives." *Evaluation* 22 (1): 72–90.

Bamattre, Richard, and E. Morris. 2016. *The MasterCard Foundation Learn, Earn, and Save Initiative: Final Report of Five Years of Longitudinal Data of the Swisscontact U-Learn Program*. Minneapolis, MN: University of Minnesota, Department of Organizational Leadership, Policy, and Development.

Bamberger, Michael. 2015. "Innovations in the Use of Mixed Methods in Real-World Evaluation." *Journal of Development Effectiveness* 7 (3): 317–26.

Bamberger, Michael, Vijayendra Rao, and Michael Woolcock. 2010. *Using Mixed Methods in Monitoring and Evaluation: Experiences from International Development*. Washington, DC: World Bank.

Befani, Barbara. 2013. "Between Complexity and Generalization: Addressing Evaluation Challenges with QCA." *Evaluation* 19 (3): 269–83.

Befani, Barbara, and John Mayne. 2014. "Process Tracing and Contribution Analysis: A Combined Approach to Generative Causal Inference for Impact Evaluation." *IDS Bulletin* 45 (6): 17–36. http://onlinelibrary.wiley .com/doi/10.1111/1759-5436.12110/abstract.

Bhaskar, Roy. 2008. *A Realist Theory of Science*. London: Routledge.

Blackman, Tim, Jonathan Wistow, and Dave Byrne. 2013. "Using Qualitative Comparative Analysis to Understand Complex Policy Problems." *Evaluation* 19 (2). http://oro.open.ac.uk/37540/2/5C07E325.pdf.

Byrne, David, and Charles Ragin. 2009. *The Sage Handbook of Case-Based Methods*. Thousand Oaks, CA: Sage Publications.

DeJaeghere, Joan, and Aryn Baxter. 2014. "Entrepreneurship Education for Youth in Sub-Saharan Africa: A Capabilities Approach as an Alternative Framework to Neoliberalism's Individualizing Risks." *Progress in Development Studies* 14 (1): 61–76.

DeJaeghere, Joan, E. Morris, and R. Bamattre. 2019. "Moving beyond Employment and Earnings: Reframing How Youth Livelihoods and Wellbeing Are Evaluated in East Africa. *Journal of Youth Studies* 23 (5): 667–85.

DeJaeghere, Joan, V. Morrow, D. Richardson, B. Schowengerdt, R. Hinton, and A. Boudet. 2019. *Guidance Note on Qualitative Research in Education: Considerations for Best Practice*. London: Department for International Development.

Delahais, Thomas, and Jacques Toulemonde. 2012. "Applying Contribution Analysis: Lessons from Five Years of Practice." *Evaluation* 18 (3): 281–93.

Dryden-Peterson, Sarah, and Bethany Mulimbi. 2017. "Pathways toward Peace: Negotiating National Unity and Ethnic Diversity through Education in Botswana." *Comparative Education Review* 60 (1): 58–82.

Garbarino, Sabine, and Jeremy Holland. 2009. *Quantitative and Qualitative Methods in Impact Evaluation and Measuring Results*. London: Department for International Development, Governance and Social Development Resource Center.

Goldberg, Roberta J., Eleanor L. Higgins, Marshall H. Raskind, and Kenneth L. Herman. 2003. "Predictors of Success in Individuals with Learning Disabilities: A Qualitative Analysis of a 20-Year Longitudinal Study." *Learning Disabilities Research and Practice* 18 (4): 222–36.

Greene, J. C., and V. J. Caracelli. 2003. "Making Paradigmatic Sense of Mixed Methods Practice." In *Handbook of Mixed Methods in Social and Behavioral Research*, edited by Abbas Tashakkori and Charles Teddlie, 91–110. Thousand Oaks, CA: Sage Publications.

Guba, Egon G., and Yvonna S. Lincoln. 1989. *Fourth Generation Evaluation*. Thousand Oaks, CA: Sage Publications.

Krause, Brooke L., Aine Seitz McCarthy, and David Chapman. 2016. "Fueling Financial Literacy: Estimating the Impact of Youth Entrepreneurship Training in Tanzania." *Journal of Development Effectiveness* 8 (2): 234–56.

Leeuw, Frans. 2012. "Linking Theory-Based Evaluation and Contribution Analysis: Three Problems and a Few Solutions." *Evaluation* 18 (3): 348–63.

Leeuw, Frans, and Jos Vaessen. 2009. *Impact Evaluations and Development: NONIE Guidance on Impact Evaluation*. Washington, DC: The Network of Networks on Impact Evaluation.

Maxwell, Joseph A. 2012. "The Importance of Qualitative Research for Causal Explanation in Education." *Qualitative Inquiry* 18 (8): 655–61.

Oxfam. n.d. "Process Tracing: Draft Protocol." Oxfam. http://policy-practice.oxfam.org.uk/~/media/Files/policy_and_practice/methods_approaches/effectiveness/Process-tracing-draft-protocol-110113.ashx.

Pawson, Ray. 2002. "Evidence-Based Policy: The Promise of Realist Synthesis." *Evaluation* 8 (3): 340–58. http://citeseerx.ist.psu.edu/viewdoc/summary?doi=10.1.1.132.1507.

Pawson, Ray. 2013. *The Science of Evaluation: A Realist Manifesto*. Thousand Oaks, CA: Sage Publications.

Pawson, Ray, and Nick Tilley. 1997. *Realistic Evaluation*. Thousand Oaks, CA: Sage Publications.

Pellowski Wiger, N., D. W. Chapman, A. Baxter, and J. DeJaeghere. 2015. "Context Matters: A Model of the Factors Associated with the Effectiveness of Youth Entrepreneurship Training." *Prospects* 45 (4): 533–47.

Pellowski Wiger, N., J. DeJaeghere, and D. Chapman, with K. Chachage, E. Morris, A. Nikoi, B. Krause, R. Bamattre, M. Sikenyi, H. Eschenbacher, and C. Johnstone. 2015. *The MasterCard Foundation Learn, Earn, and Save Initiative: Longitudinal Evaluation of Year 4 Cross-Program Report.* Minneapolis, MN: University of Minnesota, Department of Organizational Leadership, Policy, and Development.

Ragin, Charles C. 2014. *The Comparative Method: Moving beyond Qualitative and Quantitative Strategies*. Oakland, CA: University of California Press.

Rihoux, Benoit. 2006. "Qualitative Comparative Analysis (QCA) and Related Systematic Comparative Methods: Recent Advances and Remaining Challenges for Social Science Research." *International Sociology* 21 (5): 679–706.

Saldana, Johnny. 2003. *Longitudinal Qualitative Research: Analyzing Change through Time*. Thousand Oaks, CA: Sage.

Saldana, Johnny. 2015. *Coding Manual for Qualitative Research*. Lanham, MD: Rowman Altamira.

Stern, Elliot. 2015. *Impact Evaluation: A Guide for Commissioners and Managers*. London: Big Lottery Fund, Bond, Comic Relief, and Department for International Development.

Tashakkori, Abbas, and Charles Teddlie. 1998. *Mixed Methodology: Combining Qualitative and Quantitative Approaches*. Thousand Oaks, CA: Sage Publications.

Tikly, Leon. 2015. "What Works, for Whom, and in What Circumstances? Towards a Critical Realist Understanding of Learning in International and Comparative Education." *International Journal of Educational Development* 40: 237–49.

Trujillo, Tina, and Sarah Woulfin. 2014. "Equity-Oriented Reform amid Standards-Based Accountability: A Qualitative Comparative Analysis of an Intermediary's Instructional Practices." *American Educational Research Journal* 51 (2): 253–93.

Vaessen, Jos, Sebastian Lemire, and Barbara Befani. 2020. *Evaluation of International Development Interventions: An Overview of Approaches and Methods*. Independent Evaluation Group. Washington, DC: World Bank.

Vaessen, Jos, and Estelle Raimondo. 2012. "Making Sense of Impact: A Methodological Framework for Assessing the Impact of Prizes." *Evaluation* 18 (3): 330–47.

Westhorpe, Gill. 2014. *Realist Evaluation: An Introduction*. London: Methods Lab, Overseas Development Institute. http://www.odi.org/sites/odi.org.uk/files/odi-assets/publications-opinion-files/9138.pdf.

White, Howard. 2009. "Theory-Based Impact Evaluation: Principles and Practice." *Journal of Development Effectiveness* 1 (3): 271–84.

CHAPTER 23

Cost-Benefit Analysis and Cost-Effectiveness Analysis

Introduction

The focus of this book up to this point has been on how to estimate the impacts of particular programs, policies, or projects. However, the decision about whether a program, policy, or project should be implemented also depends on its cost, as well as the cost of alternative interventions that have impacts on the same (or similar) outcomes. This chapter shows how to combine information on program costs with estimates on program impacts to make decisions about which program, policies, or projects are worth funding.

In general, two types of approaches can be used to combine cost information with estimated impacts to make policy decisions. The first is *cost-benefit analysis*, which assigns monetary values to both the benefits and the costs of programs (or policies or projects). When funds are scarce, governments should choose the programs that have the highest ratio of benefits to costs. If funds are less scarce, all programs for which the value of the benefits is greater than the value of the costs should be funded.

The second approach is *cost-effectiveness analysis*, which assigns monetary benefits only to the costs, and compares programs with very similar outcomes to see which programs have the largest impact per dollar spent. Although this approach dispenses with the difficult task of assigning monetary values to program benefits, it cannot be used to compare programs with different types of outcomes.

This chapter provides an introduction to, and practical advice for, both cost-benefit analysis and cost-effectiveness analysis. The first section considers how costs should be calculated, which is necessary for both types of analysis. The following section compares the two types of analysis. The next two sections describe the basic characteristics of cost-benefit analysis and cost-effectiveness analysis, respectively, followed by a short concluding section.

Calculation of costs

Both cost-benefit analysis and cost-effectiveness analysis require a monetary calculation of the costs of the program, policy, or project. At first glance this may seem to be a simple task, but many complications can arise. In practice, there are two steps:

1. Specify all of the goods and labor services needed to implement the program.[1]
2. Calculate the costs of each of those goods and services.

A helpful approach to the first step is the *ingredients method.* This is quite intuitive; the analyst needs to record all goods and labor services needed to implement the program. This list should be made carefully to prevent overlooking some goods or labor services, which would lead to underestimation of the program's costs. See Levin and McEwan (2001) for a practical discussion of how to conduct this process.

The second step is to calculate the costs of the goods purchased (or otherwise acquired) and of different kinds of labor, both skilled and unskilled. Local prices and wages can generally be used, but the process may not be straightforward, as discussed in the following subsection.

Problems with, and useful principles for, setting prices and wages

At first glance, the second step—calculating the costs for the goods and services required to implement a program—seems to be relatively simple: just go to the sources of those goods and services to obtain their prices. However, an apparently simple task can lead to numerous difficulties. The most common complications that can arise are described below, after which recommendations are provided for how to resolve them.

Common complications for calculating costs

First, market distortions may affect prices and wages in ways that cause them not to represent the true costs of the associated goods and labor. The simplest example of this is a tax on a certain type of construction material, such as metal pipes for plumbing. The price paid for those pipes includes the cost of production, which is the true cost, plus the tax. The tax portion of the price is a shift in funds from the agency that is funding the program to general government revenues and is not a cost to society as a whole. Ideally, costs should be valued by their "true" costs to society as a whole, which implies subtracting costs attributable to taxes and adding to the true cost any subsidies that may be applied to the specific good or type of labor. More generally, many other market distortions could cause prices paid not to reflect the true costs to society of goods and labor used to implement a program. The true costs are called *shadow prices*, which for any good can be defined as the change in a society's overall level of welfare from the addition (or subtraction) of one unit of the good from the society.[2]

Second, the costs of imported goods (and perhaps imported labor services) could be distorted by manipulations in the exchange rate. In some countries the exchange rate may be overvalued or undervalued for purposes that have nothing to do with the program, which implies that the costs of imported goods, and perhaps imported labor services, are distorted. The best approach in this situation is to adjust the exchange rate by using an estimate of the degree of overvaluation or undervaluation.

Third, programs may have unintended consequences, such as an increase in pollution, that are not accounted for in calculations of the cost of implementing the program. The extent of these unintended consequences must be measured, and a value must be assigned to those consequences. Assigning such a value can be complicated, and the methods for handling this exercise depend on the type of consequence. On a more optimistic note, some programs may have unintended consequences that are beneficial; for example, an increase in education levels may lead to a reduction in crime rates. Ideally, these benefits should be assigned a monetary value and then be subtracted from the costs.

A fourth complication is that many costs can be incurred over several years, and a discount rate of some kind is needed to compare costs at different times. This difficulty also applies to calculations of the benefits, which almost always accrue over several years. The most common approach is to use the market interest rate for the discount rate, assuming that this interest rate is not distorted. Several other considerations also need to be taken into account when deciding what discount rate to use. A worthwhile and accessible discussion can be found in Boardman et al. (2010).

Another complication is that the costs may affect some members of the population more than others, for example, if the funds are collected using specific taxes. If so, judgments may be needed regarding whether welfare weights should be used. For example, tax revenue may be deemed more costly if collected from lower income groups. However, the calculation of welfare weights is not always straightforward, so welfare weights must be used carefully and transparently. In many cases, two sets of costs should be calculated: one with welfare weights and one without.

A sixth potential complication is general equilibrium effects. If goods and services are purchased on a large scale, their prices could increase, which would increase the cost of the program *and* have effects on the general welfare of the population, including those who do not participate in the program. For brevity, general equilibrium effects are not considered in this chapter. Ignoring general equilibrium effects can be justified by invoking the assumption that the program is small relative to the overall economy and by the fact that incorporating such effects in general entails a complicated modeling exercise that is beyond the expertise of most evaluation agencies.

A final issue is whether cash transfers should be considered to be a cost (or user fees should be considered to be a benefit) of the program. The general answer is "no," because such transfers constitute the redistribution of funds as opposed to a cost to society in terms of the resources required to implement the program. But this is still a matter of debate; see Dhaliwal et al. (2013, 307–9) for a discussion of this issue.

General principles for addressing complications of cost calculations

These complications may seem daunting, and perhaps even insurmountable, but some general principles are useful for addressing them, the three most useful of which are discussed in the following paragraphs.

Perhaps the most important, but also somewhat abstract, principle is that, when calculating the costs of a program, the relative prices used to compare the costs of any two goods should be equal to the relative costs of producing those two goods. In economic terminology, the relative costs of any two goods are the marginal rate of transformation in an aggregate production function for the entire economy. If the relative prices are not equal to the relative costs, then the use of those goods may be set at levels that are inefficient in the sense that the program will use too much of any good for which the relative price (among the prices used to calculate costs) is lower than the relative cost of producing that good (and will use too little of any good for which the relative price is higher than its relative cost).

A second general principle is much less abstract: in an economy with few or no market distortions, both the relative and absolute prices of goods and services can simply be their market prices. The main difficulty in applying this principle is determining whether it is true that there are few or no market distortions. This determination needs to be made through discussions between local economic researchers and high-level staff of the agency undertaking the evaluation, perhaps with input from knowledgeable officials at the ministry of finance.

A third principle is that, in the presence of numerous market distortions, the best choice is likely to be to use international prices (excluding any national tariffs or subsidies) as relative prices. Although this principle is relatively easy to apply for traded goods, it provides little information on how to set prices for nontraded goods, which may include most types of labor used in the program.

More practical recommendations

On the basis of these principles, as well as others, this section provides more specific practical advice on how to calculate the costs of a given program. The first recommendation pertains to the cost of constructing buildings such as health clinics or schools. Ideally, a well-functioning rental market for similar buildings would allow the rental prices for those buildings to be used to estimate the total cost of constructing buildings for a program. However, without a well-functioning rental market for similar types of buildings, estimating the cost on the basis of general construction costs in the community, including both material costs and labor costs, is usually feasible.

The second practical recommendation pertains to labor costs. In most countries, the market wage can be used to value most types of labor required to implement a particular program. The markets for most types of labor are unlikely to be affected by market distortions. For example, very little effective regulation of labor markets is in place in rural areas of developing countries, which is also the case for informal labor markets in urban areas. However, more formal labor markets in urban areas may be affected by some distortions that lead the cost of labor to be higher than the true cost, such as professions with powerful unions or for which the main employer is the government (given that the government can set wages without direct competitive pressure to keep costs low). Unfortunately, no simple solutions to valuing labor when labor markets are distorted are at hand, so there may be little alternative to using actual wages for those types of labor. However, if a plausible range for labor costs can be established, then two cost estimates can be conducted, one using the labor cost at one end of that range and the other using the labor cost at the other end. If these two sets of estimates lead to the same decision, then there is no need to know the exact "true" value of the labor within that range.

A third recommendation is to count materials that are already available as a cost, even if they can be obtained at no cost. For example, some schools may have computers that are not being used, or some health clinics may have refrigerators with unused space that can be used to store new medicines. In most cases, the prudent approach is to include in the overall cost calculations the costs of such equipment and materials because they may not be available in other settings, and because unused equipment that is commandeered for a program has an opportunity cost in that it could have been sold or used for some other purpose. However, in some situations it may be informative to calculate two or three variants of the cost of a program, using different procedures to assign the costs of already-available materials, including one variant that assumes that the items are available at no cost for situations in which unused equipment is available that is unlikely to be sold or used for some other purpose. This general recommendation also applies to the cost of program staff, such as teachers or health workers; the time required for extra tasks that they may have to perform to implement a program should in most cases be valued at their current wages, but if there is good reason to believe that they have adequate spare time to undertake additional work, it may be useful to calculate another set of estimates that assumes that their time is available at no additional cost.

Fourth, in general the cost of donated items and labor should usually be included. The use of those items imposes costs on society as a whole (they could have been used for some other purpose, including leisure time for donated labor), even if there was no financial cost to the program. A similar point is that costs should be calculated for any time required of the beneficiaries of the program, such as time spent getting health care or obtaining job training. These costs should be included as part of the cost of the program.

A final practical note is that costs may decrease when the program is scaled up to the national level. That is, many evaluations are done on a small scale to avoid wasting resources on an initiative that in the end may not be very effective. If the program is deemed to be worthwhile and is later implemented at a regional or national level, some of the costs may be reduced. For example, the cost of designing some aspects of the program may not depend on the size of the program, so will be a smaller percentage of per unit costs if the initiative is expanded. Similarly, the costs of some materials may be lower if they are purchased in larger amounts. On the other hand, such economies of scale might be counterbalanced by less careful implementation and supervision when a program is greatly expanded, given that the pilot program may have been implemented with considerable care by staff who are committed to the value of the program.

A simple comparison of cost-benefit analysis and cost-effectiveness analysis

The rest of this chapter discusses aspects of both cost-benefit analysis and cost-effective analysis. First, a general summary of their differences and relative advantages is provided in the table 23.1.

As mentioned, both cost-benefit analysis and cost-effectiveness analysis require detailed estimation of the costs of the program. However, they diverge in other ways. The main difference is that cost-benefit analysis requires a monetary calculation of the program's benefits, which requires more work, and, even more important, more assumptions, than

TABLE 23.1 Similarities and differences between cost-benefit and cost-effectiveness analyses

	COST-BENEFIT ANALYSIS	COST-EFFECTIVENESS ANALYSIS
Requires detailed estimates of costs?	Yes	Yes
Requires monetary calculation of benefits?	Yes	No
Can be used to compare very different types of programs?	Yes	No
Can be used for programs with multiple outcomes?	Yes	Difficult
Provides a quantitative assessment of whether a program is worth the costs?	Yes	No

Source: Original table for this publication.

cost-effectiveness analysis; but if that work is undertaken and if those assumptions are credible, cost-benefit analysis has three advantages, as shown in table 23.1.

The first advantage of cost-benefit analysis over cost-effectiveness analysis is that very different types of programs can be compared because the ratio of benefits to costs can be compared for all programs. The second is that it can be used to assess programs that have multiple outcomes, which is difficult to do with cost-effectiveness analysis. Finally, it provides a quantitative assessment of whether the program is worth implementing, whereas cost-effectiveness analysis provides only information on relative effectiveness between programs, not on whether the value of the benefits is worth the costs. The following two sections explain these differences in more detail and provide additional information on both of these assessment methods.

Cost-benefit analysis (valuing the benefits)

Once the costs of a program have been estimated, cost-benefit analysis requires an additional calculation—a monetary calculation of the benefits of that program. This calculation is not a simple matter, and its complications have persuaded some analysts to prefer cost-effectiveness analysis. However, if the monetary value of the benefits can be credibly calculated, three important advantages are gained. Specifically, the researcher can (1) evaluate programs with multiple outcomes, (2) compare programs with very different outcomes, and (3) decide whether a program is worth implementing. Thus assessing what is involved in valuing those benefits is worthwhile.

Steps for implementing cost-benefit analysis

Five steps are required to undertake cost-benefit analysis, as summarized in table 23.2 and explained in detail in the remainder of this subsection.

TABLE 23.2 The five steps for implementing cost-benefit analysis

Step 1: Calculate all costs of the program.
Step 2: Estimate the impacts of the program on all the outcomes that it affects.
Step 3: Assign monetary benefits to those outcomes.
Step 4: Apply discounting to compare costs and benefits at different times.
Step 5: Calculate the ratio of the benefits to the costs.

Source: Original table for this publication.

The first step in cost-benefit analysis is to obtain estimates of all costs of the program being evaluated, including the time when each of the costs was incurred. This step is also needed for cost-effectiveness analysis. The issues involved in doing these calculations, which are not trivial, are discussed earlier in this chapter.

The second step in cost-benefit analysis is to obtain estimates of the impacts of the program on all outcomes that it affects, and the times when these benefits appear. This step is also required for cost-effectiveness analysis; the next three steps, in contrast, are required for cost-benefit analysis but not for cost-effectiveness analysis. Methods for calculating the impacts are discussed in great detail in chapters 6–17 of this book and are summarized in chapter 5, so there is no need to review them here.

The next step is the most difficult task, which is to assign monetary values to all the outcomes estimated in the second step. The next subsection discusses in more detail how to assign these monetary values. Many evaluations would like to calculate not only the total value of all of the benefits, but also how these benefits are distributed over different socioeconomic groups in the population, which requires that the estimates of the impacts obtained in the second step be calculated for the different socioeconomic groups of interest.

The monetary values obtained in the third step typically accrue at different times, and the same is true of the costs. The fourth step is to calculate the total costs and benefits during the lifetime of the program. This involves choosing a discount rate that can be used to calculate the total benefits of the program as a monetary value in a given year (often the year that the program is first implemented). This is generally referred to as the present discounted value (PDV) of the benefits of the program. The PDV of the costs is obtained using the same discount rate and calculated for the same year as the PDV of the benefits.

The fifth and final step is to compare the PDV of the benefits to the PDV of the costs. These comparisons are often presented as a ratio of the former over the latter, and are referred to as cost-benefit ratios (or sometimes benefit-cost ratios, given that the benefits are in the numerator). These ratios are then compared to see which programs have the highest ratios of benefits to costs, and these are the programs that should be given the highest priority. In principle, if funding allows, all programs with a cost-benefit ratio greater than one (meaning that the PDV of the benefits is greater than the PDV of the costs) are worth implementing and should be funded. Of course, these calculations also imply that programs for which the costs are higher than the benefits, that is, for which the cost-benefit ratios are less than one, should not be funded, or if such programs already exist they should be discontinued. If funds are limited, then all possible programs should be ordered by their cost-benefit ratios; the one with the highest cost-benefit ratio should receive highest priority, followed by the one with the second-highest ratio, and so on until all funds have been spent.

How to calculate the value of benefits

The most difficult task in cost-benefit analysis is calculating the monetary value of benefits, the third of the five steps presented in the previous subsection. A variety of different methods can be used, which is fortunate because of the wide assortment of benefits from many different types of programs, such as higher agricultural productivity, reduced infant mortality, increased school attendance, or cleaner water. The following discussion presents four common methods. Further discussion can be found in Boardman et al. (2010).

The easiest case is the one in which the program produces goods or services that are bought and sold in markets that do not have serious distortions. The current prices can be used to value these goods and services, and in some cases reliable predictions of future prices may be available. If future prices are not available, the best option is usually to use current prices. The main disadvantage of this method is that many of the goods and services produced by programs, such as years of schooling, child health, and environmental benefits, are not bought and sold in markets. The remaining three methods can be used in situations for which it is difficult to assign values to the goods and services provided by a program.

Many programs induce changes in individuals that are likely to increase their incomes. Examples of this are increased years of schooling (and, more directly, increased academic skills as measured by test scores), which should lead to higher wages throughout an individual's lifetime; job training programs, which should also lead to higher wages if the training is valuable; and improved health, which can lead to higher incomes both directly (healthier individuals are more productive workers) and, for children, indirectly via increased years of schooling induced by better health. In all three cases, the way to value these benefits is to estimate the impact of these changes in individual characteristics on wages. (Of course, health and education may confer other benefits, in which case these calculations should be viewed as lower bounds of the true value of these types of programs.) For a discussion of the impact of health on wages in developing countries, see Schultz (2010, 4804–5) and the references therein, and for a discussion of the impact of years of schooling on wages in those countries, see Orazem and King (2008) and Behrman (2010).

A third common method for valuing the benefits of a program is contingent valuation analysis. In its simplest form, this method involves conducting surveys of individuals, asking them how much they are willing to pay for hypothetical improvements in their quality of life. This method is most often used to evaluate the environmental benefits of programs, but in principle it can be used for a wide variety of benefits that are difficult to value. However, many economists are skeptical of this method. For discussions of the value of contingent evaluation methods, see Carson (2012), Hausman (2012), and Kling, Phaneuf, and Zhao (2012).

A final method for assigning the value of benefits for which there are no market prices is to infer them from consumer behavior. For example, individuals who purchase medicines that lead to a particular improvement in their health clearly value that improvement in their health at least as much as the cost of that medicine. A common example, applied mainly to developed countries, is to examine differences in housing prices for similar houses that differ in only one respect, which is where they are located; these differences in prices can, in principle, be used to determine the value that owners of housing attached to living in an area that has less pollution, or better schools, or some other aspect of the quality of life that is hard to assign a value to in other ways. Despite the many complications with this approach, it has been used in several studies in developed countries, such as Black (1999).

Discounting costs and benefits

Costs and benefits often occur at different times, and a dollar today does not have the same value as a dollar next year or 10 years from today. Once costs and benefits have been calculated for the years in which they occur, they must all be converted to a given base year value for a correct comparison. Almost always, a dollar (or any other currency) today is worth more than a dollar at some time in the future, so a *discount rate* is needed to discount the monetary value of future costs and benefits.

Once such a discount rate has been obtained, the standard formula for aggregating all future costs into the PDV of all of those costs in current (present) dollars is

$$\text{PDV of costs (base year is } t = 0) = \sum_{t=0}^{T} \frac{Cost_t}{(1+\delta)^t},$$

where δ is the annual discount rate and $Cost_t$ is the sum of all program costs at time t. Similarly, the PDV of all benefits of the program can be calculated as

$$\text{PDV of benefits (base year is } t = 0) = \sum_{t=0}^{T} \frac{Benefit_t}{(1+\delta)^t},$$

where δ is the annual discount rate and $Benefit_t$ is the sum of all program benefits at time t.

The choice of the discount rate, δ, is not simple. For robustness, calculations should be made using a plausible range for δ. Three common choices for δ are

1. The prevailing interest rate faced by the program funding agency,
2. An estimate of households' discounting of future utility, and
3. A rate set by a development agency (for example, the World Bank often uses $\delta = 0.10$).

Most organizations set δ to be between 0.03 and 0.07, with some as low as 0.00 and others as high as 0.10. Using two or three different possible values of δ to calculate the PDVs of both costs and benefits can be worthwhile to check whether the main conclusions are sensitive to changes within this range.

Another useful approach is to solve for the value of δ that makes the PDV of the benefits equal to the PDV of the costs. This value is called the internal rate of return. If the internal rate of return is greater than all plausible values of δ, then the program or project certainly has benefits that exceed the costs, whereas if this rate of return is less than all plausible values of δ, then the costs are larger than the benefits and the program or project should not be implemented, unless there are considerations that cannot be expressed in terms of monetary values of costs and benefits.

A final point is that all of the rates in the previous discussion are in "real" terms, not nominal terms. If there is significant inflation, the discount rate used should be the sum of the real discount rate plus the inflation rate. Of course, predicting future inflation is difficult, so a range of plausible predictions should be used to see whether the findings are sensitive to the different values within this range.

Cost-effectiveness analysis

In some cases it may be almost impossible to obtain monetary values of the benefits of a program, although reasonably accurate estimates of the costs can be collected. In such situations, cost-benefit analysis cannot be implemented, but cost-effectiveness analysis can be applied, providing at least partial guidance about whether some programs are more effective than others. This section provides additional discussion of cost-effectiveness analysis.

Cost-effectiveness analysis compares the costs of programs that have very similar *outcomes* (for example, increased school attendance or reduced child malnutrition). With calculation of costs having been discussed above, the main issue is to determine whether two programs really produce similar outcomes. If they do, and those outcomes are measured in the same units (or can be converted into the same units) for the programs that are being compared, for each program the cost for a one unit increase in the benefit produced by these programs can be calculated. For example, one program may reduce the incidence of child stunting (low height-for-age) by 6 percentage points at a total cost of $8 million, whereas another program may reduce it by 8 percentage points at a cost of $12 million. Thus the first program is able to reduce stunting by 1 percentage point for a cost of $1.33 million (8 ÷ 6 = 1.33), whereas the second does so at a cost of $1.5 million for each 1-percentage-point reduction (12 ÷ 8 = 1.5), so the former program is more cost-effective than the latter.

As seen in table 23.1, cost-effectiveness analysis has one big advantage over cost-benefit analysis, which is that it is not necessary to calculate a monetary value of the benefits of a given program; but it also has three disadvantages relative to cost-benefit analysis. First, it cannot compare programs that have different types of benefits. For example, one health program may reduce malnutrition among young children, whereas another one may reduce the incidence of tuberculosis in adults; cost-effectiveness calculations cannot indicate which of these programs should be given higher priority.

Second, it is difficult, and perhaps impossible, to apply cost-effective analysis when a program has more than one benefit. The only exception is when two programs both produce the same two benefits, and they do so in relatively similar proportions (for example, both programs produce about twice as much of the first benefit as they do of the second benefit), which is unlikely to be a common occurrence.

Third, cost-effectiveness analysis does not provide an overall assessment of whether a program is worth implementing. In contrast, cost-benefit analysis indicates that any program for which the costs are less than the benefits is worth implementing, whereas any program for which the costs exceed the benefits should not be undertaken. The only possible exception to this rule is the case in which the program produces no benefit at all, so it is obvious that the program should not be implemented.

Conclusion

The decision about whether a program, policy, or project should be implemented depends not only on its impact on the outcomes of interest but also on its cost. Thus the decision requires information on both program impacts and program costs. The two main approaches to combining information on estimated costs and estimated impacts are cost-benefit analysis and cost-effectiveness analysis. The former assigns monetary values to both the benefits and the costs of programs (or policies or projects), whereas the latter assigns monetary values only to the costs, which is usually easier than assigning monetary values to the benefits.

The main disadvantage of cost-benefit analysis is that it is often difficult to assign a monetary value to a program's benefits. But if benefits can be valued, then cost-benefit analysis can be used to (1) compare the relative worth of any two types of programs, including types that are very different from each other; (2) assess the merits of programs that have multiple outputs; and (3) make decisions about whether a given program is a worthwhile investment, without reference to information on other programs. The main advantage of cost-effectiveness analysis—that it does not require the calculation of the monetary value of the benefits—comes at the expense of not providing these three advantages of cost-benefit analysis.

This chapter provides an introduction, and only an introduction, to both cost-benefit analysis and cost-effectiveness analysis. Much more detailed treatments, which may be essential for making an informed decision, can be found in Boardman et al. (2010), Dreze and Stern (1987), and Levin and McEwan (2001). The decision about which approach to use will depend on the specific context; in some cases both could be applied, in which case the cost-effectiveness analysis will have more credibility because it requires no assumptions about how to value the benefits. However, cost-benefit analysis will, in principle, yield guidance on a much larger set of comparisons of different programs, although the additional assumptions may be inaccurate.

Three final practical recommendations, and one word of caution, are also worth noting. The first practical recommendation is that program impacts (both good and bad) may accumulate over many years, so initial assessments (after one or two years) are necessarily incomplete and may even be misleading. Second, the longer a program is operating, the more its initial startup costs can be spread over many years of operation, which reduces estimates of the average annual cost of the program. Third, while the program is in operation, some unexpected costs and benefits may occur that need to be quickly identified and measured to update cost-benefit or cost-effectiveness calculations, which may tip the decision regarding the merits of the program in a different direction.

The word of caution concerns external validity. Recalling the general discussion of internal and external validity in chapter 4, which focuses on the validity of estimated program impacts, the same distinction can be applied to program costs. The discussion in this chapter implicitly focuses on ensuring the internal validity of program costs. Yet any attempt to generalize cost-benefit analysis and cost-effectiveness analysis to other settings must account for not only the external validity of the estimated program benefits but also the external validity of the program costs. Quite simply, costs can vary greatly in different settings, and attempts to extend cost-benefit analysis or cost-effectiveness analysis results to other settings must consider not only whether the estimated benefits are plausible but also whether the same is true of the estimated costs. See Evans and Popova (2016) for further discussion of this issue.

Notes

1. For brevity, the rest of this chapter refers to programs, but virtually everything in this chapter also applies to policies and projects.
2. For a theoretical exposition, see Dreze and Stern (1987). The shadow price of labor can be defined as the value (measured using shadow prices) of the additional goods that can be produced with one additional unit of labor.

References

Behrman, Jere. 2010. "Investments in Education—Inputs and Incentives." In *Handbook of Development Economics,* Vol. 5, edited by Dani Rodrik and Mark Rosenzweig. Amsterdam: North-Holland.

Black, Sandra. 1999. "Do Better Schools Matter? Parental Valuation of Elementary Education." *Quarterly Journal of Economics* 114 (2): 577–99.

Boardman, Anthony, David Greenberg, Aidan Vining, and David Weimer. 2010. *Cost-Benefit Analysis,* Fourth Edition. New York: Pearson.

Carson, Richard. 2012. "Contingent Valuation: A Practical Alternative When Prices Aren't Available." *Journal of Economic Perspectives* 26 (4): 27–42.

Dhaliwal, Iqbal, Esther Duflo, Rachel Glennerster, and Caitlin Tulloch. 2013. "Comparative Cost-Effectiveness Analysis to Inform Policy in Developing Countries: A General Framework with Applications for Education." In *Education Policy in Developing Countries,* edited by Paul Glewwe, 285–337. Chicago: University of Chicago Press.

Dreze, Jean, and Nicholas Stern. 1987. "The Theory of Cost-Benefit Analysis." In *Handbook of Public Economics,* Vol. 2, edited by A. Auerbach and M. Feldstein. Amsterdam: Elsevier.

Evans, David, and Anna Popova. 2016. "Cost-Effectiveness Analysis in Development: Accounting for Local Costs and Noisy Impacts." *World Development* 77: 262–76.

Hausman, Jerry. 2012. "Contingent Valuation: From Dubious to Hopeless." *Journal of Economic Perspectives* 26 (4): 43–56.

Kling, Catherine, Daniel Phaneuf, and Jinhua Zhao. 2012. "From Exxon to BP: Has Some Number Become Better than No Number?" *Journal of Economic Perspectives* 26 (4): 3–26.

Levin, Henry, and Patrick McEwan. 2001. *Cost-Effectiveness Analysis, Second Edition.* Sage Publications: Thousand Oaks, CA.

Orazem, Peter, and Elizabeth King. 2008. "Schooling in Developing Countries: The Roles of Supply, Demand and Government Policy." In *Handbook of Development Economics,* Vol. 4, edited by T. P. Schultz and J. Strauss. Amsterdam: Elsevier.

Schultz, T. Paul. 2010. "Population and Health Policies." In *Handbook of Development Economics,* Vol. 5, edited by Dani Rodrick and Mark Rosenzweig. Amsterdam: Elsevier.

ECO-AUDIT

Environmental Benefits Statement

The World Bank Group is committed to reducing its environmental footprint. In support of this commitment, we leverage electronic publishing options and print-on-demand technology, which is located in regional hubs worldwide. Together, these initiatives enable print runs to be lowered and shipping distances decreased, resulting in reduced paper consumption, chemical use, greenhouse gas emissions, and waste.

Our books are printed on Forest Stewardship Council (FSC)–certified paper, with a minimum of 10 percent recycled content. The fiber in our book paper is either unbleached or bleached using totally chlorine-free (TCF), processed chlorine–free (PCF), or enhanced elemental chlorine–free (EECF) processes.

More information about the Bank's environmental philosophy can be found at http://www.worldbank.org/corporateresponsibility.

green press INITIATIVE